Baedeker

India

SIGHTSEEING HIGHLIGHTS ✶✶

Travellers have always been fascinated by the diversity of the people, cultures and landscapes on the Indian subcontinent. Dive into this new world with its magnificent palaces, lively cities, impressive landscapes, fragrant bazaars and heavenly beaches. There is something for everyone, be it adventurous trekking tours, stimulating encounters or relaxing Ayurveda health resorts.

First Tiger Reserve
The Corbett National Park was founded as early as 1936.

Visitors in Hampi
at the fascinating ruins of Vijayanagara

Picture postcard motif
of the Chinese Fishing Nets in Kochi

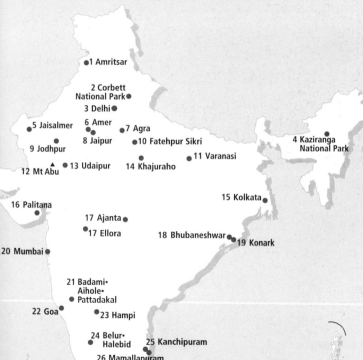

●1 Amritsar

2 Corbett National Park●

3 Delhi●

5 Jaisalmer ●   6 Amer ●   7 Agra
8 Jaipur ●   ●10 Fatehpur Sikri
9 Jodhpur ●

4 Kaziranga National Park ●

12 Mt Abu ▲ ● 13 Udaipur   14 Khajuraho
11 Varanasi

16 Palitana ●

17 Ajanta ●
17 Ellora ●   18 Bhubaneshwar ●19 Konark

15 Kolkata ●

20 Mumbai ●

21 Badami●
Aihole●
● Pattadakal

22 Goa ●

23 Hampi ●

24 Belur●
Halebid ●   25 Kanchipuram ●

26 Mamallapuram

27 Thanjavur ●

28 Kochi ●
30 Periyar NP●   ●29 Madurai
31 Backwaters ●

©Baedeker

BAEDEKER'S BEST TIPS

Of all the Baedeker tips in this book we have put together a list of the most interesting here. Experience and enjoy India from its best side!

⚠ Bollywood close up

It is a real experience to watch a Hindi film in the original and with an Indian audience, best done in the film metropolis Mumbai itself! ▶ **page 111**

Bollywood
drama, action and big emotions

⚠ Nocturnal sounds

Nocturnal repair works, temple bells, wedding music, car horns and barking dogs: light sleepers should bring ear plugs to India! ▶ **page 128**

⚠ Socks rock!

The stone slabs in India's temples, which can warm up to 30°C/86°F or 40 °C/104 °F can be quite a cause of suffering for barefoot tourists. Since shoes have to be left outside it is a good idea to bring socks so that Western visitors can walk through the holy sites as calmly as the Indian visitors. ▶ **page 136**

⚠ Lost and confused

Finding the desired hotel or restaurant can sometimes turn out to be quite an odyssey. It is easier to get to a destination by phoning the relevant establishment in advance and have the route given to the taxi-driver directly. ▶ **page 138**

⚠ A lassi please!

If Indian food gets too spicy for European tastes, extinguish the fire in your mouth with a lassi. ▶ **page 150**

⚠ Healthy thirst-quencher

They are not just a good way to quench thirst, they are also very healthy: coconuts. Vendors generally offer two varieties: »paniwalla«, which has a lot of water or »malaiwalla«, which has less milk but more of the white, sweet flesh (malai), which the vendor will get out after the milk has been drunk.
▶ **page 152**

⚠ A boat trip at dawn

One of the unforgettable experiences in Varanasi is a boat trip on the Ganges at dawn, when life on the ghats begins to stir. ▶ **page 286**

⚠ A morning stroll

The »Heritage Walk« makes its way through temples, mosques and the labyrinth of alleyways of old Ahmedabad, bringing the city's history to life.
▶ **page 301**

⚠ Warning, camel jam!

Riding a camel at sunset in the sand dunes of Sam is part of the standard programme for every tourist. However, this should be avoided on Sundays and Indian holidays. gets extremely busy at these times and tourists could find themselves stuck in a traffic jam – but with camels!
▶ **page 338**

Sunrise on the Ganges
Pilgrims come to the river early in the morning to pray and make sacrifices

■ Just your cup of tea!
Everything that happens before the golden brew finds its way into a cup is revealed during a visit of one of Darjeeling's many tea plantations. ▸ **page 381**

■ The sweet side of Kolkata
Rossogolla, Barfi, Sandesh, Gulab Jamun: Kolkata is heaven for those with a sweet tooth because Bengali sweets are famous all over India. ▸ **page 391**

■ Delicacies during Ramadan
During the Islamic month of fasting, Ramadan, some Muslim quarters turn into a gourmet's dream. Exquisitely cooked goats' tongues, syrup pancakes and spiced rice pudding are now considered fancy treats amongst connoisseurs.
▸ **page 485**

■ Pearl paradise
Leaving Hyderabad without going to one of the pearl shops north of the Charminar would almost amount to sacrilege.
▸ **page 561**

■ A peck of organic pepper
Even in India's spice plantations, organic farming is an issue. It is particularly interesting to visit the organic pepper plantations near Periyar National Park, which are cultivated by the local tribal population. ▸ **page 605**

■ Is coffee more your cup of tea?
India's answer to franchises such as Starbucks is the »Indian Coffee House«. The chain, run by the Indian Coffee Workers Cooperative, runs around 160 cafés all over India, many of which are in Kerala. Enjoy tasty Indian breakfasts and good coffee at reasonable prices.
▸ **page 622**

■ Great day trip
Anyone craving an alternative to life on the beach can hire a taxi and make a nice day trip to Kanyakumari, at India's southern tip. The wonderful wooden palace of Padmanabhapuram and the temple town of Suchindaram should definitely be included on the itinerary. ▸ **page 623**

Miniature painting
Krishna in the Basholi Style
► page 105

BACKGROUND

Price categories

Hotels
Luxury: from 58£
Mid-range: 22 – 58£
Budget: below 22£
(for one night in a double room)

Restaurants
Expensive: from 9£
Moderate: 4 – 9£
Inexpensive: up to 4£
(for one meal)

PRACTICALITIES

TOURS

Colourful clothes
are especially common in Rajasthan
► page 174

Tree nymph
on one of the stone gates at Sanchi
▶ page 435

SIGHTS FROM A to Z

Red Fort
in Old Delhi
▶ page 253

Kathakali Dancer
applying his intricate make-up
▶ page 507

Background

CONCISE AND TO THE POINT,
EASILY COMPREHENSIBLE AND
A GOOD SOURCE OF REFERENCE:
INTERESTING INFORMATION
ABOUT INDIA, ITS PEOPLE, ITS
ECONOMY, POLITICS, SOCIETY
AND EVERYDAY LIFE.

MYTH, MAGIC AND MODERNITY

India is booming. As an economic partner and a travel destination, India is in demand. Together with China, India has the world's fastest-growing economy and in recent years has established itself as a political heavyweight. Unlike its northeastern neighbour however, Gandhi's birthplace has never really let go of its old traditions and religious beliefs.

A trip to India is more than just a visit to a country with a markedly diverse landscape and culture. Visitors to India also travel back in time. There are few places on Earth where old and new collide and create such a synthesis as they do on the Indian subcontinent.

Religion dominates life for the majority of the people. At the same time, cutting-edge science and technology are fast establishing themselves in India. Software production and reincarnation need not be mutually exclusive.

Even in modern business life the gods still play a decisive role: where else in the world are they invited to the openings of company HQs? The elephant god Ganesha and the fortune goddess Lakshmi regularly bestow their blessings at the opening of a new software company, claiming a firm place between computers, crisps and Coca-Cola.

India has confidently stepped out onto the international platform, in the knowledge that it has a lot to offer the world. It boasts a millennia-old philosophy and history, *People with great hospitality* and moreover possesses knowledge that is now also being accepted by the West: yoga and Ayurveda are just two examples. The »world's largest democracy« is also proud of its scientific elite and its growing domestic market, with a huge number of potential consumers. Education and social advancement are two of the engines of this development; the growing middle class is evidence of it.

One thing the aspiring country cannot hide, however, is the fact that progress has failed to reach a large part of its population.

More than just Palaces and Palm-lined Beaches

Despite of the poverty that is very visible in many places, India is an immensely hospitable country. The people are proud of their rich

Spices
the reputation of India's cuisine depends on their variety

Temple sites
India's temple sites exhibit very varied architectural styles and types

Tropical vegetation
but also tea plantations, gentle hills and countless paddy fields shape the country's landscape

The Taj Mahal
a magical symbol of the subcontinent

Colours
*seem to be particularly luminous
and intense in India*

Elephants
*are hard-working but also sacred and
shrouded in myths*

cultural heritage and tourism is a fast-growing branch of the economy, and not just in the desert state of Rajasthan, whose magnificent Maharaja's palaces and fortresses have shaped our image of India for a long time. Goa's palm-lined beaches have been a popular tourist destination since the 1970s. But now other regions have also rediscovered their treasures. One of the leading areas is Kerala, India's tropical green state in the southwest of the country, which is also the home of Ayurveda. Kerala's visitors can enjoy some pampering in its many excellent hotels. However, the subcontinent has more to offer than just palaces and palm-lined beaches, deserts and wellness resorts. The north boasts the Himalaya, with mountains that reach an elevation of more than 8000m/30,000ft, while the south has temple cities and lush paddy fields. The west offers more than just desert; colourful festivals take place here, and there are splendid temple complexes. India's east with its tea plantations and humid jungles is no longer uncharted territory for tourists. Mega-cities such as Delhi, Bangalore, Mumbai and Kolkata, the latter two formerly, and maybe still better, known as Bombay and Calcutta, have excellent hotels and a huge range of cultural attractions to offer.

Faith *determines the daily lives of most Indians*

Anyone undertaking a trip from Rajasthan in the northwest to Tamil Nadu in the southeast will realize that India is a small continent of its own. The people, their customs and habits are every bit as varied as the country's natural environment. Hindu and Muslim traditions exist side by side and many other religious communities are also to be found. Another area in which the country is extremely diverse is its food: from hot and spicy to sugary sweet, from greasy and heavy to fruity and light. Indeed, India exhibits great variety and intensity in every way. Its tastes, colours, sounds and smells exert a powerful attraction. Overwhelmed with all this input, visitors find themselves trying to digest the wealth of experiences the country has to offer each and every day. India stimulates all the senses. It is both a fascinating and a shocking place, it invigorates and numbs, it attracts and repels. Indifference is perhaps the only emotion India will definitely not create in those who visit it.

Facts

India's rich history and culture are reflected in a wealth of imposing structures and a diverse variety of religious traditions, languages and dialects. However, India does not just live in the past: as one of the world's largest industrial nations it has already flung its gates wide open to the challenges of the future.

Natural Environment

The Indian subcontinent can roughly be divided into three main regions. The Himalaya, whose towering peaks are 7000–8000m/ 20,000–29,000ft high and under a permanent blanket of snow and ice, makes up the northern mountainous region. To the south the lowlands of the Indus, Ganges and Brahmaputra nestle in a crescent beneath the mountains. The third region is the Indian peninsula itself, a geologically very old area dominated by the Deccan plateau.

Three main regions

The Himalaya

India's northwest and northeast have something like a ten percent share of the 2500km/1500mi Himalaya mountain range (also commonly referred to as the Himalayas). The highest peak in the Indian Union is **Nanda Devi**, at an elevation of 7817m/25,646ft, in the western Himalaya (Kumaon Himalaya). The highest mountain in the eastern Himalaya (Sikkim) is **Kangchenjunga**, which reaches an elevation of 8586m/28,169ft. Snow-covered peaks, rugged cliffs, sharp pinnacles, deep gorges and V-shaped valleys characterize the appearance of the Siwalik Hills, the Lesser Himalaya and the Greater Himalaya. Like the foothills of the Alps, the southernmost Himalaya ranges only reach around 2500m/8200ft and display softer shapes.

High mountains

Between the two main Himalaya chains lies the very fertile **Kashmir valley**, through which a tributary of the Indus flows. Its capital Srinagar lies at an altitude of around 1600m/5250ft. The narrow gorge of the Jhelum river blocks access to the valley and has to be bypassed on the side. Towards the south the marked longitudinal arrangement of the Himalaya range becomes particularly noticeable. This is particularly true of the zone to the west of the Himalaya proper, known as the **Siwalik Hills**, which separate grass-covered valleys and lowlands from the actual high mountains.

Adjoining further to the east is a very humid area consisting of foothills, as well as the bases of the high mountains, which receive a lot of precipitation. This area is home to the notorious forest and grass swamps called »**Terai**« by the locals. They can be considered the original form of the jungle. The wide foothill area of the eastern Himalaya is covered by rainforest and, in particular, tea plantations. The **Darjeeling and Shimla heights**, which are subdivided by many rivers but which have very pleasant climates, became locations for health resorts known for their good air back in the colonial era. Further eastwards, the foothill area becomes narrower. The mountain range itself becomes much more strongly structured and large tracts are no longer as high in the west. North of Darjeeling, in the former Himalayan kingdom of **Sikkim**, the Kangchenjunga massif reaches an elevation of up to 8586m/28,169ft. In front of the fold mountains lie the Khasi Hills, which rise up almost 2000m/6600ft and form the backbone of **Assam**. This is one of the wettest places on earth. Around 12,000mm/470in of rain fall here every year (by way of comparison, London gets 584mm/23in of rain annually). The **Khasi Hills** separate the 700km/430ft-long and approximately 80km/50mi-wide Assam valley through which Brahmaputra river flows from the **Surma basin** in the south. While rice is cultivated almost everywhere in the Assam valley, it is the very wet hills of southern Assam that form one of the most significant tea-growing regions in the world. South of Assam are the **Sylhet depressions**, which form the transition to the vast delta landscape on the Bay of Bengal.

The most important rivers

The **Indus**, which at around 3200km/2000mi in length is India's longest river, rises on the Tibetan plateau, meanders through the western Himalaya (Ladakh range) and then flows through the highlands of Kashmir before it finds its way into the fertile lowlands. This area now largely belongs to Pakistan. The Indus flows into the Arabian Sea southeast of Karachi. Northern India's most important river and

Monastery above the Nubra valley in Ladakh

the holiest river of the Hindus, the **Ganges**, is formed in the 7817m/ 25,646ft-high massif of the Nanda Devi in the western Himalaya from the confluence of two headwaters. After flowing for around 2700km/1700mi through the Ganges Basin, it flows into the Bay of Bengal together with the Brahmaputra. The **Brahmaputra** itself, which rises in Tibet as the Tsangpo, is the most important river of eastern India. It makes its way through the Indian state of Assam and flows for approximately 2900km/1800mi before it reaches a huge 44,000 sq km/17,000 sq mi delta in Bangladesh, where it flows into the Bay of Bengal together with the Ganges. Its catchment area is no less than 670,000 sq km/260,000 sq mi. The risk of flooding exists all year round.

Indus-Ganges-Brahmaputra Basin

The huge and fertile basin of the Indus, Ganges and Brahmaputra, which encompasses an area of more than 650,000 sq km/250,000 sq mi, separates the geologically young fold mountains of the Himalaya from the »old« massif of the Deccan plateau.The **Ganges** flows through a shallow valley. In the western **Ganges basin** it is quite dry compared with the eastern basin. While a lot of rice and jute are cultivated in the wet eastern part, millet, barley, wheat and sugar cane are the crops of choice in the dry west. By now the Ganges and Brahmaputra have created a **delta** around 80,000 sq km/30,000 sq mi in size. This amphibian landscape is undergoing constant change, which can be attributed not just to the flooding of the two rivers, but also to tidal fluctuations and particularly to the storm surges caused by the Bay of Bengal cyclones. Despite the **extreme danger of flooding** the great increase in population has led to the settlement of the flat sandbanks between the individual distributaries. Annual storm surge disasters with many casualties are simply accepted. The mangrove swamps of the southwest delta region are known as the **Sundarbans**. A part of this unique ecosystem is a game reserve, which is still home to more than 250 Bengal tigers. In the western part of the delta lies the city of **Kolkata** on the Hooghly river, a navigable distributary of the Ganges. Between the Ganges plain in the east and the Indus lowland in the west is the **Delhi ridge**, whose highest point is at an elevation of almost 400m/1300ft. Located northwest of Delhi, the Punjab region (now divided between India and Pakistan) is known as the **Land of Five Rivers**, named after the rivers Sutlej, Jhelum, Beas, Ravi and Chenab. In historical times this landscape, sufficiently imbued with moisture, was covered by a light monsoon forest. Today this land is covered by arid grass steppe and even thorn bush savannah. In early summer temperatures rise to more than 40°C/104°F. Intensive irrigation cultivation takes place along the swollen rivers.

Between the Siwalik Hills, which is part of the Himalaya range, and the Indus lies the old landscape of **West Hindustan**, also shared between India and Pakistan. This arid savannah is used as pastureland

A fertile crescent

in many places. In recent decades numerous reservoirs (tanks) and irrigation systems have been built, allowing the lucrative cultivation of cereals and cotton. At the foot of the Siwalik Hills are flood plains (**Sirwah**), once rich with water, which can be used to cultivate cereals, maize and sugarcane. However, deforestation in the Siwalik Hills has had a detrimental effect on the rivers' flow.

Southwest of Delhi lies the **Thar desert steppe**, an area of around 260,000 sq km/100,400 sq mi with extremely sparse vegetation. Its western area is an actual desert with very barren salt soils and sand dunes. The most important cities, Jodhpur, Jaisalmer and Bikaner, lie along old caravan routes. The construction of the Indira Gandhi Canal has allowed at least some of the areas in the north of the desert steppe to be used for agricultural purposes. South of the Thar desert steppe and east of the Indus delta is the **Great Rann of Kutch** salt desert, which has an area of around 60,000 sq km/23,000 sq mi. During the monsoon season it becomes a marsh.

The Indian Peninsula · Deccan Plateau

Large massif formed early in earth's history

The formation of the Himalaya during the Tertiary period went hand in hand with great tectonic strain on the geologically old massif, which broke up into several parts. Its edges along the Arabian Sea and the Bay of Bengal, forced up during this process, now form the coastal mountains known as the **Western Ghats and Eastern Ghats** respectively. They fall off steeply towards the sea, whereas their incline on the landward side is much flatter and gentler.

The rivers on the Deccan plateau are very dependent on the amount of precipitation that falls during the monsoon season. As a result their water levels fluctuate greatly. The most important rivers are the Mahanadi, Krishna, Godavari and Kaveri (all four of them flow eastwards into the Bay of Bengal), as well as the Narmada and Tapi, which flow westwards into the Arabian Sea. Of the sacred Hindu rivers, the Narmada is the second most important. It became well known during the construction of the controversial Narmada Dam.

Mountain ranges and plateaus

The northwestern Deccan plateau, in the guise of the **Aravalli range**, abruptly ends to make way for the Indus lowlands. These fold mountains are about one billion years old and also form the geographical seam between the arid Thar desert steppe and the wetter hills of Rajasthan, as well as with the mountains and mesa regions of central India. Towards the southeast, horst-like mountain ranges give way to the **Malwa plateau**, which occupies the far north of the Deccan Traps, formed as the result of volcanic activity. Black, tropical soils known as »regur« allow this area to be used for very high-yielding agriculture, despite the risk of drought. The region's most important crop is cotton.

The **Deccan Traps** in the northwest and west of the Deccan plateau are of volcanic origin. Around 65 million years ago the area that is

Facts and Figures India

Area
▶ 3.29 million sq km/1.27 million sq mi
▶ Bordering states: Bangladesh, Bhutan, Myanmar (Burma), China, Nepal and Pakistan

State
▶ Form of government: Parliamentary democracy
▶ Capital: New Delhi
▶ Administration: 28 states and seven union territories
▶ Two houses of parliament: Upper House (Rayja Sabha) and Lower House (Lok Sabha)
▶ Prime minister: Dr Manmohan Singh (since May 2004), President: Pratibha Patil (since July 2007)
▶ National flag: horizontally striped tricolour in the colours saffron yellow,

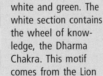 white and green. The white section contains the wheel of knowledge, the Dharma Chakra. This motif comes from the Lion Capital in Sarnath, built by Emperor Ashoka in the third century (fig. p.67)

Population
▶ 1.1 billion people
▶ Ethnic groups: 72% Indo-Aryans, 25% Dravidian, 3% Mongolians and others
▶ Population density: 358 people per sq km (916 per sq mi)
▶ Population growth: 1.7% p.a.

Economy
▶ GDP: 548 billion euros
▶ Per capita income: 441 euros p.a.
▶ Economic structure (percentage of GDP): agriculture (approx. 24%), manufacturing and mining industry (approx. 24.5%), services (approx. 51.5%)

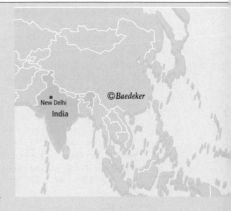

Religion
▶ 80.5% Hindus, 13.4% Muslims, 2.3% Christians, 1.9% Sikhs, approx. 1% Buddhists, 0.5% Jains, approx. 200,000 Parsi and approx. 12,000 Jews

Languages
▶ 22 recognized languages, including many regional languages and dialects
▶ Official language: Hindi; Constitution allows official use of English
▶ Lingua franca: English

Population boom
around a third of India's population are under 15

now the Deccan plateau saw the formation of a far-reaching system of crevices, from which enormous amounts of lava poured out over several hundreds of thousands of years. These lava masses solidified into plateaux with an elevation of 1000m/3300ft to 2000m/6600ft; they now dominate the landscape. Considerable mineral resources are mined in the **mountainous landscape of Bihar, Chhattisgarh and Orissa**, including iron ores, manganese and coal. The deep valleys are suitable for profitable agriculture (rice, millet and maize). The **mountainous area of Chota Nagpur**, which is rich in raw materials, has a flourishing metallurgical industry centred on Jamshedpur, a city largely maintained by Tata Steel. The railway station here goes by the name of Tatanagar. This is also where Kolkata's industry obtains its raw materials.

West of the Satpura range, the Narmada and the Tapi have created the fertile **flood plains of Gujarat**, an area that has long been highly successful in growing and processing cotton. The economic focus of this area is the city of Ahmedabad, one of the textile industry's centres in south Asia. The southern part of the Deccan plateau, including the **Maharashtra Traps plateau** as well as the Telangana plateau and the Karnataka plateau is, compared with the northern Deccan plateau, relatively uniform. Here and there rock bastions, isolated monadnocks and deep, sometimes gorge-like valleys provide some diversity in the landscape. Open monsoon forests and savannahs characterized this region until a few decades ago. Now these forests have largely been logged and transformed into grasslands and cultivated land. Since the plateau lies in the rain shadow of the Western Ghats, however, the yields are anything but rich. The construction of reservoirs (tanks) is an attempt to mitigate the situation.

Western and Eastern Ghats

The mountain range of the **Western Ghats** runs along the coastline of the Arabian Sea from the Tapi valley in the north to the tip of the Indian peninsula. The mountains fall off steeply towards the sea and intercept a large part of the rainfall; they are covered by dense tropical rainforest. The Western Ghats increase in elevation towards the south. Northeast of Mumbai they reach an altitude of 1646m/5400ft, while in the south (the Cardamom Hills) the peak of Anai Mudi towers 2695m/8842ft above sea level. Between the Western Ghats and the Arabian Sea is a narrow strip of coastline called **Konkan**, where almost anything grows and flourishes. The coast itself has little structure except for the area around Mumbai. The port city has become an outstanding metropolis and India's most important location for industry. The **Malabar Coast** along the south of the Western Ghats is characterized by its high levels of humidity.

Two important sections along this strip of coastline are Kanara and the densely populated state of Kerala in the far south. Rising up by more than 2600m/8500ft in the Kerala hinterland are the **Nilgiri Hills** (Blue Mountains), followed by the Palghat Gap, beyond which are the **Cardamom Hills**, whose highest peak is Anai Mudi at 2695m/

On the southern Malabar Coast a labyrinthine network of canals, lakes, lagoons and rivers overgrown with water hyacinths criss-cross the landscape: the Kerala Backwaters

8842ft. The proximity to the equator, the relatively consistent temperature cycles and a fairly high humidity have allowed lucrative coffee, tea and spice cultivation to thrive, at least on the mountains' windward side.

Originally the **inland plateaux** in the Ghats' rain shadow were covered by arid savannah. Further east, rivers have carved wide basins. Individual monadnocks stand out from the surrounding landscape. There are valuable raw materials to be found in several places. The gold fields east of Bangalore are quite famous. The natural conditions allow crops to be cultivated to any great extent only in certain localities. In recent decades attempts have been made to improve the opportunities for irrigation agriculture by building reservoirs, unfortunately with little success, since these »tanks« often dry up. In those areas where it is possible to farm, millet is the most important crop.

The **Eastern Ghats** follow the coast along the Bay of Bengal. North of the Godavari estuary, in the Shevaroy Hills, they reach an altitude of 1628m/5341ft and receive plenty of precipitation while the monsoon winds are blowing. Monsoon forests thus also dominate the appearance of the pristine natural landscape. In the south, the wide plains of the **Coromandel Coast** lie between the Eastern Ghats and the Bay of Bengal. Here the deltas of the three major rivers, the Krishna, Godavari and Mahanadi, run between exposed coastal plates interspersed with laterites as well as sandy coastal plains with spits and flat lagoons. This area has a long tradition of irrigation agriculture. The Godavari delta as well as the coastal area south of Chennai (formerly Madras) are now amongst India's most densely populated regions. The main crops are rice and millet, and coconut palms and cotton also play an important role.

Climate

Seasons India's climate is almost entirely tropical. The Himalayan mountain barrier protects the country from severe cold spells from the north. In January and February it is relatively dry and cool. In these months the daytime temperatures are between 20°C/68°F and 25°C/77°F, and during the night temperatures can fall noticeably below the 20°C/68°F mark. It can get quite cold in India's north and northwest. April and May are very dry and hot, and temperatures above 35°C/95°F are no rarity. Rajasthan has even seen temperatures approaching 50°C/122°F. Dust and sand storms can develop in India's arid environments.

A blessing and a curse for India: living with the monsoon

By the beginning of June the **summer monsoon** (also known as the southwest monsoon) arrives along the Malabar Coast and around Mumbai. The monsoon causes thunderstorms and severe rains to rage over the country after the long dry period. Until September the climate is tropically hot and humid. During this time most regions in India receive around 80 to 90 percent of their annual precipitation. However, the intensity of the rainfall fluctuates greatly depending on the region and the time of year. One typical feature of the monsoon season is the rapid change between rainy days and drier spells. The heaviest rains fall along the Malabar and Konkan coasts, in Assam, Bengal and Chota Nagpur as well as on the southern slopes of the eastern Himalaya. On the other hand, central India, the western Deccan plateau, the southeast (Tamil Nadu) as well as the west and northwest (Thar desert)

India *Regional Climates*

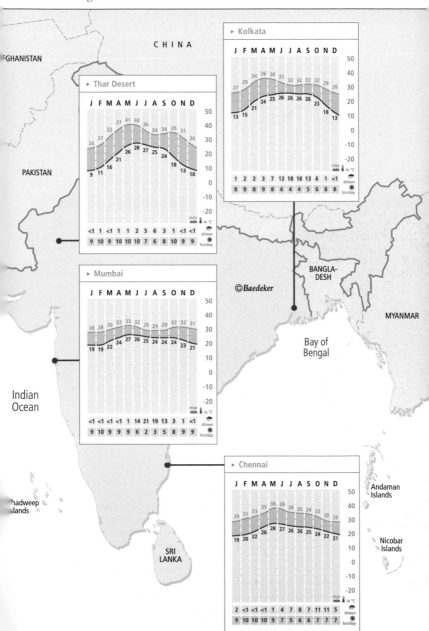

are relatively dry. Temperatures in July range between 28°C/82.4°F in the Ganges lowlands to 30°C/86°F in New Delhi. After the gradual end of the summer monsoon, i.e. a change in the prevalent wind direction, there is a relatively dry transitional period usually lasting from October to December. During this time only the Coromandel Coast can be subject to significant rain. Areas of low pressure over the southern Bay of Bengal can develop into disastrous cyclones (»Bengal cyclones«) and devastate the lowlands of Orissa, Andhra Pradesh and Bengal. From December to February/March the **winter monsoon** (northeast monsoon) is dominant; it brings particularly large quantities of rain to some parts of the Himalaya, such as Kashmir.

Flora and Fauna

Species-rich jungle, species-poor agricultural land

Depending on location and climate conditions visitors will find different natural and agricultural landscapes with a corresponding flora and fauna. India has virtually **all levels of vegetation**, from tropical mangrove swamps along the coast to humid rainforests and dry bush steppes to the meadows and rocky regions of the high mountains. The classic Indian jungle, as it has been portrayed in many an adventure film, with bamboo thickets, lavishly flowering climbing plants and roving tigers, can now only be found in the less populous regions. The vast majority of the country has been transformed into agricultural land. As a result India has seen a great **reduction in its biodiversity**, particularly on the Deccan plateau. According to reputable estimates India is home to 45,000 different plant species, including 15,000 flowering plants. Around a third of these flowering plants are endemic, i.e. they only occur in India. To date, more than 1500 plant species have been registered as threatened. In the light of these figures, it is not difficult to imagine the danger to genetic potential.

Flora

Mountain region

Alpine meadows can be found in the **Himalaya** between altitudes of 4000m/13,000ft and 5000m/16,500ft (snow line). The forest line lies somewhat above 4000m/13,000ft. At lower elevations there are temperate coniferous mountain forests. Characteristic plants include rhododendron, birch, fir, pine and cedars. Coming down to altitudes of approximately 2700m/8900ft we encounter the mixed forest zone and below that, up to around 2000m/6600ft, the dominant flora is a humid, evergreen mountain forest, mainly consisting of oak, bamboo and pines. Cereals can be cultivated up to elevations of 2600m/8500ft, maize to almost 3000m/9800ft, while rice can be grown up to around the 2000m/6600ft. Between 1000m/3300ft and 2000m/6600ft

Banyan trees can reach huge dimensions. In India they are worshipped

a subtropical forest grows, with oak trees, pines, chestnuts, laurels and magnolias. Further down is a tropical monsoon forest (rainforest) with deciduous trees. In addition to tree ferns, many kinds of lianas, rubber trees and fig trees, this region is also home to various tropical hardwoods, such as teak. Dry bush vegetation is no rarity in the leeward basins and valleys of the high mountains. In front of the southern foot of the Himalaya is a wet and thus often marshy region with wholly impenetrable bamboo thickets and grasses up to 2m/6ft high. A few dwarf palm species also grow well here.

The **Thar desert** is one of India's most arid areas. Succulents, thorn bushes and hardy grasses as well as wild date palms grow here. Irrigated areas, such as the **Punjab** plains, can sustain the cultivation of rice, wheat, cotton and dates. While the western lowlands are still dominated by steppe vegetation, the flora becomes denser and more biodiverse towards the east, corresponding to increasing precipitation. First come the dry deciduous forests. Along the river channels there are evergreen riparian forests. The **Ganges-Brahmaputra lowlands** are used intensively for agriculture. Around 70 to 80 percent of this region is under cultivation, the most important crops being wheat, rice, sugarcane, cotton and jute. The hills of **Assam** in the eastern Himalayan foothills are among Asia's wettest regions. Large

Great diversity

WORSHIPPED AND DESTROYED

Nature worship and the worship of its many guises such as the sun, the moon, the mountains, rivers, plants and animals, was already widespread in India 5000 years ago. In popular religion and the beliefs of the Adivasis, Indian tribespeople, it is still alive and well today, and in Hinduism, too, nature also plays a central role.

Some of the Hindu deities who receive daily sacrifices of flowers and leaves have favourite plants: Vishnu prefers Tulsi, Shiva the Bilsa tree. Generally they also have vehicles in the shape of animals that are also considered holy: Brahma rides on a goose, Shiva on a bull, Durga on a lion, Vishnu on a sea eagle and Ganesha on a rat. For many thousands of years human beings' survival was very much dependent on plants. Trees offered protection from the hot sun and provided raw material for tools, hunting equipment, huts and palaces as well as firewood to prepare food. Healers founded many plants in the Indian flora whose roots, resin, leaves and seeds they used as remedies against diseases. Indians, whose agriculture is closely linked to the monsoon, already knew millennia ago that the mountain forests attracted the rain and at the same time put a brake

on its destructive power, which is why these forests were believed to be **dwelling places of the gods**. It was not just individual trees, but also certain species, groves and entire forests that were worshipped. This cult offered the necessary protection against short-sighted use by individual people. Only in special cases, e.g. for medical purposes, were leaves, branches and seeds allowed to be taken from holy trees and forests.

Sacred groves

The popular deities' shrines usually lie outside villages in remote locations. Even today such sacred groves can still be found in the vicinity of many villages. The people avoid cutting down trees and hunting animals there even in times of great need, so as not to attract the deity's wrath. The small woods are not just an **oasis for plants and animals** and a place of worship

Sacred groves are believed to be shrines of the popular deities

for humans, but also nature's medical treasure trove. Some people travel long distances, not because of the deities who are worshipped there but because of the rare plants. They do not just know the plants' names, they also know their medicinal uses. They gather leaves, bark, resin, blossoms and seeds from which they produce highly effective medications.

Even in India the development of modern society, i.e. individualization and modern consumer behaviour, are resulting in a slow decay of ancient beliefs and in a disregard for traditional authorities. The sudden breaking up of village structures usually has a destruction of the sacred groves as a consequence. Where there is no village community, there is also no care or protection for the village groves. Traditional authorities, who punished any disrespect of the religiously rooted prohibitions, are losing their influence. Thus wood is now sometimes gathered in sacred groves, and trees are also being cut down in them. Owners of adjacent fields are expanding them year after year to the detriment of the groves, without protests coming from the villages. Within just a few decades, millennia-old woods will be completely destroyed because of a desire for short-sighted financial gains (exotic wood, wood for paper production etc.).

Destruction of the natural environment

The Indian state is exacerbating this destruction through large-scale projects: dams, nuclear power plants and leather tanning works are ruining the structure of the natural environment forever. The Narmada Dam alone, which incorporates 30 large and 3000 smaller reservoirs, has flooded more than 100,000ha/250,000ac of land. This caused 40,000ha/100,000ac of forest to be destroyed and 200,000 people from 50 villages to be resettled. The dam project is meant to allow owners of large estates to modernize their agriculture.

Nevertheless the actions and beliefs of the Indian population are still marked by **great respect for all living things**. A case in point: individual trees that are considered holy are left standing in paddy fields even though they make modern cultivation more difficult. The Adivasis' resistance to dam construction on the Narmada river originates from a deep-rooted nature worship.

The **Chipko Movement**, one of the best-known environmental organizations in the world, has been trying to reduce environmental destruction in India for 30 years. They justifiably draw attention to the fact that ecology is nothing but sustainable economy.

parts of the natural forests have been logged and replaced by huge tea plantations. Characteristic of the **Ganges-Brahmaputra delta** are wholly impenetrable bamboo thickets and extensive mangrove forests, such as the **Sundarbans**. Further inland sundri trees, growing up to 30m/100ft, form entire forests. The **Malabar Coast**, which receives plentiful precipitation as a result of the summer monsoon, and the corresponding flood plains are covered by a particularly thick and varied flora. Numerous palm species, including coconut, areca and oil palms, a diverse shrub and bush vegetation (including tea, coffee and various spices such as cinnamon and tamarind) as well as sandalwood (Santalum album) and bamboo are all typical of this strip of coastline. Teak (Tectona grandis) also plays an important role. The typical natural forms of vegetation on the **Deccan plateau** are savannah, bush and steppe with teak, mahogany, Shorea robusta, acacias, flamboyant and date palms. The most important crop plants are cotton, sugarcane, rice, millet, chickpeas, hemp, linseed, peanuts and tobacco. Since the **Eastern Ghats** also receive rainfall in the winter because of the northeast monsoon, this area still has a large tropical rainforest. A lot of wet rice is cultivated here. Coconut palm forests shape the coastal landscape. The area around the mouths of the rivers are home to mangroves. Casuarinas do well along the sandy stretches of the **Coromandel Coast**. Irrigation agriculture takes place further inland. The most important crops are coconut palms, tobacco and peanuts.

Fauna

In light of the diverse natural and agricultural landscape it is not surprising that India also has a very biodiverse fauna, where all of the animals are perfectly adapted to the environment in which they are living. Between the snowy peaks of the Himalaya and the mangrove swamps of southern India there are **several thousand species** including far more than 300 mammalian species and more than 1200 species of breeding birds.

Cat and dog families

Anyone turning their thoughts to India's fauna will immediately think of **Bengal tigers**. Although they are at the top of south Asia's food chain, their population has fallen dramatically as a result of excessive hunting. It is estimated that there are only around 1400 of them still living in India today. Just a few decades ago India was home to tens of thousands of tigers. Their survival can however only be secured in special protected areas because of the continued destruction of their habitat. In 1973 »Project Tiger« (see also p.37) was set up and as a result several reserves were created in which it is prohibited to hunt tigers. It occasionally happens that tigers leave their reserve and attack livestock, such as buffaloes and cows, in which case the owner is provided with compensation. Tigers that attack or kill humans are either shot or brought to a zoo. In addition to the

As curious as any baby: a small elephant in the Training Centre in Korny

few remaining tigers India also has a few **lions**, **leopards** and **cheetahs**. However, these latter representatives of the big cat family have withdrawn to the thorn bush steppe of the west Indian state of Gujarat (Gir Wildlife Sanctuary).

India is also home to more than a dozen species of civet. Closely related to the civets are **mongooses**, which are much sought after because of their ability to fight snakes. There are still a few **striped hyenas** to be seen in the west Indian Gir sanctuary. The main territory of canine species, however, is the Deccan plateau, where packs of dholes (also known as Indian wild dogs) and numerous Bengal foxes still hunt. Some of the last few Indian **wolves** still live in Veldavar National Park and the grasslands are home to the **golden jackal**, one of the last important scavengers.

Three bear species call India home, the most famous being the endemic **sloth bear**. With a bit of luck members of this species can be seen in the west Indian Gir sanctuary as well as in the Kumbhalgarh Wildlife Sanctuary.

Bears

Deer, antelopes and gazelles

Still widely distributed and appreciated as quarry by both big cats and humans are the even-toed ungulates, of which there are more than 30 species at home in India, such as the four-horned antelope (chousigha) and the blackbuck. The latter is now threatened by extinction due to over-hunting. One species worth particular mention is the **nilgai**, which, with a shoulder height of 1.50m/5ft, is amongst the largest antelopes in the world. In the grass and marsh landscapes surrounded by monsoon forests there are also barasinghas with their powerful antlers, as well as chitals and hog deer. Other cloven-hoofed animals include various wild goats and wild sheep. Even today the marsh grasslands of the Himalayan foothills are home to numerous **gaur** (wild cattle), buffaloes and wild boars.

Pachyderms: rhinoceroses and elephants

Elephants and rhinoceroses enjoy the impenetrable bamboo thickets and marshy grasslands. The **Indian rhinoceros** is, however, threatened with extinction. The only populations of note live in Kaziranga National Park. **Indian elephants** are becoming rarer and rarer in the wild, since their habitat, the jungle, has been greatly reduced in size. The Asian elephant was domesticated as a riding and working animal as early as the third millennium BC. Indian elephants still prove their value today in impenetrable terrain, for example for the forestry industry. They grow to a height of 3m/10ft and can weigh between three and five tons. The head, ears and tusks are smaller than those of their African relatives. Indian elephants live as couples or in small herds comprising around a dozen animals (Baedeker Special p.606).

Monkeys

There are still more than a dozen different species of primate living in India. Those most frequently sighted are langurs, macaques, bonnet macaques and **rhesus monkeys**. This latter species enjoys special protection in some temples and can even be found in quite large numbers in the towns and cities.

Birds

As has already been mentioned, India boasts a particularly rich birdlife. Of the more than 1200 breeding bird species at least 160 are endemic. During the winter the number of bird species increases to more than 2000, when the migratory birds from central Asia arrive. India's national bird is the **peacock**, which can still often be seen in the wild, but which is also kept as a »pet«. These large birds lose their impressive plumage during the wintertime moult, and as a result souvenirs covered in peacock feathers can be obtained everywhere.

Snakes and crocodiles

More than 500 species of reptile call the south Asian subcontinent home. Snakes make up the largest reptilian group, containing more than 200 species, of which more than 50 are venomous. Wherever small game can be hunted, **cobras** are not far away. India's most famous snake, the very poisonous cobra is a synanthrope, i.e. it thrives in areas inhabited by humans. On the one hand these are highly revered animals, on the other they are also put on display by many snake charmers. Cobras can grow to several metres in length and are considered to be quite aggressive. India's largest venomous snake is the king cobra, which can grow up to 5m/16.4ft long and is particularly at home in the country's dense jungle. Watch out, too, for kraits (bungaruses), carpet vipers and in particular for the many pit vipers and other vipers that live practically everywhere. Common inhabitants of the large wetlands are **mugger crocodiles**. The same is true of **saltwater crocodiles**, which particularly like the remote mangrove forests near the river mouths on the Bay of Bengal.

Fish

Indian waters provide a habitat to more than 2000 different species of fish. The best-known is probably the mullet. Sharks are also fairly common, including hammerhead and whale sharks.

Why cows are sacred in India

It is hard for Europeans to understand why cows are considered sacred, inviolable animals. However, cows were not always worshipped in India. Vedic texts report that beef was eaten and cows were sacrificed. However, when Indo-Aryan settlers came to the region and

Not just beautiful, but loud too: thanks to their good hearing and sense of smell peacocks can give each other early warning of danger

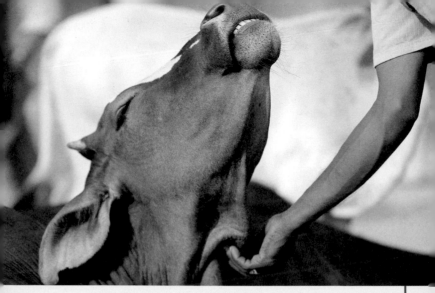

Holy animal, hard worker, beloved pet: cows in India

started farming, cows developed a central significance. Humans did not just benefit from them as working animals that pulled the plough; cows also provided milk, as well as dung, which was used as a building material and fuel. In addition to these purely pragmatic reasons there was the Buddhist influence of ahimsa, a tenet barring violence to living beings. Both of these components ultimately led to a prohibition on killing cows. The costs and benefits of cows are also the subject of new studies, particularly with regard to the fact that many people in India are suffering from famine: an Indian farmer needs at least three cows to survive, namely two draught animals and one cow to supply calves. If this farmer then has to sell or even slaughter one of these cows during a period of drought to make ends meet, he does not have many options the following year but to also sell his land – without animals he cannot cultivate his land and does not have the money to buy new cattle. The conclusion is obvious: cattle are worth significantly more as working animals than they are as food on the plate, quite regardless of the fact that the meat would be too expensive for most people in India, given the cost-intensive nature of rearing cows. What is more, the necessary pastureland is also absent.

Animal Protection and National Parks

History The concept of animal protection is a very old one in India. As early as the third century BC Emperor Ashoka, who had converted to Buddhism, passed laws to protect animals. Plants and animals play an important role in all of India's significant religions. Many animals, such as cows, monkeys, elephants, cobras, eagles and peacocks have enjoyed religious worship for millennia.

Under Mughal rule hunting became a royal privilege that was kept up by the Rajput rulers and the British. In addition to blood sports, the destruction of forests and an intensification of agriculture led to a severe fall in the number of species living in India. The first sanctuaries were set up under the British (Vedanthangal), while the Jim Corbett National Park or Corbett Tiger Reserve, founded in 1936, was the country's first national park. After India's independence many of the princes' and maharajas' former hunting grounds were converted into sanctuaries, but it was not until the **Indian Wildlife Protection Act** came into effect in 1972 that a legal framework was set up to ensure a comprehensive protection scheme of the natural environment.

Sanctuaries and national parks

There is a distinction made in India between »sanctuaries« and »national parks«. Sanctuaries are designed to protect the plants and animals living in it, but the areas are often also inhabited by people. National parks are core zones reserved just for animals, with extra protection provided by a buffer zone. In addition sanctuaries and national parks have been designated as tiger reserves within the framework of »Project Tiger«, which receive extra money for staff and equipment.

Project Tiger

It has only been thanks to the big »Project Tiger« campaign that the complete extinction of this beast of prey has been prevented. The project, the means for which were primarily raised in India itself, is considered as one of the most successful examples of saving a threatened species in the world. The approach here was not to focus on tigers alone, but rather to support a complex natural system. That was the only way in which the tiger, at the end of a long food chain, could be protected effectively. The likelihood of setting eyes on a tiger is greatest in the Jim Corbett, Kanha and Bandhavgarh national parks.

Population · Politics · Economy

More than a billion people

India is currently home to 1.1 billion people. This makes India the **second most populous country in the world after China**. 2.4% of the world's surface is occupied by 17% of the Earth's population. The population density is 348 inhabitants per sq km/901 per sq mi (2004); for comparison, the United Kingdom has 249 inhabitants per sq km/644 per sq mi. This statistic does not, however, say much about the actual distribution of the Indian population. The fertile river valleys (Ganges, Brahmaputra, Krishna etc.) and the rainy coastal landscapes of the Malabar and Coromandel Coasts have population densities of up to 1000 people per sq km/2590 per sq mi. Amongst India's states West Bengal (904 per sq km/2341 per sq mi) and Kerala (819 per sq km/2121 per sq mi) are the most densely populated, whereas Arunachal Pradesh has the lowest population density (13 per sq km/33 per sq mi). India has a **high proportion of young people** in its population: 32.7% were younger than 15 at the time of the 2001 census; only 4.7% were older than 65. The life expectancy in India increased from 32 years (1951) to 62 (men) and 63 (women). Population is growing at a rate of 1.9%. In around 2050 India will pass China as the world's most populous country. The average life expectancy in India is 64 years.

Ethnic composition

Like almost no other country on Earth, India is characterized by its **ethnic, cultural and linguistic diversity**. The majority of the population is of Indo-Aryan origin (descendants of ethnic groups who migrated here from central Asia); the other important group, the Dravidian population, is concentrated in the southern states of Tamil Nadu, Karnataka, Andhra Pradesh and Kerala. In addition Mongolian peoples (Naga, Bodo and Mizo) inhabit the northeastern Himalayan regions. There are also numerous other tribal groups in central India. It is estimated that these groups (Adivasis) comprise around 80 million people.

22 Indian languages

There are 22 main and regional languages in India recognized by the constitution. They can be divided into two main groups: the Indo-Aryan languages prevalent in northern India (e.g. Hindi, Bengali, Gujarati, Marathi, Urdu) and the Dravidian languages (Tamil, Telugu, Malayalam and Kannada) spoken in the south. In addition there are many more languages and dialects. **Hindi**, spoken primarily in northern India and written in the Devanagari script, is one of the country's official languages. The central government's attempt to make Hindi the official language in the whole of India has not, however, been overly successful. The states in southern India have always resisted the spread of Hindi as a lingua franca.

In fact, the colonial language **English** is the lingua franca. Important newspapers are published in English and many schools and universities also teach in English. The introduction of satellite television with English and/or American stations has further accelerated this development. The relative pervasiveness of the English language makes it easy for travellers to be understood almost everywhere in the country.

Education

Education in India is marked by stark contrasts. More than a third of the population are still unable to read or write. The 2001 census showed **an average literacy rate of 64.8%**, the figure being approximately 75% for men and approximately 54% for women. This census also determined that 65 million 6–14-year-olds do not attend

Going to school: not yet self-evident for all children

school. There are, however, great regional differences here. Attendance is particularly low in the poor, populous states such as Bihar and Uttar Pradesh; in Kerala, which is comparatively rich, almost all children go to school. The figures also vary greatly depending on whether the region is rural or urban, because many rural areas have only few schools and classes may not take place on a regular basis.

While on the one hand India's primary schools are in much need of improvement, the country boasts **excellent higher education institutions** and is already being called an »educational power of the future«. Around ten million students attend the approximately 300 universities in India. Some of them are elite universities, such as the Indian Institute of Technology (ITT) and the Indian Institute of Management, which are among the best universities in the world. Indian specialists with excellent qualifications can now be found in many professional sectors, particularly in the software industry – in terms of numbers Indians are the second largest group in this sector after Americans. Until recently many Indian experts emigrated, but the tide is turning because the salaries for experts have risen in India. The country's high population and the continuing large-scale investments into higher education will bring about a rapid increase in highly qualified Indian workers over the next few years, so that the term »educational power« could be exceptionally appropriate. One crucial factor in determining the country's development across the entire social spectrum will be to what extent the state will invest in better education and training of the disadvantaged members of society and in particular the degree to which it will fund the neglected primary school sector.

Indian society displays great social differences. The rapid economic development of recent decades has led to a growing middle class in India. It is estimated that it now comprises 300 to 400 million people. Their buying power expresses itself in the rapidly rising number

Social differences

Glittering dreams of the future and sobering reality

of cars and the booming shopping and entertainment centres as well as a growing tourism industry, amongst other things. On the other hand in 2004 44% of the Indian population lived below the poverty line as defined by the UN. These people have no firm roof over their head, no access to sufficient healthcare, no clean drinking water and a non-existent or inadequate education. Here too there are large regional differences. Richer states such as Kerala or Punjab provide significantly better care for their population than for example the poorer states of Bihar and Rajasthan.

The Indian population has quadrupled over the past century. Of the more than a billion people around 70% live in villages and around 30% in towns and cities. Mega-cities such as Mumbai with 16 million people or Kolkata with 13 million pose a manifold of challenges to the state. However, the improvements in infrastructure are hardly keeping up with the **growth of the cities**. Supplying water and energy to the urban population is becoming increasingly difficult and the traffic situation in some places is close to collapse, such as in Bangalore for example.

Child labour Poverty also expresses itself in India in the number of children that work because they have to contribute to the family income. According to the 2001 census the figure has risen by more than a million to 12.66 million since 1991. However, unofficial estimates suggest this number is more likely to be around **25 to 30 million**. Around 90% of them live in rural areas. The number of working children is particularly high in India's most populous state of Uttar Pradesh. They work in agriculture, but also in glass factories, weaving mills and especially in the carpet industry. Non-governmental organizations and the state have tried for decades to improve the situation of children here. Indian and foreign non-governmental organizations have been running a campaign for more than ten years, fighting child labour in carpet industry.

Women in India

There is no shortage of famous and highly educated women in India. Indira Gandhi was India's prime minister for many years, and author and activist Arundhati Roy fights for the rights of the disadvantaged population. The airline Air India has seventeen female pilots, and operated an »All Women Flight« from Mumbai to Singapore on 8 March 2004, International Women's Day. In 1997 Kalpana Chawla (by then a naturalized American) became the first Indian woman in space, part of the crew of six on the Space Shuttle Columbia. Women in India are ministers and software specialists, they run business empires and make films. However, just like their fellow women in the west, they are underrepresented in the leading areas of politics and the economy. A growing number of women and girls are now enjoying higher education. Unfortunately however the majority of Indian women are still subject to immense **sexual discrimination**: this is expressed for example in the higher illiteracy rate amongst

An initiative to support women and children

women (46%) compared with men (25%) in the 2001 census. The good news is that the number of women who are learning to read and write is growing faster than the corresponding figure for men.

One particularly severe form of discrimination can be seen by the fact that there are **more men than women** in India. In 2001 there were 933 women for every 1000 men. This gender ratio is even wider in children under the age of six. In 2001, 927 girls were born for every 1000 boys; in 1991 it was still 945 girls for every 1000 boys. The increasing number of abortion clinics has correlated with an increasing number of aborted foetuses that were female, a sign of the continuing discrimination against women in a society in which the birth of a daughter is still considered a misfortune by many because it is looked on as a financial burden, while the birth of a son is celebrated as a joyful event. The consequence of all this, i.e. that there are not enough women out there for the marriageable men, has allowed a particular crime to flourish: the trafficking of women. Girls from poor families are sold to families in which no wife has been found for the son or sons.

Most marriages in India are still arranged, as is the country's tradition. This means the families of the prospective bride and groom negotiate and make the decision, not the man and woman entering the marriage. One burden for the woman's family is often the demand of a **dowry**, i.e. financial or material gifts for the groom and his family, where she will live after the wedding. Indian newspapers regularly report one of the shocking by-products of this system: dowry murder. Since the demands for material goods and money continue in some families even after the marriage ceremony, the woman is subjected to many kinds of harassment. In the worst cases it ends in a so-called dowry murder, where the woman is killed by the husband or parents-in-law out of greed.

Many Indian women, however, have been raising their voices **against oppression, humiliation and disadvantage**. Having set up their own organizations and with the support of the many non-governmental organizations active in the whole country, women are trying to change their lives and achieve more self-determination.

Healthcare   Life expectancy in India has risen continuously in recent decades. In 2004 the infant mortality rate (under one year) was 62 deaths per 1000 births. Bad hygienic conditions, particularly contaminated drinking water, still cause around 400,000 children under the age of five to die of diarrhoea-related problems every year. According to UNICEF figures only 30% of the population have access to adequate sanitary facilities; there is a big gap in this regard between urban and rural areas (58% in urban areas, 18% in rural areas). Diseases like hepatitis A, tuberculosis, typhoid and malaria are widespread. AIDS is a steadily increasing threat. Every third child in India is classed as malnourished. The **link between poverty and disease** becomes particularly clear here. When it comes to healthcare there is once again

Street dentist in Rajasthan

a big regional gap between richer and poorer states as well as the cities. Metropolises such as Mumbai, Delhi and Bangalore have excellently equipped hospitals, and some of them even solicit patients from overseas.

India has several **traditional systems of medicine**, the most famous being **Ayurveda, Siddha and Unani**. The Indian state supports traditional medicine and it plays a major role in the country, particularly amongst the rural population, which often has little or no access to modern medicine. Not least because of Western interest in it, Ayurveda has seen a revival in its country of origin. Ayurvedic treatment is available all over India, particularly in Kerala (▶ Practicalities, Ayurveda).

Politics

The Republic of India (Bharat Juktarashtra) is a **parliamentary federation** whose federal framework retains significant centralized elements. It consists of **28 federal states** and seven centrally governed union territories (see map p.44). The capital of India is New Delhi. The federal states are further subdivided into districts, which in turn are split into tehsils and then villages. Many federal states also use a political arrangement known as the panchayat system, where administrative issues are dealt with on a village level by village councils (panchayats) and village parliaments (gram sabhas). Decision-making authority is distributed according to these different levels. With 1.1 billion inhabitants, India is the most populous democracy in the world.

Most populous democracy in the world

Constitution India's new constitution came into effect on 26 January 1950. Large sections of it make use of the draft formulated in 1935. For that reason its main features bear great similarities to the British constitution. The Indian constitution is based on the **basic notion of a secular democracy**. The freedoms of thought, expression and religion are laid down in it. The right to equality of status and opportunity were

India States · Union Territories

© Baedeker

also included and a special article deals with the abolition of »un-touchability«, an issue where principle and reality are still far apart. The state is trying, however, to improve the opportunities for "scheduled (i.e. disadvantaged) castes and tribes" in the public service sector by introducing quotas.

Legislation is enacted by the parliament, which consists of **two chambers**, the Lok Sabha (House of the People) and the Rajya Sabha (Rajya Sabha). The place where political decisions are actually made is the Lok Sabha. In addition to the general courts there are **special arrangements in civil law for the individual faith groups**. This means that judicial decisions about marriage, divorce, inheritance, alimony, guardianship and adoption can be settled within the individual religious groups, a concession on the part of the state that leads to constant political controversies. The Indian army is a **professional army** with 1.3 million soldiers. The problem of competition between the state machinery and the military or even the danger of a military coup has never surfaced in India. The army's commander-in-chief is the defence minister, whose post is as a matter of principle only given to civilian politicians, i.e. never to generals or ex-generals. Since 1974 India has been a **nuclear power**. *Legislative, judiciary and military*

India has a colourful array of political parties. In the last elections of 2004, 220 parties and 5435 candidates ran for the 543 seats in the Lok Sabha. In addition to the two major parties, the Indian National Congress and the Indian People's Party or BJP (Bharatiya Janata Party), many regional parties and groups representing the interests of certain sections of the population or castes also ran. *Parties and government*

The party the most rich in tradition is the **Indian National Congress**. It is currently in charge of the government under Prime Minister Manmohan Singh in a coalition with the United Progressive Alliance. Since India's independence in 1947 it has provided most of the country's prime ministers, several of which have come from the Nehru-Gandhi dynasty (Jawaharlal Nehru, his daughter Indira Gandhi and her son Rajiv Gandhi).

The **Bharatiya Janata Party** is currently the second largest party in India. It was in government between 1998 and 2004, when it was replaced by the Indian National Congress. The BJP is the parliamentary arm of the Hindutva movement (Hindutva means »hindu-ness«), which puts the cultural interests of Hindus above those of other religions and wants to undermine the secular state. The third largest influence is the **Communist Party of India**. It has formed the governments in the states of Kerala and West Bengal for many years.

Amongst the various **regional parties** and groups representing the interests of certain castes or segments of the population are the Samajwadi Party and the Rashtriya Janata Dal as the representatives of the lower castes and the Bahujan Samaj Party as the representative of the scheduled castes, scheduled tribes and other disadvantaged

Election campaign event of the Congress Party in Delhi:
the old leaders are brought out

groups. The Dravidian parties, led by the DMK (Dravida Munnetra Kazagham) from Tamil Nadu, also have political clout.

Aspiring new global power India is the most significant regional power in south Asia. As an aspiring new global power the country has also made a bid to become a permanent member of the UN Security Council. It now has a close relationship to the United States, as well as to the EU and also to Russia. The most difficult foreign-policy issues for India are its relationship to its neighbour Pakistan and the **unresolved Kashmir dispute**. In recent times the two states have made some small inroads regarding this matter. Domestically, India has struggled with the **issue of communalism**: certain parties such as the above-mentioned BJP regularly attempt to pit various religious groups against each other. This results in a flare-up of confrontations, some of them violent, between Hindus and Muslims in particular, which rattle the state's secular foundations.

Economy

After independence Centuries of colonial rule left India's economy in a largely desolate state. After becoming independent India, under its first prime minister Jawaharlal Nehru, decided to pursue socialistically-oriented economic policies. Important key industries such as heavy industry, mining, transport, communication and energy were nationalized.

Other economic areas such as the consumer-goods industry and agriculture were left to the private sector. This »mixed economy« was supplemented by protectionist measures that shielded the domestic market from the world market.

The first phase, from 1947 to 1966, was shaped by India's push to promote heavy industry through massive investment, an attempt at **rapid industrialization**. Nehru saw the new industries as the Indian population's future temples, while the agricultural sector was largely ignored. However droughts in 1965–66 and the 1965 war with Pakistan led to a famine, which drew dramatic attention to the neglect of agriculture, and after the revision of the five-year plans **agriculture was given more support** in the second phase, starting in 1966. A raft of different measures was aimed at increasing production. Modernization of agriculture in the 1970s, a phenomenon termed the **Green Revolution**, brought about a significant expansion of the irrigated area, increased mechanization and an intensified use of artificial fertilizers, pesticides and modern high-yielding crops. Success expressed itself in constantly growing food production. In contrast to earlier years in which India had to import grain, it can now export it. However, the Green Revolution also had its downsides. Despite increased yields and the subsidized sale of staple foods, many people spend their lives on the edge of the subsistence minimum. One of the causes for this is the unequal distribution of land. Since the colonial period a small group of landowners have controlled a large proportion of the country's agricultural land.

After decades of economic policies oriented to socialist principles and the domestic market India underwent an **economic liberalization** in 1991. As the result of a balance of payments crisis the Rao government decided to open India to the world market, using parameters set by the IMF. After initially timid growth India has achieved growth rates of 6 to 8% in recent years and **is expected to become a leading economic power in the future together with China**. Around a third of India's 1.1 billion inhabitants are considered middle class. Around the world, boom regions such as the southern Indian metropolises of Bangalore and Hyderabad stand for India's outstanding role in the software industry – almost one in three IT experts now comes from India. The aerospace industry and the field of genetic research, as well as that of nuclear research, are all areas where India has become a market leader. However, the economic centres that have developed around the country's big cities stand in stark contrast to the many neglected and underdeveloped rural regions. The social reality of large parts of society is trailing far behind the country's successful economic balance sheet. The newly founded states of Chhattisgarh and Jharkand, which are inhabited mainly by indigenous tribes (Adivasis), have so far not felt much of the economic and social improvements. The average per capita income in 2004 was stated to be US$ 572, but to put this into perspective it

Transformation into a market economy: India as a new economic power

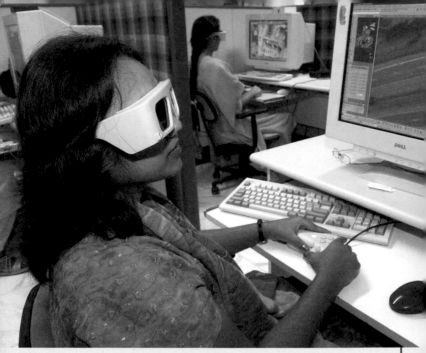

Growing trend: one IT specialist in three currently comes from India

should be added that more than 35% of the population still have to make do with less than a dollar a day.

Important economic sectors

India is still a country of villages; that is where 79% of its inhabitants live, and two-thirds of all economically active people work in **arable and livestock farming**. 43% of the country's land area is agricultural land, but less than a third of the country's GDP is generated here, most farmers working solely to meet their own needs. Rice is the most important crop. Other grains such as wheat and millet as well as oilseed crops are also significant, and further typical crops include sugarcane, cotton, tea and jute. Fluctuations in yield are common, since they are greatly dependent on the monsoon rains. Livestock farming is also important in India. It is estimated there are almost 200 million cattle in India, which is more than in any other country on Earth. Buffalo, goats and camels also play a big role, both as working animals and as a food source.

Inshore and open sea fishing have become increasingly significant. The fleets were modernized within the framework of the Blue Revolution, while fish-farms have been set up along the coasts. The export of fish and crabs brings in much sought-after foreign currency. Freshwater fishing plays an important role for Indians as it provides them with a good source of protein.

Forestry is also flourishing: India's forests are increasingly being cut down for industrial purposes (paper and furniture) and the poorer people in society are cutting down trees to cover their own need for firewood. Since state-run afforestation programmes can hardly keep up with the logging activities the proportion of land covered in forest is constantly decreasing. It is estimated that 2.5 million ha/620,000ac (0.76% of the land area) of forest are lost in India every year. For that reason the mountainous regions are already displaying **significant damage caused by erosion**. While the government's target is to maintain 33% of India's land area as forest, only 23% of the country is still forested. Time and again the inhabitants of the forest regions protest against the destruction of the forests through peaceful resistance. In some cases, as in the case of the **Chipko movement**, the campaigns have been successful.

Rich coal deposits allow the country to be relatively self-sufficient with regard to **energy** (almost 90%). In addition to coal, petroleum products, water and nuclear power all play an important role. Crude oil is mainly imported, despite increased extraction, thus straining the balance of payments.

It takes many hands to shoe a cow

The **industrial sector** employs around 14% of the economically active population and produces around a quarter of the GDP. Among India's highly developed industries are aerospace, arms, pharmaceuticals and of course software. India's key industries are the steel and cotton industries, the chemical industry and the textiles industry. Sugar, tobacco, leather goods and paper are also produced in large quantities.

The booming **service sector** employs around a fifth of the workforce. This sector is, however, responsible for **half of the annual GDP**. This is partly due to the many »outsourcing« offers Indian service companies make to foreign businesses. From operating call centres to writing bills for insurance companies and filing tax returns, India's services now reach customers all around the world.

One area of the Indian economy that should not be overlooked is the **huge informal sector** of self-made service jobs, from street vendors and shoe shiners to maids. Around 300 to 400 million people work in this sector.

Religion

India's faiths The vast majority of the Indian population (80.5%) are Hindus. However, almost all other world religions are also represented in India. Of these religions Islam has the most followers (with 13.4%) followed by Christianity, Sihkism and Jainism. Buddhists,and Parsis are represented as small religious communities.

Hinduism

The term Hinduism was coined by Europeans and is a **collective term for the many faiths** held by the inhabitants of the subcontinent. For that reason it is also difficult to offer a precise description of Hinduism. These days this faith, in its traditional expression, incorporates Shaivism, Vaishnavism and Shaktism as well as further elements such as the worship of nature and traditional deities. It has been stressed many times that Hinduism is more of a way of life than a religion. In contrast to other world religions Hinduism has **no founder or prophets and no fixed doctrine**. Hinduism is rather characterized by a diversity that often perplexes Western visitors.

History Hinduism is one of the world's oldest religions. Its roots reach back to the 3rd millennium BC. Thus, a famous soapstone seal from the **Harappa period** (2500–1700 BC), which depicts a three-faced man with horns in a meditative posture, is interpreted to be a prototype of the Hindu god Shiva. The originally nomadic **Aryan immigrants**

The diversity of India's religions shapes the subcontinent →

settled northern India's river valleys around 1000 BC. Over the course of several centuries their beliefs merged with those of the **original Dravidian population groups** into a collective whole now called Hinduism. The first stage of this synthesis process is labelled the **Vedic period** because the beliefs of that time were written down in the holy scriptures, the Vedas (knowledge). Originally the Vedas were passed down through oral tradition by rishis (seers); later, between 1000 BC and AD 500, the important texts were written down. The oldest of these works is the **Rig Veda**, a collection of more than 1000 hymns written in the old Indo-Germanic language Sanskrit, addressed to important nature deities such as Indra, Agni and Varuna. Later on, the **Brahmanas** were created, which describe how certain rituals in honour of the gods have to be performed. These scriptures were reserved exclusively for Brahmins, i.e. the priests. They alone had the power to perform these rituals and thus to appease the gods. The last works to be created were the Aranyakas (aranya = forest), whose secret character meant they were taught in lonely areas such as forests. Among the Aranyakas are the **Upanishads**, which focus less on ritual than on philosophy.

Samsara, karma and moksha A central and recurrent theme in the extensive scriptures of the Upanishads is the idea of the **oneness of the universal soul and the indi-**

Tree temple with Shiva, Parvati and Nandi

vidual soul, as well as other important ideas such as **samsara (rebirth)**, **karma (repayment for actions)** and **moksha (salvation)**. The cyclical notion of birth, death and rebirth is a fundamental part of all Indian religions. An individual soul (atman) changes bodies and goes from one life to the next until it finally becomes one with the universal soul (Brahman), which brings salvation (moksha), whereby it is liberated from this cycle of rebirths. The cycle of birth and rebirth is determined by karma, the principle of cause and effect. Thoughts and actions in this life are responsible for one's fate in the next life. In order to achieve salvation Hindus have to **fulfill conscientiously and completely all of the duties (dharma) imposed on them**. People's duties are dependent on their caste, as is illustrated in the Bhagavad Gita, a classical work of later Brahman Hinduism.

The old Dharma Shastra scriptures, which were written down at the same time as the Vedas, contain descriptions of four social groups, each labelled by a **varna (colour)**. Each of these groups has a fixed place in society as well as certain religious and social duties. The Aryans, who had conquered the country at the time, naturally put themselves right at the top of the social hierarchy. The four varnas are Brahmins (priests), Kshatriyas (warriors and rulers), Vaishyas (merchants and farmers) and Shudras (servants). The first three groups are those who have been born twice in the eternal cycle of birth and rebirth. Performing the rituals and studying the scriptures is reserved for them. The last group is outside of the Hindu social system; the people allocated to this group are the ones performing impure tasks. In addition to the varnas there are also **jatis (castes)**. Since there are around 3000 of them, jatis allow for more detailed classification. Every jati, which is always associated with an occupation, places a large number of rules on its members, such as the choice of foods, the religious duties to be performed and the correct way to treat members from other castes. Initially it was not permitted to marry someone from another case and a breach of this rule was severely sanctioned.

Hindu social system

After the end of the Vedic period (approximately 800 BC) the Puranas and the **great epics the Mahabharata and the Ramayana** were created, which glorify the deeds of the deities and describe the central ideas of Hinduism. The two central deities Vishnu and Shiva became more important. However, many other deities and their vahanas (vehicles), which make the Hindu pantheon so confusing for the uninitiated, were also developed during this time. These Brahman deities, which Hindus worship directly in religious devotion (bhakti), still have a great significance today.

Brahman Hinduism

Vishnu is considered to be the god of mercy and benevolence. He is the **supreme god, who maintains the eternal order of the universe**. In his various incarnations (avatars), Vishnu keeps returning to the

Vaishnavism

world to save it when it is being threatened by demonic powers. Vishnu is worshipped in all of his **ten incarnations**, which are frequently represented in Vishnu temples. The first three incarnations are Matsya (fish), Kurma (tortoise) and Vahara (boar), the fourth being Narashimha (half lion, half human). After that, Vishnu appeared in human form as Vamana (dwarf) and Parashurama (hero). Vishnu's seventh and eighth incarnations as Rama and Krishna are the most popular. In the ninth he was Buddha and the tenth incarnation as Kalki is still to come. Vishnu took on the incarnation of **Krishna** in order to save the world from an evil demon. He is a key figure in the Mahabharata where, acting as a charioteer, he helps the Pandyan dynasty fight the Kauravas. The flute-playing blue Krishna was worshipped by Hindu women and the relationship with his lover Radha has served as a popular subject for poetry and the visual arts.

Shaivism Shiva is one of India's oldest deities and was already worshipped by non-Aryans 3000 years ago in the form of Rudra. In the age of the Brahmanas and Upanishads (800–300 BC) he was unified with other deities and has since embodied various aspects in his different forms (Murtis). Thus it is not surprising that he is called by 1008 names by believers. He is considered to be the **great yogi, god of fertility, master of the dead and of destruction**. In contrast to Vishnu he is represented in his fundamental form as the great yogi, dressed in nothing but a loincloth made of a tiger's hide and decorated with a crescent moon. His **accompanying animal, the bull (Nandi)**, is often set up in front of the main temple for Shiva. Further animals with which he is associated are the snake, a symbol of fertility and life energy, and the gazelle, which carries him as the master of all animals and living things, particularly in southern Indian depictions.

One of his most popular forms in southern India is **Nataraja**, the Lord of Dance. This form was represented in masterly fashion in the bronze art of southern India. It is said he created the world through his cosmic dance and will one day destroy it again. He holds a flame in one hand, a symbol of destruction and renewal; in the other he holds a drum in the shape of an hourglass, with which he sets the rhythm of the universe. He is dancing on a dwarf, interpreted as a demon of uncertainty. Shiva is the enlightened one, who has understood the inner truth of the world through meditation, a fact which is symbolized by his third eye. Another form in which Shiva is worshipped is that of **Linga**, the phallic symbol, which projects out of the Yoni, a ring-shaped pedestal symbolizing the female sexual organ. Linga and Yoni are venerated in many Shiva temples.

Shaktism Shaktism is the name given to a branch of Hinduism that developed relatively late; it ascribes all divine action to a **female force**. According to this principle the forces behind the male deities such as Shiva and Vishnu are also female. This theology was fully developed between the 5th and 7th centuries AD. It generally identified activity (potency) with Shakti, who stands in the polar contrast to consciousness, which is said to be male. Many local goddesses and mother deities widespread amongst India's tribal population were unified in the Shakti cult. In the 11th century Shakti was defined by her followers as the highest power of all, with Shiva and Vishnu subordinate to her. To this day the Shakti cult is still very influential in regions such as Bengal, Assam, Orissa and Gujarat.

The four-headed **Brahma** is the personification of the universal spirit Brahman and one of the three highest deities (trimurti). He is believed to be the creator god. These days there are hardly any temples specially designated for Brahma; he is usually worshipped together with other deities. The annual Pushkar festival in Rajasthan is celebrated in honour of Brahma. Various female deities are called **Devi** (goddess). The most important of her numerous guises are **Uma, Parvati, Durga, Kali and Bhairavi**. She unifies both motherly and loving as well asghastly aspects. Her destructive side is most clearly reflected in the bloodthirsty Kali, who is particularly worshipped in Bengal. One of the most common representations of her shows her as a Mahishasuramardini, as she kills Mahisha or Mahishasura, a demon in the guise of a buffalo. **Ganesha**, son of Shiva and Parvati, is doubtless the most popular god in India. There is almost no temple in which

Further important deities

Mahishasuramardini: Durga, sitting on a lion, kills the buffalo demon

he is not worshipped. He is considered the great helper of people overcoming obstacles, which is why he is also invoked at all major events such as weddings, journeys, the building of a house or exams. In addition he is also the god of wisdom and learning. His two wives are called Siddhi (success) and Buddhi (intuitive intelligence) and his vehicle (vahana) is a rat (▶ Baedeker Special p.606). **Hanuman** is the advisor of the monkey king Sugriva from the Ramayana. As Rama's loyal servant he helps him in his battle against the demon king Ravana. **Lakshmi** is Vishnu's consort and is considered the goddess of wealth and affluence. She is depicted on a lotus blossom, either in a standing or sitting position; gold coins fall out of one of her four hands. She has many different guises, of which Sita and Radha are the most important. **Sarasvathi** is the personification of a sacred river that has now run dry. She became Brahman's first wife and is thought to be the goddess of knowledge and the arts. She is holding a musical instrument in her hand. **Skanda**, Shiva's second son, is worshipped as the god of war (also under the names Kartikeya, Subramaniya or Murugan). The six-headed deity carries different weapons in his many arms, but the lance is the most characteristic. His vehicle is a peacock on which he flies through the air. **Surya**, the sun god, is depicted as a handsome youth in a chariot. Important temples in his honour can be found in Modhera and Konark.

Priest preparing the pujas

Many Hindus have a corner or a room in their house containing a **Hindu worship**
small shrine with depictions of deities they particularly worship. **Rit-**
uals (pujas) are performed on a daily basis or on holidays in honour
of the gods. In addition to singing and reading from sacred texts,
flowers and food can also be given as an offering. Fire and water,
being purifying elements, play an important role. The numerous
temples are visited by pilgrims on a more or less regular basis. Priests
(pujaris) perform rituals, recite Sanskrit dictums and share out **pra-**
sad (consecrated food) amongst the believers. In return the believers
give the temple money or natural produce such as coconuts and ghee
(clarified butter). **Pilgrimages** are a central component of the practice of the Hindu faith. Since Hinduism does not have regular sermons or prayers they are the only way to participate in collective religious experiences. Hundreds of thousands set off every year to seek
out particularly holy places, which are mostly located along a river
or by the sea and which are associated with the central deities Vishnu
and Shiva. The most holy place is **Varanasi** on the banks of the
Ganges. A bath in the holy river or cremating the dead here, subsequently dispersing the ashes, are believed to offer good prospects of
being saved from the eternal cycle of birth and rebirth (► Baedeker
Special p.290). In addition to Varanasi, India has seven holy cities,
which are Haridwar, Mathura, Ayodhya, Ujjain, Dwarka and Kanchipuram. However, many other towns are important centres of pilgrimage, such as Puri, Rameshwaram, Srirangam and Pushkar. Anyone going to these places can still feel the vital force of Hinduism
there.

Jainism

The founder of Jainism, Mahavira (born 599 BC) was a near con- **Mahavira**
temporary of Buddha. He is considered to be the last of **24 ford-**
makers (Tirthankaras), who have found salvation. Like Buddha, he
came from a noble household and was dissatisfied with the outdated
caste system and the special standing of the Brahmins, who performed sacrificial rituals to mediate between humans and the gods.

Like Hinduism, Jainism recognizes the cycle of rebirths and the exis- **Salvation**
tence of a universal soul, but in contrast to Hinduism Jainism be-
lieves plants and animals also have souls. Jainas do not believe in a
god who controls world events; instead, they believe only in the law
of karma. The only way to overcome the **eternal cycle of birth and**
rebirth is through asceticism, meditation and the performance of
pure deeds. The significance of meditation for this faith can be seen
in the depictions of the Tirthankaras, who are all shown in a meditative pose.

This is also the reason why ahimsa, the **avoidance of violence to liv-** **Ahimsa**
ing beings, is a central element of this teaching. Some Jain monks

Some Jains wear a mask to prevent them inhaling an insect by accident

cover their nose and mouth to prevent themselves from inhaling an insect by accident. They also keep a broom with them at all times to clean the place they want to sit from any small living things. There are two types of monks, **Digambars (air-clad)**, who go without clothing and usually stay in the monasteries and **Shwetambars (white-clad)**. Their respect for all living things prevents Jainas from taking up various jobs, including agricultural ones. Many of them have turned towards intellectual activities or trade and have a significant amount of influence despite their small number of approximately 4.5 million. Most of them live in Gujarat.

Places of pilgrimage The Jain temples, which believers travel great distances to visit, contain the various Tirthankaras, which all look very similar and can only be distinguished by small symbols. Important temples can be found in Gujarat (Shatrunajaya and Girnar) and Rajasthan (Ranakpur, Jaisalmer and Mount Abu), as well as in Karnataka (Sravana Belgola). Generally speaking, since **leather is impure** to Jainas, all leather objects (including belts) have to be removed before entering one of their temples.

Buddhism

Buddha During his 80-year life Buddha, the enlightened one, developed and proclaimed a teaching that now has far more followers outside of India than it does in the country where it originated. Buddha's teachings, like Hinduism, build on the idea of **rebirth** and cosmic cycles, but deny the existence of a god who is supposed to be responsible for creation and could bring salvation to human beings. **Siddharta Gautama** was born the son of a prince around 560 BC in Lumbini (Nepal). He left his family at the age of 29 and went in search of the knowledge that would bring salvation. Initially he tried to achieve this through self-mortification and severe asceticism, but to no avail. Then finally, after many years of wandering, while he was meditating under a Bodhi tree in Bodhgaya (Bihar), he managed to discover the cause of suffering in the world and the way to escape the eternal cycle of rebirths. He first announced his teaching of the **four noble truths and the noble eightfold path** to break the cycle in Sarnath, not far from Varanasi (formerly known as Benares), thus setting the wheel of his teaching in motion. The first two truths say that all life is suffering and the cause of suffering is people's desire. The third truth says that salvation is possible and the fourth shows the way to **Nirvana (meaning »extinguishing« or »blowing out«)**, namely by following the eightfold path. Buddha's eightfold path consists of right view, right intention, right speech, right action, right livelihood, right effort, right mindfulness and right concentration (meditation).

Over time monks gathered around Buddha and he wandered across the Ganges plain, teaching as he went. His teachings were written down only several centuries after his death by his students. According to Buddhist tradition the »Enlightened One« entered Nirvana at the age of 80. The rural upper class donated money and food to the monks, hoping for a blessing. Thus Buddhism developed into a major movement that spread through all of India. Buddhism was greatly promoted by Emperor Ashoka (268–239 BC), after which it became a world religion. Ashoka had countless stupas built and sent missionaries to spread the word in places near and far.

Spreading the teachings

Over time different schools developed within Buddhism. The **Hinayana School**, also called »the low vehicle«, sees salvation as a process only the individual can guide. Buddha was usually only repre-

Different schools

sented by symbols, such as a footprint, a wheel (for the teaching) or the Bodhi tree (for enlightenment). This religious orientation was replaced in India by **Mahayana Buddhism**, which developed later on. This began in the 1st century BC and is also referred to as the »great vehicle«. Boddhisatvas play an important role in this school in the people's striving for salvation. Boddhisatvas are enlightened beings who do not, however, enter Nirvana; instead, they linger on earth to

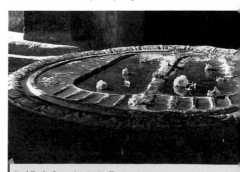

Buddha's footprint in Bodhgaya

support humans in their efforts. Mahayana Buddhism depicts Buddha in many different poses, and he is increasingly being worshipped as a god. In the second half of the first millennium **Vajrayana Buddhism** (»diamond vehicle«) developed, which attempted to use magic formulae and practices to achieve heavenly salvation.

Important Buddhist **places of pilgrimage** are Bodhgaya, Sarnath and Kushnagar, the place where Buddha died. Songs and meditations play an important role during the pilgrimages.

Sikhism

Content of the faith The founder of this movement was Guru Nanak (1469–1539); he was born in the Punjab region. The religion he founded is based on a **synthesis of Islamic and Hindu ideas**. Sikhism, like Islam, is monotheistic and non-pictorial. The element taken over from Hinduism is the belief in rebirth, but miracles and the caste system are rejected. The way to salvation is via sermons, devotion to god (Bhakti) and meditation, and is open to everyone, regardless of race, caste or gender. In Punjab, Sikhs are the economically most successful group, which has in turn led to prejudice and persecution. In contrast to India's other world religions the religious works of the Sikhs were not written in classical languages, but in Punjabi, the local language. Male Sikhs (disciples) can be recognized by their turban and five characteristics: uncut head hair and beard, a comb, a small sword, a metal bracelet and knee-length trousers.

Guru The Sikh community has a guru (teacher) as its religious leader, while the Sikhs are the students. The tradition of gurus, who were considered to be the incarnation of earlier gurus, is a long one. The fourth guru, Ramdas, laid the foundation stone of the **Golden Temple in Amritsar**, the modern-day centre of Sikhism. Guru Ramdas was held in high regard by the Mongol ruler Akbar, and Sikhs enjoyed religious freedom. When several gurus were tortured and killed by Muslim rulers in subsequent periods, the community became a militant order with the goal of defending their faith by force of arms, if need be. The tenth guru, Gobind Singh (1675–1708) finally declared the guru tradition over, whereupon the holy scripture of the Sikhs, the **Adi Granth**, was directly venerated as a guru. For this reason the sacred text has since also been called the Guru Granth Sahib.

Islam, Zoroastrianism and Christianity

Amongst the religions that came to India from the outside are Islam, Christianity, Zoroastrianism (Parsis), the Bahai faith community and Judaism.

Islam The youngest of the world religions, which was preached by the **Prophet Muhammad** (AD 570–632) and the content of which was written down in the Qur'an, reached India as early as the seventh century through merchants and isolated military attacks. From the twelfth century onwards Muslim conquerors came to India in several waves, where they first founded the Delhi sultanates and later the Mughal Empire. This caused Islam to be become widespread in India. **Sufis**, holy men, who sought experience of God through meditation and mysticism, were instrumental in this. Islamic practice includes several rules Muslims have to follow: Muslims have to be capable of voicing the creed, they have to pray facing Mecca five times a day, they have to uphold Ramadan, the month of fasting, they must give alms to the poor and they must not eat pork, drink alcohol or participate in any gambling activity.

Even though the Muslim conquerors were constantly at war with the Indian kingdoms, these were **not wars of faith**, but rather wars of influence and power. Thus Mughal rulers married Hindu princesses without concern, and often had commanders of a different faith leading their armies. For centuries both religious communities lived peacefully with each other and the **one culture stimulated the other**, in architecture (Indo-Saracenic style), in the synthesis of Arabic and Indian medicine (Unani medicine) and in the culinary sphere (Mughal cuisine). However, the country's partition into India and Pakistan led to numerous acts of violence and a **mass exodus** of In-

Delhi's Jami Masjid is India's largest mosque

dian Muslims to Pakistan and Hindus from Pakistan to India. Post-colonial India, which sees itself as a secular state without a state religion, has been the scene of confrontations between Muslims and Hindus for years. In 1992 the Babri mosque in Ayodhya was destroyed by militant Hindus, leading to fighting all over the country. The terrorist attacks of 2008 on hotels in Mumbai were blamed on the Pakistan-based militant group Lashkar-e-Taiba. The Pakistani government eventually accepted that Ajmal Amir, the only gunman to be captured alive, is indeed a Pakistani national.

Zoroastrianism In 1500 BC the Persian prophet **Zoroaster** announced the core-beliefs of the religion named after him. It was Persia's state religion for more than 1000 years, from the fifth century BC to the seventh century AD, until the Muslim conquerors of the country forced the followers of Zoroastrianism to flee. One group of fugitives managed to get to northwest India at the time. They are called **Parsis** in India, after their place of origin. Most of the approximately 100,000 believers live in Mumbai and Gujarat. The Parsi faith is shaped by the notion that the two opposed forces, which are identified with the creatures **Ohrmuzd (good) and Ahirman (evil)**, are in a constant battle. The entire universe is divided into opposite pairs such as good and evil, day and night, death and immortality etc., with the two rivals each responsible for one side of the opposing pair. The Parsi people associate death with Ahirman, which is why dead bodies are believed to be inhabited by demons and thought to be unclean. To prevent the sacred elements of earth, fire and water from becoming polluted, the dead person is brought to a funerary site, i.e. to one of the **Towers of Silence**. Once there, the dead body is undressed and left to the natural forces of wind, weather and vultures. This custom, which stems from this people's nomadic way of life in Persia, is not without its problems in Mumbai, where the vulture population is in decline because of pollution.

Despite Hindu and Muslim rule the Parsi people were able to practice their faith in peace in India. From the mid-18th century onwards they developed into a very successful merchant group, working closely with the British. They are still amongst the richest population groups in India.

Christianity Even before Christianity came to Europe, it had already spread in India. The Syrian Christians in Kerala cite early proselytization by **Thomas the Apostle**, who is said to have visited the Malabar Coast in the first century, during which time he allegedly founded Christian communities before he died as a martyr near Madras. The monk Cosmas Indicopleustes, who visited southern India in the sixth century, reported on Christian communities there. They were most likely Nestorians who had come from Persia. Christianity experienced a renewed revival in the 16th century when the **Portuguese** chose Goa as their base for a Catholic proselytization programme.

The Portuguese destroyed Indian temples within their sphere of influence and they forcibly converted the population. Under colonial rule Christian missionaries were also very active; they were particularly interested in the tribal population and the lower castes. Even though Christians only make up 3.5% of the population today, they are nevertheless highly influential in some regions (Kerala, Goa) and have made a significant contribution to India's education and health-care systems. Interestingly the newly converted Christians in India often did not reject the caste system and their liturgy also took over several elements of Hindu rituals.

History

Did you know that the Aryans conquered northern India in around 1750 BC? Who were the Mughal Emperors? What did Gandhi want to achieve with the now legendary Salt March? Who was India's prime minister for 17 years after the country obtained independence? What was the origin of the Kashmir conflict that is still smouldering today?

Indus Valley Culture

3rd century BC	Urban civilizations of Mohenjo Daro and Harappa in the Indus valley

More than 4000 years have passed since the first civilization devel- **Early metro-**
oped on the soil of the subcontinent along the banks of the Indus in **polises on**
what is now Pakistan. Around 1000 settlement sites have been un- **the Indus**
earthed by archaeological digs so far. Since their discovery in the
1920s **Harappa and Mohenjo Daro** have been the focal points of archaeological research. They were the urban centres of a farming culture that had settled along the Indus and its distributaries, cultivating
wheat, barley and pulses as well as mustard, sesame and cotton on
the fertile flood plains. These two metropolises, which are 600km/
370mi apart, achieved their great wealth through intensive trade with
the Arabian peninsula. The Indus was used as a convenient transport
route.
Little is known about the people's governance and religion. Excavations have brought **large residential and production sites** to light
without clear signs of a particular governmental or religious architecture. Further discoveries show god figures, which could imply a connection with the Hinduism of later times. Since however the script
of this people has still not been deciphered, many questions regarding this early civilization still remain unanswered. There is also speculation about the fall of this civilization. It is thought to have come
to a **violent end** in around 1750 BC, with unburied bodies in the
upper layer of Mohenjo Daro cited as evidence for this. Whether bellicose conflicts or a great flood were the cause of the downfall is just
one of the many mysteries surrounding the Indus valley civilization.

Aryan Immigration

around 1750 BC	Aryan invasion of northwest India, rise of Hinduism

The **immigration of the Aryans**, nomadic cattle herders from central **Arya, the noble**
Asia, in around 1750 BC caused the most dramatic event in India's **ones**
history to date. The exact origin of the conquerors, who proudly
called themselves Arya, the noble ones, is unknown. They invaded

← *Nehru with his grandsons Sanjay and Rajiv,*
  who were both to have political careers and die tragically

India from the northwest via the Khyber Pass and first settled in Punjab. The Vedas, the collected knowledge of this people, provide information about their customs and habits.

Conquest of the subcontinent to the east

Only after several centuries did the Aryans push further eastwards into the Indian subcontinent, **gradually settling on the Ganges plain** (1000– 600 BC). Whether or not they encountered and subordinated the Dravidians during this period remained a controversial matter of debate among scholars for a long time. More recent research however strengthens the theory that the Dravidians only came and settled in southern India by sea from Iraq and Iran after the Aryans had already arrived and that they then mixed with the local population. Over time, many smaller ruling states developed in the north and northeast of the country. These feuded with each other.

Creation of the great epics

This was also the time the two great epics, the **Mahabharata** and the **Ramayana** were created. The mythical city of Ayodhya, the seat of Lord Rama, portrays the ideal image of government by a just king.

Role of priests

In addition to the king, the priests were also a highly influential group. Their monopoly of all the religious rituals made them indispensable mediators between the gods and the people. Kings also received legitimation through the regular sacrifices for which they required the priests known as Brahmins. Thus their role was upgraded, which also expressed itself in the society's social structure. It was during this time that the **caste system** was developed, with the Brahmins at the top; its effects are still present in modern-day India.

First Indian Empire

272–231 BC	The Buddhist emperor Ashoka (Maurya) rules almost the entire subcontinent.

Cultivation of the Ganges plain

Around the year 500 BC there were a number of new developments that would significantly change the face of the subcontinent. The use of iron fully asserted itself and allowed improved methods of cultivation in agriculture. This ultimately led the Ganges plain to be transformed into a fertile rice landscape. However, important developments were not restricted to the material sphere. This was also the hour of the new religions **Buddhism and Jainism**, which questioned the power monopoly held by the priestly caste.

The Mauryas

All this prepared the way for the rise of the Maurya dynasty (322–185 BC), which was to become India's first empire. The great **Emperor Ashoka** (c272–232 BC) was particularly successful in consolidating the realm and extending his sphere of control. After his violent submission of the Kalinga kingdom located in modern-day Orissa, he converted to Buddhism, which he subsequently made the state religion.

Numerous monastic communities developed under his protectorate, which then brought their ideas to all areas of the sizeable empire. **Uniform administrative institutions** were created for the first time under Ashoka, which he used to rule the country through centralized government from the capital Pataliputra (Patna in modern-day Bihar). He had his political and ethnical ideas publicized by means of edicts on rocks and columns all over the country. Even though they tended more towards pacifism in line with his new **Buddhist worldview**, he did not hesitate to point out the real power structure. Thus the messages chiselled in stone all the way between Kandahar in modern-day Afghanistan and the southern Deccan plateau are not just testament to his ethnic and religious missionary spirit, they also bespeak his imperial claim to power, which reached far beyond the borders of his territory. The great empire only survived Ashoka's death by 50 years; however he was the first ruler to create a cultural unit at a supraregional level.

Ashoka's rule

Ashokan pillar
model for India's national emblem

Rise of Regional States

| 185 BC | Empire breaks up into individual states |
| AD 50–320 | Kushan Empire: promotion and development of Buddhism |

After the decline of the Maurya dynasty **Brahmin orthodoxy underwent a revival**, since patronage for the Buddhist monasteries and their monks disappeared. In the many small kingdoms that developed in their place, priests once again took on the role they had held in earlier times. As the keepers and agents of an old tradition they had a crucial role at the courts and often determined a state's fate.

Decline of the Maurya dynasty

The Brahmins' migration to the south also led to their religious and social ideas being spread through the whole country, thus bringing about a **harmonization of regional cults and beliefs**. It was during this time that Hinduism was created. In addition to many insignificant states this period had four main players: the Sungas in the north, the Kalingas in the east, the Satavahanas on the Deccan plateau and the Sakas (Scythians) in the northwest.

Rise of Hinduism

However, not all of the rulers adopted the old beliefs again. Kanishka, the great Kushan king, who created an empire in the subconti-

Kushan period

nent's northwest during the first century, was a follower of Buddhism and aided its distribution. His state was also the birthplace of a unique synthesis of Indian and Greek cultural beliefs, which found their expression in **Gandhara art**.

Hindu Empires

320–510	The Gupta dynasty dominates northern India
980–1250	The Chola Empire in southern India

Development of arts and culture

A certain amount of internal stability was created by the conditions needed for the unequalled flourishing of arts and culture during this period, which has gone down in the history books as **the golden age of Hindu empires** and during which one of India's most beautiful monuments was created. Apart from the Huns, who settled in large parts of northern India during the fifth and sixth centuries, no other foreign peoples advanced into the subcontinent. This led to a gradual standardization of the kingdoms' ruling style and to generally binding rules for recognizing allies and engaging in conflicts.

Sculpture of Ganga (Gupta period, 5th century)

The **Gupta dynasty** (AD 320–500) grew to become the most important power in the north and its court was considered an exemplary model of **courtly culture**. After this empire was broken up by the Huns several new centres of power were formed in its place, of which that of King Harshavardhana (AD 606–647) gained supremacy. At the same time the south also began taking the stage of historical and cultural processes to a greater extent.

A surprising event was the rapid **rise of the Chalukyas** of Badami, who obtained a significant amount of power under their great kings Pulakeshin I (AD 543–566) and Pulakeshin II (AD 609–642). The **Pallavas** under their king Narasimhavarman (AD 630–660) also developed into a significant power in the south. However, it was not long before other dynasties shaped the course of history again. The **Rashtrakutas** from Ellora (AD 757–973) threw out the Chalukya dynasty and made themselves the rulers of the Deccan. The Pallava dynasty was kept in check by the resurrected **Cholas** (from 985 to the end of the 13th century). The unparalleled Chola bronzes and the golden age of Tamil literature, whose tireless supporters they proved to be, were to their credit. The appearance of the **Hoysalas** (AD 1110–1310) with their capital Halebid marks a further high point in the ups and downs of the various dynasties. Their civilization, which created the unforgettable monuments in the temples of Halebid, Belur and Somnathpur, also signified the end of the period of classical arts and culture. **Political fragmentation and lively rivalries as well as Hindu dominance** marked this period, whose dynasties created some of India's most beautiful cultural monuments as a result of power-political and religious competition. The process of the »Hinduization« of regional cults also ran its course and, while retaining regional and local variety, led to a further harmonization of beliefs.

The awakening of the south

At the same time Hinduism spread to Southeast Asia. Vietnam, Cambodia, Java and Sumatra all took over the subcontinent's religious ideas as well as its ruling style, architecture and writing. The millennium of Hindu empires came to an end with increasing invasions by Islamic conquerors from the 12th century onwards. It was replaced by the renewed clash between various cultures, which led to both agreement and synthesis as well as fighting and destruction over the centuries.

The spread of Hinduism to Southeast Asia

The Delhi Sultanate

| 1206–1526 | Muslim rule, first over northern India, then over other parts of the subcontinent |

Spread of Islam The inevitable result of the gradual spread of Islam and the territorial conquests of its advocates was a confrontation with the rulers of the subcontinent. The raids undertaken by Mahmud of Ghazni (997–1030), a Turkish military commander, in northwest India were the prelude to the later firm establishment of Islamic rulers in India. This took place when the Delhi sultanate was established by Qutb-ud-din-Aibak (1206–10) in 1206. The Ghurids' armies from Afghanistan, led by Muhammad of Ghur (1150–1206), had previously brought large parts of northern India under their control. Aibak was made governor in Delhi and after his master's death he became independent. This was the **beginning of a 200-year rule by the Delhi sultans**, who fought their way ever further southwards with their strong armies. Under the commander Malik Kufur the Muslim rulers' armies conquered several Hindu kingdoms, that of the Yadavas on the northern Deccan, the Warangalim in the east and the area of the Hoysalas on the southern Deccan.

The Empire under Tughluq This prepared the ground for the establishment of an empire of unrivalled dimensions, governed by Sultan Muhammad bin Tughluq (1325–51). At the same time the empire had reached such proportions that it could barely be governed from faraway Delhi. In 1327 the ruler moved his capital to the stronghold of Daulatabad (former Devagiri) on the northern Deccan. However, just two years later the ruler had to leave his new seat of government because of the threat of losing control of the north, his real power base. This marked the **end of the heyday of the Delhi sultans**, since efforts to keep the empire together were unsuccessful in the long run.

Limits of power Tughluq's retreat to the north was the signal for the founding of the last Hindu Empire of **Vijayanagar** by the brothers Harihara and Bukka in 1336 and the creation of an independent **sultanate under Ala-ud-din Bahman Shah** on the Deccan in 1347. The frontiers were also crumbling in the north and as a result the subsequent Sayyid dynasty (1414–51) and the Lodi dynasty (1451–1526) had to limit their ambitions to the area around Delhi. The Delhi sultans finally abdicated when the Mughal ruler **Babur** (1483–1530) invaded India in 1526 and laid the foundation for the second Islamic empire.

Mughal Rule

1504–1739	Rule of the Muslim Mughal emperors

Humayun Babur had been the ruler in Kabul since 1504 and conquered the northern Indian plain in several military campaigns (1526–30). His son Humayun's (1530–56) attempts to consolidate the area were less successful however. He had to relinquish the conquered territory to the Afghan commander Sher Shah after being defeated and fleeing to Persia. It was only after the death of Sher Shah and the consequent confusion that Humayun managed to gain a foothold in India again. However, it would be Humayun's son **Akbar** (1556–1605) who would write the most glorious chapter of Mughal rule on the Indian subcontinent.

Under Akbar's rule an empire developed that with regard to its concept and its claims can only be compared to that of the Maurya emperor Ashoka. Akbar's policies were surely influenced by the prag-

Akbar's empire

matic notion that permanent Muslim rule in India could only assert itself if the beliefs of the Hindu majority were respected. As a result of this insight Akbar did not try to seek his fortune through confrontation, as some of his predecessors had done. He was able to bind the Rajputs, Hindu rulers, to his court by creating many different relationships, such as a **directed marriage policy**. The great tolerance with which he was credited ended however when power-political interests were threatened. Nevertheless Akbar went down in the annals of history as **an enlightened mind for his time**. Thus there are reports about the arrangement of religious debates in his intermittent residence Fatehpur Sikri, where followers of different faiths could engage in argument with each other about the truth. The syncretist **Din-i-Illahi religion** he proclaimed was probably not welcomed by the Islamic orthodoxy either.

Akbar's trump card in governing the large country lay in his lean, centrally-run administration with which he governed areas he had subdued. In addition to introducing the rupiya to the empire and adopting taxation policies to facilitate inter-regional trade, it was particularly his strategic superiority through the use of firearms that se-

Scene from the Akbarnam, a collection of miniatures relating the emperor's deeds: Akbar crossing the Ganges

cured his power. He governed his country from his capital Agra; it included Punjab, parts of Rajasthan as well as a section of the Ganges plain and later also Bengal. In the south his empire was bordered by the Deccan sultanates and the huge Vijayanagara Empire.

Akbar's heirs While Akbar primarily went down in history as a political strategist, his successors **Jehangir** (1605–27) and **Shah Jahan** (1628–58) stood out for their promotion of the arts. Jehangir's decisions were largely influenced by his politically able wife **Nur Jahan**; the memory of Shah Jahan is also linked to the role of his wife. He had the famous mausoleum the **Taj Mahal** built in Agra in honour of his wife Mumtaz. It was ultimately the enormous financial burden associated with the construction of such pompous structures that pushed the state into bankruptcy. This was a welcome motive for Shah Jahan's son Aurangzeb (1658–1707) to oust his father, hold him captive and put himself at the pinnacle of the empire.

Aurangzeb Aurangzeb's method of securing his rule stood in stark contrast to that of his predecessors. Particularly his destruction of Hindu temples showed him to be a **ruthless agent of an aggressive fundamentalism**. Under his rule the Mughal Empire reached almost the same dimensions as it had had in Tughluq's day. In pursuing his ambitious power-political goals Aurangzeb had however stretched his state's resources to the absolute limit and while he was fighting on the southern frontier the neighbours in the north, burdened with high taxes, rebelled against the central government.

The **gradual dissolution of the empire** could no longer be prevented. The **rise of the Marathas**, adversaries who could no longer be subdued, also became too much for the Mughal Empire. Launching their attack from Pune in the highlands southwest of Mumbai, they conquered large parts of the surrounding areas under their leader **Shivaji**. Aurangzeb's weak successors were no longer able to defend themselves and with Nadir Shah's invasion form Persia in 1739 Mughal rule over India, which had lasted for more than two centuries, finally came to an end. Once again the country fragmented into many small regions, because neither the Marathas nor any other power were able to fill the political vacuum that had developed. This situation created ideal conditions for the expansionist European powers, which had long had their eyes on India.

European Colonial Rule

1498	Vasco da Gama's landing in Calicut
1600	Founding of the English East India Company
1757	Start of British domination after the Battle of Plassey

Kappad beach near Kozhicode: this is where Vasco da Gama stepped on to Indian soil for the first time

After Vasco da Gama discovered the sea route to India in 1498, the **First European** Portuguese began founding trading posts on the subcontinent's west-**conquerors** ern coast as early as the first half of the 16th century. They were fol-lowed by the British, Dutch and French. The Europeans' goal was to gain access to India's sought-after spices, but also to its cotton, indi-go, silk and saltpetre.

By 1600 the **East India Company** had already been given the mono-poly for English trade with India and it soon made a huge fortune. The coastal towns of Surat and Bombay in the west as well as Madras and Calcutta in the east became the bases for the ever increasing en-gagement of the British on the subcontinent. Over time they man-aged to defeat all the other colonial powers in numerous conflicts. France had developed into the strongest opponent of British inter-ests, but after three wars in the 18th century was put in its place. Ini-tially the colonial powers were primarily focused on purely **economic interests**, but over time **power-political motives** also came into play. A military conquest of India was the only guarantee that there would be a continuous, secure exploitation of India's raw materials in the long term. This process was set off when the Nawab of Bengal, who had become suspicious of the increasing presence of the British, took the British trading-post of Calcutta. One year later the British army, led by General Clive, decisively defeated the Bengalis.

This victory, which went down in history as the Battle of Plassey **Military conquest** (1757), marked the beginning of the political and military conquest **of India**

Coronation of George V as Emperor of India in Delhi on 12 December 1911

of India. From their new bastion in Bengal the British succeeded in advancing to all parts of the country over the following decades, subduing the regional and local rulers, whose disunity was no small factor in the British success. **They formally let the maharajas keep their independence, but in fact they were subject to British suzerainty** and were unable to make their own political or economic decisions. Growing commitment in India led an increasing number of people in Britain to demand that the power of the East India Company be limited to purely economic issues.

India under the British crown   A law to that effect was passed in 1784; it handed over military, civilian and financial affairs to a representative of the British crown. The systematic expansion of the administration by means of salaried officials and increased infrastructure measures, and later particularly the construction of a railway network to facilitate access to and from the country's interior, were rigorously pursued. **In addition to India's administrative unification a uniform set of laws and a universally valid currency were also introduced.** These achievements, with which the colonial power liked to show off, were, however, overshadowed by the **disastrous economic consequences** which the centuries-long European presence had for India. The **continuous removal of raw materials** without any adequate compensation, the control of the Indian domestic market by the British using customs policies that severely disadvantaged the Indian population, and the British monopoly of the country's salt production are just a few examples of **economic policies which were solely focused on British interests**. The social consequences, such as unemployment as a result of entire job sectors being destroyed, migration into the cities and mass poverty, were even more disastrous.

This system could not, however, have been maintained without the **collaboration** of many local rulers and those who had already been dependent on the patronage of those in power in earlier times, the Brahmins and the scribe caste, who took jobs in the British administration. The demand for native qualified workers also led to the adoption in the early 19th century of Western educational institutions, where young Indians could get training to become officials, lawyers or teachers. The spirit reigning in these institutions was best expressed by the words of Thomas Babington Macaulay, in effect the British minister of justice in India, who said in 1835: »We must at present do our best to form a class who may be interpreters between us and the millions whom we govern; a class of persons, Indian in blood and colour, but English in taste, in opinions, in morals, and in intellect.« The failure of this plan became clear a little while later. It was the graduates of these schools and universities who were the first to speak up against the British rulers and demand participation and freedom.

Beginning of the Struggle for Iindependence

1857–58	The Indian Mutiny
1885	Founding of the Indian National Congress

Nationalist thinking was already developing in the mid-18th century amongst the new Indian upper class that was slowly developing. The first organized, violent resistance came from another quarter, however. **In 1857, a large section of the British-Indian army in India, in league with northern India's landlords, rebelled** against the colonial power. The so-called Indian Mutiny, which had its centres in

Indian Mutiny

Lucknow, Delhi and Meerut, was however suppressed after a few months because of a lack of leadership and co-ordination. British rule had been under serious threat for a short period and far-reaching conclusions were drawn from this incident: the East India Company was abolished and **India came under the direct rule of the crown**. The governor-general, who until then had been the commander-in-chief, was given the title of Viceroy and the British government was expanded to include a dedicated cabinet post, the Secretary of State for India. Increased British distrust of their subjects, particularly of the new educated class, followed.

Nationalist ideas The Indian Mutiny was more of a rebellion of India's traditional forces, but the new generation of intellectuals oriented itself on **Western ideas of participation, democracy and nationalism**. As a result they demanded Indian participation in law-making, access to higher administrative positions and lower taxes. These demands were finally institutionalized when the **Indian National Congress was founded** in Bombay in 1885. This union of leading Indian politicians, dominated primarily by liberals, worked hard for a continuous development of the country within the framework of the British Empire. However, the Congress soon became a platform for more radical ideas, particularly the demand for complete independence from the colonial power. A **return to India's old traditions** also took place; these, for many, were identical with Hindu thoughts and beliefs. As Muslims were not able to agree to these ideas, it was thus inevitable that the national movement would split. This ultimately led to the formation of the **Muslim League** in 1906 and the Hindu Mahasabha one year later, while politicians of all religions continued collaborating in the National Congress. The Congress was divided into the moderates, who were hoping for reform, and the radicals, who wanted to boycott the forthcoming constitutional reform; as a consequence of this division, the National Congress also split in 1907.

Mahatma Gandhi

1920	Gandhi takes over the leadership of the National Congress, the most important institution of the independence movement.
1930	Campaign of civil disobedience, Salt March
15 August 1947	Independence; bloody confrontation between Hindus and Muslims in Punjab and Bengal

Driving force of the freedom movement The independence movement entered the crucial phase when Mohandas Karamchand Gandhi, known as »Mahatma« (»great soul«), became its leader. Ghandi did not just possess charisma and effective political ideas, he also proved to be an **ideal unifier** who was able to bring all of the different political, social and religious groups together. In every sense he represented a stroke of fortune and became the driving force behind India's path to freedom. In 1915 Gandhi returned from South Africa and immediately became involved in the political discussions. **Non-collaboration with the British and non-violent resistance** were the slogans with which he took over the leadership of the National Congress in 1920. He also transformed the ideas of the fight for independence from a middle-class, intellectual affair into an issue of concern to the masses.

Gandhi used a number of spectacular campaigns to force the British to negotiate. The legendary **Salt March**, with which Gandhi sought to break the British salt monopoly, was only one of them. Violent suppression of the rebels and regular arrests of the rebel leaders, including **Jawaharlal Nehru**, who was to become India's first prime minister, were the routine responses of the colonial power.

Path to freedom

Nehru and Gandhi at the opening session of the Congress in July 1946

While the British did try to make constitutional reforms to accommodate the independence movement, they were half-hearted at best. Over time the differences in the ideas of the Congress and a section of the Muslims came to light, when the lawyer **Muhammad Ali Jinnah** presented himself as their spokesman.

Demands for a state designated for Muslims

The Muslims were fearful they would come off badly in a state dominated by the Hindu majority and for that reason were in favour of a federal constitution, in which the provinces were largely autonomous. This desire first found expression in the demand for separate constituencies for their religious group. The British, who wanted to counteract the growing power of the Congress by supporting the minorities, agreed to this proposal. During the first elections in 1936 the Congress obtained an overwhelming victory, the exceptions being those provinces where Muslims were in the majority. In 1940, Jinnah, who had by then become the leader of the Muslim League, first mentioned the two-nations theory, according to which Hindus and Muslims were two different nations.

The **Muslim demand for their own state, Pakistan**, was not long in coming. This put Jinnah in stark opposition to his former allies Gandhi and Nehru, who were working towards a unified, secular India that had room for all ethnic, social and religious groups. The formation of an interim government at the conference in Shimla in 1945 failed because of Jinnah's veto and his renewed demands for an autonomous state. The British greatly strengthened his position with their »**divide and rule policy**«.

Unrest between Hindus and Muslims

On 16 August 1946 Jinnah called for a »direct action day« in order to lend weight to his plan. This was followed by bloody rebellions in Kolkata, where Muslims drove the local Hindus out of the city so they could forcibly unite it with Bengal, a province in which the Muslims were in the majority. Seeking revenge, the Hindus who had fled to the province of Bihar killed several Muslims living there. Several times that year the country stood **on the brink of civil war** and the pressure on the British to allow this derailed colony to become independent continued to grow.

Lord Mountbatten as the »saviour in a time of need«

The promise of salvation came from the former commander of Britain's Southeast Asia campaigns, Lord Mountbatten, who, equipped with wide-ranging powers, was sent to India as the new viceroy. He prepared a plan of action incredibly quickly, providing for a separation of the colony into two separate states.

Partition and independence

India's independence was proclaimed on 15 August 1947, the new state of Pakistan having been founded the previous day. **Along with the joy of having at long last achieved freedom there were the awful reports of expulsion, violence and death.** In the wake of India's partition and independence more than 250,000 people lost their lives. In particular the divided provinces of Punjab and Bengal were the scenes of terrible massacres; parts of the capital, Delhi, resembled hell. The dream of freedom was paid for with the trauma of hatred and discord, a burden under which both India and Pakistan are still suffering.

Post-independence India

30 January 1948	Assassination of Mahatma Gandhi
26 January 1950	New constitution takes effect India becomes a republic

Independence

»Many years ago we signed a pact with fate and now the time for us to honour our vow is close (...). We are leaving the old for the new, an era is coming to an end and the soul of a nation so long suppressed is finding its voice.« These were the words of Jawaharlal Nehru in his speech before the constituent national assembly on the day of independence.

Assassination of Gandhi

Just six months later, Jawaharlal Nehru and the entire nation were dumbstruck when Mahatma Gandhi was shot by a Hindu fanatic on 30 January 1948. Like no other, the father of the nation, lovingly called »Babu«, was a **symbol of peace, tolerance and non-violence**, and India entered into great mourning when he died. Nevertheless the deed is a painful reminder of the seeds of violence that had become established in the young state right from the start. As soon as India had become independent war broke out with Pakistan over Kashmir, which, though inhabited by a Muslim majority, was ruled by a Hindu prince. Despite a ceasefire overseen by the UN which came into effect in 1949, the Himalayan state remained one of the main conflict areas between India and Pakistan.

Nehru as prime minister

With Jawaharlal Nehru as the prime minister of a strong Congress government, one of the great men of the independence movement was now in charge of the state and highly esteemed both in India and abroad. During his time in office his foreign policies were shaped by **policies of global neutrality and peace** in the time of the Cold War and the concurrent conflict with India's immediate neighbours Pakistan and China. A border dispute between India and China led to armed conflict in 1962.

Characteristic of Nehru's domestic policies was the attempt to promote the country's industrialization and social reforms with the help of a strong state. The incorporation of the former principalities, which made up no less than two-fifths of the entire country, and the reorganization of the states by language, also took place under his governance. When Nehru died in 1964 India lost one of the leading architects of the new state. His successor, Lal Bahadur Shastri, was only in office for a short time. His sudden death made room for Nehru's daughter Indira Gandhi, who significantly contributed to the destiny of the country for almost twenty years.

The Era of Indira Gandhi

1966	Indira Gandhi becomes prime minister
1969	Congress Party splits
1971	War with Pakistan, independence of Bangladesh
1975–77	The Emergency
1980	Landslide for the Congress I Party, Indira Gandhi becomes prime minister again
1984	Assassination by two Sikh bodyguards

»India is Indira«   »India is Indira and Indira is India« was one of the slogans with which the prime minister sought to achieve victory for her Congress Party. The modesty with which her father's generation, particularly her father himself, shaped the country's politics was to come to an end with the era of Indira Gandhi. On the domestic front with the **formation of new parties** the ruling Congress Party saw the formation of new rivals, particularly in southern India.

? DID YOU KNOW ...?

■ ... that Indira Gandhi was not related to Mahatma Gandhi? She married the Parsi Feroze Gandhi. However, the fact that she bore the same name as India's symbolic figure was of great use to her.

The Congress Party itself also had great internal problems. Here, Indira Gandhi was able to prove her power-political skills for the first time, when she brought the majority of the members of parliament to her side after she forced **a split in the Congress**. It was with this »new old« party, which now bore her initial (**Congress I**), that she won the next elections, using the populist slogan »garibi hatao« (»fight poverty«).

Military inter-   She reached the high point of her popularity in 1971 after the intervention in East   vention in the crisis region of East Pakistan, from which the **new**
Pakistan   **state of Bangladesh**, with great help from the Indian army, emerged. However, soon afterwards her star began to fade. Social unrest and several strikes reminded the government that their promise to fight poverty had not been kept. After the prime minister was expelled from parliament in 1975 for electoral malpractice, she called for a state of emergency.

Indira Gandhi with her son Rajiv

This was the most severe **breach with the rules of democracy** since India's independence. 100,000 members of the opposition were arrested, the press censored and the elections scheduled for the following year delayed. Her popularity continued to plummet when her son Sanjay imposed rigid family planning measures, conducting a campaign of forced sterilization.

When the delayed elections were finally held in 1977 the Congress (I) Party suffered a clear defeat and was beaten by the Janata Party, a coalition of five opposition parties. However, within a short time the depiction of the Congress Party as the common enemy was no longer enough to keep the coalition together. In 1980 early elections were held in which Indira Gandhi came out victorious once again. The prime minister's last government was marked by increasing in-

State of emergency 1975–77

Turbulent years

stability. Violent confrontations and an **erosion of power** in the northwestern and northeastern federal states characterized the situation. Civil war broke out in Assam between the native population on the one hand and the representatives of the Indian state, the administration and the military on the other. Indira Gandhi's downfall finally came because of **problems in Punjab**. Punjab, which had been divided between India and Pakistan in 1947, is the traditional home of the Sikhs, who had felt disadvantaged because of the central government in New Delhi right from the start. The argument between the two parties, which initially revolved around land and water rights, escalated on both sides. It came to an initial climax in the **attack on the Golden Temple of Amritsar**, the most important Sikh place of worship, by Indian troops because militant Sikh rebels had established a stronghold there. This sacrilege did not just lead to increased radicalization amongst Sikhs, it was also a decision which Indira Gandhi was to pay for with her life.

Indira Gandhi's assassination

In October 1984 Indira Gandhi was shot down by two of her Sikh bodyguards. The subsequent riots claimed the lives of thousands of members of this faith in New Delhi, who were killed out of revenge by fanatical Hindus. In order to prevent further chaos, Indira Gandhi's son Rajiv was proclaimed her successor after only short negotiations. His mother had been training the former Air India pilot to become her successor after her preferred choice, her other son Sanjay, died when the plane he was piloting crashed in 1980. The **handover of power within the Nehru-Gandhi dynasty**, on whose continued existence the influence of leading Congress politicians depended, was thus successful.

Rajiv Gandhi

1984	Rajiv Gandhi is sworn in as prime minister
1991	Assassination at an election meeting in Tamil Nadu

New hope

With Rajiv Gandhi, a member of the younger generation stepped on to the political stage for the first time and as a result the expectations placed in him, particularly by his peers and the new generation, were great. The **hope for fundamental political and social change** was immense and Rajiv Gandhi promised when he took power that he would build an »India of the 21st century«. The recipe for this great leap forward consisted of a gradual opening of the economy and increased use of modern technologies. The growing middle classes profited from his consumption-oriented, highly import-dependent economic model, but the majority of the population, in the agricultural sector, did not see any improvements.

The mountain of debt grew ever higher until, in 1991, the state faced bankruptcy. Solving the country's regional conflicts, an issue that was still of quite some urgency, also proved difficult. The young prime minister showed himself open to discussion with regard to the conflicts in Assam and Punjab and he was able to negotiate an agreement with the Assam population in 1985, which calmed down the situation, but to this day the area in the northeast has remained a trouble spot. The renewed siege of the Golden Temple in Punjab in 1988 was also a clear sign that the country was still far from solving the conflict. When civil war broke out in Kashmir in 1989, India's primary conflict zone made a loud comeback on the political scene.

Dwindling popularity

Rajiv Gandhi's image as a young, dynamic innovator, which had brought him an overwhelming mandate in form of a three-quarters majority in the elections, ebbed away. A weighty factor in this fall in popularity was the **Bofors scandal**, a weapons deal with a Swedish arms company, in which the sizeable sum of around 200 million dollars found its way into the pockets of leading members of government. As a result, Gandhi's squeaky-clean reputation suffered a severe blow. The Congress Party was taught a lesson at the subsequent elections in 1988, when it had to hand over power to a newly formed alliance under the leadership of V. P. Singh's Janata Party. However, the political strength of this coalition was also quickly spent, and by 1991 new elections had to be held. Once again Rajiv Gandhi threw himself into the election campaign as the candidate of the Congress Party and sought contact with the country's people who had abandoned him. However, pressing the flesh in this way was to be his downfall.

Rajiv Gandhi's assassination

During an election campaign event near Chennai Rajiv Gandhi was killed by a bomb in 1991. A member of the Tamil liberation organization, the **Tamil Tigers**, had thrown it into the crowd.

New Developments

1991	Introduction of economic liberalization
1998–2005	After the BJP's election victory Atal Bihari Vajpayee becomes prime minister
2005	Victory of the Congress Party and a new prime minister, Dr Manmohan Singh

End of the Nehru-Gandhi dynasty

The tragic fate of Rajiv Gandhi also marked the end of the decades of rule by the Nehru-Gandhi dynasty, at least for a while. The concentration of power in one single family had for a long time been the country's guarantee of political stability. At the same time it had led to a weakening of the democratic institutions and resulted in a **power vacuum** after the ruling period of the family came to an end.

Opening of the market

The new Congress government under **P.V. Narasimha Rao** initiated the opening of the Indian market in 1991. This free-market policy led to a growth of the middle class on the one hand and to aggravated social conflicts on the other, because the situation of the poorest got worse. One result of the social tensions was the **strengthening of Hindu nationalism** (Hindutva) and the BJP Party (Bharata Janata Party). Since the end of the 1980s the BJP had seen a steady increase in support and at the 1996 elections it became for the first time the strongest party in parliament. It failed to form a government, however. Between 1996 and 1998 a four-party coalition governed the country under prime ministers H. D. Deve Gowda and Inder Kumar Gujral.

The BJP in power

Following the elections in March 1998 the BJP finally managed to take over the government. **Atal Bihari Vajpayee** became India's new

Sonia Gandhi with her son Rahul and India's prime minister Dr Manmohan Singh at a remembrance vigil in memory of her murdered husband Rajiv Gandhi

prime minister until the party's defeat at the next elections in spring 2005. During his time in office he continued the liberal economic policies of his predecessors, but he continually took a nationalist approach. His failure to be re-elected can be attributed to the disillusionment of the poorest members of society in particular, as their situation had not improved under the BJP.

Most recent developments and the future

Since 2005 the Congress Party has been ruling the country again. India's current prime minister is the economics expert **Dr Manmohan Singh**, who took up the position after Rajiv Gandhi's widow Sonia turned down the office. However, she has chaired the Congress Party since 1998. **India's growing economic potential has caused its international political role to change.** India is not just the leading power in south Asia, it also lays claim to an appropriate role amongst the world's leading nations, such as a permanent seat on the UN Security Council. Amongst the most important subjects of Indian politics are the ongoing issue of India's relationship to its neighbour Pakistan, and the Kashmir question. A process of détente has been in place for some time now, but it has been subject to several disturbances. On the domestic front the state faces the regular challenge of minimizing communal confrontations battled out between extremists from different parties and religious communities.

Art and Culture

How do temples in northern India and southern India differ? What is the Mahabharata? Which Indian-born writer received death threats from Iranian Mullahs? And with what statistic has Bollywood long since overtaken its American counterpart?

Architecture

Indian architecture, apart from forts and palaces, mainly revolves around religious structures. While it was the defence and display function that was in the foreground when forts and palaces were constructed, religious architecture aimed at reflecting the beliefs of the different religions. Other criteria came into play only with post-independence modern architecture and the construction of urban structures.

Indian architecture can be divided into three main historical periods. Each of these periods developed certain characteristics. Until the 6th century architecture was **greatly influenced by Buddhism**, after which regional Hindu kingdoms were formed in which different types of temple buildings developed. The most important in this category are the **Nagara style** of the northern Indian temples and the **Dravidian style** of southern India. From the 12th century onwards the **Islamic building style** developed. Its main buildings were mosques, tombs and palaces. The structures built by the British were usually geared to European architecture and were built largely for prestige purposes. After India achieved independence there were only a few ambitious projects in which religious buildings (Bahai Temple in Delhi) or entire towns (►Chandigarh) were designed and built.

Buddhist Architecture

Among the oldest still extant historical buildings are the remains of the stupas, **dome-shaped monuments**, in which Buddhist relics were kept. A stupa (head of hair) consists of a base (medhi) and a hemispherical dome (anda) above it. These places of remembrance are interpreted as an image of the cosmos and the individual architectural elements as symbolic representations of the different levels of the mythical world-mountain, Meru. Stupas are crowned by a circular disc, symbolizing rule and protection, while the central axis symbolizes the axis of the earth. Sometimes stupas are surrounded by walls, which are interspersed by gates (toranas) through which pilgrims can enter. The toranas of **Sanchi** with their excellent sculptures, which symbolically represent Buddhist teachings, are a particularly good example. While stupas were nothing more than small mounds during the time of Ashoka, over time they developed into huge stone domes rising up to the sky on stepped pedestals. The stupa in Sanchi has a diameter of 36m/39yd and a height of 16.5m/54ft without its top piece.

Among other architectural developments during this time were **cave monasteries** with large prayer halls (chaitya halls) and simple living

Stupas

← »The wonderful flute melody« (Indian miniature, around 1700)

quarters for the monks (viharas). They were built during the time of Hinayana Buddhism. Buddha himself was never represented in chaitya halls, since he never wanted to be worshipped as a god; they rather contained symbols such as Bodhi trees, wheels or Buddha's footprints. In later times the Buddhist centres of northern India saw the development of monasteries. Good examples can be found around Leh.

Stupa in Sarnath

Another special feature of Buddhist architecture are **stambhas**, **monolithic columns** topped by capitals adorned by trees, bulls or elephants. Emperor Ashoka also had such stambhas with engraved edicts set up all around the country, but his columns only had lion capitals. This indicates the adoption of the lion as a symbol of power, taken over from Iran.

Hindu Architecture

The oldest Hindu temples, structures made of wood and mud, have not survived the millennia. The later stone temples tried, however, to mimic the wooden temples. Hindu temples developed into a synthesis of architecture, sculpture and painting. The Shilpa Shastras (architectural treatises) exactly laid down the floor plan and the relationships between the individual temple parts. The numerical relationships and architectural elements were attempts to transfer a complex religious system to architecture by using numerology. The entire temple thus became an architectural manifestation of symbolic thought.

The temple as the cosmos

Temples are a miniature reproduction of the cosmos and the temple tower represents the axis that connects earth to the heavens. This is also the reason why **orientation towards the sun** and the arrangement of figures symbolizing the signs of the zodiac play an important role in temple construction. Hindu temples are understood both as a representation of the universe as well as a representation of the human body. The small **cella (garbhagriha)**, which contains the central deity, corresponds to the heart or the soul. A temple's upper areas are usually populated by figures that are in motion, such as dancers, divine nymphs and musicians, as they embody the element air. The lower area contains representations of all the natural forces that are necessary to protect the temple. The depiction of lovers (mithuna figures) is also supposed to protect a temple from lightning and other forces of nature.

The garbhagriha, the shrine, in which the central deity resides, is oriented towards the east, so that the rays of the rising sun can illuminate the deity. A corridor (pradakshina patha) runs around the shrine; it is used by Hindus to walk around the deity in a clockwise direction, an important component of prayer. Above the cella is a tower known as shikhara or vimanam. There is often a prayer hall (mandapa) in front of the shrine. Typologically two main styles can be identified, the Nagara and the Dravidian styles, which particularly differ in their roofing. This is just a rough classification, since transitional forms also exist.

Basic pattern of the temple complex

The Nagara styleis most prevalent in **northern India**. Its characteristic feature is the parabola-shaped tower, the **shikhara**, above the cella. There are usually several halls in front of the cella, some of which are crowned by smaller pyramid-shaped towers. The earliest examples of this style from the Gupta period were destroyed by the first Islamic conquerors. The temples in **Osiyan** (Rajasthan) from the 8th century are amongst the few that still give an idea of what these relatively small temples looked like. Later, the Solanki rulers in Gujarat (11th century) built the Sun Temple in **Modhera**. The shikhara consists of one piece with an atrium in front. The rich sculptures along the temple's outer walls are particularly impressive. Good examples

Nagara style

An example of the Nagara style: Mukteshavara Temple in Bhubaneshwar

of the next phase of development are the temples of **Bhubaneshwar** and **Puri**. The individual temple components that were developed over time were all given names. The cella was called deul, the atrium jagamohan. Between these two parts, which are crowned by a conical, multi-part tower, is a single, narrow connection. Other areas attached to the actual temple are a dance hall (nata mandapa) and a food hall (bhog mandapa), both of which have pyramid-shaped roofs, however. The temples of **Khajuraho** (11th–12th centuries) have a very steep, conical tower, which consists of many small shikharas coming together as an organic whole. Every one of these small shikharas rises up above the depiction of a secondary deity and physically represents the hierarchical order of the Hindu pantheon. The towers in the atria also rise up slowly in the same style and together with the main tower form a complex unit. The corridor around the cella in Khajuraho is illuminated by the presence of windows and adorned with sculptures.

Dravidian style The Dravidian style mainly developed in **Tamil Nadu** some time around the seventh century. The earliest examples of it are the temples in **Mamallapuram** and **Kanchipuram**. The temples built by the Pallava dynasty had a great influence on temple construction, not just in India but also in Java and Cambodia.

Particularly characteristic of this style are the **vimana**, the towers rising up above the garbhagriha. The temple tower of the Shore Temple in Mamallapuram is still quite modest, but over time they became higher and higher: the 58m/190ft vimana of **Thanjavur** is a landmark of the town that can be seen from far and wide. It is said to have been so famous that it served as a model for Prambanan Temple in Indonesia. In front of the vimana is the ardha mandapa (atrium). New elements were added over time, such as the maha mandapa (great hall), which was used for musical events, and the kalyana mandapa (wedding hall), where the wedding of the residing deity and his companion were celebrated every year. The temple complex was protected by a wall with four gates, above which the **gopurams**, towers rising up over the temple entrance, were built. The Pandyas, who took power after the Pallavas, brought the gopurams to perfection. They were the new symbols of the growing temple complex that could be seen from great distances. Gopurams were adorned with thousands of figures, which were a visual depiction of India's legends for the country's rural population. By the end of this development entire temple cities were built, some of which took on huge proportions. Particularly good examples are the temple complexes of **Sri Rangam**, **Madurai** and **Thanjavur**.

Jain Architecture

Architecturally speaking, Jain temples do not differ significantly from Hindu temples. They do, however, have a few remarkable features.

Typical southern Indian temple complex, here in Tirukkalikundram (near Mamallapuram)

In contrast to Hindu temples they appear plain on the outside as their wealth of sculptures is unfolded in their interior. The cella is sometimes open to the north, south, east and west (caumukha). Generally speaking, Jain temples are flooded with light. Sometimes they also possess closed rooms into which believers can withdraw to meditate. The largest caumukha temple in honour of Adinatha in **Ranakpur** (Rajasthan) with its 29 halls and 1444 finely carved columns is a very good example. Other regions also saw the development of huge temple cities as a result of more and more temples being built. Mount Satrunjaya in **Palitana** (Gujarat) contains 863 temples, many of which house fine marble sculptures.

Mughal Architecture

Some Indian buildings of international stature were constructed during the Mughal period. The most important Mughal buildings are **tombs, mosques, palaces and gardens**. The gardens are often part of the palaces or tomb complexes. Some of the most elegant buildings of the Mughal period were built during the reign of Shah Jahan, the use of marble, the inlay work using semi-precious stones and the frequently fanned arches giving this architecture a lightness and elegance. The **Taj Mahal** is the real masterpiece, combining Persian and Hindu elements into a single harmonious whole. Other famous structures erected during the reign of Shah Jahan were the Red Fort and the great Jama Masjid mosque in Delhi, which set the standard for all subsequent buildings.

Basic structure of mosques

The basic structure of a mosque consists of a roofed prayer hall (haram) and a forecourt. Inside the prayer hall the wall facing Mecca is marked by a mihrab (prayer niche). The main mosques also contain a minbar or imam's pulpit. The forecourt is often surrounded by an arcade, which starts and ends at the prayer hall. There is usually a fountain in the forecourt, which is used for the necessary ritual cleaning prior to prayer. The minarets, from where a muezzin calls to prayer, are particularly striking architectural features.

Mughal mosques

The first mosques were built from the remains of destroyed Hindu temples by Indian craftsmen (p.258). The corbel arches of these

Symbol of a great love: the Taj Mahal, mausoleum for Mumtaz Mahal

mosques highlight the still very strong Hindu influence. Later Indian mosques were also fitted with domes, modelled on the mosques from the Arab area, using arch techniques with radial grooves. The Mughal rulers had craftsmen brought to India from Turkey and Persia so that their mosques would resemble those of their original homeland. In contrast to Hindu or Jain temples, mosques, following the Islamic tradition, are unadorned; only flower and plant motifs are sometimes used for decoration. The Indo-Saracenic style, in which a mosque's columns and walls possess extremely detailed relief structures, developed in Gujarat. Particularly good examples are the **Jama Masjid in Delhi** and the **Moti Masjid in Agra**.

Forts

The Mughal conquerors, who were constantly at war with their neighbours, had numerous forts and even entire cities built, the focus being on defence and display. In addition to the Red Fort in Delhi and the fort in Agra, the now abandoned city of Fatehpur Sikri is a successful example of the Mughal rulers' efforts. They were architecturally inspired by older Indian models such as the complexes of Mandu or Gwalior Fort.

Tombs

The tomb complexes for the dead were developed to perfection under the Mughals. In addition to India's most famous structure, the Taj Mahal, other noteworthy buildings of this type are Humayun's tomb in Delhi, the Itmad-ud-Daulah in Agra and the Qutb Shahi tombs in Hyderabad.

Gardens

Char Bagh (four gardens), a geometrically designed garden, is one of the main components of tombs and forts. Sometimes gardens, which were closely connected to Muslim ideas of paradise, were created in their own right. These gardens were first created in Persia and brought to India by the Mughal ruler Babur, where over the centuries they continued to develop. Important examples can be found at Humayun's Tomb in Delhi or in Shalimar Garden in Srinagar.

Colonial Architecture

Prestige buildings

In addition to forts and administrative buildings, the British built some prestige buildings in order to underline their right to rule. The **Victoria Memorial** in Kolkata, built in honour of Queen Victoria, and the city of New Delhi, which was built from scratch as an administrative centre, were two of the most ambitious British projects.

Palaces

During the colonial era new palaces were built in several cities for the Indian maharajas, which often emulated European styles. These buildings were designed by Europeans and sometimes the furnishings were also imported from Europe. Impressive examples are **Jai Vilas** (1874) in Gwalior and **Lalbagh Palace** (1880) in Indore, whose gates are a replica of the Buckingham Palace gates.

VICTORIA MEMORIAL

The Victoria Memorial is one of the most important relics of the time when Kolkata was still British and went by the name of Calcutta. The building of white marble with its formal gardens and pools was planned by the British foreign minister Lord Curzon (1859–1925) to give the empire a monument of its golden age. It was designed by Sir William Emerson and completed in 1921.

🕐 Open:
daily except Mon 10am–5pm. Photography is not permitted inside. The English-language sound-and-light show takes place at 7.15pm (Oct–Feb) or 7.45pm (March–Sept).

① Bronze Statue
In front of the north entrance there is a statue of Queen Victoria, in whose honour the memorial was built. From 1877 to 1901 she was Queen of England and Empress of India.

② Structure
The romantic statues above the entrance, the Mughal corner domes and the elegant high colonnades at the sides make the structure seem like a mix of classical European architecture and the style of the Mughal period. Its harsher critics label it a failed attempt to build a better Taj Mahal. The foundation stone for the 103m/340ft-long building was laid in 1906 by the Prince of Wales, the future King George V.

③ Central Dome
The 5m/16ft rotating victory statue on top of the magnificent dome weighs three tons.

④ Museum
The museum mainly exhibits works relevant to British-Indian history. They include a genuine Reynolds, Queen Victoria's rosewood piano, and a model of Fort William, as well as jewellery, armour, weapons and original contracts of the East India Company. Paintings depict Indian landscapes and buildings as well as portraits of British colonial officers and scenes from military conflicts. There is a painting showing the magnificent entry of the Prince of Wales (later Edward VII) into Jaipur (1876) as well as French guns that were captured at the Battle of Plassey. The museum also possesses the black throne of the Nabob, who was defeated by Clive in 1757. In addition there are some very nice Indian and Persian miniatures and rare books and manuscripts. Furthermore there is a lot of information about Indians' lives, where visitors can read about how the average British family used to live in Calcutta. Having more than 100 servants, from cooks to gardeners and from nannies to punkah wallahs (servants to fan fresh air), was commonplace. Visitors should not miss the section about the Indian independence movement.
Tip: There is a particularly lovely view to be had of the park (Maidan) from the balcony over the entrance.

»A Game of Cricket in Calcutta«
(Colour lithograph, 1861)

Indo-Saracenic Style   In addition to the European copies, another style developed known as the Indo-Saracenic Style, a mixture of Indian and European architectural elements. The Victoria Memorial in Kolkata, the High Court in Chennai and the **Victoria Terminus** (Chhatrapati Shivaji Station) in Mumbai are just three examples. In addition there are interesting variations such as Umaid Bhavan in Jodhpur, a new interpretation of Indian architectural design, and Lalgarh Palace in Bikaner, which has a very Indian air.

Post-independence Architecture

Since India's independence, architecture has been shaped by the attempt to meet the growing need for residential and commercial premises. Two projects should be mentioned in this context: firstly **Chandigarh**, the newly built capital of Punjab; and secondly Haryana. Both were meant to express the idea of a modern, democratic India. The architect **Le Corbusier** designed a city with wide streets, large squares and districts divided up according to function. Even though the concrete buildings have now become grey and weathered and have lost a lot of their symbolic power for a new, independent India, they have nonetheless become models for subsequent generations of Indian architects.

Another noteworthy structure is the **Indian Institute of Management** in Ahmedabad. The complex was designed by American architect **Louis Khan**, and built between 1962 and 1972 using the ruins of Mandu and Fatehpur Sikri as inspiration. The brick buildings on the site, which covers an area in excess of 25ha/62ac, have been constructed in such a way as to accommodate the special climatic conditions. They provide protection from the heat of the sun, but let wind in. The buildings have large galleries and courtyards, since Khan assumed that learning should not just take place in lecture halls, but also outside.

Literature

Beginnings   The oldest traditions, which provide insight into the early cultures of the subcontinent, are more than 3000 years old. They were handed down orally from one generation to the next. They were captured in writing only much later, which is true of the majority of examples from that time. For that reason it is often difficult to attribute works to a single author.

When speaking of »Indian literature« it should be noted that this term can in no way be compared to »English literature« for example. India's poets and authors did not and do not write in »Indian«. The old texts were written in Sanskrit, Pali, Prakriti or Tamil.

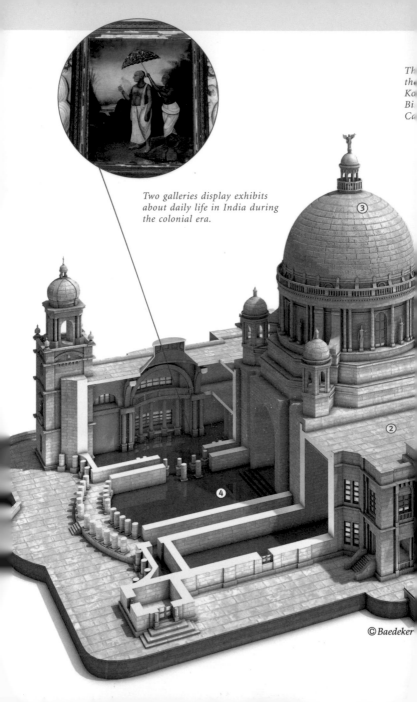

Two galleries display exhibits about daily life in India during the colonial era.

Th...
the
Ko...
Bi...
Ca...

③

②

④

© Baedeker

The Victoria Memorial stands at the southern end of the Maidan, Kolkata's green lung, close to the Birla Planetarium and St Paul's Cathedral (both on the left).

Bronze statue of Empress Victoria in front of the north entrance

①

It was only much later that Hindi, which is based on different dialects, and Urdu, which has an Arabic-Persian influence, developed as important literary languages. Modern Indian authors, however, have to face the burning question of how to reach the multilingual readership of their country.

The oldest literary works of the subcontinent, the **Vedas** (veda = knowledge), were written in Sanskrit, whose Indo-Germanic roots are evident in many words. The Vedas are a **collection of religious texts**, which were developed between 1200 and 500 BC. The oldest section, the **Rigveda**, contains 1028 hymns for the different gods of the nomadic Aryan people of the time. Bit by bit the **Samaveda** followed, a compilation of songs, some of which are identical to the Rigveda, and the **Yajurveda**, a collection of formulae that were recited during sacrifices. The final section is the **Atharvaveda**, which mainly consists of spells to ward off demons and diseases. The **Brahmanas**, texts containing complicated sacrificial rituals (900 to 400 BC), fall into the transitional period from Vedism to Hinduism. This was also the time in which the role of the priests as mediators between god and the people greatly grew in importance.

Excerpt from the Indian national epic, the Mahabharata

In contrast, the Upanishads (secret teachings), which were developed around 600 BC, contain the **philosophical views** of the Indians. They do not form a definite philosophical system, since many thinkers and schools participated in its development. | **Upanishads**

Two works that have become really popular – in the true sense of the word – are the two great epics, the Mahabharata and the Ramayana. The time they were conceived cannot be clearly defined, since they were presumably the work of many generations. One period is commonly cited by Western historians, lasting from the 4th century BC to the 4th century AD. However, in India both epics are considered to be the works of particular poets: according to this theory the Mahabharata was written by the sage Vyasa, while the Ramayana is said to have been penned by the poet Valmiki. Both works were to have a | **Mahabharata and Ramayana** decisive influence on the subjects of future literature right up to the modern age. This is particularly true of the famous didactic poem, the **Bhagavat Gita**, which forms the heart of the Mahabharata. To this day every child in India grows up with the images and stories of the five Pandava brothers of the Mahabharata. The most popular stories are still the ones about the great hero Rama, his consort Sita, the monkey leader Hanuman and the evil demon Ravana. The characters of the Ramayana, whether making appearances in bedtime stories, street theatre productions or a pan-Indian television series, continue to represent both reprehensible and judicious patterns of behaviour, and even in the age of satellite television and the internet many people orient themselves by them.

Different languages of literature

Even though many texts were written in **Sanskrit**, it was not the only literary language of its time. Thus many Buddhist and Jain texts have been handed down in both **Sanskrit** and **Pali**. There are also rich collections of texts in **Tamil**, India's second oldest language. The conquests of large parts of India by Muslim rulers brought Persian-Arabic literary traditions to India during the Middle Ages. Some of India's most beautiful love poems were written in the new language, Urdu, a blend of Persian and Arabic with the dominant Hindi. The main patrons of that art were the Mughals of northern India; it was at their courts that the poets usually lived. **Urdu poetry** had its golden age during the 18th and 19th centuries, with famous names such as Meer, Zafar and, in particular, Ghalib.

Bhakti literature

The religious literature of the Hindus also saw great changes from the 10th century onwards. Thus a counter-movement formed to the very exclusive Sanskrit literature, which was only understood by a few. This new literature was called Bhakti literature. This term is used to describe **devotional religious expression** written in the various regional languages, thus making it accessible to the people. The most popular and influential amongst the many Bhakti poets was **Tulsi Das** (1532–1623), but a female name also won great fame: **Mirabai** (c1500–c1550) achieved immortality with her passionate verses to the god Krishna. The words of the radical critic **Kabir** (1440–1518), who attacked the cemented rituals of Hinduism and Islam, sound positively modern: »If I can be guided by a stone idol / then let me go and worship an entire mountain« or »The mullah caws from the tip of the mosque / as if Allah were deaf«.

Western influence

One crucial factor for the developments in modern Indian literature was the introduction of the Western system of education and the English language. This led to diverse reactions amongst Indian intellectuals. Many of them soon felt so at home with English that they also wrote their works in that language, while others chose this time to focus anew on a national identity and wrote in their mother tongues such as Hindi, Bengali, Marathi or Tamil.

The most famous Bengali poet is also considered to be India's greatest modern poet: Rabindranath Tagore (1861–1941). He was awarded the **Nobel Prize in Literature** for his work *Gitanjali* in 1913 (▶Famous People).

Rabindranath Tagore

As of the 1930s more and more Indian authors started using the language of their colonial rulers, which had become a second mother tongue for many of the country's intellectuals. Amongst this group are the great novelists **R. K. Narayan**, **Raja Rao** and **Mulk Raj Anand**. By and large, all of them make use of subjects that are primarily populated by Indian characters in largely native terrain. Other authors writing in English include Kamala Das, Anita Desai and Shashi Deshpande, whose novels, tales and short stories mainly focus on the role of women in modern India. Another author of great critical acclaim is U.R. Ananthamurthy from Karnataka; his novel *Sanskara* was made into a successful film.

English-language Indian literature

More recent developments: a new generation of authors that has been helping to shape the literary scene since the early 1980s has a

More recent developments

Salman Rushdie

more cosmopolitan style. The most noteworthy individuals in this category are **Salman Rushdie** (▶Famous People) and **Amitav Ghosh**. Rushdie became famous as a result of his bestseller *Midnight's Children*, which earned him the Booker Prize in 1981. Many novels followed. After the publication of *The Satanic Verses*, Ayatollah Khomeini issued a fatwa requiring Rushdie's execution, forcing the author to go into hiding for nearly a decade and resulting in a break in diplomatic relations between the UK and Iran. Amitav Ghosh is one of the younger generation of Indian authors. His novels, such as *The Circle of Reason*, *The Calcutta Chromosome* and *The Glass Palace* made him world famous. Another member of this group is the politically active author **Arundhati Roy**, who had a surprise success with her book *The God of Small Things* (▶Famous People). The »NRIs« (Non-Resident Indians) living in the United States or in Canada, the UN diplomat **Shashi Tharoor**, the Parsi author **Rohinton Mistry** and **Jhumpha Lahiri** from Bengal, are also all part of the circle of younger successful authors.

Translation and international significance

At the same time writing in the mother tongue is and always will be the only way for many authors to express Indian reality and Indian ideas in a worthy manner. Unfortunately only a few of these often brilliant works manage to obtain a larger readership that transcends regional or even national boundaries, since good translations are difficult and rare, especially into languages other than English.

Music

Classical Indian Music

Our perception, it is said, is shaped by culture. If this statement is true this must also be true of hearing. Familiar with opera houses or open-air concerts, Westerners are not usually uplifted when they hear classical Indian music for the first time.

Foundations

What is it about classical Indian music that sounds so strange to Western ears? Why is it so different from other familiar sounds, from Bach to hip hop? India's classical music has always been court and temple music. This fact has shaped its **contemplative and meditative character**, which is often felt to be nothing but monotonous and boring when listened to with ignorance and through the filter of Western musical traditions. It is not just the tuning system that is alien to Western ears, other unfamiliar aspects are its melodies, rhythms and instruments. Attentive concert-goers will notice immediately that there is always a solo instrument accompanied by one or more other instruments. This already highlights one of its most important characteristics: Indian music is **monophonic**, and has no

Ravi Shankar, the master of the sitar

polyphonic elements or harmonies. Its basis is the human voice. Song lyrics form the foundation of the musical pieces and as a result the instruments make use of the same three octaves or so that the human voice can master.

Tuning system

The Indian tuning system is based not on equal temperament, but rather on "just" intonation (with intervals based on whole-number ratios). The sangama, the Indian scale, like the European, possesses **seven main notes**. However there is a much more differentiated system of 22 intermediate intervals. It is the relationship of these intervals around a freely chosen keynote that give Indian music its timbre. An accompanying instrument, often the four-stringed tambura, provides the keynote, its perfect fifth and their octaves. This chord is the base on which the musicians construct their playing.

Raga and tala

Like all music Indian music also has its roots in religion. It can be traced back to the melodies of Vedic songs and sacrificial rituals, in which it was the main component. The Samarveda, the collection of texts that also contains some of the musical works of the Aryans of the time, provides insight into its theory and its basic terms. **Raga (melody)** and **tala (rhythm)** form the music's framework. Every raga is based on a succession of five to twelve notes, which can be combined with each other by following certain rules, conveying **specific**

moods. Thus morning ragas, evening ragas, ragas for the different seasons and, last but not least, male ragas and female raginis can be created. Depending on the time at which they are played they will unfold their special effect. The talas, of which there are several hundred, form the basic structures of Indian rhythm. They are, like European music, divided into bars. A tala's most important accent is always on the first beat. An **onomatopoeic syllable**, recited by the musician, accompanies every single beat. The development of a raga is usually divided into three parts. The first part, called alap, does not have any rhythmic accompaniment. In the second part, the gap, the melody starts to be accompanied by drums; it is governed by fixed compositions. The final part is the jhala; it ends at a fast pace in a climax. Of course different developments occurred in classical music over time.

Amongst the various styles there are two main directions. In northern India the dominant sound is **Hindustani music**, a style pervaded by Islamic elements. The southern-Indian variant, known as **Carnatic music**, is closer to the original form. The same fact that held true for Indian literature for a long time was also true of the country's music until the 20th century, namely that it was not written down and played from the score, but transmitted orally. This took place within the family tradition, as it still does today. India's musicians come from old musician families in which artistic skills are directly passed on to the next generation.

More recent developments
How alive this tradition is becomes clear on visiting a classical Indian concert. However, Indian sounds have long found their way into Western music as a result of globalization. Back in the mid-1960s, George Harrison added sitar to the recording of the Beatles' *Norwegian Wood*, and in 1971 was joined on stage by Ravi Shankar and a star-studded cast for the Concert for Bangladesh. These days Indian sounds can be heard in clubs and bars around the world. Moreover, the popular Indian music that forms the soundtrack to Bollywood films has found new fans as a result of the Indian film industry's increasing fame.

Dance

Divine imitation
Dance is the imitation on stage of the divine world. Its themes and subjects come from the seemingly endless collection of Indian myths and legends. The great epics, the Mahabharata and the Ramayana, have always been particularly popular sources of inspiration for dance artists.

There are no individual characters; instead the dances feature the typical characters of Hindu society: the ascetic, the priest, the king, the princess and, of course, the entire world of gods.

The compendium of classical dance literature is the Natyashastra, **Natyashastra** which dates back to the second century AD. The collection of texts can supposedly be traced to the sage Bharata. However, it does not just address dance, but also its »accompanying arts«, music and singing. It identifies the complicated language of a dancer's steps, gestures and looks. The book is also a treatise about the point and purpose of the performance itself. The Natyashastra distinguishes between two kinds of dance: the purely rhythmic dance (nritta) and theatrical dance (natya).

Movements and sequences are presented very precisely and in detail: from the head via the neck, chest, stomach, hands, fingers and buttocks to the feet. **108 different postures** are known to classical dance as well as **64 hand gestures** and **36 forms of gaze**, with seven different

One of the 64 hand gestures of Indian dance

ways of raising the eyebrows. In this way, gods, humans, animals and objects can be represented; it is difficult even for Indians to understand the complicated language of the body straight away. The permitted movements are strictly specified and improvisations are not allowed.

The work is not just a manual for artists' practical use. It addresses the **effect the dancers have on their audience** in great detail. The question arises of how a performer can possibly express an emotional attitude (bhava) in such a way that the audience feels the right emotions (rasas) as a result. The answer is that it takes years of training before an artist can do this. The most convincing dance artists are those who manage to produce the full range of emotions, from being in love, to anger, to fear, in the audience.

It is thanks to the perseverance of a few families and dancers that the **Revival of classi-** art of classical Indian dancing has not fallen into oblivion. Today **cal dance styles** there are schools all over the country which teach the classical dance styles. A by-product of these institutions has been the development of a modern theatre movement, which combines traditional elements with modern choreography. The most important and best-known forms of classical dance are in southern India, **Bharata Natyam** from Tamil Nadu, **Kathakali** from Kerala and **Kuchipudi dance theatre** from Andhra Pradesh. Northern India is the home of **Kathak**, Orissa is the birthplace of **Odissi**, and the mountain peoples of the eastern Himalaya developed **Manipuri**.

Crafts

Craft tradition For dancers, musicians, sculptors and painters, but also weavers, potters and dressmakers, Sanskrit has only one word: shilpa. All these professions are seen as having derived from Vishvakarma, the architect of the gods. Traditional Indian society made no distinction between arts and crafts. Craftsmen were artists, and artists in turn were always craftsmen. India's wealth of arts and crafts traditions is as inexhaustible as the diversity of its landscapes. From the archaic and lively expressiveness of its Dravidian population, to the 3000 year-old aesthetic code of the Vedas, to the innovations of the Islamic conquerors: this treasure of artistic knowledge built up over the millennia contributes to the subcontinent's great artistic wealth.

In the villages the **skills to perform these arts and crafts have always been handed down within certain castes and families**. From a simple clay pot to a meticulously proportioned, chiselled temple sculpture, India's art ranges from the profane to the religious. Rules and laws passed on from generation to generation determine the production process. Materials, shapes, colours, patterns and proportions are all fixed. However, artisans are not considered mechanical producers, a fact that is often hard for Westerners to understand; artisans' work is rather an expression of their creative and, in particular, their spiritual powers.

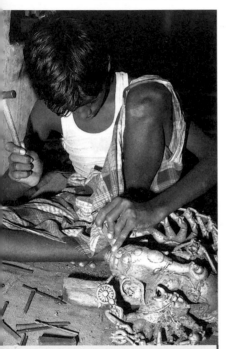
Working on a bronze sculpture

The shilpis were very much supported in the past by the courts and temples, who gave them contracts or who employed them directly. Both India's colonization and the industrial revolution have caused the status of artisans to suffer quite severely. The competition from machines and the flooding of the Indian market with British ready-made goods have brought about the near destruction of entire professions, such as that of the weaver. Mahatma Gandhi managed to save Indian arts and crafts from collapse with his concept aimed at strengthening the village economies. The simple spinning wheel became the symbol of self-confidence and political resistance. India's arts and crafts traditions have thus not yet been banished to museums and books. They are still there, the castes of the potters, basketmakers, woodcarvers, blacksmiths, goldsmiths and of course sculptors. Symbols of cultural and social continuance and strength, they are carrying on their own traditions in every region of this vast country (►Practicalities, Shopping).

Painting

The archaeological digs of the period of the Indus valley civilization (3000 to 1500 BC) have brought many ceramics with depictions of peacocks, deer and flower motifs to light. A few particularly interesting objects can be seen in the museum in Delhi and in the small museum in Lothal in Gujarat, the place where the objects were found. Original paintings are not extant, however, either because there were few such objects made or because they have not managed to survive all these years.

Indus valley civilization

The cave paintings of Ajanta are outstanding examples that prove India had a highly developed art of painting from very early on. The **artistic frescoes** usually depict stories from the life of Buddha. The

Cave paintings of Ajanta (3D image p.436)

Example of the Basholi school: Krishna talks about his love

masterpieces of Mahayana Buddhism were created bit by bit between the first and eighth centuries AD.

The **Mughal rulers** supported large painting studios, in which the country's best artists were gathered. The sponsored painters addressed various subjects depending on a ruler's preferences; miniature painting was developed to perfection. Right from the start, the rulers used this form to depict their deeds and thus have themselves immortalized. Alongside this, the **art of portrait painting** also developed. Akbar had his court painters create portraits of all the important people of his empire. The court painters went so far in their efforts to portray every detail that they worked with brushes so fine they consisted of a single hair. They thus managed to paint individual hairs in a beard, hairs that can only be seen when inspecting the portrait with a magnifying glass.

Miniature painting

In contrast to the Mughals' aristocratic paintings, **Rajput miniature paintings** used almost no shading; instead they consisted of large areas of pure colours without any drawings within them. Rajput pictures often seem like stage backdrops. A tree signifies a forest, a pink spot stones, wavy lines water and a peacock the monsoon. Rajput painters used a collection of symbols for particular objects of reality or moods. This alphabet used by the painters can only be read by those who know it. Since painting was often used to illustrate religious texts, it is impossible for someone who doesn't know the legend or story depicted to understand the meaning of the pictures. Legends from Krishna's life became the most popular subject of Rajput painting. Important **regional schools developed in Mewar, Bundi, Kotaha and Malwa**. During the 13th and 14th centuries, Hindus fleeing from the Islamic conquerors settled in the western Himalaya and founded the Pahari (mountain) states. Here, in this sparsely populated, remote area, the miniature painting of the **Pahari school** reached its zenith in the 18th century and became known far and wide as the Basohli and Kangra schools. **Kangra paintings** are characterized by their soft depictions of landscapes and few figures, while **Basohli paintings** on the other hand have bright, contrasting colours and keenly traced figures. Amongst this school's most popular motifs are stories from the life of Krishna and the goddess Durga.

Painting in India was and is more than just an art of rulers and the rich, it also belongs to the people. Particularly in rural regions various traditions have been kept alive. The spectrum ranges from pictures at house entrances that created anew every day (**rangolis**) to house paintings that are renewed every year. The **Madhubani paintings** from Bihar are not just drawn on houses, they are also put on paper and sold as paintings in the cities. The **rich painting tradition**

Folk painting

← *House painting is an art form practised by women in many parts of India*

of the tribal populations is seeing increasing recognition both in India and internationally. The filigree paintings of the Warlis from Maharashtra or the Gonds from Madhya Pradesh are on show in numerous galleries around the world.

Western influence and continuation of the tradition

British rule had a great impact on the painters from the urban middle and upper classes during the 19th century, but with different effects. Painters like **Ravi Varma** tried to imitate the Western, realistic style, while others, such as **Abanindranath Tagore**, were at pains to develop their own style from the purely Indian traditions of Ajanta and Ellora, the Mughal style and the miniature paintings. Amongst the important modern Indian painters are **Jamani Roy** with his still lifes and **Amrita Shergil** with her pictures of Punjabi farmers, in which she exhibits much empathy with her subject. She tried to develop a synthesis of Western and Indian painting traditions in her images.

Contemporary painting

In light of the wealth of traditional art forms still alive today it is easy to overlook the fact that there is still room for modern art in India. This is particularly true of the paintings by those whose most important representatives have established reputations far beyond their country's borders. Two large galleries, one in Mumbai, the other in New Delhi, have now been dedicated to modern Indian painting. The pictures of the most outstanding artists in this genre are now being auctioned off by Christie's and Sotheby's in London and New York and fetch sizeable sums.

Progressive Artists Group

The birth of contemporary Indian painting approximately coincides in time with that of the Indian state. Several artists came together in Mumbai and joined forces under the name Progressive Artists Group. They were intent on going their own way in the confrontation with traditional Indian and Western painting. Several of India's great modern painters, such as M. F. Husain, Raza, F. N. Souza and Gaitonde, came from this group, and these painters had a significant impact on the next generation. **M.F. Husain**, the best-known name of the group, did not just receive critical acclaim as a painter. His film *Through the Eyes of a Painter* won the Golden Bear at the Berlin International Film Festival in 1967.

Today's art scene in India

During the 1950s a new generation of painters made a name for themselves. Tyeb Mehta, Akbar Padamsee, Anjolie Ela Menon and Nalini Malani, along with past master Husain, are just some of the artists who have a crucial impact on the scene to this day. Amongst the younger generation of Indian painters known beyond their country's borders are Jogen Chowdhury, Manjit Bawa, Meera Mukherjee and Arpita Singh. However, there are many even younger artists who are competing for attention. The works by a husband and wife team, Atul and Anju Dodiya, are considered particularly promising.

Sculpture

Indian sculpture has a tradition going back several thousand years and has produced some world-class works. Finds dating back to the Indus valley civilization have uncovered terracotta, stone and bronze sculptures and seals of outstanding quality. They point towards an early development of Indian art of sculpture.

Indus valley civilization

The earliest large-scale sculptures date back to the Maurya period, which was established by Chandragupta in 322 BC. The military conquests of Alexander the Great and particularly the subjugation of the Achaemenid Empire caused many artists to flee the Middle East to the Indian cultural sphere. This influence is seen particularly clearly on sculptures such as the famous monumental **Lion Capital**, which once adorned the columns set up by Ashoka. A masterpiece of such a lion capital, which became one of India's national emblems, can be found in the museum in Sarnath.

Maurya period (322–104 BC)

In the complexes of Khajuraho the temples seem to exist solely as a backdrop for the wonderful figures and ornaments.

Kushana period (2nd–3rd cent. AD)	The Kushana Empire, which stretched from Pataliputra to modern-day Pakistan under Kanishka, profited greatly from the Greek artists who had immigrated from the Alexandrian empire. The **Gandhara School**, which developed from this synthesis, left behind Buddha sculptures which resemble Greek sculptures to an astonishing degree.
Gupta period (320 – end of 5th cent.)	During the rule of the Guptas (AD 300–600), sculpture came to an artistic zenith. The masterpieces of that time usually depict **Buddha** in a standing or sitting position. They functioned as role models far beyond India's borders, all the way to Southeast Asia.
Pallavas and Cholas (AD 500–1050)	The sculptors' town of Mathura played a pioneering role in the making of sculptures for the entire Indian area from the sixth century BC until the fifth century AD. The most important development after the Gupta period took place 1000km/600mi further south, in Mathura in southern India. The Pallava dynasty, which controlled large parts of southern India between the fourth and ninth centuries, initiated great building works in their capital Kanchipuram and the port of Mamallapuram, in which sculptures played a major role. A special masterpiece is the 12m/39ft by 18m/59ft **granite relief in Mamallapuram**, a wonderful composition of animals, humans, saints and gods. The successors of the Pallavas, the Cholas, took bronze casting to new levels of perfection. The **southern-Indian classical bronze sculptures** are amongst the most significant sculptures in the world. One important motif in bronze sculptures produced using the cire perdue method is **Nataraja**, the dancing Shiva (fig. p.1).
Wealth of sculptures in temples (11th–12th cent.)	In contrast to Chola sculptures, which were conceived as individual objects, large temple complexes started using countless sculptures as a Western design tool from the 12th century on. Good examples are those of the temples built by the Hoysala dynasty in Somnathpur, Belur and Halebid, the complexes in Khajuraho and the Jain temples of Ranakpur, Mount Abu and Palitana.
Delhi sultanates (1206–1526)	Islamic rule led to a dramatic reduction in the manufacture of sculptures, since hardly any Hindu or Jain temples were being built and Islamic religious buildings used almost no sculptures. Artistically chiselled stone windows are interesting exceptions; a good example can be found in Sayyid mosque in Ahmedabad.
Present	Since Jain and Hindu temples are still being built today, the art of sculpture in India is alive and well. It continues to take its motifs and styles from its tradition and the classical writings about sculpture. It is possible to admire the skills of Indian sculptors in numerous workshops in Mamallapuram, for example. Younger artists also take their cues from Western aesthetics. Their works can be seen in city galleries or in the artists' colony Cholamandal, not far from Chennai.

Film

The **popularity of Bollywood movies**, even on European television, has made Indian films well-known in this part of the world, too. The fan-clubs of **Shah Rukh Khan** and **Amitabh Bachchan** have spread all the way to Europe. However, Indian film is not only Bollywood, even though the latter productions are the best-known. The southern Indian cities of Chennai and Hyderabad make just as many melodramatic romance movies as the studios of Mumbai, maybe even more. India also has an interesting alternative film scene and can look back on a long and eventful cinematic history.

D.G. Phalke (1870–1944), a painter and photographer, is considered the founder of Indian cinema. In 1913 he made his first movie, *Raja Harishendra*, which was inspired by an episode from the Mahabharata. He formed his own production company and made more than a hundred films over the next few decades. Early Indian film history is also associated with the name of the German cinematographer and director **Franz Osten** (1876–1956), who worked on numerous German-Indian co-productions and participated in setting up the famous film company **»Bombay talkies«** in the 1930s. At the same time the typical Indian musical developed and more than a hundred films were being produced every year. Until that time only entertainment movies were being made, but in the 1950s a greater differentiation developed: joining the genre of popular films were socio-critical and artistically challenging films. The absolute market leaders (and still popular today) were the melodramas by the all-round genius **Raj Kapoor**, who was not just able to sing, dance and act, but also direct and produce his own films. His sad-funny outsider character in *Awaara* (*The Rogue* 1951), *Shree 420* (*Mr. 420* 1954) and the famous latecomer *Mera Naam Joker* (*My Name is Joker*, 1971) filled cinemas for years and enchanted audiences not just in India but around the world.

Several masterpieces of 1950s' Indian cinema were also made by the directors **Guru Dutt** and **Bimal Roy**.

International recognition was achieved in particular by the two Bengali filmmakers **Satyajit Ray** and **Mrinal Sen** (► Famous People). Ray's *Apu Trilogy* (*Pther Panchali/Aparajito/Apur Sansar*), which was made between 1955 and 1959, achieved international fame. It is about the various stages in the life of a boy on his way to becoming a

Producers, directors, actors

Baedeker TIP

Bollywood close up

It is a real experience to watch a Hindi film in the original and with an Indian audience, best done in the film metropolis Mumbai itself. The old Art Deco cinemas, such as the »Regal«, the »Eros« and the »Metro«, are all located in south Mumbai and are well known to every taxi driver. Anyone who cannot handle the length of these films can leave the cinema during the interval.

»Sex and Crime«
Indian style

DREAM FACTORY BOLLYWOOD

A scene of hilly terrain, burned by the sun. Thick thorn bushes line the asphalted road. Suddenly the bushes are filled with movement and there is a call of »action!«.

No, this is not Hollywood. We are at the northern tip of Mumbai, where the mega-city ends and the rolling hills that go to the coast begin. Film City is the name of the place where dozens of heroes win battles, while heroines are wooed and evildoers lose their lives. Here, at the border between sad suburbs and bleak no man's land, India's dreams are produced. At **more than 950 films a year**, the subcontinent's film output is number one in the world, even ahead of the United States. An entire sector of industry makes its living off the big screen and India's cinematic fairy-tales are exported across the globe, from Russia to South Africa and of course Britain. Millions of dollars, or rather, billions of rupees flow into the pockets of the film bosses every year, because despite DVDs and satellite television the cinema is still number one amongst the preferred entertainments of the poor. Mumbai is the Mecca of commercial film production and is called »Bollywood« by many. The film studios are busy all year round. Almost no day goes by without some corner of the city centre being closed because of filming in progress. Despite the supremacy of Hindi films there is competition from elsewhere in India. In such a multilingual country not everyone can or wants to speak and understand Hindi. This is particularly true in the south and so Chennai, Hyderabad, Bangalore and Thiruvananthapuram have seen the creation of **regional varieties** of the popular blockbusters. Kolkata also has its own film industry – but Kolkata's taste has always been a little bit different.

»Collective fantasies«

is the name given by the Indian psychoanalyst Sudhir Karkar to the stuff dreams are made of. Yearnings are awakened in the half-light of packed cinemas and satiated again before the audience is released into India's generally harsh reality. Commercial films usually only use the format of **good triumphing over evil**, love triumphing over lies and hatred, in short the classic happy ending. For a long time the Indian film industry used Hollywood as a model, but now it has its own style. Popular films

encompass melodrama, action, comedy and thriller in one, »Indified« through songs and dance performances that are an indispensable component of all productions and give them an average length of three hours.

As in traditional popular theatre, the big screen only uses characters everyone knows. There is the young hero wooing the beautiful lady who has captured his heart and the evil villain who is trying to throw a spanner in the works. In the background is the usually suffering mother and then there is the father who always creates problems, and this cast is spiced up by all those supporting actors who either help good prevail or who have formed a pact with the dark powers. The excited audience egg on the courageous hero with their applause and angrily shake their fists against the evil gangsters; they cry with empathy for the death of the old mother and are thrilled about the wondrous end to the story.

The recipe is as old as curries and masalas in India's cuisine and, indeed, is popularly called »**masala film**«. Yet this alone does not yet fill cinemas, it does not enrage an audience, it does not bring in the millions. It is the stars that make every story a permanent hit; it is their songs everyone is singing the next day from Delhi to Chennai. They can also be the reason that the flicks are shelved and join the other flops after just ten screenings.

The big celebs of the film industry are greatly sought after, but as suddenly as their stars have risen they can sink again. It is not just film stars who are born here: the industry also creates gods, gangsters and politicians and the line is not always clearly drawn. Fame will buy a comfortable life for a while. But if all the money runs out and getting into private business has failed, there are still enough connections between the film world and the underworld for actors to increase their pocket money in other ways. From drug dealing to gun running, we have seen it all. It often happens that India's big screen gods canvass voters for earthly parties, in exchange for good money of course, and many a Rambo has found his way into parliament or even on to a premier's seat. And thus they carry on in their well-known roles, from heroic hunks to villains hated by all, proclaiming the good news that Hindi films are just like real life after all.

Film poster for Mira Nair's »Salaam Bombay«

man. His work was called poetic and realistic, sensitive and competent, multifaceted and observant. During the decades until his death Ray's films were part of the staple repertoire of international film festivals.

Mrinal Sen's name is closely associated with the **New Cinema movement** he brought into existence. Most of the young filmmakers who joined this group were united in their great dissatisfaction with the commercial films that were dominating the entire scene. Social criticism, political engagement and the development of a new film aesthetic were their primary goals. Even though sophisticated films have been sentenced to an existence in the shadows in India because there are only very few art-house cinemas, an alternative film scene has developed, which is standing up to the dominant Hindi films and is making a name for itself internationally. India's cultural metropolis, Kolkata, keeps delivering new impulses and a lively film movement has also developed in Kerala in southern India, whose productions are known beyond India's film enthusiasts. Even Mumbai, the stronghold of commercial Hindi films, still has enough room for the avant-garde, for aesthetics and other outsiders.

One of the best-known Indian filmmakers of today is **Mira Nair**, whose productions *Salaam Bombay*, *Monsoon Wedding* and *Kamasutra* played in cinemas around the world. She attempts to take serious subjects and make them into films using Bollywood elements. A British film, director Danny Boyle's *Slumdog Millionaire*, was set in Mumbai and featured a largely Indian cast. It achieved phenomenal success, being nominated for ten Academy Awards in 2009 and winning eight, as well as four Golden Globes, and seven BAFTA Awards.

Famous People

Which Indian poet received the Nobel Prize in Literature in 1913? Who did Churchill disrespectfully call a »half-naked, seditious fakir«? Who changed from being a literary hopeful into a political activist? And did you know that the families of conductor Zubin Mehta and pop singer Freddie Mercury come from Mumbai?

Sri Aurobindo (1872–1950)

Anyone reading Sri Aurobindo's life story and following his amazing **Philosopher** **transformation from an active revolutionary in the freedom movement to a spiritual yoga practitioner, philosopher and master** will have the feeling of having delved into an adventurous coming-of-age novel. According to his family's wishes, Aurobindo spent his school and university years in England, the intention being for him to have a career in the Indian civil service. In 1893 he returned to India, making contacts to a part of the Bengali liberation movement that was considered particularly radical. He moved to Kolkata in 1906 and became actively involved in the events there. Two years later he was arrested by the British in connection with a series of bombings, but in the absence of proof that he had been involved he was released again in 1909. Aurobindo was nevertheless perceived as one of the biggest enemies of the state and was put under constant surveillance. In order to avoid a second arrest he fled to the French enclave of Puducherry in southern India in 1910. This escape also marked the end of his political activities. The transformation undergone by the former revolutionary was not a sudden one. There had been a run-up to his retreat to immerse himself in the practices of yoga and meditation. During his years in Baroda, Aurobindo was already occupying himself with spiritual ideas and had used his prison stay in Kolkata to study yoga. Surrounded by a small circle of disciples, he gradually developed the spiritual and philosophical network of his ideas and his specific practice of yoga. Every year the number of followers coming to Puducherry grew, amongst them the French national **Mira Richard**, who was to become his right-hand woman and who continued his work under the name of »the mother«. In 1926 Aurobindo withdrew into seclusion and handed over the leadership of his followers to »the mother«.

Indira Gandhi (1917–84)

Indira Gandhi, **daughter of Nehru**, headed the Indian state for almost 16 years, making her one of the few women to have been successfully stood their ground in this male-dominated role. She married Feroze Gandhi in 1942, and in 1944 and 1946 she gave birth to her **sons Rajiv and Sanjay**. In 1948 she moved to New Delhi with them and accompanied her father on trips abroad, gathering her first political experiences. In 1959, after Nehru's death, she became the president of the Congress Party. In 1964 she was appointed the minister for information and broadcasting and just two years later she had become prime minister. Her deliberately populist policies using the slogan »garibi hatao« (»stop poverty«) allowed her to win the support of the masses and after the successful intervention of the In- **Long-standing prime minister**

← *To this day Indians speak respectfully of »Gandhiji«: Mahatma Gandhi*

Nehru with his daughter Indira (around 1940)

dian army in eastern Pakistan, 1971 saw her at the peak of her popularity. It was not to last, however; a period of drought and the resulting unrest and strikes ended with a state of emergency being proclaimed on the 26 June 1975. Mass arrests of awkward opposition politicians, censorship of the press, and a prohibition on strikes and demonstrations, as well as the forced sterilization campaign run by her son Sanjay, cost Indira Gandhi her office in the belated elections of 1977. However, the new government also fell into disrepute, which allowed Indira Gandhi to become **prime minister for the third time in 1980**. Her final years were marked by the conflicts in Assam and Punjab. Communal conflicts between Hindus and Sikhs brought about President's Rule, when the government was run from New Delhi. This culminated in the **storming of the Golden Temple in Amritsar**, the holiest Sikh shrine, by the Indian army, since militant Sikhs had barricaded themselves inside it. »Operation Blue Star« did not just cost thousands of soldiers and Sikhs their lives, it ultimately also led to the death of the prime minister herself. Seeking revenge for her actions, two of Indira Gandhi's Sikh bodyguards shot her on 31 October.

Mahatma Gandhi (1869–1948)

Advocate of non-violent resistance

Mohandas Gandhi was called Mahatma (great soul) by the poet Rabindranath Tagore, and the people called him Babu (father). Today, Indians still respectfully call him »Gandhiji«.

Gandhi's journey to becoming a key figure in the Indian struggle for independence and being dubbed the »**Father of the Nation**« was a long one that first took him halfway round the world. He was born in Porbandar (Gujarat) in 1869, the son of a merchant family. After studying law in England, Gandhi returned to India in 1891 and after several unsuccessful attempts to set up as a lawyer there he left for South Africa in 1893. He was to remain there for 20 years; the experiences he had shaped both his political ideas and his practical political skills. Humiliation and merciless discrimination against his fellow Indians drove Gandhi to declare war on racism in South Africa. He worked tirelessly for the interests of the Indians, both as a lawyer and through political campaigns, and they quickly came to see him as a leader. It was here that Gandhi developed his concept of **satyagraha** (staying firm to the truth), the practice of **non-violent resistance to the authorities** that was to become the model for so many later actions.

When Gandhi returned to India he was already a well-known political leader and it was not long before he also stood at the **head of the Indian liberation movement**. The methods of resistance he had tested in South Africa became a powerful engine on the path to independence. The Mahatma's programme consisted of a great campaign of non-collaboration with the British and various boycotts, as well as the famous Salt March. As a result he obtained widespread support both from the country's intellectuals and from the masses of poor farmers, who enthusiastically supported his cause.

However, Gandhi did not just confront the colonial power, he also addressed the problems of India's own system. Even though he never worked to abolish the caste system, he fought unflinchingly **against unequal treatment of the untouchables**, whom he called Harijans (God's children). He stood for integration, because thanks to his charisma and his exceptional political abilities he was able to mediate between the camps. His top priority was to achieve mutual respect and peace between the religions. He fought for this goal until his death and was thus able to prevent many a bloodbath during the upheavals before and after India's independence. »Death would be an overwhelming liberation for me. I would prefer to die than to witness the destruction of India, Hinduism, the Sikh religion and Islam. I'm in God's hands.« These words, uttered by the 78-year-old during his last fast for peace between the religions, tragically came true just a short while later. On 30 January 1948 Mahatma Gandhi was shot by a Hindu fundamentalist.

Jiddu Krishnamurti (1897–1986)

Many consider Jiddu Krishnamurti to be the most important Indian philosopher of the 20th century. This great spiritual teacher did not want to be seen as such and **resisted any cult of his person** while he was still alive. He was very different from the traditional image of an Indian guru. Krishnamurti offered neither firm teachings nor any clear beliefs and definitely created no sect for the path to wisdom and enlightenment. The way through the »pathless land of truth«

Philosopher

had to be found by everyone personally, a notion Krishnamurti developed not least because of his own path of development, which was riddled by numerous obstacles.

Jiddu Krishnamurti was born in Madanapalle (Andhra Pradesh) on 11 May 1895. His life took a crucial turn through his father's association with the Theosophical Society, an esoteric group influenced by Buddhist thought. The group's president, Annie Besant, saw the future saviour in 14-year-old Jiddu and made him the head of the newly founded eastern Order of the Star, a role he initially accepted without resistance. The older he grew, however, the clearer his doubts about the entire project became. In 1929 he finally brought about the dissolution of the order. His justification at the time already contained the core of what he started preaching from then on: »I maintain that truth is a pathless land, and you cannot approach it by any path whatsoever, by any religion, by any sect. [...] Truth, being limitless, unconditioned, unapproachable by any path whatsoever, cannot be organized; nor should any organization be formed to lead or coerce people along a particular path.«

Krishnamurti now moved to Ojai in California. This was to serve as his base for his travels around the world. He gave lectures and engaged in conversations with his listeners. **Krishnamurti Foundations** were founded in England and the United States. His dislike for any kind of personality cult and his belief that puts the individual at the centre of any spiritual development and emphasizes personal responsibility brought him more followers and fame in the West than in his home country. Krishnamurti died at the age of 90 in 1986.

Zubin Mehta (born 1936)

Conductor   Zubin Mehta was exposed to classical Western music in his parents' house in Mumbai. His father was a renowned concert violinist and

the founder of both the Bombay Symphony Orchestra and the Bombay String Quartet. As a child Mehta was given piano lessons and learned how to play the violin; by the age of 16 he was given his first opportunity to play for his father in the Bombay Symphony Orchestra. In 1954 his family sent him to the Vienna Conservatoire. Four years later Mehta took his first exam and won first prize in the conducting competition in Liverpool, which earned him his first post as assistant conductor at the Liverpool Philharmonic Orchestra. Between 1960 and 1967 Mehta

Celebrated all around the world: Zubin Mehta

worked as music director for the Montreal Symphony Orchestra. In 1962 he took on the same position at the Los Angeles Philharmonic Orchestra. Guest performances in Europe's biggest concert halls, such as in 1961 with the Berlin and Vienna Philharmonic Orchestras, were also on the programme. There is also a close link between the great conductor and Israel: the Israel Philharmonic Orchestra is one of Mehta's favoured ensembles. For a long time, seventeen years in total, his focal point was his work with the Los Angeles Philharmonic Orchestra. He stayed there until 1978 and then went to the New York Metropolitan Opera. In September 1998 Mehta became the **music director of the Bavarian State Opera**. He conducts both the Bavarian State Opera and the Bavarian State Orchestra.

? DID YOU KNOW ...?

■ ... that Freddie Mercury's family came from Mumbai and belonged to the Parsi faith community? The famous singer of rock giants Queen was actually called Farrokh Bulsara.

Jawaharlal Nehru (1889–1964)

First Indian prime minister

Only Mahatma Gandhi enjoyed more renown and popularity amongst the Indian people than his political colleague Jawaharlal Nehru. The **dedicated freedom fighter** who later became prime minister of India embodied the continuity of the political ideas and the uncompromising ethics of the independence movement of the new India like no other. He was exposed to nationalist thought from a young age, since his father, Motilal Nehru, was one of the leading figures of the Indian National Congress. After completing his law degree in Cambridge he returned to India in 1912 and soon became actively involved in his country's liberation movement. He became a firm defender of the notion of complete independence as well as one of the main leaders of the movement beside Gandhi. Following India's independence in 1947 Nehru became the head of government as India's prime minister and remained in that position until his death in 1964. From a foreign-policy point of view he gained respect and recognition during the time of the Cold War as a **central figure of the Non-Aligned Movement (NAM)**. When Nehru died India lost one of the most outstanding and active personalities involved in creating the new state.

Ramakrishna (1834–86)

Hindu reformer

Ramakrishna came from a poor Brahmin family. He was born in Bengal in 1836. His spiritual exercises as a priest brought him divine experiences that shaped his teachings. Ever-returning states of trance gave him visions of the divine in the form of the goddess Kali, Rama, Krishna and later even Muhammad and Jesus. Ramakrishna was a **mystic**, a follower of the bahkti, the total devotion to the divine. His insights and wisdom, which he spread in several graphic stories and sayings, could also be understood by the people, a fact that played a significant role in his popularity One of Ramakrishna's particular concerns was the **harmony of the religions**. Basing his ideas on an intensive confrontation with the different faiths he preached tolerance, because for him all religions led to the same goal. Over time the master surrounded himself with an ever larger number of disciples. His favourite student was to be Narendranath Datta, the future Vivekananda, who was to continue Ramakrishna's work after his death by founding the **Ramakrishna Mission**. This reformist Hindu organization is still active in India and other countries today, and spreads Ramakrishna's thoughts throughout the world.

Satyajit Ray (1922–92)

Film director

The Bengali scriptwriter and director Satyajit Ray is internationally seen as one of the greatest film artists and as **India's most famous filmmaker**. Ray founded the Calcutta Film Society, and assisted Jean Renoir in 1950 in his famous film about the Ganges, *The River*. In 1955 the first part of the film trilogy *Pather Panchali* was completed, which received an enthusiastic reception at the Cannes Film Festival in 1956. A year later Ray received the Golden Lion of Venice for the second part, *Aparajito*, and in 1959 he completed the trilogy with *Apu Sansar*. From the 1960s on his works won numerous national and international awards, including several Golden and Silver Bears at the Berlin Film Festivals, where he was a member of the jury several times.

Arundhati Roy (born 1961)

Writer and political activist

Arundhati Roy shot to worldwide fame overnight with her first novel ***The God of Small Things***. It has remained her only literary work to this day; nonetheless the socially committed author keeps hitting the headlines even outside her own country.

Roy was born in India in 1961; her father came from Bengal, her mother from Kerala, the tropical state on India's southwest coast, where she grew up and found the material for her future novel. After running away from home when she was 16 and keeping herself alive in her new home of Delhi by collecting old bottles, she began studying architecture. She found her way to writing in the 1980s. She wrote scripts and plays together with her husband, director Pradeep Krishen, an activity she later also pursued on her own. She wrote *The God of Small Things* between 1992 and 1996 and won the Booker Prize for it in 1997. The book topped the bestseller lists for a long time and was published in more than thirty countries. It made Roy a highly sought-after personality. Since then she has been using her fame to work against war and injustice. She is considered one of the most vehement critics of the Narmada Dam in western India and is

From literature to fighting war and globalization

fighting together with the local population against the social and ecological consequences of this large-scale project. Roy's style as a political journalist is committed, passionate and sometimes very subjective, an approach that has often been criticized. She is now one of the most famous activists of the **anti-globalization movement**, which is fighting against the negative consequences of increasing internationalization.

Salman Rushdie (born 1947)

British author born in India (fig. p.99)

»The next day, amid the continuing conversions, Salman the Persian is dragged into the prophet's presence. [...]›Salman Farsi,‹ the prophet begins to pronounce the sentence of death, but the prisoner begins to shriek the qalmah: ›La ilaha illallah. La llala!‹ Mahound shakes his head. ›Your blasphemy, Salman, can't be forgiven. Did you think I wouldn't work it out? To set your words against the Words of God.‹« These lines from Salman Rushdie's controversial novel ***The Satanic Verses*** are not the only ones that bear a striking resemblance to the author's fate in real life.

Like his fictitious namesake in the story, the author had to hide from pursuers who were threatening to kill him because of allegedly blasphemous utterances, and like Salman the Persian Salman Rushdie also tried to apologize in retrospect for his »lapse«. As a result of the **fatwa** pronounced by the Iranian leader Ayatollah Khomeini on 14 February 1989 requiring Rushdie's execution, he was suddenly in the public eye and had to seek out anonymity.

All this even though the author, who was born in Mumbai in 1947, came from a Muslim household himself. He spent his childhood in the city of his birth and later moved to the Pakistani city of Karachi. He studied history at Cambridge University. After several attempts at writing his second work earned him his breakthrough: his historical novel *Midnight's Children*, which tells India's story after its independence, won Rushdie the Booker Prize in 1981. His subsequent book *Shame* was also widely praised.

Finally, in 1989, the book was published which put an end to Salman Rushdie's ordinary life and forced the author to move from one hiding place to another. Even though the former Iranian government officially revoked the death sentence at the end of the 1990s, the author still receives threats from fundamentalist circles. This has not stopped him from writing new novels and stories, however, the most notable being: *Haroun and the Sea of Stories* (1990), *The Moor's Last Sigh* (1995), *The Ground Beneath Her Feet* (1999), *Fury* (2002) and *Shalimar the Clown* (2005). His latest novel is *The Enchantress of Florence* (2008).

Ravi Shankar (born 1920)

Sitar player and composer (fig. p.101)

That the sitar is an Indian stringed instrument and the raga a musical form became known amongst Western audiences as a result of countless concerts by the sitar virtuoso Ravi Shankar.

Born in Varanasi in 1920, since 1938 the musician has devoted himself completely to studying classical music. During a tour of the United States in 1957 the audience were thrilled with both the classical Indian music they heard and with Shankar himself. Since that time the Indian sitar virtuoso has not only captured Western audiences with the sounds of ragas, he has also inspired various different musicians with Eastern sounds. Through the Beatles the sitar even found its way into pop music. Nor did Shankar shy away from classical Western music. His series of concerts with the violinist Yehudi Menuhin under the title »East meets West« has become quite famous. Ravi Shankar is considered **the best-known Indian musician**, but his flirtation with Western music has also brought him a lot of criticism amongst purists in India.

Rabindranath Tagore (1861–1941)

Poet and philosopher

Poet and painter, feudal lord and teacher, father and loner, hermit and cosmopolitan: it seems hard to capture all of the personality facets of Rabindranath Tagore, **India's most famous poet of the modern age**.

A Bengali, Tagore was born in Kolkata in 1861. He published his first poem at the tender age of 14. At the age of 20 he wrote his first novel and from that point until his death a never-ending flood of literary works followed. One source of enrichment, into which he put a large part of his energy, was the **school in Santiniketan** (place of peace), north of Kolkata, which Tagore had founded in 1901. Here he was able to put his ideas of a reformist education into practice. »Living and working together« was his motto. Teachers were meant to be more than just providers of knowledge; they were also meant to be role models for the students. The practical, intellectual and spiritual areas of life were not separated. Thus the curriculum also included singing, dancing, theatre and crafts.

On numerous lecture journeys to other countries Tagore advertised his ideas and held poetry readings. His biggest success came with the poetry collection *Gitanjali* (an offering of songs). It was written between 1907 and 1910 and his very own English translation into prose earned him the **Nobel Prize in Literature** in 1913. Tagore's constant urge to discover new horizons did not wane, even as he grew older. When he was 60 he started painting and in 1939, when he was 78, he appeared in his own dance drama. Tagore died two years later in the house where he was born.

Rabindranath Tagore being visited by Gandhi in his ashram in Santiniketan (1940)

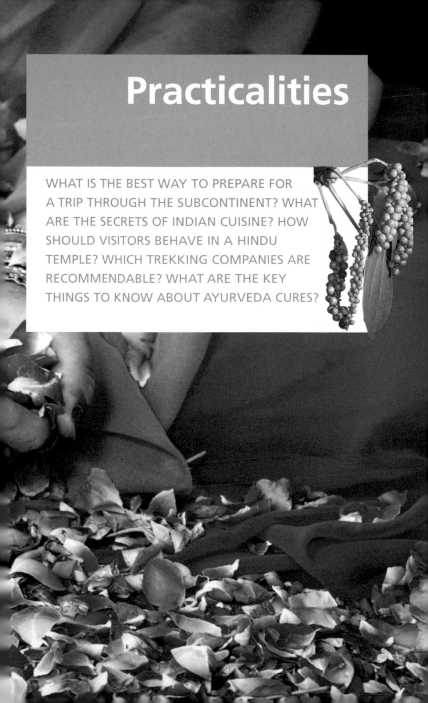

Practicalities

WHAT IS THE BEST WAY TO PREPARE FOR
A TRIP THROUGH THE SUBCONTINENT? WHAT
ARE THE SECRETS OF INDIAN CUISINE? HOW
SHOULD VISITORS BEHAVE IN A HINDU
TEMPLE? WHICH TREKKING COMPANIES ARE
RECOMMENDABLE? WHAT ARE THE KEY
THINGS TO KNOW ABOUT AYURVEDA CURES?

Accommodation

Recommended accommodation in the larger towns and tourist centres is listed in the section »Sights from A to Z«. An in-depth, up-to-date list of hotels can be found online on the homepage of the Federation of Hotel & Restaurant Associations of India (www.fhrai.com).

The homepage of India Tourism also has a link to an extensive list of hotels (www.incredibleindia.org). Most hotels in the higher price categories have their own websites or at least email addresses. They can change from time to time, while telephone numbers tend to remain more constant, making them the safer bet.

House boats House boats can be hired for a day or more in the backwaters of Kerala. The sizes of the boats vary: there are smaller boats for two people and larger boats for up to twelve people. Full board is generally included in the service. In addition to the captain there is usually also a cook and a deckhand on board. Further information about such boat trips can be obtained from the Kerala Tourism office in Kerala and from their website, www.keralatourism.org.

Youth hostels Youth hostels in India provide comfortable, inexpensive places to stay for trips, hikes and mountain tours. Every hostel has a capacity of around 40 beds (female and male dorms). Beds with bed sheets, blankets, lockers, electric lighting, a communal kitchen and parking are available. Information can be found under www.yhaindia.org, the website of the Youth Hostel Association of India.

Rest houses Many of the smaller, less well known places in rural areas that are of interest to tourists do not have any hotels. Government rest houses (facilities with a hotel-like character for government officials who are passing through) are often the only places to stay. These governmental rest houses (also known as circuit houses or Dak bungalows) are open to tourists. They tend to lie close to the national roads.

Staying in private family accommodation known as **homestays** is becoming increasingly popular. Information and addresses are available from tourist offices.

! _Baedeker_ TIP

Nocturnal sounds

Nocturnal repair works, temple bells, wedding music, car horns and barking dogs: the average sounds of an Indian night are not the same as those in Europe, so light sleepers should bring ear plugs as a precaution.

Arrival · Before the Journey

The international airports of Delhi and Mumbai are serviced by al- By air
most all major European airline companies. There are a host of regular flights from London Heathrow to Mumbai or Delhi, and a number of airlines, such as British Airways, Air India, and Jet Airways, fly
there non-stop. Flights are also available from London Heathrow to
India's other international airports, Kolkata, Chennai, Hyderabad
and Bangalore, but these often involve changing planes. Such airlines
as Lufthansa, KLM, All Italia, Air France, Austrian Airlines, Swiss,
Gulf Air, Qatar – the list goes on – also operate services from London to India. A non-stop flight from western Europe to India takes
around eight hours. The time difference and the prohibition on
night flights in Europe mean most aeroplanes land in India around
midnight.
Air India also flies direct from JFK in New York to Mumbai and Delhi. Qantas flights from Sydney to India involve a change of planes,
often in Singapore. British Airways offer flights from Dublin to India
with a stop at London Heathrow; Air France's Dublin to Mumbai
service stops off at Paris Charles de Gaulle.
Depending on the season, various airlines offer discounted fares. The
peak season between December and January is the most expensive
time to fly. Those wishing to travel to India at this time should book
as early as possible – a minimum of six months in advance is advisable.
Larger airports such as Delhi, Mumbai, Bangalore, Chennai and Kolkata have a special **taxi service** (Prepaid Taxi Service), which will take
passengers to their destination after the correct fee is prepaid at the
counter. All the taxi driver is then given is the receipt and a tip.

No passenger ships sail to India directly. There is the possibility of By sea
taking a cargo ship to India, for example from Southampton with
NSB Freighter Cruises. Information is available from The Cruise
People Ltd., tel. +44 (0)20 7723 2450, www.cruisepeople.co.uk.

Before planning an overland trip by car travellers are strongly ad- By car
vised to make detailed inquiries about the current political situation
in all of the countries along the route.

Entry and Exit Regulations

All visitors travelling to India will need a valid passport and an entry Visa required
visa. Visas can be obtained in Indian consulates and through travel
agencies. There is also a form that can be downloaded from the internet at the following URL addresses: in.vfsglobal.co.uk (UK);
www.travelvisapro.com/?apply_visa,do.visa_information,to.India
(USA).

Areas with special status

The following federal states and union territories currently require special entry permits: Manipur, Andaman and Nicobar Islands, Sikkim, Arunachal Pradesh and Mizoram. Such permits are no longer required for Darjeeling, Assam, Meghalaya, Nagaland and Tripura. Since the rules and regulations on this issue are subject to frequent change it is best to inquire about the current status.

Special permits can be obtained from Indian consulates and embassies.

Tip

It is advisable to make photocopies of all important travel documents and to keep them separate from the originals. If documents are lost or stolen, having copies will make things considerably easier.

Customs regulations

All personal items are exempt from duty. This includes personal jewellery, 200 cigarettes, 50 cigars and 0.95 litres of alcoholic beverages. High-value items, such as video cameras or laptops, can only be brought into the country duty-free if travellers make a declaration that these items will be exported again.

Travel insurance

It is recommendable to take out travel insurance. Indian hospitals generally expect to be paid in cash for any treatment, which is why it is important to keep all bills and receipts. In addition any travel insurance should include repatriation. Other sensible inclusions are insurance against the loss or theft of luggage. However, travel insurance companies usually expect a report from the Indian police, which is often difficult to come by.

Ayurveda

Traditional healing

In recent years interest in Ayurveda, one of India's traditional healing methods, has greatly increased in the west. Ayurveda (**knowledge of life**), like Chinese medicine, uses a holistic picture of human beings. According to Ayurveda, following a lifestyle in accordance with the old instruction is the prerequisite for health. Eating correctly has a central significance. In addition to diets that are specially tailored to a person's clinical picture, Ayurvedic therapies mainly centre around essential oil treatments, particularly oil massages, as well as medications obtained from old Indian medicinal plants. Ayurvedic therapies have proved to be particularly successful in treating conditions such as asthma, liver problems, allergies and a large array of psychosomatic problems.

Tip

Anyone wishing to take advantage of Ayurvedic resorts or treatments in India has two options. The first is to book a stay in one of the

► AYURVEDA

WELLNESS RESORTS AND CLINICS IN KERALA

► **Arya Vaidya Sala**
676503 Kottakal
Tel. 04 93 – 74 22 16
www.aryavaidyasala.com
The best-known of the public
Ayurveda clinics in northern
Kerala.

► **Sahyadri**
Peermade
Tel. 048 63 – 320 97
and in Kottayam
Tel. 04 82 – 87 20 47
and Kochi
Tel. 04 84 – 34 65 06

► **Coconut Lagoon**
P. B. 2
Kumarakom
Kottayam
Tel. 04 84 – 301 17 11
www.cghearth.com

► **Surya Sadmudra Beach Garden**
Pulinkudi Mullur
P. O. Thiruvananthapuram
Tel. 04 71 – 248 04 13
www.suryasamudra.com

► **Kairali Health Resort**
Kodumbu
Pallakad District
Tel. 04 92 – 232 25 53
www.kairali.com

► **Nagarjuna Ayurvedic Resort**
Thannipuzha Okkal P. O.
Tel. 04 84 – 248 33 50
nagarjuna@giasmd01.usnl.net.in

► **Kalari Kovilakom**
Kollengode – 678 506
Palakkad, Kerala
Tel. 04 84 – 301 17 11
www.cghearth.com

► **Spice Village**
Thekkady
Kumily Road
Tel. 04 84 – 301 17 11
www.cghearth.com

► **Marari beach**
Mararikulam, Allapuzha – 688549
Tel. 0478 – 286 38 01
www.cghearth.com

► **Somatheeram Ayurvedic Health Resort**
Chowara P. O.
Thiruvananthapuram – 695501
Tel. 0471 – 226 65 01
www.somatheeram.org

many wellness resorts offering Ayurvedic treatments; the other is to arrange a session in an Ayurvedic clinic. Those visitors choosing the hospital option should not expect to find the same kind of organizational, technological and hygienic conditions that would be the norm in Europe. There are a large number of wellness resorts in Kerala, but other states have them too. India's Ministry of Tourism has published a list of recommended Ayurvedic clinics and wellness resorts in India (cf.: www.india-tourism.com, link: Wellness, Ayurveda).

OLD KNOWLEDGE REDISCOVERED

Ayurveda has been in style for quite some time now. Ayurvedic cookbooks and massage courses, natural cosmetics and tea blends all make use of the ancient treatment method with all of its traditions. The home of Ayurveda, India and Sri Lanka, where its methods have been used to heal people for thousands of years, has seen more and more hotels attract their guests with Ayurvedic cures and wellness offers.

Some of Ayurveda's medical insights are at least as old as the Indians' earliest written documents. Plants and their healing powers were already praised in the Rigveda, the oldest collection of manuscripts from around 1200 BC. Today it is believed that the Ayurvedic body of experience contains knowledge gathered over many millennia. Most manuscripts date from 500 BC–AD 1000.

»Science of Life« is the meaning of the Sanskrit word, and the description does not just incorporate insights from the medical domain. Ayurveda is a philosophy of the proper treatment of human beings and their environment. Internal as well as external harmony and balance are the fundamental goals. The holistic approach of the teachings includes physical and mental aspects as well as emotional and spiritual ones.

Powers of self-healing

According to the Ayurvedic school of thought, human beings are seen as a reflection of the universe. The same elements exist in both: earth, water, fire, air and ether. They shape the human constitution and manifest themselves in the three Doshas: Vata, Pitta and Kapha. Vata or wind/ether is associated with movement and related to the body's nervous system, circulation, breathing and eliminating processes. Pitta or fire is associated with the body's metabolism, digestion

Herbs and spices not only make food tasty, they also aid digestion.

Classic treatment: shirodhara

and heat balance. Kapha or water/earth relates to the body's liquid balance and its natural defences. A person is healthy when the three Doshas are in balance with each other. Illnesses are expressed in their imbalance. By means of pulse diagnosis and examining the tongue and eyes, but also by studying an in-depth medical history, Ayurvedic doctors examine their patients and can determine which Dosha or which two Doshas predominate.

This gives them insight about the state of their patients and the cause of their complaints. Ayurvedic therapy is not interested in treating symptoms. It looks at the person as a whole. Treatment takes time and involves more than just taking medicine. It is a network of different methods with the goal of increasing the body's power to self-heal. This includes massages and other treatments with oil, enemas, heat treatments and, most importantly, the proper diet.

»Food is medicine«

is one of the guiding principles. The menu is determined depending on the predominant Dosha. A person with too much fire or Pitta has to stay away from chillies and pepper because the heat in the body has to be reduced. A proper diet does more than just heal; it prevents many ills. The ancient Indians knew ways of combating the diseases of modern society such as obesity, heart attacks and strokes. Health through proper diet and sufficient exercise are old Ayurvedic principles because what matters is right living. Emotional and spiritual matters are part of this, so meditation and yoga are often integrated into any treatment plan.

Ayurvedic treatment

Many patients and medical practitioners from the West are looking at India's millennia-old knowledge with interest and hope. In many cases Ayurvedic medicine can demonstrate successes, particularly in the treatment of chronic diseases. However, the recent popularity has also sometimes led to abuses of the label »Ayurvedic doctor«, which is not regulated in many countries. Anyone interested in proper treatment should take a good look at the doctor's training. It should have lasted for at least six years and cannot be acquired in weekend courses. Upon request, reputable hotels and resorts will provide information about the training of their medical staff.

Beach Holidays

The Indian subcontinent has **5000km/3000mi of coastline**, the majority of which is untouched by tourism. The beaches frequented by holidaymakers are concentrated around Goa, but there are also beaches with tourist infrastructure in Kerala, Karnataka, Maharashtra and Gujarat along the west coast, in Tamil Nadu and Orissa on the east coast, and around the Lakshadweep islands in the Arabian Sea and the Andaman and Nicobar Islands in the Bay of Bengal. In **Goa** almost the entire coastline, with its beautiful sandy beaches, has been developed with tourism in mind. Three noteworthy beaches here are Calangute, Baga beach and Colva beach. They are lined by five-star hotels with private beaches as well as by less luxurious hotels, tourist cottages and youth hostels. Amongst the most important seaside resorts in **Orissa** is the up-and-coming town of Gopalpur-on-Sea with various beach hotels. In addition Puri, one of the main Hindu centres of pilgrimage, also has a fine beach to offer; it also has three and four-star hotels, tourist bungalows and a single youth hostel. In **Gujarat** there are beaches and hotels in Diu and Daman, but Chorwad, Dahan, Dwarka and Mandvi also have accommodation ranging from basic to luxurious. Further south, along the coast **between Mumbai and Goa** in Maharashtra, there are also several beaches with accommodation nearby, such as in Alibag, Murud Janjira, and Ganapatipule near Ratnagiri for example. So far there is not much tourism infrastructure in place along the coast of **Karnataka**, but very nice beaches can be found in Karwar and Ullal (cottages), Malpe, Udipi and Mangalore, for example. The beaches near Gokarna in northern Karnataka and Om beach in particular with the newly built SwaSwara hotel complex are considered a real insiders' tip. The best-known beaches in **Kerala** are Kovalam and Varkala. However,

Vagator beach: one of the most beautiful beaches of Goa's north coast

there are also very nice beaches near Allapuzha (Marari beach) and Kozhikode (Kappad beach), which also have good hotels. **Tamil Nadu's** resorts are located in Kanyakumari, Tiruchendur, Rameswaram, Karikal, Puducherry and Mamallapuram.

The beaches on the **Andaman Islands**, such as near Corbyn's Cove (South Andaman Island) and on Havelock Island are outstanding. Another wonderful destination is the islands of **Lakshadweep** with their white sandy beaches and, on Bangaram Island, a wealth of diving opportunities.

Children in India

India is a very child-friendly country. Families with children are welcome everywhere. However, a family holiday in India has to be well-planned. The hottest time of year, i.e. summer, should be avoided; the same applies to the rainy season. Families wanting to go to the beach will be well served by the flat beaches of Goa. Zoos, camel and elephant rides will be real highlights for the little ones. The website **www.travelforkids.com** has tips for activities that children will enjoy in the various regions and cities of India.

Electricity

India generally uses 220-volt alternating current; some regions use   Tip direct current, however. Since the voltage can vary quite significantly, it can sometimes be risky to use certain sensitive equipment such as laptops (surge protection indispensable!).

Indian plugs have three pins. Anyone travelling to rural regions or staying in cheap hotels should bring a torch, since power cuts are not uncommon. Better hotels do not have this problem because all of them are fitted with their own emergency generators.

Emergency

USEFUL TELEPHONE NUMBERS

Fire brigade: tel. 101 Police: tel. 100
Ambulance: tel. 102

Etiquette and Customs in India

When travelling to a country with a completely different culture the opportunities for putting one's foot in it are particularly plentiful. The following code of conduct presents the accepted etiquette in India so that travellers can avoid the main pitfalls.

How to Dress Appropriately

In big cities such as Mumbai, Delhi, Bangalore or at the beaches of Goa and parts of Kerala the Western fashion of dressing in shorts and mini skirts has long become accepted. However, generally speaking, shorts and mini skirts in particular, low-cut tops and uncovered shoulders are frowned upon. This is especially true for rural areas but also of course when **visiting religious sites**. Before entering a mosque or temple, shoes have to be removed at the entrance. Some religious sites will only let members of their religious community enter; this is true for example of the many temples in Kerala and Tamil Nadu, as well as some temples in Orissa. In some temple complexes, particularly Jain temples, leather items (such as handbags) are prohibited. Anyone accepting a priest's blessing in a temple is expected to make a donation. Alms after visiting a temple or a mosque for the needy sitting in front of them are also customary.

! *Baedeker* TIP

Socks rock!

The stone slabs in India's temples, which can get as hot as 30°C/86°F or 40°C/104 °F can be a cause of some suffering for barefoot tourists. Since shoes have to be left outside it is a good idea for Western visitors to bring socks so they can walk through the holy sites as calmly as their Indian counterparts.

Beach holidays and swimming are not typical Indian customs. Traditional Indians only go into the water during a ritual cleansing and they stay dressed during that process. Away from the holiday beaches and hotel swimming pools tourists in bathing trunks or bikinis are considered a rare attraction. Naked swimming is forbidden in India and may well incur punishment.

Coming into Contact with Poverty

There are more than one billion people living in India and a large percentage lives below the poverty line. Government aid for poor, sick or old people does not exist. Looking after those in need is usually done by family members. However, as in many other countries, the social fabric is changing, leaving many people by the wayside, helpless and alone.

Sharing, in the form of **alms** for example, after visiting a temple or mosque is a firm part of the culture and is practised by many Indians

Going topless is taboo on all Indian beaches

as a matter of course. It is difficult for foreigners to act »properly«, particularly on their first confrontation with such huge poverty. It is a personal decision how much to give to whom in a particular situation.

However, the following information can be used as a guideline: **begging** in the large tourist centres is often organized. The people who receive the money have to hand it over later to a boss and only get a small fraction of it. This is particularly true of begging children, who are sent out onto the streets by their parents to contribute to the family income. Thus it is impossible for them to learn a trade or even attend school. If old people are forced to sit on the streets and hope for alms it is generally because of great plight. Disabled and sick people often have no other way of getting their hands on any money apart from begging.

Handling Money

It is customary in many **bazaars** and shops to haggle for goods; indeed, it is positively expected. Before making any major purchases it is best to enquire in advance in various places about relevant prices. Street vendors in particular are very communicative. Their offers should not be misunderstood as »come-on«. Anyone enquiring about the price of an item is considered genuinely interested.

Haggling

A large proportion of Indians are employed in the service sector. Labour is cheap, which is why services are inexpensive. Tips supplement the small income of employees in hotels and restaurants so this is an area where it is nice to be generous. Travellers staying in luxury hotels are naturally expected to part with greater amounts of money than backpackers.

Tips

Staff in **hotel restaurants** of the five-star category expect a tip of 10%. In normal **restaurants** it depends on the size of the meal and the number of people served but 5% should be an absolute minimum. Good, friendly service has its value everywhere. It is particularly inappropriate to be stingy in cheap restaurants because the waiters here are paid significantly less than their counterparts in luxury hotels.

It is also expected that guests pay a tip for services in the **hotel**, from carrying luggage to room service. Anyone staying in a hotel for an extended period of time should also not forget the room attendants and bellmen.

Taxi drivers do not generally expect a tip, but sometimes expect to be allowed to keep small quantities of change. If they are helpful in loading and unloading luggage, a tip should be given.

> ! **Baedeker TIP**
>
> **Lost and confused**
>
> Finding the desired hotel or restaurant can sometimes turn out to be quite an odyssey. It is easier to get to a destination by phoning the relevant establishment in advance and have the route given to the taxi driver directly.

Taking Photographs

With all of its colours, India is a photographer's dream. However, when taking pictures **people's feelings should be respected**. Most people do not have a problem with having a picture taken. However, it is always polite to ask beforehand when taking a close-up. It is important to remain very low key when taking photographs of religious ceremonies and no pictures should be taken without getting consent from the relevant people first. It is also polite to ask the priest for permission before taking pictures in a temple in which ceremonies are still taking place. Taking pictures of people and fobbing them off with alms afterwards is a widespread evil amongst tourists travelling to poor countries. This behaviour promotes begging, particularly amongst children.

Anyone wanting to take pictures of certain archaeological monuments with a flash or a tripod may need a permit from the Archaeological Survey of India, New Delhi, Janpath. Taking pictures in game reserves is allowed in exchange for a fixed fee; in tribal areas it is generally forbidden.

It is not a problem to obtain photographic material and film in the cities and near tourist attractions. However, it is a good idea to check the production date and the display area (not in the hot sun!).

Visiting an Indian Family

When entering a home the **shoes should be removed**, unless the hosts specifically say you can keep shoes on. Shaking hands as a greeting is not customary in traditional families, it is however very widespread in most Westernized families, particularly amongst the men. The traditional welcome gesture involves pressing the hands together in front of the face and then bowing slightly with the head.

Anyone invited to dinner should still any hunger pangs with a snack beforehand. Indian families tend to eat very late. If there is any alcohol it will be drunk before the meal. This can last until 11pm or later. It is customary to go home after the meal is finished.

It is traditional to **eat with the right hand** in India. If faced with the dilemma of not having any cutlery available, which can happen in rural areas for example, it is important to stick to this rule. The left hand is considered impure, since it is used for other purposes (toilet).

Alcohol can only be ordered in restaurants with a bar. All vegetarian restaurants are strictly alcohol-free zones. A bowl of fennel seeds is handed out after a meal to help with digestion. Their effect should definitely be tested, particularly after a heavy northern Indian meal, which may well have been prepared with clarified butter (ghee) or cream.

Table manners

When photographing people, particularly women, use tact and ask permission first

Further Sources of Misunderstanding

An important gesture that is easy to misunderstand... The kinds of misunderstanding that can arise as a result of the incorrect interpretation of gestures are illustrated by this small anecdote by the famous jazz musician Duke Ellington about an incident that occurred while he was staying in the Taj Mahal Hotel in Mumbai, which he describes in *Music is my Mistress*: »…as the chronic room-service type I rang for a page and started asking him for the menu. I start listing my favorite foods and finally end up with roast chicken, but every time I choose a meal he reacts by shaking his head. Even though I'm right on the sea, he even shakes his head when I say the word ›fish‹. Since I didn't know any better I settled for a lamb curry for four days, after which I discovered that shaking the head means ›yes!‹.«

Festivals · Holidays · Events

India has some secular holidays and a large number of religious holidays, which can take place on different dates as a result of various calendar calculations. Banks, authorities and larger shops usually close on these dates. However, different states have different policies when it comes to public holidays and it also depends on the significance of a particular religious community in a particular location (▶ Baedeker Special p.392). www.india-tourism.com has a link to a page listing the exact dates of the festivals.

 RELIGIOUS HOLIDAYS

HINDU FESTIVALS

▶ **Pongal**
Harvest festival celebrated in southern India and particularly in Tamil Nadu (13–16 January).

▶ **Makar Sankranti**
is also celebrated under many other names, particularly in northern India. It always takes place on 14 January. The kite-flying competitions held in Ahmedabad on this day are quite famous.

▶ **Kumbha Mela (p.240)**
The largest Hindu festival (and the world's largest festival). It takes place every twelve years, following the cycle of Jupiter around the sun, in four different places in India: Allahabad (Prayag), Haridwar, Ujjain and Nashik (January / February).

▶ **Shivratri**
Celebration in honour of the god Shiva, involving music and sing-

Holi is one of many spring festivals in India, but it is the jolliest and most colourful by far

ing, observed in all of India (February / March).

▶ **Holi**
Lively festival at the beginning of spring. The day is best spent in old clothes since it is traditional to throw around coloured powder and bags of water (February / March).

▶ **Rath Yatra**
Celebrated in Orissa and mainly in Puri (June / July). Three large temple floats are decorated in honour of the god Jagannath (from which the word »juggernaut« is derived), which are taken on a procession through the town.

▶ **Teej**
Colourful festival for the goddess Parvati to welcome the monsoon. It is mainly popular in Rajasthan (July / August).

▶ **Ganesh Chaturthi (p.475)**
is dedicated to the popular elephant god Ganesha (also known as Ganapati in Maharashtra). Statues

are taken through the town in a procession and then thrown into the sea / river. Particularly big celebrations take place in Mumbai and other parts of Maharashtra (August / September).

▶ **Onam (p.509)**
Harvest festival, mainly observed in Kerala, accompanied by the famous snake boat races in the Backwaters and colourful elephant processions (August / September).

▶ **Dussehra (p.382)**
(called Navaratri in southern India, Durga Puja in Bengal): this festival is celebrated in memory of goddess Durga's victory over a demon after a nine-day battle. The best known procession on this occasion is in Mysore (September / October).

▶ **Diwali (p.393)**
Festival of light (October / November), celebrating the beginning of the New Year according to the Hindu calendar. Houses are decorated with colourful lanterns

and oil lamps and firework displays are held everywhere.

MUSLIM FESTIVALS

These festivals change their dates every year since Muslims observe a lunar calendar.

▶ Id-ul-Zuha (Bakr Id)

Sacrificial festival in memory of Abraham's sacrifice. It is considered the most important Islamic festival in which an animal (often a lamb) is slaughtered and parts of the animal are handed out to people in need.

▶ Id-ul-Fitr (Ramzan Id)

The festival of breaking the fast after the month of Ramadan

▶ Muharram

Shiite commemorative festival in honour of Imam Hussain's martyrdom. It is mainly observed in Lucknow.

FESTIVALS OF OTHER RELIGIOUS COMMUNITIES

▶ Easter and Christmas

Quite a large percentage of Christians can be found in the states of Goa and Kerala, thus these two festivals are particularly celebrated there.

▶ Mahavir Jayanthi

Day of celebration in honour of Mahavir, the founder of the Jain religion, particularly in Gujarat and Rajasthan, since they are home to many Jains (March / April).

▶ Jamshed Navroz

21 March, Parsi New Year festival. This religious community has strong representation in Mumbai.

▶ Buddha Jayanthi

In memory of Buddha's birth, enlightenment and death, which all took place at this time of year (April / May). The main place of celebration is Sarnath.

▶ Baishakhi

The Sikhs in Punjab celebrate the beginning of the harvest season (April / May) with music and dancing.

CULTURAL EVENTS

During the winter months, particularly in December / January, cultural events such as music, dance, theatre and film festivals take place all over the country. Particular treats are the festivals hosted by the state tourist offices in historical locations, which are held every year.

Food and Drink

North Indian Cuisine

Indian cuisine, in all its diversity, is like no other. There are some general characteristics that differentiate northern Indian cuisine from its southern counterpart. The general belief that all Indian cooking is hot and spicy and is accompanied by tea is not entirely true.

The people of northern India prefer **bread as a side dish** instead of rice. The food here is relatively greasy, often contains meat and is **not particularly spicy**. It is customary to drink tea after meals. In southern India however coffee is much more popular and the food is lighter, usually vegetarian and significantly spicier. Northern Indian restaurants will often feature the dishes listed below on their menus:

i **Price categories**

- Expensive: from £9.50/700 INR
- Moderate: £4.50/330 INR – £9.50/700 INR
- Inexpensive: up to £4.50/330 INR
  (price for one meal)

MENU

Vegetarian dishes

Aloo Gobi	potatoes with cauliflower
Aloo Mattar	potatoes and peas
Aloo Palak	potatoes and spinach
Baingan Bharta	aubergines in sauce
Bhindi Masala	okra in sauce
Channa	chick peas
Dal	lentils in a spicy sauce
Malai Kofta	veggie balls in sauce
Mulligatawny soup	traditional Anglo-Indian soup with a lentil base
Navrattan Korma	mildly spicy vegetables
Paneer Palak	cheese with spinach
Paneer Mattar	cheese with peas
Shahi Paneer	cheese in a spicy sauce

Methods of preparation

Tandoori dishes and foods, in which vegetables or meat are coated in a mix of spices and yoghurts and baked in a special oven, e.g. tandoori chicken.

dopiaza	with a lot of onions, moderately spicy
jalfrezi	with tomatoes and green peppers, spicy
keema	dish with a minced meat base
kofta	meat balls
kurma	sauce with yogurt, mild
malai	creamy sauce, mild
masala	hot spice mix

muglai	Mughal-style, i. e. with cream, often with almonds and raisins, mild
tikka	meat chopped up into small chunks

Meat dishes

Chicken Masala / Muglai	chicken in a hot / mild sauce
Shahi Chicken	chicken in a mild sauce
Kheema (Khima)	mince sauce
Mutton Masala	lamb in a hot sauce
Mutton Muglai	lamb in a mild sauce
Mutton Rogan Josh	lamb in a hot sauce

Rice dishes

Biryani	rice dish with a special spice mix, considered meal for special occasions (e.g. chicken birya also available with lamb, egg, vegetables etc.)
Pulao	mild rice dish, e.g. chicken pulao. Also available in combination with vegetables, crab, fish or as »Kashmiri Pilao«, enriched with raisins and almonds.

Breads

Bhatoora	large, leavened pitta bread
Chapati	round, thin pitta bread made from wheat flour
Naan	thick, firm pitta bread (similar to a pizza base)
Papad, papadom	very thin flat bread made of lentil flour, deep-fried in oil
Paratha	thick flat unleavened bread, fried, sometir stuffed with vegetables (stuffed paratha)
Puri	small deep-fried dough cases made from wheat flour
Roomali Roti	very thin flat bread
Roti	round flat bread, usually like chapati

Sides and snacks

Raita	spiced yoghurt, as a side
Samosas	deep-fried dough cases stuffed with meat vegetables (potatoes, peas, spinach etc.)

Pakoras .... vegetables coated in chickpea flour, then deep fried

South Indian Cuisine

Southern Indian restaurants often offer a dish known as thali. Thali, meaning plate, consists of a **platter with various vegetables, yogurt and pickles** (veg thali); some of them also contain meat (non-veg thali); it is served together with chapattis or puris and rice. The snacks served in southern Indian restaurants, which are traditionally eaten as a late breakfast or in the afternoon, are very tasty. Southern Indian cuisine is **generally more spicy** than northern Indian cooking. Restaurants in southern India often have menus featuring the following dishes:

Thali

Snacks

Dosa	flat bread made of rice and lentil flour cooked in oil, usually eaten with coconut chutney and sambar (spicy sauce)
Masala Dosa	dosa with a potato filling
Paper Dosa	especially thin, large dosa
Idli	small cooked cakes made of rice flower, served with coconut chutney and sambar
Appam	small rice cakes, usually served with a spicy sauce, Kerala speciality
Uttapam	thick pitta bread made of rice and lentil flower, usually prepared with onions or tomatoes and served with chutney and sambar as a side
Wada	small cakes made of lentil flower cooked in oil, served with chutney and sambar on the side

Traditional dishes

Lemon rice	rice flavoured with lemons
Pongal	mildly spiced rice with yogurt
Rasam	very hot soup on a tomato base
Sambar	very spicy sauce on a lentil base, usually enriched with some vegetables

CURRYING FLAVOUR

»If I go abroad, I always carry my own kitchen with me.« This comment characterizes the relationship most Indians have towards their food like no other, because in their opinion Indian cuisine is unrivalled.

To this day strict Brahmins refuse to eat outside of their homes. Most vegetarian restaurants have traditionally been in the hands of this caste because only its members are able to cook according to the extensive and diverse purity requirements. The dabbawallahs or »food bringers«, who can be recognized by their white caps and by the mountains of silver pots which they carry with ease on foot, on a bike or in a bus through the crowds, can only survive where »home-made food« has priority, where a hard-working wife or her cook prepares lunch for the husband and services are so cheap that it is less expensive to have a meal delivered through a vast city than it is to go to a canteen.

No curry, please, we're Indian!

There is one word that usually comes to mind when thinking about Indian food: curry. Curry is everything that's hot and gives food that unique »Indian« flavour. Curry powder is yellow and a pinch of it improves any meal in the West, from mild fish dishes to zesty salad sauces; it gives an otherwise boring meal an exotic touch. Curry is surely the most »Indian« of all spices and can be found all around the world, with one exception: India itself. Anyone ordering curry with rice here and expecting that yellow-coloured rice with meat or vegetables will be sorely disappointed, and indeed their request will fall on deaf ears. A particularly understanding soul might come back with a few twigs from the sweet neen tree, sometimes called the »curry tree«. Maybe the unsuspecting traveller will even lucky enough to come across a waiter in a five-star hotel who is in the know about Western customs. But the man or woman on the street, the many owners of small restaurants, the countless operators of the dhabas, India's street stalls, will not have heard of curry. The creators of this confusion were the British colonial rulers, who in their ignorance labelled the real secrets of Indian cuisine and the customary mixtures with one word: »curry«. Those who know their onions, however, are aware that it is the countless, usually freshly ground spices, mixed with each other in a whole variety of combinations and then fried in ghee, that give Indian dishes their incomparable taste and variety.

Masala is the name Indians have given to the mix of different ingredients and every household has its own recipe for preparing a dish, even though instant powders have also found their way to Indian kitchens. The basis of northern Indian cuisine is cumin, cardamom,

A symphony of spices and aromas

Fresh ingredients ar the most important factor in Indian cui

ginger, cinnamon, cloves, coriander and turmeric (the powder that gives dishes their yellowish colour). Mustard seeds, sweet neen, wild onion, tamarind and of course the white flesh of coconuts are the basis of many southern Indian dishes. One thing that should not be forgotten are the red, dried chillies, or the fresh, green variety, that give the food in both the north and the south its well-known and sometimes dreaded spiciness. The closest thing to »curry« is garam masala, a mix of cardamom, cinnamon, cloves and pepper, which is used when preparing meat dishes and chick peas and is also available on our spice racks at home.

Mild or spicy?

Indian cuisine is marked by great regional differences. The tasty breads fried in ghee, parathas and naan, are popular in northern India. Many meat and vegetable dishes also require the use of ghee, clarified butter. Creamy-mild dishes, usually fitted with the attribute »muglai«, refer to the time when the Mughal emperors ruled in the north and gave the cuisine a Persian-Arabian touch. The food in southern India is lighter, but usually spicier. Here, rice really develops its significance and is indispensable both in the afternoon and in the evening. In addition to very many tasty vegetable dishes there are also delicious fish dishes, particularly in Kerala. These treats can only be appreciated when the taste buds have significantly increased their tolerance for the hot chilli peppers. Anyone whose palate cannot come to terms with the delicacies of Indian cuisine can take refuge in the comparatively mild Chinese food or even in familiar European dishes, an option that is available in many places, but that is no substitute for the diversity of the local Indian cuisine.

Desserts

Those visitors to India with a sweet tooth will have no trouble going without chocolate for a time, given the amount of different sweets and desserts Indian cuisine has to offer. It should be said that these desserts contain a lot of sugar, so those who do not have a stomach for it should stay away. The desserts tend to be very sweet to European tastes, but that should not stop anyone from trying barfi, halva or similar treats.

Deserts

Barfi	dessert on a milk base with cardamom and many other spices, nuts (sometimes coated in a thin silver foil)
Gulab Jamun	little balls cooked in oil and dunked in syrup, extremely sweet
Halva	milk with various spices and sugar (cooked until it becomes firm). Halva is available with various ingredients; the most famous variety is Gajjar Halva made from carrots; this is best tried in the bazaar of Old Delhi, where it is for sale during the winter in large iron pans.
Jalebi	orange-coloured sweet made of syrup, fried and very sweet
Kulfi	Indian ice cream in cardamom or pistachio flavour (can be eaten in all good restaurants without hesitation!)
Laddu	a sweet based on wheat flour with a lot of sugar and raisins
Ras Malai	dessert made of milk and cheese (Paneer) in cooked milk with cardamom and other spices
Rasgulla	dessert on a cheese base with rose water and dunked into syrup
Basundi and Payasam	deserts on a milk base with spices

There is a large **selection of fruit** available at any market. Certain varieties can only be obtained when they are in season or if they are grown regionally, while others, such as bananas, are available everywhere all year round. Ideally all fruit should be peeled or, if this is not possible, placed into an iodine solution or potassium permanganate for half an hour. India is famous for its mangoes, such as Alfonso mangoes from Mumbai and the Konkan Coast; however, they only really taste good when they are in season (March–June). Papayas, pineapples, melons, oranges and pomegranates are widely available. Sitafal, a round green fruit with a wavy surface, and chiku, a small round fruit with a brown peel, are also tasty. The flesh of the huge jackfruits is also worth trying.

? DID YOU KNOW ...?

■ ... that there are around 1000 different mango varieties in India and that this fruit is a symbol of love (and sex)? The best mango variety is the Alfonso mango; it grows along the coast between Mumbai and Goa and is best eaten in the months of April and May.

Drinks

The main drink of the Indian population, water, should only be drunk by tourists after it has been boiled or well filtered. Several types of mineral water are available at the markets. When buying bottled water it is important to make sure the seal is not broken, since some sly traders sometimes refill bottles and resell them.

Tea and coffee on the other hand can be drunk everywhere without hesitation. Tea is traditionally drunk with milk and sugar and it is also served in this way except in Western standard hotels or restaurants, and the same is true of coffee. While drinking tea is quite widespread in all of India, coffee has a long tradition in southern India and is particularly tasty there; the coffee served in the north is usually instant. Another drink to try is **masala chai**, a tea enriched with spices. It is mainly offered in simple restaurants. **Alcohol consumption** is allowed in India with the exception of a few states; alcoholic drinks are served in bars and restaurants that have permits. There is a total prohibition on alcohol in Gujarat; a number of other states have restrictions in place.

! *Baedeker* TIP

A lassi please!

If a certain dish is too spicy, a good way to extinguish the fire in your mouth is by drinking a lassi. The Punjabi yoghurt drink does not just sooth a burning tongue, it also tastes good: lassi can be ordered salty, sweet or natural. Mango lassi and lassi with almonds and pistachios (badam-pista lassi) are available in most restaurants in northern India.

Irresistible fruit: pomegranates →

Health

The horror stories in the news about the plague, cholera, malaria, typhoid and other contagious diseases sometimes afflicting the Indian subcontinent definitely do not have the most inviting effect on anyone considering coming to India. The reports of epidemics that continue to make their way though our media should however be taken with a pinch of salt, since the situation is often exaggerated.

On the other hand it cannot be denied that the hygienic conditions are bad in many places. The alarming state of health of a large proportion of the population is mainly due to their poverty and a lack of commitment from those in politically responsible positions. The average visitor will not generally spend any time in those places where a significant part of the population have to spend their lives: in the slums of the big cities or villages with polluted well water.

Precautions Various precautions are however indispensable for every traveller. The primary imperative of avoiding diarrhoea requires the following rules: all boiled drinks such as tea, coffee or soups can be consumed without hesitation. The same is true of soft drinks and the products of well-known alcoholic beverage companies. In all other cases the general rules are:

1. Only drink boiled water or bottled mineral water. Check mineral water bottles to make sure the seal is still intact since empty bottles are sometimes refilled with normal water.
2. Do without ice cubes in drinks.
3. Only eat ice cream in very good restaurants or hotels.
4. Don't swallow any tap water when brushing your teeth.
5. When ordering fresh fruit juices, check that they are not being mixed with water.

Further information is available at www.cdc.gov.

Generally speaking, all cooked meals can be enjoyed without hesitation. Vegetarian food is particularly safe. The freshness of meat and fish, however, cannot always be guaranteed, and these foods should only be eaten in good hotels and restaurants. Other recommendations include:

1. Avoid salads and other raw foods.
2. Either peel fruit or clean it in a potassium permanganate solution (for half an hour is best).
3. Even though the snacks being sold in the streets look and smell tempting it is best to avoid them.

> ! **Baedeker TIP**
>
> **Healthy thirst-quencher**
>
> They are not just a good way to quench thirst, they are also very healthy: coconuts. Vendors generally offer two varieties: »paniwalla«, which has a lot of water or »malaiwalla«, which has less milk but more of the white, sweet flesh (malai), which the vendor will scoop out after the milk has been drunk.

When buying fruit it is a good idea to stick to whole fruits with peel

The most common ailment travellers to India have to battle is diarrhoea. It is usually just a harmless reaction of the body to the unfamiliar spices (particularly to the spicy chilli) and can be reduced or avoided by getting used to the new foods gradually. In worse cases it is the result of an intestinal infection that can occur in various degrees of severity and is caused by ingesting rotten foods or polluted water. **Avoiding diarrhoea**

Malaria is one of the diseases that has greatly increased on the subcontinent in recent years. Thus it is absolutely necessary for all travellers to take precautions against malaria, except for those exclusively visiting the higher Himalayan regions. Your GP or an institute of tropical medicine will be able to provide more information. Additional protection can be obtained by using a mosquito net, which is a particularly good idea for those travellers wishing to stay in more basic accommodation. Rooms with air conditioning do not guarantee a 100-percent mosquito-free environment. The »Indian method« of keeping these pests away indoors is by having ceiling fans running at full speed. Protective creams and long clothing can also provide additional protection. **Malaria**

Travellers are also often plagued with the typical cold symptoms such as a sore throat, a runny nose, coughing and a stiff neck. Draughts, fans, open windows in trains, buses and taxis or the unavoidable change from tropical heat to air-conditioned hotel rooms and restaurants can cause some trouble in the nose, throat and chest area. In addition to the relevant medications a cotton scarf is also very useful. **Colds**

Heat, dirt and humidity make the perfect breeding place for all kinds of bacteria. For that reason it is particularly advisable to pay atten- **Hygiene** tion to personal hygiene in this tropical climate. Washing hands before every meal is an absolute must.

In addition to the standard traveller's first-aid kit and the above mentioned anti-diarrhoea drugs everyone coming to India should bring a set with sterile hypodermic needles, alcohol and antiseptic bandages. This should be viewed as a precautionary measure when travelling in rural areas, where medical care sometimes leaves a lot to be desired.

Bugs
Hotels attempt to wage war on all kinds of bugs that could be hiding in the beds with chemical means, but the odd flea or bug bite may still occur, particularly if staying in cheap accommodation.

Sun protection
India is a tropical country. In some parts of the country temperatures can rise to over 40ºC/104ºF, particularly before and after the monsoon. Sun protection in the form of creams, a sun hat and sun glasses are an absolute must for every visitor. In addition visitors should avoid spending too much time in the blazing sun.

Vaccinations
There are currently no required vaccinations for India. Institutes of tropical medicine give recommendations in light of the current situation. They generally include vaccinations against meningitis, typhoid and hepatitis B. If necessary, polio vaccinations should also be refreshed and a tetanus vaccination can do no harm.

Anyone spending time in a country that has yellow fever six days before entering India has to have a valid vaccination certificate (the list of affected countries can be obtained from consulates).

After the holiday
Some diseases, such as malaria, have a long incubation period. If any kind of symptoms, particularly a high temperature, gastrointestinal infections etc. should appear after returning home, a doctor should be consulted and informed about any recent trip immediately. A safety check in an institute of tropical medicine is only advised after longer stays.

Medical Help

Most doctors in India's cities speak English. Larger hotels often employ a doctor who is there specifically to look after the guests. Examinations generally take place fully clothed. Regardless of the size of the town patients have the choice between being treated by allopathic, homeopathic and Ayurvedic physicians.

Emergency and in-patient treatments
Taking out travel insurance that covers repatriation in the event of an emergency, as well as other costs, is recommended. In the event that in-patient treatment is unavoidable it is advised to get information from the nearest consulate about good-quality clinics in the area. If a blood transfusion is necessary it is an absolute must to check whether the donor blood has been tested for HIV.

Information

 USEFUL ADDRESSES

INDIAN EMBASSIES AND HIGH COMMISSIONS

► **Indian High Commission in the UK**
India House, Aldwych
London WC2B 4NA
Tel. 20 7836 8484
www.hcilondon.net

► **Indian High Commission in the Republic of Ireland**
6 Leeson Park
Dublin 6
Tel. 01 497 0843
www.indianembassy.ie

► **Indian High Commission in Canada**
10 Springfield Road
Ottawa, Ontario K1M 1C9
Tel. 613 744 3751
www.hciottawa.ca

► **Indian Embassy in the USA**
2107 Massachusetts Avenue NW
Washington DC 20008
Tel. 1 202 939 7000
www.indianembassy.org

► **Indian High Commission in Australia**
3-5 Moonah Place
Yarralumla, Canberra ACT 2600
Tel. 2 6273 3999
www.hcindia-au.org

► **Indian High Commission in New Zealand**
180 Molesworth St, Wellington
Tel. 04 473 6390
www.hicomind.org.nz

DIPLOMATIC REPRESENTATION IN INDIA

► **UK High Commission in New Delhi**
Shantipath, Chanakyapuri
New Delhi 110021
Tel. 011 2687 2161
www.ukinindia.com

► **UK High Commission in Chennai**
20 Anderson Road
Chennai 600 006
Tel. 044 42192151

► **UK High Commission in Kolkata**
1A Ho Chi Minh Sarani
Kolkata 700071
Tel. 033 2288 5172

► **UK High Commission in Mumbai**
Naman Chambers
C/32 G Block Bandra Kurla
Complex
Bandra (East) Mumbai 400 051
Tel. 022 6650 2222

► **Embassy of Ireland**
230 Jor Bagh
New Delhi 110 003
Tel. 011 2462 6733
www.irelandinindia.com

► **High Commission of Canada**
7/8 Shantipath, Chanakyapuri
New Delhi 110 021
Tel. 011 4178 2000
www.india.gc.ca

▶ **United States Embassy in India**
Shantipath, Chanakyapuri
New Delhi 110021
Tel. 011 2419 8000
http://newdelhi.usembassy.gov/

▶ **Australian High Commission in India**
1/50 G Shantipath, Chanakyapuri
New Delhi 110021
Tel. 011 4139 9900
www.ausgovindia.com

▶ **New Zealand High Commission**
Sir Edmund Hillary Marg
Chanakyapuri
New Delhi 110 021
Tel. 011 2688 3170
www.nzembassy.com

FURTHER INFORMATION

▶ **India Tourist Office (in the UK)**
7 Cork Street
London, WIX 2AB
Tel. 020 7437 3677
www.incredibleindia.com

▶ **Indian Ministry of Tourism (in India)**
Transport Bhavan
Parliament Street
New Delhi 110 001
Tel. 91 011 23 71 19 95
Fax 91 011 23 71 05 18
www.incredibleindia.org

▶ **India Tourist Office (in the USA)**
1270 Avenue of Americas
Suite 1808, New York NY 10020
Tel. 212 7516840
Fax 212 5823274
www.incredibleindia.com

INTERNET

The major website for tourist information about India is www.incredibleindia.com. A second site with a wealth of well presented information is www.india-tourism.com. Up-to-the-minute news can be found at www.indiatimes.com. Those requiring more detailed information about the individual states can look on the relevant websites. The hotel directory on the website of the Federation of Hotel &Restaurant Associations of India (www.fhrai.com) is constantly updated.

Literature · Film

Fiction **Forster, Edward Morgan**: *A Passage to India* (Penguin Classics 2005). E. M. Forster's classic tale tells the story of a young British girl, Adela, and her desire to escape the prejudiced British community of Chandrapore and find the »real India«.

Ghosh, Amitav: *The Circle of Reason* (Penguin 2008, first pub. 1986). The story of Alu's odyssey, a tragicomical story between reality and magic.
The Glass Palace (HarperCollins 2001). Colonial history and a love story are intertwined in this family saga set in Burma, Malaya and India.

The Hungry Tide (HarperCollins 2004). The author uses great story-telling power to describe the fateful meeting between Piyali Roy, a woman of Indian descent who nonetheless feels American, the entrepreneur Kanai Dutt from Delhi and the fisherman Fokir in the Bengali Sundarbans. Nature and culture and love and death all collide in this book.

Kaye, M. M.: *The Far Pavilions* (Viking 1978, reprints). Entertaining story set in the 19th century about an officer who grew up in India, and an Indian princess.

Lahiri, Jhumpha: *Interpreter of Maladies* (Houghton Mifflin 1999). Collection of short stories about Indians living in other countries. Lahiri's debut was awarded the Pulitzer Prize in 2000.

Lapierre, Dominique: *The City of Joy* (Arrow 2003). This novel, first published in 1985, tells of the experiences of a Polish priest and an American doctor in the slums of Kolkata. A proportion of the royalties go to a charity working in the city.

---

i India in Film

- *Apu Trilogy*: by Satyajit Ray: a masterpiece by the Bengali filmmaker from the 1950s, which tells the life story of a village boy on his way to the big city. The trilogy consists of the films *Pather Panchali*, *Aparajito* and *Apu Sansar*.
- *Salaam Bombay*: Mira Nair's award-winning film about a street child in Mumbai
- *Monsoon Wedding*: also by Mira Nair, an Indian wedding as a mirror of society and its contradictions
- *Fire, Earth, Water*: In this trilogy filmmaker Deepa Mehta addresses the subjects of lesbian love (*Fire*), the consequences of India's partition (*Earth*) and the fate of widows in Varanasi on the Ganges (*Water*).
- *The River*: Jean Renoir's legendary 1951 film about the Ganges
- *Gandhi*: The story of the great Indian freedom fighter by Richard Attenborough starring Ben Kinsley
- Good Bollywood films: *Lagaan* is a four-hour epic about colonialism and cricket with big emotions. The situation of ethnic minorities in modern India is the subject of the thriller *Dil Se* (*From the Heart*) with superstar Shah Rukh Khan. The committed but stubborn teacher of a deaf-mute girl is played by Bollywood's ex-champion Amitabh Bachchan in the film *Black*.

Nagarkar, Kiran: *Cuckold* (HarperCollins 1999). The kingdom of Mewar in 16th-century Rajasthan provides the backdrop to this novel in which the crown prince and his wife, the poet Mirabai, are at the centre of intrigue and jealousy.

Nair, Anita: *Ladies Coupé* (Vintage 2003). Six women tell each other their life stories during a night-time train journey.

Roy, Arundhati: *The God of Small Things* (Harper Perennial 2004). The rhythm of life in rural Kerala and the love for an »untouchable« are the central subjects of this prize-winning novel, first published in 1997.

Rushdie, Salman: *Midnight's Children* (1981, Vintage 2008), *Shame* (1983, Random House 2008), *The Satanic Verses* (1988, Consortium

1992), *Haroun and the Sea of Stories* (1990, Puffin 2001), *The Moor's Last Sigh* (1995, Vintage 1998), *The Ground Beneath Her Feet* (1999, Vintage 2007), *Shalimar the Clown* (Cape 2005). Rushdie's imaginative novels sway between historical« reality and magical dream worlds. His fitful heroes are drawn from Mumbai to London and Mecca or from Kashmir to California. They are just as at home in modern India as they are inhabiting the old legends and myths.

Seth, Vikram: *A Suitable Boy* (1993, Phoenix 1995). On 1500 pages Seth describes the lives of four extended families in post-independence India and provides insights into the social and political realities of the subcontinent.

Film poster for »Gandhi« with Ben Kingsley in the lead role (1982)

Suri, Manil: *The Death of Vishnu* (Bloomsbury 2001). His whole life is flashing past as Vishnu, who lives on the stairs of a tenement in Mumbai, is battling with death. Suri's much praised debut.

Tagore, Rabindranath: *The Tagore Omnibus* (Penguin Classics 2001). Poetry, prose and drama. The works of the Bengali poet and winner of the Nobel Prize in Literature in a new edition.

Tharoor, Shashi: *Riot: A Love Story* (2001, Penguin 2003). The American member of an international aid organization is murdered during religious unrest in a small town east of Delhi. What is behind this murder?

Dalrymple, William: *City of Djinns. A Year in Delhi* (Penguin Books 2003). Dalrymple intertwines the history of India's capital with encounters in modern Delhi. His humour and gift for observation are a joy.

Non-fiction

Frater, Alexander: *Chasing the Monsoon: A Modern Pilgrimage Through India* (Penguin 1991). The Observer correspondent writes about a trip he took from Kanyakumari in South India to Cherrapunjee in the northeast during the monsoon.

Gandhi, Mahatma: *An Autobiography: Or the Story of My Experiments with Truth* (Penguin 2007). Gandhi's memoirs.

Kakar, Sudhir: *The Colours of Violence: Cultural Identities, Religion and Conflict* (South Asia Books, 1995). Confrontations between various religious groups in Hyderabad are taken by the Indian psychoanalyst Kakar as the reason to explore the causes of the conflicts in India.

Keay, John: *India, a History* (HarperCollins 1999). A readable work on the subject.

Michaels, Axel: *Hinduism: Past and Present* (transl. Barbara Harshav, Princeton University Press 2003). The India expert describes India's largest religion in a clear and competent manner. For readers who want a deeper insight into Hinduism.

Tharoor, Shashi: *India: From Midnight to the Millennium and Beyond* (1997, Arcade 2006). An introduction to India's history since its independence.

Travellers to India will generally get a long way with English. However, anyone wanting to get to know the diversity of the Indian languages in more detail will get a first impression with the **Lonely Planet Phrasebook** *Hindi, Urdu and Bengali*.

Language guide

Media

Daily newspapers
English-language newspapers make up about a quarter of India's total daily newspapers. They are outnumbered only by Hindi publications, whose market share lies at 30%. The remainder is made up of printed material in the various regional languages.

The best-known, supra-regional daily newspapers are *Indian Express*, *The Times of India*, *The Statesman*, *The Pioneer*, *The Asian Age*, *The Hindu* and *The Hindustan Times*. Particularly interesting are the Sunday editions of the *Times of India* (*Sunday Times*), the *Indian Express* and the *Asian Age* with background reports and supplements about culture and society. There are some very reputable regional daily newspapers such as *The Telegraph* (Kolkata) or the *Deccan Herald* (Bangalore).

Magazines
The best-known and most important news magazine is still *India Today* from New Delhi, which is published weekly. In addition there is a broad spectrum ranging from reputable specialist publications to tabloids.

From business papers to fashion magazines: the entire spectrum of Indian print media

Money

India is a cheap travel destination for visitors from countries with hard currencies. The price of a cup of coffee in Europe will buy a good meal in India. Services are extremely inexpensive and goods of all kinds are cheap to buy. Indians, particularly those from tourist areas, know very well how easy it is to live with dollars or euros in their home country. Thus it is not surprising that services and goods are sometimes offered to foreigners at inflated prices. In these situations it is worth considering whether an argument over a few rupees is really worth the trouble. This can best be avoided by finding out about prices in advance for purposes of comparison. On the other hand haggling for a fair price is often part of the deal, particularly amongst street vendors of all kinds, and if foreigners constantly pay excessive prices it can also cause the costs for locals to shoot up, in Goa for example. The entry fees for many tourist attractions are often significantly more expensive for foreigners than for Indians.

Value of money

i Exchange rates

- 1 EUR= 68.50 INR
  1 INR = 0.015 EUR
  1 GBP = 72.84 INR
  1 INR = 0.014 GBP
  1 USD = 50.05 INR
  1 INR = 0.20 USD
  (as of March 2009)

India's currency is the rupee. One rupee is the same as a hundred paisa. Coins of 1, 5, 10, 20, 25 and 50 paisa are issued. The main ones used in monetary transactions are the 25 and 50-paisa coins. Rupees are issued in the following notes: 1, 2, 5, 10, 20, 50, 100, 200, 500, and 1000; the three smallest of these units are also issued as coins.

Currency

Banks are generally open Mon–Fri 10am–2pm, Sat 10am–noon, foreign exchange offices are usually open until the evening. International airports offer a 24-hour service.

Opening hours

Travellers' cheques are the safest solution on any trip. A number of banks, foreign exchange offices and hotels will convert them into cash. The best port of call is the State Bank of India, which exchanges both travellers' cheques and cash. The same is true of foreign exchange offices and many of the more expensive hotels, but in the latter case the exchange rate may be calculated to tourists' detriment. Large airports also have foreign exchange offices. Money should best be exchanged in larger cities or tourist centres. Remote or small towns rarely have facilities to do this.
Rupees are usually handed out in 50 or 100-rupee quantities. The **receipt issued must be kept**. In some cases it is used as proof for an official exchange having taken place, for example when buying train or plane tickets.

Exchanging money

● CONTACT DETAILS FOR CREDIT CARDS

In the event of lost bank or credit cards you can contact the following numbers in the UK and USA (phone numbers when dialling from India):

▶ **Eurocard/MasterCard**
Tel. 001 / 636 7227 111

▶ **Visa**
Tel. 001 / 410 581 336

▶ **American Express UK**
Tel. 0044 / 1273 696 933

▶ **American Express USA**
Tel. 001 / 800 528 4800

▶ **Diners Club UK**
Tel. 0044 / 1252 513 500

▶ **Diners Club USA**
Tel. 001 / 303 799 9000

Have the bank sort code, account number and card number as well as the expiry date ready.
The following numbers of UK banks (dialling from India) can be used to report and stop lost or stolen bank and credit cards issued by those banks:

▶ **HSBC**
Tel. 0044 / 1442 422 929

▶ **Barclaycard**
Tel. 0044 / 1604 230 230

▶ **NatWest**
Tel. 0044 / 142 370 0545

▶ **Lloyds TSB**
Tel. 0044 / 1702 278 270

Indian rupees

Torn bank notes should be given back at once since it is hard to get rid of them again.

When exchanging money it is wise to ask for a number of smaller notes (10 and 5-rupee notes) in order to have the right amount of money at hand for tips or change.

Credit cards Credit cards are accepted by all the better hotels and a growing number of shops and restaurants as well as by airline companies. Visa, American Express, MasterCard and Diners Club are the most widespread. The Bank of Baroda will pay out cash on a credit card of up to 20,000 rupees a day.

It is advisable not to enter into a transaction with one of the many black-market traders who can be found in all the tourist strongholds. Apart from anything else, it is prohibited.

Black-market transactions forbidden!

It is also not permitted to bring rupees in or out of the country. Travellers wanting to bring more than US$2500 as well as more than US$10,000 in travellers' cheques or cash (total amount) have to declare this on the currency declaration form when entering the country.

National Parks · Wildlife Sanctuaries

There are **93 national parks and almost 500 wildlife reserves** in India. These parks, which play an important role in conserving India's flora and fauna, make up approximately 4.7% of India's total area. In order to preserve and research the unique diversity of India's ecosystems **15 biosphere reserves** have been set up. A few of the most significant will be briefly described in the following section. It is advisable to book accommodation in advance. Information is available from the local State Tourism Development Corporations or the parks' administrative authorities.

► NATIONAL PARKS

► 1 Bandhavgarh National Park

Madhya Pradesh (175km/110mi northeast of Jabalpur)
Size: 449 sq km/173 sq mi
Season: beginning of Nov–mid-June; closed Tue.
Forest and marshy grassland; very good wildlife-watching opportunities (gaur, chital, monkeys, many different birds, such as great hornbills).
Trips in Jeeps, elephant rides, hiking trails, observation towers. Accommodation: Forest Lodge in the park. Information: Bandhavgarh National Park, Director, Umaria – 486 661, Dist. Shahdol, Madhya Pradesh.

► 2 Corbett National Park (p.240)

Uttarakhand in the Himalayan foothills (294km/183mi northeast of Delhi)
Size: 520 sq km/200 sq mi
Season: Nov–May
Oldest national park and famous animal conservation area. Broad-leaf forest and grassland. In addition to tigers the park is populated by elephants, various deer species, leopards, jackals and various monkey species. Birds of prey, herons and other bird species as well as mugger crocodiles also live here. Trips by Jeep or elephant rides. Accommodation within the park. Information: Corbett National Park, Field Director, Ramnagar, Dist. Nainital, Uttarakhand.

Chitals in Bandhavgarh National Park

▶ **3 Dachigam Wildlife Sanctuary**
Kashmir (20km/12mi north of
Srinagar)
Season: June–July
Wide valley, mountain slopes.
Home to the rare Kashmir stag,
bears, leopards, heron eyries. Ac-
commodation: house boats on the
Dal and Nagin lakes. Information:
Jammu & Kashmir Tourist Re-
ception Centre, Srinagar – 190 001,
Kashmir.

▶ **4 Dandeli National Park**
Karnataka (140km/87mi south of
Belgaum)
Park with bison, tigers, panthers
and sambar deer. Easy to get to
from Goa. Accommodation:
guesthouse in Kulgi Forest and
Mandurli as well as bungalows
with views of the river in Dandeli.
Information: Government of India
Tourist Office, KFC Building, 48
Church St., Bangalore – 560 080,
Karnataka.

▶ **5 Dudhwa National Park**
Uttar Pradesh, on the border to
Nepal (430km/265mi northeast of
Delhi)
Size: 815 sq km/315 sq mi
Season: Dec–May
Wet broad-leaf forest, grass steppe.
Home to the rare barasingha deer,
settlement project for Indian rhi-
noceros, known for its species-rich
bird world, and particularly for its
many owl and stork species. Trips
by Jeep, elephant rides, observa-
tion towers. Accommodation in
the park. Information: Dudhwa
Project Tiger & National Park,
Field Director, Lakhimpur, Dist.
Kheri, Uttar Pradesh.

▶ **6 Govind-Sagar
Bird Sanctuary**
Himachal Pradesh (135km/85mi
northwest of Chandigarh)
Home to cranes, ducks and geese.
Accommodation available in
Bhakra. Information: Chandigarh

National Parks Map

3 Dachigam

6 Govind Sagar

33 Valley of Flowers
20 Naina Devi

2 Corbett

27 Sariska   5 Dudhwa
15 Keoladeo Ghana   8 Jaldapara   14 Kaziranga
26 Ranthambor   18 Manas
29 Shivpuri

17 Little Rann of Kutch   7 Hazaribagh
19 Marine   21 Nal Sarovar   1 Bandhavgarh 22 Palamau
35 Velvadar   31 Sundarbans
28 Sasan Gir   13 Kanha
                                30 Similipal
16 Sanjay Gandhi   32 Tadoba   Bay of
   (Borivili)   Bengal

Indian
Ocean

4 Dandeli

25 Pulicat
9 Rajiv Gandhi   34 Vedanthangal
   (Nagarhole)
12 Wyanad   10 Bandipur
11 Mudumalai   24 Point Calimere
23 Periyar

Tourism, Sector 17, Chandigarh, Himachal Pradesh.

► **7 Hazaribagh National Park**
Bihar (100km/60mi north of Ranchi)
Season: Feb–March
Sambar and nilgai, tigers and leopards, occasionally muntjac deer. Accommodation in the park.

Information: Government of India Tourist Office, Sudama Palace, Kakarbagh Rd., Patna – 800 020, Bihar.

► **8 Jaldapara Wildlife Sanctuary**
West Bengal (150km/95mi east of Bagdogra)
Season: March–May
Tropical forest and grassland.

Out and about with an elephant guide

leopards, jackals, monkeys, mugger crocodiles, tortoises and waterfowl. Trips in Jeeps, boat trips on the lake. Accommodation: visitor bungalows.

10 Bandipur National Park
Southern Karnataka (80km/ 50mi south of Mysore)
Size: 865 sq km/335 sq mi
Hilly terrain with dry broad-leaf forest and grassland, reservoir. Tiger reserve; large elephant herds, chitals and sambar deer, leopards, Deccan red dogs, various monkey species, mugger crocodiles, water turtles and waterfowl. Trips in minibuses, elephant rides. Accommodation in the park.

11 Mudumalai National Park
Tamil Nadu (70km/45mi northwest of Ooty)
Size: 321 sq km/124 sq mi
Hilly terrain, marshes, wet and dry broad-leaf forest. Elephants, chitals, sambar deer, gaurs, tigers, various monkey species, Deccan red dogs. Trips in Jeeps or cars, elephant rides, hiking trails close to the park's perimeter, outdoor camps, observation towers. Information: Mudumalai Wildlife Sanctuary, Mahalingam Building, Coonor Road, Ooty – 643 001, Tamil Nadu.

12 Wyanad National Park
Kerala (110km/70mi northeast of Kozhicode)
Accommodation in a forest rest house. Special permit required. Information: DTPC (District Tourism Promotion Council), Kalpetta, tel. 049 36 – 20 21 34.

Large bird stocks, rhinoceros and elephant. Accommodation: guesthouse in Jaldapara. Special permission is needed to visit the park. Information: Government of India Tourist Office, »Embassy«, 4, Shakespeare Sarani, Kolkata – 700 071, West Bengal.

▶ **9 – 12 Jawahar National Park (p.565)**
Jawahar National Park contains Bandipur and Nagarhole National Parks as well as Mudumalai and Wyanad Wildlife Sanctuaries. It is characterized by extensive mixed forests and has India's largest elephant population.

9 Nagarhole National Park
Southern Karnataka (100km/60mi southwest of Mysore)
Size: 640 sq km/245 sq mi; dry broad-leaf forest and grassland, reservoir. A good place for elephant watching; the park is also home to gaurs, tigers, chitals,

▶ **13 Kanha National Park**
Madhya Pradesh (170km/105mi southeast of Jabalpur)
Size: 940 sq km/365 sq mi

Season: Nov–June
Forested areas and grassland. Tigers (good observation opportunities), leopards and other wild cats, home to barasingha deer and gaurs, species-rich bird world. Trips in Jeeps or by car, elephant rides, walks. Accommodation in the park, in Kanha or Kisli. Closed on Tue. Information: Kanha Tiger Reserve, Field Director, Mandla – 481 661, Madhya Pradesh.

▸ **14 Kaziranga National Park**
Assam, on the banks of the Brahmaputra (220km/135mi east of Guwahati)
Size: 430 sq km/166 sq mi
Season: Nov–April
Marsh landscape between rivers and lakes with grassy and forested areas. The national park is famous for its Indian rhinoceroses. It is also home to elephants, deer, wild boar and many waterfowl. Impressive elephant rides, trips by Jeep or car, watch towers. Accommodation in the park. Special permits are required to visit the park. Information: Kaziranga National Park, Director, Bokkhat – 785 612, Dist. Jorhat, Assam.

▸ **15 Keoladeo-Ghana Bird Sanctuary (p.232)**
Rajasthan, between Jaipur and Agra
Size: 29 sq km/11 sq mi; Season: Sept–Feb. Well-known bird sanctuary. Winter home for many migratory birds, a natural wetland with additional artificial lakes and canals as well as bush land and forest. In addition to many monkey and deer species the park is home to approximately 370 bird species, of which 130 are breeding

birds. In the winter months ducks, geese, various birds of prey and the rare Siberian cranes arrive. Ideal for walks and bike rides. Accommodation in the park. Information: Keoladeo National Park, Director, Shanti Kutir, Bharatpur – 321 001, Rajasthan.

▸ **16 Sanjay Gandhi National Park (Borivili)**
Maharashtra (20km/12mi north of Mumbai)
Season: Oct–June
Nature conservation area, also known as Borivili Park, with Kanheri caves and the Tulsi and Powai lakes. Watefowl and smaller wild animals. Information: Bombay National History Society, www.bnhs.org

▸ **17 Little Rann of Kutch Wildlife Sanctuary**
Gujarat (195km/120mi west of Ahmedabad)
Season: Oct–June
Salt desert, herds of Indian wild donkeys, wolves, caracals. Accommodation in the wildlife sanctuary / Dhrangdrha. Information: Gujarat Tourism, HK House, Ground Floor, Opp. Gandhi Ashram, Ashram Road, Ahmebad – 380 009, Gujarat.

▸ **18 Manas Wildlife Sanctuary**
Assam, on the border to Bhutan (180km/110mi west of Guwahati)
Size: 2837 sq km/1095 sq mi
Season: Jan–March
Riparian landscape with grassland, dry and wet broad-leaf forest. Tigers, elephants, Indian rhinoceroses, gaurs, various deer species as well as the rare Gee's golden langurs. Trips by jeep, elephant rides, boat trips. Accommodation

in the wildlife sanctuary. Special permits required to visit the park. Information: Manas Project Tiger, Field Director, Barpeta Road, 781 315, Assam.

▸ 19 Marine National Park

Gujarat, coastal region in the Gulf of Kutch (between Okha in the west and Jodia in the east)
Offshore islands with coral reefs and mangroves. In the winter it is home to many migratory birds, some islands have breeding colonies. Information:
Director, Marine National Park, Forest Department, Pradashan Ground, Jamnagar, 361 005, Gujarat.

▸ 20 Naina-Devi Wildlife Sanctuary

Uttarakhand (280km/175mi from Rishikesh)
Season: June–July. »Roof garden« in full bloom. A special permit is required to visit the park.

▸ 21 Nal-Sarovar Bird Sanctuary

Gujarat (65km/40mi west of Ahmedabad)
Season: Nov–Feb
Lake, flamingoes and migratory waterfowl. Accommodation close to the lake. Information: Nal Sarovar Bird Sanctuary, Range Forest Officer, Vekaria, P. O. Sanand, Dist. Ahmedabad, Gujarat.

▸ 22 Palamau Tiger Reserve

Bihar (155km/95mi northwest of Ranchi)
Season: Feb–March
Forested hills.
Tigers, leopards, elephants, occasionally wolves. Accommodation in Betla. Information: Palamau Project Tiger, Field Director, Daltonganj – 822 101, Bihar.

▸ 23 Periyar Wildlife Sanctuary (p.604)

Kerala, in the Western Ghats (190km/120mi southeast of Kochi)
Size: 350 sq km/135 sq mi
Humid, tropical broad-leaf forest, grassland and branching reservoir; attractive park with very good opportunities to watch wild animals. Elephants, sambar deer and chitals, gaurs, various monkey species, species-rich bird world. Boat trips, limited amount of walking possible. Accommodation: various hotels in the vicinity. Information: Periyar Ecotourism Centre, Thekkady, www.periyartigerreserve.org

▸ 24 Point Calimere Bird Sanctuary (Kodikkarai)

Tamil Nadu (200km/125mi southeast of Tiruchirapalli)
Season: Nov–Jan
The bird sanctuary (25 sq km/10 sq mi) is mainly known for its flamingoes, but also for its herons, teals, curlews, waders and wild boar. Accommodation in the forest rest house. Information: Point Calimere Wildlife Sanctuary, Kadampadi, Nagapattinam – 611 001, Tamil Nadu.

▸ 25 Pulicat Bird Sanctuary

Andhra Pradesh (60km/35mi north of Chennai)
Flamingoes, pelicans, herons and terns. Accommodation in Nellore. Information: www.aptourism.com.

▸ 26 Ranthambor Tiger Reserve (p.349)

Rajasthan (130km/80mi southeast of Jaipur)

Gaur live in small herds to better protect their young from tigers

Size: 392 sq km/151 sq mi
One of the best-known tiger reserves. Season: Nov–May. Hilly landscape with dry broad-leaf forest and grassland as well as some rugged cliffs and narrow valleys. In addition to tigers, various deer species, of which sambar deer are the most famous, also live here. Mugger crocodiles, pythons and tortoises as well as many different bird species also call the reserve home. Trips by Jeep. Accommodation in the park. Information: Ranthambhore National Park, Field Director, Sawai Madhopur – 322 001, Rajasthan.

▶ 27 Sariska Wildlife Sanctuary
Rajasthan, in the Aravalli Hills between Delhi and Jaipur (40km/25mi southwest of Alwar)
Size: 800 sq km/309 sq mi
Season: Feb–June
Dry broad-leaf forest and bush landscape; artificial watering holes along the road allow visitors to see the animals from the car; one of the tiger sanctuaries. Home to various hoofed animals such as sambar deer, chitals, leopards, jackals, caracals, various monkey and bird species, particularly peacocks. Trips by Jeep or car. Accommodation varying in price available in the park. Information: Sariska Wildlife Sanctuary, The Field Director, Project Tiger, Dist. Alwar, Rajasthan.

▶ 28 Sasan Gir National Park (Gir National Park, p.324)
Gujarat (400km/250mi southwest of Ahmedabad)
Size: 259 sq km/100 sq mi
Season: Jan–May
Hilly terrain with dry broad-leaf forest and thorn bush. Retreat for the last Asiatic lions (currently around 350), also home to leopards and other wild cats, deer, antelopes and many bird species. Trips by Jeep, walks, watch towers. Accommodation in the park. Information: Sasan Gir National Park, Sanctuary Superintendent, Dist. Junagadh, Gujarat.

▶ 29 Shivpuri National Park
Madhya Pradesh (120km/75mi southeast of Gwalior)
Season: Feb–May
Forest area with a lake. Antelopes, tigers, leopards and waterfowl.

Accommodation: forest rest house, hotel in Shivpuri. Closed on Tue. Information: MPTDC Tansen, 6A, Gandhi Road, Gwalior, Madhya Pradesh, and under www.mptourism.com.

▸ **30 Simlipal Tiger Reserve**

Orissa, on the border to Jharkhand (220km/135mi northeast of Bhubaneshwar)
Size: 2750 sq km/1062 sq mi
Season: Nov–June
Hilly terrain with dense broad-leaf forest, valleys and waterfalls. Tiger reserve, also home to elephants, deer, wild boars and many birds such as hill mynahs. Trips by Jeep. Accommodation in tourist guesthouses near the park. Information: Similipal Project Tiger, Field Director,
Baripada – 757 002, Orissa.

▸ **31 Sundarbans Tiger Reserve (p.398)**

West Bengal, Ganges river mouth (60km/35mi south of Kolkata)
Size: 1330 sq km/514 sq mi (core area)
Season: Feb–March
Mangrove swamps and a highly branching river system. Sanctuary of the royal Bengal tiger (currently 270), approximately 260 bird species, water snakes, saltwater crocodiles, tortoises. Boat trips. Visitor permits required. Information: Sundarbans Tiger Reserve, Field Director, Canning, Dist. 24 Parganas, West Bengal or www.wbtourism.com.

▸ **32 Tadoba National Park**

Maharashtra (208km/130mi south of Nagpur)
Season: March–May
Teak forests and a lake. Tigers, leopards, nilgai antelopes, gaurs and crocodiles. Accommodation in the park. Information: Government of India Tourist Office, 123 M. Karve Rd., Opp. Churchgate, Mumbai – 400 020, Maharashtra.

▸ **33 Valley of Flowers National Park**

Uttarakhand (160km/100mi northeast of Rishikesh)
Season: July–August is the main period of bloom
Size: 87 sq km/34 sq mi
Wonderful flower valley, home to potentillas, meconopsis, cypripedia and gentian. 4km/2.5mi long and up to 2km/1mi wide, located at 3400m/11,150ft–3700m/ 12,140ft in the mountains of the Garhwal Himal. Website of the Garhwal Mandal Vikas Nigam: www.gmvnl.com.

▸ **34 Vedanthangal Water Birds Sanctuary**

Tamil Nadu (85km/55mi southwest of Chennai)
Season: Oct–March
One of the most important breeding sites in India; cormorants, herons, storks, pelicans and many more; accommodation in the forest guesthouse. Information: Wildlife Warden, 50, Fourth Main Road, Gandhi Nagar, Adyar, Chennai – 600 020, Tamil Nadu.

▸ **35 Velvadar National Park**

Gujarat (65km/40mi from Bhavnagar)
Season: Oct–June.
New delta grassland, large gathering of blackbucks. Accommodation in the park. Information: Deputy Conservator of Forests, Bhavnagar Division, Multistory Building, Bhavnagar, Gujarat.

Personal Safety

There is no particularly high risk to personal safety in India if travellers stick to some generally accepted rules. Remote areas and parks should be avoided at night – this is particularly true for women. Slums should either not be visited at all or only in the company of locals, and in the event of such a trip it is best to leave the camera in its bag.

Tips on behaviour

When travelling it is best to leave valuable jewellery, particularly gold, at home. Money (avoid large sums) and documents should always be carried in a pouch around the neck. It is important to be on one's guard in large crowds, particularly at stations and markets. As in other places the world over, these areas attract thieves. Slitting open handbags in full buses and trains is a particularly widespread method.

Under no circumstances should any luggage be left unattended anywhere at any time.

Valuables must be stored in a safe place in a hotel, i.e. in the hotel safe or in a lockable cupboard or suitcase. Taking a small padlock is a good idea, but they can also be bought everywhere in India. Room doors should best be locked.

Hotel

There are occasional reports about attacks on buses or trains during the night-time hours, but during the day there is no problem using these forms of transport. These attacks are much more likely to occur in India's poorest state, Bihar. Visitors there should definitely avoid travelling by night. During overnight train journeys luggage should be kept closed and tied to something.

Travelling by bus and train

Women travelling alone are no rarity in India, but they may face some harassment. This is truer of the north of the country than of the south.

Safety tips for women

Wearing inconspicuous clothes, particularly Indian clothes (such as salwar kameez), can be a great advantage. There is generally no problem sleeping in overnight trains. Some trains have special »ladies' compartments«.

Travellers to Kashmir face personal safety issues owing to the unstable political situation. Official Indian tourism offices, one's own government and the Indian embassies and consulates can provide information about the most recent developments.

Kashmir

Even though hashish, called ganja in India, is an old cultural drug in this country, any possession of hashish, marihuana and other drugs (with the exception of alcohol, apart from in a few states) is illegal and will be severely punished.

Drugs

Post · Communications

Post It currently (2008) costs eight rupees to send a postcard to Europe, while a letter costs 15 rupees. Only a five-rupee stamp is needed to send a letter within India. Most post offices are open from 10am to 5pm, Saturdays from 10am to 4pm. Variations may occur.

Making telephone calls in the hotel The telephone connections within India and to other countries are generally very good. Anyone staying in a more expensive hotel will always have the choice between dialling directly or through an operator. Most better class hotels also have internet connections.

Private telephone stations Telephone calls made from one of the numerous service stations, which have now also found their way to remote villages, are significantly cheaper. They can be recognized by the sign ISD / STD. ISD means that an international connections are available, while STD means domestic long-distance calls can be made.

Many of these stations are now also fitted with fax and internet connections. Anyone wanting to surf the web should inquire about prices; a unit counter will be available for telephone calls.

▶ DIRECTORY ENQUIRIES AND DIALLING CODES

▶ **Dialling codes to India**
from the UK and Republic of Ireland: tel. 00 91
from the USA, Canada and Australia: tel. 00 11 91

▶ **Dialling codes from India**
to the UK: tel. 00 44
to Australia: tel. 00 61

to the Republic of Ireland:
Tel. 00 353
to the USA and Canada: tel. 00 1

▶ **Directory enquiries in India**
Tel. 186

▶ **International directory enquiries**
Tel. 197

Prices

▶ WHAT DOES IT COST?

Taxi ride
4–6 rupees
per km

**Overnight stay
(pension)**
from 500 rupees

Simple meal
from 50 rupees

**Water
(1-litre bottle)**
20 rupees

Shopping · Souvenirs

It is a good idea not to come to India with full suitcases. As regards shopping, travellers will be faced with great temptations. Excellent commodities and materials, the country's **high-quality arts and crafts with their millennia of tradition** and, last but not least, the low prices will make the heart of many a shopper hunting for a bargain or a souvenir beat a little bit faster. Every region in India has its own specialities, based on the local raw materials and skills. Fans of precious silks will find precisely that in Varanasi and Chennai, but not so much in Mumbai and Delhi. Silver jewellery is more available at the bazaars and in the antique shops of Jaipur and Jodhpur than in the south of the subcontinent, and carvings made of Mysore sandalwood are obviously most prevalent in the area of the same name. However, all of these items can be bought in all the big cities and tourist centres.

Indian Treasures

Silk and cotton fabrics from India enjoy a great reputation around the world. The silk fabrics from Chennai (Kanchipuram Silk), Bangalore, Mysore and Varanasi are famous. An abundance of all kinds of cotton fabrics is available. Colours, patterns and production methods vary depending on where a product was made and a trained eye can tell by a specific pattern from which region the item came. Embroidery from Gujarat and Rajasthan are well known far beyond India's borders. Often they are adorned with tiny mirrors. **Saris, scarves and bedspreads**, particularly those made using the tie-dye method, which are called **bandhni** by the locals, are further specialities of these two states. Ikat fabrics are also highly popular. **Ikat**, geometric patterns produced using a special weaving method, are put on blankets, saris and other garments and are specialities of Orissa and Andhra Pradesh.

> **? DID YOU KNOW ...?**
>
> ■ ... that the sari, the traditional Indian dress for women, is at least 5.5m/18ft long and that its pattern and border gives away the region or town in which it was made?

Those looking for a fine garment that is also warm need look no further than a **cashmere scarf**. The top product in this category is called shah tush or the »king of wool«, where said wool comes from a rare Tibetan antelope. Its material is so soft that it fits through a ring and is said to be able to withstand temperatures of -40ºC/-40ºF. It is now illegal to purchase shah tush. However, products made of **pashmina wool**, which comes from a mountain goat and is known as cashmere wool around the world, is both legal and affordable. Scarves made of normal sheep's wool, embroidered and in a multitude of colours, can be bought both in Kashmir and in other Himalayan states. Scarves known as kulu scarves from Himachal Pradesh are sold all over India.

Buying carpets in India is both controversial and popular. A millennia-old tradition of knotting carpets exists in Kashmir, but it is also widespread in Punjab, Rajasthan and Uttar Pradesh. The uncertain political situation has pushed many traders from Kashmir to the south of the country. Thus their carpet shops can be found in all the large cities and tourists centres now. **Kashmir carpets** are hand-knotted and made either of silk, of wool, or of wool incorporating a little silk in order to give them a silky feel. A label on the underside will provide information about the material and the number of knots per square inch. 150 knots per square inch signifies average quality, while more than 300 knots singles out the carpet as high quality. The carpets have Persian names since the designs come from Persia.

In order to combat the terrible working conditions for children in India's carpet industry, the initiative RugMark was set up in collaboration with the organisations Misereor, Brot für die Welt, and Terre des Hommes, and also enjoys the support of Western governmental organizations, charities and corporate sponsors. Carpets that bear this label have been made by producers who are committed to not employing children and to allowing international inspections. Such carpets are also available in Europe and North America (see www.rugmark.net).

Carpets and rugs

For many Indian women the gold jewellery they are given at their wedding means the same to them as a savings account or life insurance means to their counterparts in the West. Gold is usually sold in 22 carat quality and because of the large amount of tax placed on it, it is not exactly one of the Indian market's bargain buys. However, silver jewellery is incredibly diverse and comparatively inexpensive. **Bracelets, necklaces, rings, some of them set with precious stones** dominate the shop windows of many jewellers. A large proportion of the goods are made in Rajasthan, Bengal, Tibet and Nepal. Fans of old silver jewellery will find what they are looking for in Jaipur and Jodhpur. There is a large selection available for low prices. Necklaces, bracelets and rings made with real **pearls** are manufactured in Hyderabad, where a particularly inexpensive and large selection is available.

Gold and silver jewellery

The bronze sculptures that were made by the Chola dynasty and can still be admired in India's museums achieved great fame. The descendants of the former masters still produce **statues of gods** using the cire perdue method, which then find their way to temples and households as well as to a growing number of art lovers. South India, particularly Tamil Nadu, is the home of bronze casting. Pots, plates, beakers as well as oil lamps and statues of gods are made of copper and brass in many parts of the country.

Bronze sculptures

← *The women of Rajasthan wear particularly colourful clothes*

Reproductions of old miniature paintings are common

Wood and stone Walnut bowls from Kashmir, bamboo chairs from the northeast, sandalwood figures from Mysore, teak and rosewood furniture – the list of wood products is endless. Despite the high shipping costs, **furniture**, from folding screens with Jali carvings to painted, low tables from Rajasthan to heavy cupboards, trunks and beds with traditional designs, are in high demand and are shipped all around the world. The main production site for **inlay works** made of wood and marble is Agra. A small model Taj Mahal made of white marble, adorned with precious stones, a wooden side table with inlaid floral patterns or just cooking utensils produced in the same way are all reminiscent of the mastery of the builders of this magnificent tomb.

If a shop is selling **figures of gods** made of stone it is very likely that they came from the town of Mamallapuram, south of Chennai. The town is home to numerous workshops in which the old craft of stone carving is alive and well and the artists create the entire Hindu pantheon in all sizes over and over again. Anyone with a liking for these goods should not be put off by the enormous weight of the statues. Larger statues, which can easily weigh more than 50 kilograms, can be shipped if need be. Poompuhar Emporium, owned by the state-run Handicraft Development Corporation, is particularly reliable.

Silver jewellery from Jodhpur

The list of India's traditional arts and crafts would not be complete without one of the oldest handicrafts. **Clay pots** in all shapes and sizes, simple or lavishly adorned, can be bought all over India.

A popular souvenir of an India trip is a **miniature painting**. This tradition, which developed to perfection at the courts of the Mughals and Rajputs, is still cultivated in Rajasthan. A painting's price depends on the work the painter invested in it and of course on the artist's skill. A painter may have worked for weeks or even months on a particularly sophisticated and complicated picture. Anyone wishing to buy older miniatures should not rely solely on the trader's word, but ask someone with knowledge on the subject.

In addition to antique shops, which are often located in the tourist districts or the large luxury hotels, there are numerous antique markets. When buying antique goods it should not be forgotten that artificially aging new items has itself developed into a real art in India. Larger shops also see to shipping goods overseas.
Those wishing to take antiques or other art objects home should contact one of the offices of the **Archaeological Survey of India**

(www.asi.nic.in), who can provide expert's opinions as well as export permits. Visitors should be aware that it is illegal to export items more than 100 years old or items such as skins or products made from protected animals. Information is available in New Delhi, tel. 23 01 74 43.

Food   Food items such as pickles, spices (turmeric, cardamom, ginger, coriander, nutmeg, poppy seeds) and tea can be bought at reasonable prices at all larger markets.

Sport and Outdoors

Sports Activities

India has a large selection of sports activities, from trekking and winter sports in the north to water sports on the coast, as well as golf, polo, hockey and much more. Detailed information is available from www.incredibleindia.org.

Diving   In **Goa** organized tours by boat to interesting diving locations are offered by various companies, such as Water-Sports Bogmalo Beach (tel. 08 32 – 51 23 05).

On the **Lakshadweep islands**, Poseidon Neptun Professional on Bangaram Island (c/o Casino Hotel, Willingdon Island, Kochi - 68 20 03, tel. 04 84 – 266 82 21, www.cghearth.com) is the best choice for an introductory course or for a six-day certification course. Organized boat trips to the reefs and individual diving lessons are also possible (season: Oct–May). Information is available from Lakshadweep Tourism (tel. 04 84 – 66 83 87, www.lakshadweeptourism.com).

Magnificent coral reefs around the **Andaman and Nicobar Islands** provide a splendid environment for divers. Some hotels organize courses or have founded diving schools, such as Dive India: Village No. 3 (Havelock, tel. 031 92 – 28 21 87, www.diveindia.com). The oldest diving school in the Andaman Islands has its headquarters at Havelock and offers daily trips and excursions. Also on offer are diving courses at various levels. Barefoot Scuba, the diving school of the Barefoot hotel at Havelock, offers beginner's and intermediate courses during the season (www.barefootindia.com). Further information is available from the Directorate of Tourism Andaman and Nicobar (Port Blair, tel. 031 92 – 23 84 73, www.tourism.andaman. nic.in).

Trekking   India's northernmost border, formed by the Himalaya mountain range, is a popular destination for trekkers and mountaineers from all around the world. Trekking tours are organized in the Garhwal region (Uttarakhand), in Himachal Pradesh, in Jammu and Kashmir, in Ladakh, in Zanskar, in Darjeeling and in Sikkim.

The best trekking season in **Garhwal** is before and after the monsoon, i.e. in April–May and in September–October. This region, which is home to many myths and legends, also contains the source of the Ganges. Other rivers originate here too. The hill station of Mussoorie is a good starting point for treks to the valleys of Yamunotri and Gangotri rivers. Departing Rishikesh via the wonderful Valley of Flowers (bloom: August) will bring trekkers to the holy place of pilgrimage of Badrinath. Almora, the starting location for hikes to the surrounding pine and rhododendron forests, is another trekking centre. Further information is available on the website of Uttarakhand Tourism (www.uttaranchaltourism.in), under www.gmvnl.com or kmvn.org. The landscapes of **Himachal Pradesh** range from infertile rocks and fast-flowing streams in the Spiti and Lahaul valleys in the north to the fertile orchards in Kangra and Chamba. Some particularly interesting sites are Kullu Valley, Rohtang Pass, Chamba and the former summertime capital of the British, Shimla. There are many trekking routes covering all levels of difficulty. Season: mid-June–end of October. Information available from Himachal Pradesh Tourism Development Corportation in Shimla or on the websites www.himachaltourism.nic.in and hptdc.nic.in.

The best trekking time in **Jammu and Kashmir** is mid-June–end of October; rain is very likely in the summer months. Popular starting locations are Srinagar, Gulmarg and Pahalgam.

Information about trekking tours around **Darjeeling** is available from the Department of Tourism in Darjeeling, Silver Fir Building, Banu Sarani. Tours are offered ranging in elevation and level of difficulty. Speciality treks for plant and animals lovers are also available. Information can be found under www.wbtourism.com.

Sikkim: treks departing from Yoksum in western Sikkim go to Dzongri with wonderful views of the Kangchenjunga range. Authorized agencies in Gangtok offer various routes.

The season in **Ladakh / Zanskar** runs from the end of June to the end of October. Ladakh lies in the rain shadow of the mountain ranges and does not receive any monsoon rains. Zanskar, however, does see some rainfall during the summer months.

The best trekking opportunities start in Leh. Information and equipment is available from the Jammu &Kashmir Tourist Office in Leh.

Ideal starting bases for the **Western Ghats** are the small town of Mahabaleshwar in the north and the Coorg region in the south. Information is available from the tourist offices of Maharashtra (for Mahabaleshwar) and Karnataka (for Coorg).

Additional information and permits for trekkers and mountaineers: ◄ Tip
Indian Mountaineering Foundation, Benito Juarez Road, New Delhi – 021, tel. 011– 241 11 12 11, www.indmount.org.

Rajasthan's desert can be explored on horseback or on a camel. **Horseback and** Tours lasting several days are offered and the nights are usually spent **camel safaris** in tents. Popular starting locations are Jodhpur, Jaisalmer and Bikaner. Information is available from the Rajasthan Tourist Office (www.rajasthantourism.gov.in) and in the travel agencies of the places cited.

Whitewater rafting

One of the newer sports in northern India is river rafting. Whitewater rafting is possible on a number of Himalayan mountain rivers. They include the Zanskar, Indus, Chenab and Lidder in the Kashmir-Ladakh region, the Beas and Sutlej in Himachal Pradesh, the Ganga, Bhagirathi, Tons and Sarda in Uttarakhand and the Teesta and Rangit in Sikkim. Further information is available from the relevant tourist offices.

Winter sports

Gulmarg (2730m/8957ft) in Kashmir is the best-known and best-developed winter sports resort in India (guaranteed snow from December to April, various pistes). Josimath in Garhwal, which is actually a place of pilgrimage, is being developed into a winter-sports

A major inspiration for many travellers: meditation courses in India, the cradle of yoga

resort. A cableway leads to the pistes of Auli and Gorsain near Kuari Pass, from where there are magnificent views. The season runs from January to March, during which time snow is guaranteed.

Information and offers about motorbike trips through southern India, Rajasthan and Ladakh can be found under www.wheelofindia.com.

Motorcycle trips

Yoga

A large part of Hinduism's philosophical tradition is finding increasing numbers of followers in the West: yoga, which literally translated means »to unite«. It is a method by which human beings can develop spiritually. Mental and physical exercises are used in yoga as instruments of liberation from the material world. Amongst the many schools of yoga the practice of hatha yoga has found the most followers. Exactly specified body positions (asanas), breathing exercises (pranayama) and mental concentration exercises are the three main pillars of hatha yoga, which is now being taught in many yoga centres in the West.

Those wanting to learn or practise yoga in India have a large number of yoga centres to choose from in almost every larger town. Ashrams also often offer yoga courses as well as other courses with meditative exercises. An extensive list can be obtained from India Tourism (www.incredibleindia.org, links: Wellness, Yoga) and from the Government of India tourist offices.

Time

Despite its size India is entirely located within a single time zone. India is 5 hours 30 minutes ahead of Greenwich Mean Time. There is no summer or daylight-saving time, so the time difference may vary according to the time of year. India does not generally use the 24-hour clock; as in the UK and elsewhere, times are expressed as am or pm.

Time difference

Tour Operators

Many operators offer good round trips and study trips to India. The following section is a small selection of recommended operators. A longer list can be found on the Incredible India website (www.incredibleindia.org)

TOUR OPERATORS

IN THE UK

▶ **Discovery Initiatives Ltd.**
51 Castle Street, Cirencester
Gloucestershire, GL7 1QD
Tel. 01285 643333
Fax 01285 887888
www.discoveryinitiatives.co.uk
Wildlife holidays, tiger watching,
ecotourism

▶ **Global Link Travel &Tours**
Capricorn House
1 Mandeville Place
London , W1U 3AW
Tel. 020 7224 7766
Fax 020 7224 7733
www.globallinktravel.co.uk
Low budget student tours, wildlife,
gourmet and historical tours, Pal-
ace-on-Wheels, steam railways

▶ **Mountain Kingdoms**
Old Crown House, 18 Market
Street
Wotton Under Edge, Gloucester-
shire, GL12 7AE
Tel. 01453 844400 or 0845 330
8579
Fax 01453 844422
www.mountainkingdoms.com
Trekking in the Himalaya

IN THE USA

▶ **Unique Journeys**
71 Keystone Ave
Reno NV 89503
Tel. 775 323 0110
Fax 702 323 6914
www.uniquejourney.com
Trips to India with a personal
touch, homestays

▶ **Wilderness Travel**
1102 Ninth St.
Berkeley Ca 94710
Tel. 510 558 2488
Fax 510 558 2489
www.wildernesstravel.com
Organized tours of between two
and three weeks taking in India's
highlights

IN INDIA

▶ **Jungle Lodges and
Resorts Ltd.**
2nd floor, Shrungar Shopping
Centre, MG Road, Bangalore
Tel. 080 – 25 59 70 21/24/25
www.junglelodges.com
Specializes in nature trips and
jungle safaris.

▶ **L'Orient Travels**
3, June Calls Vidyanagari Marg
Kalina, Mumbai – 098
Tel. (022) 26 65 06 16
www.orienttravelsindia.com
offers trips such as »Smiling Buddhas, Changing Landscapes« to
Ladakh and a trip to Bhutan as
well as Jeep safaris through the
Himalaya and round trips such as
through Kerala, Rajasthan and
Gujarat and nature walks in Borivili Park near Mumbai.

▶ **Indo Asia Tours**
Tel. (011) 24 69 17 33
www.indoasia-tours.com
Offers cultural and study trips, but
also individual itineraries; including trips to the neighbouring
countries of Nepal, Bhutan, Sri
Lanak, Bangladesh and Myanmar.

▶ **Pioneer Travels**
Pioneer House, 5th Cross Road,
Kochi-003
Tel. 04 84 – 266 61 48
www.pioneertravels.com
Organizes Backwater trips, house-
boat stays; has its own taxi fleet.

Transport

India's spectrum of means of transport ranges from rickshaws that are still pulled by men in Kolkata to supersonic jets. In between, there is a variety of ways to get about. There are bicycle rickshaws and their modern counterpart, scooters, a three-wheeled vehicle with a high-pitched horn, which visitors to India will be able to hear in their minds' ear long after their trip has come to an end. Then come the spacious, robust Ambassadors, vintage in design but still without any significant competition on the roads as far as taxis are concerned, and the red double-decker buses, reminiscent of the London Routemasters, that make their way through Mumbai's traffic chaos every day. Coaches, ranging from shaky, dented tin boxes to luxury models with air conditioning, video and a fridge bring masses of people north, south, east and west, year after year, and a very well developed, very comfortable railway network, which does have some safety issues, accesses the entire subcontinent.

Hovercraft bring travellers in just a few hours from Mumbai to the tourist stronghold of Goa. Finally, there is plenty of competition for air space between the state-owned Indian Airlines and various private companies.

Road Traffic

India's roads are ruled by the law of survival of the fittest. The indisputable kings of the road are the many lorries, and only reckless bus drivers would dream of challenging the big trucks to risky evasive manoeuvres, which often lead to accidents. Passenger cars are third in the pecking order, followed by motorized rickshaws and cyclists. At the bottom of this hierarchy are pedestrians, who should follow certain rules of behaviour that could be a matter of life and death.

Important tips for pedestrians

The following are generally applicable: a green traffic light for pedestrians does not automatically mean that vehicles will stop. Anyone wanting to cross a street should not expect cars or bicycles to brake – the drivers will usually try to avoid the tiresome biped by swerving. This is mostly successful but assumes that said pedestrian crosses the road in the »Indian« manner, i.e. slowly and with the expectation that a wait in the middle of the road will be necessary before the second half of the street can be crossed. Under no circumstances should visitors run across a street. Newcomers really should wait for a very favourable situation. North Americans should not forget that the people in India drive on the left. The only creatures exempt from these safety rules are the numerous cows, which are considered sacred in India. They often take their time on six-lane highways, safe in the knowledge that even the most reckless lorry driver will respect their special status.

City traffic Buses and taxis are the main forms of transport within cities. In Mumbai, the fastest way to get to the northern suburbs, particularly during the day, is to take one of the suburban trains. Kolkata has a tram, which can only move very slowly in the city's traffic chaos. It also has a modern underground, which presents an alternative for certain districts. Delhi has also recently acquired a modern underground. City buses are generally overcrowded, but very cheap. One alternative is to use taxis, usually Ambassadors, or motorized rickshaws. In smaller towns bicycle rickshaws and horse-drawn rickshaws can also be used. Taxis and motorized rickshaws are usually fitted with a counter attached to the outside of the vehicle. This measures the units travelled and is used to calculate the fare. Ideally the driver will have a list of current journey prices available.

This is however only the ideal (Mumbai is a model in this case, but there are black sheep everywhere). In many places the price has to be negotiated in advance and so it is good to have some idea about the price level. Large airports and train stations often offer a prepaid taxi service, where the passenger pays for the distance in advance, thus avoiding the trouble of having to negotiate a price in a completely alien city. International airports have a private and public prepaid taxi service. The public one is generally a lot cheaper than the private one and just as good.

Bus connections Those places that cannot be accessed by rail can at least be accessed by road. Especially the many Himalayan valleys and hill stations can only be reached by bus or taxi. Generally, travelling by bus is not as comfortable as travelling by train in first or second class. Sometimes buses are faster or take shorter routes because the train tracks can be quite winding.

Car Rentals and Tourist Taxis

Actively participating in India's traffic requires knowledge of all the special rules, as well as great skill in dealing with masses of vehicles, pedestrians and cows and other animals which may be on the roads, particularly in rural areas. Tourists do not generally have either the knowledge or the skill. For this reason car rental companies usually offer their vehicles with chauffeurs. On trips lasting several days the driver will sleep in the car or in designated rooms in the hotel. The same is true for tourist taxis, which can be hired through tourist offices and travel agencies. It is recommended to hire a taxi through the governmental tourist offices, but there are also many private car rental companies.

i **Car rental companies**

- Car Rental India, Delhi, tel. 011 – 29 81 22 00
- State Express, Delhi, tel. 011 – 26 85 54 83
- Hertz, Mumbai, tel. 022 – 65 70 16 92
- Hertz, Chennai, tel. 044 – 22 32 51 14
- Pioneer Travels, Kochi, tel. 04 84 – 266 61 48

India's holy cows aren't bothered by traffic

Rail Travel

India has the sixth-largest railway network in the world. 63,000km/
39,000mi of track run all over the subcontinent, even to its most remote corners. Exploring the country by rail is a good idea, particularly for those travellers who come with enough time. It is the only
way to get a real impression of India's size, its geographic diversity
and, not least, of the people's everyday lives – impressions frequent
fliers largely have to forgo.

Train connections

There are several trains a day between the big cities, usually called
express or mail trains, which differ greatly in the amount of time
they take to complete a trip. The fastest are the **Rajdhani Express
Trains**; they run between all the major metropolises and can be twice
as fast as ordinary trains, but they are also very expensive.

Classes and prices

The main trains usually have a first class (with or without air conditioning) and a second class (with or without air conditioning), and
passenger trains also have a third class. The number of passengers
admitted to the air-conditioned first and second-class coaches is
limited and the prices are several times higher than those of the regular second class. The compartments of the first and second classes
AC are very spacious and have two to four beds. For night trips bed
sheets are provided, sometimes for free, sometimes for a fee, and the
same is true for all meals. »Second AC« is highly recommended.
Much cheaper and less comfortable, though with better views since
the windows can be opened, are the carriages of the regular second
class, which are divided into normal carriages and sleeping cars.

TRAVELLING LIKE A MAHARAJA

Journey back into the days of pomp and luxury, into the fairy-tale world of Arabian Nights, embedded in the comfort of five-star luxury: all of these things are promised by the operator of the Palace on Wheels.

Rajasthan's palaces and forts and India's greatest attraction, the Taj Mahal, are all on the agenda of the one-week tour of the »Palace on Wheels«, a super-modern luxury train, whose interior is reminiscent of the ambience of old Rajput chambers.

Pure luxury on rails

Every Wednesday, from September to April, 14 carriages leave New Delhi and make their way westwards into the desert. Jaipur, with its Palace of Winds, is the first stop on the trip. From there the train makes its way through the Thar desert to Jaisalmer. The medieval desert town with its sandstone fort, palaces and havelis is one of Rajasthan's great attractions. Continuing further to the west, the Palace on Wheels next reaches Jodhpur with its bluish-white houses, above which Meherangarh Fort rises up. Next in line is Rathambore National Park, famous for its tigers, then it's on to the magnificent fort of Chitaurgarh and finally to Udaipur. Passing through the bird paradise of Keoladeo Ghana National Park near Bharatpur the train reaches Agra, home to the famous Taj Mahal. A visit to the deserted palaces of Fatehpur Sikri is also on the itinerary before the train arrives back in its home station of New Delhi.

In addition to all of the entrance tickets the tour includes lunch in the famous palace hotels of the aforementioned cities as well as other extras. The train is equipped with two dining cars, a bar and luxuriously furnished double rooms with a bathroom, air conditioning and other five-star standards. Those wishing to delve into this fairy-tale world will not need the riches of a maharaja, but it does take a deeper dip into the wallet to purchase this pleasure.

Further information on this dream journey on rails is available at travel agencies, at »Palace on Wheels« itself (Tourist Reception Centre, Bikaner House, New Delhi, tel. 011 – 23 38 18 84) and online at www.incredibleindia. org or www.palace onwheels. com.

Some trains on the main routes have what are known as AC Chair Cars, which resemble the open-plan carriages of European intercity trains. Many trains provide ladies' compartments for women travelling alone, but these are only available in second class.

Indian Railways publishes an updated timetable every year, listing all of the trains and their departure times as well as fares. *Trains at a Glance* is the name of this brochure, which is available from the information offices of the major railway stations. The timetables and most important connections can also be found on the website of India's state railway company »Indian Railways« (www.indianrail.gov.in) and also on www.railtourismindia.com.

Timetables and tickets

Purchasing a train ticket is generally a lot easier for foreigners than it is for Indian travellers, who often have to book their trips months in advance. All the very big cities and many of the main tourist destinations with train connections have **special tourist counters**, which are often in the stations themselves or nearby. Finding the right place often takes more time than buying the ticket. It is best to ask for the exact address at the station's information office or the tourist office and not shy away from returning two or three times.

? DID YOU KNOW ...?

■ ... that tickets can still be obtained for many sold-out trains? The magic word here is TATKAL. Unfortunately the counter staff do not point out this option. Five days before the date of departure this quota, known as the Tatkal quota, goes on sale. The tickets are then a bit more expensive and are non-refundable.

To make travelling more comfortable for tourists the government has introduced a tourist quota available to travellers in larger towns and cities with important tourist attractions. It allows travellers to buy train tickets for a certain journey from the departure station to another place on the day before or the morning of the departure, as long as the train is scheduled to leave in the evening. This does not, however, apply to all trains and stations. Although it is possible to get on Indian trains without a reservation it is not recommended, particularly not for night journeys. Travellers are not permitted to use the first and second class AC coaches without reservations.

Tourist quota

An Indrail pass allows its owner to use all of the railway connections within India. It can be obtained abroad from travel agents specializing in India, or from large Indian train stations. Its price depends on the train class required and the length of time the pass is valid for (maximum 90 days).

Indrail pass

After the »Palace-on-Wheels« luxury train in Rajasthan proved to be an extremely successful undertaking, other states have followed suit with similar services (►Baedeker Special p.186), such as Maharashtra with its »Deccan Queen«.

Luxury trains

AIRLINE COMPANIES

INTERNET

▶ **Indian Airlines**
www.indian-airlines.nic.in

▶ **Jet Airways**
www.jetairways.com

▶ **Deccan Air**
www.deccanairlines.in

▶ **Spice Jet**
www.spicejet.com

▶ **Kingfisher Airlines**
www.flykingfisher.com

INDIAN AIRLINES TELEPHONE NUMBERS

▶ **Mumbai**
Tel. 022 – 22 02 30 31

▶ **Delhi**
Tel. 011 – 24 63 13 37

▶ **Kolkata**
Tel. 033 – 22 11 68 69

▶ **Chennai**
Tel. 044 – 23 45 33 02

▶ **Bangalore**
Tel. 080 – 22 97 84 06

Air Travel

Those wishing to visit the Taj Mahal and the beach of Kovalam on the same trip who do not have much time should consider taking domestic flights for the longer distances. The journey from Delhi or Mumbai to Chennai takes 26 hours by train, but the flight takes just 90 minutes. Tickets for domestic flights can also be bought at travel agencies outside India or via the internet.

India is covered by an increasingly dense flight network. Several private airline companies now compete with the national one, Indian Airlines. The most important private carriers are Jet Airways, Air Sahara, Deccan Air, Kingfisher Airlines and Spice Jet.

Boat Travel

Boat connections There are boat connections between Chennai and Sri Lanka and to the Andaman Islands and from Kochi to the Lakshadweep islands. Panaji in Goa can be reached from Mumbai by boat. There are several boat routes on the Kerala Backwaters.

The **main passenger ports** in India are Mumbai, Kolkata, Kochi, Chennai, Kozhicode, Panaji and Rameshwaram.

There are connections between Kolkata and Chennai to Port Blair on the Andaman Islands. They are seasonal, however, and during the monsoon they do not generally run (information: Shipping Corporation of India, www.shipindia.com).

The **Backwaters excursions** around Kochi in Kerala are particularly attractive. Several different tours are on offer, such as Kozhicode – – Kochi and Alapuzzha – Kottayam.

Travellers with Disabilities

There are almost no travellers with disabilities in India, so it is hardly surprising that the country does not yet have much infrastructure to accommodate such visitors. Only a few international hotels are reasonably equipped to meet the needs of disabled travellers. Anyone travelling to India with a disability should thus not come alone, and discuss all the details about accommodation and transport in advance with the help of a tour operator at home.

► **RADAR**
12 City Forum, 250 City Road,
London EC1V 8AF
Tel. (020) 72 50 32 22
www.radar.org.uk

► **SATH (Society for the Advancement of Travel for the Handicapped)**
347 5th Ave., no. 610
New York, NY 10016:
Tel. (21) 4 47 72 84
www.sath.org

Weights and Measures

India uses both Imperial and metric units. Weights and temperatures are usually given using the metric system.

The term **1 lakh** is used in India for the number 100,000. Thus one million corresponds to 10 lakh. The number 10,000,000 is also called **1 crore**.

UNITS OF MEASURE

► **Area units**
1 square inch (in²) = 6.45 cm²
1 cm² = 0.155 in²
1 square foot (ft²) = 9.288 dm²
1 dm² = 0.108 ft²
1 square yard (yd²) = 0.836 m²
1 m² = 1.196 yd²

1 square mile (mi) = 2.589 km²
1 km² = 0.386 mi²
1 acre = 0.405 ha
1 ha = 2.471 acres

► **Volumes**
1 cubic inch (in³) = 16.386 cm³

1 cm³ = 0.061 in³
1 cubic foot (ft³) = 28.32 dm³
1 dm³ = 0.035 ft³
1 cubic yard (yd³) = 0.765 m³
1 m³ = 1.308 yd³

▶ **Liquids**
1 gill = 0.118 l
1 l = 8.474 gills
1 pint (pt) = 0.473 l [[American pint]]
1 l = 2.114 pt
1 quart (qt) = 0.946 l

1 l = 1.057 qt
1 gallon (gal) = 3.787 l
1 l = 0.264 gal

▶ **Lengths**
1 inch (in) = 2.54 cm
1 cm = 0.39 in
1 foot (ft) = 30.48 cm
10 cm = 0.33 ft
1 yard (yd) = 91.44 cm
1 m = 1.09 yd
1 mile (mi) = 1.61 km
1 km = 0.62 mi

When to Go

Best time to go: Oct–March

The best time to go to India is from October to March. The weather is particularly pleasant during the winter months. The nights are cool and the daytime temperatures are bearable. However, in northern India visitors should expect cold nights, particularly in January. Another attractive time to go is the period immediately following the monsoon in September–October, since the country is particularly green at that time of year. The rainy season itself is not ideal for tourists. Heavy rain, extreme humidity, tropical heat and flooding all work against any travelling. Nonetheless this time of year still has its appeal because rainfall is generally limited to a few hours a day, except for in the coastal regions. Southeastern India can see some rainfall during November and December as a result of the northeast monsoon.

Travelling to India in the month of May is not recommended. This is the hottest month in India: in Rajasthan and parts of central India the thermometer can often climb to almost 50°C/122°F. In addition May is the main holiday time for Indians, so hotels will be full and means of transport packed.

The right clothes

Depending on the region and time of year different clothing is appropriate. It can get quite chilly in parts of northern India in January for example. Temperatures here drop to a few degrees above freezing; in the Himalayan regions they naturally drop even lower. Woollen pullovers, warm jackets and socks should definitely be packed. In large parts of South India the temperatures do not fall below 15°C/59°F–20°C/68°F even in the winter. During the day it gets very hot, as it does in North India: 25°C/77°F–30°C/86°F and higher in the interior. Light cotton clothing is the most pleasant to wear. Stout shoes should also be packed.

The pre-monsoon months are the hottest time of year in India. Light cotton clothing is best for both this and for the post-monsoon period. A scarf is indispensable, since drafts, fans and the constant change between air-conditioned restaurants and hotels and the outside can stress the body.

The rainy season generally lasts from June to September and in southern India it can also be wet in November and December. The heavy rains, particularly in the coastal regions and mountains, make very good rain gear a necessity.

Tours

ANY TRIP THROUGH INDIA IS SURE
TO UNCOVER A NEW FACET OF THIS
WONDERFUL, CHAOTIC COUNTRY –
AND IT IS NOT JUST THOSE IN
SEARCH OF CULTURE, THE BEACH OR YOGA WHO
WILL GET THEIR MONEY'S WORTH!

TOURS THROUGH INDIA

India's diversity is exciting and inexhaustible. Anyone can find their personal paradise here: stunning sandy beaches, adventurous trekking tours, magnificent palaces, lively cities, holy temples, breathtaking landscapes and fragrant spice bazaars, as well as meditation and relaxing Ayurveda resorts.

■■■ **TOUR 1** **Indian Grand Tour**
A trip to the most outstanding sights the Indian subcontinent has to offer ► **page 200**

■■■ **TOUR 2** **The Exotic South**
This tour focuses on old India, which, almost untouched by the Mughals in the north, has remained the legendary tropical dream destination. ► **page 202**

■■■ **TOUR 3** **Land of the Kings**
Rajasthan shows its fairytale side: magnificent palaces, unassailable forts, proud Rajputs, women in wonderfully colourful saris and masterly arts and crafts. ► **page 206**

■■■ **TOUR 4** **Through Gujarat**
This state, which has woken from its 100-year sleep, draws visitors in with its wonderful Jain temples, palaces, nature reserves and fabled beaches lined by palm trees. ► **page 209**

■■■ **TOUR 5** **Places of Pilgrimage in the Northeast**
Following in Buddha's footsteps to rarely visited Hindu temples ► **page 210**

■■■ **TOUR 6** **On the Deccan Plateau**
Even those who know a lot about India will find there is plenty to discover on this tour. ► **page 212**

Star-shaped
Keshavara Temple in
Somnathpur

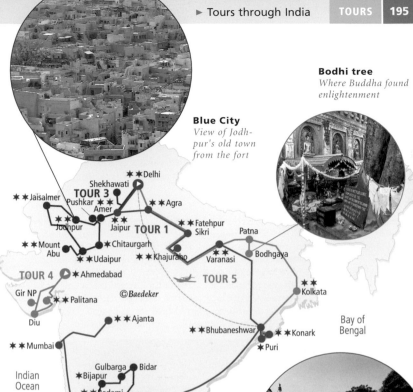

Bodhi tree
Where Buddha found enlightenment

Blue City
View of Jodh-pur's old town from the fort

Giant relief
It describes the creation myth of the Ganges

India's southernmost point
This is where the Arabian Sea, the Bay of Bengal and the Indian Ocean meet

Delhi
Shekhawati
Jaisalmer
Pushkar
Amer
TOUR 3
Jodhpur
Jaipur
Agra
TOUR 1
Fatehpur Sikri
Patna
Mount Abu
Chitaurgarh
Khajuraho
Varanasi
Bodhgaya
Udaipur
Ahmedabad
TOUR 4
©Baedeker
TOUR 5
Gir NP
Palitana
Kolkata
Diu
Ajanta
Bhubaneshwar
Konark
Mumbai
Puri
Bay of Bengal
Indian Ocean
Gulbarga
Bidar
Bijapur
Badami
TOUR 6
Goa
Hampi
Bangalore
TOUR 1
Sravana Belgola
Kanchi-puram
TOUR 1
Belur
Chennai
Mysore
Mamallapuram
Somnathpur
Puducherry
Tiruchirapalli
Chidambaram
Periyar NP
Thanjavur
Kochi
Madurai
Backwaters
TOUR 2
Thiruvanantha-puram
Kanyakumari

Travelling in India

It is more than 3000km/1800mi between Kashmir's snow-covered peaks and Kanyakumari, India's southernmost tip. Itanagar, the capital of Arunachal Pradesh, the easternmost state, is also separated by a distance of almost 3000km/1800mi from the desert town of Jaisalmer in the west on the border to Pakistan. Between these extremities lie India's 28 federal states and seven union territories. The country is about the same size as Europe, and just as varied.

The northwest: deserts, palaces and festivals Deserts and palace-like fortifications, camel safaris and colourful dress: all of these things are associated with Rajasthan and Gujarat, the two Indian states furthest to the northwest. **Rajasthan is still India's number one travel destination**. Its excellent tourist infrastructure with a large number of places to stay, from palace hotels to tent camps in the desert, and its many historic cities, led by Jaipur, Udaipur and Jaisalmer, attract hordes of visitors every year. The annual Pushkar Mela, a two-week festival held in Pushkar, a place of pilgrimage, is famous far beyond India's national boundaries.

The fairy-tale interior of Jodhpur's Umaid Bhavan palace

In addition, **Gujarat** has now awoken from a hundred-year sleep, and it too is presenting its sights and attractions in an advantageous light. The famous Jain temples of Palitana, the Sun Temple of Modhera and the desert region of Kutch are just three of the state's great attractions. It gets quite cold here in the winter and very hot in the summer, so suitable clothing is particularly important.

India's mountain regions are as interesting to those seeking salvation as they are to those who wish to get some peaks under their belt. Spiritual sites such as Haridwar and Rishikesh, Dharamsala with its Tibetan influence, the places of pilgrimage at the sources of the Ganges and the monasteries of Ladakh and Sikkim attract Indian tourists and foreign visitors alike. The mountains of the Himalaya range are perfect for **trekking tours** of all kinds. The states of Himachal Pradesh and Uttarakhand offer a large number of activities ranging from hiking to rafting. Darjeeling and Sikkim are also excellent starting locations for mountain excursions.

The Himalayan region: high peaks and sacred sites

India's most famous structure, the **Taj Mahal in Agra**, is an absolute must for anyone visiting northern India. As it is just four hours from Delhi by train, visiting the Taj Mahal can easily be combined with a stay in the capital. The capital itself has plenty of buildings dating back to the Mughal period. **Old Delhi**, with its busy bazaars, is a completely different world from **New Delhi**, with its excellent hotels and many different restaurants. These two parts of the city have recently been connected by the new Metro. Punjab is home to the famous city of **Amritsar** with its Golden Temple, the largest place of worship of the Sikh community.

Northern India: from the Mughals to the metro

Until recently the northeast states were considered uncharted territory on a tourist map of India. This has gradually been changing. Following Assam, with its national parks and tea plantations, other regions such as Meghalaya and Tripura are opening their doors to foreign visitors. Tourism is now even being encouraged in Nagaland. **Unspoilt nature** makes this a great region for hiking, mountaineering, rafting, fishing and other activities.

The north-eastern states: tea plantations and trekking

The fertile Ganges plain is a significant area for Hindus and Buddhists alike: it is the location of **Varanasi**, a centre of Hindu spirituality, and of places where Buddha lived and taught: **Bodhgaya** and Nalanda. At the mouth of the Ganges lies the city of **Kolkata** with its millions of inhabitants, its rich historic heritage and lively cultural scene. Tropical Orissa, with its lavish vegetation, is also home to a number of important religious sites, first and foremost the temple cities of **Bhubhaneshwar** and **Puri** as well as **Konark** with its sun temple, which is an outstanding example of Hindu religious architecture. Buddhists have also left their mark on Orissa with many buildings and monasteries.

The Indo-Gangetic plain and the east: sacred land

Central India: home of the Adivasis	Large parts of central India are **tribal areas**, inhabited by indigenous peoples, the Adivasis. The tribes are particularly numerous in Madhya Pradesh, the new states of Chhattisgarh and Jharkhand, as well as in parts of Bihar and Orissa. Large **nature reserves** can also be found here, such as Bandhavagarh Park and Kanka National Park, where tigers may be encountered. Madhya Pradesh is home to the famous temples of **Khajuraho** with their esoteric sculptures as well as other interesting places, such as the Maharaja cities of Gwalior and Orchha.
The Deccan plateau: historical sites and high tech	The Deccan Plateau has seen many rulers over the centuries, and a large number of them have left their mark here. The old temple cities of Badami, Aihole and Pattadakal are amongst the oldest evidence of this. The ruins of **Hampi**, which bespeak the brilliance of the medieval Vijayanagar Empire, are also quite magnificent. Both are Hindu sites. However, Muslims also left impressive cities and structures behind, for example in Bijapur, Bidar and Gulbarga, as well as in **Hyderabad**. The latter has been nicknamed Cyberabad, because, like **Bangalore**, the largest city on the Deccan plateau, it has become a centre of the software industry.
India's west coast: a place to get lost	From Gujarat's coast in the north to India's southern tip via the millionaire city of **Mumbai** there are around 2000km/1200mi of beaches, palm trees and tropical vegetation. The popular holiday destination of **Goa** with its long sandy beaches is a wonderful place to relax. The most southwesterly state, **Kerala**, lures visitors with lavish tropical vegetation to the backwaters and the Western Ghats, where spices such as pepper, cardamom and many others are cultivated. **Lovely beaches** in Kovalam, Varkala and other places as well as many very good hotels will provide all the necessary rest and relaxation. **Ayurvedic treatments** have a long tradition in Kerala and are offered in many resorts. Last but not least the region draws in visitors with its cultural diversity and countless traditional festivals.
The southeast: land of a thousand temples	Nowhere in India are there so many old temples and temple cities as there are in **Tamil Nadu**, because the subcontinent's foreign conquerors never made it this far. Thanjavur, Chidambaram and Kanchipuram are just three of the best-known examples. Parts of **Andhra Pradesh** also have many holy sites travellers can visit. Fertile paddy fields characterize the region. Between Tamil Nadu's capital **Chennai** and Kanyakumari's southern tip there are plenty of interesting places to see along the coast, such as the temple city of Mamallapuram and the former French colony of Pondicherry. Nice sandy beaches make for inviting places to take a dip.
India for nature lovers	Large parts of the subcontinent have been declared **nature conservation areas**. These are home to tigers, elephants and many other wild animals. Jawahar National Park in the south, the largest in India, has

the biggest elephant population in the country. India is also a paradise for bird watchers. Nature reserves such as the sanctuary of Bharatpur in Rajasthan are ideal for watching many different species.

Beach holidays in India

The most attractive beaches are to be found in **Goa**. However, other maritime states have also developed their beaches for tourists. The best-known in Kerala are **Kovalam** and Varkala, but appealing facilities have also been built on the other stretches of coastline. The union territories of Daman and Diu, former Portuguese colonies along the west coast with white sandy beaches, are attractive. Along the east coast, seaside resorts are developing along the beaches of Orissa, Andhra Pradesh and Tamil Nadu. The Andaman and Nicobar Islands, as well as the Lakshadweep Islands off India's southwest coast, are a **veritable paradise for divers**.

Ayurveda in India

Many excellent hotels and resorts offer Ayurveda spas and treatments. In this regard, no other federal state can compete with tropical **Kerala** in the southwest of the country, where the practice has a long tradition. However, Goa and some places in the Himalaya also have some attractive resorts catering to visitors' wellbeing.

Trekking and mountaineering in India

The **Himalaya** provide excellent locations for trekking and mountaineering. The mountain states of Himachal Pradesh and Uttarakhand attract particularly large numbers of trekkers. High mountain tours can be organized from Ladakh, Darjeeling and Sikkim. However, anyone wanting to climb to greater elevations in the Himalaya mountains will need a special permit (▶ Practicalities, Sport and Outdoors).

The right mode of transport

India has a very well developed civil aviation network and one of the longest railway networks in the world. These days travellers can choose amongst many different airline companies to travel longer distances within the subcontinent. Taking the train in India is also quite comfortable if travelling first class. Hiring a taxi including a driver is ideal for overland journeys and this is possible in every larger town. Taking the bus is cheap but uncomfortable and exhausting.

A good alternative: tours by taxi

Tour 1 Indian Grand Tour

Start and destination: from Delhi to
Ajanta and Ellora

Duration: min. 30 days

For some, it is an appealing idea to explore the entire subcontinent in one single trip. This is possible but it does require a lot of time, at least if travelling without a tour operator. Tour 1 should serve as a guideline for those who do have sufficient time. The trip is not free of stress and requires good preparation. Those wanting to travel in a more pleasant and comfortable manner should book with one of the many tour operators specializing in India. This is not the cheapest option but it does save a lot of time and worry.

India's
highlights

The starting point of this tour is ❶✱✱ **Delhi**, India's capital. With its countless museums, its forts and mosques dating back to the Mughal period, and its beautiful gardens, the city gives visitors plenty of time to acclimatize to India. From here visitors can easily explore the »golden triangle«: Jaipur, Agra and Delhi. ❷✱✱ **Jaipur,** with its well-preserved palaces and its pink houses in the city centre, offers an insight into the lives of the Maharajas of Rajasthan. Jaipur is a vibrant bazaar city, and the starting point for a trip to the country's most famous monument, the legendary Taj Mahal in ❸✱✱ **Agra**. The Red Fort and the abandoned palace complex of ❹✱✱ **Fatehpur Sikri** approx. 40km/25mi away are also worth visiting.

There is a direct flight between Agra and the small temple town of ❺✱✱ **Khajuraho**. Its numerous temples from the Chandella period are known for their outstanding erotic stone sculptures. A further short flight from Khajuraho then takes travellers to the next destination, ❻✱✱ **Varanasi**, the most sacred city of the Hindus. It is situated along the impressive banks of the Ganges and possesses numerous temples visited by thousands of pilgrims every day.

The tour continues on to ❼✱✱ **Bhubaneshwar**, Orissa's old temple city, whose main attractions are the many well-preserved temples from the eighth to twelfth centuries decorated with high quality sculptures. This is a good place to go on a day trip to the famous Sun Temple of ❽✱✱ **Konark** and the pilgrimage centre of ❾✱ **Puri** with its Jagannath Temple.

Next on the itinerary is a flight from Bhubaneshwar to ❿✱ **Chennai**, Tamil Nadu's capital, formerly known as Madras. A tour of the city should definitely include a visit to the Government Museum with its collection of southern Indian bronzes. Day trips to the old Pallava capital of ⓫✱✱ **Kanchipuram** and to the beach temples in ⓬✱✱ **Mamallapuram** are particularly worthwhile. ⓭✱✱ **Madurai**, the site of Meenakshi Temple, a large temple complex built in the classical southern Indian Dravidian style with tall gopurams, is the next destination on this tour.

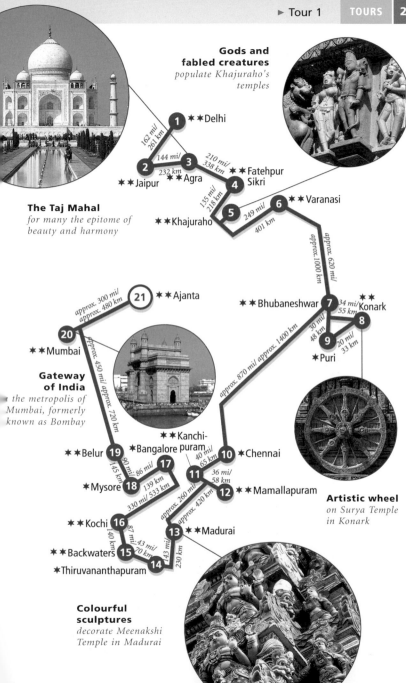

Gods and fabled creatures
populate Khajuraho's temples

The Taj Mahal
for many the epitome of beauty and harmony

1 ★★Delhi

162 mil/ 261 km

2 ★★Jaipur   144 mil/ 232 km   **3** ★★Agra   210 mil/ 338 km   ★★Fatehpur Sikri

4

135 mil/ 218 km

5 ★★Khajuraho   249 mil/ 401 km   **6** ★★Varanasi

approx. 620 mil/ approx. 1000 mil

21 ★★Ajanta

approx. 300 mil/ approx. 480 km

20

★★Mumbai

approx. 450 mil/ approx. 720 km

★★Bhubaneshwar   **7**   34 mil/ 55 km   ★★Konark

8

30 mil/ 48 km   **9**   20 mil/ 33 km

★Puri

approx. 870 mil/ approx. 1400 km

Gateway of India
the metropolis of Mumbai, formerly known as Bombay

★★Belur **19** ★Bangalore   ★★Kanchi-puram

17   40 mil/ 65 km   **10** ★Chennai

90 mil/ 145 km   86 mil/ 139 km

18   330 mil/ 533 km   **11**   36 mil/ 58 km

★Mysore

12 ★★Mamallapuram

approx. 260 mil/ approx. 420 km

★★Kochi **16**   87 mil/ 140 km   43 mil/ 70 km   **13** ★★Madurai

Artistic wheel
on Surya Temple in Konark

★★Backwaters **15**   43 mil/ 230 km

14

★Thiruvananthapuram

Colourful sculptures
decorate Meenakshi Temple in Madurai

To get to ⑯ ✶✶ **Kochi**, probably the most interesting city along the entire coastline of Kerala, travellers will have to fly via ⑭ ✶ **Thiruvananthapuram**. If this journey is done by taxi it will take a day (eight hours), but the roads make their way through wonderful mountain landscapes. The city, built on seven islands, used to be the most important spice port of the Malabar Coast, and colonists and traders from all around the world have left all kinds of different buildings behind here. Kochi is also a good base for a boat trip to the fascinating world of the ⑮ ✶✶ **Backwaters**, a labyrinth of countless lagoons, rivers and canals.

The next tour destination is ⑰ ✶ **Bangalore**, Karnataka's capital. It is well situated to be the starting location for an approx. three-day tour to the old Maharaja town of ⑱ ✶ **Mysore**, as well as to ⑲ ✶✶ **Belur and Halebid**. Mysore's showpiece is the Wodeyar palace, the Wodeyar dynasty having ruled the princely state from 1399 to 1947. Good examples of the architectural style favoured by the Hoysala rulers are the temples of Belur and Halebid from the eleventh and twelfth centuries. They can be visited in the context of a one-day tour from Hassan.

Leaving Bangalore, the tour continues by plane to the city of ⑳ ✶✶ **Mumbai**, with its 16 million inhabitants, which is also the country's economic centre. Visitors should not be put off by the Moloch that is Mumbai: in particular the quarters Colaba and Fort in the south of the city and the old town with its bazaars reveal special facets of an Indian city to those who visit.

Those who have not yet seen enough can take a short flight to Aurangabad on the Deccan plateau, from where it is possible to go on a day trip to the famous cave temple of ㉑ ✶✶ **Ajanta and Ellora**. The very well preserved drawings and the impressively worked sculptures of the temple site are some of the best that Indian art has to offer. Mumbai and Delhi are both good cities from which to fly home.

Tour 2 The Exotic South

Start and destination: from Chennai to Bangalore   **Duration:** approx. 30 days

An alternative for individual travellers to the mammoth programme laid out in tour 1 would be to visit just a part of the country. Routes 2–6 are suggestions for regional tours, which take two to four weeks to complete and can be combined with such extensions as a beach holiday in Goa.

The starting location of the second tour is Tamil Nadu's capital ❶ ✶ **Chennai**, an important economic and cultural metropolis of southern India. The museums, temples and the famous Marina

Beach offer plenty of opportunities to discover the diversity of Tamil Nadu. A trip to the »Golden City of a Thousand Temples«, ❷ ★ ★ **Kanchipuram**, approx. 70km/45mi away, should not be missed.

There are two possible options here in the old Pallava capital. Travellers can either go back to Chennai or continue straight to ❸ ★ ★ **Mamallapuram** via Chengalpat. The extremely pleasant stretch along India's east coast from Chennai to Mamallapuram is lined by coconut plantations. Around 20km/12mi south of Chennai, travellers can visit the artist colony of Cholamandal. The crocodile farm 42km/26mi along the route is also worth a visit. The small town of Mamallapuram with its beautiful temples from the Pallava period and a pleasant beach is a good place to relax after a stay in busy Chennai.

The next leg of the tour to the south is the former French colony of ❹ ★ **Puducherry**, formerly known as Pondicherry, approx. 100km/60mi away, with the Aurobindo ashram as a spiritual and cultural centre for his followers who are dotted around the world. The town

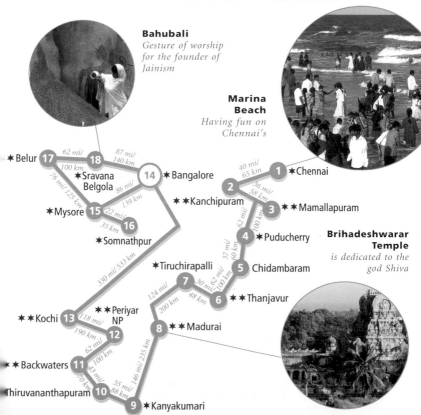

Bahubali
Gesture of worship for the founder of Jainism

Marina Beach
Having fun on Chennai's

Brihadeshwarar Temple
is dedicated to the god Shiva

★ Belur 17 62 mi/ 18 87 mi/ 140 km
100 km ★ Sravana Belgola 14 ★ Bangalore 40 mi/ 65 km 1 ★ Chennai
76 mi/ 125 km 86 mi/ 139 km 2 56 mi/ 58 km
★ Mysore 15 22 mi/ 35 km 16 ★ ★ Kanchipuram 3 ★ ★ Mamallapuram
★ Somnathpur 62 mi/ 100 km 4 ★ Puducherry
330 mi/ 533 km ★ Tiruchirapalli 37 mi/ 60 km 5 Chidambaram
7 30 mi/ 62 mi/ 48 km/ 100 km
124 mi/ 200 km 6 ★ ★ Thanjavur
★ ★ Kochi 13 ★ ★ Periyar NP 118 mi/ 190 km 12 8 ★ ★ Madurai
★ ★ Backwaters 11 62 mi/ 100 km 146 mi/ 235 km
Thiruvananthapuram 10 55 mi/ 88 km
70 mi/ 43 mi/ 9 ★ Kanyakumari

Don't miss the banana market in Kochi!

has been able to preserve much of its French flair and makes for a nice change.

Leaving Puducherry a good fast road leads via Cuddalore to ❺ **Chidambaram**, the city with the impressive temple for Nataraja, the dancing Shiva. Nature lovers should make an excursion to Piccavaram 25km/15mi away, with its mangrove forests. From Chidambaram the tour now makes its way westwards towards the interior through the fertile Kaveri delta towards ❻ ✱✱ **Thanjavur**. Paddy fields, houses covered in palm leaves, and lotus ponds shape the landscape. Thanjavur is home to Brihadeeshvara Temple, perhaps the most beautiful temple in Tamil Nadu. The city of ❼ ✱ **Tiruchirapalli**, 56km/35mi to the west, is an ideal starting location for a visit to Sri Rangam, a huge temple city located on an island in the river.

From Tiruchirapalli travellers can take a bus, train or plane to the city of ❽ ✱✱ **Madurai** in the heart of Tamil Nadu. Its Meenakshi Temple is one of the best places to witness Hindu religiosity, which is still alive today, close up. The journey from Madurai to India's southern tip, ❾ ✱ **Kanyakumari**, passes almost exclusively through the dry interior until the mountainous foothills of the Western Ghats can be spotted. The Arabian Sea, the Indian Ocean and the Bay of Bengal all come together south of Kanyakumari, a city of pilgrimage that is particularly popular with Indian tourists.

From there a picturesque road lined with many palm trees and lotus ponds leads to ❿ ✱ **Thiruvananthapuram**. Along the way a good place to visit is Padmanabhapuram, the wonderful wooden palace of the Rajas of Travancore. The journey continues through a lush green landscape to the beach of Kovalam, Kerala's best-known seaside resort. This is a great place to relax after the challenges of the trip so far. Kerala's capital, Thiruvananthapuram, is only 13km/8mi to the north. Apart from its interesting museums with their impressive collection of sculptures and excellent carvings, as well as Padmanabhaswami Temple, the city does not have many sights of interest to tourists.

The trip now continues northwards by train or bus to Kollam. Those travelling by taxi can also make a detour to the beautiful beach of Varkala. In Kollam, Kerala starts presenting itself from its best side: stretching from here northwards is one of India's most fascinating landscapes, the ⑪ ✳ ✳ **Backwaters**. They consist of a labyrinthine network of lakes, rivers and canals. Travelling by ferry or hiring a houseboat to the next destination, Allapuzzha, is now an alternative to using a bus or taxi. The old merchant town, now a centre of coconut processing, can be reached more quickly by land.

The Backwaters are even more diverse and beautiful between Allapuzzha and Kottayam, the next destination. The boat trip through the web of countless waterways takes two-and-a-half hours. Kottayam itself does not have much worth seeing; it is however a good starting point for a visit to ⑫ ✳ ✳ **Periyar National Park**. The bus route makes its way through a densely populated green hilly landscape with paddy fields and palm, cocoa and banana plantations. All kinds of spices, coffee and tea are cultivated in the adjoining Cardamom Hills. Periyar Wildlife Sanctuary lies at an elevation of 750m/2460ft to 1500m/4920ft and is one of India's largest protected areas. It is known for its large elephant herds and its many different species of water birds. A direct bus connection through lavish tropical landscape leads back to ⑬ ✳ ✳ **Kochi** on the coast. The city built on seven islands is probably the most interesting place along the entire Malabar Coast. Many traces have been left behind by the different conquerors who came to these parts. They give Kochi its unique flair.

Now a train or a plane can be taken to ⑭ ✳ **Bangalore**, Karnataka's capital. The city of 6.5 million inhabitants is better known for its excellent shopping, hotels and restaurants than for any outstanding attractions. Bangalore serves as the base for the last tour segment, the trip to the Maharaja city of ⑮ ✳ **Mysore**. It is an approx. four-hour drive by bus or taxi through the quite dry, slightly hilly terrain of the southern Deccan plateau to Mysore. The city's main attraction is the large Maharaja's palace. Also very interesting is the Hoysala temple in ⑯ ✳ **Somnathpur**, 40km/25mi east of Mysore and best reached by taxi. Next, visitors should take a bus to Hassan further north, a 120km/75mi trip that will take around three hours. The sights here are the Hoysala temples in ⑰ ✳ ✳ **Belur and Halebid** with their unique architecture and their ornately worked sculptures, which can be visited comfortably on a day trip (bus or taxi: 30km/20mi–40km/25mi).

The return journey from Hassan to Bangalore can either be completed directly or via ⑱ ✳ **Sravana Belgola**. The holy Jain site houses the 17m/56ft statue of a Tirthankara, which is believed to be the biggest sculpture in the world. From here ⑭ ✱ **Bangalore** can be reached by bus in around three hours.

Alternative Those not wishing to travel all the way to India's southernmost tip can shorten the tour by taking a direct bus or taxi from Madurai to Periyar Wildlife Sanctuary.

Tour 3 Land of the Kings

Start / destination: Delhi   **Duration:** 7–14 days

Despite its barren landscape, the desert state of Rajasthan is one of the most popular destinations in India. Its fairytale palaces, filigree Jain temples and medieval cities invoke the magic of past epochs. A visit to Rajasthan, the land of kings, is best begun in Delhi, heading then to Jaipur. The trip described below makes use of aeroplanes, trains, buses and taxis. Those travellers who wish to avoid the sometimes tedious train or bus journeys or who have limited time can also visit the most important cities of Jaipur, Jodhpur and Udaipur by plane within a week.

The journey begins in ❶ ✱✱ **Delhi**; the first destination is ❷ ✱✱ **Jaipur**, Rajasthan's capital. Travelling to Jaipur on the Pink City Express (five hours) is highly recommended. Five days should be taken to visit the city's attractions (Jal Mahal, Hawa Mahal, observatory) and the highlights of the surrounding area such as ❸ ✱✱ **Amber Fort** and Samode Palace. Anyone wishing to see not just the cities but rural areas too can use Jaipur as a base to travel around the region of ❹ **Shekhawati** (taxi from Jaipur to Nawalgarh three hours), which is known for its painted havelis (merchant houses). A round trip takes several days, and it is a good idea to hire a taxi for the tour.

The next destination after Jaipur is ❺ ✱✱ **Jodhpur**, the city on the edge of Thar Desert with its impressive Meherangarh Fort and Umaid Bhavan Palace. The nearby old capital of Mandore and the old temple city of Osiyan can be visited by taking day trips from Jodhpur.

Jodhpur is also the starting point for a trip to the medieval caravan city of ❻ ✱✱ **Jaisalmer** in the middle of the desert. Far removed from the big cities, visitors have an opportunity here to admire a large fort, Jain temples and elaborately decorated merchant houses or to wander through winding alleyways. It is just as exciting to participate in a camel tour to the sand dunes and to witness the sunset. There are several ways to get to Jaisalmer from Jodhpur: by bus /

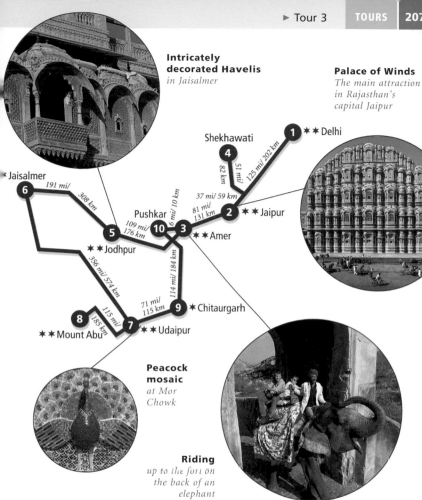

Intricately decorated Havelis
in Jaisalmer

Palace of Winds
The main attraction in Rajasthan's capital Jaipur

Peacock mosaic
at Mor Chowk

Riding
up to the fort on the back of an elephant

train (six hours), by train (ten hours) or in a small propeller aircraft. Since the roads are very good and little used, the most pleasant form of travel is by bus or car. Leaving the arid desert behind, the tour makes its way southwards via Jodhpur to ❼ ✶✶ **Udaipur** with its enchanting lakes and palaces. Those who are not in a hurry and do not want to fly should definitely take a bus or car to Udaipur and stop to visit the Jain temple of Ranakpur on the way. There is also the option of spending the night here to recover after the excitement of the journey.

It is just another 185km/115mi from Udaipur to ❽ ✶✶ **Mount Abu**, Rajasthan's southernmost tourist attraction. With its lush vegetation and cool mountains, the town of Mount Abu is a pleasant contrast to the hot desert city of Jaisalmer in the north. Take a look at the Dilwara Temples in the town.

Leaving Mount Abu, the tour returns to Udaipur and then onwards to ❾✷ **Chitaurgarh**, the once glorious fort of the Rajput rulers, in which every last man and woman sacrificed themselves during the Muslim conquest. The huge ruined fort is a reminder of the attempts – sometimes heroic, sometimes suicidal – of the Rajput kings to withstand Islamic conquest. From Chitaurharh the best way to get back to Delhi is via ❿**Pushkar**, the sacred city of the god Brahma. Apart from November, when the famous Pushkar Fair takes place, the city is quite idyllic, situated by a lake with countless temples where visitors can experience the deep religious devotion of the Hindus here. It is only another 140km/85mi from here to ❷✷✷ **Jaipur**, and from there it is easy to return to Delhi. An alternative would be to shorten the trip and return directly to Delhi or Mumbai from Udaipur by air.

Tips for extensions There are a couple of options for extending a trip to Rajasthan. One option would be to visit Gujarat, another would be to spend some time on the beaches of Goa. Those wishing to prolong the trip with a tour of the less well known state of Gujarat should drive from Mount Abu to Ahmedabad by bus or car or take the train from Abu Road.

The fort built on a hill stands high above Jodhpur

Those taking the overland route to Ahmedabad should try to visit the Sun Temple in Modhera. The best way to reach Goa is from Udaipur via Mumbai. The alternative to flying is a very long journey by train or bus.

Tour 4 Through Gujarat

Start / destination: Ahmedabad   **Duration:** 10 days

The land of the Jains and Gandhi's birthplace is now one of the most modern industrial regions in India. At the same time the state's far west still has pockets that have hardly been touched at all by modern civilization. So far Gujarat is only visited by few tourists even though there are many outstanding temples, palaces, nature reserves and palm-lined beaches in close proximity, which in addition have good road access. The choice of hotels is not quite so well developed but it is quite a bit cheaper to travel here than it is in neighbouring Rajasthan.

The tour is best begun in ❶ ✱ **Ahmedabad**, which can easily be reached from Mumbai and Delhi by plane. There is also a good train and bus connection from Mumbai. Ahmedabad has some interesting

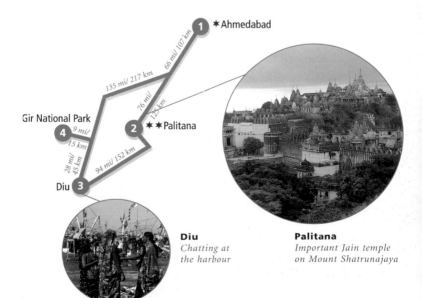

Diu
*Chatting at
the harbour*

Palitana
*Important Jain temple
on Mount Shatrunajaya*

museums, the Gandhi Memorial Institution and several mosques. In addition it is a good starting point for excursions to Modhera and Lothal. Modhera has one of India's finest Hindu temples, while in Lothal relics from the Harappa period, the oldest traces of civilization in India, were discovered during archaeological digs (approx. four days).

Leaving Ahmedabad the journey continues by bus to Bhavnagar (180km/110mi to the southwest), where it is possible to sleep in a palace hotel. From here it is not far to ❷ ✳ ✳ **Palitana**, the Jain temple city on Mount Shatrunajaya. A walk to these temples is surely one of the best experiences in India. There is the possibility of driving to ❸ **Diu** (152km/94mi) from Palitana, which is interesting because of its Portuguese atmosphere and lonely sandy beaches. The beaches and hotels here are not comparable to those in Goa, but the lives of the locals are still authentic – hardly any tourists come here and visitors will often have a beach to themselves. The next destination after Diu is the old temple city of Somnath. The famous ❹ **Gir National Park**, which is still home to Asiatic lions, can be reached via the town of Keshod (56km/35mi). After a night spent here, the tour continues via Junagadh (40km/25mi) and a detour into the Girnar Mountains via Rajkot (102km/63mi) back to Ahmedabad (226km/ 140mi).

Further excursions

Further places to visit: from Rajkot travellers can visit Dwarka (108km/67mi from Rajkot), a place of pilgrimage for devotees of Krishna, via Jamnagar (88km/55mi); another option is to fly from Jamnagar to the remote desert town of Bhuj, the centre of the Kutch region, and return from there to Mumbai.

Tour 5 Places of Pilgrimage in the Northeast

Start / destination: Delhi   **Duration:** 21 days

The route through India's northeast is a great way to visit some of the most important places of pilgrimage for Hindus and Buddhists. Around three weeks should be set aside for this round trip, which makes use of planes, trains and buses.

The trip begins in India's capital ❶ ✳ ✳ **Delhi**. After acclimatizing and visiting the many sights of the city, fly on to ❷ ✳ ✳ **Bhubaneshwar** on the east coast and explore the region from east to west. Bhubaneshwar, Orissa's capital, is said to have once been home to 7000 temples, many of which can still be seen today. One particularly famous example is Mukteshavara Temple; other noteworthy sites are

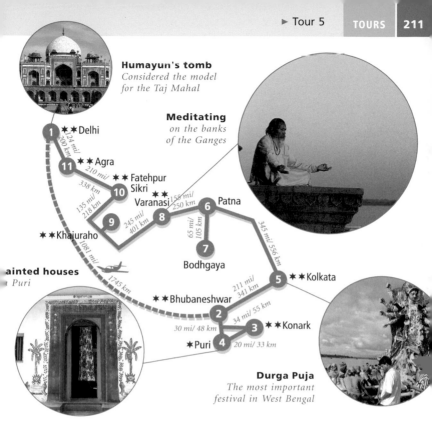

Humayun's tomb
*Considered the model
for the Taj Mahal*

Meditating
*on the banks
of the Ganges*

1 ✶✶Delhi
11 ✶✶Agra
✶✶Fatehpur Sikri
10
✶✶Varanasi
✶✶Khajuraho
9   8   6 Patna
7
Bodhgaya
5 ✶✶Kolkata
✶✶Bhubaneshwar
2
3 ✶✶Konark
✶Puri 4
34 mi/ 55 km
30 mi/ 48 km   20 mi/ 33 km
211 mi/ 341 km
345 mi/ 556 km
65 mi/ 105 km
155 mi/ 250 km
245 mi/ 401 km
135 mi/ 218 km
338 km
210 mi/
24 mi/ 200 mi
1081 mi/
1745 km

ainted houses
Puri

Durga Puja
*The most important
festival in West Bengal*

the Jain cave monasteries on the nearby twin mountains Udayagiri and Khandagiri. Around Bhubaneshwar visitors can also see the remains dating from Orissa's Buddhist period in Ratnagiri. In addition Bhubaneshwar is a good starting location for day trips to the Sun Temple of ❸✶✶ **Konark** and Jagannath Temple in ❹✶ **Puri** (60km/37mi). Next on the itinerary is Gopalur-on-Sea, where several days can be spent relaxing on the beach.

Leaving Bhubaneshwar, the next destination is ❺✶✶ **Kolkata**. The city on the Ganges has many buildings dating back to the British colonial era, such as the Victoria Memorial. Do not pass up this chance to visit to the Indian Museum.

After Kolkata the trip continues to ❻**Patna**. This is the base for a visit the important Buddhist cities of ❼**Bodhgaya**, Nalanda and Rajgir. Bodhgaya, where Buddha found enlightenment, is quite impressive with Mahabodhi Temple. Bodhgaya is best reached via Gaya (12km/7mi), which has good connections to Patna by bus and taxi (105km/65mi). Nalanda (90km/55mi southeast), once a university city with

2000 teachers, is now a city of ruins. Only 12km/7mi to the south lies the town of Rajgir, which Buddha is said to have loved greatly. After his death the first Buddhist council was held here.

Leaving Patna, the tour continues by bus (250km/155mi, five hours) or train (just under five hours) to the sacred Hindu city of ❽ ✶ ✶ **Varanasi**. The main attraction of this city is the Ganges, the sacred river with its bathing steps. A worthwhile excursion from Varanasi is to visit Sarnath (10km/6mi), where Buddha preached for the first time.

Return journey The flight from Varanasi to Delhi allows stopovers in Khajuraho and Agra: ❾ ✶ ✶ **Khajuraho** is famous for its many temples from the Chandela period and their outstanding stone sculptures. The wonderful complex is particularly well known for its erotic depictions. Those with time to spare should definitely make a detour to the abandoned imperial city of ❿ ✶ ✶ **Fatehpur Sikri**. ⓫ ✶ ✶ **Agra**, with India's most famous monument, the Taj Mahal, is then the crowning finale of the trip.

Tour 6 On the Deccan Plateau

Start / destination: Goa   **Duration:** 10–12 days

This tour can be begun in Mumbai, Goa, Bangalore or Hyderabad and takes in places on the Deccan plateau less frequented by tourists. It is also suitable as an addition or substitute for those travellers who have already seen India's best-known highlights.

The starting point of the route described here is ❶ ✶ ✶ **Goa**. It is a day's drive by taxi or bus (via Dharwad / Hubli), the tour's first destination. The drive to the famous caves and temples of ❷ ✶ ✶ **Badami, Pattadakal and Aihole** makes its way through the fertile Western Ghats up to the more arid Deccan plateau. The best base for visits to the temple sites is Badami, which has several hotels to choose from. The next two days can be spent visiting the impressive sites of the Chalukyas.

On day four the trip continues by bus or taxi across the plateau to ❸ ✶ **Bijapur**, 140km/87mi to the north. The old Muslim city can be seen from a long way off because of the huge dome of the Gol Gumbaz memorial. The mosques, tombs and citadels spread out over the rambling, green city are worth visiting, so several days can be spent here.

The trip continues from Bijapur to another stronghold of the former Deccan sultanates, ❹ **Gulbarga**. The city is famous for the unique architecture of its mosque and is a real highlight for lovers of Islamic art. Those with sufficient time should make a detour to ❺ **Bidar** to the northeast. Bidar also has plenty of remains from the time when the Muslim dynasties were making history.

It is a day trip by bus, train and / or taxi to the former capital of the Vijayanagar rulers, the great adversaries of the Deccan sultans, to ❻ ✳ ✳ **Hampi**. Once little known, Hampi is now being visited by increasing numbers of tourists despite the exhausting trip to get here. There are regular connections to the ruins for those based in Hospet. Visitors should set aside two days to visit the old city, situated in an impressive rocky landscape. Leaving Hampi, visitors can either choose to travel to Bangalore or Mumbai by train from Guntakal or (return) to Goa by bus or taxi.

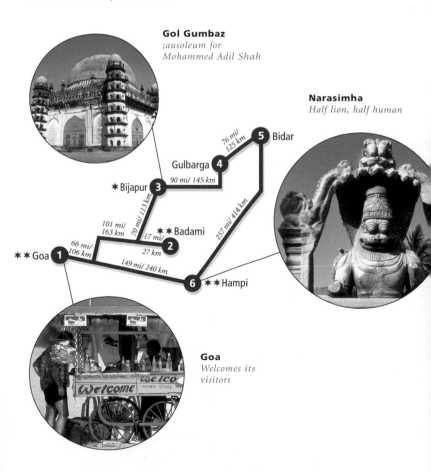

Gol Gumbaz
;ausoleum for Mohammed Adil Shah

Narasimha
Half lion, half human

76 mil 125 km — ❺ Bidar

Gulbarga ❹
90 mil/ 145 km

✳ Bijapur ❸

101 mi/ 163 km
70 mil 113 km
257 mil 414 km

✳ ✳ Badami ❷
17 mil 27 km

✳ ✳ Goa ❶
66 mil 106 km

149 mil 240 km

❻ ✳ ✳ Hampi

Goa
Welcomes its visitors

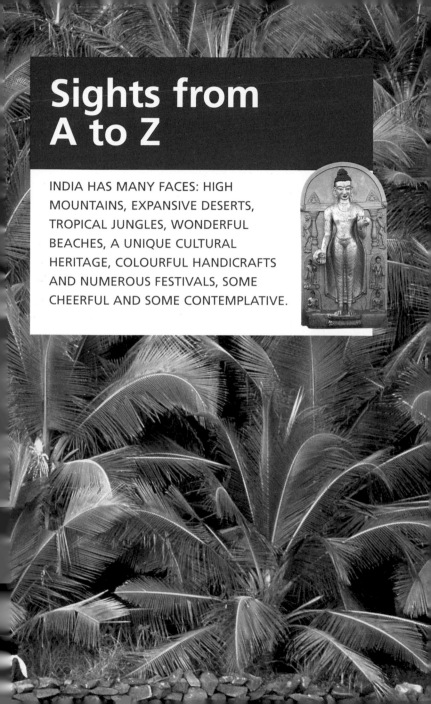

Sights from A to Z

INDIA HAS MANY FACES: HIGH
MOUNTAINS, EXPANSIVE DESERTS,
TROPICAL JUNGLES, WONDERFUL
BEACHES, A UNIQUE CULTURAL
HERITAGE, COLOURFUL HANDICRAFTS
AND NUMEROUS FESTIVALS, SOME
CHEERFUL AND SOME CONTEMPLATIVE.

NORTH INDIA

STATES AND UNION TERRITORIES
Chandigarh: union territory
Delhi: union territory
Haryana: capital Chandigarh
Himachal Pradesh: capital Shimla
Jammu and Kashmir: Capital Srinagar
Punjab: capital Chandigarh
Uttar Pradesh: capital Lucknow
Uttarakhand: capital Dehra Dun

India's north is dominated by the high mountains of the **Himalaya** and the Indo-Gangetic plain shaped by the rivers flowing through it. The Himalaya mountain range crosses the northern states of Jammu, Kashmir, Himachal Pradesh and Uttarakhand. Kashmir and Uttarakhand are home to the **highest peaks**, quite a few of which exceed 7000m/23,000ft. The southern part of northern India is dominated by the magnificent Ganges and its tributaries. Over thousands of years people have lived along the banks of these rivers, developing an intensive agriculture that secures the survival of many millions of people. The two smaller states of Punjab and Haryana between the Himalayan foothills and the desert of Rajasthan have a climate marked by cold winters and hot summers. Both have become **intensively used agricultural regions** with enormous surpluses. The states of Himachal Pradesh and Jammu & Kashmir are sparsely populated, extensively cultivated regions, in which arable farming only takes place in a few high valleys and on terraces. Uttar Pradesh contains the fertile Ganges plain, which is intensively used and quite densely populated. Delhi has a special status. It has been the Indian subcontinent's most important centre of government for 400 years. Delhi's hot climate prompted not just the Mughals but also the British to develop numerous hill stations in the Himalaya into summer residences.

From the heights of the Himalaya to the lowlands of the Ganges

The states of Punjab, Haryana and Uttar Pradesh are primarily agricultural regions. The main crops in Haryana are rice, wheat, sugarcane, cotton and oilseed; in Punjab all of these are cultivated as well as maize and lentils. India's agriculture, which underwent modernization in the course of the »**Green Revolution**«, is characterized by the heavy use of tractors, fertilizers and pesticides. These states are

Economy

← *Bathing in the Ganges is said to wash off all sins and liberate believers from the cycle of constant rebirth.*

the country's front-runners with regard to rice and wheat production. The affluent farmers of Punjab supply the city of Delhi and other cities with their agricultural products. Haryana is known for electronics, tractors, agricultural machinery and sanitary goods. Despite being irrigated by the Ganges, **Uttar Pradesh, the most populous state**, is one of India's poorest regions. In addition to wheat this state's crops are sugarcane, potatoes and oilseed, which are also industrially processed here. The major industrial branches are concentrated on food processing and manufacturing fertilizers, cement and glass. The **new state of Uttarakhand** was created in the year 2000. Its area is around 60,000 sq km/20,000 sq mi, and it was formerly part of the Himalayan region of Uttar Pradesh.

History

According to Hindu legend the region north of Delhi was once the centre of mystic kingdoms. Thus the battle from the Mahabharata between the brothers of the Kaurava and Pandava dynasties is said to have taken place in Kurukshetra near Panipat in Harayana. Buddha preached for the first time in Sarnath not far from Varanasi. **In addition to Buddhism, Jainism also developed in the area that is now Uttar Pradesh**. Both religions were a response to the stagnancy of orthodox Hinduism at the time. Sikhism developed in northern Punjab in response to the violent confrontations between Muslims and Hindus. In ancient times the Maurya Empire (321–185 BC) covered the whole of northern India. Under the ruler Ashoka, Buddhist missionaries were sent all the way to Kashmir. The Kushana Empire (AD 50–320) and the Gupta Empire (AD 320–535) left lasting marks on the region.

India's northwest has always been the route by which conquerors came into the country. From Parthians to Huns, Persians, Afghans and Greeks, many peoples attacked India and usually left after plundering the country. In the first half of the 16th century, the Islamic ruler Babur founded the Mughal Dynasty, which controlled the whole of northern India from Delhi for 150 years. Guru Nanak (1469–1539) founded Sikhism in Punjab. As a result of a confrontation with the Mughal rulers, a Sikh empire was formed between 1799 and 1830, which was, however, defeated by the British. The British made **Delhi the capital of their empire once again in 1911**. Since India's independence Delhi has been the centre of Indian democracy. Uttar Pradesh, as the most populous federal state, carries particular weight in parliamentary elections. With two exceptions, all prime ministers to date have come from this region. Claimed by both India and Pakistan, Kashmir, the northernmost state, has been a trouble spot for decades.

Rich in cultural monuments

The region is rich in cultural monuments from various periods and possesses important centres of several religions, such as Hinduism (Varanasi), Buddhism (Sarnath), Islam (Delhi) and Sikhism (Amritsar). The outstanding attractions in the Delhi area are relics of the

Mughal dynasty: forts, mosques and tombs are testimony to the flourishing architecture of that time. India's capital has more to offer than just the Red Fort, Humayun's tomb and the Friday Mosque. It has imposing colonial buildings built by the British as well as outstanding museums. The now abandoned capital of Fatehpur Sikri, built by Akbar, is proof of the architectural visions of India's greatest Mughal ruler. Located along the Ganges are the **important cities of Hindu pilgrimage**, Rishikesh, Allahabad and Varanasi. Varanasi, which sees a great influx of Hindu pilgrims in search of salvation all year round, is doubtless India's most impressive city of pilgrimage. Just outside Varanasi lies Sarnath, where Buddha set »the wheel of doctrine« in motion through his first sermon. While Sarnath now has nothing more than the remains of its former Buddhist heyday, there are countless monasteries to be seen in **Ladakh**, in which Buddhism has remained alive and well to this day. One place of particular significance is Dharamsala, where Tibetan refugees have settled, including the **Dalai Lama**, the religious leader of the Tibetans. Finally, the capital of Punjab, Amritsar, is the religious centre of Sikhism and is also the location of the Golden Temple.

In addition to its many cultural attractions, India's north also has many natural sights to offer, first

Varanasi: steps to the holy river

and foremost the **magnificent mountains** of the Himalaya. Himachal Pradesh, Uttarakhand, and Jammu and Kashmir have wonderful flower meadows, orchards and lakes and lure visitors to extremely barren regions far removed from civilization. Shimla, Kullu, Manali and Srinagar are good starting locations from which to explore the world of the Himalaya. The **Jim Corbett National Park, the oldest nature reserve in India**, is an absolute must for nature lovers.

★★ Agra

State: Uttar Pradesh
Population: 1.45 million

Altitude: 169m/554ft
Distance: 204km/127mi south of Delhi

There is one thing everyone associates with Agra, namely India's most famous building, the Taj Mahal. Every year, millions of visitors from India and around the world come to this city on the western bank of the Yamuna river.

The Taj Mahal: famous the world over

The first historical knowledge of any certainty regarding Agra, a place some even connect to legends about the god Krishna, dates back only to the 16th century. During this time the Lodhi ruler Sikander (1489–1517) moved his residence from Delhi to Sikandra, which received its name later in his honour, approx. 10km/6mi away

To die for: the view of the Taj Mahal from Shah Jahan's private chambers in the Red Fort

▶ VISITING AGRA

INFORMATION

UP Tourism
64, Taj Road
Tel. 05 62 – 222 64 31
www.up-tourism.com

SHOPPING

Agra is famous for marble objects with inlays, such as vases and bowls. Large selections of leather goods are also sold here. In Shilpagram, an old »artisan village« with stalls near the East Gate, visitors will also find handicrafts from all around India. Cultural events also take place here. Well known shopping streets are the Mall, MG Road and Munro Road.

WHERE TO EAT

▶ Expensive

① *Nauratna*
In the Mughal Sheraton
Tel. 05 62 – 233 17 01
Excellent northern Indian Mughal cuisine and a pleasant ambience.

▶ Inexpensive

② *Dasaprakash*
Meher Theater Complex
1, Gwalior Road
Tel. 05 62 – 236 35 35
Those who fancy some dosas, idlis or wadas here in the north will be very happy with this southern Indian restaurant.

WHERE TO STAY

▶ Luxury

① *Welcomgroup*
Mughal Sheraton
6 B, Fatehabad Road
Tel. 05 62 – 233 17 01
www.itcwelcomgroup.in
Exclusive hotel with many sports and recreation services. Also known for its very good cuisine.

② *Taj View*
Fatehabad Road
Tel. 05 62 – 223 24 00 / 418
www.tajhotels.com
As the name implies, some of the rooms have views of the legendary Taj Mahal. Pool, several restaurants and bars are also available.

▶ Mid-range / Budget

③ *Grand Hotel*
137, Station Road
Tel. 05 62 – 222 75 11
Clean, middle price range hotel with a restaurant and bar.

▶ Budget

④ *Amar Yatri Nivas*
Fatehabad Road
Tel. 05 62 – 223 30 30
Only 1km/0.6mi from the Taj Mahal. Basic, clean rooms with air conditioning. Multicuisine restaurant.

from Agra. Agra itself only gained significance after the Mughal rulers and primarily the powerful ruler Akbar (1542–1605) had recognized that they would be able to cleverly defend their sphere of power against invaders from the south from the fort erected on the banks of the Yamuna river. While Akbar's grandson **Shah Jahan** (1592–1666) made this city unique by building the famous mausoleum, the political centre was transferred back to Delhi. The founding

Agra Map

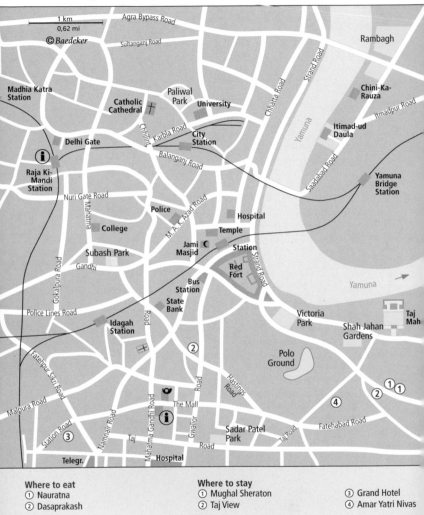

Where to eat
① Nauratna
② Dasaprakash

Where to stay
① Mughal Sheraton
② Taj View
③ Grand Hotel
④ Amar Yatri Nivas

of Shahjahanabad, Delhi's seventh city, and the construction of the Red Fort there, made this relocation of the centre of power clearly visible for all to see. No longer capable of defending itself, Agra, abandoned by its defenders, was subsequently plundered twice, once in 1761 by the Jats and then in 1770 by the Marathas, as a result of which significant damage was caused to the city's buildings. Today the primary threat to the monuments of that time is increasing pollution, which has already caused irreversible damage.

Agra is made up of the old town in the north and the new town, Agra Cantonment, in the south. Located here are the most important sites, most hotels and Agra Cantonment station, where the trains from Delhi arrive. Tajganj, the winding old bazaar district, is situated to the south of the Taj Mahal.

✳ Taj Mahal

Nobody will ever forget the moment they set foot into the garden and see the famous Taj Mahal for the first time. Even though smaller than the photographs usually taken with wide-angle lenses make it seem, it is nonetheless impressive. The symmetry of the shapes of both the mausoleum and the garden, meticulously observed to the smallest detail, imparts an **impression of perfect harmony** to onlookers. Emperor Shah Jahan wanted this magnificent mausoleum to be a monument to his favourite wife Mumtaz Mahal, who died at the age of 38 giving birth to her 14th child. The Taj Mahal has its back turned to the Yamuna river and is situated at the end of a garden (Char Bagh), which is divided into four parts by canals. The garden's entrance is a richly ornamented, almost 30m/100ft gate made of red sandstone. At the centre is a pool which reflects the entire dome when the light is right. The dome rises up from a marble platform that measures 100 sq m/1076 sq ft in size and is 6.7m/22ft thick. It is flanked by four 42m/138ft minarets, one located in each corner, as well as by two mosques somewhat further away.

The building is strictly guarded. The entrance, where a **security check** is conducted, is located on the right next to the main gate. No metal objects or food items are allowed in the complex. The ban on photography only applies to the burial chamber's interior.

The mausoleum, an octagonal structure 56m/184ft square and 58m/190ft high, is vaulted by a magnificent central dome (pinnacle 74m/243ft) and four smaller domes on the sides. The building was made of brick and subsequently clad in white **marble**, which was brought here from Makrana in Rajasthan and contributes significantly to the awe-inspiring impact of the structure. The stone exterior makes the Taj Mahal shimmer in many different colours depending on the time of day and the light conditions. Highly detailed inlay works (pietre dure) using semi-precious stones adorn parts of the exterior façade and large areas of the mausoleum's interior. The southern gate leads to the burial chamber. Lattice windows filter the bright light of day, shrouding the interior in a diffuse half-light, which is perfect for looking at the beautiful magnificent ornamentation on all the walls. Located here are the two grave replicas covered in wonderful flower motifs. The real tombs of Mumtaz and her husband Shah Jahan,

Garden with an enchanting mausoleum

⊙ Opening hours: from sunrise– 7.30pm (and at night during full moon), closed Fri

Mausoleum

TAJ MAHAL

✳ ✳ Wherein lies the magic of this marble mausoleum that poets have labelled »a teardrop upon the cheek of time« and »a sigh made stone«? To this day the Taj Mahal (built 1631–53) is not only visited by tourists from all around the world but also by newly-wed Indian couples to make their union last forever, because it is considered the monument of eternal love.

🕐 Open:
daily except Fri sunrise 7.30pm
(open at night at full moon)

① South Gate

The complex is accessed through a gate of red sandstone, decorated with imaginative calligraphy and arabesques. The 22 small domes stand for the number of years it took to build the Taj Mahal. The perfect harmony of its proportions have meant that the Taj Mahal is considered one of the most beautiful and significant buildings of the Mughal style.

② Flower Garden

Symmetry was the most important factor when planning the complex. It follows the model of classical »Char Baghs«, gardens laid out in a geometric pattern, typical of the Mughal style. A river channel divides a square into four parts. There is a 6m/20ft marble platform at the centre.

③ Taj Mahal

More than almost any other building, the Taj Mahal, towering on a pedestal, has become a symbol of an entire country. The spandrels which elegantly solve the difficult problem of transition from square ground plan to round dome are considered a particular tour de force. Four smaller domes surround the magnificent main dome under which the tombs are located. To ensure that they fall away from the main building in the event of an earthquake the minarets lean slightly outwards. More than 20,000 people are said to have participated in the construction of the building, which is a UNESCO World Heritage Site. Specialists were even commissioned from Europe (pietra dura, see fold-out) to work on the semiprecious-stone inlays.

④ Tombs

The richly adorned coffins of Shah Jahan and Mumtaz Mahal stand in the main hall. Originally the Mughal emperor had been planning to build a second Taj Mahal in black marble for himself. In fact he was entombed next to his wife in 1666. Their »real« tombs are underground and are not accessible to the public.

The Mughal emperor Shah Jahan had the magnificent mausoleum built in memory of his favourite wife Mumtaz Mahal

© Baedeker

Approach via the southern portal

①

②

Marble inlays give the Taj Mahal a different coloration depending on the time of day.

Cenotaphs in an artistic false tomb

who also found his final resting place here, are located one floor below in the **crypt**. They are covered in the **finest floral ornaments** of the entire monument, which, even though they are barely 3cm/1in in size, consist of up to sixty precisely cut individual pieces. There is a certain amount of mystery surrounding the builder of this architectural marvel. It is clear that the Taj Mahal conforms to the long and rich tradition of Mughal domed tombs and has a direct model in Humayun's tomb erected in Delhi 100 years earlier. The building works were begun in 1631, shortly after Mumtaz Mahal's death, and more than 20 years passed before the mausoleum was completed. The fact that it swallowed vast sums of money was probably also one of the reasons why Shah Jahan's son Aurangzeb (1618–1707) violently seized power from his father. He had his father thrown into prison in 1658, where he died in 1666.

Taj Museum
⊙

To the right of the main entrance is the small Taj Museum with an exhibition on the monument's history (open: daily except Fri 10am–5pm).

✷ ✷ Red Fort

Fort
⊙
Opening hours:
daily
sunrise–sunset

In 1556 the Mughal ruler Akbar started with the construction of a fort, which was further extended by his successors Jehangir and Shah Jahan. He built a 2.5km/1.5mi double wall made of red sandstone as protection. Two gates led inside: the Delhi Gate in the west, the former main entrance, and the Amar Singh Gate, which is the gate visitors now use to enter the complex.

It leads to a large garden bordered on the right by the **Jehangir's palace** (Jehangiri Mahal), a two-storey structure also made of red sandstone. It is one of the older buildings still extant from Akbar's time. The many elements of Hindu architectural tradition used on this building are a reminder of Akbar's openness to that religion. Going through the wine garden (Anguri Bagh) to the north, visitors will get to the Khas Mahal, the **private rooms** of the emperor and his daughters, which were commissioned by Shah Jahan in 1636. The elegant marble pavilions with their golden Bengali style roofs use lattice windows permitting views of the Yamuna river and the Taj Mahal. Other structures located by the wine garden are the Mina Masjid, the ruler's tiny private mosque and the palace of mirrors (Sheesh Mahal) in the northeast corner, which is decorated with tiny mirrors on the walls and ceiling.

There are some wonderful views to be had of the fort's exterior façade, the river, and the Taj Mahal to the south from the **octagonal tower** (Mussaman Burj), which joins on to the Khas Mahal in the north. In the tower's deep dungeons Aurangzeb kept his father Shah Jahan captive until his death. A few steps north of the tower is the **Private Audience Hall** (Diwan-i-Khas). Spreading out in front of it is the fish palace (Macchi Bhawan), which is nothing

The large audience hall with its cusped arches

but a courtyard that once contained a fish pond. Situated on its northwest side is **Gem Mosque** (Nagina Masjid), which was specially designated to women.

Leaving Macchi Bhawan via the stairs on its western side, visitors will get to a large garden with the **Large Audience Hall** (Diwan-i-Am). Buried in the tomb in front is the British governor John Russell Colvin, who died of cholera in Agra in 1857 during the Indian Mutiny. North of the courtyard is the famous **Pearl Mosque** (Moti Masjid), to which access has not been permitted for some years now. The same is true for all other parts of the fort, which are used by the Indian military.

Further sights in Agra

Less well-known, but still clearly worth a visit, is the tomb of Itimad-ud-Daula, a minister under the emperors Akbar and Jehangir. His daughter Nur Jahan, who was married to Jehangir, is responsible for having this little jewel amongst the local mausoleums built.

✷
Itimad-ud-Daula

The tomb is located on the eastern banks of the Yamuna river and can be reached via a nearby bridge. In the midst of a tranquil garden the small marble resting place, **one of the most beautiful examples of Mughal architecture**, rises up on a rectangular platform. It was built between 1622 and 1628 as a quadrangular structure (20m/65ft) with a minaret located in each corner and a quadrangular pavilion at its centre. The wonderful marble latticework and the magnificent pietre dure work on the exterior façade and the interior walls are quite remarkable. They provided the impulses for the later covering of the Taj Mahal (open: sunrise–sunset).

Chini-ka-Rauza

Around 800m/875yd from the mausoleum is the Chini-ka-Rauza, the tomb of Afzal Khan, a minister under Shah Jahan. Chinese tiles decorate this site in Persian tradition with attractive geometric patterns (open: sunrise–sunset).

Around Agra

✶
Sikandra

Opening hours:
sunrise–sunset

Around 10km/6mi north of Agra, along the road to Mathura, is Sikandra. All that is left of the city of the Lodhi ruler Sikander (1489–1517), apart from a few insignificant monuments, is the famous **tomb of Akbar**. The building seems very unusual because of the mix of Buddhist, Hindu and Islamic architectural elements, and is testament to the open mind of the ruler buried here. Many of the Islamic elements were subsequently added under Jehangir and Shah Jahan. The garden, at the centre of which is the mausoleum, a five-storey building made of red sandstone and white marble, is accessed through the richly adorned south gate. The mausoleum is 25m/82ft tall and each of the storeys is a little smaller than the previous one, giving it a step-effect. They are framed by domes covered by pavilions that are reminiscent of the palaces in Fatehpur Sikri. On the fifth floor is a **marble monolith with the 99 names of Allah**; Akbar's real tomb lies hidden in a small crypt on the ground floor.

Ram Bagh

Experts believe one of the earliest examples of a Mughal garden is Ram Bagh, 11km/7mi from Agra. It was planted under the ruler Babur in 1526 (open: sunrise–sunset).

Mathura

Mathura (54km/34mi north of Agra, population 250,000) is **one of the seven holy cities of Hinduism**, which the members of this religion also call Braj Bhoomi. The popular god Krishna is said to have been born here in a prison cell and to have spent his youth in the surrounding area. For that reason there are **countless sites and temples consecrated to Krishna** here. The Hare Krishna sect also has its headquarters in nearby Vrindaban. However, the city was not just a significant centre of Hinduism. Buddhists also settled here. The Buddhist emperor Ashoka had various stupas built here. Between the first and third centuries the central Asian Kushana dynasty made Mathura the capital of its empire and into a centre of Buddhist art. The Chinese traveller Hiuen Tsang reported the existence of 20 monasteries and 2000 monks in the seventh century. Over the course of the Islamic conquest of northern India the city was subjected to repeated destruction and plundering, from Mahmud of Ghazni's raid in 1017 to Sikander's invasion in 1500 and Aurangzeb's presence in the mid-17th century. He had Jama Masjid, the city's most important mosque still extant, built in the city centre.

One of the significant places of pilgrimage for Hindus is the **Sri Krishna Janmbhoomi** temple, which was built over a prison cell, Krishna's legendary birthplace. The ghats on the banks of the Yamuna, first and foremost Vishram Ghat, where the god is said to have killed the bloodthirsty ruler Kamsa, are important places for believers. Another favourite visitor attraction is Dwarkadheesh Temple, which is also dedicated to Krishna.

The **archaeological museum** with a significant collection of sculptures from the Kushana period is also very worthwhile (open: daily except Mon 10.30am–4.30pm (July–mid-April) and 7.30am–12.30pm (mid-April–June).

Vrindaban

Vrindaban (69km/43mi north of Agra) is said to be the place where the god Krishna had his legendary erotic adventure with the gopis (cow girls), stole the clothes of bathing women and plotted many other adolescent pranks. The town has countless temples dedicated to him, most of them not particularly old.

✴ Fatehpur Sikri   E 6

On a hill approximately 40km/25mi west of Agra is the abandoned imperial city of Fatehpur Sikri, one of the most imposing remnants of the Mughal Empire. One legend recounts the story of its founding at this remote place, where happiness is in the air. It was the seat of the famous Sufi saint Shaikh Salimfrom the Chishti Order in the 16th century. In 1569 Emperor Akbar, who had remained childless until that time, turned to the holy man who prophesied that the emperor would have not one but three sons. When his first heir was born a year later, Akbar called him Salim (the later Jehangir) and had a huge mosque built out of gratitude. The building work for Fatehpur Sikri (city of victory) in memory of Akbar's conquest of Gujarat began in 1572. However, as soon as it was completed the seat of government was abandoned again. A lack of water and incidents along the empire's northwest border led to this city being given over to decay and plunder. Akbar moved his seat of government to Lahore and Jehangir subsequently withdrew to Agra, which was more secure. By 1590 Fatehpur Sikri was a dead city.

Layout of the city

Fatehpur Sikri is divided into **two separate complexes**: the palace area and the mosque somewhat to the southwest. The entire complex, adapted to the topographical circumstances, stretches out along a rocky hill and was surrounded by an approx. 10km/6mi defensive wall, which can still be recognized in places.

Palace area

Coming from Agra, the extensive palace area is accessed via the Public Audience Hall (Diwan-i-Am), an inner courtyard surrounded by

Fatehpur Sikri *Map*

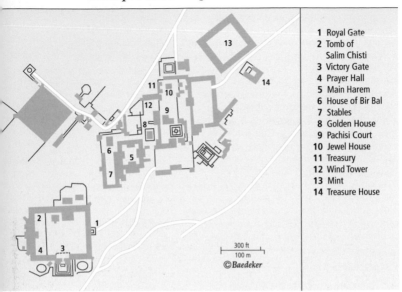

1 Royal Gate
2 Tomb of Salim Chisti
3 Victory Gate
4 Prayer Hall
5 Main Harem
6 House of Bir Bal
7 Stables
8 Golden House
9 Pachisi Court
10 Jewel House
11 Treasury
12 Wind Tower
13 Mint
14 Treasure House

300 ft
100 m
©Baedeker

columns, which then leads into the interior of the second palace courtyard (Pachisi Court). The two-storey detached sandstone building on its north side is now called the Private Audience Hall of the emperor (Diwan-i-Khas); its original purpose, however, is not known. Pavilions on the roof's four corners adorn the structure, while its interior is dominated by a mighty central column with rich relief work and a splayed capital. At the pool's (Anup Talao) north-west corner is a small, elegant, richly adorned building, which is called the House of the Turkish Sultan. Pachisi Court is dominated by the **Panch Mahal**, an airy, five-storey pavilion, which towers above the entire palace complex. There is a magnificent panorama to be had from the top floor. The tower, which is supported by 176 columns, narrows towards the top. The ground floor rests on 84 columns, while the top, roofed pavilion is only supported by four columns.

✱
Pavilion ▶

Southwest of the Panch Mahal is the **harem area** with the women's residences. There is a small residence in front of them, which is known as Maryam's House or Golden House (Sunahra Makan), in which Akbar's mother Maryam, a Christian, lived when she was in the city. Directly beyond it is the entrance to the harem, above which two stars of David can be found. The number of women who lived here is unknown, but it is clear that many of its inhabitants came from courts in Rajasthan and were Hindus. **Akbar's preference for Hinduism** did not just express itself in his choice of wife, but also in his palaces' architecture and interior designs. This is particularly evident in the harem area, whose decorations and ornaments are often reminiscent of temples and thus offer a stark contrast to its roofs made of blue tiles, which was a Persian tradition. Outside the harem, on its northwest side, stands the House of Birbal. Birbal was a minister under Akbar, but he did not live here. The building was also inhabited by Akbar's wives.

The palace area is exited via a narrow path, which leads directly to the Emperor's Gate (Badshahi Darwaza), one of two entrances that lead to the mosque's large inner courtyard. One of its noticeable features is the small marble mausoleum that Akbar had built in memory of Sheikh Salim Chishti. To this day the tomb of the Sufi saint is a **popular place of pilgrimage**, particularly for women who want to have a child. They plait strings into the mausoleum's marble lattice work, which is considered unsurpassed in its quality in all of

Sacred area

◄ Mausoleum

Pilgrims at the tomb of the Sufi saint Salim Chisti

India. Along the courtyard's western side is the prayer hall. It is supported by pillars that are based on the style of Hindu temple architecture. At first glace the monumental 54m/177ft Buland Darwaza, or High Gate, resembles a **triumphal arch** of classical antiquity. The gate, with three rounded archways and elaborate ornamentation made of sandstone and marble, was built as the mosque's main entrance to commemorate Akbar's victory over Gujarat. A steep stairway leads down to a small square populated by local traders.

✳ ✳
◀ Buland Darwaza

✳ Keoladeo Ghana National Park　　　　E 6

Bird paradise　The 52 sq km/20 sq mi Keoladeo Ghana National Park (55km/34mi west of Jaipur) is situated in a natural depression and its lakes and marshes make it ideal for birds. To date, more than **350 species** have been spotted in the national park. Many birds come from northern countries to overwinter and raise their young here. The best time for bird-watching is August–October. The vegetation is mainly made up of acacias, shrubs with berries, and capers. The local mammal population includes sambar deer, chital, nilgai antelopes, wild boar and rhesus monkeys. The area can be explored on foot or by bicycle. It is also possible to hire rickshaws and go out on the lake in a boat.

Rose-ringed parakeet

Since the protected area lies along the main route between Delhi and Mumbai it can easily be accessed by train from Jaipur and Delhi. There are also bus connections from Jaipur, Agra and Fatehpur Sikri for example. Information and inexpensive accommodation is provided by RTDC Hotel Saras (Agra Road, tel. 056 44 – 22 542).

Another good option is the more comfortable Bharatpur Forest Lodge right in the park (tel. 056 44 – 22 27 60).

A good starting location for a visit to Keoladeo Ghana National Park is the formerly fortified city of **Bharatpur** (3km/2mi to the north). Its Lohargarh Fort, which is protected by two clay walls and ditches, was founded by the Rajput king Suraj Mal in 1732 and was never conquered by the British. There are three palaces in the fort complex, of which the Maharaja's palace and the Kamra Palace (which houses a museum) are the most impressive.

✳ Allahabad

State: Uttar Pradesh
Population: 1.05 million

Altitude: 98m/322ft
Distance: 583km/362mi southeast of Delhi

The confluence of the major rivers, the Ganges and the Yamuna, has always been considered a particularly holy place and as a result there are countless myths and legends associated with it. Devout Hindus believe three rivers come together here, not just two: according to legend the (invisible) Sarasvati joins her two sisters here.

The place where the rivers meet is known as Sangam. Every twelve years (the next time is 2013) the Allahabad **Kumbha Mela** is held here, the largest festival of pilgrimage, which takes place in a three-year rhythm alternating in Allahabad, Nasik, Ujjain and Haridwar (Baedeker Special p.392).

✳ Festivals of pilgrimage

Allahabad goes back to Emperor Akbar, who had a fort and settlements built in the place where once the old town of Prayag had stood. In 1801 the British took over the city. Allahabad became a centre in Uttar Pradesh in 1858; it played an important role in India's battle for independence.

History

What to See in Allahabad

The fort is still extant; however, it can only be viewed from the outside since the military is stationed there. For this reason there is also no access to the **Ashokan pillar** (around 230 BC), which is decorated with edicts and which was presumably brought here by Akbar.

Allahabad Fort

❯ VISITING ALLAHABAD

INFORMATION

Tourist Office
Hotel Ilawart
35, MG Marg
Civil Lines
Tel. 05 32 – 260 18 73

GETTING THERE

By rail (lies along the main line between Delhi and Kolkata) or bus

WHERE TO EAT / WHERE TO STAY

▶ **Mid-range**
Yatrik
33, Sardar Patel Marg
Tel. 05 32 – 260 17 13
Centrally located with a restaurant, a nice garden and pool. The rooms are spacious and nicely furnished; they are fitted with air-conditioning and some have bathtubs.

Visitors can get deeper insight into Allahabad's more recent history by visiting Anand Bhavan. The former **Nehru family home** was given to the state in 1970 by Indira Gandhi and made into a museum (open: daily except Mon 9.30am–1pm and 2pm–5.30pm). ⊙

Anand Bhavan

Also worth a visit is Allahabad Museum, situated in the middle of a park. It has local finds (terra cotta figures, stone sculptures) as well as a respectable collection of miniature paintings from Rajasthan and pictures by the Russian painter Nicolaus Roerich (open: daily except Mon 10.30am–4.30pm). ⊙

Allahabad Museum

✳ Amritsar

D 4

State: Punjab
Population: 1.01 million

Altitude: 234m/768ft
Distance: 446km/277mi northwest of Delhi

Amritsar, only 26km/16mi from India's neighbour Pakistan, is Punjab's second-largest city. The only land connection from India to Pakistan leads through Amritsar and used to be part of the Silk Road.

The city's modern section is located to the northeast of the station. Its shopping streets can be found here around The Mall and Lawrence Road. The Ram Bagh gardens contain a small museum with a weapons collections and portraits of some of Punjab's rulers. With its many temples and mosques, the old town extends to the south of the railway lines. The famous **Golden Temple** is the centre of this part of town.

The Mughal ruler Akbar the Great gave the area around Amritsar to the fourth religious leader of the **Sikhs**, Ram Das (1574–81), who founded a town at this important land trading route between East and West. His youngest son Guru Arjun enlarged the artificial lake Amrit Sarovar; between 1589 and 1601 he built the first temple in the middle of the lake. However, this temple was occupied and desecrated by the Afghan conqueror Ahmed Shah Durani in 1757. Although the Sikhs managed to regain control of the temple they were defeated four years later and it was blown up. After the conquerors departed, the temple was rebuilt. Maharaja Ranjit Singh (1780–1839), the Sikhs' greatest secular ruler, donated the **100kg/ 220lbs of gold with which the roof was covered in 1830**, hence the name »Golden Temple«.

History

← *Every twelve years Allahabad, at the confluence of the sacred Ganges and Yamuna, becomes the centre of the Hindu universe*

▶ VISITING AMRITSAR

INFORMATION

Tourist Office
In Pegasus Palace Hotel
Queens Road
Tel. 01 83 – 240 24 52
or on the website of Punjab Tourism:
www.ptdc.com

GETTING THERE

By air or rail from Delhi and Chandigarh

FESTIVALS

Baisakhi is celebrated in April. It is the New Year's festival according to the solar calendar and also the harvest festival. Guru Govind Singh founded the Sikhs' Brotherhood of Saint Soldiers, Khalsa, on this day. The birthdays of the first guru, Nanak (October / November) and the last guru, Govind Singh (December / January), attract a large number of visitors.

WHERE TO STAY / WHERE TO EAT

▶ Mid-range

Mohan International
Albert Road
Tel. 01 83 – 222 78 01
One of the top hotels, restaurant serving Punjabi cuisine.

▶ Mid-range / Budget

Mrs. Bhandari's Guest House
10, Cantonement
Tel. 01 83 – 222 85 09
12 rooms (with stove heating upon request) in a nice old building with a garden and pool, restaurant. Camping in the garden is possible for a fee.

▶ Budget

Grand Hotel
Opposite the station
Tel. 01 83 – 256 24 24
Very centrally located with basic, clean rooms.

Amritsar came to fame in more recent times when a militant group of Sikhs led by Sant Jarnail Singh Bhindranwale barricaded themselves in a part of the Golden Temple, the Akal Takht, demanding an autonomous state for Sikhs. On the orders of Indira Gandhi the army stormed the temple district and killed the rebels in July 1984. 1200 innocent pilgrims also lost their lives in this large-scale attack. This operation led to great outrage amongst the Sikh population, and four months later the prime minister was shot by Sikhs who were part of her own team of bodyguards.

✳ ✳ Hari Mandir – the Golden Temple

Temple complex
The Golden Temple, also called the Darbar Sahib, Hall of the Lord, is situated in an almost square lake measuring around 130m/140yd on each side. There is a marble walkway surrounding the lake, and a marble bridge of almost 30m/33yd connects the temple to the western shore. According to legend the lake, which bears the name Amrit Sarovar (Lake of the Nectar of Immortality), possesses **healing**

powers; for this reason, to this day many pilgrims come to the steps of the lake's eastern shore to clean themselves.

The temple's main entrance is located on the north side next to the tower. Immediately after crossing the entrance area, visitors can see the Golden Temple and the lake glittering in the sunshine. Here they can do as the pilgrims do and walk clockwise around the lake on the wide marble walkway (Parikrama). The first place visitors reach are the bathing steps and the many shrines, which represent 68 of India's important holy places. To the east, outside the actual temple complex, stand the buildings that provide accommodation and food for thousands of pilgrims every day. Continuing along the walkway around the lake, visitors get to the shrine built in honour of Baba Deep Singh

The holiest Sikh temple: Hari Mandir

on the southern shore; he lost his life in the fight against Ahmad Shah Durani in 1758.

On the western shore there is a marble bridge that leads to the Golden Temple. Directly opposite stands the second holiest building, the **Akal Takht**. Every day, early in the morning, the Sikhs' holy book (Guru Granth Sahib), a collection of more than 3000 hymns in honour of their god, is brought from the Akal Takht to the Hari Mandir in a solemn ceremony and brought back again in the evening. The Akal Takht was built by Guru Har Govind in 1609, but in the 18th and 19th centuries it underwent great changes. When Indian soldiers stormed it in 1984 parts of the building were destroyed. It has largely been rebuilt now with the help of donations.

The **Hari Mandir**, the **Sikhs' holiest temple**, is accessed via a 60m/66yd marble walkway. The entire building except for the ground floor is covered in copper plates and the onion dome is gold plated. The copper plates are engraved with texts from the holy book. Oriels and pavilions break up the temple's rather compact appearance. The **Sikhs' holy book** is kept inside the temple. At the temple's eastern entrance a priest recites texts from the book and the many pilgrims sing along. On the first floor visitors will also see Sikhs practising the ritual of Akhand Path, the continuous recitation of the holy book.

The pilgrims offer flowers and money in the vicinity of the book and for a donation they can have an excerpt read out to them. A professional reader needs two days to recite the book in its entirety.

Further Sights in Amritsar

Jallianwalla Bagh Jallianwalla Bagh is a memorial commemorating 379 civilians who were murdered under British rule. This group of unarmed people were shot at by British soldiers in 1919 because they had assembled without permission. In a desperate attempt to escape the bullets many threw themselves into the fountain, where they died. Anyone taking a closer look will still be able to see the marks on the fountain where it was hit by bullets. The Amritsar massacre was the immediate cause of the non-co-operation movement led by Mahatma Gandhi (►Famous People), which in turn led to India's independence. Today a sign and a small museum with photographs commemorate this dark chapter of India's colonial rule.

Durgiana Mandir This Durga temple with gilded temple towers and silver portals is an important Hindu shrine.

✶ Chandigarh

E 4

State: Punjab / Haryana
Population: 642,000

Altitude: 1250m/4100ft–1980m/6496ft
Distance: 250km/155mi north of Delhi

Chandigarh, which is the capital both of Haryana and of Punjab, is famous for its city architecture. The modern capital does not have any special attractions, except for the buildings by Le Corbusier, which attract architecture enthusiasts from around the world.

The town is quite sprawling and divided into 48 sectors, which makes orientation relatively easy. Otherwise Chandigarh is a necessary stopover for all those travelling to the Himalaya by land. Chandigarh is situated in a valley in the middle of the Siwalik Hills. When Pakistan separated from India, the state of Punjab was also divided. Lahore, together with the state's western territory, went to Pakistan. In return Chandigarh was voted the new capital. It was the desire of the prime minister of the time, Jawaharlal Nehru, that the capital, which was considered »progressive, modern and open«, would be a symbol of the new democratic India.

What to See in and around Chandigarh

✶ Townscape by Le Corbusier The first plans for the city were designed by Albert Mayer and Matthew Nowicki in New York. When one of the architects died in an aeroplane crash in 1950, all the remaining designs were handed over to the famous Swiss-born French architect Le Corbusier. Under Le Corbusier's leadership and that of his colleagues Pierre Jeanneret, Jane Drew and Maxwell Fry, the city was built in the period between 1951 and 1964. Le Corbusier created a completely modern **architecture oriented to Western aesthetics**, which had no Indian stylistic elements.

The city blocks divided into 48 sectors with wide roads and extensive green spaces are dominated by the large buildings such as the High Court, the government building and the state legislature. All of these prestigious buildings are located in Sector 1 in the city's north. Though they have already lost some of their beauty, their powerful shapes are still impressive. Le Corbusier's city had a big impact on India's architects who favoured Western styles, and gave such architecture a major impetus in India.

The Rock Garden near the High Court is one of India's most bizarre landscaped gardens. The artist **Nek Chand** spent a large part of his life creating **surrealist sculptures and objects** from objets trouvés. The garden, almost 2ha/5ac in size, has become a labyrinth of figures as a result of decades of work and is a lot of fun for children and adults alike.

★
Rock Garden

The museum exhibits fossils from prehistoric times, while he Fine Art Gallery has a collection of Indian miniatures from the Rajasthan, Kangra and Mughal schools. In addition it has some sculptures from the Hellenistically inspired Gandhara school. The museum and the gallery are both located in Sector 10.

Museum and gallery

▶ VISITING CHANDIGARH

INFORMATION

Chandigarh Tourism
Interstate Bus Terminus
Sector 17
Tel. 01 72 – 270 46 14
www.chandigarhtourism.gov.in
This building also contains offices of Himachal Tourism and Punjab Tourism. Another office is located at the Plaza, Sector 17.

WHERE TO STAY / WHERE TO EAT

▶ **Luxury**
Taj Chandigarh
Sector 17/A
Tel. 01 72 – 551 30 00
www.tajhotels.com
An elegant hotel with several restaurants.

▶ **Mid-range / Budget**
Aroma
Himalaja Marg
Sector 22/C
Long-established two-star hotel with many works of art. It also has a 24-hour coffee-shop as well as an elegant restaurant with a waterfall and live music in the evening.

Zakir Hussain Rose Garden This garden between Sectors 16 and 17 has **one of Asia's largest facilities for breeding roses**. Visitors can admire around 1000 different rose varieties over almost 10ha/25ac. The roses are in bloom in the winter.

Pinjore Garden Around 32km/20mi from Chandigarh is Pinjore Garden, a garden built on a terrace, dating back to the 17th century.

✶ ✶ Corbett National Park

F 5

State: Uttarakhand
Distance: 295km/183mi northeast of Delhi

Altitude: 400m/1310ft–1000m/3280ft

At the foot of the Himalaya, crossed by three hill ranges running east to west, is India's oldest animal sanctuary, Jim Corbett National Park.

India's first tiger reserve, Jim Corbett National Park, was created in 1936. It became known far beyond the country's borders through »Project Tiger«

The 520 sq km/200 sq mi protected area is home to more than 50 species of mammal, 25 reptile species and around 580 bird species. It is particularly famous for its tiger population. When a flood was caused by an ambitious dam project, flooding a tenth of the park, all of the animals except for the water birds were forced to escape to higher regions.

The tigers of Corbett National Park were hunted by locals and the British alike until the 1930s, causing their population to be decimated. Then, of all people, a hunter had a change of heart and saw to it that the **first protection zone for the endangered animals was set up in 1936**. In honour of Jim Corbett's work the park was later named after him. In 1973 **»Project Tiger«** was started here with the support of the World Wildlife Fund (now the Worldwide Fund for Nature); the experiment was later expanded to 18 other parks in an attempt to keep the endangered big cats from extinction. In addition to tigers, the park is also home to other wild cats such as leopards and leopard cats. Another great attraction is the park's **elephants**, which move through the area in herds. The park is also home to several species of deer, such as sambars, chitals and many more.

The park has several rest houses, which are a good base for animal watching. The best known is in Dhikala. More information is available from Uttarakhand Tourism in Delhi. Organized tours are offered from Delhi and Nainital, from Garhwal Mandal Vikas Nigam and Kumaon Mandal Vikas Nigam. Season: mid-November–mid-June.

Tip

▶ VISITING CORBETT NATIONAL PARK

INFORMATION
Project Tiger Office
Ramnagar
Tel. 059 47 – 25 14 89
For visitor permits, accommodation and park tours.

GETTING THERE
By rail or bus from Delhi

SEASON
Mid-November–mid-June

WHERE TO STAY
Good accommodation in the park through »Project Tiger«, through Uttarakhand Tourism in Delhi and www.ua.nic.in

▶ Luxury
Infinity Resorts
Ramnagar
Tel. 059 47 – 280 41 03
Situated on the banks of the Kosi river with many different ways in which to explore the natural environment.

▶ Mid-range
Corbett Inn
Ramnagar
Tel. 059 47 – 25 17 55
Clean, spacious rooms. Only five minutes from the visitor centre.

✶ ✶ **Delhi** (Union Territory)

India's capital
Population: 12.8 million

Altitude: 216m/709ft
Distance: 1408km/875mi northeast of Mumbai, 1896mi west of Kolkata

India's capital, like the country's other cities, is a reflection of its rapid economic development. Multi-lane highways criss-cross the city on several levels and thousands of cars race past the tombs of the Mughal rulers. Delhi's modern Metro was recently opened, and will be extended further in the coming years. No other place in Delhi makes visitors quite so aware of the co-existence of tradition and modernity as Chawri Chowk Metro station, where the masses are released from the cool world of air-conditioning, digital displays and glass fronts into the tumult of Old Delhi's bazaars.

Delhi is made up of **Old Delhi**, which, with its narrow, winding alleys and large number of shops and markets, is always overcrowded, and spacious **New Delhi** around the parliament building, which was designed by the English architect Sir Edwin Lutyens as the capital of colonial India. There are several famous buildings to be seen resulting from the Delhi's 1500 years of history; however, the city is huge and the attractions are far apart from each other. Delhi is a good place to learn about the various facets of Indian culture, boasting excellent museums and staging outstanding events. India's more recent art is also on display in many galleries in the city.

History

approx. 1500 BC	Legendary city of Indraprastha
12th century	Significant Hindu centre in northern India
1206–1526	Sultanate of Delhi
1526–1857	Rule of the Mughal emperors
1857	Beginning of British colonial rule
1911	Delhi becomes India's capital
since 1947	Post-independence: economic boom and expansion into a global metropolis

The **capital of the world's largest democracy** can look back on more than 3000 years of history. According to legend the site of modern-day Delhi was once the location of Indraprasatha, the capital of the Pandava kings in around 1500 BC. The site on the banks of the Yamuna has always been considered strategically favourable, which is why cities were repeatedly founded, conquered, destroyed and rebuilt here. The Roman geographer and astronomer Ptolemy,

View over the city's roofs from the Friday Mosque

who visited this region in the second century AD, wrote about a town called **Dilli** in his travel reports. Many cities were founded here, seven of which are considered significant. The earliest historically proven settlement goes back to the Tomara Rajputs, who built a city by the name of Lal Kot here in AD 736. Only a few walls from this city are still extant near the Qutb Minar (tower of victory). The Tomaras were driven away by the Chauhans, who built Quila Rai Pithora in 1180, which is considered the first city of Delhi. However, in 1191 it was captured by the Afghan conqueror Muhammad of Ghur. His general, Qutb-ud-din, founded the first **Delhi Sultanate**. The Qutb Minar, which can still be seen in southern Delhi, is an architectural masterpiece dating from this time. The next conquerors, who founded the second city of Delhi under the name of Siri, were also of central Asian origin. Siri, near modern-day Hauz Khas, was extended by a fort further to the south and renamed Tughluquabad by Ghiyas-ud-din Tughluq, the self-proclaimed sultan, in 1321. This third city and also the fourth city, Jahapanah, which lay between Siri and Lal Kot, were only short lived. In 1328 the Mughal rulers moved their capital from Delhi to Daulatabad on the Deccan plateau 1000km/620mi away, a better-protected location. The fifth city, Firozabad, founded by Sultan Firoz Shah when the capital was moved back to Delhi, was plundered by the central Asian Turkic king Timur

(Tamburlaine) in 1398. For a short period the Sayyids (1414–51) were able to establish themselves in Delhi, but they were driven out by Dhulul Lodhi, who founded the **Lodhi dynasty** (1456–1526). There are some wonderful structures from this time still extant in the Lodhi Gardens. The rulers were defeated by the Afghan king Babur at a battle north of Delhi in 1526. His dynasty, with the name Mughal, derived from the word »Mongol«, was to have a great influence on the whole of India.

Of the 19 **Mughal emperors**, Humayun, Akbar, Jehangir, Shah Jahan and Aurangzeb are the most famous. In Aurangzeb's day their empire encompassed almost all of India. Delhi was considered India's most magnificent city and many monuments, now big tourist attractions, were erected during the time of the Mughals. Humayun, Babur's son, had Din-Panah citadel built, which was later called Purana Qila (Old Fort). Today it is one of Delhi's most important sights. Humayun had to flee after just ten years from the Afghan king Sher Shah. The conqueror Sher Shah built the sixth city, Shergarh, around Humayun's fort. Humayun, however, managed to reconquer Delhi in 1555 and from then on there was peace in the city for several centuries. Shah Jahan built Shah Jahanabad, the seventh city, with Jama Masjid as the religious and Purana Qila as the governmental centres. The Mughals' wealth attracted many conquerors. The Persian ruler Nadir Shah finally managed to conquer Delhi in 1738. During the subsequent plunder he did not just take the famous Peacock Throne, he also took many women from the harem, capable architects and craftsmen, 1000 elephants, 7000 horses and 10,000 camels back to his empire. The famous diamond Koh-i-Noor also fell into his hands. The Mughal Empire never recovered from this looting. The weakened city was conquered by the British in 1803 and the incumbent Mughal emperor Shah Alam II (1759–1806) of the time was thrown into prison, where he died.

! *Baedeker* TIP

Delhi's spirits come alive

William Dalrymple's *City of Jinns* is still well worth reading. The author peels back the layers of the Indian capital like those of an onion and uncovers Delhi's various facets and periods with plenty of humour, copious knowledge and an unerring sense for detail.

			Where to eat	Where to
1 Kashmiri Gate	9 Vir Buhmi	17 Lalitkala Gallery	① Punjabi by Nature	① Imperia
2 Bus Terminal	10 Rauoa Begum's Tomb	18 All India Fine Arts &	② Spice Route	② Oberoi
3 St James' Church	11 International Dolls	Crafts Society	③ United Coffee	③ Nirula'
4 Delhi Municipal	Museum	19 National Archives	House	④ YWCA
Corporation	12 Gandhi Memorial Hall	20 National Museum	④ Karim's	⑤ Ajanta
and Town Hall	13 State Emporia	21 National Gallery of	⑤ Sagar Ratna	⑥ Shrawa
5 Bhagirath Palace	14 Sacred Heart Cathedral	Modern Art	⑥ Chandni Chowk	Fort Vie
6 Digamber Jain Temple	15 Jantar Mantar	22 National Stadium	Basar	
7 Shanti Vana	16 Museum of	23 Crafts Museum		
8 Shakti Sthal	Natural History			

Delhi Map

1 km
0,62 mi
©Baedeker

Grand Trunk Road

Delhi University

Old Secretariat

Sharmat Road

Mahatma Gandhi

Rashanara Garden

Ashoka's Pillar

Mutiny Memorial

Ladakh Boudh Vihar

Rani Thansi Marg

Bihari Marg

Zorawarsingh Marg

2
× 3
1

Road

Govind Singh Marg

Delhi Station

4   5
6   6

Red Fort

Vijay Ghat

Yamuna

Yamuna Bund Marg

Desh Bandhu Gupta Road

Fatehpuri Mosque

Jami Masjid

OLD   4

7

Bahadur Shah Zafar Marg

8

9

amai Road

Ajmeri Gate

10

DELHI

Turkman Gate

Raj Ghat

5

New Delhi Station

Ferozshah Kotla

Community Hall

Lakshmi Narayan Temple

Road

Mandir Marg

Kardinail Stadium

5

Connaught   3
Place   3

Bhel Bhavan

Yamuna Velodrome

11   IG Stadium

Mahatma

14   13

15

Baba Singh

Khatak Marg

Talkatora Garden

Ashoka Road

16
4   1
17   2

18

Curzon Road

Deen Dayal Upad Marg

12

19

Rashtrapati Bhavan

Sansad Bhavan

20

27

Wellington Crescent

21

23
Raj

Path

24

India Gate

26

Mathura Road

Old Fort

Gandhi

dha
anti

Polo Ground

22

NEW DELHI

Road

25

Dr. Zakir Hussain Road

Zoo

6

Nehru Memorial Museum

Akbar

Delhi Golf Club   2

4

ANAKYAPURI

Nehru Park

Safdarjung's Tomb

Prithviraj Road

Lodi Gardens

Lodi Road

Tibet House

Humayun's Tomb

Isa Khan

Road

28   29

DILLI HAAT

Sir Aurobindo Marg

Vasant Vihar, Hauz Khas Qutb Minar Complex ↓

Darya Khan's Tomb

1

↓ Bahai Temple

Lala Lajpat Rai Path

Ring Road

In 1857 Indian soldiers tried to drive out the British in a rebellion. However, the uprising was put down in a bloody fight and many members of the royal family were murdered. For that reason the entrance to the Red Fort is still known as the Khuni Darwaza, the bloody gate. This marked the end of the Mughal dynasty and the **beginning of British colonial rule** in northern India. In the following year the rule of India was handed over by the East India Company to the British crown. Kolkata became the colony's new capital. King George V however declared Delhi the capital of the Indian crown colony once again in 1911 and had many buildings erected for the government and administration. Only two years later the foundation stone of colonial India's new capital was laid. It took almost 20 years for the elaborate buildings to be completed. Delhi was finally inaugurated as the capital of Britain's largest colony in a great celebration in 1931. After India's **independence** on 15 August 1947, Delhi remained the capital. Since then Delhi has been constantly expanding and is now truly amongst the world's great cities.

 ## VISITING DELHI

INFORMATION

Information Office of Delhi Tourism
N-36 Connaught Place
Middle Circle
Open: daily 7am–9pm
Tel. 011 – 23 31 53 22 or 23 31 42 29
www.delhitourism.nic.in

India Tourism Office
88, Janpath
Tel. 011 – 23 32 00 05 / 08

»The Delhi City«
City magazine published every fortnight

FESTIVALS • TRADE FAIRS

Garden festival (end of Feb), Qutub Festival for classical music and dance (Oct), large Suraj Kund arts and crafts fair in Haryana (8km/5mi south of New Delhi (beginning of Feb)

SHOPPING

Delhi has many shopping streets, bazaars and markets. Here are a few popular addresses:

Baedeker recommendation

Ethnic food and goods
Textiles from all over India as well as the country's culinary specialities can be found in Dilli Haat in the south of the city. The government-run market with almost 200 stalls and snack bars is open all year round from 11am–10pm (Sri Aurobindo Marg, opposite the INA Market).

New Delhi
There are shops selling Western clothes at Connaught Place, and there are small shops along Janpath with cheap textiles, shoes, jewellery and souvenirs. Khan Market, the market in the Defense Colony and Hauz Khas Village with its small boutiques and galleries, all in the south of New Delhi, are also popular. Sunder Nagar Market south of Purana Quila sells antiques.

Old Delhi
Those who love the bazaar atmosphere

will find everything they desire in Chandni Chowk, Old Delhi's bazaar district; it has jewellery, printed paper, arts and crafts and a lot more; however, anyone who does not know the place runs the risk of getting lost in these labyrinthine alleyways. It is best to use Chandni Chowk's main road or Chawri Bazar Metro station for orientation. In the evenings and at night women in particular should avoid this area.

Khadi Gramodyog
A shop selling goods form the Gandhi production sites: textiles, cosmetics and food (24 Regal Building at Connaught Place).

Fab India
Indian textiles from blouses to curtains (Khan Market).

Book shops
Good selection and advice in »Bahri-sons« (Khan Market) and »The Bookworm« (B 29, Connaught Place).

Emporium Complex
Shops from India's various states: visitors will find a large selection of arts and crafts, from cashmere scarves to bronze sculptures (Baba Kharak Singh Marg).

Cottage Industries Emporium
Arts and crafts on several levels including a café (Janpath, opposite Imperial Hotel).

WHERE TO EAT
► Expensive
① *Punjabi by Nature*
Vasant Vihar
Priya Cinema Complex
Tel. 011 – 51 51 66 66
Currently considered the best restaurant for northern Indian cuisine in Delhi.

Preparing tasty malpuras (syrup pancakes)

② *Spice Route*
In the Imperial Hotel
Janpath
Tel. 011 – 23 34 12 34
One of Asia's top restaurants, top
notch southeast Asian cuisine.

▶ **Moderate**
③ *United Coffee House*
15-E, Connaught Place
Restaurant, bar and café in one, very
good Tandoori dishes, snacks and
coffee.

④ *Karim's*
2 locations:
Gali Kababian, near the south entrance
of Jama Masjid in Old Delhi
(tel. 011 – 23 26 98 89)

and in New Delhi »Dastarkhwan-e-
Karim«, 168/2 Nizamuddin West
(tel. 011 – 24 35 54 85).
Famous establishment for kebabs and
other tasty Mughal dishes.

▶ **Inexpensive**
⑤ *Sagar Ratna*
K-15, Outer Circle
Connaught Place
Tel. 011 – 23 41 24 70
Vegetarian dishes from southern and
northern India.

⑥ *Chandni Chowk Bazaar*
Delhi has many famous sweets; they
can be sampled at the bazaar where
they are cooked in large vats. Particularly well known are the carrot
halva (gajar-ka-halva), a traditional
winter sweet, and the orange-coloured
Jalebis.

WHERE TO STAY
▶ **Luxury**
① *The Imperial*
Janpath, New Delhi
Tel. 011 – 23 34 12 34

www.theimperialindia.com
Traditional luxury hotel with several
very good restaurants and bars, centrally located.

② *The Oberoi*
Dr. Zakir Hussain Marg-3
near Humayun's Tomb
Tel. 011 – 24 36 30 30
www.oberoihotels.com
Luxury hotel with five restaurants and
two bars.

▶ **Mid-range**
③ *Nirula's Hotel*
L-Block, Connaught Circus
New Delhi
Tel. 011 – 23 41 74 19
www.nirulas.com
Centrally located three-star hotel with
two restaurants, a bar and an internet
café. All the rooms are fitted with air
conditioning.

▶ **Mid-range / Budget**
④ *YWCA*
10, Sansad Marg
New Delhi
Tel. 011 – 23 34 02 94, 23 34 52 35
www.ywcaindia.org
Pleasant rooms, breakfast buffet
and dinner. Budget for its central
location.

⑤ *Ajanta*
36, Arakashan Road
Ram Nagar
Tel. 011 – 23 62 09 27
Located close to the station, large
rooms, internet café and restaurant.

⑥ *Shrawani Fort View*
11, Sunder Nagar
Tel. 011 – 24 35 96 70
Pleasant, inexpensive hotel with a view
of the zoo in the district of Sunder
Nagar.

Highlights *Delhi*

Red Fort
The largest building from the time of the Mughal rulers in the heart of Old Delhi

Humayun's Tomb
Wonderfully designed mausoleum

Jama Masjid
The Friday Mosque is best visited at sunset

National Museum
Largest museum with a significant collection of sculptures and miniatures

Qutb Minar
The 72.5m/238ft tower is the oldest structure left over from the Muslim rulers.

Connaught Place
The heart of New Delhi with many restaurants and shops. There are wide tree-lined avenues departing the square in every direction.

Jantar Mantar
Maharaja Jai Singh's observatory

Chandni Chowk
A stroll through the alleys and bazaars of Old Delhi

Lodi Gardens
A green oasis in the city

Crafts Museum
Traditional handicrafts in a building by Charles Correa

Kebab at Karim's
The art of Muslim cooking traditions

New Delhi

Connaught Place consists of three concentric ring roads and several other roads radiating from the centre. It is the beating heart of the aspiring business city, in which many banks, well-known jewellery and fashion shops as well as offices of the most important airline companies can be found.

★
Connaught Place

Follow Sansad Marg (Parliament Street) from Connaught Place for five minutes to get to a small park with red buildings with a futuristic air.
The buildings are part of an **observatory**, which Maharaja Jai Shing had built in 1724 to calculate astronomical data for the Hindu calendar and astrological nomographs. Maharaja Jai Singh of Jaipur was an enthusiastic astronomer. He built four other observatories, in Jaipur, Mathura, Varanasi and Ujjain. With the help of these instruments the movements of the sun, the moon and other celestial bodies could be determined, as could the exact time.

★
Jantar Mantar
🕐
Opening hours:
daily 9am–5pm

Lakshmi Narayan Temple

West of Connaught Place is Lakshmi Narayan Temple, which was donated by the industrialist Birla family and dedicated to the god Vishnu in 1938. It is one of the few large Hindu temples in Delhi and is visited my many Hindus every day.

✳ **India Gate**

Southeast of Connaught Place stands the India Gate. Its walls contain more than 3000 names of Indian soldiers who lost their lives fighting on the side of the British in the First World War. The sandstone monument (1931) was designed by Sir Edwin Lutyens.

✳ **National Gallery of Modern Art** ⏱

Not far away is the National Gallery of Modern Art in Jaipur House. It has an **excellent collection** with works by contemporary Indian artists (open: daily except Mon 10.45am – 5.15pm).

✳ **Old Fort (Purana Qila)**

On a hill southeast of the India Gate stand the remains of the Old Fort built by the Afghan ruler Sher Shah. According to the most recent archaeological digs the old Indraprastha is said to have been located here. Entering the complex through the south gate, visitors come across the octagonal Sher Mandal sandstone tower, which the Mughal emperor Humayun used as a library. The place became his downfall, literally, when he slipped on the stairs and fell to his death in 1556.

✳ **Crafts Museum** ⏱
Opening hours: daily except Mon 9.30am–6pm

Located in close proximity, on Pragati Maidan, is the interesting Crafts Museum. It is an attempt to **preserve India's diverse arts and crafts tradition** and to show it to the public. The building, designed by Charles Correa, really accentuates the exhibits, which come from all over India. Numerous events with music and dance take place here as do performances of traditional crafts, which allow spectators to experience the skills of the potters and weavers amongst others.

✳ ✳ **National Museum** ⏱
Opening hours: daily except Mon 10am–5pm

Delhi's largest museum, the National Museum, was only built in 1960. Its core goes back to an exhibition that was held in London in 1947–48, in which some of the **most significant exhibits of Indian culture** were brought together. Today the museum contains a comprehensive collection from India's early history (2400–1500 BC) to the miniature paintings of the 18th century. The various sections also show finds from the Indus valley civilization, stone figures from the Maurya dynasty, terra cotta figures from the Gupta period, southern Indian bronze sculptures and several wood carvings from Gujarat. It is worth planning to spend a few hours here to enjoy this unique collection at your leisure.

Sansad Bhavan (parliament of India)

On the way to the Presidential Palace, visitors will pass a circular building surrounded by columns at the southwest end of Parliament Street. This is India's Parliament House. The elected representatives from the states meet here in two houses, the lower house with members by direct election, and the upper house, with members elected indirectly by the states and territories.

Architecturally speaking, Humayun's tomb was a model for the Taj Mahal in Agra

Continue westwards to get to Rashtrapati Bhavan, formerly the seat of the British viceroys. The buildings are connected to each other via Rajpath, the wide ceremonial avenue that is lined with gardens on both sides. At the independence celebrations (26 January) crowds of hundreds of thousands gather here to admire the parades. During the turbulent times prior to India's independence **Lord Mountbatten** resided here. Once again the British architect Sir Edwin Lutyens was responsible for this building, which is very European in its character. Together with Herbert Baker, Sir Edwin designed New Delhi's entire government district after King George V announced in 1911 that the capital would be moved from Kolkata to Delhi. Today the huge building serves as the Presidential Palace.

To the south lies the **diplomatic district of Chanakyapuri** with its embassies that are often designed in the style of the country to which they belong.

Rashtrapati Bhavan (Presidential Palace)

Railway enthusiasts will very much enjoy the Rail Transport Museum. It has maharaja carriages and some old trains on display (open: daily except Mon 9.30am–5pm).

Rail Transport Museum
🕐

Humayun's Tomb, which his widow Bega Begum had built in 1565, **is one of Delhi's most beautiful Mughal structures**. This building is the first mature example of a garden tomb, i.e. the synthesis of a garden and a tomb. The most perfect example of this type of tomb was

✱✱ Humayun's Tomb

built in Agra, namely the world-famous Taj Mahal. The square, four-part garden (Char Bahg) is divided into further squares by canals, which are in turn divided up by smaller water channels. Humayun's Tomb is situated on a high platform, making it appear even more monumental. The building, made primarily of red sandstone with **black and white marble inlays**, is crowned by a white marble dome. Below the building in a crypt are the remains of Humayun and his wife Bega Begum. The last Mughal emperor Bahadur Shah sought refuge here, but he was captured by the British in 1857 and thrown into prison.

Bu Halima's Garden
Bu Halima's Garden is situated in front of Humayun's Tomb. It also contains the older tomb of Isa Khan, which combines Hindu and Mughal stylistic elements.

Tibet House Museum
🕐
The Tibet House Museum in Lodhi Road has an interesting collection of Tibetan art (open: daily except Sun 10am–5pm, closed for lunch.

✴
Safdarjung's Tomb
Safdarjung's Mausoleum in the middle of a large garden was built by Nawab Shauja-ud-Daula in 1753 for his father and is an excellent example of late-period Mughal architecture. To this day the building with its gardens is a **popular destination** for the city's inhabitants.

The cool **Lodhi Gardens** with some 15th-century tombs are an **oasis in the hectic city of Delhi**. The largest of the tombs, the tomb of Sikandar Lodhi, possesses some very nice columns and archways and is situated beside an artificial lake.

The 72.5m/238ft red sandstone tower in the **Qutb Minar complex** with verses from the Qur'an is **the oldest structure of the Muslim rulers in Delhi**. The tower's first floor was built as a victory tower by Qutb-ud-din in 1199 and later completed by his successor. Firoz Shah had part of the top renovated and during this process parts of the sandstone façade was replaced by marble plates. It was from this tower that the muezzin called to prayer.

Not far from Qutb Minar are the **relics of India's first mosque** (12th century), which was built from the remains of

Hindu relics in Qutb Minar complex

Hindu temples with the help of Indian craftsmen. Upon closer inspection visitors will still be able to recognize **various Hindu symbols of good fortune** (mangalas), such as the motifs of the overflowing jug and the laughing Face of Glory. The builder, Qut-al-Din Aibek, does not seem to have been very satisfied with the result, which is why he had a stone »curtain« built in front of the prayer hall in 1198, probably to stop it from looking like an Afghan mosque.

There is an **iron column** in the courtyard with inscriptions from the Gupta period. This non-rusting column is 7.2m/23.6ft tall and has a diameter of 37cm/14.5in. It is a testament to the incredible mastery of metalwork in ancient India.

This lotus-shaped temple made of white marble and situated in the middle of a very large, landscaped garden is considered a successful example of modern temple architecture. The temple on Kalkaji Hill is the religious centre for members of the Bahai religion, and was donated by Mirza Husain in 1868.

Bahai Temple (Lotus Temple)

Old Delhi

The city of Shahjahanabad, which was originally protected by a 7km/ 4mi wall with 15 gates, is what is now known as Old Delhi. Those with strong nerves and a desire to plunge into the adventure that is »Old Delhi« will find what they are looking for in the main shopping street, **Chandni Chowk,** and in the narrow, busy markets of Kinaari Bazaar, Naya Bazaar and Meena Bazaar. Some buildings, like the Red Fort and Jama Masjid, can easily be visited. They convey a lively image of Delhi's former heyday under the Mughal emperors.

Townscape

The Red Fort is the **largest monument the Mughal rulers have left behind**. Its construction lasted from 1639–48 and the remains of the older cities of Firozabad and Shergarh were generously used to build it. The fort's 1km/1100yd by 500m/550yd complex runs along the Yamuna river (north-south axis) on the eastern edge of the former town of Shahjahanabad. A high sandstone wall and a deep moat that got its water from the Yamuna protected the fort from attackers.
The fort is accessed via the massive three-storey **Lahore Gate** at the centre of the western wall. First visitors will walk through **Chatta Chowk**, a bazaar protected by wind and weather by high arcades. Where merchants now try and sell their goods, exclusive shops once sold silk, jewellery and gemstones in the time of Shah Jahan. The original architecture can only be seen in a few places these days, for example at the shop with the number 19. After walking through this busy market visitors will arrive at Naqqar Khana (**drum house**), where everyone with the exception of the royal family had to leave their mounts behind. The building got its name from the musicians who played here five times a day in honour of the Mughal emperor. Newly arriving princes were welcomed with a special melody,

★★ Red Fort (Lal Qila)

enabling the palace's inhabitants to recognize exactly who was approaching. The four-storey drum house made of red sandstone is decorated with pretty plant motifs, which have however lost the gold plating they once had.

Between the first and second courtyard is the Audience Hall, **Diwan-i-Am**. This is where the emperor used to meet the nobles of his country. Thus the hall that now seems quite plain used to be adorned with everything that highlighted the monarch's splendour. The floor was covered in precious carpets, the bare walls had a white coating that was polished in such a way to make it shimmer like marble. Colourful flower motifs were painted on it. There are some **attractive inlay works with birds and plants** to be seen on the hall's back wall.

In front of it is the platform for the emperor's throne. Balustrades made of gold and silver divided the nobility according to their ranking. A third balustrade made of sandstone was designated for less significant visitors.

Behind the Audience Hall are six **private palaces** and a huge garden. The palaces were built in an elevated location right by the riverbank. This afforded them protection while at the same time exposing them to a cool breeze from the river.

Immediately east of the Audience Hall (Diwan-i-Khas) in the direction of the river is the Palace of Colours, the Rang Mahal, and south of it is the Mumtaz Mahal, the Palace of Jewels. Both palaces were once reserved for the women of the harem and the princesses. The **Rang Mahal** contains some finely worked marble windows and rooms with mirrored walls, which the Mughals took over from Rajasthan's palaces. The **Mumtaz Mahal** now houses a very worthwhile museum with a collection of weapons, carpets, textiles and chess boards.

To the left of the Rang Mahal is **Mussaman Burj**, a part of the Khas Mahal, the ruler's private palace, with an octagonal room on the fort's east wall. The ruler showed himself to his people on the Jharokah-i-Darshan (balcony). The Tosh Khana has an excellent filigree marble wall. All of these palaces were connected to fountains via a canal, which cooled the rooms.

Further north is the large **Diwan-i-Khas**, where guests were received for private audiences. This was once the location of the famous Peacock Throne, which was brought to Persia after Delhi was plundered by Sher Shah. Opposite the Diwan-i-Khas is the small, very attractive **Moti Masjid**, which was only built later under Aurangzeb.

The **archaeological museum** has objects and artworks from the Mughal period on display (open: daily 10am–5pm). In addition an English-language **light and sound show** takes place at 7.30pm and 8.30pm.

✶✶
Jama Masjid (Friday Mosque)

Shah In 1650 Jahan started building the Jama Masjid on elevated ground not far from the Red Fort. It took 5,000 workers six years to complete this huge mosque. The Mughal ruler visited it every Friday with his entourage to say his prayers. This is **India's largest mosque**, and the third largest in the world.

With its two onion towers above the main mosque, the minarets and the huge courtyard, it is considered a perfect example of Mughal architecture. Of the three entrance gates the east gate, the largest, was reserved for the Mughal rulers. There are four 40m/130ft minarets, two on the complex's north side, two on the south side. The main hall is oriented towards Mecca. The west side contains the niche (mihrab) from where the imam reads. The mosque is visited by particularly large numbers of believers every Friday, who come to pray in the courtyard. It houses a few relics such as the sandals of Muhammad, beard hairs of the prophet and a chapter of the Qur'an which he allegedly dictated himself. The mosque once impressed the conqueror Timur (Tamburlaine) so much that he had a replica built in Samarkand.

North of the Friday Mosque stands one of the Ashokan pillars. This 14m/46ft column from the 3rd century BC proclaims **Ashoka's edicts** in Brahmi script. It was brought from the region around

Ashokan pillar

The Red Fort rises up imposingly over Old Delhi

Life in such a busy city can be quite exhausting: having a rest after work

Meerut to Delhi by Firozeshah Tughlaq in the 14th century and now stands among the remains of Firozabad, the fifth city that was built at around 1354. Today there are nothing but ruins left of this settlement, including the remains of its Jama Masjid.

Monuments for political leaders Old Delhi also has some modern structures worth seeing, including the monuments to independent India's political leaders. They are located between Mahatma Gandhi Road and the Yamuna river south of the Red Fort. The best-known tomb,, **Raj Ghat**, a black block of marble, is dedicated to **Mahatma Gandhi**, who was cremated here in 1948. In addition there are Shanti Vana, the memorial to **Jawaharlal Nehru**, India's first prime minister, Vijay Ghat for Lal Bahadur Shastri and memorials to **Indira Gandhi** (Shakti Stala, all ►Famous People) and her son **Rajiv Gandhi** (Vir Bhumi).

Dolls Museum Quite nearby, in Bahadur Shah Zafar Marg, Shankar's International Dolls Museum has a collection of dolls from all around the world (open: daily except Mon 10am–6pm).

Around Delhi

Dehra Dun (235km/145mi northeast of Delhi, population 535,000), capital of the new state of Uttarakhand, is located in a broad valley between the Siwalik Hills to the south and the Himalayan foothills to the north. Tourists usually use this town as a starting point for visits to the places of pilgrimage ►Haridwar and Rishikesh on the upper Ganges or as the first base for trekking in the mountains.

Dehra Dun

A nice excursion goes from Dehra Dun to the hill station of Mussoorie 34km/21mi to the north and already in the foothills of the Himalaya. The British called this place »Queen of the Hills«. They came here to seek refuge from the sweltering heat of the Indian summer. In a **picturesque location**, Mussoorie (269km/167mi northeast of Delhi, population 20,000) stretches out along a mountain ridge, already part of the Himalayan foothills, which drops off steeply into the valley of Dehra Dun. The year-round pleasant climate and the healthy air were probably the main reasons why numerous well-known elite boarding schools chose to locate here; thus groups of uniformed students are seen all over the town. In addition to relaxing walks there are also some worthwhile excursions to the surrounding area, such as to Kempty Falls (15km/9mi) or to the picturesque little town of Dhanolti (28km/17mi). From Mussoorie's second-highest elevation, Gun Hill, which has a cableway running up it, in clear weather visitors will have splendid views of the snow-covered six-thousanders of the Himalaya to the north. Mussoorie can be reached from Dehra Dun by taxi or by bus.

Mussoorie

★ # Dharamsala (Dharmsala, Darmshala)

State: Himachal Pradesh
Population: 17,000
Distance: 520km/325mi north of Delhi

Altitude: 1250m/4100ft – 1800m/5900ft

Dharamsala is situated on the slopes stretching from the Kangra valley to the Dhauladhar range (4750m/15,584ft). The town, which thanks to its fresh air was declared a climatic health resort by the British, was completely destroyed by an earthquake in 1905.

Today it consists of two strikingly different parts. The lower town is dominated by shops, administrative buildings and bus stations and does not have much of interest to offer tourists. The upper town, McLeodganj, almost 600m/1970ft above the lower town, can be reached via a 9km/5.5mi road. McLeodganj has had a lot of Tibetan influence and is **home to the Dalai Lama**, the spiritual leader of Ti-

▶ VISITING DHARAMSALA

INFORMATION
Tourist Office
In McLeodganj
Tel. 018 92 – 22 12 32
Also take a look at the websites of
Himachal Pradesh Tourism
(www.himachaltourism.nic.in); for
specific information about hotels see
Himachal Tourism
(www.hptdc.nic.in).

GETTING THERE

There is a plane connection between
Dharamsala and Delhi. In addition
buses come here from Delhi, Manali,
Kangra, Pathankot and Mandi.

WHERE TO STAY/
WHERE TO EAT

▶ **Mid-range**
Chonor House
Near Thekchen Choeling Gompa
Tel. 018 92 – 22 10 06
Part of the Norbulinka Institute of
Tibetan Culture; very nice rooms and
an excellent restaurant.

▶ **Mid-range / Budget**
HPTDC Dhauladhar
Dharamsala
Tel. 018 92 – 22 49 26
Large rooms with balcony and great
views, restaurant, bar and pleasant
terrace.

betan Buddhists. Even though the town only has few architectural
monuments it is an important centre for all those interested in Tibetan culture.

What to See in Dharamsala

McLeodganj Upper Dharamsala owes its name to the British lieutenant-governor
David McLeod, who founded it in 1848. The church of St John in
the Wilderness with the tomb of
Lord Elgin, one of India's viceroys,
illustrates the significance of Dharamsala as a hill station for the British. It is a 15-minute walk from
the bus stop to the new Tsuglagkhang **Buddhist temple**, which
is located opposite the Dalai Lama's residence. Sermons are held
in this temple daily and visitors
can look at **thangkas**, religious
scroll pictures. When the Dalai Lama is here he preaches sermons in
the Tsuglagkhang.

Meditating monks

The **Tibetan library** on the road
from Dharamsala to McLeodganj

has some excellent, sometimes very old Buddhist texts as well as a collection of Buddha figures. This is a good place for anyone wanting to find out in more detail about Buddhism (open: Mon–Sat ☉ 9am–1pm and 2pm–5pm, closed on the 2nd and 4th Sat of the month).

Around Dharamsala

There are some good hiking trails around Dharamsala. Trips to Dal **Hiking trails** Lake (3km/2mi, 1837m/6027ft) are popular; it has good views of Dharamsala and the Kangra valley. The Tibetan children's village is also located by the lake. It looks after orphaned refugee children from Tibet. A hike via Bhagsunath (2km/1mi from McLeodganj), with a well and a temple, to Dharamkot (3km/2mi from Bhagsunath) offers quite varied scenery.

When it comes to mountaineering, Dharamsala has many diverse **Mountaineering** opportunities on offer. The pre-monsoon season from April to June is the most suitable. Information is available from the Himachal Tourism Development Cooperation, Kotwali Bazar, tel. 01892–22 42 12 or at www.hptdc.nic.in.

Haridwar

F 5

State: Uttarakhand
Population: 200,000

Altitude: 294m/965ft
Distance: 214km/133mi northeast of Delhi

At the foot of the Siwalik range, where the Ganges leaves the mountains and enters the plains, lies Haridwar, one of the subcontinent's most sacred places.

Every twelve years the **Kumbha Mela**, the most important festival of pilgrimage for Hindus, takes place here. Held every three years, it alternates between the cities of Allahabad, Nashik, Ujjain and Haridwar.

There is another legend associated with this small town: it is said that Prince Bhagirath lived here as an ascetic for many years to give salvation to the souls of his ancestors who had died at the hands of a curse by the sage Kapila. His penitence was answered by the god Shiva, who sent the Ganges to the Earth; its waters cleansed the souls of the 60,000 dead, thus freeing them (Baedeker Special p.290). All year round therefore, the ghats on the riverbanks are an **important destination for pilgrims**, who trust in the particularly cleansing and redemptive power of the Ganges at this spot. River water is packaged into large plastic containers for those who remained at home.

▶ VISITING HARIDWAR · RISHIKESH

INFORMATION
Uttarakhand Tourist Office
In Haridwar
Tel. 013 34 – 26 53 04

In Rishikesh
Railway Road
Tel. 01 35 – 243 02 09

See also the website of Uttarakhand
Tourism (www.uttaranchaltourism.net)

GETTING THERE
By rail or bus to Haridwar or Rishi-
kesh. The nearest airport is Jolly
Grant, 18km/11mi from Rishikesh.

SPORT AND OUTDOORS
Trekking
Uttarakhand Tourism has two organ-
izations that conduct trekking tours
and run accommodation: there is the
Garhwal Mandal Vikas Nigam
(www.gmvnl.com) for the Garhwal
region and the Kumaon Mandal Vikas
Nigam (www.kmvn.org) for the
Kumaon region.

Yoga
Rishikesh is a centre of yoga. There are
many ashrams in which yoga can be
practised and in which visitors can stay
for extended periods of time. Two

particularly famous ones are Shivananda Ashram founded by Swami
Shivananda in 1936 and the Academy
of Meditation formerly run by
Maharishi Mahesh Yogi.

WHERE TO STAY / WHERE TO EAT
▶ Luxury
Ananda in the Himalayas
Rishikesh, tel. 013 78 – 22 75 00
www.anandaspa.com
An internationally renowned spa with
all the comforts anyone could ask for,
including an Ayurveda centre, Thai
massages, reiki, yoga, many sports
opportunities and excellent cuisine.

▶ Budget
There are many ashrams offering
inexpensive accommodation in
Rishikesh.

**Tourist Bungalows owned by GMVN
(Garhwal Mandal Vikas Nigam)**
In Rishikesh
Tel. 01 35 – 243 30 02
Basic rooms with a balcony; garden
and restaurant are also available.

In Haridwar
Tel. 01 33 – 422 64 30
The equally basic rooms are clean, and
there is a restaurant.

Anyone wanting an insight into Hindu religious life, into the many
ceremonies and daily tasks in the lives of the believers, is in the right
place here. As is the case at all religious sites it is recommended to
use cameras only sparingly.

What to See in Haridwar

✱
Bathing steps

The bathing steps and particularly the **Harki Pairi Ghat**, where visitors can see one of Vishnu's footprints on a stone, are particularly in-

teresting. Bathing mainly takes place in the early hours of the morning, but people also gather by the river during the day and particularly in the evening to hold the **Aarti ceremony**, in which a small boat made of folded leaves is filled with flowers, incense sticks and an oil lamp and sent on its way.

As is to be expected, there are countless temples dedicated to various deities in and around Haridwar. In the centre of town is Mansa Devi Temple, in which one of the manifestations of Durga is worshipped. The temple can be reached via a cableway.

Mansa Devi Temple

A little way outside town, around 3km/2mi downriver, is Daksha Mahadevi Temple. It is said that Daksha, the father of Sati, held a sacrificial ceremony here, without, however, inviting Sati's husband, the god Shiva. Sati, according to tradition, was so outraged that she immolated herself.
In addition to a visit to these religious sites, a stroll through the winding, narrow streets of the old town is pleasant; it is so small that nobody will get lost.

Daksha Mahadevi Temple

Every twelve years the Kumbha Mela takes place in Haridwar, alternating with Allahabad, Nashik and Ujjain

Searching for spiritual experiences in Rishikesh

Rishikesh   F 4

Yoga, meditation and starting location for mountain excursions

While Haridwar is mostly visited by Indian pilgrims, Rishikesh (25km/15mi to the northeast) is also well known amongst Western fans of yoga and meditation. The name of the place, which is surrounded by the hills of the Siwalik range alludes to its purpose: **Rishikesh is the place of the Rishis, the wise, holy men**. On their search for inner wisdom and spiritual experiences more and more people from all around the world are drawn to the ashrams here. Even the Beatles came here seek the path within, under the guidance of their guru Maharishi Mahesh Yogi. However, a large number of Indian pilgrims also come here: their destinations are primarily the countless temples lining the banks of the Ganges and the holy places near the sources of the Ganges in the Himalayas, which can be reached by bus from Rishikesh.

Centres of pilgrimage at the sources of the Ganges and Yamuna   F 4

Places of pilgrimage

The places of pilgrimage along the headwaters of the Ganges and Yamuna are amongst the most important destinations **a devout Hindu**

should visit over the course of a lifetime. However, it is not just the sources that are considered particularly sacred; the entire mountain region is also thought of as a holy place, believed to be the favourite **residence of the gods** with its more than 50 peaks above 6000m/ 19,500ft. In the Mahabharata, the legendary Sanskrit epic, the famous Pandava brothers undertook pilgrimages to the sacred shrines in the high mountains on various occasions – that tourism has an age-old tradition here is undeniable.

Travelling to the places of pilgrimage is possible during the **season between the beginning of May and the end of October** and is organized by the national tourist offices in Rishikesh and Delhi. Those wanting to make their way to the sites independently by taxi should be aware that they get very busy during the summer months and so it is better to book accommodation with the tourist office in advance. It is also mandatory to be vaccinated against cholera if visiting Badrinath, Kedarnath, Gangotri and Yamunotri. There are no roads fit for traffic leading all the way to the sacred sites. The final miles usually have to be completed on foot.

Pilgrims at the holy river

Yamunotri (227km/141mi north of Rishikesh, 3185m/10,449ft) lies in the shadow of the 6315m/20,719ft Bandarpunch and is the place **where the Yamuna has its source**. The sacred river originates from a glacial lake at 4400m/14,436ft. On the left bank stands Yamuna Temple, which was built in the 19th century. There are a few hot springs nearby, which are the main attraction besides the temple in Yamunotri. The pilgrims use the boiling water of the »sun springs« (Surya Kund) to cook their rice. The temple is open from the beginning of May to Diwali (end of October). Yamunotri can be accessed via a vehicle road to Hanumanchatti (2400m/7874ft). From Hanumanchatti there is a footpath (approx. 13km/8mi) – mules and horses can be hired.

Surrounded by a cedar forest, the village of Gangotri (248km/154mi **Gangotri** north of Rishikesh, 3048m/10,000ft) is situated on the banks of the Bhaghirathi, one of the Ganges's headstreams.

It gets its name from the legendary Prince Bhaghirath, whose many years of asceticism were rewarded by Shiva, who sent the Ganges down to Earth. In order to dampen the power of the plummeting masses of water the god caught them with his curls. Thus they fell to Earth as many little streams and one of them was named after the famous prince (► Baedeker Special p.290). On the right bank of the Bhaghirathi stands **Ganga Temple**, on the left there are several dharamsalas (hostels for pilgrims) and ashrams. The main destination of the pilgrims is the **source of the Bhaghirathi**, known as Gaumuk (face of a cow), which originates on the Gangotri glacier around 19km/12mi above the village.

Opening hours: beginning of May–Diwali (end of October)

Kedarnath

Opening hours: beginning of May–Diwali (end of October)

The Shiva temple of Kedarnath(3584m/11,759ft, 226km/140mi northeast of Rishikesh) is situated in a high valley at the foot of the 7500m/24,606ft Kedarnath Dome. The shrine got its fame from the **Jyotirlingam**, the natural rock lingam that is worshipped here. The temple was probably built in the eighth century. Some of Gandhi's ashes were scattered 6km/4mi away in the lake known as **Gandhi Sarovar**.

Badarinath

Opening hours: beginning of May–Diwali (end of October)

Since time immemorial pilgrims have been coming to the small village of Badarinath (294km/183mi northeast of Rishikesh, 3133m/10,279ft) on the banks of the Alaknanda, another headstream of the Ganges. A shrine had already been built here in the early Buddhist period and in the eighth century the reformer Shankaracharya had a Shiva temple built, presumably in the same location. Today the **temple** is consecrated to the god Vishnu. In addition to a few hot springs, the particular appeal of the place is its **breathtaking scenery**. Badarinath is close to the Tibetan border and the snow-covered peaks of Nilkantha, Nar and Narayan tower overhead. It is not far from here to the famous Valley of Flowers (see below).

One worthwhile excursion would be to visit the village of **Mana** 4km/2.5mi away, the last place before the Tibetan border. The Vasudhara Falls are in the vicinity. The source of the Alaknanda is located around 15km/9mi above Badarinath at the Alakapuri glacier. The path leading up to it is quite difficult to negotiate.

Along the road from Badarinath to Josimath is **Lake Hemkund**, a glacial lake that is sacred to Sikhs. There is a small temple on its shore, where master Govind Singh is said to have meditated.

Garhwal and the Kumaon region

Tip Trekking tours are organized by Garhwal Mandal Vikas Nigam Ltd in Rishikesh. Bookings can be made via the national tourist offices in Delhi, Kolkata and Mumbai. The ideal season is before and after the monsoon (April–May and September–October).

Valley of Flowers Flower lovers all around the world have heard of the 10km/6mi Valley of Flowers, situated at an altitude of more than 3000m/9800ft. This is a worthwhile place to visit during the monsoon months; the display of colour of the more than 2000 species, some of which are very rare, is especially beautiful in August.

The Kumaon region, whose eastern border meets Nepal, is a popular **Kumaon** holiday spot for Indian tourists in search of a refuge from the hot **mountains** summer months. The most important holiday towns are Nainital, Almora and Ranikhet. In addition the ► Corbett and Dudhwa national parks are located here.

The small town of **Nainital** (around 150km/95mi east of Rishikesh, 1933m/6342ft) is a particular attraction for Indian tourists as it has a big range of sports and leisure activities to offer. The governmental enterprise Kumaon Mandal Vikas Nigam runs organized tours in the surrounding area.

By the late 15th century **Almora** (1646m/5400ft), 67km/42mi from Nainital, was the capital of the Chand kingdom. Numerous hiking trails and viewpoints surround the town, which also has a number of cultural sights to offer itself. These include for example the old temples of Kasa Devi (8km/5mi) and Chital (6km/4mi), the sun temple of Katarmal (17km/11mi) somewhat further out of town, as well as a group of temples that the Chand rulers had built in Jageshwar (34km/21mi).

Ranikhet (1829m/6000ft) is a particularly picturesque mountain town with good opportunities for excursions and a nice panoramic view of the western Himalaya.

Jammu and Kashmir (state)

Area: 222,236 sq km/85,806 sq mi　　**Population:** 10.1 million
Capital: Srinagar

The region of Jammu and Kashmir is dominated by the high Himalaya mountains. This region can be subdivided into the following seven geographic regions. From the southwest to the northeast these are the lowlands, the foothills, the Pir Panjal range, the Kashmir plateau, the Central Himalaya, the upper Indus valley and the Karakorum mountain range.

The narrow plain gets less than 500mm/20in of rain a year, meaning its vegetation is quite sparse. The foothills rise up from 600m/1950ft–2250m/7400ft. They receive more rainfall and the rivers have created some very fertile valleys. The Pir Panjal range reaches elevations of up to 5000m/16,400ft and above the tree line there is nothing but pastureland. The Kashmir plateau, which has an average altitude of 1800m/5900ft, is blessed with the sediment-rich soil of the Jhelum river and is very fertile. Cedar forests, pines, walnut trees and rhododendron meadows shape the landscape. The Central Himalaya, with peaks of more than 6500m/21,300ft and remote valleys, is very arid. The monsoon climate gradually transforms into continental climate here. The upper Indus valley, the location of the town of Leh, is notorious for its extreme climate, which is characteristically cold and dry. Alpine vegetation dominates here. The Karakorum mountains contain some of the world's highest peaks and are also called the »**Roof of the World**«. As if in contrast to the peaceful landscape, the region's political situation is very unstable. Daily life here has been marked by bomb attacks and military raids for decades.

Legend   According to legend the land was once ruled by a water demon, who terrorized the region. However, the powerful Rishi Kashyapa managed to conquer the demon by draining the lakes, which made later settlement possible. For this reason the area was called Kashyapamar, which later became Kashmir.

History   India's northernmost region came under the rule of Indian kings early on. It was already part of the large Ashokan Empire in the third century. Buddhism was Kashmir's state religion, too. During the 13th and 14th centuries the region fell under Muslim rule, causing Islam to spread. The great Mughal ruler Akbar managed to annex Kashmir to his empire in 1586. Akbar had the Hari Parbat Fort built in Srinagar and his son Jehangir also commissioned the construction of many buildings. Kashmir experienced an almost 200-year golden age. Since the Mughal rulers were never able to get used to Delhi's heat they built roads to Kashmir so they could escape the hot Indian summers. They were the first to discover this region as a hill station and they beautified it by laying out gardens. The British and rich Indians later followed suit.

After Mughal rule in Kashmir came to an end, the region was conquered by the Afghan ruler Ahmad Shah Abdali in the mid-18th century. Later, from 1818 onwards, the region fell into the hands of the Sikh king Maharaja Ranjit Singh. After the first Anglo-Sikh War (1845–46) the British won influence over Kashmir. The British East India Company sold Kashmir for 7.5 million rupees to the King of Jammu, Gulab Singh, in 1846. His realm consisted of Jammu and Kashmir as well as Ladakh and Baltistan.

When India and Pakistan became independent states in August 1947, the Maharaja of Kashmir, Hari Singh, was undecided to which state he wanted to belong. A short while later the tribal populations of Baltistan and Gilgit managed to separate from Jammu and Kashmir and join Pakistan. At the same time the Muslims also demanded that Jammu and Kashmir join Pakistan, and Pakistani troops invaded Kashmir. Faced with this situation, the Maharaja of Jammu and Kashmir asked the Indian armed forces for help.

Indian military units were able to drive out the Pakistani troops, and the Pakistani attempt to annexe the region failed. To this day India and Pakistan have not been able to solve the Kashmir question. No

The Dal lake in Srinagar mainly appears to consist of a labyrinth of canals, lotus ponds and silting

agreement has been found as to where the border should run. Three wars, in 1948, 1965 and 1971, have not resulted in any change in this situation.

Kashmir is currently still a place where violent confrontations take place between militant separatist groups and the Indian army. **Visiting this region is therefore risky.**

Current situation

✱ Srinagar   D 2

Srinagar (population 980,000) at the heart of the Kashmir plateau has more to offer than just forts and mosques and some very attractive Mughal gardens. It has fresh air and many places of natural beauty. According to legend this place, which is situated along the old inner-Asian trading route, had already seen the founding of a town called Srinagri by Emperor Ashoka before the start of the Common Era. There is a historical account of a town being founded by King Raja Pravarasen in the sixth century. After centuries of serious fighting between Hindu and Muslim rulers the town was incorporated into the Islamic Empire by Shah Mir. Srinagar experienced a golden age after Kashmir was conquered by Akbar (1568). The various Mughal rulers from Delhi laid out gardens which have retained their beauty to this day.

Mughal gardens and other places of natural beauty

★ ★ **Townscape**	The picturesque town on the meandering Jhelum river is surrounded by green mountains and lakes. The **Dal lake** and the Nagin lake with their houseboats, floating markets and countless lotus flowers are a major reason that Srinagar is one of northern India's most attractive towns. The **houseboats** on the waterways are particularly famous. Some of them are quite luxurious. One of the nicest experiences in Srinagar is taking a trip on one of the narrow boats known as shikara.
Old town	Srinagar's old town extends to both sides of the Jhelum river. The two parts of town are connected by seven bridges (kadal).
Shah-i-Hamadan mosque	Shah-i-Hamadan, **Srinagar's oldest mosque**, is situated on the eastern bank of the Jhelum river and was built by Sultan Qutab-ud-din.
★ **Mughal gardens**	The Mughal rulers who came to Kashmir to escape Delhi's heat had many symmetrical gardens with fountains laid out, which are still well-preserved today. When the British commissioned gardens for the President's Palace, Rashtrapati Bhavan, when New Delhi was being built, they were inspired by the gardens in Kashmir. The following are amongst the most important gardens.

The garden laid out by Mughal ruler Jehangir for his beloved wife Nur Jahan in 1619, **Shalimar Bagh** (16km/10mi northeast of the centre) is one of the most beautiful in the whole of Srinagar. At the foot of the Zabarvan massif opposite the eastern shore of the Dal lake is the Garden of Joy, **Nishat Bagh** (11km/7mi northeast of the centre), which was laid out by the brother of Queen Nur Jahan. Compared to the others, **Chasma Shahi** is rather modest in size at 108m/118yd x 38m/42yd. It was laid out by Ali Mardan Khan around a spring said to have healing powers in 1642. The former Buddhist monastery of **Pari Mahal** is not far from Chasma Shahi. It was transformed into a place of learning by Shah Jahan's oldest son, Dara Sikah.

i Trouble spot

■ Srinagar, Kashmir's capital, has been a political trouble spot for decades. Fighting between separatists demanding independence and the Indian army means there are frequent violent incidents. Before planning to visit Srinagar it is essential to obtain detailed information about the political situation. There is a security risk for anyone travelling to this region. Information about safety can be obtained from Indian embassies and high commissions; further tourist information is available on the website of Jammu and Kashmir Tourism (www.jktourism.com).

Hazrat-bal-Dargah	The large mosque made of white marble, Hazrat-bal-Dargah, is **one of the most important religious centres for Muslims**. One of the Prophet Muhammad's beard hairs is kept here. It is said to have been brought here from Biajpur in Karnataka by Khwaja Noor-ud-din in 1700.

Ladakh

State: Jammu and Kashmir

Distance: approx. 890km/555mi north-east of Delhi

This region in India's far north formerly known as West Tibet is now called La-dvag (land of passes). The extremely barren region only drops to 3000m/9800ft at its lowest point.

In the north the region is bounded by the mountains of the Karakorum and in the south and west by the Himalayan massif. Ladakh has the world's largest glacier outside the polar regions. The climate is marked by extreme aridity, with annual precipitation only 50mm/2in on average. The days are extremely hot, but during winter nights temperatures can drop to -50°C/-58°F. In contrast to the spectacular snow-covered mountain landscape of the Himalaya, Ladakh is characterized by a **stony landscape**, which is only occasionally interrupted by houses or monasteries. The manmade stone walls, which can be up to 1km/0.6mi long, are also part of the landscape. The uppermost stones of these so-called **mani walls** have the most significant and oldest mantra of Tibetan Buddhism engraved in them. The syllables »om mani padme hum« (Sanskrit, literally »OM«, jewel in the lotus) express the fundamental attitude of empathy; their recital is the desire to be liberated to Nirvana. These stones were usually donated by dignitaries.

Mani stones bearing the mystical formula »Om Mani Padme Hum«

History   The region was probably already inhabited thousands of years ago by nomadic pastoralists. It grew in significance later on as a trading post along the Silk Road. Around the 10th century the Thi dynasty ruled over Ladakh from its capital of Shey, but the Tibetan Buddhists also had great influence over the area and built more than 100 monasteries (gompas).

In 1533 Soyang Namgyal managed to unite this region all the way to Lhasa and create a kingdom. This dynasty was put under pressure by Tibet's fifth Dalai Lama, Nawang Lobsang Gyatso (1617–82) with Mongolian support. It was only with the help of the Mughal rulers from Kashmir that Delegs Namgyal managed to drive off the conquerors. However, he had to pay dearly for this assistance: Ladakh became dependent on the Mughals and later it fell under British rule.

Ladakh is the only part of what was once Tibet that has escaped the Chinese occupation of 1950. While the original Tibetan culture and

 VISITING LADAKH

INFORMATION

Director of Tourism
Leh
Tel. 019 82 – 25 22 97

Jammu and Kashmir Tourist Office
Delhi
512-512A Tolstoy House
Tolstoy Marg
Connaught Place
Tel. 011 – 23 71 49 48
www.jktourism.com

GETTING THERE

During the summer months (approx. end of June–mid-September) the Manali Leh Highway is open; taxis and buses drive along the breathtaking route, which is almost 500km/310mi in length. In addition there is a regular flight service between Delhi and Leh. However, the flights are cancelled in poor weather. Leh has the world's highest airport (3505m/11,500ft), thus anyone wanting to travel by air should plan for this difference in altitude and take it easy for the first few days.

EVENTS

Ladakh Festival (Aug / Sept)

SHOPPING

There is a very large selection of semiprecious stones (particularly turquoise), jewellery and thangkas on sale here.

WHERE TO STAY / WHERE TO EAT
► Mid-range / Budget
Lumbini
Fort Road
Tel. 019 82 – 25 25 28
Pleasant rooms, food included in the price.

Omasila
Changspa
Tel. 019 82 – 25 21 19
Terrace with a great view, good restaurant.

Padma
Ghirghir / Fort Road
Tel. 019 82 – 25 26 30
Rooms of various price categories with garden and roof terrace restaurant.

Instruction in Buddha's teachings

Tibetan Buddhism are persecuted with ruthless severity in occupied Tibet, they have been preserved in Ladakh to this day. Since the 1962 border conflict between China and India, Indian armed forces have been stationed in Ladakh.

Among the region's most important sites are Leh, the palace of Stok and the Shey and Tikse monasteries.

Destinations

✳ Leh   E 2

The once rich town of Leh is situated on the fertile floodplain of the upper Indus. Although located on the Silk Road, the town has lost its function as a trading post for caravans. Today Leh is a **military base for Indian troops** defending the border from China. It is best not to venture too far away from the main roads; those visitors that do are liable to be mistaken for spies and arrested. Leh is an ideal starting location for discovering many monasteries in Ladakh.

Old capital of Ladakh

History	Leh became King Senge Namgyal's new capital in the 17th century when, for strategic reasons, he moved it here from Shey only 15km/9mi away. Thanks to its location along the Silk Road, Leh quickly became an affluent town. However, when the Chinese borders were closed in 1950 as a result of tension with India, Leh lost its function as a trading post. Since Ladakh was opened to tourists in 1974 the main visitors to Leh and the surrounding monasteries have been **backpackers**.
Leh Khar Palace	Standing on Mount Tsemo is the old eight-storey palace of the king of Ladakh, constructed under King Senge Namgyal **and modelled on the famous Potala Palace in Lhasa**. It was built in the 16th century when Ladakh oriented itself more closely towards Tibet during a time when it was religiously and culturally dominated by the Gelug sect. It was already severely damaged in 1815 by Kashmiri attacks, and renovation work is progressing only very slowly. There are some old thangkas, Buddha statues and depictions of the goddess Durga on display on the ground floor.
Namgyal Tsemo Gompa ⏀	Above the palace, on the »mountain of victory«, is the Namgyal Tsemo Gompa, a monastery with its Maitreya Temple and its Gonkhang, dedicated to the guardian divinities. The monastery is only open in the mornings from 7am to 9am and sometimes in the afternoons from 5pm. There is a lovely view from the monastery of the town and the mountains.

Around Leh

Sankar Gompa	This monastery 2km/1mi from Leh is the centre of the Gelug sect. The building contains wall paintings and a hundred-head depiction of Avalokiteshvrara.
Stok Palace	Around 16km/10mi south of Leh is Stok Palace. A part of the four-storey palace, which was built in the 19th century, is still inhabited by the royal family. One of the wings houses a very worthwhile museum with attractive thangkas and Buddhist ritual objects.
Shey	The palace and temple of Shey (15km/9mi southeast of Leh), Ladakh's old capital, are largely in ruins. However, in addition to an impressive Buddha statue there are also some restored wall paintings to be admired in the temple. In addition Shey has a monastery as well as Buddha statues carved from the rock.
✱ **Tikse**	Around 19km/12mi southeast of Leh there is a **15th-century Tibetan monastery**. The impressive gompa, which stands atop a mountain, has a breathtaking view of the valley. In its interior the monastery houses **Ladakh's largest golden Buddha**. To the right of the monastery courtyard is the new Maitreya Temple, which was inaugurated

Stony path to Tikse monastery

by the Dalai Lama in 1980. Across the courtyard is the somewhat higher Chokhang (Dharma Hall) with wall paintings portraying the bhavacakra, the Tibetan calendar and Buddha. Adjoining the Chokhang is Tsangkhang (Hall of the Peaceful Deity) with depictions of Shakyamuni, Maitreya and the eleven-headed Avalokiteshvara. Immediately to the right is the main Chokhang with a red façade. Inside there are wall paintings and statues dating back to pre-Buddhist history as well as from the Buddhist canon. South of the monastery complex are the **Dukhang Karpo** (White Assembly Hall) with old Tibetan paintings and **Chomo Lhakhang** (Nun Temple) somewhat higher up, both of which are worth a visit.

Ladakh's largest monastery, the Hemis Gompa, is located 45km/ 28mi south of Leh. It is famous for the **masked dances** (Cham dances) that illustrate Buddhist history and take place in June–July. Every twelve years a huge **thangka** is unrolled here. The next time will be in 2016. The monastery was founded by the Tibetan monk Stagtsang Raspa in 1638. It consists of a large complex of buildings behind a large monastery courtyard. The rooms contain ritual objects, Buddha statues and wall paintings. The pictures in the Old Temple (Lhakhang Nyingpa) show moments from the life of the historical Buddha as well as the family tree of the sect's saints. The lhakhang in the northeast has some attractive Buddha statues on display.

Hemis Gompa

✳ Lucknow

Capital of Uttar Pradesh
Population: 2.5 million

Altitude: 123m/404ft
Distance: 514km/319mi north of Delhi

The capital of Uttar Pradesh has some historical and political significance, but its historical attractions, usually remains from the Mughal Empire, cannot compete with those of ►Delhi or ►Agra. However, all those who enjoy northern India, and Muslim architecture in particular, will find this city on the banks of the Gomti has some interesting buildings in store.

Lucknow is a busy city with wide avenues and parks, but also with winding bazaar districts. The Urdu spoken here is still considered exemplary. In other respects this city also shows its Muslim character by its Shiite population, which is unusually high for India. Lucknow gained significance from 1775 as the **capital of the Nawabs of Oudh**, former provincial governors of the Mughal Empire, who made themselves independent when that empire fell. Lucknow was the centre of the courtly culture, which was already falling apart, for almost 100 years until the British dethroned the last ruler, Wajid Ali Shah in 1856, annexing the province of Oudh and stationing themselves here. Just a few years later the city became the centre of attention once again, this time as the **scene of the Indian Mutiny**, the revolt of Indian troops against the British.

What to See in Lucknow

There are attractions all over the city, but the most important ones are clustered in the northwest. Bara Imambara, a **three-storey mausoleum** built by Nawab Asaf-ud-Daula in the Chowk bazaar district (1775–97) as the family tomb. The mausoleum is accessed via the huge »**Turkish Gate«, Rumi Darwaza**, which is modelled on the Sublime Porte in Istanbul. The 50m/55yd long, 16m/17yd wide, 15m/49ft high building has an impressive arched roof. A stairway leads up to the labyrinthine first floor with its many narrow hallways.

On the west of the courtyard stands **Asafi Mosque** (entry for Muslims only), which has a minaret on either side.

Somewhat to the northwest of Rumi Darwaza is the 67m/220ft bell tower from the year 1881 and directly opposite is the Hussainabad Imambara, also called Chota (small) as opposed to Bara (large) Imambara (1837–42). This is the **tomb of the ruler Ali Shah,**

✳
Bara Imambara

🕐
Opening hours:
daily 6am–5pm

✳
Hussainabad Imambara

🕐
Opening hours:
daily 6am–5pm

← *Bara Imambara in Lucknow*

Lucknow Map

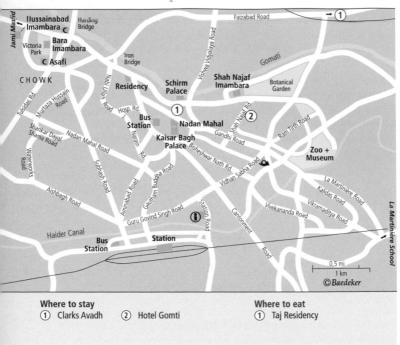

Where to stay
① Clarks Avadh ② Hotel Gomti

Where to eat
① Taj Residency

which is adorned with many towers and minarets. The courtyard surrounding the tomb has a pool with small replicas of the Taj Mahal on either side.

Immediately to the west is the Jama Masjid with three domes and two minarets. Admission is reserved for Muslims only.

Residency Around 3km/2mi to the southeast is the Residency (1800), which was besieged for months during the great mutiny by Indian troops in 1857. Impact holes made by the cannon balls during this event can still clearly be seen.

Shah Najaf Imambara Shah Najaf Imambara, the tomb of Ghazi-ud-Din Haidar, was built in 1827 and named after a Shiite place of pilgrimage in modern-day Iraq. The majority of the valuable interior decoration and furnishing has fallen victim to looting (open: 8am–5pm).

Nadan Mahal The Nadan Mahal, the tomb of Lucknow's first governor, dates back to around 1600. The red sandstone dome is an example of early Mughal architecture.

⏵ VISITING LUCKNOW

INFORMATION

Tourist Office of UP Tourism
10, Station Road
Tel. 05 22 – 263 81 05
www.up-tourism.com

WHERE TO EAT

► Expensive

① *Taj Residency*
Gomti Nagar
Tel. 05 22 – 239 39 39
Excellent Avadhi cuisine (local, famous Lucknow cuisine); the kebabs are a must!

WHERE TO STAY

► Luxury

① *Hotel Clarks Avadh*
8 M. G. Marg,
Tel. 0522-262 0131
Centrally located modern hotel with good food.

► Budget

② *UPSTDC Hotel Gomti*
6, Sapru Marg
Tel. 05 22 – 221 47 08
Run by the Uttar Pradesh State Tourism Development Corporation, clean rooms.

A few yards east of the Nadan Mahal is the Sola Khamba. The red sandstone pavilion houses five graves and also dates back to the early Mughal period.

Sola Khamba

Another remarkable building here is the La Martinière School, which was donated by the Frenchman Claude Martin, who originally had wanted to build his house here but died before its completion. The building, which is an architecturally colourful mix of styles, is now a private school. Kim, the eponymous hero of Kipling's novel, was among its early »alumni«.

La Martinière School

The State Museum has significant collections from the Kushana and Gupta periods (open: 10.30am–4.30pm, closed Mon). The gallery displays portraits of the Nawabs of Oudh (open: 10am–5pm).

Museums
⏱
⏱

★ Shimla

E 4

Capital of Himachal Pradesh
Population: 123,000

Altitude: 2160m/7087ft–2213m/7260ft
Distance: 280km/174mi north of Delhi

Shimla, located at an altitude of more than 2000m/7000ft, is one of India's most popular hill stations and offers a broad spectrum of sports activities ranging from fishing to hiking, riding, skiing and golfing. This place is frequented by large numbers of tourists during the high season from April to June.

The town is also an important trading centre for agricultural products from Himachal Pradesh (especially fruit) and for handicrafts. Carpets, woollen shawls, embroidered winter clothes and silver jewellery from Shimla are so sought after all over India that almost nobody who comes to the town leaves without making some purchases.

 VISITING SHIMLA · KULLU VALLEY · CHAMBA

INFORMATION

Shimla
Tourist office by the station or at the Victory Tunnel
Tel. 01 77 – 265 45 89

Manali
The Mall
Tel. 01 91 – 25 21 75

Dahalpur
Tel. 019 02 – 22 23 49

GETTING THERE
Bus connections from Delhi and Chandigarh for example, narrow-gauge railway from Kalka.

SHOPPING
Himachal Pradesh is famous for its woollen products: shawls, pullovers, blankets and much more can be bought in Shimla and the surrounding area directly from the makers.

TREKKING
Himachal Pradesh Tourism offers a large number of tours, which can all be viewed and booked on their website:
www.himachaltourism.nic.in

WHERE TO EAT / WHERE TO STAY
▶ Luxury
Woodville Palace Resorts
Raj Bhavan Road
Shimla
Tel. 01 77 – 262 39 19

Nice building full of character dating back to the 1930s with a stylish interior and a large garden.

Chapslee
Lakkar Bazaar
Shimla
Tel. 01 77 – 280 25 42
Nice colonial building that keeps the days of the Raj alive; located on the outskirts of town in green surroundings.

▶ Mid-range / Budget
White
Lakkar Bazaar
Shimla
Tel. 01 77 – 265 61 36
Centrally located with pleasant rooms and good views.

HPTDC Hotel Rohtang Manalsu
Manali
Tel. 019 02 – 25 23 31
On the road to Hadimba Temple with a view of the old village of Vashisht.

HPTDC Hotel Sarvari
Kullu
Tel. 01 92 – 22 24 71
Rooms in various price categories, restaurant, bar, good view.

HPTDC Hotel Iravati
In Chamba
Tel. 018 99 – 226 71
Centrally located accommodation with a garden and restaurant.

The name of this relatively young town probably comes from Shya- **History**
mala, a local form of the goddess Durga. Until 150 years ago there
was nothing but a small village here. From 1822 onwards the British,
in search of a refuge from the hot Indian summers, built the first sol-
id houses here. Later they even moved their capital to Shimla for
some months each year. When the railway line was built in 1904 the
speedy development of the sleepy village became inevitable. **Until the
First World War Shimla was closed to Indians because the Europeans wanted to keep themselves to themselves**. Only Indian servants were permitted. After India became independent in 1947 Shimla
was **temporarily proclaimed the capital of Punjab**, until the new city
of ►Chandigarh was built. After new borders had been agreed, Himachal Pradesh was made into a new state with Shimla as its capital
in 1966.

What to See in and around Shimla   E 4

Shimla is situated at the top of a 12km/7mi ridge that connects sev- **The Mall**
eral mountains. The roads »The Mall« and »Ridge«, which form the
heart of the town, help with orientation. There are many hotels,
banks, shops and restaurants along these streets and since they are
pedestrianized they are ideal for a relaxed stroll. Those who have arrived in Shimla by car, bus or train can use a tourist lift, which during the day brings tourists from Cart Road in the lower town to The
Mall higher up.

The place where The Mall and Ridge meet is called Scandal Point. It **Scandal Point**
got its name because the daughter of a British officer, who had fallen
in love with an Indian prince, ran away with her lover from here. Today this place, which still has a few old colonial buildings from the
British period, is a popular **meeting place for tourists**.

Himachal State Museum, situated to the west of The Mall, was **Himachal State**
opened in 1975. It has an extensive collection of regional arts and **Museum**
crafts. The miniatures from the Pahari school and the embroidered
textiles are particularly interesting.

Viceroy Lord Dufferin had this British-style structure built in 1888; **Viceregal Lodge**
it is the largest monument of the colonial era. During the hot sum-
mer months Britain's largest colony was ruled from here. The house
can be viewed in the context of a guided tour.

Situated at the town's highest point, , at an altitude of 2680m/8793ft, **Jakhu Temple**
is Jakhu Temple, consecrated to Hanuman, the monkey god, who is
popular in the whole of India. There are live monkeys here too,
which the Indian pilgrims like to feed. The 2km/1mi path from The
Mall to the viewing point takes around half an hour. On clear days
the snow-covered Himalayan peaks can be seen.

Around Shimla   **Glen** (4km/2.5mi west of the centre) is an idyllic destination (1830m/6004ft) in a forest by a clear river. The small town of **Kufri** (2501m/8205ft) is around 16km/10mi east of Shimla (on the road to Rampur). The **ski pistes** in the vicinity of the winter sports resort are some of the best in all of India. There is an excellent golf course in **Naldera** (30km/20mi northeast of Shimla).

Kullu Valley   E 4

The idyllic valley at the southern edge of the Himalayan mountains is amongst northern India's best hiking regions. It is around 500km/ 310mi from the capital Delhi and can be reached relatively quickly. The direction of the valley is determined by the watercourse of the Beas river. It has a length of around 80km/50mi, from Larji (958m/ 3143ft) in the south to the town of Manali (2000m/6562ft) in the north. Kullu Valley is **very popular amongst trekking tourists** as well as an important station on the way to the remote high valleys of Lahaul and Spiti. The tourist centre is Manali, but the other towns along the route Mandi – Kullu – Manali also see their share of tourism.

Mandi   The town of Mandi has a population of approx. 30,000 and is located 160km/100mi north of Shimla. It has always been an important station on the way to Kullu Valley. Its name, meaning market, points to its traditional role as a trading and reloading point. Among Mandi's shrines worth taking a look at are Bhutnath Temple and Triloknath Temple.
The drive up to **Lake Rewalsar** (25km/15mi southwest of Mandi) at an altitude of 2000m/6562ft is accompanied by beautiful views of unspoilt mountain landscape. Three religious communities have sacred sites representing their faith in this small town: there is a Buddhist monastery, a Sikh temple and a Hindu temple.

Kullu   Kullu (1,219m/4,000ft; population 15,000) is the capital of the district of the same name. The town consists of two different parts: Sultanpur, where the administrative buildings, hotels and the hospital are located and Akhara Bazar, the market area by the river. Apart from a few temples in the vicinity, Kullu does not have any special attractions.
Above the main bus station is **Raghunath Temple**, the most significant religious site in Kullu. The most important event in Kullu is the

★

Dussera ►   annual Dussera Festival, held in September / October, which attracts both the locals from the surrounding mountain villages and tourists. After a ceremonial procession to the temple the images of Raghunath, the main deity of Kullu Valley, and the other approx. 360 local deities are displayed in a richly adorned tent on the festival field (maidan) for the duration of the celebrations (► Baedeker Special p.392).

Terraced fields around Shimla

High up above the valley, around 10km/6mi east of Kullu, there is a temple consecrated to Shiva towering atop a rock up which there is a steep path. Built during the middle of the eighth century, it is thought to be the region's oldest temple. Its façade is decorated with some attractive representations of various deities. The north side of **Biljaura Mahadev Temple** is adorned by a depiction of an eight-armed Mahishasuramardini, the south side by a Ganesha sculpture. The entrance, as is the case with so many temples, is covered in images of Ganga and Yamuna, which are meant to symbolically cleanse the entering believers.

The mountain village of **Manikaran** 45km/28mi east of Kullu in the Parvati valley is known for its **sulphurous hot springs**. Since healing powers are attributed to the hot spring water there are bathing facilities available here (separate for men and women).

Around 25km/25mi north of Kullu, at an altitude of 1760m/5774ft, lies the town of Naggar. There is a **stunning view** to be had of Kullu Valley from up here. It is hard to believe that the small, still very quiet village was the capital of the small kingdom for more than 1000 years. The old palace, situated on a mountain ridge, was renovated by a British major in 1846 and is now being used as a hotel. Naggar's most important religious sites are Gaurishankar Temple, the Vishnu temple and the Krishna temple, which are all in the vicinity of the palace. The **Roerich Museum** above the former resi-

✷
◀ Naggar

dence is named after the Russian artist Nicolaus Roerich (1874–1947), who left Russia after the First World War and chose Naggar as his new home.

Manali Thanks to its good infrastructure and location at the foot of the Rohtang Pass, the northernmost town in Kullu Valley (1926m/6319ft; population 2600) is considered the ideal starting point for hikes in the mountainous world of the Himalayan foothills. The increasing influx of tourists has meant that Manali is no longer the peaceful hill station it once was and the townscape has become increasingly dominated by modern concrete buildings.

In the immediate vicinity of the small mountain town the peaks of Indrasan Deo Tibba (6001m/19,688ft), Hanuman Tibba (5950m/19,521ft), Makar Beh (6052m/19,856ft) and Shiker Beh (6200m/20,341ft) rise up to the sky. They can be climbed in small groups. The equipment necessary for such **mountain tours** can be bought or rented from the **Mountaineering Institute** on the Mahali–Naggar Road. Since some of the area around Manali is a restricted military zone visitors are strongly advised to hire an experienced mountain

The only way to the Lahaul valley is across Rohtang Pass

guide, which the institute will find for a fixed price. It is difficult to find porters for these expeditions. However, they can also be organized by the Mountaineering Institute or by one of the many trekking agencies, as long as the organization is informed in advance. The local tourist office will also have more information.

According to legend, Bhima, one of the Pandava brothers, is said to have killed the demon Hadimb here and married his sister Hadimba, who had been terrorized by the demon. The **Temple of Hadimba Devi** was built in her honour. The three-storey pagoda in the middle of a cedar forest was built by Raja Bahadur Singh in the 16th century. The temple's columns and entrance gates are richly adorned with wood carvings. The interior, in which the goddess's footprints are worshipped, seems comparatively bare.

The place in the old part of Manali, where **Manu Temple** stands, is believed to be the place where Manu, the first person on Earth, set foot on land after the great flood, which he survived in a boat. It is the only temple in India that is dedicated to him.

The pretty village of **Vashisht** around 4km/2.5miManali northeast of Manali is mainly visited because of its many hot **sulphurous springs**, which are said to have healing powers. The old stone temple near the springs is dedicated to the saint Vashisha Muni.   **Around Manali**

Rohtang Pass (51km/32mi north of Manali, 4112m/13,491ft) on the route to Keylong is **the only way into the Lahaul valley**. The pass is open from June to September. Keylong (117km/73mi north) can be reached via an asphalt track and has some monasteries and gompas. The appeal of the Lahaul valley on the border to Tibet lies, despite its barrenness, in its large glaciers that are surrounded by high, snow-covered mountains.

◄ Rohtang Pass

Chamba   E 3

The idyllic town of Chamba, situated on the southern bank of the Ravi river (approx. 240km/150mi northwest of Shimla) at an altitude of 2380m/7808ft, is considered a **good starting location for trekking tours** to the surrounding area. During the summer months the gaddis (shepherds) come here to let their animals graze on the mountain meadows. There is a road from Dalhousie to Chamba 26km/16mi away, making it easy to access. Chamba can look back on a **history going back more than 1000 years**. The »middle kingdom«, founded in the ninth century, was conquered by Sikhs in the beginning of the 19th century. Its isolated location has led to a synthesis of Hinduism with the religions of the mountain peoples. The city has six stone temples in honour of Shiva and Vishnu.

The **Rang Mahal**, the palace built by Umed Singh in the 18th century, contains some nice wall paintings depicting scenes from the Krishna legend. The temples worth visiting here are **Lakshmi Narayan Temple**, in honour of Vishnu, and Hariraya Temple.

🕐 The **Bhuri Singh Museum** has a good collection of miniatures from the Kangra and Basholi schools (open: daily except Sun, 10am–5pm).

Trekking tours
In the north, the **Lauhal valley** can be reached via three high passes, Kalicho, Kugti and Chobia. There is a nice three-day trek from **Bharmaur** (60km/37mi southeast of Chamba, 1981m/6499ft) to Lake Manimahesh (3950m/12,959ft).

Chamba is the starting point for a trek over Kugti Pass (5215m/17,100ft) **to Manali** (Kullu Valley). This trek takes around twelve days to complete. Along the way there are Hindu temples, Buddhist monasteries, deodar forests and snow-covered mountains. This trek is demanding and requires a good level of fitness as well as good equipment. The best time to go is from April to August (►Practicalities, Sport and Outdoors). Information is available at the following websites: www.himachaltourism.nic.in and www.hptdc.nic.in.

★ ★ Varanasi (Benares)

H 7

State: Uttar Pradesh	**Altitude:** 80m/262ft
Population: 1.03 million	**Distance:** 677km/421mi west of Kolkata

The holiest of Hindu cities is situated on the western banks of the Ganges. With its narrow alleys, bazaars and countless temples, Varanasi plays a similar role Mecca does for Muslims, and the busy city is a magnet for Indian tourists.

History
Varanasi is **one of the oldest inhabited cities in the world**. Settlements existed here as long as 3000 years ago. Like no other region the area around Varanasi is associated with Indian religions. Not far from this holiest of Hindu cities is Sarnath, an important centre of pilgrimage for Buddhists. Varanasi gets its name from the two rivers, Varuna and Assi, which both flow into the Ganges here. Indians also know this city as Kashi, the city of spiritual light. The British called it **Benares**.

Since the city was conquered several times and razed to the ground by Muslim troops, most of Varanasi's temples and other buildings have been built fairly recently. Only after the creation of the Hindu Maratha Empire under Shivaji (1627–80) were more Hindu temples built. Almost all of Varanasi's important buildings date from the 18th century or later. Nevertheless Mark Twain wrote this about Varanasi when he travelled through India in the late 19th century: »Benares is older than history, older than tradition, older even than legend, and looks twice as old as all of them put together.«

On the ghats of the Ganges →

! Baedeker TIP

A boat trip at dawn
One of the unforgettable experiences in Varanasi is a boat trip on the Ganges at dawn, ideally from Assi Ghat to Manikarnika Ghat; from there visitors can walk back along the ghats to the starting point.

India's most spiritual city

According to Hindu belief it is thought to be particularly commendable to have visited this holy city at least once in a lifetime and to **wash off all sins by bathing in the Ganges**. Those who are fortunate enough to die on the banks of the Ganges are guaranteed salvation, which is why it has always been the case that many old Hindus make a pilgrimage here. The city is home to approximately 50,000 Brahmins, members of the top priestly caste. Many of them work, like their ancestors, as priests in the city's many temples or at the ghats on the Ganges, of which there are almost 100. They promise pilgrims support in their **search for salvation from the cycle of birth and rebirth** by reciting the holy dicta in the old language Sanskrit, a rather lucrative undertaking.

What to See in Varanasi

River banks
✷ ✷
Ghats ►

Varanasi's greatest attraction does not consist of its buildings but of the opportunity to get an **insight into the vitality and diversity of Hindu practices**, which are primarily conducted on the bathing steps (ghats). From morning till night thousands of Hindu pilgrims flood to the Ganges to bathe in it or conduct holy rituals in the hope of thereby achieving salvation. A **trip in a rented rowing boat** along the Ganges early in the morning or in the evening is particularly recommendable. **Manikarnika Ghat**, where the dead are cremated, is blackened by soot and **must not be photographed**. Failing to obey this rule can lead to problems.

Golden Temple of Vishvanath

Like many other temples in India the original structure was destroyed by the Mughal emperor Aurangzeb. The current temple was built by the queen of Indore in 1777; its gilded exterior was added by Maharaja Ranjit Singh in 1835. The temple is only accessible to Hindus, but the narrow alleys leading to it are lined by countless shops selling oblations and it is worth coming here to watch the comings and goings. Since the tensions began between Hindus and Muslims the **area around the temple has been strictly guarded**.

Aurangzeb Mosque

The large mosque situated behind Vishvanath Temple is easy to recognize from the river. It was built by **Aurangzeb**, who destroyed the

▶ VISITING VARANASI

INFORMATION

Tourist Office of UP Tourism
At the station, tel. 05 42 – 234 63 70

Tourist Bungalow
Parade Kothi, tel. 05 42 – 22 01 62

Also see the following website:
www.up-tourism.com

SHOPPING

Varanasi is famous for silk. Those who do not want to barter at the bazaars should find good products at fixed prices in the markets run by UP Tourism (addresses from the tourist office).

WHERE TO STAY / WHERE TO EAT

Anyone wanting to stay near the river should forgo alcohol and non-vegetarian fare out of respect for this site that is so sacred to Hindus.

▶ Luxury
① *Taj Ganges*
Nadesar Palace Grounds
Tel. 05 42 – 250 30 01
www.tajhotels.com

Located in a large garden with several restaurants. Its distance from the river means the above-mentioned rules regarding consumption of alcohol or meat do not apply.

② *Palace on the Ganges*
B 1/158 Assi Ghat
Tel. 05 42 – 231 50 50
22 individually furnished rooms and one roof terrace restaurant characterize the »Palace on the Ganges«.

▶ Mid-range / Budget
③ *Hotel Ganges View*
Assi Ghat
Tel. 05 42 – 231 32 18
This very well-run, pleasant hotel is right on the banks of the Ganges. A terrace leads directly to the river. In addition the vegetarian cuisine is excellent.

④ *Alka*
D 323 Mir Ghat
Tel. 05 42 – 232 84 45
Nicely furnished rooms, also directly by the Ganges, with a restaurant.

---

previous Vishvanath Temple built by Raja Man Singh in 1699. The stones of the Hindu temple were used for the walls of the new mosque. Its entrance was **modelled on the Taj Mahal**. The three-domed mosque used to have huge minarets, but they no longer exist.

Not far from the banks of the Ganges is Alamgir Mosque, which was also built by Aurangzeb in the location of a destroyed Hindu temple.   **Alamgir Mosque**

Westwards, in Vidyapeeth Road is Bharat Mata Temple, **a »secularized« temple** that does not contain any depictions of deities. Instead the floor contains a large marble relief of the Indian subcontinent. The temple inaugurated by Mahatma Gandhi is dedicated to »Mother India«.   **Bharat Mata Temple**

Varanasi Map

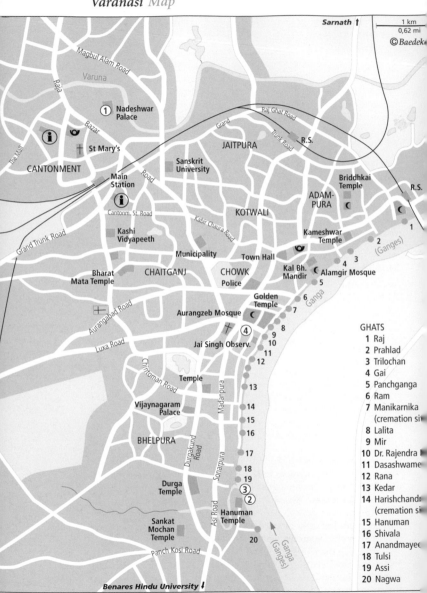

Sarnath ↑

1 km
0,62 mi
© Baedek

Magbul Alam Road

Varuna

Raja

Bazar

① Nadeshwar Palace

The Mall

ℹ

St Mary's

CANTONMENT

Main Station

ℹ

Cantonm. St. Road

Kashi Vidyapeeth

Grand Trunk Road

Bharat Mata Temple

CHAITGANJ

Aurangabad Road

Luxa Road

Chitroman Road

Temple

Vijaynagaram Palace

BHELPURA

Durgakund Road

Durga Temple

Sankat Mochan Temple

Panch Kosi Road

Benares Hindu University ↓

Sanskrit University

Kabir Chaura Road

Road

KOTWALI

Municipality

Town Hall

CHOWK
Police

Aurangzeb Mosque

Jai Singh Observ.

Madanpura

Sonarpura

Asi Road

Hanuman Temple

JAITPURA

Grand

Trunk Road

Raj Ghat Road

R.S.

ADAM-PURA

Briddhkai Temple

☾

☾

R.S.

Kameshwar Temple

Kal Bh. Mandir

Alamgir Mosque

Golden Temple

☾

④

✝

Ganga

(Ganges)

1

2

3

4

5

6

7

8

9

10

11

12

13

14

15

16

17

18

19

20

Ganga (Ganges)

GHATS
1 Raj
2 Prahlad
3 Trilochan
4 Gai
5 Panchganga
6 Ram
7 Manikarnika (cremation si
8 Lalita
9 Mir
10 Dr. Rajendra
11 Dasashwame
12 Rana
13 Kedar
14 Harishchandr (cremation si
15 Hanuman
16 Shivala
17 Anandmayee
18 Tulsi
19 Assi
20 Nagwa

Where to stay / Where to eat
① Taj Ganges
② Palace on the Ganges
③ Ganges View
④ Alka

Further south is Durga Temple, which is also known as **Monkey Temple** because of the monkeys that live here. Its tower symbolizes the entrance of all five elements into the world soul. Durga Temple is considered **one of Varanasi's most holy temples** and attracts many believers.

Directly next door is **Tulsi Manas Temple**, named after the poet Tulsi Das, who wrote his version of the great epic Ramayana, Ramcharita Manas, here.

Durga Temple

Varanasi has always been a centre of learning. In addition to Sanskrit, music and dance were taught here. Benares Hindu University, located south of the city centre, is **one of India's largest universities**. 8000 students live on its campus and the main areas of study are Hindu culture, religion and Indian history. A collection of more than 150,000 rare manuscripts can be found in the university library.

The new **Vishvanath Temple** on the university campus was financed by the industrial family Birla. The temple was designed by Madan Mohan Malaviya (1862–1942) and is open to members of all religions. Nearby, an extensive collection of manuscripts and miniatures can be seen in **Bharat Kala Bhawan Museum** (open: daily except Sun 10.30am–5pm).

Benares Hindu University

Around Varanasi

The small town of Sarnath (10km/6mi east of Varanasi) contains remains of a number of monasteries, stupas and a museum with excellent sculptures from the Maurya period. Sarnath's Isipatana Migadya Park is said to have been the location where Buddha, after his wanderings, meditation and enlightenment, **preached his first sermon in around 528 BC, thereby setting the wheel of law in motion**. The great Maurya king Ashoka had the Dharmarajika Stupa built here, but it was taken away again in 1794. All that is left are the traces of the foundations and some posts of a stone fence that were added later. An Ashokan pillar with a lion's capital, now India's national emblem, can be seen in Sarnath Museum. The lower section of the smooth column with inscriptions stands in the excavation complex. Thanks to the extensive reports by the Chinese pilgrims Fa Hsien and Hiuan Tsang it is known that Sarnath **was once a flourishing centre of Buddhism**. Hiuan Tsang (around AD 640) reported that 1500 monks lived here. The monastery is said to have had a height of 65m/213ft and in addition to Ashoka's 22m/72ft stupa there was allegedly another 90m/295ft stupa. It was later forgotten, but systematic digs since the beginning of the 19th century have uncovered the various parts of the complex that can now be seen. **Buddha Purnima**, Buddha's birthday, is celebrated in May with a procession, where the public gets to see relics to which they do not usually have access.

★
Sarnath

The **complex** is entered from the east; on the right there is a modern Buddhist temple with Japanese frescoes (1930), and in front of it is a

Meditating at one of the most sacred Hindu sites

THE HOLY RIVER

In contrast to the ocean, which is considered male, all rivers are female in India, since they look after the people like a mother, giving them fertility and wealth. All rivers are sacred, but the most sacred of them all is undoubtedly the Ganges (Ganga), which, according to Hindu beliefs, flows through all three worlds: heaven, earth, and underworld. It is the epitome of purity and millions of devout Hindus make pilgrimages to its holy sites every year.

Bhagirathi, one of the five main source rivers, originates in an ice cave at the foot of the Gangotri glacier.

It merges with **Alaknanda** in Deva-prayag to become the Ganges, which flows through the southern Himalaya and then leaves the mountains behind near Rishikesh. At Haridwar it breaks through the Himalayan foothills and reaches the lowlands.

At Allahabad it merges with the **Yamuna**. In this place (Sangam), thought to be particularly holy, the mythical underground river **Sarasvati** is also said to flow into the Ganges. Shiva is said to have settled with his wife Parvati in the old town of Benares, modern-day **Varanasi**. For that reason it has always been a destination for devout Hindus. Beggars and millionaires alike come here to find salvation.

Every morning yogis and pilgrims can be seen praising the sunrise and undergoing ritual cleansing with its water. For millennia the Brahmins on the ghats have earned their money reciting the mantras necessary for salvation.

The descent of Ganga

According to an ancient legend, Ganga came to earth from the heavenly sphere to bring salvation to the souls of dead Hindus and to give humanity fertility. The **legend of the creation of the river** illustrates not only its religious significance for devout Hindus but also the wisdom of the people who had understood the hydrological cycle, the dangers of heavy monsoon rains and the protective function of forests: »There once lived in India a wise king called Bhagiratha. He was praised all over India for his sense of justice and his love of god. As he got older he remembered the cruel fate of his ancestors. They had been burned and cursed by a powerful ascetic because of an offence. Since then their souls were lost, unable to find

the way to heaven. Bhagiratha decided to dedicate the rest of his life to his ancestors' fate. He handed over the kingdom to his minister and set off for the forests of the Himalaya. Once arrived, he sat down below a wonderful tree and devoted himself to strict asceticism. Bhagiratha was only filled with the thought of his ancestors' salvation.

catch Ganga's destructive power.‹ Bhagiratha subsequently began a second meditation. He spent more years meditating and concentrated his thoughts on the ascetic Shiva. Finally the divine Shiva appeared to him as well and said: ›Bhagiratha! I am pleased with your self-control and your strict asceticism! I will help you and protect the earth from Ganga's

Since then she has been releasing everyone from their sins and irrigating the dry land.

»After many years of deep meditation Brahma, the granter of wishes, appeared to him and said: ›Dear Bhagiratha, I have heard your heart's desire. Your ancestors can only be released from their curse if their mortal remains are washed away by the holy water of the heavenly Ganga. I have already asked her to come down to Earth and bring salvation for your ancestors. The divine Ganga has acquiesced, but has also pointed out that her power is so mighty that she will destroy the earth when she descends from heaven. I cannot help you. Only Shiva, the master of the forces of nature, can

destructive powers. Come, end your meditation and follow me to the peaks of the Himalaya!‹ Bhagiratha ended his meditation and followed Shiva. Other gods, saints, animals and people gathered together to be present at the upcoming divine event. Once arrived at the Himalaya, Shiva stood on the highest peak and invited Bhagiratha to ask Ganga to come down to earth. As soon as Ganga had heard Bhagiratha's plea, she threw herself down on to Earth from heaven with a thunderous noise. She was sure the earth would break apart under her force.

Ganga gets tangled in Shiva's long hair during her descent to Earth

However, **Shiva caught her in his hair**. The divine Ganga became entangled and tried to free herself to no avail. After a long search during which she lost her excessive power, she flowed as the holy river Ganges from his hair and slowly and peacefully made her way through India. On her long way to the sea she also washed over the remains of Bhagiratha's ancestors and released them from their sins. In this way the heavenly Ganga came to Earth. Since then she has been releasing everyone from their sins and irrigating the dry land.«

Highly esteemed purity

Since time immemorial the water of the Ganges has been considered particularly pure and is believed to help with more than just disease. Anyone who dies by the Ganges, or whose ashes are scattered in the Ganges after the body has been cremated will also be cleansed of old sins. It is considered particularly commendable if rituals performed in a temple or in the home are performed with water from the Ganges, which is why it is transported over long distances.

The esteem in which this water is held has taken on curious forms in Indian history. It is reported that the Chola king Rajendra I (1012–44) went on a twelve-year military campaign to the Ganges and had the tributary vassals transport the water to his newly built capital in the south, more than 2000km/1200mi away. This act earned him the sobriquet Gangaikondacholan (the Chola who brought the Ganges). Before his trip to England for Queen Victoria's diamond jubilee the Maharaja of Jaipur, Madho Singh II (1880–1922), even had two huge silver vessels made so he would have water from the Ganges for drinking and performing religious ceremonies.

Today respect for the Ganges has made way for **economic interests**. »Shiva's hair«, as the forests of the Himalaya are also called, are cut down without heed for **ecological consequences**. When the slopes of the Himalaya mountains slid away it was devout farmers in the early 1970s who tied themselves to the trees in order to protect them from the loggers. New dangers lurk in the form of huge dam projects threatening the fragile water ecosystem.

In addition the inflow of industrial waste has polluted the »pure« Ganga. In 1985 the Central Ganga Authority Board (CGA) was founded under Rajiv Gandhi, with the aim of reducing the amount of pollutants in the Ganges, but its success is very questionable as a result of India's urge to modernize.

Bodhi tree, which is said to be a seedling of the legendary tree from Sri Lanka. It is said that it came from the original tree from Bodhgaya, under which Buddha found enlightenment.

Turning to the left from there visitors will see Sarnath's best-preserved monument, the particularly impressive, large **Dhamekh Stupa** from the Gupta period, which has some still extant fine relief work. The stupa has a diameter of 13m/42ft and a height of 28m/92ft. Its upper part consists of brick, while the lower portion is decorated with sandstone.

Behind the stupa is the **excavation zone** with the remains of four monasteries, the foundations of the Dharmarajika Stupa and the remains of a broken Ashokan pillar. Parts of the monastery complex were only added by Queen Kumaradevi in the twelfth century, but below them monastery complexes from the Kushana period have been discovered. Most areas were, however, destroyed in the Islamic conquest of 1197. This very worthwhile museum contains the above-mentioned **lion capital** as well as some very nice Buddha statues in the Mathura and Gupta styles. There are also several Hindu sculptures on display, which indicate that this site must have once been an important place for Hindus, too (open: daily except Fri 10am–5pm).

⊕ Opening hours: daily 9am – 5pm

★ ◄ Museum

⊕

Around 500m/550yd south of Sarnath stands a stupa from the fifth century; it was, however, altered by Akbar in 1588, who added a tower to the top of it. Akbar had this tower built to commemorate his father Humayun's visit to Sarnath.

Chaukhandi

Around 100km/60mi east of Varanasi, in Sasaram, is the **mausoleum of Sher Shah Suri** (died 1545). The impressive dome has a height of 46m/151ft and a diameter of 22m/72ft. It is crowned by a golden lotus and can be seen rising up in the middle of an artificial lake. Upon closer inspection it can be seen that the building was once decorated with colourful geometric patterns. The small town is also the location of the tombs of the father and son of Sher Shah Suri as well as some other Muslim buildings.

Sasaram

WESTERN INDIA

STATES AND UNION TERRITORIES
Daman and Diu: union territories
Gujarat: capital Gandhinagar
Rajasthan: capital Jaipur

The federal state of Rajasthan with its many palaces and forts is one of India's most visited destinations. Gujarat on the other hand is only just beginning to market its own attractions, which are also very much worth seeing. Northwest Rajasthan is characterized by the **Thar desert**, which, towards the south-west, gives way to the **Kutch region** in Gujarat. Life here is dominated by a lack of vegetation and extreme climatic conditions. While the Thar desert is characterized by hot summers and dry, cool winters, part of the Kutch region, the »Rann of Kutch« salt desert, is flooded during the monsoon season, transforming it into a salt lake. In the southern part of Rajasthan are the **Aravalli Hills**, which are some of the oldest mountains in the world. The amount of rainfall here is greater and the overall climate is cooler. In the far south of western India is the **Kathiawar peninsula** in the state of Gujarat. This huge basalt platform is extremely fertile. Its highest elevations at around 640m/2100ft are near Gir; the national park here provides the last Asiatic lions with a habitat.

The region east of the Indus, which is now in Pakistan, had already been home to civilizations during the Harappa culture (third and second millennia BC). The enormous Ashokan Empire incorporated parts of both Rajasthan and Gujarat. The region was subsequently ruled by the Maurya dynasty and the Bactrian Greek kingdoms, until it was annexed by the Guptas. Remains of the old cities can still be seen in Lothal (Gujarat).

History of Gujarat

In the ninth century Gujarat flourished under the Solanki rulers, but it subsequently fell victim to pillages by Muslim conquerors on several occasions. The destruction of the temple city of Somnath by Mahmud of Ghazni (1026) is one of the saddest chapters in the history of the state. Following this event, independent Muslim rulers established themselves in Gujarat, but their territories were then incorporated into the Mughal Empire by Humayun and Akbar. In the mid-18th century Muslim rule came to an end when the Marathas took power.

← *Young women at a balcony of Jaisalmer's palace*

The father of the Indian liberation movement, **Mahatma Gandhi, was born in Gujarat** and it played an important role in his battle against the British colonial empire. Gujarat became an independent state only when it separated from the former state of Bombay in 1960.

History of Rajasthan

Starting in the seventh century, Rajasthan saw the development of **countless small kingdoms**, which were ruled by the Rajputs. They identified themselves with Hinduism to such an extent that they considered themselves descendants of the hero Rama and acted as defenders of Hinduism in the period of Muslim conquest. The initial Mughal attempts to conquer Rajasthan failed as a result of the Rajputs' ferocious resistance, which sometimes led to the complete destruction of individual kingdoms. **Their valour, which sometimes approached self-destruction, greatly contributed to their glorification**. Akbar (1546–1605) attempted to reach an agreement with the Rajput rulers though matrimonial alliances: he married daughters of Rajput kings, which brought about mutual political recognition. When British rule spread over India the Rajputs supported the British in their fight against the Maratha Empire and, as British allies, enjoyed considerable privileges. In the 1818 Treaty of Subordinate Alliance, the Rajputs **bowed to British rule** and were thus awarded advantages. After India's independence the kingdoms were dissolved and in 1956 the new state of Rajasthan was founded.

Economy

Gujarat is one of India's most industrialized regions. In addition to the traditional focal points, namely textiles and salt mining, petroleum refineries have been growing in importance in recent years. Refineries and factories for fertilizers play a sizeable role. A well-developed infrastructure and good energy supply are drawing more and more companies to Gujarat. Modern methods of cultivation are quickly taking hold in agriculture, which has caused the small state to rank second in India when it comes to peanut and tobacco production. Other crops are market fruits such as sugarcane, cotton, mangoes and bananas. The dry northwest is used only extensively, mainly for livestock farming. Gujarat is particularly famous for its handicraft traditions. Finely embroidered textiles or batik fabrics (bandhini) are amongst the most popular products alongside silver works.

Farming in **Rajasthan** is limited in the west because of a lack of rainfall. Farmers mainly plant millet and lentils, but their true wealth lies in their herds of goats, sheep and camels. Regular droughts frequently lead to famines and to a loss of these herds. Rajasthan's south on the other hand receives more rainfall. Wheat, maize, cotton, sugarcane, chilli and tobacco are cultivated here. Rajasthan is rich in mineral resources. In addition to copper, iron, zinc and silver, Rajasthan's most important resources include coal, chalk, magnesium and quartz. Important industries are the textile, sugar, cement and glass industries, as well as the production of pesticides. The processing and trading of gemstones in Jaipur attracts traders from all around the world. As in Gujarat, Rajasthan's arts and crafts are famous. Fabric prints, wooden dolls, miniature paintings, marble figures, leather and textiles are just a few of the products made by local artisans.

Attractions

Rajasthan, the land of kings, is one of India's most popular destinations. The well-preserved **Maharaja's palaces** of the past, with their extravagant opulence, portray an insight into the luxurious lives of these rulers. An additional appeal consists in the fact that many of these palaces can also be stayed in. The nicest palaces are in **Amer, Bikaner, Jaipur, Jodhpur and Udaipur**.

The desert town of Jaisalmer has a medieval fort and a centre worth seeing, as well as filigree Jain temples and attractive merchant villas. In addition visitors have the chance to ride camels into the desert on tours lasting several days. Located at the border between Gujarat and Rajasthan are the impressive Jain temples in Mount Abu and Ranakpur. The annual festival in Pushkar with a camel and funfair is one of the best in India.

Laying out the chilli peppers to dry

Gujarat does not yet receive the greatest number of tourists, but, in addition to the extensive and impressive **Jain temple cities** such as Palitana and Mount Girnar, boasts important Hindu temples (Modhera, Dwarka, Somnath). The state capital Ahmedabad is home to countless mosques, excellent museums and modern buildings by well-known architects. One very special attraction is Gir National Park, the home of the rare Asiatic lions.

Diu and Daman are sleepy towns on the Arabian Sea that have held on to their Portuguese flair. Far away from the tourist hotspots, life here can be enjoyed at a leisurely pace.

✴ Ahmedabad (Ahmadabad)

C 8

State : Gujarat
Population: 4.5 million

Altitude: 55m/180ft
Distance: 551km/342mi north of Mumbai

Ahmedabad, India's seventh-largest city and the most populous in the state, is situated on the banks of the Sabarmati river. The former capital is an important trading centre, particularly for cotton and textiles, and an ideal starting location for explorations of Gujarat with its impressive Jain and Hindu temples, its nature reserves and its coastline.

Gujarat's special development policies have made Ahmedabad one of India's most developed cities. Amongst the city's most important educational institutions are Ahmedabad University, Lalbhai Dalpatbhai Institute of Indological Research and the nationally famous Indian Institute of Management (IIM).

✴
International kite festival ▶

During the traditional **Makar Sankranthi festival** (14 January) an international kite festival is held, when the sky becomes filled with kites of all sizes and colours. The following day a competition takes place in which all the participants have to try to bring down their opponents' kites. The competitors even attach glass shards to their lines to cut those of their rivals. The city also has a kite museum.

History

Ahmedabad owes its name to Sultan Ahmed Shah, who fortified the old Hindu city of Asval in 1411, making it his capital. The city quickly grew and it was not long before artisans flocked to it from near and far. After just half a century Ahmedabad was considered one of India's richest cities. As a result of the conquest by Akbar's troops in 1572 it became part of the great Mughal Empire. Ahmedabad remained the provincial capital and was well-known as an important market for silk and brocade. These valuable goods were exported from here to places as far away as Europe. The rich mer-

Ahmedabad *Map*

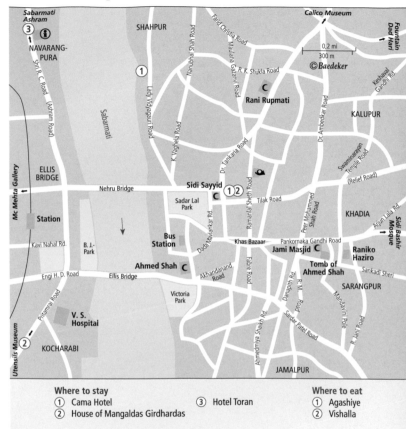

Where to stay
① Cama Hotel
② House of Mangaldas Girdhardas
③ Hotel Toran

Where to eat
① Agashiye
② Vishalla

chants built magnificent houses decorated with wooded façades, only a few of which are still extant today. From 1630 onwards the city was plagued by famines and political conflicts, causing it to lose more and more of its significance. During the period that followed, the rule of the city passed between Mughals and Hindu Marathas and back again. In 1817 Ahmedabad came under British influence and flourished a second time as a textile centre. It was even given the sobriquet »**Manchester of the East**«.

In addition to textiles the city's other important trading product was opium, which the British sold to the Chinese. Mahatma Gandhi found plenty of followers amongst Ahmedabad's underpaid textile workers. Together they set off from Sabarmati Ashram in Ahmeda-

► VISITING AHMEDABAD

INFORMATION
Gujarat Tourism
H. K. House
Ashram Road
Tel. 079 – 26 58 91 72
www.gujarattourism.com

GETTING THERE
There are plenty of connections by air, rail or bus from Mumbai and Delhi.

SHOPPING
The busy bazaar in the old town is worth a visit, particularly the streets in Manek Chowk. Here visitors will find everything from jewellery to the bandhini fabrics (batik fabrics) that are so typical of Gujarat; there is a particularly large selection available around »Raniko Haziro«. The biggest modern shopping street is C. G. Road in Ahmedabad's new town. The shops here sell clothes, shoes, jewellery and much more.

WHERE TO EAT
► Alcohol free
Gujarat is a »dry state«, meaning hotels and restaurants do not serve any alcoholic beverages.

► Moderate
① *Agashiye*
in the »Mangaldas Girdhardas« Hotel
Tel. 079 – 25 50 65 35
Excellent vegetarian specialities served in a very pleasant atmosphere (see recommendation).

► Inexpensive
② *Vishalla*
opposite Vasana Tol Naka
Tel. 079 – 26 60 24 22
Ethnic restaurant on the outskirts of Ahmedabad. Diners sit on the floor at long tables; the restaurant serves a typical Gujarati thali, a plate of many different regional vegetarian dishes. The complex also had a cultural programme and a children's programme every day with theatre and music. During a visit it is also a nice idea to look at the museum of kitchen utensils.

WHERE TO STAY
► Luxury / Mid-range
① *Cama Hotel*
Khanpur Road, tel. 079 – 25 60 12 34
www.camahotelsindia.com
This hotel is situated on the Sabarmati river (50 rooms, all with air conditioning); swimming pool and two restaurants.

Baedeker recommendation

② *The House of Mangaldas Girdhardas*
opposite Sidi Sayyid Mosque
Lal Darwaja
Tel. 079 – 25 50 66 46, fax 079 – 25 50 65 ?
www.houseofmg.com
Hotel with twelve very tastefully and individually decorated rooms in an old vil right in the centre of Ahmedabad. There a two restaurants, including an excellent roc terrace restaurant where guests can dine ! candlelight to the strains of classical Indi. music.

► Budget
③ *Hotel Toran*
Gandhi Ashram Road
Tel. 079 – 27 55 93 42
Hotel run by Gujarat Tourism, directly opposite Gandhi Ashram (Sabarmati Ashram). Basic but clean rooms; small vegetarian restaurant.

bad on 12 March 1930 on the famous **Salt March**, which initiated the struggle for freedom. After India gained its independence there were several violent confrontations in Ahmedabad between Hindus and Muslims. **International architects** such as Le Corbusier and Louis Khan as well as renowned Indian architects such as Doshi and Correa participated in the town-planning process of modern Ahmedabad.

> ! **Baedeker** TIP
>
> **A morning stroll**
> Old Ahmedabad is best discovered during a walk through the old quarters, known as the Pols of Ahmedabad. The »Heritage Walk«, which begins every morning at 8am and makes its way through temples, mosques and the labyrinth of alleyways of old Ahmedabad, brings the city's history to life. The guided tours start at Swaminarayan Temple; directly opposite is the office of the Ahmedabad Municipal Corporation (bookings directly in the office or under tel. 98 24 03 28 66 and 25 39 18 11).

What to See in Ahmedabad

On the river's eastern bank is the old town with its narrow alleys, its many mosques and its bazaars. East of Jami Masjid, around Manek Chowk, several of the famous townhouses with their wooden façades can be seen.

Cityscape

Ahmedabad is home to more than 50 mosques of which the most important are Sidi Sayyed Mosque and the Friday Mosque or Jami Masjid, which was competed by Ahmed Shah in 1524; it lost two minarets in the earthquakes of 1818 and 1957. It is an extremely successful example of the mixing of Indian and Arab architectural styles. The use of old columns from Hindu temples and the employment of Hindu craftsmen for the construction of this mosque illustrate this fact. The 260 columns that support the mosque's 16 domes also have Hindu patterns.

★ Jami Masjid

Sidi Sayyed Mosque was built by the Siddhi people, African slaves. This small mosque, which now stands on a traffic island, is famous for its **finely worked marble lattice windows**. Indeed, they are so finely worked that they belie the heavy starting material. The two windows depicting palm-tree motifs are particularly beautiful; they are considered the pinnacle of the Indo-Saracenic style.

★ Sidi Sayyid Mosque

Rani Rupmati was the first wife of the sixth Gujarati sultan Qutbuddin Ahmad Shah II (1451–58) and later the wife of the seventh sultan Mahmud Begadha (1458–1511). However, she died young. Her second husband had this beautiful mosque and tomb built in her honour. The grave immediately to the right of the mosque is a compact structure, crowned by a dome supported by 32 columns. Rani Rupmati Mosque is a very good example of the mosque architecture of the 16th century.

Rani Rupmati Mosque

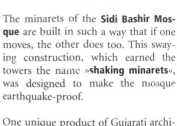

Earthquake-proof:
»shaking minarets«

The minarets of the **Sidi Bashir Mosque** are built in such a way that if one moves, the other does too. This swaying construction, which earned the towers the name »**shaking minarets**«, was designed to make the mosque earthquake-proof.

One unique product of Gujarati architecture is the stepped wells. They did not just serve as a water reservoir, but were also a retreat during the hot summer months. Various underground halls lead to the actual well, from which the water was obtained. The **Dada Hari Vav** in the district of Asarva was built like a spiral over three storeys into the ground. It is said to have been constructed according to the designs of Dada Harir, a woman from Mahmud Shah's harem, in 1499. Another, somewhat simpler and older well, the **Bhavani Bav**, is also located in the district of Asarva. Fifty-two steps lead down to the cool water. The

✳ Stepped wells

structure is attributed to the Solankis, a Rajput clan from the eleventh century. By **Lake Kankaria**, where Jehangir and his wife Nur Jahan once spent many evenings together, there is an idyllic picnic site popular with Indians.

✳✳ Calico Museum of Textiles

🕐 Opening hours: daily except Wed and holidays 2.30pm–5pm

This museum houses **one of the best collections of textiles in the world**. The sacred wall hangings with depictions of Krishna and embroidered Mughal tents are particularly interesting. In addition to textiles from Gujarat, the museum also exhibits embroidery from Kullu Valley, shawls from Kashmir and brocade from Varanasi. The processes of textile manufacturing and dyeing are clearly displayed by means of models and explanations. Founded by Gira Sarabhai, the museum is housed in a very attractive villa and its neighbouring buildings.

Utensils Museum

🕐 Opening hours: daily 10am–7.30pm

This museum, founded by Surendra Patel and located in the Vechaar Vishalla Environmental Centre, has more than 10,000 utensils from India on display. From spoons, metal lunchboxes and kitchen utensils to jugs, this museum has everything that gets used in India's various regions.

✳✳ Sabarmati Ashram

Mahatma Gandhi founded this ashram in 1918 after his return from South Africa, and he lived here until 1930. **His home** has been maintained in its original condition. The important stages of the battle for independence are displayed here through photographs. Those who are interested can use the excellent library. The ashram is located around 6km/3.5mi north of the city centre on the western bank of the Sabarmati river.

Opening hours: daily 8am–6.30pm

This gallery has an internationally famous collection of miniatures from the Gujarati Jain school, the Mughal period, the Rajasthani school and the Pahari school.

MC Mehta Gallery

The Tribal Museum and the Shreyas Folk Art Museum provide information about the tribal populations and their handicrafts.

Further Museums

Around Ahmedabad

The **Adalaj stepped well** (20km/12mi north of Ahmedabad) is one of the best examples of this type of structure, which was once common, particularly in Gujarat. The well, which spreads out elaborately over four levels, has beautifully ornamented columns and countless niches in which Hindu deities are depicted. It is said to have been built by Queen Radabhai (1489). Visitors enjoy the drop in temperature, which increases the further down the stairs they go.

★
Adalaj

The archaeological excavation site near Lothal (80km/50mi south of Ahmedabad) uncovered remains of human settlement dating back to the time of the Indus valley civilization. Visitors can see old brick houses and a large basin that was used as a dock for ships. The small archaeological museum contains jewellery, tools and ceramics from almost 5000 years ago, when Lothal traded with faraway lands such as Mesopotamia and Egypt.

Lothal

The Sun Temple of Modhera (106km/66mi north of Ahmedabad) is surely **one of India's most beautiful temples**. The temple, with a deep lake in front of it, was built by King Bhim Dev I in 1026–27. The well-proportioned structure, which stands on a plateau, is preceded by a hall with very attractive columns. Its exterior walls are ornamented with several depictions of the sun god Surya riding his horses. Parts of the temple were unfortunately destroyed by Mahmud of Ghazni. The huge temple complex is surrounded by many attractive relief sculptures and small shrines.
The Sun Temple is only rarely visited by tourists since it is somewhat difficult to get to. The trip is, however, worth the effort.

★ ★
Sun Temple of Modhera

Patan (120km/75mi north of Ahmedabad), the old capital of the Solanki dynasty, also has an **impressive stepped well**, the Rani ki Vav. The entire interior wall is adorned with very nice sculptures (Vishnu incarnations). Since the well was buried under sand until recently, the sculptures have been preserved in very good condition. In addi-

★
Patan

A very special gem: the sun temple of Modhera

tion Patan is famous for its old wooden houses and the manufacture of **saris using the double ikat technique**, in which both the warp and the weft are dyed before weaving. Clever dyeing creates the typical pattern during the weaving process.

Rajkot Mahatma Gandhi spent part of his youth in Rajkot (190km/120mi west of Ahmedabad). The house in which he used to live is now a museum. The Watson Museum owns excavation finds from early Indian civilization as well as colonial relics.

★ Ajmer

D 6

State: Rajasthan
Population: 520,000

Altitude: 486m/1594ft
Distance: 399km/248mi southwest of Delhi

The town of Ajmer is situated in a pretty valley in the Aravalli Hills and is, with its large lake, Ana Sagar, one of the holiest places for Muslims.

Although the town does not have any special architectural attractions it is visited by thousands of Islamic pilgrims coming to see the **tomb of the founder of the Sufi movement** in India every year. The six-

VISITING AJMER · PUSHKAR

INFORMATION

Tourist Offices

Ajmer: in the RTDC Hotel Khadim
Tel. 01 45 – 627 426
(inexpensive accommodation)

Pushkar: in Sarovar Hotel by the lake
www.rajasthantourism.gov.in
Since Pushkar is a very holy place for
Hindus, no alcohol is allowed to be
consumed in this town.

GETTING THERE

Ajmer is located on the rail connection between Ahmedabad and Delhi.

EVENTS

Pushkar Mela in November: camel
fair, funfair and cultural programme.
During this time accommodation
must be booked in advance.

WHERE TO STAY / WHERE TO EAT

▶ Luxury / Mid-range

Pushkar Palace
Pushkar, tel. 01 45 – 277 22 26
www.hotelpushkarpalace.com
Right on the lake with a nice terrace,
great for enjoying the sunset; vegetarian restaurant, cultural events in the
evenings.

Mansingh Palace
Ajmer
Vaishali Nagar
Tel. 01 45 – 242 57 02
The 54 rooms have every amenity,
there is an international restaurant
and a bar.

▶ Inexpensive / Budget

Sunset Café and Hotel
Pushkar (by the lake)
Tel. 0145 – 277 33 82
The Sunset Hotel has twelve rooms, a
nice garden and an internet café.

Hotel Jannat & Restaurant
Ajmer, Nizam Gate
Dargah Sharif
Tel. 01 45 – 243 01 08
Right by the bazaar, clean rooms and
good, inexpensive northern Indian
specialities.

Moon Dance
Tel. 01 45 – 277 26 06
Pushkar
(opposite the Vishnu Temple)
Small restaurant serving international
cuisine (good pasta dishes) in a
pleasant garden; sometimes tabla
concerts are held.

day festival commemorating the dead (Urs Festival) for the Sufi
monk Muin-ud-din Chishti, which is celebrated after the full moon
in the seventh month of the Islamic lunar calendar (April / May),
draws hundreds of thousands to Ajmer. This gives visitors the opportunity to listen to the religious songs of the Muslims, the Qawwalis.
Ajmer is also the starting location for the world-famous **Pushkar
Fair**, one of India's largest camel fairs during which hundreds of
thousands of pilgrims flock to the Brahma temple.

Ajmer, founded as early as the eleventh century by the Rajput Chauhan clan, was conquered by Muhammad Ghori in 1193 and thus fell

History

under Muslim rule. Muslims ruled the city until 1326. It then became a bone of contention between Rajput kings, Maratha rulers and Muslim sultans. Under Akbar's rule, who used the city as a base to defeat the Rajput kings, it enjoyed a cultural heyday.

The great Sufi master Khawaja Muin-ud-din Chishti (1143–1235) settled here in 1191 in order to spread the Islamic faith. He founded the **Chishti Order**, which is named after him and which remains one of the most influential Sufi orders. His tomb is now the city's main attraction. In 1818 Ajmer fell under British colonial rule, unlike many other towns in Rajasthan that were able to hold on to their autonomy, at least in part.

What to See in Ajmer

Tip All of the town's sights are to be found in the labyrinthine old town and are easily reached on foot.

Bazaar at Dargah Sharif, Khawaja Muin-ud-din Chishti's mausoleum

The tomb of Sufi Muin-ud-din Chishti has always been an **important place of pilgrimage for Muslims**. The saint's fame was great and widespread. Even the great emperor Akbar is said to have undertaken 14 pilgrimages to Ajmer. Well-known Mughal emperors such as Humayun, Shah Jahan, Jehangir and Akbar had mosques built here in his honour.

The centre of the complex, which is entered through a magnificent twelfth-century gate, is the Sufi's small brick tomb, which was extended several times in later centuries. Akbar Mosque (1570) and Jami Mosque, which Shah Jahan had built in 1637–38, can also be found in the complex. This beautiful place of worship consists, like the Taj Mahal in Agra, of white marble, which was brought here from the nearby Makrana quarry. The prayer hall has an attractive mihrab.

★
Tomb of Sufi Muin-ud-din Chishti

Leave the mosque and turn right after approx. 400m/440yd up the hill to get to Adhai-din-ka-jonpara Mosque, the »house of two-and-a-half days«. It got its name because the fakirs came together here during the Urs celebrations. One impressive aspect of the mosque, which is now in serious disrepair, is the **seven arches, which are masterfully engraved with words from the Qur'an**.

A Jain temple stood at this site originally, but it was partially demolished so the mosque could be built. The architectural relics give away the varied history of the place.

★
Adhai-din-ka-jonpara Mosque

This artificial lake was created under the Rajput prince Anaji during the previous millennium. Shah Jahan subsequently built five pavilions on its shore, of which four are still extant. The garden laid out by Jehangir, Daulat Bagh, is all but destroyed.

Ana Sagar

In the city centre there is a museum in Daulat Khana (Akbar's Palace), which was built by Akbar, with sculptures from Rajasthan and some finds from the time of the Indus valley civilizations (open daily except Fri 10am–4.30pm).

Museum

Also in the vicinity is the Jain Nasiyan Temple made of red sandstone. Only one hall is open to the public. It contains a gilded model of a heavenly city.

Nasiyan Temple

Pushkar

Pushkar lies just 11km/7mi northwest of Ajmer. It has **one of the few temples in India dedicated to the god Brahma**. Since this place has always been considered particularly holy, almost 400 temples have been built here over time. Once a year, during the full moon of the Hindu month Kathik (October / November) the otherwise quiet town is transformed into a huge fairground. The event being celebrated is Pushkar Mela, a **two-week festival and one of India's larg-**

★★
Pushkar Mela

Pushkar Festival attracts thousands of pilgrims every year. At the same time a huge camel market, dance performances and a large bazaar are held

est camel fairs. The ghats by Lake Pushkar draw religious pilgrims who bathe here to wash away their sins. However, traders also come here and spend days haggling over the price of cattle and camels, the greatest treasures of the desert inhabitants. As in ▶Jaisalmer, a temporary tent city is set up to provide accommodation for the many visitors. The rest of the year Pushkar is a place offering visitors relaxation and a slow exploration of the Hindu pantheon.

✶ Alwar

E 6

State: Rajasthan
Population: 230,000

Altitude: 50m/164ft
Distance: 197km/122mi southwest of Delhi

The old Rajput town on the route between Delhi – Jaipur is only visited by a small number of tourists, despite its idyllic location at the foot of the Aravalli Hills. In addition Alwar is the proud owner of one of Rajasthan's most beautiful palace complexes. The town is usually used as a base for excursions to Sariska Tiger Reserve.

VISITING ALWAR · SARISKA NATIONAL PARK

INFORMATION

Tourist Office
Alwar
Tel. 01 44 – 223 73 78
www.rajasthantourism.gov.in

GETTING THERE

Train and bus connections to Jaipur, Delhi, Jodhpur, Ahmedabad

WHERE TO EAT / WHERE TO STAY

► **Budget**

RTDC Hotel Meenal
Alwar
Tel. 0144 – 34 73 52
A basic hotel run by Rajasthan Tourism.

RTDC Hotel Tiger Den
Sariska
Tel. 01 44 – 284 13 42
Centrally located, directly next to the park entrance. The hotel has large, clean rooms.

► **Luxury**

Sariska Palace
Sariska
Tel. 01 44 – 284 13 22
www.thesariskapalace.in
The Sariska Palace is housed in a former hunting lodge owned by the Maharaja of Alwar. The very pleasant complex has a first-class swimming pool in a new extension.

History

The region around Alwar saw human settlement as long as 3500 years ago. According to legend some of the events recounted in the great epic the Mahabharata are said to have taken place here. At times the town was part of the Maurya Empire, later it became a bone of contention between the expanding Mughal Empire of Delhi and local Rajput rulers. Alwar experienced its high point under the Rajput king Pratap Singh, who made himself independent from Jaipur and made Alwar the capital of his own state in 1771. The town was at that time protected by an imposing fort situated on the nearby 300m/984ft hill. Later, Singh's successors united with the British and successfully fought against the Marathas. In return for their support, the British afforded the rulers of Alwar special treatment.

What to See in Alwar

★
Vinai Vilas Mahal

Within the walled old town, which is accessible by five gates, on the shores of a large artificial lake is the town's palace dating back to the year 1840. Maharaja Vinay Singh had a memorial built by the shore for his father Bakhtawar Singh as well as the palace on the shores of Lake Siliserh 10km/6mi away. This lake used to be connected to Alwar via a canal, thus supplying the town with sufficient water. A large part of the palace is now used by government bodies and is not open to the public. A further part, including the entrance hall, can only be viewed with a special permit available from Alwar House in Delhi.

Meeting on the streets of Rajasthan

Government Museum
🕐
Opening hours:
10am–5pm

Visitors must therefore content themselves with viewing the remaining rooms, in which the Government Museum is housed. In addition to various sculptures the museum contains objects privately owned by the royal family (including a silver table) and a very extensive manuscript collection (7000 works). The miniatures from the Alwar school (19th century) and the Bundi school are also worth seeing.

Chhatris (tombs)

At the lake's southern shore is the **cenotaph of Maharaja Bakhtwar Singh** (1781–1815), made of red sandstone and white marble. Bakhtwar Singh's consort, the maharani, is said to have committed sati (ritual suicide) here, which is why the building is also called Musi Maharani. The compact, harmonious building is reminiscent of the attempt by the Rajputs to imitate the imperial lifestyle of the Mughal rulers, who brought the tradition of cenotaphs to India.

Purjan Vihar

Purjan Vihar, also known as Company Bagh, was laid out by Maharaja Shiv Dan Singh in 1868 to make the hot summer more bearable. The park has a summer house with decorated interiors.

Around Alwar

Situated in a scenically picturesque setting on the banks of Vijay Sagar Lake (10km/6mi from Alwar) is the palace in which the royal family now lives. Upon polite request parts of the palace are often shown to visitors. Just the drive here and the palace's external appearance, however, are enough to warrant a visit.

Vijay Mandir Mahal

Around 40km/25mi from Alwar, on the road to Jaipur, lies the 480 sq km/185 sq mi national park that was founded in 1955 and is part of »Project Tiger«. Visitors to the mountainous and partially inaccessible terrain, the **former hunting grounds of the Maharaja of Alwar**, would be extremely lucky if they were to see a tiger. Those who want to try their luck anyway can find accommodation in Sariska Palace for example and immerse themselves in watching wild animals and dreaming about the lives of the hunting maharajas. The park is home to nilgai antelopes, sambar deer, chital, wild boar, grey langurs and rhesus monkeys. In addition to water birds and owls the park is also inhabited by **oriental white-eyes**, baya weavers, Indian rollers, rose-ringed parakeets, house crows and golden orioles. Wild animals such as bears, hyenas, tigers and leopards are only rarely spotted, since it is not possible to drive in the park at night.

✷ **Sariska National Park**

It is easier to spot animals during the dry season from tree hides when they come to the few watering holes. The best season to visit is February–June.

Bhuj

A 8

Federal state: Gujarat
Distance: 1270km/790mi southwest of Delhi

Population: 120,000

Bhuj is located in India's far west, in the Kutch desert region, almost on the border with Pakistan. The town was severely damaged in a disastrous earthquake in 2001, when many of its inhabitants lost their lives.

To this day the scars of this natural disaster can still be seen in many places. New settlements have sprung up on the outskirts of town, since a large proportion of the population were left without a roof over their heads. The attractions of the medieval town were also greatly damaged during the earthquake. The old palace and the new palace as well as the cenotaphs (**Chhatris**) have partially collapsed. Renovation work has now started, but the monuments can only be reconstructed in parts.

⏵ VISITING BHUJ

INFORMATION
Gujarat Tourism
Rann Resort
Mirzapur Road
Tel. 028 32 – 22 49 10
www.gujarattourism.com

GETTING THERE
Flight connections to Mumbai; train connections to Ahmedabad and Mumbai

SHOPPING
Shrujan
Shrujan is promoting the preservation of traditional embroidery in Kutch.

Nicely furnished shops sells clothes, scarves, blankets and pillows of exceptional quality (behind G. E. B. Sub Station, Post – Bhujodi, tel. 028 32 – 24 02 72).

WHERE TO STAY / WHERE TO EAT
▶ **Mid-range / Budget**
Hotel Prince
Station Road, tel. 028 32 – 22 03 70
Considered the best hotel in town. It is centrally located, has 42 rooms (most of them with air conditioning) and two restaurants. Excellent vegetarian dishes are served by Toral restaurant.

History Like the desert town of ▶ Jaisalmer in Rajasthan, Bhuj used to be a trading town that got its wealth from the caravans taking their goods along the overland route from India to Afghanistan and Persia. A local prince, Rao Khengarji I, made Bhuj the capital of a small, wealthy kingdom in 1548. When the British conquered Gujarat, Bhuj was also taken by them in 1819. As was the case in other kingdoms in the region, this one also co-operated with its conquerors. After India became independent, tensions developed between India and its neighbour Pakistan, which were followed by two wars (1965 and 1971). India was distrustful of Pakistan, and defensive activities were increased; Bhuj was developed into a large base for the Indian air force, which brought about modest development in the region.

What to See in Bhuj

Old town Bhuj's old town, with its narrow, confusing alleys in which cows and camels amble about, is worth a visit. Those who are interested in the culture and crafts of the Kutch region will be well served by the bazaars and their offerings of jewellery and textiles.

Rao Pragmalji's Palace Rao Pragmalji's Palace in the heart of the town, next to the post office and the bazaar, was only designed in 1865 by British architect Col. Wilkins.

★ Aina Mahal On the other side of the courtyard stands Rao Lakha's Palace with the famous Aina Mahal. In addition to a particularly beautiful door

Known for the manufacture of wonderful textiles and exceptional jewellery: the tribes of Kutch

adorned with ivory inlays, the palace has richly decorated rooms. The walls of the impressive mirror hall only show their true splendour in the glow of the chandeliers. The fountain in the interior was a source of cooler temperatures in the hot summers. The worthwhile **Palace Museum** displays exhibits from the possessions of King Rao Lakha, from lithographs to crystal glasses (open daily except Sat 9am–12pm and 3pm–6pm).

Gujarat's oldest museum, founded in 1877 by the future British governor of Bombay, Sir James Fergusson, has a large collection of textiles, weapons, paintings and inscriptions. The anthropological department is also very interesting; it provides an insight into the region's ethnic composition (open daily 9am–11.30am and 3pm–5.30pm, closed Wed and every second and fourth Sat of the month).

Kutch Museum (Fergusson Museum)

The cenotaphs (**chhatris**) of Bhuj's rulers lie outside the town. Many of the polygonal buildings, whose domes were supported by columns, collapsed during the earthquake. The best tomb in honour of Rao Lakha has been restored. The memorial stone has a depiction of a tradition that was widespread amongst the royal family, namely the immolation of widows (jauhar), where the wives of the kings also climbed on the funeral pyre upon his death. It is said that when Rao Lakha died his 15 court musicians also took their own lives.

Cenotaphs

Around Bhuj

Mandvi and surroundings In the small harbour town of Mandvi visitors can enjoy a tour of the harbour and at the same time watch how dhows, the traditional fishing boats, are constructed. On the outskirts of town there is a nice beach with a small holiday complex run by Gujarat Tourism. There is, however, no shade. Around 10km/6mi west of Mandvi is **Vijay Vilas Palace**, which dates back to the 1930s. Parts of the building are still inhabited by the maharaja's family. The other parts are open to the public. There is an attractive view of the surrounding area from the roof terrace. The maharaja also runs a luxury resort, located a few miles away by the beach.

Great Rann of Kutch An official permit (available through Gujarat Tourism in Bhuj) is needed to drive towards the Pakistani border in a Jeep. From there visitors will have an excellent view of the salt desert (Great Rann of Kutch) and the border to Pakistan.

Kutch is **famous for its textiles**. The inhabitants of the total of 300 villages produce exquisite embroidery that is sold all over India. Some of these places can be visited; the permit and guide required can be organized through Gujarat Tourism.

✳ **Bikaner**

C 5

State: Rajasthan	**Altitude:** 237m/778ft
Population: 420,000	**Distance:** 435km/270mi west of Delhi

As a result of its good location along the old caravan road, which connected central Asia and northern India with the ports of Gujarat and Delhi, Bikaner has always been an important trading post.

Bikaner owes its current name to the conqueror Bika, who took the desert city in 1486. For four centuries it was the centre of a kingdom ruled by Rajput maharajas. After India's independence Bikaner found itself on the edge of India because of the country's partition into India and Pakistan. It thus lost its function. Today the town is far away from the important transport routes and gives a rather sleepy impression. The old town and the palace complex, however, still portray an idea of what the once magnificent desert town must have been like.

What to See in Bikaner

Old town Near the station to the west lies the old town of Bikaner, which is still surrounded by a wall. In contrast to towns like Jaisalmer and Jaipur visitors can amble through the old town undisturbed by street vendors and simply watch the comings and goings of everyday life on the streets. The two Jain temples from the 16th century are particularly interesting.

In 1587 the Rajput king Raja Rai Singh, an influential military commander of the great Mughal Emperor Akbhar, began building this ground-level fort, which is protected by a moat and high walls. In some locations the almost 1km/0.6mi wall is 9m/30ft thick and has a height of 20m/66ft. It is thanks to these impressive defensive measures that the fort was never taken by enemy forces and is still in very good condition. Over time Rai Singh's successors erected countless structures within the walls, so that visitors can now admire **more than 30 palaces, temples and pavilions**. Large parts of the palaces are open to the public. As it is easy to get lost in the many rooms, it is advisable to make use of the guides employed by the fort to look around. Particularly impressive are **Ganga Niwas Durbar Hall** with the finely chiselled walls and ceiling, **Phul Mahal (Flower Hall)**, decorated with mirrors, and **Chandra Mahal (Moon Hall)**, painted with hunting scenes. The rooms' interiors clearly show the influence of Mughal architecture. The fort museum has an extensive collection of weapons with menacing swords, cannons and huge rifles, which soldiers once used to fire at enemies from the backs of elephants.

★ ★
Junagarh Fort

In front of Junagarh Fort in Bikaner

▶ VISITING BIKANER

INFORMATION

RTDC Hotel Dholamaru
Tel. 01 51 – 54 41 25
www.rajasthantourism.com

GETTING THERE

Train connections to Delhi, Jaipur,
Jodhpur; bus to Jaisalmer

WHERE TO STAY / WHERE TO EAT

▶ Luxury / Mid-range
Lallgarh Palace
Tel. 01 51 – 254 02 01

www.lallgarhpalace.com
The hotel is a sandstone palace more
than 100 years old. Its restaurant
serves specialities from Rajasthan as
well as Western cuisine. The hotel also
organizes camel safaris.

▶ Budget
RTDC Hotel Dholamaru
Tel. 01 51 – 54 41 25
Basic, clean hotel run by Rajasthan
Tourism.

Lalgarh Palace

Maharaja Ganga Singh (1898–1943) was a close ally of the British. His Camel Corps fought with them in Somaliland and he went to Europe several times. It was very important to him to modernize his kingdom quickly. It is therefore understandable that he hired a British architect when he wanted a new palace. In contrast to the highly popular Indo-Saracenic style, the palace designed by Samuel Swinton Jacob is typically Rajasthani. European elements were only incorporated in the interior. Part of the building is still inhabited by the descendants of the royal family. Another houses a museum and a third part has been converted into a luxury hotel. The museum owns an extensive collection of weapons and a very interesting photographic exhibition with old pictures that paint a vivid image of the lives of the kings in Rajasthan.

Ganga Golden Jubilee Museum

The Ganga Golden Jubilee Museum has a small but nice collection of terra cotta figures from the Gupta period and miniatures, manuscripts and textiles from the Mughal period. Another section has regional handicrafts (open daily except Fri 10am– 5pm).

Around Bikaner

Camel breeding farm

India's only state-owned camel breeding farm can be found 10km/ 6mi north of Bikaner. Its main purposes are breeding and research. Most of the desert animals are used in parades and film recordings but the camels for the Indian border protection troops are raised here too.

Karni Mata Temple

Deshnok (33km/20mi south of Bikaner) is home to Karni Mata Temple. Even though this temple does not have any architectural attrac-

The Rajasthani unit of the Border Security Force riding on camels

tions besides the silver entrance door, which was a donation from Maharaja Ganga Singh, it attracts pilgrims from near and far. Its main attraction is a population of **thousands of rats**. The rats enjoy complete protection within the temple and are cared for by the pilgrims and priests. They are believed to be incarnations of poets from the Charan tribe, who could become human beings again in their next lives.

Nagaur (110km/70mi south of Bikaner), an old Rajput town largely undiscovered by tourism, comes to life once a year (January/February) when it hosts India's largest cattle fair. Accommodation can be found in a tent city, making it possible for visitors to stay right in the midst of all the hustle and bustle. **Nagaur**

★ Bundi

State: Rajasthan
Population: 80,000

Altitude: 302m/991ft
Distance: 465km/290mi southwest of Delhi

Bundi enjoys a picturesque location in a valley in the midst of the Vindhya Hills in southeast Rajasthan. Towering on a rock above the town with its artificial lake and its colourful houses is the large palace complex of the former Rajput kings.

Tourism has left Bundi far more untouched than many other places in Rajasthan, and this has allowed it to maintain its original atmosphere to a much greater extent. Its attractions, bazaars and some pleasant accommodation make this an attractive place to spend some time. The dynasty of the Chauhan Rajputs under their ruler Rao De-

▶ VISITING BUNDI · KOTA

INFORMATION

Tourist Bureau Bundi
Brij Narayan ki Kothi
532 Jail Kund Road
Tel. 07 47 – 244 39 97 or
07 47 – 244 30 00

Tourist Reception Centre in Kota
RTDC Hotel Chambal
Tel. 07 44 – 232 65 27

GETTING THERE

Very good train connections from
Delhi or Mumbai to Kota. The closest
major airport is Jaipur (245km/
150mi), which offers flights to Kota.
There are regular bus connections
between Kota and Bundi (36km/
22mi).

WHERE TO EAT / WHERE TO STAY

► Luxury – Inexpensive
Haveli Braj Bhushanjee
Bundi (below the palace,
opposite the Ayurvedic

hospital)
Tel. 07 47 – 24 42-322/509/127
www.kiplingsbundi.com
The owners of the 200-year-old
Haveli, a long-established family from
Bundi, have created a pleasant hotel
in it. The 24 rooms are furnished in
the traditional style and some of them
are still decorated with old wall
paintings. There is a good vegetarian
restaurant as well as an attractive roof
terrace with a great view of the palace.

► Luxury / Mid-range
Hotel Brijraj Bhavan Palace
in Kota
Raj Bhavan Road
Tel. 07 44 – 245 05 29
Situated on raised ground above the
river is the former British Residence,
which has been transformed into a
hotel. The seven rooms, all of which
have air conditioning, and the international restaurant ensure that guests
have a very comfortable stay here.

va Haora founded their capital here in 1322 and built the fort on the
hill above the town during the second half of the 14th century. During its eventful history Bundi was an independent kingdom for a
while, but its rulers finally succumbed to the rule of the Delhi
Mughals at the start of the 17th century. From 1818 onwards it fell
into the hands of the British.

What to See in Bundi

★ ★
Palace complex
Visible from far away, the huge palace complex stands on a rock
above the former capital. Rudyard Kipling, who spent some time
here at the end of the 19th century, thought the building looked like
»an avalanche of masonry ready to rush down and block the gorge«.
This impression is primarily caused by the convoluted architecture,
which is largely the result of the palace's constant expansion by various rulers. Its oldest parts date back to the beginning of the 16th
century. The most recent ones were added around 100 years ago.

Some parts of the complex are accessible to the public, and they are particularly interesting because of their excellent wall paintings. The entrance to the palace is the massive **Hathi Pol (Elephant Gate)**. Adjoining the courtyard on the other side of the gate is **Chitra Shala**, a picture gallery fitted with columns. It contains some wonderful wall and ceiling paintings dating from the 18th century. The paintings, which are in green, turquoise and white, show courtly scenes and stories from the god Krishna's life. The **Chattra Mahal**, where the royal rooms were located, also contains some good murals as do many other parts of the palace, not all of which, however, are open to the public. The kingdom of Bundi was a centre of Rajput painting between the 17th and 19th centu-

ries. Many courts supported painters' studios, but those of Bundi were particularly famous and shaped the style of the **Bundi school**.

The **Star Fort (Taragarh Fort)**, whose remains are to be found on the mountain above Bundi, date back the town's founding days. It was built in around 1350. Some merlons, a large cannon and the water containers that were chiselled into the rock walls can still be seen. The good views of Bundi, too, make this a pleasant place to visit.

As is the case in many of the cities in Rajasthan and Gujarat, Bundi also has several stepped wells. The best example is **Raniji ki Baori**,

Typical Bundi miniature from Garh Palace

a 1699 construction commissioned by the maharani of the ruler of that time. The 46m/151ft well in the town centre is adorned with richly ornamented columns and arches.

Hidden in and around Bundi there are tombs and small palaces as well as further stepped wells. It is best to hire a rickshaw together with a knowledgeable local driver for a few hours to explore these attractions. The tombs of the Rajput rulers are located in **Kshar Bagh**, an overgrown garden, where visitors will meet no-one except for the resident peacocks. Quite nearby, in the middle of a modest wood, is the maharaja's small hunting lodge, **Shikar Burj**. Rudyard Kipling spent some time in the former summer palace of **Sukh Niwas** during his stay in Bundi.

Further attractions

Not far from the road to Kota is the **tomb with 84 columns** which was built for Rao Raja Anirudh Singh. The **old town** is also worth visiting. It is worthwhile exploring on foot the narrow alleyways with their colourful and sometimes decorated houses, the workshops, busy bazaars and the magnificent vegetable market.

Around Bundi

Kota

Kota (36km/22mi to the southeast) is home to a lot of industry and is one of the headquarters of the Indian army. The town on the Chamba river is also an important railway junction, with all of the trains between Delhi and Mumbai stopping here. Kota was once the capital of the kingdom of the same name, and some monuments from this time are still extant. The museum in the town palace enjoys particular fame because of its excellent collection of Rajput paintings. Those wanting to spend a longer time in this area would be much better off making neighbouring Bundi the base for exploring the region.

★ ★
Museum ▶
◷
Opening hours:
daily except Fri
11am–5pm

Rao Madho Singh, who was made the ruler of Kota by the Mughals, started building the **palace** in 1625. Its most recent additions were made in the 20th century. The main reason the complex is worth visiting is the famous **Rao Madho Singh Museum**, which in addition to weapons, photographs and other memorabilia from the world of the maharajas contains one of the most famous collections of works by various Rajput painting schools of the past centuries.

✴ **Diu · Daman** (Union Territories)

C 9

Population: 21,000 / 25,000   **Altitude:** Sea level
Distance: 400km/250mi northwest (Diu)/
160km/100mi north (Daman) of Mumbai

Diu, the small, sleepy town on Diu Island (3km/2mi by 12km/7mi) off Gujarat's southern coast, was long under Portuguese control. Many ruins on this palm-rich island date back to the colonial period.

History

Diu was an important port for trade with Arab countries as early as the 13th century. At the start of the 16th century the Portuguese launched two attempts to occupy Diu, both of which failed as a result of resistance by the Islamic ruler Malik Ayaz. Finally, under Nuno da Cunha, the Portuguese managed to get this strategically important island under their control in 1531. Shortly afterwards they built a fort. In 1961 the Portuguese were forced to leave the island by the Indian government, who threatened to use military force if need be. Today Diu and Daman are union territories that are under the direct administration of Delhi.

Even though the island is connected to the mainland via two bridges, Diu does not feel as it were part of India. The white churches and country villas give a Mediterranean feel to the place, which is increased by the fact that the women wear dresses and skirts instead of saris. Since there are not many tourists in Diu, it is a nice place to get away from the hustle and bustle of the mainland. **Atmosphere**

Diu has several churches; St Paul's is the largest. St Thomas's now houses a museum, containing wooden statues of angels and saints. **Churches**

The fort at the island's eastern end is protected naturally by the sea on three sides; the land access route was protected by a ditch and massive gates. Today it is a tranquil ruin strewn with cannon balls, though part of it is used as a prison. There are nice views of Diu, the sea and the coast of the mainland from the fort. **Fort**

Diu has several beaches, of which Nagoa's beach (7km/4mi westwards) is the best. Hotels of various price categories have now been built here. **★ Beaches**

The once-famous 10th-century temple of Somnath (65km/40mi west of Diu) was plundered by Mahmud of Ghazni seven times. The present temple was only rebuilt after India's independence. In comparison to the Sun Temple of Modhera it seems bare, since it has hardly any sculptures on the exterior walls. **Somnath**

 VISITING DIU · DAMAN

INFORMATION
Diu: at the harbour
Tel. 028 75 – 25 26 53

Daman: at the bus station
Tel. 02 60 – 225 51 04

GETTING THERE
Flights to Diu leave from Mumbai. There are train connections to Daman from Mumbai, and trains also run between Ahmedabad and Vapi (12km/7mi away).

WHERE TO EAT / WHERE TO STAY
► **Moderate / Inexpensive**
Gurukripa
Seaface Road
Nani Daman (Daman)

Tel. 02 60 – 225 50 46
Good restaurant serving tasty fish and seafood. Has a roof terrace and spacious rooms.

Radhika Beach Resort
Nagoa Beach (Diu)
Tel. 028 75 – 25 25 53
www.radhikaresort.com. Pleasant three-star complex with bungalows and a pool. It also has a cocktail bar and an international restaurant.

Jay Shankar
Jallandhar Beach (Diu)
Tel. 028 75 – 25 24 24
Meeting place for travellers; has a restaurant.

Diu Harbour

Daman C 9

The enclave of Daman on the Gulf of Cambay is a former Portuguese colony on India's west coast. The town, located on the mouth of the Daman Ganga river, developed into a port from 1531 onwards, when the Portuguese began trading with East Africa. It experienced its golden age at the beginning of the 19th century as a result of opium trading; however, the British put a stop to this because of their own interests in the region. As in Goa and Diu, the Indian government forced the Portuguese in Daman to give the land back to India in December 1961 by threatening them with the use of military force. Daman has subsequently always been associated with Goa, but since 1987 it has been an autonomous **union territory** that is administered from Delhi.

Townscape Daman, formerly known as Damao, is divided into the larger district of Nani Daman and the smaller district of Moti Daman by the Daman Ganga river, which is spanned by a bridge and has several ferry services connecting the two parts of town. Amongst its attractions are churches, a fort and a prison. In contrast to those in Goa or Diu, the beach here is not very attractive, and moreover there are very dangerous currents in some places. Those who nevertheless want to swim should do so on the sandy beach around 4km/2.5mi south of the town of Daman.

Nani Daman on the coast is home to the old fort with a small church and its cemetery. It does not, however, bear comparison to the large complexes in Diu and Goa.   **Fort**

Besides **Bom Jesus Church** (1559) with its large, painted wooden altar, the other church of interest is **Rosario Chapel**. The wooden panels bear depictions of biblical stories. The statue of Mary is said to have been donated out of gratitude after the town survived an attack by Maratha king Shivaji.   **Churches in Moti Daman**

Dwarka

A 8

State: Gujarat
Population: 28,000

Altitude: Sea level
Distance: 1200km/745mi southwest of Delhi

The port town of Dwarka in the far west of Gujarat is an important place of pilgrimage for Krishna worshippers. After his victory over the demon king Kamsa, Krishna is said to have left Mathura and come to Dwarka.

There, the sea itself is said to have given land to the god so he could found a new town. After his death the sea reclaimed the land. Dwarka is also the most important holy place for Vishnu followers, since Krishna is one of Vishnu's incarnations. In addition the Hindu philosopher Aid Sankaracharya, the founder of the Advaita movement, is said to have lived here.

Some time ago divers from the National Institute of Oceanography succeeded in identifying and photographing parts of a sunken city off the coast of Dwarka. It is believed that there used to be trade connections with countries on the Mediterranean. It is unclear, however, whether the city sunk because of a tectonic shift or because of a rise in sea level. Beneath today's settlement, traces of five older towns have been found. The temple complexes were built more recently; it was only under the Gaekwad kings of Baroda (twelfth century) that Dwarka became an important place of pilgrimage.   **History**

What to See in and around Dwarka

The five-storey Dwarkanath Temple, which is more than 50m/164ft tall and has five storeys, forms the town's centrepiece. It is said that a temple called Jagat Mandir stood on this site 2500 years ago. The narrow, almost elegant building is supported by 60 columns and dates from the 16th century. The pilgrims who flood here every day   ✱ **Dwarkanath Temple**

DWARKA

INFORMATION
www.gujarattourism.com

GETTING THERE
Rail connection with Jamnagar,
where there is an airport

**WHERE TO EAT/
WHERE TO STAY**
▶ **Budget**
Toran Tourist Bungalow
Tel. 028 92 – 23 40 13
Basic, clean accommodation run by
Gujarat Tourism.

access the temple via Swarga Dwar (Heaven's Gate) and leave it via Moksha Dwar (Salvation Gate).

Dwarka also has a temple in honour of Rukmini, Krishna's wife, from the twelfth century. The offshore island of Bet, to which there is a ferry connection, has some shrines and a temple dedicated to Krishna.

The old port of **Porbandar** (87km/ 54mi southeast of Dwarka) is famous for being **Mahatma Gandhi's birthplace**. An exhibition on Gandhi's life is housed in Kriti Mandir, next to the house he was born in. It also contains some of his personal effects.

Bileshwar   Bileshwar (15km/9mi from Porbandar) possesses several important Shiva temples from the seventh century. Not far from Bileshwar is a very richly adorned stepped well, the Vikia Vav, which is one of the largest in India. Wells like this one had the double purpose of supplying people with water and being a cool refuge during the hot summers.

★ Gir National Park (Sasan Gir National Park)

B 9

State: Gujarat	**Altitude:** 150m/492ft–643m/2110ft
Distance: 1280km/795mi southwest of Delhi	

The arid, hilly and forested area of the south of Saurashtra Peninsula is home to Gir National Park, which is world famous for its population of Asiatic lions.

Asiatic lions   In the past, Asiatic lions lived within a wide belt that stretched from northwest India to Persia and Arabia. The intensification of arable and livestock farming has decimated the population. During a count in 1913 the total number of lions was only 20. As a result the Nawab of Junagadh placed these animals under strict protection. These efforts were continued after India achieved independence. Today the park is home to approximately 340 lions.

Gir National Park has an area of 260 sq km/100 sq mi and lies within a 1412 sq km/545 sq mi protected area that is also used for agricultural purposes. The hilly landscape features many small valleys and depressions in which rainwater can gather. The airy mixed forests and the grassland provide an ideal habitat for sambar deer, chitals, chinkaras and nilgai antelopes. In addition the area is home to wild boar, langurs and old-world porcupines. Other predators besides lions include hyenas, jungle cats and leopards. As are many other parks, this one is inhabited by many bird species, including hoopoes, peacocks, Egyptian vultures and cattle egrets.

 GIR N.P.

INFORMATION
www.gujarattourism.com

GETTING THERE
Rail connections from Ahmedabad via Varaval or by car via Junagadh (60km/37mi to the northwest)

WHERE TO STAY
▶ **Mid-range / Luxury**
Lion Safari Camp
Sasan Gir, tel. 079 – 26 46 30 33
www.palacesofindia.com. Accommodation in luxurious tents within the

Visitors can drive through the park in a **Jeep** accompanied by a guide. There is no guarantee that this will result in lions being spotted. Those who have limited time but still want to see a lion should visit the smaller, fenced-in safari park, which was set up for that purpose.

Tip During the monsoon season (generally from mid-June to mid-October) the park is closed. The information office in Sasan provides details about possible tours and the safari park. Guides can also be hired here. The simplest option is to visit the park in a Jeep hired in Junagadh.

✳ Jaipur

D 6

Capital of Rajasthan
Population: 2.3 million

Altitude: 380m/1247ft
Distance: 261km/162mi southwest of Delhi

Jaipur is one of the corners of the »Golden Triangle« of tourism, which also includes India's capital Delhi, and Agra, home of the Taj Mahal. Large Maharaja's palaces and other buildings from the time of the Rajput rulers, the salmon-coloured old town with its lively bazaars, the excellent shopping opportunities and good hotels entice visitors to stay. Jaipur is also an ideal base for a round trip through Rajasthan.

⬤ VISITING JAIPUR

INFORMATION

Department of Tourism, Art & Culture
Government of Rajasthan
Govt. Hostel Campus
Paryatan Bhavan, MI Road
Tel. 01 41 – 511 0595
www.rajasthantourism.gov.in

GETTING THERE

Flight connections, fast trains and buses from Delhi, Mumbai and other places

FESTIVALS

Jaipur Festival (cultural festival in January)

SHOPPING

Jewellery, particularly semi-precious stones and silver, as well as textiles and traditional leather shoes are Jaipur's specialities. The bazaars of the Pink City are famous for them. Many shops can also be found on Mirza Ismael Road (MI Road) and around the Hawa Mahal. A large selection of jewellery is available at Chameliwala Market.

WHERE TO EAT

▶ Expensive

① *Peshawri*
Welcomehotel Rajputana Palace Sheraton, tel. 01 41 – 510 01 00
Excellent northern Indian cuisine.

▶ Moderate

② *Niros*
MI Road, tel. 01 41 – 237 44 93
Very good northern Indian cuisine as well as Chinese dishes, beer and wine.

▶ Inexpensive

③ *LMB*
Johari Bazar, tel. 01 41 – 256 58 44

Modern furnishings, traditional vegetarian snacks and dishes. Also famous for its sweets, which are sold at the bar.

WHERE TO STAY

▶ Luxury

① *Rambagh Palace*
Bhawani Singh Road
Tel. 0141 – 221 19 19
www.tajhotels.com. This former hunting lodge of the legendary Maharaja Man Singh II is one of the city's first hotels. Surrounded by a huge park the accommodation comprises exclusive rooms and suites.

② *Samode Haveli*
Gangapole, tel. 01 41 – 263 23 70
www.samode.com
150-year-old residence with individually furnished rooms, a handpainted dining room and a nice terrace in a green garden.

▶ Mid-range

③ *Jasvilas*
C-9, Sawai Singh Highway
Bani Park, tel. 01 41 – 220 46 38
www.jasvilas.com. Very good, small and personally run hotel in a nice villa with a swimming pool and garden. Dinner can be served on request in the cosy dining room.

▶ Mid-range / Budget

④ *Hotel Diggi Palace*
Shivaji Marg, S.M.S. Hospital Road
Tel. 01 41 – 237 30 91, 220 49 02
www.hoteldiggipalace.com
An oasis in the middle of busy Jaipur, this old palace is situated in an attractive flower garden. There is a pleasant roof terrace restaurant serving international cuisine, as well as an internet cafe.

Jaipur Map

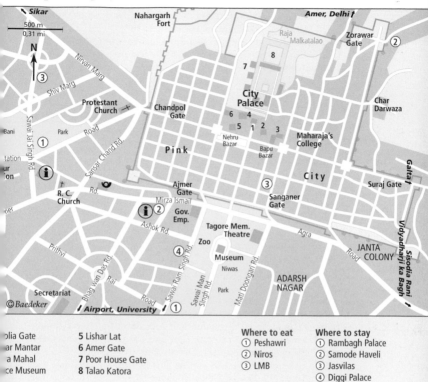

Jaipur is a relatively young city. It was built by Jai Singh II in 1728 **History**
because the old capital of Amer had become too small for him. The
city was divided into nine parts with each district being given a certain function, as is specified in Shilpa Shastra, the ancient Indian architectural teachings. The old town was protected by a high wall. **✷**
Seven gates allowed access to the city. The striking, uniformly sal- ◄ Pink City
mon-pink colour of the façades in the city centre, the reason why Jaipur is also known as »Pink City«, are more recent. By 1818 the Maharaja of Jaipur had signed an agreement which afforded him protection by the British colonial power. Thus it was no surprise that he
had the city painted in the welcome colour of red on the occasion of
the Prince of Wales's visit in 1876. Since that time all the property
owners in the important streets are required to paint the façades of
their houses in this colour. Those neglecting to do this will have their
façade painted by the city authority and be sent a bill.

Handicrafts Jaipur is known for **gemstones**, which are polished in the city. They cost a fair bit less here than they do in Europe. However, without detailed knowledge the danger of purchasing a fake is quite high. In addition to gemstones, Jaipur has a great selection of printed **textiles**, fabrics decorated with tiny mirrors, **silver jewellery**, **miniatures** and **blue pottery** to offer. The most important markets are located near the Hawa Mahal and in Johari Bazaar. The Rajasthani Handicrafts Emporium on Mirza Ismail Road is the right place to go for those wanting to shop in peace and quiet. Near to Jaipur, **Sanganer is known for its hand-printed textiles**. The patterned stamps made of wood are used according to long-standing tradition to print cotton fabrics.

What to See in and around Jaipur

★ ★
City Palace
🕐
Opening hours:
daily
9.30am–4.45pm

The vast majority of the City Palace can be seen as part of the Sawai Man Singh Museum. Only a small section is still inhabited by the royal family. The city palace was commissioned by Jai Singh (1728–32) and later extended several times.

The first free-standing building of several floors that, thanks to its finely worked façade, grabs the attention upon entering the palace is the **Welcome Palace** (Mubarak Mahal). This building contains a good collection of old textiles and the royal family's jewellery. In addition there is a weapons collection on display. **Singh Pol** (Lion's Gate), guarded by two white marble elephants and a palace guard, leads into the complex's interior. The large **Reception Hall** (Diwan-i-Khas), which is open on all four sides and was used for private audiences, invites visitors to linger. The two large 300kg/660lb silver containers were made especially for the trip of King Madho Singh II to England in 1799. He used these containers to transport water from the Ganges on his sea voyage of several months. According to legend the water remained fresh the entire time and the maharaja was able to maintain his ritual purity through the use of the holy Ganges water (▶Baedeker Special p.290).

West of Diwan-i-Khas is the magnificent **Peacock Court** (Pritam Niwas Chowk), which affords the best views of the royal family's seven-storey residence (Chandra Mahal). The gates of the courtyard are decorated with shimmering depictions of peacocks. Upon returning to the Diwan-i-Khas visitors will be able to recognize the **art gallery** and the **museum** beyond it, which are housed in the former hall of public audiences. Visiting them is highly recommendable. Particularly interesting are the collections of old manuscripts and Indian miniatures.

★ ★
Hawa Mahal
(Wind Palace)

The Wind Palace (Hawa Mahal) was built by Sawai Pratap Singh in 1799. The five-storey palace consists mainly of a **façade** and is a great illustration of the values of Rajput culture. It has **almost 900 windows**, allowing the many women of the palace to observe proces-

The Palace of Winds consists of just a façade. From here women were allowed to watch the goings on down on the street

sions and what was happening on the streets without having to be seen by others. The custom of purdah is widespread amongst Rajputs. It forbids unknown men to see women's faces. The walk through the various storeys affords wonderful views of the city palace to the west of the Hawa Mahal as well as of the city of Jaipur. The name »Wind Palace« comes from the fresh breeze that blows into the small windows.

Opening hours: daily 10am–5pm

These curious buildings were built under Jai Singh between 1728 and 1734 in order to measure the planets' movements and thus to improve the calendar. Every one of the 16 instruments had a specific function, and these are explained during the informative guided tours. The large 27m/90ft Samrat Yatra is still used during the traditional **Guru Purnima Festival** (July / August) to predict the strength of next year's monsoon.

★ ★
Jantar Mantar
Opening hours: daily 9am–4.30pm

Rambagh Palace, the maharaja's former garden palace, is now a luxury hotel.

Rambagh Palace

Leave the old town through Sanganer Gate to get to Ram Niwas Garden, an inviting place to take a break and relax. In the south of the

Ram Niwas Park

Visiting the observatory of Jai Singh.
The town's palace can be seen in the background

⏱ Opening hours:
daily except Fri
10am–5pm

park is the Indo-Saracenic Albert Hall. It houses the Central Museum with its fine collection of miniature portraits and various handicraft products made by Rajasthan's rural population. The garden also contains a zoo with a crocodile farm.

Nahargarh Fort Around 2km/1mi from the city centre, on a hill, stands Nahargarh Fort, also known as Tiger Fort. It was built by Sawai Singh in 1734 and extended by Sawai Ram Singh II in 1868. From the top there are nice views of the »Pink City«.

✶
Galta One nice excursion would be to visit the temples of Galta (approx. 5km/3mi east of the city centre). Departing from Surya Gate in the east of the city, walk along a winding path, past monkeys and cows, up to the **Sun Temple**, from where there are nice views of the city. The path descends on the other side down to Galta, past a gorge with a water basin to the temple complex, which is peacefully situated in the valley. After busy and loud Jaipur this is a **place of tranquillity and contemplation**. This excursion takes around three to four hours.

✶
Samode Turn right on the road from Jaipur to Sikar near Chomu to get to the small town of Samode after 42km/26mi. This town, surrounded by an old town wall, has a small bazaar, but its main attraction is Samode Palace, a real **gem amongst Rajasthan's many palaces**. The palace, which was built by a finance minister of Jaipur's king Jai

Singh II, is now a luxury hotel. One of the palace's highlights is **Durbar Hall (Entrance Hall)**, which is completely decorated with Meenakari tiles, paintings and gilded tile borders. Above the palace is an old fort, which is easily accessible via a staircase. There is a nice view of the region from the top. Samode can be visited on a day trip or on the way to the painted houses of ►Shekhawati.

✱ Amer   D 6

A road departs ►Jaipur heading for Amer (11km/7mi to the north), running between two ranges of the Aravalli Hills. After a sharp turn the **fort of Amer** suddenly appears on a mountainside. The fort is situated on the ridge of a mountain range called Kali Koh and is naturally protected from all sides.

Outstanding example of Rajasthan's architecture

Amer, the former capital of Kachchwaha dynasty, was built by Man Singh (1589–1614), one of Akbar's allies, in 1592 and later extended by Jai Singh (1621–67).

The fort itself is a wonderful example of Rajput architecture. Its outstanding strategic location becomes particularly clear when climbing up the narrow switchback road to the fort on the back of an elephant.

Three large gates protect the path to the palace. Behind the first gate, Jai Pol, is a courtyard, a gathering place for monkeys and elephants in which countless people and snack stalls are crowded together. Those who do not have the courage to ride up to the fort on an elephant can pluck up the courage for a short jaunt here. A steep stairway leads up to Singh Pol, the Lion's Gate. Beyond it is the Diwan-i-Am, the Audience Hall, with a double-columned colonnade and a temple for goddess Kali, who is worshipped here as Sita Mala. The palace is situated one storey higher and is accessed through the third, large **gateway, Ganesh Pol**.

A classic trip:
riding up to the fort on an elephant

🕐 Opening hours:
daily 9am–4.30pm

Ganesh Pol was built in 1640 and is rich in mosaics, whose wonderful mix of colours and patterns contributed to the fact that this gate is considered one of the most beautiful in India. Immediately to the left is the **Victory Hall** (Jai Mandir), which is made of white marble and decorated with many arabesques. This building is one of the most successful examples of the synthesis between Mughal and Hindu architecture. Detailed floral ornaments adorn the walls; the ceiling is covered in many mirrors. After walking through Jai Mandir visitors enter the small **Mirror Hall** (Shish Mahal), which only unfolds its true splendour when the doors are closed and candles are lit. The fort's guides are proud to be able to demonstrate the sparkling of the mirrors: it creates an impression of being under a twinkling starry sky. The **Entertainment Hall** (Sukh Niwas), with its sophisticated cooling techniques, gives an idea of how people tried to defy Rajasthan's hot climate centuries ago. Further inside there are many more rooms, which were inhabited by the king's many wives. Some of the walls still have remains of paintings. Radha and Krishna as lovers is a common motif.

On the drive back to ► Jaipur visitors will pass **Lake Maota**; on its shores are the geometrically laid-out Dilaram Gardens. A small archaeological museum is also part of the complex.

⁎ ⁎ Jaisalmer

B 6

State: Rajasthan
Population: 60,000

Altitude: 40m/131ft
Distance: 864km/537mi west of Delhi

The desert town of Jaisalmer is located in Rajasthan's northwest not far from the Pakistani border. Its richly adorned merchant houses (havelis), narrow streets, its impressive fort, sand dunes and camel safarisall come together to give visitors a feel for the atmosphere of a desert town that is almost without equal.

History The Bhatti prince Rawa Jaisal Singh founded Jaisalmer, the »oasis of Jaisal«, in the middle of the desert 17km/11mi from his old capital of Lodawa in 1156. The new town was built on a mountain and given additional protection against attacks by neighbouring tribes by constructing high walls around it. It managed to withstand all attacks and still has the air of a town from centuries long gone. Jaisalmer owes its great wealth to its location on the old camel route from India through modern-day Pakistan to Afghanistan.

The Jain traders and bankers earned so much money in this spot in the desert that they had **wonderful havelis** with artistically decorated balconies and painted façades built for them. The regional golden yellow sandstone was an excellent material for the stone masons, who used it to produce the finest stonework. As a result of the parti-

▶ VISITING JAISALMER

INFORMATION

Tourist Office
Station Road
Tel. 029 92 – 524 06
www.rajasthantourism.gov.in

GETTING THERE

Train connections to Delhi and
Jodhpur, bus connection to
Bikaner

SHOPPING

Jaisalmer is famous for its blankets
and pillows interwoven with gold and
silver thread, as well as for its
embroidery. Wooden puppets are also
made here. The town resembles a
small bazaar with countless shops.
The largest take up entire havelis.

CAMEL SAFARIS

Trips through the dunes on a camel
are organized by almost every hotel in
Jaisalmer. The accommodation recommended here also offers such
tours.

WHERE TO STAY / WHERE TO EAT

▶ Luxury

Fort Rajwada
Jodhpur-Barmer Link Road
Tel. 029 92 – 25 32 33
www.fortrajwada.com
The town's most luxurious hotel, with
a stylish and elegant interior and
every creature comfort. The Roopal
restaurant serves specialities from
Rajasthan as well as Western cuisine.

Jawahar Niwas Palace
1, Bada Bagh Road,
Tel. 029 92 – 25 22 08
More than 100-year-old haveli with
views of the fort. The restaurant
serves northern Indian specialities.

▶ Mid-range

Killa Bhawan
is considered the best establishment
in the fort.
Tel. 029 92 – 25 12 04
www.killabhawan.com
A great view of the sunset can be had
from the terrace; breakfast is included, no restaurant.

tion of Pakistan and India the border became impassable, causing
the town to lose its earlier significance. Jaisalmer's people took up
new jobs. Some became livestock farmers, others tried their luck
producing handicrafts and processing camel wool. Many of Jaisalmer's inhabitants left the town for the Gulf states.

What to See in Jaisalmer

Follow the narrow streets lined by houses with stone balconies to
get to the citadel, which towers atop the 80m/260ft Trikuta hill. Beyond its 9m/30ft wall with almost a hundred towers stand countless
buildings. Some of Jaisalmer's population still live within the fort.

★★
Citadel

The seven-storey palace, the Juna Mahal, in the middle of the fort is
one of the oldest in Rajasthan. It is famous for its **covered umbrella-**

Juna Mahal

The ancient caravan city of Jailsalmer is situated in the middle of an 80m/260ft rock in the middle of the Thar desert

like roof terraces and sandstone balconies. The sandstone was easy to work with and the balconies are ornamented in such great detail that they appear to be made of wood. As a result of the arid desert climate the stones have hardly weathered, meaning the buildings can be admired almost in their original state.

Havelis

★ ★

Patwon-ki-Haveli

In Jaisalmer there are many beautiful merchant houses (havelis). The most magnificent example is the Patwon-ki-Haveli. It was built by the brocade trader Patwa for his five sons and consists of a group of five houses. It lies hidden in a narrow street. The **Salim-Singh-ki-Haveli** near the fort's main entrance was built by Salim Singh Mehta, the prime minister of Mulraj II, in 1815 and is still inhabited. The detailed balcony façade around the house is a remarkable product of the art of stonemasonry. Rising up on the building's roof is the Moti Mahal (Pearl Hall), which seems to have simply been placed there. It has twelve richly adorned arches along its length and seven along its width, displaying depictions of peacocks. Those wishing to see more havelis should take a look at the **Nathmal-ki-Haveli**, an outstanding building designed by two brothers. Each brother was responsible for a part of the building and even though no motif was used twice they achieved a structure that feels very harmonious.

The group of seven Jain temples within the fort complex as well as a further temple are impressive legacies of the Jain merchants who sought refuge here from persecution by Hindu rulers in Rajasthan. The temples were built between the 12th and 15th centuries and are consecrated to different fordmakers (tirthankaras) such as Parshvanatha and Rishabha. Their richly ornamented halls with numerous figures provide an insight into the Jain understanding of the cosmos: they are populated by heavenly women (apsaras) and musicians. Of particular interest is **Parshvanatha Temple** (1417) with 52 small shrines and **Rishabha Temple** (1479) with 600 depictions of meditating fordmakers. The library (Gyan Bhandar) contains one of the most extensive collections of Jain literature.

✱
Jain Temple

Not far from Gadi Sagar reservoir is a small, private folklore museum. It exhibits musical instruments as well as small wooden altars (kawad) with depictions of gods with which storytellers used to go from village to village.

Folklore Museum

Jaisalmer is known for its wonderful palaces and havelis with their filigree balconies

Aagolaie: a village between Jaisalmer and Jodhpur

BETWEEN YESTERDAY AND TODAY

Around two-thirds of India's population live in rural locations. India has more than 50,000 villages of varying sizes and types, including clustered villages, linear villages, small hamlets, stilt-house villages, mound settlements, stone houses, mud huts and palm-leaf huts.

The **neighbourhood formation** so typical of Indian villages is the result of the country's caste hierarchy. Big landlords who are in the highest castes (Brahmins, Vaishyas) live in manors on the village's outskirts. The independent farmers, the Ryots, cultivate their own land; they are members of the farmer caste. Tenants with different usage rights come from the Shudra caste. The majority of the village population are farm workers, most of whom do not own their own land and make a living as day labourers and by taking on odd jobs. The worst off are **Harijans** (God's children, also »untouchables«), who, as landless day labourers, have to work under conditions that can well be compared to serfdom. They live in isolated quarters on the outskirts and are not allowed to move freely in the village. Access to temples is not permitted to them, neither is the use of the well. Many do not even know that »untouchability« has officially been abolished.

The efforts of the Indian government have brought schools, wells and electricity to many villages. A well-developed road network now connects even the most remote villages with the towns. Television and internet have found their way into India's villages and even farmers who have never gone beyond their village boundaries can see pictures of the outside world. Despite all of this, the daily lives of village inhabitants are determined by **tradition**, and life follows the rhythm set by nature.

An example: Aagolaie

The Rajasthani village of Aagolaie is home to approx. 2000 people; a third of them live in the old village core, while the others are scattered in individual farmsteads (dhani) on their fields. Of the almost 30 **castes** the jats (farmers), raikas (shepherds), mochis (shoemakers) and dolis (musicians) are the most important. The village centre is inhabited by craftsmen such as shoemakers, goldsmiths, carpenters, priests and barbers; the dhanis on the other hand are mainly occupied by farmers and shepherds. Only the village core has electricity and

sometimes a working water supply. Two old temples and the dilapidated market place are evidence of the time when Aagolaie had an important market function for the region. The main road has several tea places, vegetable stands and a shop with sweets and biscuits. The customers are lorry drivers or people passing through, but the village inhabitants also come to buy tea, sugar and spices here. The people in the dhanis are busy securing their survival all year round. Only by carefully stockpiling food and by applying sophisticated agriculture developed over thousands of years (cultivating many plants, using wild plants, keeping pets) are the farmers able to survive at the edge of the Thar desert.

When the **monsoon rains** come in the months of June and July the village comes to life and all of its inhabitants work tirelessly to plough the fields and sow the seeds. The seedlings have to be protected from the many peacocks and the young plants from roaming animals such as deer and antelope. Nonetheless **respect for all living things** forbids seeing these animals as pests and killing them.

Quite the opposite in fact: peacocks and deer are worshipped. The children take the pets to the meadows and make sure that they do not eat the crops. When the rains are good the crops are harvested, threshed, cleaned and carefully stored. Since this work has to be done by hand it takes several months until it is complete. From November to February festivals and weddings are celebrated, people visit each other and come together, but it is also the time when the mud huts are repaired and thatched roofs are re-done. Then comes the hot summer, when **water shortage** is the biggest problem. Sometimes the women have to walk several miles to get water from a pond. The children go with the animals to distant watering holes to let them drink. In bad years, when the monsoon stays away, the shepherds walk up to 800km/500mi with their animals in search of food and water.

The rural life is not an easy one and many villages are still dominated by a few rich landowners. Mahatma Gandhi's dream that villages would organize themselves into **democratic village councils** is still far removed from reality.

Sunset Point   On an elevation in the north of town are chhatris (cenotaphs) of Jaisalmer's rulers. Many people come together here at sunset to enjoy the magnificent view of the fort, which turns golden in the evening sun.

Around Jaisalmer

Camel safaris   Jaisalmer is home to several agencies specializing in camel safaris. The tours can last anything from a day to a week. It is best to take a few days to really be able to experience the desert on the back of a camel.

Bada Bagh   Heading northwards along the road to the left of Sunset Point the road reaches an oasis called Bada Bagh (big garden) after approx. 6km/4mi. The access road, just beyond a military camp, is a little hard to find. On an elevation beyond the oasis are many graves for the rulers of Jaisalmer. This place, hardly visited by tourists, demonstrates the decline of the former magnificence of the desert town like no other. The atmosphere is particularly pleasant in the afternoons.

All that is left of Lodruwa (9km/5mi from Jaisalmer), the former old capital, is a single Jain temple complex, which radiates a strange magic in the desert. Within the complex is a depiction of Kalpavriksha, the tree that grants wishes. Sacred cobras live right opposite in a small crack.

✷ Lodruwa

✷ Sam sand dunes   Every day numerous tourists make their way to the Sam sand dunes (40km/25mi from Jaisalmer), the large migrating dunes, in order to experience a **breathtaking sunset** over the desert. It can be admired from the back of a camel, as an entire »camel pack« is available for specifically this activity.

> **! Baedeker TIP**
>
> **Warning, camel jam!**
> Riding a camel at sunset in the sand dunes of Sam is part of the standard programme for every tourist. However, this should be avoided on Sundays and Indian holidays. It gets extremely busy at these times and tourists could find themselves stuck in a traffic jam – but with camels.

✷ ✷ Jodhpur

C 6

State: Rajasthan
Population: 930,000

Altitude: 224m/735ft
Distance: 604km/375mi southwest of Delhi

Jodhpur, the former capital of Marwar (Marwar = land of the dead), is the second largest city in Rajasthan after Jaipur. It lies on the edge of Thar desert.

● VISITING JODHPUR

INFORMATION
www.rajasthantourism.gov.in

SHOPPING
Jodhpur is a veritable paradise for lovers of Indian furniture and antiques, which can be bought here in large halls. Many items are not actually old, they have only been made to look old. However, the selection is enormous.

Handicrafts and textiles, leather and jewellery in particular, can be found at Tripolia Bazaar, on Station Road and around the clock tower.

WHERE TO STAY / WHERE TO EAT
► Luxury
① *Umaid Bhavan Palace*
Tel. 02 91 – 25 05 01

www.umaidbhavan.comThis grandiose Maharaja's palace is considered the best establishment in Jodhpur. The two excellent restaurants and an underground swimming pool contribute to the good life here.

② *Ajit Bhawan*
Near Circuit House
Tel. 02 91 – 251 04 10
www.ajitbhawan.com
The old palace is located in a very nice garden with a swimming pool.

► Budget
③ *Hotel Ghoomar*
High Court Road
Tel. 02 91 – 254 40 10
Centrally located RSTDC hotel with basic rooms.

The town was founded by the Rajput king Rao Jodha, a member of the Rathor clan, in 1459. The old town with its narrow streets, pretty sandstone houses and well-preserved fort is surrounded by a 10km/6mi town wall and still imparts a vivid impression of the lives of Rajasthan's kings. This town owes its great wealth to its special location at the edge of the desert. It was once the most important reloading point for goods being transported on the overland route from Gujarat's fertile regions to Delhi.

Today the town is an important centre for agricultural products. The High Court and the university have made it into a centre of administration and education. It is a good starting point for tourists wanting to visit the desert town of ►Jaisalmer.

What to See in Jodhpur

Meherangarh Fort, situated on a sandstone hill, was built in the 16th century and was never conquered by a foreign ruler, which is why it has remained undamaged. The seven city gates on the winding path to the fort, each one impressive in its own right, make it clear why this city was so difficult to conquer. The rock on which the fort was built rises 120m/394ft above the surrounding area and thus provides natural protection. In addition the fort is protected by a massive wall

✶ ✶
Meherangarh Fort

that reaches 36m/118ft high in places. In the walls around the gate are **sati stones with hand prints**. They commemorate the women who underwent ritual immolation after their husband's death.

🕐
Opening hours:
daily 9am–5pm

The fort contains the **Meherangarh Museum**. Its 18 departments have weapons, armour for war elephants, carpets, musical instruments, furniture and costumes on display. They bespeak the maharajas' magnificence and wealth and the great mastery of handicraft production of that time.

Blue City

The fort affords wonderful views of Jodhpur, which has an overall blue appearance because of the large number of blue houses it contains. Blue is the colour of the god Krishna, who is so popular in Rajasthan. The painted houses are usually inhabited by Brahmins. Leave the fort to go to the old town and wander through a labyrinth of narrow streets and through Gandha Ghar, Jodhpur's marketplace with the clock tower.

★
Jaswant Thada

Standing on a hill near the fort is the white marble monument for Maharaja Jaswant Singh II, who died in 1895. The pretty garden in front of the monument is a lovely place to recover from the hustle and bustle of the city. In front of Jawant Thada there are numerous

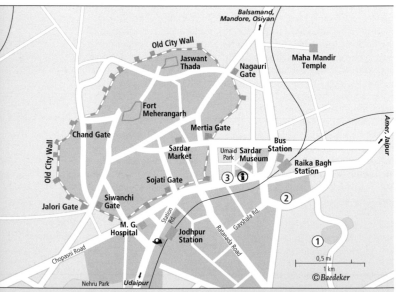

Jodhpur Map

Balsamand,
Mandore, Osiyan

Old City Wall

Jaswant
Thada

Nagauri
Gate

Maha Mandir
Temple

Fort
Meherangarh

Mertia Gate

Chand Gate

Old City Wall

Sardar
Market

Umaid
Park

Sardar
Museum

Bus
Station

Raika Bagh
Station

Sojati Gate

Siwanchi
Gate

Jalori Gate

M. G.
Hospital

Station Rd.

Jodhpur
Station

Ganshala Rd.

Ratanada Road

Chopasni Road

Nehru Park

Udaipur

Amer, Jaipur

0,5 mi
1 km
©Baedeker

Where to stay / Where to eat
① Umaid Bhavan Palace Hotel   ② Ajit Bhawan   ③ Hotel Ghoomar

The view from the fort of the old town with its blue houses, most of which are inhabited by Brahmins, is impressive

chhatris (cenotaphs) for the dead warriors from the nobility. There is a nice view from here of the city, Meherangarh Fort and Umaid Bhavan, the new palace of the king of Jodhpur.

The magnificent Umaid Bhavan palace was commissioned as a residence by Maharaja Umaid Singh in the last century (construction began in 1929). It took several thousand workers 15 years to complete the enormous palace, which had been designed by British architect H. V. Lanchester. At first glance its double dome resembles more a mix between Rome's St. Peter's Basilica and a Renaissance palace than an Indian building. The 348 rooms with huge dining halls and an underground swimming pool speak volumes about the maharajas' lifestyle before they had to relinquish their power. Tiles, baths and basins for the bathrooms were imported from Italy. The Maharaja of Jodhpur still inhabits some of the rooms. Another part of the palace houses a museum. The greater part of the building has, however, been transformed into a luxury hotel.

Umaid Bhavan (fig. p.196)

Around Jodhpur

The summer palace in Balsamand (6km/3.5mi north of Jodhpur) on the shore of the artificial lake was built by Balak Rao Parihar in 1159 and the shade provided by the large trees make the area a popular spot for picnics.

Balsamand

✴
Mandore
Mandore (8km/5mi north of Jodhpur) was the old Marwar capital before they moved it to Jodhpur. It was founded as early as the sixth century but was subsequently conquered and destroyed several times. The pretty gardens make this an inviting place to visit. In the middle of the gardens are some red sandstone chhatris, cenotaphs for the rulers of Jodhpur. The largest chhatri is dedicated to Maharaja Diraj Ajit Singh (died 1763). Its façade is adorned with outstanding sandstone sculptures. The Hall of Heroes contains 16 colourful figures, most of them popular heroes or Hindu deities.

✴
Osiyan
Scattered throughout the old town of Osiyan (64km/40mi north of Jodhpur) are **more than 20 old Hindu and Jain temples**. Dating from the eighth to tenth centuries, the temples represent an important stage in the development of the Nagara style. Harihara Temple no. 1 (AD 750–850) shows clearly how the niches have changed; Harihara Temple no. 3 is interesting because of its entrance hall, which has a vaulted roof. Situated on a hill and visible from a great way off is **Sachiya Mata Temple**, which is consecrated to the goddess Durga.

Tranquil Osiyan was once a junction along the old trading route through the Thar desert. It is worth visiting for a group of Hindu and Jain temples

Mount Abu

★ ★

State: Rajasthan
Population: 25,000

Altitude: 1260m/4134ft–1300m/4265ft
Distance: 750km/466mi southwest of Delhi

The temple town located at an altitude of more than 1200m/4100ft in the Aravalli Hillsis a popular destination all year round. At this altitude the picturesque Mount Abu enjoys a pleasant climate and its eucalyptus forests and lakes make it an ideal place to come and relax.

It is no wonder, therefore, that the only mountain station of Rajasthan, a state that is otherwise hot, is a popular destination for wealthy Indians. The famous Dilwara Temples are an **important place of pilgrimage for Jainas**. Mountains have a special significance in Jain mythology, which is why they often built their temples on elevated ground.

The four temple complexes (Mount Abu, ►Mount Girnar, ►Palitana and Ranakpur), together with the fifth imaginary mountain Astapada, form a copy of the mythical continent Nandisvaradipa. This land is said to have 52 temples. Nandisvaradipa is on a par with the conceptions of paradise in other religions.

Thus it was natural that a minister of the Solanki dynasty at the time of its golden age had a temple built for the tirthankaras of the Jainas on this high mountain between the Himalaya and the Western Ghats. The first temple was built as early as 1031, while the construction of the other three wore on for more than 400 years.

! Baedeker TIP

Leather stays outside
Jainas consider leather to be impure so all objects made of leather (including belts) have to be handed over before visiting the temples.

 ## VISITING MOUNT ABU

INFORMATION
Tourist Office
Opposite the bus station
Tel. 02974 – 351 51
www.rajasthantourism.com

GETTING THERE
Rail connection to Abu Road (located on the main line Ahmedabad – Delhi), then a bus connection (45 minutes)

WHERE TO STAY / WHERE TO EAT
► **Luxury / Mid-range**
Palace Hotel
Bikaner House
Tel. 02974 – 23 86 73
This former summer palace of the maharajas of Bikaner with its stylish rooms is a fine establishment. The complex has a park with its own lake as well as a restaurant.

Sunset Point on Mount Abu is a popular and beautiful place to see the sun go down

★★
Dilwara Temples

★
Vimala Shah
Temple ▶

The Dilwara Temples can be found 5km/3mi northwest of the town of Abu and are easily reached in a one-hour walk. All four temples are made of white marble, which was brought to the site from 30km/20mi away. The oldest, Vimala Shah Temple, is consecrated to the first tirthankara Adinath, though it is named after its donor, the Solanki minister Vimala Vasahi. The sanctum has a representation of **tirthankara Adinath** sitting in a meditative posture. In contrast to the plain exterior, the interior is decorated with filigree marble statues. 2000 craftsmen are said to have worked on the marble for more than 14 years in order to complete the temple. Some of the figures were produced by shaving blocks of stone, and the craftsmen were paid depending on the amount of dust shaved off. Large numbers of horses, elephants, heavenly women and musicians give a stunning **taster of life in paradise after salvation**. One particularly remarkable feature is the octagonal dome in the hall in front of the cella, which rests on eight columns. The roof, which is supported by goddesses and shapely dancing girls, vaults in the shape of a lotus. The white, translucent marble gives the whole building such lightness that it looks as if the figures are floating. In contrast to the confusing wealth of figures, the **floor plan of Jain temples** is straightforward. At the centre of the temple is the cella with the depiction of the fordmaker. Adjoining it is an entrance hall with two gateways in front of it. The entrance hall leads into a hall of columns. In front of this hall is the hall for ritual dances, which is covered by a self-supporting dome. The entire axial complex with the three halls and the cella are situated in a courtyard that is surrounded by a double colonnade and a border of niches. In front of the niches on the colonnade's roof are outstanding marble reliefs. The depictions show tirthankaras. In front of the temple is a hall with ten marble elephants and a rider who symbolizes the temple's donor. **Photography is not allowed** inside the temple.

Neminath Temple, the most filigree of them all, and the incomplete **Adinath Temple** correspond to the same basic structure described above. The cella of Adinath Temple has a statue of the first tirthankara made of five different metals in 1582. Only **Camukh Temple**, which is right behind the entrance to the left, has a different layout. The cella is open on all four sides and has one hall in front of it.

✶ Mount Girnar

B 9

State: Gujarat
Distance: 1220km/758mi southwest of Delhi

Altitude: 1117m/3665ft

The attractive, extinct Girnarvolcano has been an important holy centre for more than 2000 years. 4000 steps lead up the mountain, which is climbed by both Hindu pilgrims and Jainas from all over India in order to visit the many temples on its slopes. The Jain temples are particularly impressive.

Halfway up Mount Girnar (at around 600m/1970ft) there is a group of 15 Jain temples, which are walled like the ones in Shatrunaya (▶ Palitana). The first temple along the way is **Neminath Temple**, which was built between the 12th and 15th centuries. It is consecrated to the 22nd tirthankara Neminath, who is said to have meditated here before he found salvation and began being worshipped as a fordmaker. Neminath is depicted in the cella in black marble in a meditating pose. The temple consists of several halls with many columns, which are adorned with excellent sculptures, as is customary in Jain temples. Opposite stands **Mallinath Temple**, which was built by the same donors, who also had Jain temples built in ▶ Mount Abu and on Mount Shatrunajaya near ▶ Palitana.

✶ **Jain temples**

▶ VISITING MOUNT GIRNAR

INFORMATION
www.gujarattourism.com

GETTING THERE
Rail connections from Ahmedabad and Rajkot to Junagadh. There is a direct bus between Diu and Mount Girnar.

WHERE TO EAT/WHERE TO STAY
▶ **Inexpensive**
Hotel Girnar
Majewadi Darwaja
Junagadh
Tel. 02 85 – 262 12 01
Hotel run by Gujarat Tourism with a vegetarian restaurant.

Those who succeed in climbing the remaining 2000 steps to the peak will be rewarded with a **breathtaking view** of the temple complex from above and of the plain. The mountain is crowned by a temple dedicated to the Hindu goddess Amba Mata. It is sought out by young couples, who hope the goddess can bless them with a long, happy marriage.

Junagadh

Junagadh was already being ruled in the second century by the Kshattrapas and after the Rajput kings fell under Muslim rule in the 16th century. The old citadel in the east of the town has a mosque as well as two impressive stepped wells (the Adi Chadi Vav and the Navghan Kuva). A number of Buddhist caves lead to the conclusion that this town was already populated under Ashoka (approx. 268–233 BC).

Two of the town's sites are the mausoleum of Baha-ud-din Bhar and Nawab's Palace (1870), which houses the Durbar Hall Museum. Junagadh's actual significance lies in its **proximity to the sacred Jain location** that is Mount Girnar (3km/2mi to the east). The ascent begins west of the citadel behind Damodar Kund, where there also is a large stone in Pali script, which has been deciphered to be an edict by Emperor Ashoka. It takes several hours to ascend and descend the mountain, with a necessary stopover in Junagadh.

✷✷ **Palitana**

B 9

State: Gujarat
Population: 45,000

Altitude: 600m/1970ft
Distance: 1100km/684mi southwest of Delhi

Mount Shatrunajaya near Palitana is one of the four most important holy places for Jains. More than 860 temples with approx. 10,000 sculptures from the 15th and 16th centuries are scattered across the mountain's two peaks.

▶ VISITING PALITANA

INFORMATION
www.gujarattourism.com

GETTING THERE
Train connection from Ahmedabad to Bhavnagar or flight from Mumbai to Bhavnagar. Then a bus or train to Palitana (50km/31mi)

WHERE TO STAY / WHERE TO EAT
▶ **Budget / Inexpensive**
Hotel Sumeru
Station Road, tel. 028 48 – 25 23 27
Hotel run by Gujarat Tourism: 17 basic, clean rooms (some of them with air conditioning) vegetarian restaurant.

For those who find the climb difficult there are litters

As was the case on ▶ Mount Girnar, the temples and the mountain here form a synthesis, which have made them the most attractive temple complex of the Jain religious community. Both peaks of the temple mountain and the valley between them are surrounded by a wall. **This is where the Jains' 24 fordmakers are said to have achieved enlightenment**.
During Mahavir Jayanthi in the spring (March / April), held in commemoration of the last tirthankara, thousands of pilgrims come to Palitana. Climbing the more than 3000 steps (around 3.5km/2mi) requires a good level of fitness. Litters are available for people who cannot walk up themselves.

✷ Shatrunajaya Temple Complex

After having almost reached the top of the mountain the path forks and parts of the complex come into view. The left path descends slightly before it goes uphill again to Khartaravasi Tuk, which fills the northern ridge. Before entering this complex visitors can refuel with some yogurt and milk at the entrance. Eating is not permitted within the complex.
The overall impression of the **huge temple city** is quite stunning. It has more than 860 individual temples, making it the **largest complex of its kind in India**. Between the northern ridge and the higher, southern temple complex is a central group of temples. It contains Vallabhai Temple and the large Motsah Temple, both of which date back to the 19th century. It is best to take the left path to Khartaravasi Tuk first. This path also leads to the temple office, where visitors can pay the photography fee.

Place of pilgrImage with more than 860 temples

Visiting the temple complex on Mount Shatrunajaya, one of the four holy Jain mountains, is one of the highlights of Gujarat

After passing the office, visitors will pass through a gateway to the **northern temple group**. A path with many small shrines and temples leads to the complex's most important temple, Adinath Temple. It is dedicated to the first fordmaker and dates back to the 16th century. It is surrounded by countless small temples with excellent depictions of tirthankaras. The quiet prayers of the faithful and countless monks pervade the area. The monks can easily be recognized by their mouth masks and brooms, which are meant to prevent them from accidentally inhaling or trampling small living creatures. It is said that Adinath visited the mountain several times and that his son built the first temple here.

The **central group** can be visited on the way back, then there is a steep path up to the **southern temple complex**. Another option would be to walk back along the ascent route to the fork in the road and then choose the right-hand one. Vimalavasi Tuk on the southern ridge is 500m/550yd along this path. It is dominated by the two-storey Adishvara Temple. It contains a large sculpture of Rishabha (Adinath) that pilgrims come here to worship. In addition to the main temple Ramanaji Gandharia from the 16th century is also worth looking at. There is a magnificent view of the Adinath Temple complex a little way below and of Gujarat's broad landscape, its fields, mountains and lakes.

The temples are open from 7am to 7pm. After sunset even the priests leave the temple complex at an elevation of 602m/1975ft in order not to disturb the gods. Since the ascent takes around 90 minutes, it is a good idea to set off very early before it gets too hot.

Tips

⊙

Around Palitana

This town (51km/32mi northeast of Palitana), founded by Bhav-singhji Gohil in 1723, is still an important trading centre for agricultural products from Gujarat today. The town has a memorial in honour of Gandhi (Gandhi Smirti) and, in the same building, the Barton Museum with a collection of weapons and coins. There are also some old buildings from the British colonial period.

Bhavnagar

Ranthambor National Park

E 6

Federal state: Rajasthan

Distance: 350km/215mi southwest of Delhi

Ranthambor National Park is situated between the Aravalli and Vindya Ranges and has an area of 410 sq km/158 sq mi. In addition to its main attraction, tigers, it is also home to chitals, nilgai antelopes, langurs, wild boar, crocodiles and other animals. It is said that more than 270 bird species have been sighted in the park to date.

The region around Ranthambor has been inhabited for more than 1000 years. The year 944 saw the construction of the Chauhan dynasty fort, which was taken by Islamic rulers several times. Ala-uddin Khalji conquered it in 1301 and Akbar's troops in 1569. Later

 VISITING RANTHAMBOR NATIONAL PARK

INFORMATION

Project Tiger
Office in Sawai Madhopur
Tel. 074 62 – 22 02 23

Information is also available on the website
www.rajasthantourism.gov.in

GETTING THERE

Train connection to Sawai Madhopur (on the main line between Mumbai and Delhi), after which it is another 14km/9mi

WHERE TO STAY / WHERE TO EAT

▶ **Mid-range / Budget**
RTDC Castle Jhoomar Baori
Tel. 074 62 – 220 49 57
RTDC puts up its guests in a former maharaja's hunting lodge, located within the park on a hill. It also has a good restaurant.

Ranthambor fell back into the hands of the Maharaja of Jaipur, who used this rugged region as a hunting ground. In 1974 the area became a tiger reserve and in 1981 it became a national park. Visitors wishing to lay eyes on a tiger need not only luck but also plenty of time. Further park attractions are the fort with its temples, a mausoleum and an attractive pool, as well as two of India's largest banyan trees.

Shekhawati (Region)

C–E 5/6

State: Rajasthan

Distance: 280km/175mi southwest of Delhi

Shekhawati, situated northwest of Jaipur in the triangle Jaipur – Delhi – Bikaner, has only recently become a tourist destination. With almost 400 villages, the region's many merchant houses possess wonderful wall paintings. Its name comes from King Rao Shekha of Amarsar (1433–88), who successfully refused to pay tribute to the king of Amer in 1471.

Shekhawati remained independent for almost 300 years and was considered the home of highwaymen and bandits. The **caravans** with goods from Delhi and Jaipur going westwards via Bikaner and Jaisalmer had to pass through this region, which led the successful Marwari merchant group to gain good standing. It was only the East India Company that managed to get the region under their control and levy taxes from the population at the beginning of the 19th century. Several important merchant families subsequently left the region in favour of Delhi, Ahmedabad, Mumbai and Kolkata. There they became influential and wealthy entrepreneurs. Many of them spent part of their fortune on having **havelis**, large merchant houses with colourful walls, built in their villages. The result is that this remote and otherwise little developed region of India possesses a wealth of houses with large painted depictions of mythological subjects as well as motifs from modern times with aeroplanes, trains and Europeans in peaceful co-existence. Today, Shekhawati is considered the **largest open-air picture gallery in the world**.

> **! Baedeker TIP**
>
> ### Highlights off the beaten track
> Some of Shekhawati's best wall paintings are located in two remote villages: in the gold and silver shop of Mahansar (near Mandawa) and in the mausoleum in Parastampura (near Nawalgarh). It is best to go by taxi from the closest town.

Havelis As was their tradition, the Rajputs built their houses as fortresses. Since they were also intent on keeping their wives away from other men's eyes, the houses are surrounded by high walls. Walking

Entrance to Schrafta haveli in Mandawa

through a gateway visitors will first come into a courtyard, which is reserved for male guests, a kind of open-air reception hall. The walls in this area are painted. The courtyards located further inside the havelis are reserved for women and family members. They must not be entered by other men. During the first phase (1850–1900) the **wall paintings** were predominantly made from vegetable paints that were applied to the wall base when it was still damp. Later, predominantly synthetic paints from Germany were imported, and these could be painted on dry walls too (1900–1930). Like the Rajput rulers who decorated their palaces with Belgian glass and Venetian tiles, the traders decorated their estates with paints from overseas. The colourful walls with their bright pigment paints create a stark contrast to the monotonous landscape.

Round Trip through the Shekhawati Region

Almost every village in the region has painted houses. The most interesting places are listed below. The towns of Nawalgarh and Mandawa are good starting locations for exploring the region.

▶ VISITING SHEKHAWATI

INFORMATION

Tourist Office
In Jhunjhunu: Mandawa Circle
Churu By-pass Road
Tel. 01 59 72 – 54 50 83
www.rajasthantourism.gov.in

GETTING THERE
Train connection from Delhi to Na-walgarh (Shekhawati Express); the train also goes to Sikar, Fatehpur, Jhunjhunu and Churu. The most convenient option is to hire a taxi in Jaipur. The drive to Nawalgarh takes around two and a half hours.

SHOPPING
The small town of Mandawa has numerous shops selling handicrafts and antiques, since this is where most tourists come.

WHERE TO STAY / WHERE TO EAT
▶ Luxury / Mid-range
Mandawa Palace
Mandawa

Tel. 015 92 – 22 31 24
www.castlemandawa.com
Visitors can live like the maharajas in Mandawa: 70 rooms, a hand-painted dining room and a nice terrace restaurant are all there for guests' enjoyment. From the palace roof there are some wonderful views of the town and the surrounding area.

Baedeker recommendation

▶ Inexpensive
Apani Dhani
Jhunjhunu Road, Nawalgarh
Tel. 015 94 – 22 22 39
www.apanidhani.com
Mr Jangid, the owner of this small hotel, has committed himself to socially and environmentally responsible tourism. Guests stay in clay huts and are provided with excellent vegetarian dishes from the hotel' own organic garden. Guided tours of the neighbouring villages are also organized.

Nawalgarh

The town of Nawalgarh, which has a fort founded in 1737 by Thakur Nawal Singh, possesses many painted havelis, of which the most important are Surajmal Chauchhariy and the havelis of the **Poddar**, **Goenka** and **Bhagat** families. Roop Niwas Palace, now a palace hotel, displays architectural elements from Europe and Rajasthan. The tourist office with its frescoes and the clock tower are reminiscent of the British era. The small **museum**, housed in a haveli, has some nice frescoes.

✱
Parasrampura

The highly **worthwhile cenotaphs for Shardul Singh** (1681–1742), who put an end to 300 years of Mughal rule in the region by conquering Jhunjhunu and Fatehpur, can be found in Parasrampura (20km/12mi from Nawalgarh). The wall paintings with scenes from the Mahabharata and Ramayana epics as well as battle scenes are considered forerunners of the later wall paintings of Mandawa. The temple is also worth a visit.

At the heart of the Shekhawati region is **Dera Dundlod Kila Fort**,   Dundlod
which is protected by a ditch and was built by Kesari Singh in 1750.
Next to the fort are the tombs of the royal family, which are also
painted. Goenka Haveli near the fort and Satyanarayan Temple with
its religious paintings are also worth visiting.

Mandawa is the region's best-known town. It was built by Thakur   ✱ ✱
Nawal Singh in 1755. There are **many painted houses** here owned   Mandawa
by the rich Goenka and Chokani merchant families. The best havelis
are those of Ladhvam Goenka (1870), Gulab Rai Ladia (1859) and
Newatia Haveli (interesting depictions with aeroplanes). There are
great views of the old town and Rajasthan's arid plain from the fort,
which is accessed via three impressive gateways. The hotel in the
complex is a nice place to stay in the heart of Shekhawati. The palace
has a museum with a coin collection, costumes and silver objects. A
gate decorated with depictions of Krishna leads from the palace
straight to the bazaar.

The small hamlet of Mahansar can be reached via a sandy track from   ✱
Mandawa. It contains the **jewel of Shekhawati, the gold and silver**   Mahansar
shop (»Sone-ki-dukan«), a ha-
veli from around 1850. Inside
the haveli are wonderful and
extremely well-preserved frescoes decorated with gold leaf,
showing images from the lives
of the gods Vishnu and Krishna. The key for this gem can
be obtained for a fee from a
guard.

Ramgarh boasts the region's
largest number of painted havelis. Many of them have in-
teresting motifs, as the town   *Artistic detail in the gold and silver shop:*
was a stronghold for the weal-   *Krishna is riding on an elephant made of women's bodies*
thy traders. The richly deco-
rated **Shani Temple** for the god Saturn and the chhatris (cenotaphs)   ✱
of the Poddar family on the town's western edge are also worth visit-   Ramgarh
ing.

Fatehpur was also governed by Islamic rulers until the Rajput king of   Fatehpur
Sikar took over the town in 1731. It has some very nice havelis on
the main road to Sikar. In **Goenka Haveli** there are religious depictions and walls nicely decorated with mirrors. **Singhania Haveli** combines religious images and scenes from modern times with cars and
aeroplanes. There is a **small surprise**: Krishna being chauffeured
around in a limousine.

Sikar   Sikar, formerly a fief of the king of Jaipur, stands out because of the **blue Biyani Haveli** and the **Mahal**. In addition the Murarka and Somani havelis are worth visiting. In addition to the havelis the large stepped well with its sandstone sculptures is also recommendable. The town was founded by Daulat Singh in 1687 and is easily accessible via National Highway 11.

Jhunjhunu   Jhunjhunu, capital of the district of the same name, has many hotels and good transport connections; it is another ideal base for exploring the region. The town, probably founded by the Jats (farmer caste), was conquered by Islamic rulers, who were in turn driven out by the Rajputs at the beginning of the 18th century. Standing on the hill north of the bus station are remains of Islamic mausoleums and a mosque. In the north of the town is the **Merani Baori**, a stepped well, not just used for obtaining water but also as a place to find some cool shade during the hot summers. Important **havelis** are Modi, Tibrwala, Nuruddin Faroogi and the Khetri Mahal, which are all next to each other in the old town. The Khetri Mahal was built in around 1760 and resembles a palace more than a residence. **Rani Sati Temple** served to glorify sati (widow immolation). It is sought out by traditional women out of respect, but has also been the target of severe criticism by those who condemn this practice as an extreme example of misogyny.

Churu   The small town of Churu is home to the palatial six-storey **Surana Haveli**, which is definitely worth a visit.

Lachhmangarh   The view from the old fort is of the town of Lachhmangarh, which is home to the region's largest haveli. **Ganeriwala Haveli** has four inner courtyards, some of which are painted with scenes from everyday life. Rathi Haveli is situated next to the clock tower by the bazaar.

★ ★ Udaipur

D 6

State: Rajasthan	**Altitude:** 582m/1909ft
Population: 233,000	**Distance:** 670km/415mi southwest of Delhi

Udaipur, praised as the »City of Lakes«, is, with its magnificent palaces, exotic gardens and picturesque lakes, one of the most beautiful places in India.

Udaipur is situated on the slopes of the Aravalli Hills and is an ideal base for a longer stay. The city's many sights, its pleasant atmosphere and its interesting surroundings make it **one of Rajasthan's most important tourist attractions**.

⏵ VISITING UDAIPUR

INFORMATION

Tourist Office
Fateh Memorial
Suraj Pol
Tel. 02 94 – 41 15 35
www.rajasthantourism.gov.in

SHOPPING

The bazaar sells handicrafts not just from Rajasthan but from all over India. There is a great selection of embroidered fabrics and jewellery.

WHERE TO STAY / WHERE TO EAT

▶ Luxury

① *The Lake Palace Hotel*
Tel. 02 94 – 252 88 00
www.tajhotels.com
This former Maharaja's palace is located in the middle of the lake. With a stylish interior and a pretty garden, it is one of India's most famous hotels.

② *Shivniwas Palace*
City Palace
Tel. 02 94 – 252 80 16
www.hrhhotels.com
This stylish palace with its original furnishings is situated right on the shores of the lake. It has 31 suites; the service is very friendly.

Baedeker recommendation

▶ Mid-range / Budget
③ *Jagat Niwas Palace Hotel*
Lalghat
Tel. 02 94 – 242 28 60, 242 01 03
www.jagatniwaspalace.com
This white haveli from the 17th century is a lovely place to stay. Some of the rooms have views of the lake and there is a wonderful roof terrace with a good restaurant. It is nicest here during dusk, when flocks of birds soar over the water.

The luxurious Lake Palace Hotel

History

Since Chitaurgarh, the old Mewar capital, had been conquered by Islamic rulers three times despite its enormous fort, the maharana (great warrior) Udai Singh, who had to flee Chitaurgarh from Abkar's troops, searched for a new place to found a town in 1559. He finally chose the site where Udaipur is now located. Surrounded by mountains serving as a natural protective barrier on the one hand, on the other there is plenty of water here. The Mewar dynasty, the highest-ranking Rajput dynasty and successors of the Sisodias, who in turn based their authority on the legendary god-king Rama, finally moved their residence to Udaipur in 1567. However, they found no

Udaipur Map

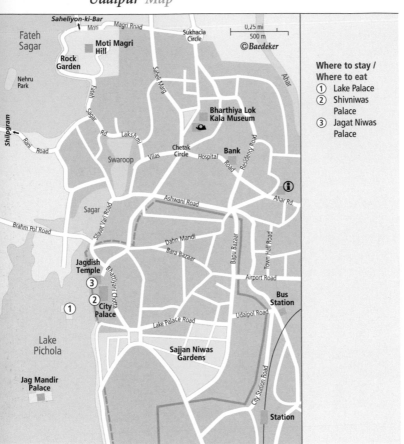

Fateh Sagar

Saheliyon-ki-Bari
Moti
Magri Road
Sukhacia Circle

0,25 mi
500 m
©Baedeker

Moti Magri Hill

Rock Garden

Nehru Park

Shilpgram

Saheli Marg

Fateh Sagar Rd

Rani Road

Laksmi

Bharthiya Lok Kala Museum

Chetak Circle

Swaroop

Vilas

Hospital

Bank

Residency Road

Ashwani Road

Sagar

Brahm Pol Road

Sikar Vari Road

Dahn Mandi

Bara Bazaar

Bapu Bazaar

Ahar Rd.

Town Hall Road

Jagdish Temple

③

②

① City Palace

Bhattiyani Chotta

Airport Road

Bus Station

Udaipol Road

Lake Palace Road

Lake Pichola

Sajjan Niwas Gardens

City Station Road

Jag Mandir Palace

Station

Where to stay / Where to eat
① Lake Palace
② Shivniwas Palace
③ Jagat Niwas Palace

peace here either because Udai Singh's son, Maharana Pratap, had to defend the town against constant attacks by Akbar. Akbar had already managed to get some of the Rajputs on his side through his marriage to the daughter of the Rajput king of Amer. He was finally able to defeat Mewar too in a battle near Haldi Ghatti (27km/17mi north of Udaipur) in 1576. However, Maharana Pratap managed to win back some of his kingdom in the following years. His son Amar Singh finally recognized Mughal rule in 1614 and the Mewar kingdom embarked on a relatively stable period of peace, during which arts and culture flourished. New palaces were built, the old palace extended and Jagdish Temple constructed. Miniature painting also reached a high point.

What to See in Udaipur

★ ★
City Palace
⊙
Opening hours:
daily
9.30am–4.30pm

Udaipur's City Palace on the eastern shores of Lake Pichola is, with a length of around 500m/550 yd and a width of 250m/275 yd, one of the largest and best-preserved palace complexes in Rajasthan. Right by the main entrance (Tripolia) there are eight arches chiselled from stone on the left-hand side. Here the maharanas, as the maharajas were called in these parts, were weighed on their birthdays against gold and silver, which was then distributed to the poor.

The **palace complex** includes several rooms and courtyards on several levels. There are many nice views of Lake Pichola, the city centre and the Aravalli Hills from the top storey. The **Moti Mahal (Pearl Palace)** with the typically Rajasthani use of mirrors is particularly worth visiting, as is the **Chini-ki-Chitra Mahal** with its Chinese tiles. Situated at a raised location of 30m/98ft is a courtyard (Badi Mahal) with trees and a hall, from where there is a pleasant view of the city. Visitors will be able to see huge marble cisterns here, which used to contain water in order to cool the air. Mor Chowk is famous for its **peacock reliefs** painted in bright colours. They are amongst the most magnificent depictions of the national bird in India. Peacocks, the vehicles (vahanas) of the god of war Skanda, enjoyed particular worship in the realm of the bellicose Rajputs. The palace also houses a **museum** (Government Museum) with a collection of stone sculptures.

Mor Chowk with its lavish peacock mosaics

Zenana Mahal

To the right of the exit a path leads to the Zenana Mahal, the **Queen's Palace**. There is an exhibition on the first floor of this building around a large courtyard displaying photographs and utensils belonging to the royal family. The cannons in the courtyard are reminders of the fact that the palace, which now seems so peaceful, was once the scene of war and violence.

Jagdish Temple

Jagdish Temple seems more like a fort from the outside and a steep stairway has to be climbed in order to get to it. Since the walled temple was never destroyed it can still be admired in its original condition. Even though the temple was only built by Jagad Singh I in

1651, it is completely committed to the Hindu architectural tradition. It contains no elements of the Mughal style, which is now the dominant style all over northern India. The Mewars, who were constantly fighting with the Mughals, deliberately wanted to avoid using any stylistic elements from their archenemy.

Bharathya Lok Kala Mandal
Opening hours: daily 9am–5.30pm

This house contains an interesting museum set up by D. L. Samar in 1952. It gives visitors an insight into Rajasthani handicrafts, contains a collection of musical instruments and explains the traditions of several tribes. In addition there are almost hourly performances of the puppet shows.

Saheliyon-ki-Bar

The former pleasure garden for the court's women located in the north of the city on the eastern shore of Lake Fateh Sagar has now lost much of its former appeal. Nevertheless the shady spot with its lotus pond is a place to while away some time.

The calm Lake Pichola is rather shallow and quickly dries up when there is not much rainfall

Lake Pichola, situated in front of an idyllic mountain range, is an ideal backdrop to the maharaja's buildings in and around the lake. The **Lake Palace Hotel** (Jag Niwas), now one of India's best palace hotels and only accessible to hotel guests, is located in the middle of the lake.

✱ **Lake Pichola**

Located on a second island is the **Jag Mandir**. It was in this palace and in the Gul Mahal, a pavilion with vaulted roofs, that young Shah Jahan found refuge in 1623 when he had to hide after a failed revolt against his own father Jehangir. During his stay he is said to have got some inspiration for the Taj Mahal, the world-famous mausoleum he would later build in ►Agra. The Jag Mandir, with is beautiful garden, is one of the most idyllic spots in Udaipur. Boat trips on the lake are offered, departing from City Palace.

✱ **Jag Mandir Palace and Garden**

This pretty lake created by Maharana Jai Singh in 1678 has a lake promenade and a boat connection to Nehru Park.

Fateh Sagar

Around Udaipur

Drive westbound along the road on Lake Fateh Sagar's southern shore for 5km/3mi to get to the artisans' village. Sponsored by the West Zone Cultural Centre, the village puts on music and dance performances and visitors can also watch craftsmen produce their goods, which can also be purchased.

Shilpgram
🕑
Opening hours: daily 9.30am–6pm

Ranakpur, on the route between Jodhpur and Udaipur (96km/60mi north of Udaipur), is famous for being **one of the largest and most beautiful Jain temple complexes** in India. The temples at the foot of the Aravalli Hills are largely in good condition and just as filigree as the Dilwara temples on Mount Abu. In addition to the main temple (1439) there are three other Jain temples, which are all almost 500 years old. The three-storey main temple with its **1444 columns of different designs**, its numerous small shrines and 29 larger halls is open from 10.30am to 5pm.

✱ ✱ **Ranakpur**

🕑

Inside this temple, known as Chaumukha (four-faced), is a representation of Adinath which looks in all four directions, as well as two smaller temples for the tirthankaras (fordmakers) Neminath and Parshvanath. The exterior walls are decorated with very beautiful sculptures made of white marble, some of which are erotic in nature. The third, somewhat secluded temple is dedicated to Surya, the sun god.

Immediately at the entrance of the temple complex on the right-hand side is a small pond with depictions of Shiva and Parvati as well as the monkey god Hanuman. These remains, along with Surya Temple, illustrate the cultic significance this place also has for Hindus. There is accommodation for the pilgrims within the complex as well as a good vegetarian canteen. In contrast to the Dilwara temple rules

Made of marble: Tirthankara in Ranakpur

visitors may photograph anything except for the statues of the tir-thankaras. The pleasant landscape with many trees, mountain streams and terraced fields make this area a good place to go walking.

✱ Chitaurgarh (Chittaurgarh, Chittor)

The first mention of Chittaurgarh's (70km/45mi northeast of Udaipur) fort on the 150m/492ft plateau, which drops steeply to all sides, was in 728. The town was the target of Islamic conquerors who repeatedly subdued it despite the heroic and desperate defensive attempts of its inhabitants.

The battle of the Rajputs against the Islamic rulers was sung about in numerous legends and stories. Sultan Ala-ud-din Khalji besieged the town for the first time in 1303 because he desired the beautiful Padmini, the queen of Chitaurgarh. When it became clear during the fighting that the fort would fall into the hands of the sultan, the **savage Rajput ritual Jauhar** was performed: women and children burned themselves on a huge pyre and the remaining men sought death in the hopeless battle. Ala-ud-din Khalji finally conquered a deserted city.

After just two centuries the city was besieged again, this time by troops belonging to the sultan of Gujarat, Bhadur Shah. Again, 13,000 women chose death and more than 30,000 men died in battle. The conquerors were not able to enjoy their victory for long, because after just two weeks they had to flee from Humayun's approaching troops. When Chitaurgarh was besieged for the third time 30 years later, this time by powerful Akbar, the young king fled with a small entourage and founded a new capital in Udaipur, from where he continued to offer resistance against the Islamic rulers.

The women had to ascend the pyre once more and the remaining troops went to battle under the leadership of the 60-year-old vassal Jaimal and Patta, who was only 16. All were killed. Akbar was so impressed by the heroic courage of Chitaurgarh's men that he had marble sculptures made of the two Rajput leaders. He had the sculptures, Jaimal and Patta riding elephants, erected outside the gates of the Red Fort in Delhi.

! Baedeker TIP

Chitaurgarh in fiction
Love, intrigue, jealousy, battle and death: 16th-century Chitaurgarh is the scene of Kiran Nagarkar's novel *Cuckold*, which tells the story of the fates of the crown prince of Mewar and his wife, the poetess Mirabai.

✴ Fort

An 11km/7mi wall encloses the remains of the once mighty and much contested fort. Viewing the fort, which is situated up on a 180m/590ft hill, takes around half a day. The stronghold is reached via a steep, winding road that used to be guarded by eight gates. There are cenotaphs for the many warriors who died in battle at every gate. After walking through Ram Pol visitors enter the sprawling complex with several ruins as well as around 50 well-preserved buildings.

Rana Kumbha Palace

The first structure on the right-hand side is the 15th-century Rana Kumbha Palace, which is unfortunately in ruins. Vaulted cellars can be made out, in which the Jauhar, the ritual burning of the women and children, took place. Udai Singh is said to have been born here and built his palace in Udaipur using this one as a model.

✴ Victory Tower

Vijay Stambha (Victory Tower) is surely the most outstanding structure of the entire complex. The nine-storey 38m/125ft tower was commissioned by Rana Kumbha after a victory against the sultans of Gujarat in 1468. In contrast to the plain tower of victory of the sultans in Delhi, the Qutb Minar, which does not have any sculptures, this tower is decorated with **depictions from the Mahabharata and Ramayana**. Interestingly, in addition to Hindu sculptures there are also figures of the Jain tirthankaras and examples of Islamic calligraphy praising Allah.

Kirti Stambha

Not far from the Victory Tower is the 13th-century Kirti Stambha, which is only 23m/75ft. It was donated by a wealthy merchant in honour of Adinath, the first fordmaker of the Jain faith. A stairway leads to the tower's roof, from where visitors can enjoy a wonderful view.

Padmini Palace   In addition to the small victory tower there is also a palace of the former princess of Sri Lanka, Padmini, which is situated in the middle of a pond. It is said the Mughal ruler Ala-ud-din Khalji (1296–1316) saw her reflection in a mirror once. He was so overwhelmed by Padmini's beauty that he besieged the city and imprisoned her husband. The queen committed Jauhar and the city was completely destroyed.

Kalika Mata Temple   Kalika Mata Temple was originally a sun temple. In 1568, however, it was consecrated to the goddess Kalika, an incarnation of Parvatis. Upon closer inspection visitors will still be able to recognize depictions of the sun god Surya on the exterior walls.

Further temples   In Kumbha Shyama Temple (eighth century) Vishnu is worshipped in his incarnation as a wild boar (Varaha). The same complex also contains the smaller Mirabai Temple. **Mirabai** was a Rajput princess, who penned many poems and ballads in honour of Krishna. To this day she is one of the most popular poets of the desert state.

Vadodara

C 8

State: Gujarat
Population: 1.5 million

Altitude: 35m/115ft
Distance: 425km/265mi north of Mumbai

Vadodara, formerly Baroda, is a fast-expanding modern city home to India's largest petrochemical production plants.

The city known all over India as an arts and university city is an old royal city. Its gardens and palaces give it a pleasant atmosphere. Unfortunately some of the palaces are not accessible to the public. Vadodara has good transport connections and accommodation, making it a pleasant place to stop between Mumbai and Ahmedabad.

Though Vadodara developed into a royal city only late on, its rise was incredibly fast. The city was founded by Gaekwads (protectors of cows), who, being the military leaders of Maratha king Baji Rao, even conquered the mighty Mughal city of Delhi. In a very short amount of time they managed to become one of the richest and most influential dynasties in India.

What to See in Vadodara

Lakshmi Vilas Palace   This palace was designed by British architect R. H. Chrisholm. The somewhat eclectic building exhibits a mix of European and Indian styles and is particularly impressive because of its size and lavish interior.

The complex also contains the **Maharaja Fateh Singh Museum**, which has copies of paintings by famous European artists such as Titian and Rubens as well as a good collection of works by the Indian painter Ravi Verma.

The **Vadodara Museum** is idyllically located in the middle of Sayaji Bagh, a picnic site very popular with the locals. The extensive collection goes back to Maharaja Syaji Rao Gaekwad III and contains art from various parts of Europe and Asia (open daily except Mon and holidays 10am–5pm).

VADODARA

INFORMATION
Narmada Bhavan
Indira Avenue; tel. 02 65 – 242 74 89

WHERE TO STAY
► **Luxury / Mid-range**
Taj Residency
Akota Gardens
Tel. 02 65 – 235 45 45
www.tajhotels.com
With two international restaurants and a swimming pool.

In the immediate vicinity of the Vadodara Museum to the west is the famous university with the very beautiful building that houses the academy of arts. It has produced **some of the most important contemporary Indian painters**. **Academy of Arts**

Around Vadodara

The millionaire's city of Surat (150km/95mi south of Vadodara) by the Tapti river was an important trading centre in the 19th century. It was dominated by the Parsi people. Between the 15th and 17th centuries Surat's harbour was the departure point for Muslim pilgrims to Mecca. Today Surat is an important centre for the textile industry and for diamond cutting. **Surat**

The old harbour town of Bharuch (73km/45mi south of Vadodara) at the mouth of the sacred Narmada river has a Dutch fort as well as a 14th-century mosque, in whose construction parts of a Jain temple were used as well as Parsi »Towers of Silence«. **Bharuch**

EASTERN INDIA

STATES AND UNION TERRITORIES

Andaman and Nicobar Islands:
union territory
Bihar: capital Patna
Jharkhand: capital Ranchi
Northeastern states: Arunachal Pradesh
(capital: Itanagar), Assam (capital: Dispur),
Manipur (capital: Imphal), Meghalaya (capital:
Shillong), Mizoram (capital: Aizawl), Nagaland
(capital: Kohima), Tripura (capital: Agartala)
Orissa: capital: Bhubaneshwar
Sikkim: capital: Gangtok
West Bengal: capital: Kolkata

The heart of eastern India is made
up of the fertile and industrially
developed West Bengal together
with the poorer neighbouring
states of Bihar, Jharkhand and Orissa. In the far northeast is the very
small Himalayan state of Sikkim as well as the group of seven northeastern states, which are largely sparsely populated and, with the exception of Assam, receive few tourists. The Andaman and Nicobar
Islands have been put into this section of the book because they can
be accessed from Kolkata.

India's east stretches from Orissa's green coastal plain across the **Natural**
mountains of the Eastern Ghats and the rather dry plateau to Bihar **environment**
and Jharkhand. The Gangetic plain of West Bengal forms the northern and eastern border to the states. West Bengal reaches northwards
all the way to the Himalayan foothills and connects Sikkim and the
northeastern states via a narrow corridor with the Indian subcontinent.
The Himalaya form the border of the northern part of the states of
Sikkim and the richly forested but hardly accessible Arunachal Pradesh. Further to the south the land gradually drops down to flood
plain of the Brahmaputra, which, lined by paddy fields, flows eastwards through Assam. South of this fertile valley is the hilly plateau
of Meghalaya, which in turn drops off to the Gangetic plain in the
south.
The Ganges' marshy river delta, which also covers large parts of the
neighbouring country of Bangladesh, is repeatedly the scene of disastrous floods. The Andaman and Nicobar Islands are situated
1500km/930mi south of Kolkata in the Indian Ocean, but they can
also be reached by air from the Bengali capital and from Chennai.

← *Colourful appliqués manufactured in Pipli*

Economy The dominant economic activity in Orissa, Jharkhand and Bihar is rice growing and the same is true of the fertile flood plains of the Brahmaputra and the Ganges. The tea plantations in northern West Bengal (Darjeeling) and in Assam are India's largest tea-growing regions and are an important source of income. The metalworking industry is concentrated in West Bengal, Jharkhand and Bihar and large steel factories are based there, as in Jamshedpur for example. The region has been nicknamed **»India's Ruhr valley«** as a result of its coal and ore. It belongs to the state of Jharkhand, which was newly formed in the year 2000. The region around Kolkata is also considered an industrial magnet. The city's steelworks and textile factories can draw on a huge pool of workers and also attract the poor populations from neighbouring states.

History The Gangetic plain is closely linked with early Indian history. The fertile banks of the river were settled by Indo-Aryan tribes as early as 3000 years ago. They had come to this area from the northwest. Many temples in the modern-day state of Bihar point towards the signs of Buddha in that region. Patna, the capital of Bihar, was the ruling seat of the great Emperor Ashoka (274–232), who created the first Indian empire from here. Evidence of Hindu rule is particularly well preserved in the magnificent temples of Orissa, which were built around the tenth century. Kolkata, the regional metropolis on the Hooghly river, was the starting point for the British conquest of India and the signs of its colonial past are still visible in the city in many places. The northeastern states with their large proportion of

Konark: a temple in the shape of a solar chariot

tribal populations are amongst the country's areas of tension. Ethnic conflicts and political differences of opinion with the central government in Delhi frequently lead to violent confrontation.

The Andaman and Nicobar Islands have for a long time been home to aboriginal tribes, some of which have little contact with outsiders to this day, but are now populated predominantly by settlers from the mainland. The islands were used by the British as penal colonies.

Attractions

Eastern India is one of the subcontinent's less visited regions, but it has a broad spectrum of attractions on offer. Orissa boasts outstanding temples in **Bhubaneshwar** and **Konark**, as well as the **city of pilgrimage, Puri,** the state's »Golden Triangle«, as it is advertised by the local tourist offices. Interesting Buddhist monasteries can usually also be found nearby.

Bihar, too, has its own treasures: **Bodhgaya and Nalanda** are important historic Buddhist sites. West Bengal's capital Kolkata does not enjoy a particularly good reputation amongst travellers, but upon closer inspection it does offer a large number of interesting sights and activities. Hikers will find what they are looking for in the **mountains of Darjeeling** in the far north of West Bengal and in **Sikkim**.

The northeastern states are not yet well developed for tourism. **Assam** with its famous **Kaziranga National Park**, home to the rare Indian rhinoceros, and the hill station Shillong in Meghalaya are the best-known destinations. The Andaman and Nicobar Islands are considered a Mecca for divers.

Andaman · Nicobar Islands (Union Territory)

M/N 12–16

Capital: Port Blair
Distance: 1000km/620mi east of Chennai

Population: 100,000

Lined up in the Bay of Bengal like a string of beads are the more than 300 islands of the Andaman and Nicobar island group. They are the tips of an ancient mountain range that once ran from Myanmar to Sumatra.

The Andaman island group consists of the three main islands, North, Middle and South Andaman, with Little Andaman to the south and countless smaller islands. The Nicobar Islands are even closer to the equator. Their main islands are Great and Little Nicobar; they, too, have numerous smaller islands. During the **tsunami disaster** in December 2004 many of the islands were flooded and a third of the inhabitants were killed.

Thick jungle, a large number of rare birds, white sandy beaches, crystal-clear water, and an incredibly diverse and colourful underwater world attract nature lovers, divers, snorkellers and travellers, who come in search of the last paradise on earth. Only a few of the islands are inhabited. Their original population resisted every kind of contact with the outside world, in one case successfully. Fishing, hunting and, on some islands, agriculture (cultivating rice and coconuts, keeping pigs) as well as copra production are the inhabitants' main food sources.

 VISITING ANDAMAN & NICOBAR ISLANDS

INFORMATION

Directorate of Tourism
(Andaman and Nicobar)
Port Blair
Tel. 031 92 – 232 69 94
www.tourism.andaman.nic.in

India Tourism Office
VIP Rd. 189
Junglighat
Port Blair
Tel. 031 92 – 23 63 48

GETTING THERE

Planes fly to the islands from Kolkata and Chennai. The Andaman Islands can also be reached by boat from Kolkata, Chennai and Vishakapatnam (Shipping Corporation of India, Chennai tel. 044 – 25 22 08 41 or Kolkata Tel. 033 – 22 48 23 54).

Visitor's permits
A permit is necessary for those wanting to come to the islands. Travellers arriving by air will be given one when arriving at the airport in Port Blair. Those coming by ship have to organize the permit in advance from the Indian embassy or in one of the Foreigners Registration Offices in Delhi, Kolkata and Chennai.

WHERE TO STAY / WHERE TO EAT

▶ **Luxury / Mid-range**
Fortune Resort Bay Island
Port Blair

Tel. 031 92 – 23 41 01
www.fortuneparkhotels.com
Elegantly furnished rooms with balconies and great views, good restaurant as well as a nice garden with a seawater pool.

Barefoot at Havelock
Beach No. 7
Radhanagar
Havelock
Tel. 031 92 – 28 21 51
(in Chennai: tel. 044 – 24 34 10 01)
www.barefootindia.com
Situated on one of the nicest beaches; has many activities such as diving, fishing, hiking and yoga to offer.

▶ **Mid-range**
Wild Orchid
Beach No. 5
Vijaynagar
Havelock
Tel. 031 92 – 28 24 72
www.wildorchidandaman.com
Rustic cottages with a lot of bamboo, just a few metres from the water, good food.

▶ **Budget**
Megapode Nest
Haddo Hill
Tel. 031 92 – 23 22 07
www.aniidco.nic.in
Accommodation run by Andaman and Nicobar Tourism, garden and good restaurant.

Heavenly beaches on the Andaman Islands

The exact origin of the islands' aboriginal population is unknown. The dark-skinned population of the Andaman Islands is of Negroid descent while the population living on the Nicobar Islands can trace their origins back to the Burmese. For a long time the various tribes lived on the islands and survived off hunting and fishing. One of the first Western travellers to lay eyes on the coasts of the remote islands was **Marco Polo**. He was followed in the 17th and 18th centuries by missionaries, who tried and failed to convert the islands' inhabitants to the Christian faith.

The next people to come to the islands were the British. It was they who set up a **penal colony** on South Andaman in 1858. A relic of this time is the old prison in Port Blair. Until 1945 the former colonial power brought its particularly disagreeable opponents to this prison; the last to be sent here were many Indian freedom fighters, who met their deaths under appalling conditions.

After India's independence the two island groups were incorporated by the state as a **union territory**. These days the majority of the population consists of settlers who have come to the islands from India's mainland, particularly from Bengal, and of the descendants of the former prisoners, while the aboriginal population is in the minority. A large part of the population was wiped out by disease in the 19th century. The destruction of their natural habitat by deforestation worsened the situation. In the meantime some of the island territory has been put under protection but the deforestation of the vulnerable tree population still continues under the Indian government. While the inhabitants of the Nicobar Islands have come closer to the Indian settlers, the tribes on the Andaman Islands keep their distance. The Sentinelese people in the north of the island group still manage to defend themselves with bows and arrows against »civilization« and prevent strangers from setting foot on their island.

Port Blair

Capital of the Andaman Islands and largest town of the island group

Port Blair (population 100,000, 1255km/780mi from Kolkata and 1191km/740mi from Chennai) is located in the southeast of South Andaman. This is where all travellers arrive and where most of the hotels, the information office for tourists and the private companies offering cruises through the archipelago are located. The small town stretches out over several hills.

A reminder of South Andaman's past as a penal colony is the **old prison** in the town's northeast. A small museum and a light-and-sound show commemorate the many freedom fighters who were incarcerated by the British here (open: daily except Mon 9am–12pm and 2pm–5pm).

In the **Aquarium Marina Park** to the south visitors can explore the islands' fascinating underwater world. A crocodile farm adjoins the museum (open: daily except Sun 8.30am–5pm). Insights into the lives of the aboriginal population are provided at the **Anthropological Museum**, which exhibits weapons, tools, traditional dress and dugouts of the first island inhabitants (open: daily except Thu 9am–4pm).

The **Forest Museum** provides interesting information about the diversity of the local timbers. Right next door, the precious, increasingly rare timbers are processed in **one of the oldest and largest sawmills** in Asia. Those who are interested may watch but not take pictures (open: daily except Sun 9am–1pm and 2pm–5pm).

Places to Visit on the Andaman and Nicobar Islands

Beaches

The white beaches of Corbyn's Cove and Wandoor on South Andaman are inviting places for a spot of sunbathing. It should be borne in mind, however, that scantily-clad tourists are not a typical part of the locals' everyday experience.

Swimming and diving opportunities

Attractive Swimming and diving opportunities are available on the islands of Havelock, Neil and Cinque, all of which are accessible from Port Blair via regular boats. Tourists can also go on organized boat trips, giving them the opportunity the get to know the islands better. The best time to visit is from October to April. In November / December the islands may be grazed by the edge of the **northeast monsoon**.

National parks

The Andaman and Nicobar Islands are home to many rare animal species. Some of the areas have been designated national parks and are home to dugongs and sea turtles, saltwater crocodiles and monitor lizards. Many bird species, some of which live only in these latitudes, also find protection here, including Andaman woodpigeons and Sunda teal, white-headed starlings and common mynas, green imperial pigeons and white-bellied sea-eagles.

Bhubaneshwar

19

Capital of Orissa
Population: 650,000

Altitude: 54m/177ft
Distance: 438km/272mi southwest of Kolkata

Together with ▶ Puri and Konark, Bhubaneshwar, Orissa's capital since 1950, forms the state's »Golden Triangle« of tourism.

Bhubaneshwar means »place (bhuba) of the god Shiva (Ishvara)«. Life here is still very slow-paced compared with other Indian cities. It is said that the god was worshipped in 7000 temples in the city, of which roughly 500 are still extant. Most of them are in ruins, but they also contain **some of the best temples in the whole of India**. They were built between the eighth and 13th centuries during the rule of the **Kalinga kings**. Even though their architectural style is clearly based on the northern Nagara style, the local characteristics are also immediately obvious. The main feature is the arrangement of the halls and temple tower in an extremely horizontal manner with a simultaneous vertical structuring of the conical tower. The latter effect is mainly achieved through the symmetrical arrangement of figures and ornaments. The elements of Buddhist architecture on the older temples are also noteworthy.

 VISITING BHUBANESHWAR

INFORMATION
Department of Tourism
Paryatan Bhawan
Museum Campus
Tel. 06 74 – 243 21 77

There are also tourist offices at the airport, at the station and in Lewis Road. Further information is available from the website of Orissa Tourism (www.orissatourism.gov.in).

WHERE TO STAY / WHERE TO EAT
▶ Luxury
Trident Hilton Bhubaneswar
Nayapalli
Tel. 06 74 – 230 10 10
www.hilton.com

Sophisticated hotel set in a large garden with a jogging trail and a swimming pool.

▶ Mid-range
Swosti
103, Janpath
Tel. 06 74 – 253 57 78
www.swosti.com
Centrally located with well-furnished rooms and fine cuisine.

▶ Budget
Panthanivas
OTCD
Ltd. Lewis Road
Tel. 06 74 – 243 23 14
www.panthanivas.com
Hotel run by Orissa Tourism.

What to See in Bhubaneshwar

There are many temples in the city, the most important of which will be described here. They are easily found with the help of a city map or a guide and can comfortably be visited in a single day.

Parasura Mesh-vara Temple

✱ This small, very decorative temple is considered the most attractive and best-preserved example of the early temples and dates back to the seventh century. The 13m/43ft temple tower, which rises up above the square sanctum, has a rectangular hall (jagamohan mandapa) in front of it. Its roof has only one step, a mark of early temple architecture. Amongst the rich sculptural display on the four external façades, the seven mother goddesses on the north side of the hall as well as a **very attractive depiction of Durga** on the north side of the temple tower as she kills the buffalo-demon Mahisha (Mahishasuramardini) stand out. The depiction on the south side above the figure of Ganesha is also interesting: Shiva is shown as a beggar receiving fruit from Parvati. Astute visitors will notice that several of the Shiva figures bear the face of Buddha, which can be explained by the ongoing **Buddhist influence**. The column hall inside the small temple is more reminiscent of a Buddhist chaitya hall than of a Hindu temple. However, the lingam in front of the temple is entirely in honour of the god Shiva. It **consists of 1000 small lingams**.

Bhubaneshwar Map

Station
Orissa Museum
0,25 mi
500 m
©Baedeker
Udayagiri
Kandagiri
Baddandasahi Road
Vivekananda Marg
Puri Canal
Parasura-meshvara Temple
Vaital Temple
Raja Rani Temple
Mukteshvara Temple
Bindu Sarovar
Brahmeshvara Temple
Lingaraja Temple
Puri Cuttack Road
Old Town
Dhauli

Vaital Temple The figures and ornaments on Vaital Temple from the eighth century are exquisite. The small temple on the west side of the Bindu Sarovar lake bears the name »pumpkin temple« because of its unique shape. In this case there is no conical roof rising up above the sanctum, instead it is a pyramid-like construction reminiscent of a southern-Indian temple tower. Rising up from it in turn are three small pointed towers.

The magnificent ornamentation on the temple's front wall is deserving of admiration. The temple is consecrated to the goddess Chamunda, one of Durga's incarnations. She can be admired on the façade in the guise of Mahishasuramardini defeating the buffalo demon.

A milestone in the development of Orissa's temple architecture is Mukteshvara Temple from the tenth century. It stands on the edge of a complex that also contains other temples and is surrounded by a small, decorated wall.

★ ★
Mukteshvara Temple

In front of the temple there is a **richly adorned entrance gate** with a round arch supported by two columns and decorated with figures of women. The structure itself consists of a 10.5m/34ft conical tower above the sanctum and a square hall with a stepped roof in front of it, both of which have been masterfully sculpted. This temple owes its special air not just to its harmonious blending of architectural form and inlaid figures; its ceiling decoration, too, consisting of an eight-leafed lotus into which the seven mother goddesses and Shiva have been chiselled, is very impressive.

The arch in front of Mukteshvara Temple shows Buddhist influences

Lingaraja Temple from the eleventh century with its 46m/151ft temple tower, which is visible from afar, is the central focal point of a larger walled complex that is **only accessible to Hindus**. A platform on its north side gives visitors insights into the microcosm of the countless temples. The stylistic development on Lingaraja Temple, which was to be seminal for future generations, is plain to see. The temple no longer consists of two parts. Two further buildings, a dancing hall and the offering hall were later added to the conical tower with the hall in front of it (jagamohan mandapa). Over time the temple's functions were expanded and thus a new dance tradition was created as a form of worship, which was then performed in the new halls. The dance created at the time, still known today under the name Odissi, continues to be nurtured as a classical dance in India and is performed both within the country itself and abroad.

★
Raja Rani Temple Pay a visit, too, to Raja Rani Temple from the eleventh century. Made of shimmering reddish-golden sandstone, it represents a different style. The 18m/60ft tower is longer here and consists of many small towers, an element that is also represented on the temples of ▶Khajuraho. The **entrance gate**, which is protected by two guards, is particularly impressive. Above the guard figures are Nagas and Naginis as well as the nine planet gods. Along the external façades visitors will recognize the eight guards of the different points of the compass. Not far away is **Brahmeshvara Temple** with its erotic sculptures.

Museums **Orissa State Museum** displays exhibits from the state's rich history
🕑 (open: daily except Mon 10am–4pm) on display. A collection of cult objects, huts and wall paintings, which will give interested visitors an insight into Orissa's tribal inhabitants, is exhibited by the **Museum**
🕑 **of the Tribal Research Center** (open: daily except Sun 10am–5pm).

Around Bhubaneshwar: Near Vicinity

★
Hirapur Hirapur is located around 15km/10mi east of Bhubaneshwar. There, visitors will find one of the rare **Yogini temples**. Only four of them are known to exist in India. The 64 Yoginis, the manifestations of Durga, are worshipped here.

Pipli Around 8km/5mi south of Bhubaneshwar, where the road forks
(fig. p.364) towards ▶Konark and ▶Puri, lies the small town of Pipli, known for its **handicrafts**. This is where the bags, wall hangings and temple parasols decorated with colourful appliqués and sometimes also with small mirrors come from.

Buddhist sites Orissa's old Buddhist tradition goes back to the great **Emperor Ashoka**. After his bloody conquest of the empire of Kalinga (Orissa's old name) in the third century BC, the famous ruler converted to Buddhism. This was the beginning of the lengthy golden age of Buddhist culture in this region.

On the small hill of **Dhauli** (8km/5mi southwest of Bhubaneshwar) is one of the first pieces of evidence of this Buddhist influence, namely the rock edicts Emperor Ashoka set up throughout his empire. Here there are only eleven instead of the usual 14, as he deliberately dispensed with three edicts that described the gruesome conquest of Kalinga. Instead he conveyed reconciliatory messages such as »all human beings are my children« to the people. A symbol of wisdom and strength and thus of Buddha himself is the stone elephant nearby, half of which is protruding from a rock. The Shanti Stupa, the peace pagoda on the hill, is also a reminder of the peaceful message of Buddhism. It was donated by the Japanese sect Nippon Buddha Sangha.

Jain monasteries On the twin peaks of Udayagiri and Khandagiri (8km/5mi northwest of Bhubaneshwar) there are several caves. Some of them were used as early as the first century BC as cells of a Jain monastery. The donor of this particular complex was Orissa's king Karavela (168–153 BC), a follower of Jainism. The most interesting sites are the caves on **Udayagiri** to the right of the road. At the foot of the hill is Rani Gumpha (Royal Cave, no. 1), a two-storey structure where each storey has 13 cells. The entrance gates bear attractive reliefs. Quite close by are Chota Hathi Gumpha (Small Elephant Cave, no. 3) and Vijaya Gumpha (Victory Cave, no. 5) with a Bodhi tree relief above the entrance. Up on the hill is Hathi Gumpha (Elephant Cave, no. 14) with an inscription about the deeds of King Karavela. Also quite nearby is Ganesha Gumpha, in front of which there are two elephants. Its entrance has however been closed off.

Nava Muni Gumpha (New Monk's Cave, no. 7) is on **Khandagiri**. Figures of monks have been chiselled into the cave's walls. It is sealed off, and can only be viewed from the outside. The small Durga rock temple is also worth a visit. It has the 24 tirthankaras (fordmakers) of Jainism chiselled into the rock, a relic of earlier times. Ananta Cave (no. 3) with its richly adorned entrance should not be missed.

Monasteries

The three most important centres of Buddhism were located in the hilly landscape northeast of the town of Cuttack (40km/25mi north of Bhubaneshwar). In a radius of just 20km/12mi several monasteries were built here, whose remains have been uncovered in archaeological digs. Even though all three sites are worth visiting, **Ratnagiri** has the most to offer. On a small hill near the village of the same name remains of two monasteries were found during archaeological digs, whose origins can be traced back to the sixth century AD. The ruins of Maha Vihara (large monastery), a single-storey brick structure on a pedestal, can be visited. The real gem of the complex is the **richly decorated and very well-preserved granite entrance gate** that leads into an inner courtyard. As is traditional for a vihara there are cells for monks on both sides and the sanctum in the back houses a 2.5m/8ft sitting Buddha statue with his companions Vajrapani to his left and Padmapani to his right.

5km/3mi from Ratnagiri there are the remains of another monastery complex and a brick stupa, which can also be visited: **Udayagiri**. According to current information from the archaeologists this is the largest Buddhist complex in Orissa, which experienced its golden age from the seventh to the twelfth

Impressive discoveries were found in the ground around Udayagiri

centuries and of which only parts have been uncovered to date. The location the monks chose for their abode is impressive: the site is harmoniously nestled into the U-shaped hills that surround it, while it maintains an open view to the east.

Of the three sites, **Lalitagiri** is the oldest. It was founded in the first century BC. Excavations are under way here too. So far, archaeologists have found the remains of seven monasteries, one chaitya hall and several stupas. Smaller discoveries can also be viewed in the museum (open: sunrise–sunset). Human remains were found in a number of repositories on the top of the hill, which caused much speculation, some of which went so far as to suggest they could be the remains of Buddha himself.

Around Bhubaneshwar: Further Afield

Similipal National Park Located at the border to Bihar is Similipal National Park (220km/ 135mi northeast of Bhubaneshwar), one of India's new tiger reserves. It has a total area of 2750 sq km/1060 sq mi. The forested hills with their valleys and waterfalls are home to many animals. In addition to almost 100 tigers the park is inhabited by leopards, elephants, sambar deer and numerous bird species. The best starting locations for a visit are the towns of Baripada (train connection to Balasore, on the Kolkata–Chennai main line) and Joshipur in the west of the park. There are also bus connections from Bhubaneshwar and Kolkata to both towns.

Bodhgaya (Bodh Gaya)

| 7

State: Bihar
Population: 22,000

Altitude: 113m/371ft
Distance: 600km/375mi west of Kolkata

For the world's Buddhists, Bodhgaya is the most sacred place on earth, and the Buddhist faith is still very much alive and well here.

To this day Bodhgaya has remained a peaceful city and even though all of the sites are located closely together and can comfortably be visited in a single day, it is an appealing prospect to spend a little bit more time here. The very clean, basic monasteries offer inexpensive accommodation. Visitors should, however, be aware that the rules in place in the monasteries have to be properly followed. In December the exiled head of Tibetan Buddhism, the **Dalai Lama**, comes to Bodhgaya, and with him come thousands of Buddhists.

History Siddharta Gautama came to this place (Uruvela) after long wanderings in search of enlightenment. He meditated for seven days under a Bodhi tree on the banks of the Nairanjana river. In this way he

● VISITING BODHGAYA

INFORMATION

Tourist Office
Corner of Bodhgaya Road / Temple
Street
Tel. 06 31 – 220 06 72

Information is also available on the
Bihar Tourism website
(www.bstdc.bih.nic.in).

GETTING THERE

Train connection to Gaya, from there
by bus or by taxi (13km/8mi).

WHERE TO STAY / WHERE TO EAT

► **Luxury**
Royal Residency
Tel. 06 31 – 220 01 24
Modern hotel with all the amenities
imaginable.

► **Budget**
There are many monasteries in
Bodhgaya offering inexpensive rooms,
such as Gelupa Tibetan monastery,
Bhutanese monastery, Daijokyo Tem-
ple and Root Institute.

achieved complete insight into the laws of life and gained the knowledge of how to overcome suffering. Visitors will still be able to see
the remains of a stone wall with relief works around the Bodhi tree
dating back to the Sunga period (first century BC). Mahabodhi temple was built as early as the second century AD and comprehensively
renovated in the late 18th century.

What to See in Bodhgaya

This temple was built directly in front of the Bodhi tree under which
Buddha achieved enlightenment and **Buddhists consider it their
most important shrine**. The pyramid-shaped structure was given its
current form in the 14th century. The 55m/180ft temple contains a
gilded statue of Buddha. The temple's exterior, which is structured
into seven steps, is decorated with countless Buddhas. The frieze,
which runs around three sides of the temple base, contains 85 sandstone Buddhas attributed to the Sunga period.

✷ ✷
**Mahabodhi
Temple**

The old Bodhi tree **under which Buddha meditated and found enlightenment** is said to have been destroyed by Emperor Ashoka prior
to his conversion to Buddhism. The current tree goes back to a seedling of the original tree, which had been taken to Sri Lanka by missionaries. The red sandstone under the sacred tree, Vajrasila, marks
the place (diamond throne) where Buddha found enlightenment.
Pilgrims come here to tie colourful ribbons on to the tree and the
stone fence that surrounds it as a sign of worship.

✷
Bodhi tree

Lake Mucalinda in the southern part of the complex is one of seven
holy places commemorating Buddha's presence. Others include one

✷
Lake Mucalinda

Pilgrims are decorating the site under the Bodhi tree where Buddha found enlightenment with colourful scarves, flowers and small votive gifts

of Buddha's footprints and the lotus path. During his deep meditation a massive storm is said to have broken out on the sixth day. A **cobra** is said to have curled up beneath him and held out its head above him for protection. A statue in the middle of the lake is a reproduction of this scene.

Buddhist centre   Mahabodhi Temple served as a model for many temples in Southeast Asia. Many pilgrims from all around the world have made the temple into a Buddhist centre again. Believers have donated a large number of **votive stupas**. Many Buddhist states such as Bhutan, Myanmar, China, Japan, Thailand and also Tibet have built temples here, thus making Bodhgaya a vibrant, international centre of Buddhism. Around 1km/0.6mi from Mahabodhi Temple is Magadha University, a centre of Buddhist studies.

Further temples   Of the numerous further temples of different Buddhist communities, the two the most worth visiting are the **Japanese temple** with its polished marble floors and golden Buddha statue, and the Tibetan temple. The **Tibetan temple**, painted in vibrant colours with the big dharma chakra (wheel of doctrine) that can be set in motion by believers, conveys a piece of Tibetan culture. It is said that those who turn the wheel three times will be washed clean of their sins. The temple also contains Buddha and Bodhisattva statues. The depiction of Avalokitesvara, Tibet's patron, is particularly attractive.

Archaeological Museum   West of Mahabodhi Temple near the game preserve is the archaeological museum, which has local finds as well as ninth-century bronze statues of Hindu and Buddhist deities on display.

Buddha statue   Visible from afar, the 20m/65ft Buddha statue on the road leading to the Tibetan temple was unveiled by the Dalai Lama in 1989.

Around Bodhgaya

Only around 12km/7mi to the north is the town of Gaya, one of the **Gaya** seven sacred places of Hinduism. According to legend the giant Gayasura is said to have lived here. He had more purifying powers within him than all of the country's sacrificial locations put together. Vishnupad temple in the centre is a place of pilgrimage; it is, however, only accessible to Hindus.

In the vicinity of Hazaribagh (139km/86mi southeast of Bodhgaya), **Hazaribagh** which literally translated means »thousand gardens«, there are forests **National Park** with sal trees. The reserve's animal population includes sambar deer, nilgai antelopes, chitals and the rare muntjac, a red deer species. Leopards or tigers will only be spotted with a lot of luck. Distributed throughout the park are ten observation towers, from where the animals can be watched. The season lasts from October to March. The park contains basic accommodation.

✶ Darjeeling

State: West Bengal
Population: 345,000

Altitude: 2134m/7001ft
Distance: 650km/404mi north of Kolkata

Every teadrinker has heard of Darjeeling, but very few are able to locate the origin of their favourite brew on a map.

The British brought the tea plant to India's northeastern mountain region, which is now the province of Darjeeling, part of West Bengal. Though it is one of the most famous tea-growing regions in the world, these days Darjeeling's good reputation comes not only from the excellent orange pekoe; it has also made a name for itself as a desirable destination for nature lovers and trekking tourists. A well-developed tourist infrastructure and highlights such as the view of the Kanchenjunga range and Mount Everest attract travellers from all around the world.

The area of what is now the province of Darjeeling was once a much **History** fought-over strip of land that often changed hands. Before it came under British rule it was governed by the kings of Sikkim, Bhutan and Nepal.
Like many a place along the Himalaya chain, Darjeeling's location made it a place of refuge for the British troops who were plagued by heat and disease. By the mid-19th century the town already had a permanent population of 10,000, of which the majority were Nepalis who worked on the newly established tea plantations. Much later on this migration led to great tensions between their descendants and

▶ VISITING DARJEELING

INFORMATION

Tourist Office
Government of West Bengal
1, Nehru Road
Tel. 03 54 – 225 40 50
Information about trekking tours can be obtained there or on the website www.wbtourism.com

GETTING THERE

To get to Darjeeling take the narrow-gauge railway from Siliguri or a bus or taxi. The closest airport is Bagdogra (100km/60mi to the south).

SHOPPING

Tea galore!

WHERE TO STAY / WHERE TO EAT

▶ **Luxury**
Windamere Hotel
Observatory Hill

Tel. 03 54 – 225 40 41
www.windamerehotel.com
An old colonial hotel in a wonderful location with all kinds of amenities.

▶ **Luxury / Mid-range**
Fortune Hotel Central
Tel. 03 54 – 225 87 21
www.fortuneparkhotels.com
40 rooms, distributed throughout a modern complex and an old colonial building with a lot of flair. An excellent international restaurant is also part of it.

▶ **Mid-range**
Planters Club
Tel. 03 54 – 225 43 48
Traditional club in Darjeeling with a billiard room and bar. The view of the Kanchenjunga massif is breathtaking and cold feet can be warmed on the hot-water bottles.

the West Bengal government. The majority of the Nepali-speaking population, Gurkhas, felt discriminated against by the Indian authorities in many ways. Only in 1988 when they were granted autonomy, albeit to a limited extent, did peace return to the troubled region.

The best **times to go** are the months immediately preceding the monsoon and those immediately afterwards, i.e. April–mid-June and September–November. Those visiting the region in spring will have the good fortune of witnessing the magnificent rhododendron and magnolia blossoms. It can get painfully cold in winter.

What to See in and around Darjeeling

Townscape
The small town is situated on a mountain ridge. Its lower part contains a railway station, a bus station and a taxi stand. The main connection between this part of the town and the more elevated assembly square (Chowrastra) is Laden La Road, called Nehru Road along its upper section. There are several hotels, shops, the Tourist Office of West Bengal, the post office and a bank along this road.

The view of the magnificent mountain landscape, particularly that of the Kanchenjunga range, can be enjoyed by visitors during a walk along one of the circular trails. The view from Observatory Hill is particularly stunning.

✱ ✱
View of the Kanchenjunga range

Around 3km/2mi outside of town is India's first **ropeway** (Darjeeling Rangeet Valley Passenger Ropeway) on which visitors can travel and explore the landscape for 8km/5mi.

The **Himalayan Mountaineering Institute**, which is located in the middle of a zoo, lies on an approximately 10km/6mi circular route. The exhibition there provides insights into the history of mountaineering (open: daily 9am–4.30pm).

> **!** *Baedeker* TIP
>
> ### Just your cup of tea!
>
> Everything that happens before the golden brew finds its way into a cup is revealed during a visit of one of the region's many tea plantations, such as Happy Valley Tea Estate in Darjeeling (Tue–Sat 8am–12pm and 1pm–4.30pm, Sun 8am–12pm). Those interested in organic, fair trade produce should head to Makaibari Tea Estate near Kurseong. Accommodation can also be found there (tel. 03 54 – 233 01 81, www.makaibari. com).

Those interested in handicrafts can visit the Tibetan Refugee Self Help Centre. The centre was set up in 1959 by refugees from nearby Tibet. Nice carpets, woollens and wood and leather goods are for sale here. The centre is closed on Sundays.

Tibetan Refugee Self Help Centre

Several Buddhist monasteries can be visited in the vicinity. After a short 15-minute walk from Chowrasta visitors will reach Bhutia Busty monastery. In the town of Ghoom (around 8km/5mi away) is Yiga Choling monastery, whose shrine contains a 5m/16ft statue of the future Buddha Maitreya and Samten Choling monastery.

Buddhist monasteries

An excursion to Tiger Hill (2590m/8497ft) 17km/11mi away is a worthwhile trip. This is a particularly good spot to watch the sun rise over Kanchenjunga. One option is to join an organized trip run by the Tourist Office in Darjeeling.

Tiger Hill

Since 1881 a narrow-gauge railway, which has been added to **UNESCO's list of World Heritage Sites**, has been servicing the 75km/47mi stretch between the valley station of Siliguri and Darjeeling. Originally created to take tea and wood from the town, the train now transports tourists to Darjeeling and back again. Via countless loops the steam train masters the altitude difference of 2000m/6560ft between the two towns.
The very scenic journey through the changing vegetation from hot and humid Siliguri to cool Darjeeling takes about 6 hours and trains run all year round, though there can be disruptions during the monsoon.

✱
Narrow-gauge railway (Toy Train)

An excursion to the busy bazaar town of Kalimpong (51km/32mi east of Darjeeling, population 40,000) is particularly recommended on Wednesdays and Saturdays, when markets are held in the town. The people of the surrounding towns flock to Kalimpong to buy their goods. The town itself has three 20th-century monasteries: Tharpa Choling monastery (1937), Zong Dong Pairi Fo Brang monastery (1975) and Thongsa Gumpha monastery (founded in 1962, but whose buildings are more recent).

Kalimpong

The main attraction for many tourists is the wide range of trekking opportunities in this area. Depending on personal fitness, hikers can choose between easier, lower-altitude regions and high-altitude trekking, which requires a lot more stamina. The range of tours on offer includes day trips to others lasting a week or more as well as speciality treks for those with an interest in flora and fauna. More detailed information is available from the youth hostel in Darjeeling. During the season trekking tours are regularly organized from there, too. Visitors also have the option of using the Tourist Office in Darjeeling.

★
Trekking tours

★ # Kolkata (Calcutta)

K 8

Capital of West Bengal
Population: 13 million

Altitude: 6m/20ft
Distance: 1442km/896mi east of Delhi

Many travellers who have found their way to the city on the Hooghly river have tried to put the phenomenon that is Kolkata into words: Kipling called it »city of dreadful night«, Dominique Lapierre, author of the famous eponymous novel about the city, described it as »city of joy«, while Günter Grass, Germany's Nobel Prize winning author, thought it was nothing but »a pile of shit that God dropped«.

Like no other city in the so-called Third World, Kolkata is considered a symbol of social and ecological disaster and a warning example of what the uncontrolled growth of modern cities can result in. In actual fact, the poor of Kolkata live in the same humiliating conditions as those in Delhi and Mumbai, the latter having overtaken Kolkata when it comes to population. Nonetheless Kolkata is considered **India's poorhouse**, which can also be explained by the large number of refugees from the neighbouring country of Bangladesh as well as from the poor states of Bihar and Orissa. Both the state and many non-governmental organizations are trying to improve the situation of the poor. The city's social institutions that were founded by **Moth-**

Facets of a city

← *Tea pickers*

In West Bengal and its capital Kolkata, Durga Puja,
the festival in honour of the great goddess, is the most important of the entire year

er Teresa and her Missionaries of Charity have already become legendary.

But Kolkata is quite definitely better than its reputation, and it would be an injustice if all that was said about the city was how bad conditions are here. In addition to an **extremely diverse and vibrant cultural scene** and very interesting parts of town such as the old colonial quarters or the artisan quarter Kumar Tuli, it is particularly the friendliness and helpfulness of the Bengalis that make a stay in Kolkata a very special experience.

Cultural centre

By as early as the 19th century Kolkata had acquired a reputation for being **India's cultural centre**. Many significant artists and authors have been produced by the city, the most famous being the poet and Nobel laureate **Rabindranath Tagore** (▶ Famous People). Kolkata's cultural scene is still much talked about, be it its sophisticated film and theatre productions, its major music festivals, or its highly valued literature. Along with Mumbai and Delhi the city is also the third large centre of contemporary painting.

Legend and history

1690	Trading post of the East India Company
1757	Battle of Plassey
1858	Capital of British India
1947	Capital of the state of West Bengal since India's independence

Kolkata's origins lie in the merging of three villages into a trading post of the East India Company in 1690. On the banks of the river stood a famous temple consecrated to the goddess Kali, and it was this that gave Kolkata its name. According to legend, the god Shiva

Rickshaw pullers can still be seen in the centre of Kolkata

flew into a rage upon the death of his wife Sati (Kali) and began destroying the world. The other gods, shocked by his actions, asked Vishnu, the preserver of the world, for salvation. Vishnu threw his divine discus, which split the body of the dead Kali into 51 pieces. He scattered them and dissuaded Shiva from continuing his destructive fit of rage. Wherever pieces of Kali fell to ground, temples sprung up in which the goddess was worshipped. One of them arose on the banks of the Hooghly river, where Kali's right toe had landed. The name Kalikata or Kolkata in Bengali can thus be traced back to **Kalighat (place of Kali)**.

Thanks to its favourable location, the new **trading post** developed quickly; it was protected from enemies by Fort William. This aroused the mistrust of Nawab Siraj-ud-Daulah, who ruled Bengal at the time. He was extremely unhappy about the British building forts. In 1756 he occupied the city and held the British in a dungeon, the notorious »Black Hole of Calcutta«. His rule over Kolkata only lasted a year, however, because he was defeated by British troops under Robert Clive at the Battle of Plassey in 1757. This victory strengthened British rule over Bengal and led to increased building activity within the city. The new Fort William was completed in 1774 and the **»Black City« of the locals** was built to the north of the **»White City« of the British**, the area around what is now »BBD Bagh« square. The centre of the »Black City« was Bara Bazar, originally a thread market that is now the most sprawling wholesale market in India. The **»Grey Quarter«** between the two cities was inhabited by merchants from all around the world. This was also the time the city was given its sobriquet »village of palaces« because the newly rich merchants showed off their affluence by building magnificent villas and palaces.

»White Kolkata« got a new boost after it became the **capital of British India** in 1858. A large number of prestige buildings were designed to underline its character as a centre of government. The move of the seat of government from the politically tense Bengal to the more central Delhi in 1911 caused Kolkata to lose its outstanding position, but it still remained one of India's most important cities. The class of Bengali intellectuals that developed in the 19th century was one of the most severe critics of British colonial rule right from the start and thus a **centre of national opposition** formed in the city, from which crucial impulses emanated for India's subsequent liberation.

Kolkata on foot Anyone really wanting to get to know Kolkata should try to explore parts of the city centre on foot. The best time to do this is in the mornings because the air is particularly heavily polluted with emissions in the afternoons. It is best to use a street map for orientation and rely on the helpfulness of the Bengalis, who are happy to assist strangers.

Kolkata Map

1 Marble Palace	8 Town Hall
2 Nakhoda Masjid	9 Government House
3 Asutosh Museum	10 Fairlie Ghat
4 Writers Building	11 Birla Planetarium
5 St John's	12 St Paul's
6 BBD Bagh	13 Academy of
7 High Court	Fine Arts

Where to eat
① Grain of Salt
② Aaheli
③ Kewpies
④ Flury's
⑤ Chennai Kitchen

Where to stay
① Oberoi Grand
② Taj Bengal
③ Kenilworth
④ Fairlawn
⑤ YWCA

Highlights *Kolkata*

Indian Museum
The best collection of Buddhist
Gandhara sculptures and much more
▶ page 391

Victoria Memorial
Marble memorial from the British colonial
period
▶ page 389

Howrah Bridge
The world's busiest bridge
▶ page 395 f.

Kali Temple
Temple dedicated to Kali, Kolkata's patron
goddess
▶ page 391

Kumar Tuli
Clay gods are made here.
▶ page 395

Rabindra Bharati Museum
The famous Bengali poet and recipient of
the Nobel Prize in Literature, Rabindranath
Tagore, was born in this house.
▶ page 395

Marble Palace
Private museum with a colourful salma-
gundi of exhibits, including a Rubens
▶ page 391

New Market
Contrary to the name, the bazaar that has
everything is not new.
▶ page 391

K. C. Das
Try traditional Bengali sweets.
▶ page 391

BBD Bagh and the Southern City Centre

The centre of the former »White City« is BBD Bagh (Benoy-Badal-
Dinesh-Bagh), also known under its former name Dalhousie Square.
Grouping around the pool fed by natural springs are some of the
large colonial buildings dating from the time of the British Raj. On
the north side stands the Writers' Building, the former workplace
and home of the writers, the young employees of the East India
Company. These days the red brick building is the **seat of West Bengal's government**. The main post office with its dome ceiling can be
found on its west side.

**BBD Bagh,
Writer's Building**

Further south, on the corner of Hastings Street / Old Council House
Street, is St John's Church, which was consecrated in 1784. It contains the mausoleum of the city founder Job Charnock, who was an
envoy of the East India Company.

St John's

Further south, along the Esplanade West, stand the Gothic towers of
the High Court, a replica of Ypres town hall.

High Court

A few metres to the east is Kolkata's Town Hall, built in 1813, and
Raj Bhavan, formerly the British government building and now the
seat of the governor of West Bengal, built between 1799 and 1805.

Town Hall

Maidan Along the Hooghly, Maidan, Kolkata's green lung, stretches out for around 5km/3mi. The **Shahid Minar** rises up at its northern end. The 48m/157ft Doric column was called the Ochterlony Monument prior to India's independence. It commemorates Sir David Ochterlony's victory over the Nepalis.

Maidan's southern end is marked by the race course. In between these two points is the former **Fort William**, several playing fields, assembly places and, in the northwest corner of the park, Eden Gardens with a small Burmese pagoda.

► VISITING KOLKATA

INFORMATION

Tourist Office of India Tourism
4, Shakespeare Sarani
Tel. 033 – 22 82 14 75,
www.wbtourism.com
Current tips can be found in the city listings magazine *Cal Calling*.

FESTIVALS

Durga Puja in honour of the goddess Durga (Sept / Oct); Dover Lane Music Festival with the best Indian musicians (Jan / Feb)

RIVER CRUISES

The Assam Bengal Navigation Company River offers cruises on the Hooghly or the Ganges lasting four to 14 days. Passengers stay in air-conditioned cabins on a motor vessel and visit various cultural sites (tel. 03 61 – 260 22 23, www.assambengalnavigation.com).

SHOPPING

Handicrafts and textiles from the Indian state can be bought in Dakshinapan Shopping Complex in Gariahat Road. In the New Market in Lindsay Street, which is now more than 130 years old, visitors will find a large selection of clothes and a lot more. The state-run Central Cottage Industries Emporium can be found at 7, JL Nehru Road.

Sasha
27, Mirza Ghalib Street
Tel. 033 – 22 52 15 86
Handicrafts and attractive accessories from village cooperatives.

Fab India
16, Hindustan Park
Tel. 033 – 24 65 69 54
Clothes, pillow cases, blankets, curtains and much more

WHERE TO EAT

► **Expensive**
① *Grain of Salt*
Block D, 5th floor
22, Carnac Street
Tel. 033 – 22 81 13 13
Chef Sanjeev Kapoors serves dishes to please the palate on several floors: very good Bengali specialities, as well as »basic« world cuisine. Grain of Salt also has a bar and a café.

► **Moderate**
② *Aaheli*
12, JL Nehru Road
Tel. 033 – 22 28 03 01
Bengali specialities. Our tip: try the Hilsa fish!

③ *Kewpies*
2, Elgin Lane

Kolkata's best-known attraction, the **Victoria Memorial** can also be found in the southern part of the park. The domed building completed in 1921 is made of white marble and is **one of the last pieces of monumental evidence of the British claim to power in India**. In the haze of the morning mist over Kolkata the complex, with its elements of Renaissance and Mughal architecture, seems more like a fairy-tale castle cast in sugar than a symbol of political strength.

In front of it is a huge statue of Queen Victoria, while the interior houses an extensive collection of paintings and memorabilia from the time of the British Raj (open: daily except Mon, in summer 10am–5pm, in winter 10am–4.30pm, light-and-sound show: 7.15pm and 8.15pm).

★ ★
Victoria Memorial (3D image p.94)

Tel. 033 – 24 75 98 80
Tasty Bengali dishes are prepared here to traditional recipes.

► Moderate / Inexpensive
④ *Flury's*
18, Park Street
Tel. 033 – 22 29 76 64
Opens at 7am.
The cake served in this newly renovated café is a tasty treat.

► Inexpensive
⑤ *Chennai Kitchen*
P15/1 Chowringhee Square
Tel. 033 – 22 48 85 09
South Indian cuisine, the large selection of dosas is the house speciality.

WHERE TO STAY
► Luxury
① *The Oberoi Grand*
5, JL Nehru Road
Tel. 033 – 22 49 23 23
Old, stylish colonial hotel with a lot of flair and good cuisine in a central location.

② *Taj Bengal*
34 B, Belvedere Road
Alipore
Tel. 033 – 22 23 39 39
www.tajhotels.com

An oasis of calm and a comfortable alternative to the Oberoi. The hotel has a swimming pool as well as several restaurants and bars.

► Mid-range
③ *The Kenilworth*
162, Little Russell Street
Tel. 033 – 22 82 39 39
Modern hotel in the city centre with a garden, bar and restaurant.

④ *Fairlawn Hotel*
13 A, Sudder Street
Tel. 033 – 22 52 15 10
www.fairlawnhotel.com
Mrs. Smith and her daughter run this British-style hotel, where afternoon tea is served in the garden. It is reminiscent of days gone by in many other ways too.

► Budget
⑤ *YWCA*
1, Middleton Row
near Park Street
Tel. 033 – 22 29 70 33
Centrally located south of Park Street, the YWCA has a pretty green courtyard and a restaurant. When demand is high the clean, light and friendly rooms are only let for longer periods of a week or more.

The hustle and bustle on Nehru Road

St. Paul's Cathedral

🕐 Opening hours: daily 9am–12pm and 3pm–6pm

East of it visitors will find St. Paul's Cathedral from the year 1847. It is one of India's most important churches. Its tower is a replica of that of Canterbury Cathedral. The mosaics on the glass windows and the **memorial tablets** inside the church are quite interesting. They provide an insight into the often short but eventful lives of many an India traveller of days gone by.

Birla Planetarium

Immediately in front of it is the Birla Planetarium, whose equipment includes the Celestron C14 telescope and the Carl Zeiss universal planetarium projector. Presentations in English are held every day.

★ **Academy of Fine Arts**

🕐

The Academy of Fine Arts, just a short distance away, is also worth a visit. In addition to medieval miniature paintings it exhibits drawings and manuscripts by Tagore as well as a collection of works by the famous Indian painter **Jamani Roy**. Changing exhibitions by contemporary artists are also shown here (open: daily except Mon 3pm–8pm).

Nehru Road (Chowringhee)

The city's modern shopping street, formerly known as Chowringhee, is now called Nehru Road and borders the eastern end of Maidan. It has many interesting shops, and banks and airlines have their offices here.

Mother Teresa Street (formerly Park Street)

Mother Teresa Street with shops and the old café Flurys can be accessed via Nehru Road. Many British found their final resting place under pavilions, obelisks and (nowadays) weathered tomb stones in the old **Park Street Cemetery**.

The big Bazaar New Market in Lindsay Street, another one of Nehru Road's side streets, is also worth visiting. The halls of the 1874 building sell clothes and jewellery, household goods, suitcases, books, food and a lot more.

Bazaar
New Market

The imposing Indian Museum, built in 1875, also has its entrance on Nehru Road. In addition to the departments of mineralogy, zoology and numismatics, it is particularly famous for its **collection of Buddhist Gandhara sculptures**, which is considered to be the best in the whole of India. The Buddhist sculptures from Bharhut in Madhya Pradesh from the second century BC are also outstanding. Otherwise, the department of handicrafts, which displays textiles, sculpture and jewellery from all over India, is particularly recommendable (open: daily except Mon, in summer 10am–5pm, in winter 10am–4.30pm).

★ ★
Indian Museum

> **!** **Baedeker TIP**
>
> **The sweet side of Kolkata**
> Rossogolla, Barfi, Sandesh, Gulab Jamun: Kolkata is heaven for those with a sweet tooth because Bengali sweets, which have a milk base, are famous all over India. They can all be sampled one after the other at K. C. Das on Esplanade / East.

Around 3km/2mi to the south is the temple of Kolkata's patron goddess, Kali. Kali represents a destructive aspect of the goddess Durga and demands daily sacrifices. Even today, young goats are sacrificed in her honour. The temple houses an **image of the goddess** wearing a necklace of skulls as she sticks out her bloody tongue.

★
Kali Temple

In the temple's immediate vicinity is an ochre-coloured building which houses the **Mother Teresa Home for the Dying** (Nirmal Hriday).
The legendary missionary many consider the epitome of charity was buried in the mother house in AJC Bode Road under a marble stone with the inscription »Love one another as I have loved you«.

Nirmal Hriday

Northern City Centre

Since some of the following sites are very well hidden it is a good idea to hire a taxi or a knowledgeable guide.

Tip

North of BBD Bagh is Nakhoda Mosque, the main mosque in Kolkata. It is built of red sandstone, modelled on Akbar's tomb in Sikandra. Its minarets have a height of 46m/150ft.

Nakhoda
Mosque

Marble Palace, further north on Muktaram Babu Lane, was built in 1855. It is a relic of the time when Kolkata was called the »village of

★
Marble Palace

New lamps at Diwali are supposed to help the souls of the dead to find their way to heaven

DIWALI, DUSSERA, HOLI

As befits a country of such size and with such a diversity of religions India has countless festivals. Many, however, are only of regional significance or only play an important role for a certain religious group. Their exact dates can be looked up under www.incredibleindia.org.

The most important dates in the Hindu festival calendar are those of **Diwali** (Dipawali). This four-day festival during the last two days of the Hindu month of Ashvin and the first two days of Kartik (Oct/Nov) is celebrated in almost all of India. It is thought that the **festival of light** goes back to pre-Aryan rituals for the end of the monsoon period. Vishnu's followers celebrate it in honour of Rama, Vishnu's seventh incarnation. Everything is concerned with new beginnings: entrepreneurs take stock, houses are cleaned and given a fresh coat of paint. Lamps are lit at night. The people dress in new clothes and spend the time visiting each other and playing games. Even before the festival large quantities of the sweets popular in India are made and eaten.

The ten-day festival of **Dussehra** ends with the Durga Puja on the first night of the Hindu month of Ashvin (Sept/Oct) and is celebrated in honour of female forces, the goddesses. In the preceding nine nights the following incarnations of the goddess Devi are celebrated: Mahakali, Mahishasuramardini, Chamunda, Nanda, Raktadanti, Sakhambari, Durga and Labhramari. It is customary to set up and worship depictions of goddesses in houses and in public places. During the nights pandits (teachers) tell stories about the deeds of the goddesses. Thus the great legends are passed on from one generation to the next. Dussehra is a particularly important festival in Bengal, where Durga is highly esteemed (fig. p.384). However, the maharajas of Rajasthan also celebrated this festival with a lot of pomp, since Durga, being the goddess of war, was very popular with them. In southern India, female

forces are also honoured, but not just Durga; all three main goddess of the Indian pantheon are worshipped: Durga, Lakshmi and Sarasvati. For three nights each, elaborate altars with figures of deities or humans are set up. This custom very much resembles the way nativity scenes are set up at Christmas in the West.

Welcoming spring

One of India's jolliest, gayest and most colourful festivals is **Holi**, celebrated on the day of the full moon during the Hindu month of Phalgun (Feb/March). It is customary for the people to splash each other with paint and tease each other. Sometimes they also throw water balloons or manure. For this reason it is advisable to avoid the old town quarters during this festival. It is celebrated in honour of Krishna and Kama. In the night before Holi, wood is gathered everywhere, whereupon large fires are lit at junctions considered to be magical; this is meant to expel spirits. Holi marks the end of winter and the beginning of spring and has many similarities to the European carnival.

Ganesha and other gods

Ganesh Chathurthy is celebrated on the fourth day of the Hindu month of Bhadrapad (Aug/Sept) in honour of the elephant god Ganesha, who enjoys great popularity in the whole of India. Ganesha is said to have been born on this day, which is why large figures of the god are set up and worshipped in public places three days before the festival. Districts and streets compete to have the largest and most beautiful Ganesha. This festival is particularly impressive in Maharashtra and specifically in Mumbai, where, in one great procession, thousands of Ganesha figures of all sizes are carried to the sea and immersed (fig. p.475).

Sivarathri (Feb/March) is a festival held in honour of the ascetic Shiva. It involves strict fasting. The night before is spent telling stories and legends. **Janmashtami** (July/Aug) is

believed to be Krishna's birthday and is celebrated with songs and dancing. This festival is particularly popular in the region around Mathura, where Krishna is said to have spent his youth.

Rama's birthday, **Ram Navami**, is celebrated on the ninth day of the Hindu month of Chaitra (March/April). It is customary to read to others from the Ramayana or to perform plays about the life of the hero Rama. This festival has a special significance in Uttar Pradesh.

The temple in Puri consecrated to the master of the universe, Jagannath, is the site of one of India's most spectacular **temple festivals**, held annually. Hundreds of thousands of pilgrims from all over India come to be there when the temple's three deities, Jagannath, his sister Subhadra and his half-brother Balarama, are pulled to their country house on huge temple chariots and pulled back to their temple a week later. The largest temple chariot has a height of almost 14m/46ft and it requires thousands to set the three chariots in motion. The attraction of the annual three-day festival of Meenakshi Temple in Madurai, which takes place in April, is also the procession of the gods in a huge temple chariot that is pulled along the processional road around the temple. Followers of Vishnu make pilgrimages to the ten-day Vaikuntha Ekadesh Festival in Sri Rangam Temple in December. During this festival a Vaikunta Vasal (paradise gate) is set up that the pilgrims then walk through in order to obtain salvation.

Ritual cleansing

The **Kumbha Mela**, the largest Hindu festival, is also one of the most unusual mass events in India. It only takes place every three years and is held in four different towns (Allahabad, Haridwar, Ujjain and Nasik), i.e. each of these towns holds the festival every twelve years. These towns are considered the most holy because it is said that each of them received a drop of the immortality nectar Amrita. In Allahabad the Maha Kumbha Mela attractions millions of believers. All of the important representatives of Hindu groups meet here in order to discuss religious questions.

palaces«. The builder, Raja Rajendra Mullick, a rich merchant, collected everything from old Chinese vases to a real Rubens (*Betrothal of St Catherine*) here. A **permit** to visit this cabinet of curiosities, which has been transformed into a private museum, can be obtained from the Tourist Office on Shakespeare Sarani. Photography is not permitted.

Opening hours: daily except Mon and Thu 11am–4pm

Not far away, also to the north, stands the **house where Rabindranath Tagore, the famous Bengali poet and Nobel laureate, was born** (▶ Famous People). The adjoining Rabindra Bharati Museum provides an insight into the life and activities of Tagore (open: Mon–Fri 10am–5pm, Sat 10am–1.30pm).

Rabindra Bharati Museum

Further east, in College Street, are the buildings belonging to the University of Kolkata. Here visitors will also find the small Ashutosh Museum of History with a remarkable collection of typically Bengali handicrafts as well as rare Buddhist manuscripts (open: Mon–Fri 10.30am–5pm).

Ashutosh Museum

Further northwest is the district of Kumar Tuli, the residential quarter and workplace of the mrit shilpis, the clay workers. They make **statues of gods in all sizes** from clay from the Hooghly and straw. The statues are fired in the traditional manner in a clay oven and subsequently painted. They ultimately get used in the great religious festivals such as Kali Puja and Sarasvati Puja.

Kumar Tuli

In the northeast of the city, in a playful little park with fountains and stone sculptures is the 1867 Jain temple. It is completely covered with mirrors and glass mosaics.

Jain temple

Howrah

Howrah, Kolkata's sister city, is best reached via Howrah Bridge, also known as Rabindra Setu. The iron bridge, completed in 1943, spans the river without any supporting pillars in the water. It is said to be the **busiest bridge in the world**. Masses of vehicles, from double-decker buses to bicycle rickshaws, make their way across the river every day, mostly at a crawl. The bridge also connects Kolkata with the large Howrah Station. Below the bridge columns is a **large flower market** that impresses visitors with its many colours and scents. There is a magnificent view of Howrah Bridge from the riverbank. Believers conduct their rituals on the ghats.

Howrah Bridge

On this side of the river visitors will also find the Botanical Gardens. They can be reached from the opposite riverbank via a ferry from Fairlie Ghat or Chandpal Ghat somewhat further south. The park's main attraction is the approx. 200-year-old banyan tree, which is thought to be the **world's largest tree**. It has more than 1400 aerial

Botanical Gardens

HOWRAH BRIDGE

✴✴ **One of Kolkata's most famous landmarks is Howrah Bridge, which connects the city with the town of Howrah on the western bank of the Hooghly. Its official name is Rabindra Setu. It is a monument to the final days of colonial India: built in 1943 during the Second World War in order to give the Allied troops access to the front in Burma, it replaced an older pontoon bridge.**

Note:
photography is strictly prohibited from the middle of the river!

① Steel Cantilever Bridge
Howrah Bridge was one of the last steel cantilever bridges to be built. Since it was thought that the river could silt up and people were worried about an alteration to the river's course, its construction was controversial for a long time. For that reason it was decided to build a cantilever bridge that did not have any piers in the river.

② Girders
The 656m/717yd bridge spans the Hooghly, a distributary of the Ganges, in a single gigantic span of 457.5m/500yd. It has a height of 82m/267ft and most of the girders were made in India, but more complicated components were manufactured in Britain.

③ Traffic across the Hooghly
Millions of commuters use Howrah Bridge every day, as do an estimated 100,000 vehicles, making it the world's busiest bridge. There are two alternatives available, removing some of its traffic: the ferry Fairlie Ghat – Howrah and a new, second Howrah Bridge. Those wanting to get across the river as fast as possible are actually best off with the ferry, but that costs money, as does the new bridge a few miles downriver, which charges a toll. Hence most people prefer to throw themselves into the usual traffic chaos of the old bridge.

Usually congested: very many pedestrians as well as rickshaws, ox carts, cyclists and cars try to find their way between the buses

Large flower market below the bridge piers

Ghats, where many pilgrims and sadhus congregate

© Baedeker

There is a nice view of the impressive bridge from the shore. Since it has military significance it is strictly prohibited to take photographs.

roots and covers an area of 14,000 sq m/16,700 sq yd. The main trunk was removed in 1925 after it had died. The 100ha/247ac garden complex has around 12,000 plant species. The palm tree and orchid houses are particularly worth taking a look at.

Ramakrishna Mission
Drive northwards for 12km/7mi along Grand Trunk Road in Howrah to get to Belur Math, the centre of the Ramakrishna Mission, which was founded by **Swami Vivekananda**, the great propagator of Sri Ramakrishna's ideas. **Belur Math Temple**, by blending various stylistic elements of the major religions, symbolizes one of the philosopher's central ideas, namely the tolerance and co-existence of the various faiths. The residential building behind it contains Sri Ramakrishna's room, which is open to the public.

There are two further temples on the banks of the Hooghly, consecrated to Ramakrishna's wife Sharada Devi and his student Swami Vivekananda. Photography is not permitted within the complex.

Dakshineswar Temple
Cross the Hooghly further north via Vivekananda Bridge to get to Dakshineswar Temple. Dedicated to the goddess Kali, the temple was built in 1855 with the help of money donated by the rich widow Rani Rashmoni. Dakshineswar is an important place of pilgrimage.

In the Near Vicinity

✱ Sundarbans
South of Kolkata, the countless arms of the Ganges reaching out into the oceans form the **world's largest river delta**: the Sundarbans. They cover an area of 9600 sq km/3700 sq mi and consist of islands criss-crossed by channels of water. They are largely covered by mangroves. 36 species of mangrove have been counted here. The main part of the Sundarbans lies in Bangladesh, while the smaller part is in West Bengal. A **national park and a tiger reserve** were set up here. In fact, seeing one of the rare tigers in this mangrove forest requires a lot of luck; nature lovers and bird enthusiasts are far more likely to find what they are looking for. There is a bird sanctuary in Sajnekhali.

! Baedeker TIP

The Sundarbans in print
The Bengali marshes were immortalized in Amitav Ghosh's gripping novel *The Hungry Tide*. A landscape comes to life and with it so do the inhabitants of this strip of land.

Before visiting it is important to get information from the Tourist Office in Kolkata and if necessary book accommodation and acquire a permit for the reserve (information is also available on the website of the state of West Bengal). Upon request the Tourist Office also organizes group trips, but there is also the possibility of travelling to the Sundarbans alone. The best starting point is Canning river harbour (train connections from Kolkata, Sealdah Station). From here, visitors can also go on tours of the Sundarbans on steam ships.

Further Afield

From the eighth to the 18th century Vishnupur (152km/94mi northwest of Kolkata) was the capital of the Malla kings, a ruling Hindu dynasty. During its heyday (16th–18th centuries) they had a number of **Bengali-style temples** built. Characteristic of these structures are the gabled roofs and the cladding of the exterior walls with terra cotta, which usually contain depictions of scenes from mythology. The shapes of the arches on the exterior façades are an indication of the synthesis of Hindu and Muslim architecture, which is visible in many places. Outstanding examples are Shyam-Rai Temple (1643) and Jor-Bangla Temple (1655). Vishnupur can be reached by train from Howrah Station or by bus from Esplanade Terminus.

Vishnupur

»The most beautiful place on Earth I could ever hope to find«: that's how **Rabindranath Tagore** described the bare strip of land around 200km/125mi north of Kolkata, where in 1901 he started the pedagogic experiment of a system of progressive education on the basis of ancient Indian educational ideals. Students and teachers were to live together. Handicraft and artistic talents were particularly fostered and, according to the tradition, classes took place outside. Later the school became a university (Vishva Bharati), and Santiniketan is still **one of the country's largest cultural centres**. In addition to the university of visual arts there is a department of music and dance, a Tagore Museum and a centre of agricultural development.

Cultural events take place here all year round (information available from the Tourist Offices in Kolkata). Accommodation can be found in the International Guesthouse in Santiniketan. There is a direct connection from Howrah via the Santiniketan Express.

Santiniketan

◄ Tip

Murshidabad (225km/140mi north of Kolkata) was once Bengal's capital (from 1704) and the seat of government of Nawab Murshid Quli Khan and his successor Siraj-ud-Daulah, whom the British defeated at the historic Battle of Plassey. Murshidabad lies on the banks of the Bhagirathi and is home to some of the inheritance of the Bengali Nawabs, including Hazarduari Palace with its thousand doors, which now contains a museum (collection of weapons, porcelain and paintings). Immediately next to it is the Great Imambara, a mausoleum. The city's founder, Murshid Quli Khan, is buried next to the ruins of Katra Mosque. There is a train connection between Murshidabad and Kolkata departing from Sealdah Station.

Murshidabad

On the way to Darjeeling lies the town of Maldah (350km/217mi north of Kolkata), a good starting point for visits to Gour and Pandua.

Maldah

Gour 12km/7mi south of Malda is Gour, once the capital of the Buddhist Pala dynasty, the Hindu Sena dynasty and the Islamic conquerors in the 13th century. Almost all of the fort complexes and mosques are in ruins. Pay a visit to Bara Sona Mosque and Qadam Raisul Mosque, which is said to contain a footprint made by Mohammed.

Pandua Pandua (18km/11mi north of Malda), which took the place of Gour in the 14th century, is nowadays considered a significant town for Islamic architecture in Bengal. In particular the remains of Adina Mosque, built above a Hindu temple, deserve attention.

Northeastern States

K–O 12/13

A small tongue of West Bengal connects India to its seven northeastern states. Bordered by Bhutan and Tibet in the north, Myanmar in the southeast and Bangladesh in the southwest, this group of small states, namely Assam, Meghalaya, Arunachal Pradesh, Nagaland, Manipur, Mizoram and Tripura, lies some distance away from the subcontinent's major transport routes.

The fate of these often very sparsely populated states has long been closely linked to that of the rest of India, but their culture is largely shaped by the many different tribes inhabiting this region. These tribes are primarily peoples who came here from the mountains of Thailand, Laos and Myanmar, or Sino-Tibetan groups from the northeast.
Tensions between the distant central government in New Delhi and the indigenous populations who feel their cultural heritage is being threatened frequently lead to escalations, even to civil war. This is also the main reason why travelling to this region is subject to restrictions.

The region was inaccessible to foreigners for a long time. The Indian ministry of tourism is now trying to attract visitors to these states, which have so far remained largely untouched by tourism. It has also made **travelling into this region easier**. Information is available from the websites of India Tourism (www.india-tourism.com) and those in individual states (www.assamtourism.org, www.manipur.nic.in, www.meghalaya.nic.in, www.mizoram.nic.in, www.nagaland.nic.in).

Assam

The Brahmaputra, the only male river in Hindu mythology, flows for 700km/435mi through Assam from the northeast to the southwest. The river is the life blood of the small state, but also brings dis-

Northeast States *Map*

aster to the fertile valleys on the edge of the Himalaya at regular intervals. When the water of the great river bursts its banks during the monsoon, there is no stopping it: disastrous floods threaten the people, the animals and the region's agricultural production. There are **more than 1000 tea plantations** in Assam and almost a third of India's tea crop is now harvested here. The warm, humid climate and the torrential rains give rise to a strong, malty tea.

As early as the 13th century tribes from Thailand settled on the river's banks in the country's northeastern corner. They called themselves Ahom, after the landscape that had become their new home. The name means »undulating land« and it is still the local name for Assam. Over time the Buddhist Ahom mixed with the Hindu Bengalis. In the 18th century an official conversion of the tribal kings to Hinduism caused a revolt that was put down with the help of Burma, modern-day Myanmar. The eastern neighbour subsequently seized power until the region fell to the British in 1826. After India's independence, the state of Assam was founded. It quickly developed into one of the Indian government's trouble spots. Even though the small region is India's largest tea producer and even though it contributes to the country's industrial growth with its oilfields, the economic development of the volatile border region stagnated. The simultaneous immigration of refugees from crisis-ridden Bangladesh led to an explosive situation. It culminated in the creation of ULFA, the United Liberation Front of Assam, which demanded independence. During the 1980s the small state was often shaken by civil war and unrest and to this day the situation has not entirely calmed down. The presence of the Indian army has brought order, but it does not pacify the minds of the worried population, who feel their cultural identity and independent economic development are impaired.

Guwahati

Guwahati (1150km/715mi northeast of Kolkata, population 900,000), Assam's most important city, which is located immediately next to the capital Dispur, has a key position for visitors to the northeastern states. It is connected to its sister city, North Guwahati, on the banks of the Brahamaputra, via a bridge and ferries. The area around the station makes up the heart of the city. At Guwahati's eastern end is **Navagraha Temple**, the seat of the nine planetary gods

VISITING GUWAHATI

INFORMATION

Directorate of Tourism
Station Road, tel. 03 61 – 254 71 02
www.assamtourism.org

RIVER CRUISES

River cruises on the Brahamaputra
river lasting several days are organized
by the »Assam Bengal Navigation
Company« (tel. 03 61 ? 260 22 23,
www.assambengalnavigation.com).

WHERE TO STAY / WHERE TO EAT

▶ **Luxury / Mid-range**
Hotel Brahmaputra Ashok
MG Rd

Tel. 03 61 – 254 10 64
Considered the best hotel in town,
with every possible comfort and in a
central location.

Diphlu River Lodge
Kaziranga National Park
Tel. 03 61 – 260 22 23
www.diphluriverlodge.com
Excellent location right on the river.
Very nicely furnished bungalows
made with a lot of bamboo.

and an old centre of astrology and astronomy. The central shrine
contains a lingam, which is surrounded by nine more, a constellation
intended to represent the planetary gods. On an island in the middle
of the Brahmaputra a further **temple** was built that is consecrated to
Shiva. It can be reached by boat from Umananda ghat. **Kamakhya
Temple**, which is located around 8km/5mi to the west on a hill outside the city, is worth visiting. It is considered one of the most important Kali temples in India. According to legend, this is where the
yoni, the genitals of the goddess Kali, fell to earth after her dead body
had been dismembered (see also p.390). The temple tower, which is
shaped like a beehive, is a typical feature of sacred buildings in
Assam.

★★
**Kaziranga
National Park**

Assam's largest protected area (217km/135mi east of Guwahati) is famous largely because of its **Indian rhinoceros** population. As early as
1926, the hunting of this threatened animal was prohibited. Today,
in spite of the fact that poachers ruthlessly hunt down these rare
mammals, the population has risen to more than 1000. Its horn,
when ground to a powder, is said to have an aphrodisiac effect and
fetches extremely high prices on the black market. The reserve on
the southern banks of the Brahmaputra contains an area of 430 sq
km/166 sq mi. Since it was established with its current borders in
1974 the river, which regularly spills over its banks, has reclaimed
around a fifth of the original area. The park is dominated by high
elephant grass, shallow lakes and marshes, but it also contains forested areas. Unlike many other reserves visibility is not obscured by

The Indian rhinoceros is hunted down for its horn

dense jungle here and so watching wildlife can become a particularly fascinating experience. The **safari** through the extensive open grass landscape can be enjoyed on the back of an elephant or in a Jeep. The chances of seeing one of the famous single-horned rhinoceroses close up is not at all unlikely. They have become used to the presence of humans and are not fazed by them. In addition to rhinoceroses the park is also home to elephant herds, various deer species and wild boar. It is less common to spot leopards or leopard cats. The extensive marshy areas provide a habitat for various waterfowl, and herons, bar-headed geese, storks and osprey also inhabit the park. Visitors can choose from accommodation of varying price categories. The reserve closes its gates from mid-April–mid-October.

On the border to Bhutan, crossed by the rivers Mana, Beki and Hakua, is a 2837 sq km/1095 sq mi protected area (176km/109mi west of Guwahati) that is part of »Project Tiger«. It is, however, unusual to actually see this rare inhabitant. On the other hand, with a bit of luck, visitors can see two very rare monkey species here, **Gee's golden langurs** and **capped langurs**. Surilis, other monkeys, elephants, water buffalo, gaur, hog deer and chitals, as well as a few rhinoceroses, populate the reserve's grassland and forests. Bird lovers in particular will have a lot to look at: ornithologists are less attracted by rhinos than by **great hornbills**. Herons, eagles, bulbuls (a type of songbird) and pelicans also live here. The park can be explored on the backs of elephants or by boat. The best time to visit is from November to April. The park is closed during the monsoon from July to September.

Manas Tiger Reserve

Remaining Northeastern States

Area of tension The other northeastern states have **not yet been affected as much by tourism** because some of the areas have been designated military no-go zones, such as for example the north of Arunachal Pradesh. In 1962 this region saw confrontations with China, and conflicts keep flaring up. Separatist movements, ethnic and cultural reasons (a large part of the area is tribal land) and communal conflicts between the various population groups have meant that foreigners only rarely gain access and only with a special permit.

Meghalaya The small state of Meghalaya was created in 1972 from the southwestern part of Assam. The British called this region »**the Scotland of the East**« because of its hills, and the frequently foggy, wet weather probably contributed to this nickname too. A large part of the rain clouds that form over the Bay of Bengal empty themselves here during the monsoon. This makes Meghalaya one of the wettest places on Earth, with lavish forests and countless waterfalls.

Shillong (100km/60mi south of Guwahati), the capital of the small state, is also its best-known tourist attraction. Used as the seat of government by the British in Assam, the hill station was founded in 1874 in the place where a larger settlement of Khasi, the state's aboriginal population, had existed. In the centre is a large garden complex as well as Ward Lake. Some of the older hotels built in the colonial style can also be found there. The State Museum provides interesting insights into the cultural traditions of the local tribes. The Meghalaya Museum of Entomology allows visitors to look at butterflies and moths in all shapes, sizes and colours from close up. Just 1km/1100yd outside of town is Lady Hydari Park (with a zoo), which was laid out using the style of Japanese gardens as a model.

A trip to **Cherrapunjee** (56km/35mi south of Shillong) makes for a nice excursion. Its local bazaar is famous for its honey and traditional tribal jewellery. The Meghalaya Tourist Office in Shillong (Police Bazar) organizes day trips to Cherrapunjee.

> **? DID YOU KNOW ...?**
>
> ■ ... that Cherrapunjee has the highest levels of precipitation in the world? This is because the mountain slopes here receive huge amounts of water every year during the monsoon.

Arunachal Pradesh India's most northeastern state is characterized by untouched landscape, a lavish flora and fauna and the different tribal peoples who still live here largely undisturbed. Only rarely have strangers set foot in this wild and impassable terrain, which is bordered in the west by Bhutan, in the north by Tibet and China and in the east by Myanmar. There are only a few roads in Arunachal Pradesh that are fit for traffic. Most of them have been built for the army to protect India's northern border against its neighbour China. The capital, **Itanagar**, 400km/250mi northeast of Guwahati, is relatively new.

On the border to Myanmar is the 1800 sq km/695 sq mi **Namdapha National Park**, which is both large and difficult to access. The impenetrable forests are home to tigers, leopards, clouded leopards and many prosimians, including the rare hoolock gibbon. Hornbills and red pandas are also amongst its inhabitants. The park authority can provide basic accommodation. The best time to visit is October–March.

As the name Nagaland implies, this mountainous land is home to Nagas, a population group originally from Tibet. It in turn consists of several different tribes. Despite outside interference the Nagas have largely held on to their traditional customs and beliefs. The small state borders on Arunachal Pradesh in the north, on Myanmar in the east, on Assam in the west and on Manipur in the south. Its capital is **Kohima**. This is where Indian troops halted the Japanese advance into the subcontinent in 1944, and the military presence is still unmistakable today. Separatist tendencies have been kept in check somewhat but the region is still one of the Indian government's »problem areas«.
Nagaland

Nagaland is increasingly opening up to tourism. One of its interesting projects is Touphema Tourist Village 40km/25mi north of Kohima. Here, visitors can find out more about the traditional lives of the inhabitants (www.nagenvis.nic.in).

The area in the south of Nagaland, which borders on Myanmar in the east, became an independent state in 1972. Beforehand it had only been a union territory. Fans of classical Indian dance will know this region as the home of the famous **Manipur dances**. In this mountainous state, now only patchily forested, communal confrontations and a separatist movement provide plenty of ammunition for conflict. The capital of Manipur is **Imphal**, 470km/292mi southeast of Guwahati.
Manipur

Mizoram, the southernmost of the northeastern states, was only formed in 1987. Its capital is **Aizawl**. This region, too, is often shaken by political unrest. The inhabitants of the mountainous state, covered in bamboo and mixed forest, are known as Mizos (highlanders). They originally came from Myanmar to the south. Those who are unfamiliar with the region will find the many white churches here unusual. The majority of the Mizos are Christians, which can be attributed to the intensive activities of Christian missionaries in the area.
Mizoram

Valleys and mountainous forest regions characterize the state of Tripura. The Manikyas, the former rulers of this area, traced their ancestry back to the Rajputs. Uday Manikya (1585–96) founded the city of Udaipur. To this day it contains remains of that period. The San-
Tripura

dari temple 5km/3mi from the centre is famous, being one of the most important centres of Shakti worship in India. The capital, **Agartala** (50km/30mi north of Udaipur), is, on the other hand, a modern business and administration centre.

Patna

1 7

Capital of Bihar
Population: 1.7 million

Altitude: 53m/174ft
Distance: 598 km/372mi northwest of Kolkata

The city of Patna on the southern banks of the Ganges is an ideal starting point for discovering Buddhist temples in Bihar.

The capital of the state is now a hectic city and has very good transport connections to all Indian cities. The large square, Gandhi Maidan, divides Patna, which stretches out along the Ganges, into an eastern and a western part. During the monsoon season it can happen that parts of the city are flooded. Patna serves as a starting point for visits to Nalanda and Rajgir and it is also a good place to make a stop on the way to Kathmandu (Nepal).

Stupa in the ruins of Nalanda

The area where the Son and Punpun rivers flow into the Ganges has always been important. The region grew further in significance as a result of Chandragupta, the first ruler of the Maurya dynasty, who had his legendary capital **Pataliputra** built here in 31 BC. Megasthenes, the successor of Alexander the Great in India, was deeply impressed by the efficiency of the administration of the Chandragupta Empire and by the wealth of Pataliputra. Today, however, there is not much left of its former magnificence. The most famous ruler of ancient India, **Ashoka** (268–232 BC), succeeded his father on the throne in Pataliputra. He is said to have consolidated his power through ruthless military cam-

▶ VISITING PATNA

INFORMATION

Tourist Office
At the airport, at the station and in Fraser Rd.
Tel. 06 12 – 222 52 95

WHERE TO STAY / WHERE TO EAT

▶ **Luxury**
Maurya Patna
Fraser Rd.
South Gandhi Maidan

Tel. 06 12 – 220 30 40
First hotel in the city serving good cuisine and with all the amenities.

▶ **Mid-range**
Pataliputra Ashok
Beer Chand Patel Path
Tel. 06 12 – 222 62 70
Good middle price range hotel with a swimming pool and a restaurant serving international cuisine.

paigns and murders until he converted to Buddhism, whereupon he put an end to the horror. After Ashoka's death the ancient Indian Maurya Empire collapsed. Pataliputra experienced a first renaissance under someone who shared his name with the first Maurya ruler, Chandragupta (320–335) from the Gupta dynasty. His successors Samdragupta (335–380) and Chandragupta II Vikramaditya (380–414) succeeded in creating another empire. Art, handicrafts and poetry also flourished. Kuaragupta, the son of Chandragupta II, endowed the large university **Nalanda**, which became the **intellectual centre of Buddhism** for a number of centuries. More than 1000 years later the city flourished once more under the Afghan ruler Sher Shah Suri (1540–45), who also had Sher Shah Mosque built.

What to See in Patna

The city centre west of Gandhi Maidan is home to Patna's most distinctive building. This singular 29m/95ft structure was built by the British in 1786 as a granary, following a devastating famine in 1770. Two staircases lead up the tower, from where visitors can enjoy a nice view of the city.

Golghar

The Patna Museum is located on Buddha Marg south of Golghar. During the 1930s the museum moved into this building, which contains both European and Indian stylistic elements. The collection is among the best in India; however, in places its presentation leaves a lot to be desired. Its stone and terra cotta figures from the Maurya period and Buddhist bronze sculptures are particularly interesting.

★
Patna Museum
⊙
Opening hours: daily except Mon and holidays 10.30am–4.30pm

With life-sized figures, the Martyrs' Memorial commemorates the seven young men who lost their lives in the battle for independence in 1942.

Martyrs' Memorial

✶
Har Mandir

The Sikh temple (Gurudhwara) built by Maharaja Ranhit Singh is dedicated to the tenth guru Govind Singh, who was born in Patna in 1660. Har Mandir is considered **one of the holiest centres of Sikhism** and can be found in the eastern part of Patna around 6km/4mi from Gandhi Maidan.

Sher Shah Masjid

Built by Sher Shah Suri, this mosque is considered one of the most important examples of Islamic-Afghan architecture in India.

Padri-ki-Haveli

North of Sher Shah Mosque is the Roman Catholic church (1775) with a cemetery, which is known as Padri-ki-Haveli.

Kuda Bakhsh Oriental Library

The library, which was established at the start of the 20th century, possesses a rare collection of Arabic and Persian manuscripts and miniature paintings. Kuda Bakhsh Oriental Library also owns the only books that were saved during the pillage of the library of Córdoba in Spain.

Around Patna

Ruins of Pataliputra
🕐

Some **remains of the legendary capital** Pataliputra can be seen near the excavation site in the vicinity of the village of Kumrahar 7km/4mi southeast of the city centre (open: 9am–5pm).

✶
Nalanda

Nalanda (55km/34mi southwest of Patna) has been an **intellectual centre of Buddhist and Jain thought** since the fifth century BC and a university city known far beyond India's borders.

The Chinese traveller Hiuen Tsang spent twelve years here during the seventh century in order to study Buddhism. He left exact descriptions of Nalanda behind. According to his account thousands of students from India, China and Southeast Asia came here to study subjects such as logic, metaphysics, medicine, prose and rhetoric. The large excavation site illustrates the impressive extent of the former institutions. In addition to the great stupa, visitors will also be able to see the foundation walls of monasteries that provided accommodation for around 10,000 students and 2000 teachers in the sixth century. All of the university buildings were completely burned to the ground by Islamic conquerors during the twelfth century. This led to the loss of the unique library, said to have contained nine million works. In the long term this was a heavy blow to the spread of Buddhism in India.

Rajgir

Around 12km/7mi south of Nalanda, situated in an idyllic location between green mountains, lies the former capital of the Megadha Empire (sixth century BC), Rajgir. **Both Buddha and Mahavira taught here**. Many places recall the founder of the religion: the bamboo wood Venuvana, where Buddha lived with his followers, the pond in which he bathed, the garden Jivakamarvana and Mount

Grighakuta, where he gave sermons, as well as the Sattapani Caves, in which the first Buddhist council took place after his death. Today Rajgir is popular amongst Indian tourists as a **spa town** because of its hot springs. The bath, which can be overlooked from the street, looks more like a temple than a swimming pool.

The Japanese built the Vishwa Shanti Stupa on Mount Ratangiri near Rajgir. All four sides of the **World Peace Pagoda** contain gilded depictions of Buddha. The stupa can be reached via a shaky chairlift or on foot (approx. 30 minutes).

From the World Peace Temple it is also possible to see some Jain shrines on the surrounding hills

✴ Puri

I 10

State: Orissa
Population: 300,000

Altitude: Sea level
Distance: 520km/323mi southwest of Kolkata

Puri offers a stark contrast to Konark, where visitors can enjoy the tranquillity and contemplation of the place despite the many tourists. Puri is one of the largest centres of pilgrimage in India and attracts masses of believers.

Puri is located right on the coast along the Bay of Bengal and attracts not just pilgrims but also many tourists both from within and outside India as a result of its fine sandy beaches. The vast majority of Puri's visitors have only one goal in mind, though: visiting the famous Jagannath Temple and worshipping the resident deities Jagannath (ruler of the universe), his sister Subhadra and his brother Balarama.

The god behind the **Jagannath cult** is none other than Krishna, to whom, as Jagannath in the form of an archaic-looking wooden figure, offerings are made. There are varying theories on the origin of this cult. It is thought that an old local deity was absorbed into the Hindu pantheon.

What to See in Puri

During a walk across the large temple forecourt, along the main road and down its side streets, visitors will get a good impression of the

Centre of pilgrimage

▶ VISITING PURI · KONARK

INFORMATION

Tourist Office
Station Rd.
Tel. 067 52 – 22 26 64
www.orissatourism.gov.in

GETTING THERE

There are various rail connections servicing Puri. Konark is only 35km/ 22mi away and can be visited on a day trip.

EVENTS

Every year in June / July hordes of pilgrims gather in Puri for Rath Yatra, the chariot festival. The gods' idols are brought from the temple to a small house on huge chariots or carts (the original "juggernauts") of up to 14m/ 46ft in height, where they are exhibited for a week, after which they are brought back to their original location in a procession.
The Konark Festival (beginning of December) is also well-known; it features lovely music and traditional dancing.

WHERE TO STAY / WHERE TO EAT

▶ **Luxury**
Toshali Sands
Village Resort
Puri, Marine Drive
Tel. 067 52 – 25 05 71
Nice holiday complex by the sea with bungalows and cottages.

▶ **Mid-range / Budget**
BNR
Chakratirtha Road
Puri
Tel. 067 52 – 22 20 63
34 rooms in an old colonial villa with a garden, a restaurant and the »Raj atmosphere«. Quiet location near the beach.

▶ **Budget**
Panthanivas OTCD
Near CT Road, Puri
Tel. 067 52 – 22 25 62
Hotel run by Orissa Tourism: large, clean rooms, restaurant and garden.

hustle and bustle of this busy place of pilgrimage. A little experience in how to deal with beggars is needed, as are plenty of paisa coins!

Jagannath Temple

The large Jagannath Temple is **not accessible to non-Hindus**. Even Indira Gandhi was refused entry because she was married to a Parsi. It is possible to look over the temple walls from the platform of the library opposite. The temple was built towards the end of the twelfth century and features the **typical characteristics of the Orissa style**. In front of the 58m/190ft conical tower, the prayer hall, dancing hall and, quite a way in front of that, the hall of offerings are all arranged on the same longitudinal axis. However, this temple cannot compete with its predecessors in Bhubaneshwar or Konark. The comparatively sparsely decorated exterior façades illustrate the fact that the golden age of local architecture was over. The temple is surrounded by two walls. In order to feed the hordes of pilgrims, the temple complex houses **one of the largest kitchens in the world**. There are also several smaller shrines. In front of the main temple gate in the east visitors can see the pillar from Konark, whose tip is made up of the bird Garuda, Vishnu's »vehicle«.

The **old palm-leaf manuscripts** kept here can be admired in the library.

Library

At the other end of the main road is the Gandicha Mandir summer house, to which the depictions of the gods are brought during the **Ratha Yatra festival**. Every one of the chariots has sixteen wheels and is pulled by around 1000 people. In earlier times this event often involved deaths because believers threw themselves in front of the chariots' wheels and allowed themselves to be run over.

Gandicha Mandir

Those who have had enough of the masses of people can find some respite at the nearby sandy beaches, which extend for many miles. However, care should be taken when bathing, since there are some dangerous underwater currents here. There are many hotels of varying price categories near Puri beach.

Beach

View of the entrance area of Jagannath Temple

In Puri's side-streets visitors can discover houses with traditionally painted façades

✳ ✳ Surya Temple in Konark

Best-known temple in Orissa (fig. p.366)

Orissa's greatest treasure is undoubtedly the Sun Temple in Konark (36km/22mi northeast of Puri), a small village 3km/2mi from the Bay of Bengal. For some years now the temple has been on the list of **UNESCO World Heritage Sites**. An open-air theatre has been built near the complex for the annual **Konark Dance Festival**.

This temple is dedicated neither to Shiva nor to Vishnu; it is consecrated to the sun itself, the great **sun god Surya**. Even though the building is somewhat dilapidated, nobody who looks at it can escape the immense attraction emanating from its archetypal shapes, a veritable **mythology in stone**. In earlier times people imagined that the sun travelled across the sky on a large chariot drawn by seven horses, and it is this idea that underlies the construction of the Sun Temple in Konark. The place name is also connected to the sun: Kona (corner) and Arka (sun). The **sun chariot**, consisting of a sanctum and vestibule, has twelve wheels on either side and is drawn by seven horses. The numeric symbolism is a further pointer to the sun as the keeper of time: the wheels contain 16 spokes, which measure the sections of the day in 90-minute intervals and can be used as sun dials.

Temple complex

The temple complex, which in places shows strong signs of weathering by the elements, was built in the mid-13th century under King Narasimha Deva. The temple is also known as the »Black Pagoda«

and is considered to be the **pinnacle of temple architecture in Orissa**. The collapsed sanctum adjoins the square jagamohan mandapa, whose 38m/125ft roof rises in three steps in a pyramid shape above the building. A few metres to the east stands the isolated building of the dancing hall (nata mandapa). Between these two buildings there was once a pillar topped by a figure of Arun, a charioteer of the sun, but it was removed and given a new home in front of Jagannath temple in Puri. The main temple is surrounded by a wall, which contains a secondary shrine.

One of the twelve wheels of the solar chariot

The temple deserves its reputation as an unsurpassed masterpiece of local architecture primarily because of the **excellently fashioned sculptures** that are in particularly good condition at the base of the chariot. Here visitors can see animals and fabled creatures, lovers, nymphs and gods, entwined by finely worked ornaments. On the higher levels there are impressively designed couples in lovemaking; the figures are reminiscent of those on the temples of Khajuraho. There are also depictions of musicians and of animals. The dancing girls and musicians at the base of the dancing hall are particularly good. Visitors should take their time to absorb everything from the diversity of the details to the relaxed expressions on the faces of the lovers.

Sculptures

Outside the surrounding walls is a small museum that displays additional finds from the temple (open: daily except Fri 10am–5pm).

Museum
⏱

Broader surroundings of Puri

Chilka Lake (approx. 50km/30mi southwest of Puri), which stretches along the coastline and covers an area of 1100 sq km/425 sq mi, is a paradise for bird lovers. This freshwater lake, dotted with small islands, is the destination of many migratory birds in the winter and they come here in huge flocks.

Chilka Lake

Gopalpur-on-Sea (approx. 130km/80mi southwest of Puri), one of Orissa's oldest harbours, is an up-and-coming seaside resort.

Gopalpur-on-Sea

✳ **Sikkim** (State)

Area: 7069 sq km/2740 sq mi
Capital: Gangtok

Population: 540,000

The small Himalayan state of Sikkim in the northeast of the sub-continent borders on Tibet in the north, on Nepal in the west, on Bhutan in the east and on West Bengal in the south.

Immense differences in altitude and therefore also great differences in vegetation characterize this state, which is only 7000 sq km/2700 sq mi in area. It extends from the paddy fields of the Teesta valley, which lies only a few hundred metres above sea level, to orchards at moderate elevations and the bare, snow-covered peaks of the Kanchenjunga range in the far north.

History

Presumably tribes from the east, who are known as Lepchas but who called themselves Rongpas (gorge inhabitants), came to the area that is now Sikkim in the 13th century. In the 15th century they were followed by Tibetans, who brought Buddhism with them. From 1641 a Buddhist king ruled this impassable state in the southern Himalaya. At the time it was larger than it is today but it suffered under the very much larger neighbouring states. In several bellicose confrontations Sikkim was the weaker party and had to cede territory to Nepal and Bhutan. Sikkim became a British protectorate in 1861 under a treaty designed to give it greater security. The British were also responsible for the mass immigration of Nepalis, whom they employed on their newly established tea plantations. This would later give rise to social conflict in other states in northeastern India too. Sikkim obtained its independence in 1918, long before British India. Another protection treaty was signed in 1950, however: this time with the three-year-old Indian Union. Over the decades India increased its influence on the small state in the northeast, which was so often shaken by unrest. Increased tensions with China made the region more interesting to the military. In 1975 Sikkim became the **22nd state of the Indian Union** in controversial circumstances.

Current situation

Nepalis make up 75% of the population. The indigenous people, the Lepchas, make up almost 20%; the rest of the population consists of Bhotias and other tribes. Sikkim is famous amongst travellers thanks to its many Buddhist monasteries as well as its many features of natural beauty. Green river valleys, rhododendron forests, a lavish flora, and, first and foremost, the countless species of orchid and remote trekking routes make Sikkim a **paradise for outdoor enthusiasts**. However, here too the consequences of deforestation and overexploitation of resources cannot be overlooked. These issues have become huge problems in the Himalayan states and are also partly responsible the regular disastrous floods of the coastline further south. The best time to visit is March–May because of the rhododendron blossom or in September–October.

Gangtok

In good weather the five snow-covered peaks of the Kanchenjunga range make up the northern backdrop of the mountain town of Gangtok (1547m/5075ft, 724km/450mi north of Kolkata) in the southeast of Sikkim. However, fog often rises up from the valleys,

► VISITING SIKKIM

INFORMATION
Tourist Office
MG Marg
Gangtok
Tel. 035 92 – 22 16 34

GETTING THERE
The closest airport is Bagdogra near Siliguri; from there it is possible to take a helicopter to Gangtok. Buses and Jeeps depart from Siliguri, Darjeeling and Kalimpong.

Entry permit
A permit is needed to travel to Sikkim. It can be applied for together with the visitor's visa or from Airport Immigration in Mumbai, Delhi, Kolkata and Chennai as well as from the Foreigners Regional Registration Offices.

WHERE TO STAY / WHERE TO EAT
► Luxury / Expensive
Nor-Khill
Palijor Stadium Road
Gangtok
Tel. 035 92 – 20 56 37
www.elginhotels.com
Former guesthouse of the king with a stylish ambience and a good restaurant.

Shambhala Mountain Resort
Rumtek
Tel. 035 92 – 25 22 40
Main building and cottages in a nice big garden, vegetarian restaurant.

► Mid-range / Moderate
Tashi Delek
MG Marg, New Market
Gangtok
Tel. 035 92 – 20 29 91
www.hoteltashidelek.com
Centrally located with a sun terrace and a fabulous view, local specialities served in the restaurant.

Netuk House
Tibet Road, Gangtok
Tel. 035 92 – 22 67 78
Small family-run hotel with very good cuisine and attractive furnishings.

shrouding the town in a white veil and plunging it into a diffuse light.

Gangtok was built on a mountain ridge and is now a small modern town as well as **Sikkim's capital**. Particularly since its incorporation into India it has experienced a building boom and the urban area has been covered with concrete buildings, which do not necessarily conform to the romantic ideas of an idyllic Himalayan town that exist in the heads of many a traveller. The town centre is in the vicinity of Mahatma Gandhi Road. This is also where the Tourist Information Centre can be found.

The former ruler's palace cannot be visited; however, occasionally it is possible to obtain a permit to see the royal chapel, Tsuklakhang, which has attractive wall paintings and a collection of Buddhist cult objects.

Ruler's palace

Institute of Tibetology ✱ ⏱ Those interested in Buddhism should not miss out on visiting the Institute of Tibetology. It has exquisite thangkas, rare manuscripts and religious cult objects of all kinds on display (open: Mon–Sat 10am–4pm, only during the season).

Orchid Sanctuary In the park that belongs to it, the Orchid Sanctuary, almost 450 different orchid species (blossom: April–May) wait to be admired.

Do Drul Chorten Not far away the white stupa of the Do Drul Chorten rises up to the sky. This stupa was only built during the 20th century by the Nyingmapa Order and is surrounded by 108 prayer wheels. Two large statues recall the sect's patron saint, Padmasambhava, who proclaimed Buddhism in Tibet.

Enchey monastery The Nyingmapa Order also owns the Enchey monastery in the northeast of town. The small, two-storey building with its richly decorated vestibule dates back to the last century. Every year at the end of January the monastery becomes the site of colourful masked dances on the occasion of the Chaam ceremonies.

Cottage Industries Institute The sales location of the Cottage Industries Institute provides an insight into Sikkim's traditional handicrafts.

Around Gangtok

Tashi Viewpoint Visitors will have a magnificent view of the Kanchenjunga range from Tashi Viewpoint, 8km/5mi from Gangtok.

Rumtek monastery The two famous monasteries Rumtek and Phodong can be reached in a daytrip from Gangtok. Rumtek (24km/15mi southwest of Gangtok), the monastery of the Kagyupa Order (also known as the »black hut«) was founded as early as 1740. The head of the Buddhist Kagyupa sect found refuge in Sikkim during the Chinese invasion of Tibet. When he was granted land for the construction of a monastery, a replica of the Tibetan Tsrupuhu monastery was built here in the 1960s. Red columns support the roof of the prayer hall, which is decorated with magnificent thangkas and wall paintings. Right up to his death in 1982 Karmapa Rinpoche, the 16th incarnation of Karmapa, who in turn embodies Bodhisattva Avalokiteshvara, worked here.

The **Institute of Buddhist Studies** behind the monastery also contains good wall paintings and a collection of valuable cult objects. This is also where the Tibetan New Year (January / February) is celebrated with dancing and colourful costumes. On the occasion of the summer festival (May / June) episodes from the life of Padmasambhava, who brought Buddhism from India to Tibet in the eighth century, are told. The monks in Sikkim worship him as Guru Rinpoche. Rumtek can be reached by bus or taxi. The tourist office also runs sightseeing tours.

Continue past Tashi Viewpoint to get to Phodong monastery (38km/ 24mi north of Gangtok), one of the country's most important monastic complexes, which also belongs to the Kagyupa Order. The monastery is worth visiting for its **wonderful views** alone, but the drive past the big prayer wheels and Tashi Viewpoint are also a special experience. It traces its origin back to the 16th century and over time new buildings were added. Some way away and higher up is the old Labrang monastery, which was only recently restored. Phodong can be reached by bus or by taxi.

Phodong monastery

West Sikkim

West Sikkim is home to the famous monastic complexes of Pemayangtse and Tashiding. Trekking tours to Dzongri are organized from the hamlet of Yuksom. Anyone wanting to visit this part of the country requires a special permit. It is recommended that visitors take part in one of the officially organized tours.

Prayer flags blowing in the wind and an open view from Tashi Viewpoint

Pemyangtse monastery

High up on a mountain ridge above the Rangit river is the impressive Pemyangtse monastery (120km/75mi west of Gangtok). It was founded in the 17th century by Lama Lhatsun Chempo and then extended under his successor in 1705. Pemyangtse monastery is considered the most important monastery of the Nyingmapa Order and is one of Sikkim's oldest Buddhist centres. Only a few monks live in this very remote, quiet place. Further buildings, decorated with fine wood carvings, are grouped around the modest main building. Amongst the monastery's treasures are wonderful thangkas and wall paintings. The Chaam dances that take place every Tibetan New Year attract spectators from all over the country. There is a bus connection between Gangtok and Ghezing, from where there is another bus connection to Pelling 9km/6mi further north. Here and right by the monastery 1.5km/1mi away visitors will find accommodation.

Tashiding monastery

Even more remote in the monastery of Tashiding. The small town can be reached by bus from Yuksom and can provide basic accommodation. The monastery towers around 2km/1mi above Tashiding. It was built in 1717 after a rainbow had been sighted, which connected the site with Kanchenjunga.

Prayer wheels at Rumtek monastery

The sleepy town of Yuksom (40km/25mi north of Pemyangtse) has a special place in Sikkim's history. It was once the location of the state's first capital and it was from here that Buddhism was spread throughout Sikkim. Not much is left to remind visitors of those important days. The small hamlet is now mainly of interest as a base for trekking tours to Dzongri in the shadow of the Kanchenjunga range. Authorized agencies offer various routes in the area. Information is available in Gangtok (►Practicalities, Sport and Outdoors).

Trekking tours departing from Yuksom

CENTRAL INDIA

STATES
Chhattisgarh: capital Raipur
Goa: capital Panaji
Madhya Pradesh: capital Bhopal
Maharashtra: capital Mumbai

The states of Maharashtra and Madhya Pradesh have been attracting increasing numbers of travellers in recent years. Nevertheless, it is the small state of Goa that is still considered one of India's greatest tourist magnets. In contrast to the highly modernized coastal region, the heart of India still has areas serving many tribes as places of refuge, which is why they have not been developed for tourism. The new state of Chhattisgarh is one example of this.

Environment

Maharashtra's west coast is characterized by a coastal zone 80km–100km (50m–60mi) in width. Inland from this coastal region lie the Western Ghats, a precipitous mountain range that reaches elevations of up to 1400m/4600ft and catches almost the entire southwest monsoon. In the rain shadow of this range is the open, largely flat Deccan plateau. The arid, volcanic, rocky terrain is mostly used for arable farming and animal husbandry. Chhattisgarh is to the east of this region, while Madhya Pradesh to the west. This area of the heart of India is traversed diagonally from the southwest to the northeast by the 800km/500mi Vindya mountain range. Forests cover this sandstone range, which reaches elevations of up to 600m/2000ft and is intersected by the powerful Narmada river. The region is very wet, receiving between 1000mm/40in–2000mm/80in of rainfall.

Economy

Agriculture forms the backbone of the region's economy; in the coastal area of Maharashtra and Goa fishing also plays an important role. Forestry is a significant factor in Madhya Pradesh. Maharashtra is **heavily industrialized**, being responsible for almost a quarter of India's industrial production. Mumbai is India's economic metropolis, giving it a paramount position. In addition to important raw materials such as coal, iron, manganese, bauxite, silicon, sand and kyanite, the state also possesses crude oil and natural gas. Several sectors

← *Resting in front of Raj Mahal Hotel in Mumbai*

of industry have located here. In addition to the traditional textile industry, the chemical, pharmaceutical and electronics industries are now also highly developed. The most important agricultural products are rice, millet, wheat, lentils, peanuts, cotton, sugarcane, tobacco, sunflowers and vegetables. Maharashtra has an annual sugar production of 3360 tons, making it the biggest producer of sugar in India. Madhya Pradesh is still primarily an agricultural region, its most important crops being rice, millet, sugarcane, wheat, cotton, oilseeds and soy beans. Its rich forests also yield teak, sal wood and bamboo. Natural resources include diamonds, gold, iron, manganese, bauxite, copper, phosphorus and asbestos. So far mining these resources has been small-scale, since the area lacks infrastructure and energy. Important industries are electronics, telecommunications, aluminium, fertilizers, construction materials and paper. Goa's economy is based on agriculture (fruit, vegetables, coconuts) in large areas, as well as on fishing on the coast. Particularly well-known products include cashew nuts and alcohol. However, the main source of income is tourism.

History

Historically, the region around Maharashtra and Madhya Pradesh was under the influence of the Maurya, Sunga and Gupta dynasties. Later the region was controlled by Chalukyas and Rashtrakutas. Today the cave temples of Ajanta and Ellora are evidence of the region's changeful history. During the previous millennium regional kingdoms developed here, of which the best-known are the Kachawaha Rajputs and the Chandellas. The region subsequently came under Islamic rule. Under the military strategist Shivaji (1627–80) the **Maratha Empire** formed around what is now the town of Pune, which was able to free itself from the Mughal rulers and subsequently conquered large parts of northern India. Its expansionist attitude was thwarted in the decisive battle of Panipat in 1761. During the reigns of the Scindias and Gaekwads, successor dynasties of Shivaji, the Hindu kingdoms flourished until they were defeated by the British in 1818. After India's independence Madhya Pradesh was formed in 1956 and Maharashtra in 1960. The former southeast part of Madhya Pradesh was made into the new state of Chhattisgarh in 2000.

Goa has experienced an eventful history involving Satavahanas, Rashtrakutas, Chalukyas and the Kadamba dynasty. In the 14th century the region fell into the hands of Vijayanagar for a good 100 years (1335–1469). Subsequently, during the Bahmani dynasty, it was an important trade connection to Arab countries. Pilgrims set off to Mecca from here and there was much trading of spices, horses and weapons. The **Portuguese conquered Goa in 1510** and made it the most important Portuguese enclave in Asia. Only after a 450-year rule were they driven out of Goa by the Indian army in 1961. In 1987 Goa was given state status. Its capital is Panaji and it is the smallest of India's 28 states.

The commercial and cultural centre, Mumbai, is India's most modern city and is an ideal starting point for an Indian holiday. Mumbai is home to numerous galleries and museums as well as many buildings from the colonial period, during which it became India's most important port when the Suez Canal was built (1856–69). The small Elephanta Island off the coast of Mumbai is famous for its cave temples. Mumbai is also a good starting place for a trip to the cave temples of Ajanta with their outstanding paintings, and to those of Ellora, which have lovely relief sculptures. 500km/310mi south of Mumbai is Goa, whose never-ending palm beaches, green landscapes and relics of the Portuguese colonial era make it one of India's most-visited destinations. Madhya Pradesh, India's large heartland, has not yet woken up to the potential of tourism, even though it possesses some excellent old cultural monuments. The only exceptions are the magnificent temples of Khajuraho with their famous erotic sculptures. The huge fort of Gwalior and the palaces of Mandu and Orcha are amongst medieval India's impressive achievements. Sanchi, with its stupas, is a special attraction. It is one of the most important Buddhist sites. Nature lovers should definitely plan to visit Kanha National Park. The new state of Chhattisgarh consists mainly of tribal areas belonging to the Adivasi, India's aboriginal population.

Attractions

Goa welcomes its tourists

Aurangabad

D 10

State: Maharashtra
Population: 1.02 million

Altitude: 513m/1683ft
Distance: 401km/249mi northeast of Mumbai

Aurangabad, the capital of the district of the same name, is located on the hilly plateau in central Maharashtra, the Sahyadri range or Western Ghats. It has several sights of its own, but mainly serves as a starting point for visits to the famous cave temples and monasteries of Ajanta and Ellora.

History The city was founded in 1610 by Malik Ambar, a minister of the sultan of Ahmadnagar, under the name Khadke. It was later renamed by Mughal ruler Aurangzeb, who lived here for several decades, to reflect his name. Aurangabad and the surrounding area have a large number of more or less well preserved buildings, particularly from its golden age in the 17th century. Remains of the former 7km/4.5mi city wall and its 52 gates can still be seen in various places.

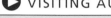 VISITING AURANGABAD, AJANTA, ELLORA

INFORMATION

MTDC Holiday Resort
Station Road
Aurangabad
Tel. 02 40 – 233 12 17

GETTING THERE

Air, rail and bus connections from Mumbai to Aurangabad

SIGHTSEEING

Daily sightseeing tours of Ajanta and Ellora are organized by the Maharashtra Tourism Development Corporation and the Indian Tourism Development Corporation, departing from Aurangabad. The Ellora tour also includes sightseeing in the surrounding area. Those who just want to focus on the caves should hire a taxi and a personal guide (who can be hired from MTDC) and explore them independently.

WHERE TO STAY / WHERE TO EAT

▶ **Luxury**
Taj Residency
Aurangabad; CIDCO
Tel. 02 40 – 238 11 06
One of the best hotels here, on the outskirts of town, with sports facilities.

▶ **Mid-range / Budget**
Hotel Kailas
Near the caves in Ellora
Tel. 024 37 – 24 45 43
Huts in a garden with many birds and views of the caves; bar and restaurant.

▶ **Inexpensive**
MTDC Holiday Resort
Station Road; Aurangabad
Tel. 02 40 – 233 11 98
Spacious, basic rooms, centrally located.

»Little Taj Mahal«

What to See in and around Aurangabad

In the northwest of the city is a water mill from the 17th century with a number of water basins arranged one above the other. The marble shrine of Baba Shah Muzaffer, Aurangzeb's spiritual teacher, can also be found here (open: sunrise–8pm).

Panchakki

Around 5km/3mi from Aurangabad, on the road to Ellora, is the memorial Aurangzeb built to his favourite wife Banu Begum. Based on the Taj Mahal in its appearance and design, it is but a pale imitation of the original in ►Agra. Even though the complex's elements (mausoleum on a plateau, four minarets, long ponds and an entrance gate) are almost identical to those of the Taj Mahal, they do not convey the impression of perfect harmony and size that captivates the beholder. This is mainly due to the disproportionately large minarets and to the use of bad building materials that are clearly feeling the effects of time (open: sunrise–10pm).

Bibi Ka Maqbara

Neglected because of their famous neighbours in Ellora and Ajanta, the nine Buddhist caves of Aurangabad are not really on the tourist map and can only be reached independently (by taxi or motorized rickshaw) . They are located 7km/4mi north of the city on a steep slope in the hills behind the Bibi-ka-Maqbara. The group consisting of the first five caves is around 1.5km/1mi from the second group to the east. They were created **between the second and ninth centuries**; the caves in the east are the more recent ones.

No. 1 is an incomplete vihara, which has a veranda with very nicely decorated pillars and reliefs. A 3m/10ft statue of a seated Buddha

★
Caves of Aurangabad
Opening hours: sunrise–sunset

making a teaching gesture can be found in cave no. 2. At the shrine's entrance are bodhisattvas with nagas and ghandharavas (snakes and heavenly creatures). The entrance of vihara no. 3 is guarded by the river goddesses Ganga and Yamuna. The hall with its twelve lavishly decorated pillars contains a shrine with a sitting Buddha statue surrounded by followers. A very dilapidated Chaitya hall from the second century is in cave no. 4. All that is left of no. 5 is the cella with a Buddha statue seated between bodhisattvas. The first cave of the eastern group, no. 6, also contains a sitting Buddha. No. 7 has a richly ornamented vihara with a depiction of Buddha on the lion's throne in the main shrine and further secondary shrines located on the veranda. No. 8 is incomplete and not worth visiting. Cave no. 9 also possesses a central shrine flanked by statues of women and bodhisattvas. There is a large Padmapani in the entrance hall.

✳
Daulatabad

A further 6km/3.5mi to the northwest lies Daulatabad. The fort was built by the Yadava ruler Bhilam Raja on a free-standing 70m/230ft rock and was known as Deogiri. In the 14th century, Mughal emperor Mohammed-bin-Tughluq renamed it Daulatabad (City of Fortune). This fort has several clever contrivances making it **impregnable to enemies**, and it was from here that he ruled his dominions. However, he only did this for a short while because the fort soon had to be abandoned for lack of water. Apart from the fort itself, the view of the surrounding hills with their table mountains also makes the climb up to the complex worthwhile. Special attention should be given to the Chand Minar, the second-highest victory minaret in India and evidence of the Islamic claim to power at that time.

Khuldabad

On the road to Ellora (26km/16mi northwest of Aurangabad) is the tomb of Emperor Aurangzeb, which was kept very modest, just as he had requested.

✳ ✳ Ellora **D 9**

Carved from the rock

The magnificent cave temples and monasteries of Ellora (30km/19mi northwest of Aurangabad, 100km/60mi southwest of Ajanta) that were carved from the rock are, next to those of Ajanta (p.435), the

Ellora Caves Map

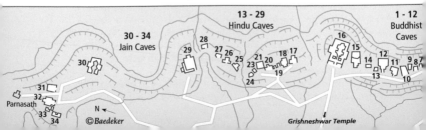

30 – 34
Jain Caves

13 – 29
Hindu Caves

1 – 12
Buddhist Caves

Parnasath

N ←

© Baedeker

Grishneshwar Temple

second highlight among Maharashtra's attractions and rank alongside **India's most important cultural monuments**. In contrast to Ajanta only twelve of these temples are of Buddhist origin (fourth–sixth centuries); the others were created by contemporary Hindus or by Jains several centuries later. They are thus evidence of the religious tolerance of this period, which saw the peaceful coexistence of different faiths as quite natural. Buddhist caves that were later used as Hindu temples remained intact. Likenesses of the Hindu deities stand next to Buddhist sculptures, such as in cave no. 11 for example.

Opening hours:
Wed–Mon
sunrise–sunset

While Ajanta's greatest strengths are its wall paintings, which were executed with the utmost artistic talent and finest psychological sensitivity, Ellora impresses with its **rich collection of sculptures**, which reveals great mastery and captivates those who see it. The caves, which are located at the base of a chain of hills running in a north-south direction, should be viewed in the afternoon because that is when they get the sun. Of particular interest are caves nos. 5, 6, 10, 12 (Buddhist caves), 14, 15, 16, 21 and 29 (Hindu caves), which include the famous **Kailash Monolith** (no. 16) as well as the Jain caves (no. 32).

The oldest caves (nos. 1–12) are of Buddhist origin (fourth century). It is believed that stonemasons who worked in Ajanta received further contracts in Ellora after Ajanta's decline. As is the case with the larger caves, the various Hindu sites dedicated to the god Shiva (nos. 13–29) were also created in the sixth century. They can be subdivided into an older group that does not yet possess any cult objects (nos. 20–24) and a more recent group with a lingam and sanctum (nos. 13–19 and 25–29). They lie around 50m/55yd north of the Buddhist group. Even further to the north are the four Jain caves (nos. 30–34), which were only created between the ninth and eleventh centuries.

Cave temples and monasteries

Visitors usually start their tour with the oldest temples, the Buddhist caves. **No. 5** is the group's largest vihara. Its floor plan is unusual: the long hall that goes far back into the rock is divided into three aisles by two long, stone benches and rows of columns running parallel to them. Twenty cells have been sunk into the wall. At the back is the shrine with a seated Buddha surrounded by helpers. **Cave no. 6** is also a large vihara. The entrance hall is decorated with many sculptures from the Viajrayana pantheon (to the left Tara with retinue and opposite Mahamayuri, goddess of scholarship). It leads into the Buddha shrine, whose doorposts are decorated with the river goddesses Ganga and Yamuna. The only Chaitya, **cave no. 10** was not created until the eighth century. It has an open courtyard and three entrances. The lavish, two-storey façade and the shape of the Chaitya window, which was sunk into the façade as part of a clover-leaf-like motif, a significant deviation from the original architectural style, are

Buddhist caves

Ellora's greatest attraction is Kailash Temple

Cave no. 12 ▶

among the interesting features. Cave no. 12 is a three-storey (tin tal) vihara. Beyond its powerful but plain façade is an entire army of figures belonging to Mahayana Buddhism. It is definitely worth climbing up to the second floor, which has Buddha under the Bodhi tree with Padmapani and Avalokiteshvara, reliefs of the seven earthly Buddhas and the seven Dhyani Buddhas. There are 18 images of Buddha in the entrance hall. Twelve female figures decorate the panel below.

Hindu caves

Cave no. 14 is also known as »Ravana's Cave«. It was given this name because of the impressive painting on the right-hand side of the cave depicting Ravana lifting Mount Kailash, the home of Shiva. Next to this painting are Shiva as Nataraja, Shiva and Parvati playing chess and Durga as Mahishasuramardini. The cave's left side is populated by Vishnu deities. Two of the easier ones to recognize are Lakshmi being splashed with water by two elephants, and Vishnu in his incarnation as a wild boar. **Cave no. 15** was called Dasavatara after the ten (das) incarnations (avataras) of Vishnu that can be seen here amongst many Shiva idols. It is thought that it was originally a Buddhist vihara that was transformed into a Hindu temple. An inscription on the door lintel indicates it was a gift of the Rashtrakuta ruler Dantidurga (AD 725–755).

Kailash Temple ▶

No. 16, the famous Kailash Temple, is **Ellora's architectural and artistic masterpiece**. This monolith, 30 sq m/36 sq yd in area and 60m/197ft tall, which represents the divine mountain Kailash in the

Himalaya, is considered **India's greatest cave temple**. A total of 150,000 to 200,000 tons of basalt were removed from around the rock. The result of this large-scale, long-lasting effort was a complete temple in the south-Indian style with a Vimana tower, halls and entrance halls, a Nandi shrine and two mighty pillars on each side. The area left free between the temple and the rock wall served as an ambulatory. The rock left in front of the courtyard was carved into a gate in the shape of a two-storey gopuram and it is from here that a bridge leads to Nandi shrine. The main temple, which stands on a pedestal, contains an entrance hall as well as a hall divided by 16 columns arranged in groups of four, and the cella with a lingam as cult image. A three-storey Vimana rises up above the sanctum. Further secondary shrines were carved into the rock face. To the left of the main temple, on the upper level, is the later Lankeshvara Temple. The complex's rich sculptural work takes visitors into the never-ending world of Hindu myths and epics.

Of the four Jain caves from the ninth/tenth centuries, no. 32 is worth seeing. It is known as Indra Sabha (Indra's Assembly Hall). The temple is a **miniature version of Kailash Temple**. Tirthankaras and the naked figure of a Gomateshvara were sculpted from a rock.

Half a kilometre (550yd) from Ellora is Grishneshvar Temple, an important place of pilgrimage for Hindus. The temple is one of the twelve places in India where a temple was built around a natural stone lingam (jyotirlingam).

○
Opening hours:
Wed–Mon
6am–6pm

Jain caves

Grishneshvar Temple

✴ ## Ajanta   D 9

In the remote gorge of the Waghora stream (106km/66mi northeast of Aurangabad) are the famous caves of Ajanta carved out over 550m/600yd in a semicircle in the steep rock face . This place became known far beyond India's borders because of its almost **unique combination of architecture, sculpture and painting**, whose expressiveness, dynamics and love of detail fascinate all who lay eyes on it. The complex is not just evidence of the history of the Buddhist religion; it is also an insightful study into life at the royal courts of the time.

UNESCO World Heritage Site
○
Opening hours:
Tue–Sun
9am–5.30pm

The 29 viharas (cave monasteries) and five chaityas (cave temples) were created between the second century BC and the sixth century AD by itinerant Buddhist missionary monks as places of protection and rest during the extreme periods of rain and heat.
The oldest caves are chaitya no. 10 and vihara no. 13. Chaitya no. 9 and viharas 8, 12, 13 and 15 can also be attributed to this early period. They were probably created as a result of gifts by the Satavahana and Kshatrapa dynasties who had converted to Buddhism. After a long period of inactivity, construction began again in the fifth cen-

History

AJANTA

✶✶ It is only thanks to a fortunate coincidence that a British officer rediscovered the Buddhist monastery complex that had already been abandoned two centuries earlier in the thickets of a valley near Ajanta. These cave monasteries and temples, recognized as a UNESCO World Heritage Site since 1983, date back to 200 BCAD 650 and are older than those in Ellora 100km/60mi away. Besides the impressive feat of carving out the rock, the wall paintings and sculptures are unique.

🕐 Open:
daily except Mon 9am–5.30pm

① Cave no. 1
This Vihara from the Mahayana period was the last to be uncovered but it is considered one of the most beautiful. To the sides of the central Buddha sculpture are the bodhisattvas Avaloki-teshvara and Padmapani.

② Cave no. 2
The pillars and capitals are richly adorned and the wonderful wall paintings are also quite eye-catching. They depict scenes from Buddha's life and stories about his birth. Among the well-known images are those of the 1000 Buddhas and the Maya's dream of an elephant with six tusks that announced Buddha's conception.

Wall paintings reveal what daily life was like in ancient India

③ Cave no. 17
This cave contains Ajanta's best-preserved wall paintings. The scene in which Vishvantara tells his wife of his banishment is particularly sensitive as is Prince Simhala's expedition to Sri Lanka.

④ Cave no. 19
The façade is quite striking with its large horseshoe-shaped, richly decorated Chaitya window. To the left of the cave is an attractive stone figure of the Naga king with his wife and servant. Seven cobras frame his head.

⑤ Cave no. 26
The Chaitya contains some attractive sculptures, including the impressive »Parnirvana Buddha«, Buddha entering the highest Nirvana (fig. p.433). Mourning students crowd around on the plinth.

1000 Buddhas: similar but all different in their details

© Baedeker

Likeness of ...admapani

Cave temple with a three-stepped stupa

Naga king with wife and servant

tury with vihara no. 6, then viharas no. 4, 16, 17, 5, 9 and 11. Inscriptions in caves 16 and 17 indicate they were donated by the Vakataka dynasty. The entire wealth of sculptures in Mahayana Buddhism can be seen in the newly built monasteries and temples nos. 1, 2, 18–20 as well as no. 9 and no. 10, which were altered in this spirit.

A layer of plaster made of mud and various organic materials was applied to the smoothed walls, which were painted when they were dry (**al secco**). The paints were formed on the basis of, among other substances, cinnabar, lapis lazuli, terra verde and kaolinite.

Tour through the cave temples

Visitors should try and take a full day to explore the caves of Ajanta and it is best to be accompanied by a knowledgeable guide. The best caves are nos. 1, 2, 10, 17, 19 and 26, which are described below.

✱ Cave no. 1 ▶

Cave no. 1 is dominated by its shrine with a Buddha figure surrounded by helpers and flying heavenly creatures. Together with the two large wall paintings depicting bodhisattvas **Vajrapani** (right) and **Padmapani** (left) it forms the centre of the vihara. The very insightful depiction of these two figures shows the high level painting had reached at the time. Further examples are »Buddha's refusal of the throne« and the »temptation by Mara and his daughters« as well as numerous further legends on the remaining walls. The wonderful ceiling painting with motifs from the world of animals and plants is also remarkable.

✱ Cave no. 2 ▶

Cave no. 2 is a smaller vihara with richly adorned pillars and ten cells. On the inside, to the side of the shrine, visitors can admire the impressive representation of the **1000 Buddhas** with different gestures and gazes. In this cave the ceiling was also carefully painted.

What is probably the oldest **cave, no. 10**, was, as is stated in a donor inscription, built as early as the second century BC. The floor plan of this chaitya temple is typically early Buddhist: triple-aisled with 39 octagonal pillars, apse with a stupa and a ceiling that imitates the original wooden construction. Two layers of paint, one over the other, can still be made out in fragments: from the older period the Samal legend and the legend of the bodhisattva who was born as an elephant with six trunks, and from the more recent period (fifth century) most of the Buddha statues.

✱ Cave no. 17 ▶

Rock temple no. 17 is an exceptionally richly sculpted and decorated vihara with very attractive paintings. Some of the depictions are considered to be particularly outstanding examples of the detailed and **delicate portraits of human emotional states**, such as the Vishvantara Jataka (left), in which Prince Vishvantara tells his wife he was banished or the depiction of »Simhala's conquest of Sri Lanka«, one of Ajanta's greatest wall paintings.

No. 19 contains the huge **7m/23ft statue of the dying Buddha** with mourning disciples on his left. Particular attention should be paid

Buddha entering Nirvana (no. 26)

to the facial expression of the saved Buddha, which is relaxed all the way down to the lips. Buddha's temptation by Mara and his daughters is also depicted.

Bhopal

Capital of Madhya Pradesh
Population: 1.45 million

Altitude: 523m/1716ft
Distance: 741km/460mi south of Delhi

Bhopal is now a modern industrial and administrative centre. As a result of its location amongst gentle hills and with its two lakes it has maintained a pleasant atmosphere compared with other Indian cities.

One special feature of Bhopal is that it was **ruled by women** between 1857 and 1926 and many of its structures were built on their orders. Bhopal has lately also become known as an art centre. The city hit the headlines in 1984 as a result of a **toxic gas disaster** at the factory of the American company Union Carbide. It cost very many people their lives, while thousands were caused lifelong health problems.

The city is said to have been founded by Raja Bhoja in the eleventh century and the two lakes are thought to be artificial. It was called Bhoj Pal (lake), which later turned into Bhopal. One of the Afghan vassals of the Mughal emperor Aurangzeb, Dost Mohammed Khan, exploited the disorder after his master's death and made himself independent in 1707. Throughout the 18th century Bhopal's rulers were loyal to the British. From the mid-19th century the city was **History** ruled by women for an extended period, first by Sikander Begum (1857–1901) and later by Shah Jahan Begum (1901–26). These two women are responsible for the creation of some of Bhopal's most significant buildings.

What to See in Bhopal

Taj-ul-Masjid ✳

Construction of this huge mosque was begun by Shah Jahan Begum, but the immense project kept wearing on, being only completed after 70 years of building works. With its three large white domes and huge minarets, it is **Bhopal's most imposing monument and one of India's largest mosques**. The prayer hall with the courtyard in front is particularly impressive. The Taj market is held around the mosque's exterior walls.

Jama Masjid is said to stand on the foundations of a Hindu temple. The Friday Mosque is the oldest in Bhopal and was built early in 1837 under Begum Kudsia. **Moti Masjid** was commissioned by Sikander Jahan in 1860 as a small replica of Jama Masjid in Delhi. A wonderful view of the city can be had from the new **Vishnu temple**, a modern building built by the Birla Foundation.

► BHOPAL

INFORMATION

MP Tourism
4th floor Gangorti Complex
T. T. Nagar
Tel. 07 55 – 277 83 83
www.mptourism.com

WHERE TO STAY / WHERE TO EAT
► **Mid-range**
Hotel Lake View Ashok
Shamla Hills; tel. 07 55 – 266 00 90
Modern hotel with good views on a hill above the lake. Bar and restaurant.

Bharat Bhavan ✳
🕐 Opening hours: daily except Sun 10.30am–5pm

Bharat Bhavan (House of India), designed by Charles Correa, has become a significant cultural centre with a library, theatre and various rooms for music events. It also contains a **very good collection of artworks created by the tribal population** (terra cotta statues, bronze figures, puppets and religious objects) and some of India's modern art.

Museums
🕐

The archaeological museum has miniatures and Buddha figures from various parts of Madhya Pradesh on display. The Tribal Habitat Museum in the Shamla mountains gives visitors a good insight into tribal architecture (open: Mon–Sat 10am–5pm, closed every 2nd Saturday).

✳✳ Sanchi

Spiritual centre of Buddhism

Sanchi (approx. 50km/30mi northeast of Bhopal) was a spiritual centre of Buddhism between the third and thirteenth centuries. As is traditional for Hinayana Buddhism, Buddha is only depicted by

Depiction of a tree nymph

means of symbols here. The lotus stands for Buddha's birth, the pipal tree for enlightenment and the wheel for his teachings. This important centre of Buddhism was only rediscovered by a British officer, General Taylor, in 1818. The complex can be easily reached on foot from the station. It takes around three hours to explore it fully.

Located on the hill is the **Great Stupa**. Its core consists of a relic stupa donated by Emperor Ashoka. During the middle of the second century it was given a casing by the Sunga rulers. The four entrances were adorned by the Satvahana dynasty (second – first centuries BC) with four magnificent Toranas (gates). Besides the Great Stupa, these **four stone gates with their fine relief ornamentation** are Sanchi's main attraction. The gates have depictions of animals, trees and people that illustrate Buddhist stories. The extremely vivid and detailed figures show the level of mastery achieved by stonemasons in ancient India.

The eastern gate depicts Buddha's mother's dream heralding his birth and predicting his farewell from the parental home. The western gate displays Buddha's various incarnations, while the southern gate shows his birth. Finally the northern gate depicts the wheel as a symbol of Buddhist teachings and several miracles from Buddha's life.

To the north of the Great Stupa is a **smaller stupa** (15m/16yd diameter) from the second century BC (stupa no. 3) with a richly adorned gate. It houses relics of two of Buddha's disciples, Sariputra and Mahamaudgalyana. At the southern gate of the Great Stupa are remains of an **Ashokan pillar** with inscriptions. To the south of it is temple no. 17 from the fifth century. Also known as **Gupta Temple**, it has a small cube-shaped cella and a columned portico. It is believed to be one of the oldest temple constructions in the Indian subcontinent. Immediately next to it is temple no. 18 (seventh century), a chaitya hall with a semi-circular apse. The western part of the complex has various monastic structures. A small path from the eastern gate of the Great Stupa leads to stupa no. 2, which was probably built some distance away from the Great Stupa since it was dedicated to ten saints who were not Buddha's immediate students.

The **Archaeological Museum** has a very good collection of coins and sculptures that was found during the excavations. The Buddha sculptures and a lion's capital from Ashoka's time, like the famous specimen in the museum of Sarnath, are particularly noteworthy. Open: Sat–Tue 10am–5pm.

Archaeological Museum

✶ Goa (State)

Area: 3701 sq km/1429 sq mi   **Population:** 1.34 million
Capital: Panaji

Sandy beaches stretching for miles, palm trees, breathtaking sunsets, and an excellent tourist infrastructure including international airports make Goa one of the subcontinent's most attractive travel destinations. The absence of extreme poverty and the familiar Mediterranean way of life of many of its inhabitants only add to its charm.

According to legend Goa, like its southern neighbour state of Kerala, also owes its origin to divine machinations. Parasurama, Vishnu's sixth incarnation, so it is written in the manuscripts of the Puranas, wrestled the land of Gomanta from the sea. Historical evidence giving information about the fate of this strip of coastline goes back to the third century BC. It is thought that this area was under the dominion of the great emperor Ashoka. Goa was only able to assert itself as an independent kingdom at a very much later date. During the tenth century the Kadambas seized power and built their capital in Chandrapur (modern-day Chandor). They also laid the foundation for the construction of Govapuri (Old Goa), the town to which they moved their seat of government a century later. Intense economic relationships with the Arabian peninsula made the town into a prospering trading centre with many temples and palaces. Time and again invaders such as the Delhi sultans, but also Hindu **History**

> **!** *Baedeker* TIP
>
> **Not just for Christmas**
> Goa is best during the off-peak months of October/November and February/March. Those who absolutely want to travel during the peak season of December/January should be sure to book in time.

clans, tried to conquer Goa. Thus the area belonged to the kings of Vijayanagara for 100 years before it fell into the hands of the Bahmani sultans in 1469. However, this Muslim rule did not last long. In 1510 the Sultan of Bijapur, who had come to power by then, was defeated by the Portuguese. That year marked the beginning of **Portuguese rule that lasted for several centuries** and was destined to end only when Indian troops invaded in 1961.

The occupying forces were threatened several times by their European rivals, the British and the Dutch, during the 17th and 18th centuries, but they were just as unable to get their hands on Portuguese possessions in the long term as the up-and-coming Marathas, who stood outside of the gates of Goa several times during the 17th and

← *Sun-worshippers, traders and cows on Vagator beach*

Goa Map

Where to eat
① Casa Portuguesa
② Fernando's Nostalgia
③ Lila Café

Where to stay
① Taj Exotica
② Fort Aguada Beach Resort
③ Coconut Creek
④ Marbella Guesthouse
⑤ Placete Rodriguez
⑥ L'Amour Beach Resort
⑦ Panjim Peoples/ Panjim Inn/ Panjim Pousada
⑧ Bhakti Kutir

1 Vagator Beach
2 Calangute Beach
3 Candolim
4 Reis Magos
5 Aldona
6 Pomburpa
7 Mayem Lake
8 Arvalem Falls
9 Miramar Beach
10 Siridao Beach
11 Pilar Seminary
12 Sri Manguesh Temple
13 Sri Mahalsa Temple
14 Sri Ramnath Temple
15 Sri Shanta Durga Temple
16 Khandeapar
17 Opa Water Works
18 Usgao
19 Tiskar
20 Dudhsagar Falls
21 Sri Chandreshwar Bhutnath Temple

18th centuries. Since their numbers were so small, the Portuguese saw themselves forced to engage in colonial policies that differed from those of the British. Mixed marriages were not just tolerated, they were encouraged. The fact that this tolerance was a means to an end and not a general political principle can be seen most clearly when looking at how the new masters treated the religion of their subjects. Particularly during the time of the Inquisition, temples were destroyed and Hindus were forced to convert. The Muslims had already left the area. Even during the 20th century the fate of the colony was closely connected to events in Portugal. The dictator Salazar who had come to power in Portugal in 1933 did not relinquish Goa even after the rest of India had become independent. The people's

▶ VISITING GOA

see maps p. 441 & . 444

INFORMATION

Tourist Office
Communidade Building
Church Square
Panaji
Tel. 08 32 – 222 34 12
www.goatourism.org

GENERAL FACTS

The whole of Goa has now found its way on to the tourist map. During the winter months there are even direct flights from Europe to this sun and sea destination. There are plenty of hotels and resorts in every price category. Those in search of the beach and party scene will be best served in the north, particularly in Anjuna, Calangute and Baga. Those who prefer peace and quiet should aim to visit the more southern beaches, such as Benaulim. However, in the peak season from December to February it is busy everywhere. During this time the prices can also be significantly higher than in the off season.

WHERE TO EAT

▶ Expensive

① *Casa Portuguesa*
Baga; tel. 08 32 – 227 70 24
Sophisticated Portuguese cuisine in an old bungalow. Sometimes the owner accompanies dinner with fados on the guitar.

④ *Horseshoe*
E-245 Rua de Querem; Panaji
Tel. 08 32 – 243 17 88
Top-quality specialities from Goa served in an elegant setting.

▶ Moderate / Inexpensive

② *Fernandos's Nostalgia*
608 Raia
Salcette

Tel. 08 32 – 277 70 54
This restaurant's interior alone is worth seeing and the specialities from Goa receive high praise.

③ *Lila Cafe*
North side of Baga river
Tel. 08 32 – 227 98 43
Diners here enjoy breakfast with home-made bread, croissants and cake, and lunch and dinner with salads, pasta and other tasty dishes.

▶ Inexpensive

⑤ *Viva Panjim*
178, Rua 31 de Janeiro. Panaji
Behind Mary Immaculate High School
Tel. 08 32 – 242 24 05
Dine by candlelight in the romantic garden or even come for breakfast, since it opens at 8.30am. Large menu, the typical dishes from Goa come particularly highly recommended.

WHERE TO STAY

▶ Luxury

① *Taj Exotica*
Calwaddo, Benaulim
Tel. 08 32 – 277 12 34
The nice bungalows of Taj Exotica stand right by the beach to the south of Benaulim, in the middle of a large garden. Several restaurants and bars, tennis court, golf course; there are also many other sports and leisure programmes on offer.

② *Fort Aguada Beach Resort*
Sinquerim; Bardez
Tel. 08 32 – 564 58 58
The hotel enjoys a picturesque location within an old fort; it has several restaurants and a private beach.

▶ Luxury / Mid-range

③ *Coconut Creek*
Bogmalo
Tel. 08 32 – 253 81 00
Small, family-friendly hotel with 20 rooms in a pleasant and quiet ambience.

⑦ *Panjim Peoples, Panjim Inn, Panjim Pousada*
Panaji
Tel. 08 32 – 222 65 23
Stay overnight in the picturesque part of Fontainhas. Choose either the Panjim Peoples (Luxury / Mid-range), an old, nicely renovated school, or the Panjim Inn or Panjim Pousada (Mid-range / Inexpensive), 31st January Road. All three hotels belong together and are just a few metres apart. They are furnished in Goa's traditional style. The Panjim Inn also has a restaurant and a pleasant veranda.

▶ Mid-range

④ *Marbella Guesthouse*
Sinquerim-Candolim

Tel. 08 32 – 22 47 95 51
Very small, but high quality Heritage Hotel with a personal atmosphere.

▶ Budget

⑤ *Placete Rodriguez*
Anjuna
Tel. 08 32 – 227 33 58
Visitors will even be able to find some peace and quiet in Anjuna in Mrs Da Costa's 200-year-old house.

⑥ *L'Amour Beach Resort*
Benaulim
Tel. 08 32 – 277 05 62
Small bungalows in a pretty garden by the beach in Benaulim.

⑧ *Bhakti Kutir*
Palolem
Tel. 08 32 – 64 34 69
Complex with bamboo huts; yoga and meditation classes, restaurant serving organic food.

---

struggle for liberation led to mass arrests, deportations and even claimed lives during the 1950s. The rebellions only ended when the Indian army intervened in December 1961. During the 1967 referendum regarding Goa's future role within India the majority of Goa's inhabitants voted for the option of becoming a separate state and not for the second option of being integrated into the neighbouring state of Maharashtra. Following its recognition as a union territory it was proclaimed the 25th state of the Indian Republic in 1987.

✴ Panaji (Panjim)

Capital of Goa If it were not for the motorized rickshaws honking their horns, the green coconut palm trees, the façades of the buildings washed out by the monsoon and the unmistakable smells ranging from curry and sandalwood to less pleasant odours, Panaji may well not be recognized as the capital of an Indian state. The town's face is still shaped by its colonial past and life here is less hectic than elsewhere in India. Panaji (population 100,000, 595km/370mi south of Mumbai) is situ-

Panaji Map

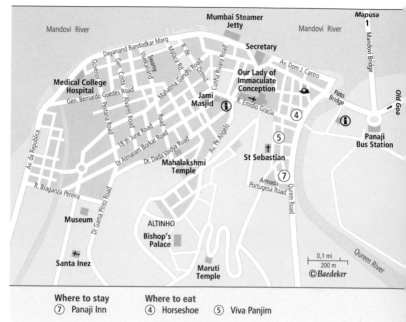

Mumbai Steamer Jetty

Mapusa

Mandovi River

Mandovi River

Mandovi Bridge

Dayanand Bandodkar Marg

Secretary

Govenor

Gen. Costa

Swamy Vivekanand

Malaka rd.

R. de

Av. Dom J. Castro

Old Goa

Mahatma Gandhi Road

Cunha Rivara Road

Cunha Rivara Road

Ormuz

Our Lady of Immaculate Conception

Pato Bridge

Medical College Hospital

Gen. Bernardo Guedes Road

Alvares Road

Road

Jami Masjid (i)

R. Emidio Gracia

(4)

(i)

Panaji Bus Station

Pestana Road

18 th June Road

Av. Pe Angelo

(5)

Dr Atmaram Borkar Road

Dr. Dada Vaidya Road

Mahalakshmi Temple

✝ **St Sebastian**

(7)

Av. da Republica

R. Braganza Pereira

Armada Portugesa Road

Qurem Road

Dr. Gama Pinto Road

Museum

ALTINHO

Bishop's Palace

0,1 mi

200 m

©*Baedeker*

Qurem River

⚓ **Santa Inez**

Maruti Temple

Where to stay	Where to eat	
(7) Panaji Inn	(4) Horseshoe	(5) Viva Panjim

ated on the southern banks of the estuary of the Mandoviriver. The town beneath Altinho Hill is connected with the northern riverbank via the modern Nehru Bridge. Around the heart of town, the Municipal Gardens and the Church of Our Lady of Immaculate Conception is the old district of Fontainhas in the east, which is largely inhabited by Christians, the commercial centre in the west and the Hindu residential district and Mahalakshmi Temple in the south.

History

In 1759 the Portuguese moved their seat of government from Old Goa (Velha Goa) 10km/6mi to the east to New Goa (Nova Goa), modern-day Panaji, taking over the former summer palace of sultan Yusuf Adil Shah. Over time the entire administration was moved to the small town, but it was never to achieve the magnificence of its predecessor. In 1843 Panjim was officially declared the capital of Portuguese India. Goa's current government still has its seat here and the sultan's old summer palace is still used for governmental purposes. These days some of the city administration is housed in it.

★
Our Lady of Immaculate Conception

To the northeast of the central square, the Municipal Gardens, is Panaji's largest church, Our Lady of Immaculate Conception, situated on a small hill. It dates back to the year 1619. Wide steps lead

Our Lady of Immaculate Conception

up to the snow-white Baroque façade and the main portal. Inside the single-nave hall is the high altar dedicated to the church's patron, as well as three further altars.

Visitors keeping to the north will get to Yusuf Adil Shah's former summer palace, today known as the **Secretary**, in which parts of Goa's administration are housed. A walk along the river promenade leads past the ferry landing stages. Here visitors can book river cruises for many different times of day. Turn left at the Indian Airlines Office in Dempo House to get to the large **Municipal Market**. Market women already offer Goa's extensive supply of fruit and vegetables outside of the gates of the bazaar, where visitors can wander amongst fire-red chillies and other spices, saris and salwar kameez, aluminium suitcases and sweet treats. Continue further in a southward direction to get to **Mahatma Gandhi Road**, Panaji's main shopping street. Restaurants, boutiques and liquor stores line the street and visitors will be able to buy Feni, Goa's famous cashew schnapps, to their heart's content here.

The picturesque old residential quarter of Fontainhas is in the east. It is also home to **Saint Sebastian's Chapel**, which dates back to 1888 and contains a crucifix from the 16th century. Altinho Hill rises up in the south. On it stands the **Bishop's Palace** (19th century). Its gallery of paintings has portraits of India's bishops. At the hill's northern foot, at Doctor Dada Vaidya Road, visitors will find the colourful Hindu **Mahalakshmi Temple** from 1817. The temple houses an id of the goddess Lakshmi made of black stone. The **State Museum of Goa** south of Kadamba bus station contains exhibitions on the country's culture and history, particularly from its pre-colonial days.

⏱ Opening hours: Mon–Fri 9.30am–5.30pm

On the opposite side of the Mandovi river-mouth from Panaji stands another Portuguese fort: **Fort Reis Magos**. Sultan Yusuf Adil Shah had already had a military bastion built at this strategically favourable location. It was then expanded and renovated by his successors in around 1704. Of the 33 cannons that defended the small garrison, nine can still be seen today. At the foot of the fort is Reis Magos Church, which was built in 1771 and renovated in 1945. It is dedicated to the Three Kings. It was here that the Portuguese viceroys took their oath before they assumed office. Seven of them were also buried here, as can be seen on the tomb slabs.

Around Panaji

✱ Old Goa (Velha Goa)

For those interested in culture a visit to Old Goa is highly recommended. The former capital and glittering Portuguese city lies 10km/ 6mi east of Panaji on the southern banks of the Mandovi river. It is easily accessible by bus or taxi. The city has several hundred thousand inhabitants and in its heyday was larger than Portugal's own capital Lisbon; indeed, it was even larger than London and at certain times boasted more churches than Rome.
Today there are more churches gathered together in one location here than anywhere else in India. Apart from these interesting buildings little is left, however, of the city's former glory, and it requires a healthy dose of imagination to picture its former size. Only a few clergy live here now and in the evenings, after the last tourist buses have left, the stage on which history was played out for hundreds of years falls quiet again.

Glittering Portuguese city

The ruling Hindu dynasty, the Kadamba, moved their capital here from Chandrapur (Chandor) around the mid-eleventh century and called it **Govapuri**. Under their government this place became a flourishing trading centre with a port, many temples and palaces. Numerous foreign conquerors had an eye on the kingdom of the Kadambas and tried to take the city. In the 14th century, the powerful rulers of Vijayanagara succeeded. They used Govapuri's harbour to import Arabian horses and other goods.
In 1469 the area fell into the hands of the Bahmani sultans and from 1488 it was in the possession of the Adil Shah dynasty of Bijapur. They made Govapuri their second residence and Sultan Adil Shah had a huge palace built near the banks of the Mandovi river. After the Portuguese had driven off the Muslim rulers in 1510 they quickly expanded their new possession. Private homes and public buildings were constructed and soon **many different religious orders, particularly the Franciscans**, settled in Old Goa and built their churches here.

History

Old Goa Map

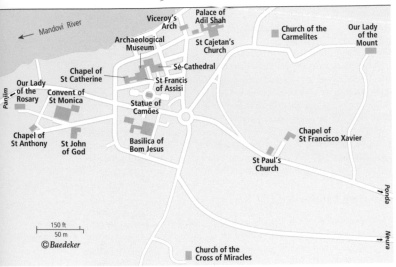

← Mandovi River

Viceroy's Arch
Palace of Adil Shah
Archaeological Museum
St Cajetan's Church
Church of the Carmelites
Our Lady of the Mount
Chapel of St Catherine
Sé-Cathedral
St Francis of Assisi
Our Lady of the Rosary
Convent of St Monica
Panjim
Statue of Camões
Chapel of St Anthony
St John of God
Basilica of Bom Jesus
Chapel of St Francisco Xavier
St Paul's Church
Ponda
Neura

150 ft
50 m
© Baedeker

Church of the Cross of Miracles

The main reasons for the decline of Old Goa at the end of the 16th century were political problems in Portugal, economic exploitation by the Inquisition and the drop in population as a result of the plague. In 1759 the Portuguese seat of government was moved to neighbouring Panjim. The repressive religious policies of the colonial rulers finally led to many religious orders, who until then had been living in Old Goa, being driven out in 1815. All they left behind were their large churches, which are the last pieces of evidence testifying to the city's proud past.

Sightseeing A tour of the monuments is best started on the banks of the Mandovi river. To do that visitors have to walk down Rua Direita to the river from the road where the buses stop. This used to be the location of the large city's harbour. One surviving structure is the **Viceroy's Arch**, the arch through which those arriving entered. It was built under Governor Francisco da Gama (1597–1600) to commemorate the discovery of the naval passage to India by his grandfather. There is a sculpture of the seafarer and conqueror in a niche along the façade and on the other side in the same spot there is a female figure, presumably St Catherine.

★
St Cajetan Walk back along Rua Direita, Velha Goa's former main boulevard, which was lined with many shops and large houses, to see the church of St Cajetan on the left. It was built by Theatines or Clerks Regular between 1650 and 1661 and named after the order's founder, Cajetano da Thiene, also known as Gaetano dei Conti di Tiene. The façade

shows the model the architects had in mind when designing this church: it bears a striking resemblance to St Peter's in Rome. The two side towers are, however, part of traditional Portuguese architecture. The building's floor plan is in the shape of a Greek cross and the dome rises up above its centre. In addition to the high altar, which is consecrated to Our Lady of Divine Providence, there are six further altars. Under the church's floor there is a well, which has given rise to much speculation. It is now believed that a temple used to stand here and that the well was the temple basin.

A closer look at the plentiful wall paintings and sculptures is quite interesting. European architects were in control of the church's construction, but the works were created by local artists. Details such as **Indo-oriental facial traits** of some of the people depicted bear their unmistakable stamp.

Outside the church, on the square's north side, are the meagre remains of Adil Shah's palace. All that is left of the once largest building in the city is its entrance gate. It was originally part of a Hindu temple before being integrated into the palace. The Portuguese governors resided here until 1695, but after that the building was left to fall into ruin. At the start of the 19th century the ruins were removed and used to build houses in Panaji.

Palace of Adil Shah

Turn westwards from Rua Direita to get to the imposing Sé Cathedral. Construction of this Dominican church began in 1592 and ended in 1619. It is consecrated to St Catherine of Alexandria and is thought to have been Asia's largest church at times. Its orientation to the west is unusual for a Christian church.

It originally had two bell towers, of which one is still present; the other was destroyed in 1776 during a monsoon storm. The huge, barrel-vaulted interior has a nave and two aisles, each of which has four chapels along the sides. The transept contains the richly gilded high altar of St Catherine, flanked by wooden sculptures of St Peter and St Paul with three further altars on each side.

★ Sé Cathedral

Sé Cathedral's choir adjoins the church of St Francis, which was built in 1661. The Franciscans had built a church in this location in 1521. However, all that remained of it was the entrance gate, built in Manueline style. This gate was integrated into the subsequent building. The church's **richly decorated Baroque interior** stands in stark contrast to the plain exterior of its façade.

There are three chapels on either side of the aisle-less nave. The high altar has a richly adorned tabernacle supported by the four evangelists; above it are two large statues of Christ and St Francis of Assisi. On both sides of the altar there are wooden images depicting events in the life of the saint. Here, too, various details, such as the floral patterns on the walls, indicate that Indian artists performed the work.

★ ★ St Francis

The Muslim portal of St Francis is a relic of the previous building

Archaeological Museum The former Franciscan convent on the church's north side, which was built between 1701 and 1765, now houses the Archaeological Museum. It displays finds from Goa's history, from Hindu sculptures to portraits of Portuguese governors, on two levels. The statue of the Portuguese national poet Luis Vaz de Camões, which used to stand on the square outside, is also housed in this museum (open: daily except Fri 10am–12pm and 1pm–5pm).

St Catherine Somewhat further west stands the chapel of St Catherine. It was only built in 1952 on the ruins of a church built by Alfonso de Albuquerque in 1510. The previous building was a reminder of the victorious entrance of the Portuguese into Adil Shah's city.

★ ★
Basilica of Bom Jesus On the south side of the road to Panaji is the bare laterite structure of the Basilica of Bom Jesus, which was once coated in a layer of white limestone. The magnificent three-storey façade of the Jesuit church that was constructed between 1594 and 1605 is a **typical example of Mannerist architecture**. The double towers so typical of many of the churches here are absent. Instead the uppermost pediment at the centre contains the christogram IHS in large writing, which the Jesuit order incorporated into its seal. Beyond the imposing façade is a single-nave building in the shape of a cross. The choir contains the gilded high altar with the divine infant and above it the larger-than-life sculpture of the order's founder Ignatius of Loyola. The south transept has the richly ornamented chapel in which Francis Xavier was buried in 1659. His remains are kept in a silver reliquary set with gemstones. The walls are decorated with pictures from the saint's life.

Southeast of the Basilica of Bom Jesus along the road to Ponda is the gate of the once famous St Paul's college, which is all that remains of it. The widely known university opened its gates in 1543 and had space for 300 students. Francis Xavier also taught here during his stay in the city. In addition to a large library the structure also contained a printing press.

St Paul's

Not far away is the small chapel for St Francis Xavier. It was built in 1884. The church that had stood here previously had fallen into ruin in 1545.

St Francis Xavier

To the south of the road to Panaji are more churches and monasteries in various states of decay, such as St John of God, a monastery founded by the Order of Saint John in 1685, which was used as a hospital. The church next to it was completed in 1721. In 1835 the order had to abandon the complex. It was later transformed into a convent. The current building was renovated in 1953.

St John of God

North of St John's is the Convent of St Monica, once the largest convent for nuns in the whole of south and east Asia. The three-storey laterite building is laid out around a large courtyard with a cloister. Several rooms still contain frescoes with Biblical scenes. The building, which was constructed between 1606 and 1627, now houses the worthwhile **Museum of Christian Art**.

Convent of St Monica

Even further west is the Chapel of St Anthony, the national saint of the Portuguese, which was built at the beginning of the 17th century. It was closed in 1835 due to disrepair, but restored in 1961.

St Anthony

One example of the Manueline style is the church of Our Lady of Rosary. The two-storey portico with a tower rising above it as well as the round towers at the corners give the building a fort-like appearance. Inside the church there are two chapels and three altars, of which the main altar is consecrated to the church's patron. The interior exhibits Gothic influences mixed with Indian ones, as can be seen on the twisted columns, for example. Our Lady of Rosary is a votive building donated by Alfonso de Albuquerque in 1510 after the victory of his troops over the sultan of Bijarpur. The church was built only later, between 1526 and 1543.

Our Lady of Rosary

There is a small church on a hill several hundred metres to the east from where visitors will have wonderful views of the surrounding area.

Our Lady of the Mount

Beaches and Towns North of Panaji

In 1612 the Portuguese built Fort Aguada in an exposed location on a rocky peninsula at the northern mouth of the Mandovi river. From

Fort Aguada

here, together with the fort on Cabo Raj Bhavan opposite and Fort Reis Magos further inland, they monitored everyone and everything entering the harbour of their capital. The fortified rock also marks the southern end of Candolim beach. The fort got its name from the mineral springs surfacing here. Built on the rock's highest point is a lighthouse, whose beam can still be seen 40km/25mi away; somewhat below it is an old cistern.

Those holidaymakers who love luxury will find that the Fort Aguada Beach Resort hotel complex within the fort's walls has some special amenities. Not far away in another part of the complex many are forced to enjoy the view: Goa's central prison is located here. Outside of the walls to the east is Linhares Church, dedicated to St Lawrence. The Count of Linhares, who was Goa's governor from 1629 to 1635, donated the church.

Candolim North of Fort Aguada lies the small village of Candolim, with a population of around 600, and the beach of the same name. Most of the former fishing families now make their living from tourism. The village has two temples, dedicated to Shantadurga and Ghangreshvar, and the church of Nossa Senhora d'Esperança (Our Lady of Hope). The beach is lined by dunes, as is almost all of Calangute beach.

Calangute and Baga The place where the Rolling Stones, the Beatles and other cult bands of the pop scene gave concerts in the 1960s and 1970s is now used by middle-class Indian tourists, British pensioners and package tour holidaymakers to lie in the sun. There is not much left here to remind visitors of the hippie and traveller beach Calangute was a few decades ago. In the last ten years hotels of all price categories have mushroomed, transforming the former fishing villages of Calangute and Baga into tourist strongholds. Nevertheless most of the accommodation comes in the shape of smaller hotels, no higher than two storeys, and they often cannot be seen from the beach as they are obscured by the dunes.

Calangute, with its 10,000 inhabitants, is one of the larger tourist towns. Many restaurants, bars and shops have opened in the centre along the road to Baga and towards the beach. Traders from Kashmir, Rajasthan and other parts of the subcontinent sell their goods here, from embroidered blankets and pillows to fashionable T-shirts and batik trousers.

The **sandy beach stretches for 15km/9mi** from Fort Aguada in the south to the mouth of Baga, a little stream, in the north. The actual Calangute beach near the town merges seamlessly into Baga beach. The entire strip of coastline is largely protected from the hinterland

> **! Baedeker TIP**
>
> **Ingo's Saturday Night Market**
>
> In Arpora, between Baga and Anjuna, a large market takes place during the season on Saturday evenings from 6pm. It has hundreds of traders, stalls selling food and drink, and live music.

Indian tourists on the beach of Anjuna

by sand dunes. There are no palm trees here, such as can be found in smaller bays. Instead there are countless beach bars and cafés all the way to Baga.

The sandy bay of Anjuna beach, lined by rocks and palm trees, is a few miles north of Baga. For many, it resembles heaven on earth. This was the place to which the freaks and hippies fled when tourism started establishing itself in Baga and Calungute. Even though the flower-power heyday is long gone, there is still much here to recall Anjuna's former role as a Mecca for alternative living, particularly the **flea market that takes place every Wednesday** and the beach festivals that are held every year around Christmas / New Year.

✴
Anjuna

Those who felt they were no longer getting the peace and quiet they hoped for in Anjuna withdrew to the north, to the two beaches of Vagator for example and particularly to the southern palm-lined Oz-ran Vagator beach. The neighbouring village of Chapora to the north has bars, cafés and shops, all proof that tourism is arriving here too, but many of the inhabitants still pursue traditional occupations such as fishing and boatbuilding. The small town's landmark is **Chapora Fort**, standing on a small rocky outcrop above the harbour. Adil Shah of Bijapur had a military post set up here, which was later extended by the Portuguese and rapidly conquered by the Marathas. The pan-oramic views from the fort, which can be accessed on foot from Va-gator beach Resort to the south, are very beautiful. There is a regular bus connection to Mapusa as well as the odd direct connection to Panaji.

**Vagator beach
and Chapora Fort**

Arambol beach and Terekhol Fort

In order to reach these destination in Goa's far north it is quite a journey. Departing Mapusa, visitors will travel through the village of Siolim, then to the north there is a ferry across Chapora river. The white sandy beaches of Morjim, Mandrem and Arambol (Harmal) seem endless. Arambol beach with its **freshwater lake**, fed by hot springs, on the other side has always been an attraction. To get to Terekhol Fort, the last bastion before the border to Maharashtra, visitors have to take a ferry from the village of Querim. Terekhol now has a nice hotel.

Mapusa

The most important trading and transport centre in the north of Goa is the small town of Mapusa (population 30,000, 13km/8mi from Panaji), approximately 10km/6mi inland. All of the buses from Mumbai and other cities in Maharashtra go via Mapusa. The town does not have any sights of interest. However, those who would like to visit the town should do so on a Friday, the day when the colourful **weekly market** takes place, which has managed to hold on to its authenticity compared with many a tourist market elsewhere. Fish, vegetables and spices are sold here alongside the inevitable T-

Margao's market sells clothes and jewellery in addition to food

shirts, sunglasses and leather sandals that decorate the façades of many beach villages. Those who felt Old Goa did not provide enough Christian-Portuguese architecture should visit the Franciscan church of Our Lady of Miracles, built in 1594 and restored in 1839.

Around 9km/6mi southeast of the district capital of Bicholim are **Goa's oldest rock temples**, the caves of Arvalem (third – fifth centuries). They are named after the neighbouring Arvalem Falls. There are five caves of varying sizes, which all lie hidden behind an entrance hall with monolithic columns. Some of them are fitted with a platform on which a Shiva lingam can be seen.

Caves of Arvalem

Beaches and Towns South of Panaji

The fast-growing industrial town of Vasco da Gama (population 110,000, 29km/18mi southwest of Panaji), with its Mormugao Harbour and Dabolim Airport to the east, is the economic heart of Goa. It is located on Mormugao peninsula, which stretches out into the ocean. It is also one of Goa's eleven provinces. Mormugao harbour is one of the most important and largest along India's west coast. It provides the people from the surrounding states with bread and work. The town has nothing of particular interest to tourists.

Vasco da Gama

Only 3km/2mi from the airport, on the south coast of Mormugao peninsula, is the small Bogmalo beach. This sandy bay is dominated by the high-rise building of a five-star hotel. The typical souvenir shops have established themselves in front of the hotel. There are a few bars and cafés on the beach but the bay does not seem crowded, in contrast to many other strips of coastline.

Bogmalo beach

The village of Colva, whose inhabitants mainly make a living from tourism but still engage in fishing, has a population of around 3500. Guests can choose amongst the countless hotels and restaurants to find ones to their liking. Colva's inhabitants are predominantly Christian and the village has an old church, Our Lady of Mercy (1581) in which a sculpture of the Christ child is venerated on the main altar.

Colva

The wide sandy beach of Colva extends for **30km/19mi**. Its individual sections are named after the villages along it. Many holidaymakers and individual tourists in particular who felt the beaches of Calungute and Baga were overcrowded moved to the sheer endless strip of coastline in the south. Although hotel construction is now booming here too, particularly in the villages of Colva and Benaulim, it is still much quieter here than it is in the north. One very pleasant pastime is to walk along the shore; those who leave the village beaches behind may even have the pleasure of being alone on the beach with the fishermen unloading their catch or repairing their nets. The spectrum of accommodation covers every price category, from spartan

✱
◄ Beach

huts to five-star complexes. Most of the accommodation, however, consists of smaller hotels and guesthouses somewhere in the middle.

Benaulim Just 2km/1mi south of Colva is Benaulim with its 10,000 inhabitants. Benaulim has a good choice of hotels and guesthouses and is a popular destination for many visitors travelling alone.

Varca A few years ago a luxury hotel complex was opened on Varca beach. The village behind it has a population of 4000 and possesses two churches, a post office and a bank.

Cavelossim and Mobor The southernmost section of Colva has seen a lot of building work in recent years. Several luxury hotels and larger complexes have been built here.

Cabo da Rama The name of the headland stems from a legend: Rama is said to have searched for his partner Sita here when she was abducted to Lanka (modern-day Sri Lanka). The Portuguese built their southernmost fort on the remains of an older complex. Those exploring this area by moped or taxi should visit this old fort.

Palolem Until a few years ago the nicely curved, palm-lined bay near the fishing village of Palolem was considered a place of refuge for those in search of tranquillity, who, in return, did not mind compromising when it came to comfort. However, this beach is now also lined with bars, cafés and many small hotels.

Margao

Trading centre in the south of Goa Those taking the train from Mumbai to Goa should not get out at the terminal station, Vasco, but in Margao (33km/20mi south of Panaji, population 80,000). The small town in the heart of southern Goa largely has a more pleasant atmosphere than the industrial location in the far west and the beaches to the south, apart from Bogmalo beach, can be reached more easily and quickly. Margao existed long before the Portuguese came to Goa. Hindu schools and monasteries (mathagrama) made the place into a centre of religious scholarship and piety. Following the arrival of the Portuguese the Jesuits came here in 1564 and just one year later they built a church on the foundations of a Hindu temple. It, like the many old Portuguese villas dotted everywhere in the town, is a reminder of the many years of colonial rule.

Municipal Gardens The Municipal Gardens with their flowerbeds and shrubs mark the town's centre. The town hall is to the south of the square. Opposite it stands the main post office (GPO). Two further important establishments for tourists, the State Bank of India and the tourist office, can be found to the west of the square.

In addition to the many retail stores, Margao has two markets, the **Markets** old Vasco da Gama Market and the new Alfonso de Albuquerque Market. The above-mentioned Jesuit Holy Spirit Church can be found on a square approximately 1km/0.6mi northeast of the Municipal Gardens. The original building was destroyed and rebuilt in 1675. At the centre of the square, opposite the church, is a large white cross. The Baroque church has ten altars. The vestry houses a precious monstrance, a gift from the Spanish king Philip III. The church square is lined by some nice old houses with balustrades and carvings. The Hindu temples Hari, Vithal and Damodar Mandir were all built in the 20th century.

Chandor (population 7000, approx. 10km/6mi southwest of Margao) **Chandor** can look back on a long history. It was here that the Kadambas built their capital in the tenth century before they moved it to Govapuri (Old Goa) later on. Chandor's visitors will find less here to remind them of its period of Hindu rule than of the presence of the Portuguese.

Evidence of their occasionally luxurious lifestyle is provided by the **double villa of the de Meñezes Bragança and de Bragança Pereira families**. A part of the 18th century villa decorated with countless antiques from Goa is open to the public between 9.30am and 5pm (tel. 08 32 – 278 42 01). There is a small Baroque Jesuit church (1645) on the square in front of the villa, which was renovated in 1945.

Opening hours: daily 9.30am–5pm

Faded pomp in the villas of the Portuguese families de Meñezes Bragança and de Bragança Pereira

Ponda and the Temple Complexes of the Surrounding Area

Ponda

Ponda (30km/19mi southeast of Panaji, population 20,000) is the administrative centre of the district of the same name and is worth visiting, particularly because of its many places of pilgrimage for Hindus in the surrounding area. The most interesting attraction in the town itself is the old Muslim Safa Shahouri Mosque. It was built in 1560 under the Adil Shah dynasty of Bijapur.

Places of pilgrimage

When the Portuguese started destroying Hindu and Muslim places of worship after conquering the coast, the believers brought their sacred objects to safe places. The inaccessible hinterland saw the construction of new temples for the Hindu idols that were being threatened by the enthusiasm of Christian missionaries and domineering colonial behaviour.

The village of **Bandora**, approximately 5km/3mi northwest of Ponda, is home to three important temples. Vishnuites and Shivaites alike make pilgrimages to Sri Ramnath Temple. The large complex, which also contains accommodation for believers, dates back to 1566 and was restored in 1905. Mahalakshmi Temple, in which Vishnu's wife is worshipped, is located in the centre of the village. The cult image of black marble was brought here from the fishing village of Colva in the 16th century. Not far away is a third temple, Sri Nagesh, dedicated to one of Shiva's incarnations. The oldest parts of the complex date back to the Vijayanagara period, as an inscription from 1413 at the temple's entrance confirms. The sanctum contains a Shiva lingam and a Nandi, the god's vehicle. The assembly hall has some nice wood carvings from the Ramayana. The entire building was comprehensively refurbished in the 18th century.

One much visited place of pilgrimage is Sri Manguesh Temple near **Priol** (9km/6mi north of Ponda). This cult site is located at the foot of a hill and also contains a temple pond. The oldest parts of the temple date back to 1565, additions and remodellings took place during the 18th–19th centuries. The temple is consecrated to Sri Manguesh, one of Shiva's incarnations, whose lingam can be seen in the cella. The complex's newer parts reveal European influence, thus in particular the glass candleholders and wall decorations.

Around 1km/0.6mi away, in the village of **Mardol**, is Sri Mahalsa Temple. Sri Mahalsa, one of Lakshmi's incarnations, is worshipped here, as is Vishnu as Mohini, his female incarnation. The sanctum contains an image of the goddess, who is extremely popular in Goa. It was one of the many that was saved from Portuguese vandalism. Beautiful wood carvings with Vishnu's ten incarnations can also be admired.

Quite a bit older than the nearby temples of Bandora, Priol and Mardol are the four rock temples that were chiselled out of laterite near the village of **Khandepar** (5km/3mi east of Ponda). They date back

Goa's paddy fields give high yields

to the tenth / eleventh centuries. Cult figures are no longer present. All that is left of the original decorations is a lotus motif on the ceiling of the first temple.

The small temple of **Tambdi Surla** (16km/10mi north of Molem) is considered the only well-preserved relic from the time of the Kadamba rulers. It dates back to the 13th century and is situated in a picturesque setting near the village of Tambdi Surla within Mahaveer National Park. The two-storey temple tower rises up above the square sanctum; the roofed mandapa (hall) is open to three sides. The cella houses a lingam, symbol of the god Shiva, to whom this temple is dedicated. The small temple can only be visited as part of a trip to the national park.

Nature Reserves

A day trip to Goa's forested hinterland leads to Bhagwan Mahaveer Sanctuary, around 30km/20mi east of Ponda. The protected area on the slopes of the Western Ghats has a size of around 240 sq km/90 sq mi. The park is home to leopards but it requires a lot of luck to spot one. It is more likely visitors will encounter herds of gaur, various deer species, monkeys, wild boar and jackals. Countless bird species, including raptors such as eagles, falcons and buzzards, as well as many kingfisher and woodpecker species, live in the park.

Bhagwan Mahaveer Sanctuary

Goa's smallest national park, Bondla Sanctuary, approximately 10km/6mi northeast of Ponda, is only 8 sq km/3 sq mi in size. Its orchid and cactus houses and its zoo make it a popular place for excursions, particularly amongst Indian tourists.

Bondla Sanctuary

Cotigao Wildlife Sanctuary in the south near Palolem has a size of 105 sq km/40 sq mi, making it the second-largest reserve in Goa. It too is home to many animals, including almost 150 bird species. The Forest Department's information centre is located at the entrance to the park. Here visitors will also find basic accommodation in small bungalows (tel. 08 32 –263 92 65).

Cotigao Wildlife Sanctuary

Gwalior

F 6

State: Madhya Pradesh
Population: 830,000

Altitude: 215m/605ft
Distance: 319km/198mi south of Delhi

Gwalior, the former capital of the Scindia dynasty, had a strategically favourable location on the Indian subcontinent's great north-south axis. The impressive 3km/2mi medieval fort on a 90m/295ft rocky plateau is evidence of the city's golden age under the Scindias, who brought a large part of the northwest under their dominion during the second half of the 18th century.

This is India's largest fort and it contains six palaces, several temples, one mosque and eight artificial lakes. Today Gwalior, with its new district of Lashkar, is an important centre for agricultural products.

It is said that a recluse by the name of Gwalippa healed the sick king Suraj Sen here, who was so grateful he founded this city. It was later plundered by the slave king Shah-ud-din Iltutmish (1211–36). From the 14th century the Tomara Rajputs ruled here until they were defeated by the Mughals. Gwalior then became a constant bone of contention between the Marathas, the Jat kings and the expanding British. It finally fell into the hands of the British after they crushed the Indian Mutiny.

View from Gwalior Fort

⏵ VISITING GWALIOR

INFORMATION

MP Tourism
At the station
Tel. 07 51 – 254 07 77
www.mptourism.com

EVENTS

Tansen Music Festival
Classical Hindustani music, every
year in Nov / Dec

WHERE TO STAY / WHERE TO EAT

▶ **Luxury**
Usha Kiran Palace
Jayendraganj Lashkar
Tel. 07 51 – 244 40 00,
www.tajhotels.com
This 120-year-old heritage hotel is

situated in the middle of a large park
and is very comfortable; good cuisine.

▶ **Budget**
MSTDC Tansen
6 A Gandhi Road
Tel. 07 51 – 234 03 70
Centrally located hotel run by Madhya Pradesh Tourism, in a large
garden. The hotel has a restaurant.

What to See in Gwalior

★
Fort complex

Standing high on a large sandstone rock called Gopagiri in the north
of Gwalior is one of India's most impressive forts. Contained within
the fort's walls are six palaces, several Hindu temples, a school and a
Sikh temple. Since the fort is several miles long it is a good idea to
access it via the Urvahi valley on its southwest side and leave it again
towards the old on the northeast side at Man Mandir Palace. There
is a group of Jain tirthankaras chiselled from the rock in the Urvahi
valley. The largest figure depicts Adinath, the first fordmaker, and is
almost 20m/65ft high. These relief figures were destroyed by Babur's
army In 1527 and later restored. Turn right on the plateau to reach
the Suraj Kund pond. It is said that it was here the city's founder
Suraj Sen once went bathing, the event that cured him of his illness.
Immediately next to it is Teli-ka-Mandir.

Teli-ka-Mandir and Man Mandir

Of all the buildings within the fort complex Teli-ka-Mandir and
Man Mandir are the most important. Teli-ka-Mandir, the oldest
structure (AD 750) was originally a Vishnu temple, as can be seen by
the Garuda above the entrance. The roof of the curious 25m/82ft
building probably took its shape from the Buddhist chaitya halls.
The British used the temple as a soda factory. Maharaja Jaya Rao
Scindia of Gwalior, a British ally, was able to do little against this disregard for Hindu culture.

Man Mandir Palace	The palace of the Tomar ruler Raja Man Singh (1486–1516) was built in around 1500 and was considered one of India's most beautiful palaces. It is also called Chit Mandir (painted palace) since its **exterior façade**, very unusually for India, is decorated with colourful mosaics of tigers, peacocks and elephants. In contrast to the colourful exterior the interior is surprisingly empty. There is only the odd lattice window. The round underground rooms were originally designed as places of refuge from the hot summers. The great Mughal emperor Akbhar was so impressed by the palace that he let himself be inspired by it in his own buildings. The Mughal rulers used the palace as a dungeon as did Aurangzeb, who kept his brother imprisoned here for five years before he was executed. Not far away is Vikram Mandir (1516) and north of it Karam Mandir. From here, after passing the five gates, visitors can leave the fort and reach the city after a steep, somewhat laborious descent.
Sas Bahu Temple	Around 200m/220yd south of Man Mandir Palace are the twin temples (late eleventh century) dedicated to Vishnu. A stairway leads up to the temples situated on pedestals. With their three-storey main halls and richly adorned façades they are considered masterpieces of Indian medieval architecture.
Archaeological Museum ⊙	Situated along the road leading to the fort is the Gujari Mahal. The archaeological museum it houses contains terra cotta figures, sculptures, replicas of the cave paintings of Bagh as well as miniatures (open: daily except Fri 10am–5pm).
✱ **Jai Vilas Palace**	Maharaja Jayo Rao Scindia, who ruled from 1843 to 1886, commissioned a British architect – as had become the fashion amongst the maharajas – to build one of the largest palaces in India for him. The three-storey building by Lt. Col. Sir Michael Filose, completed in 1874, resembles a Tuscan palazzo more than an Indian palace. It has some superlatives in store in its impressive interior, which highlight the inconceivable wealth of the maharajas. One of them is the **world's largest chandelier** in the entrance hall, which weighs 3 tons and is fitted with 248 candleholders. In 35 rooms a museum displays exhibits such as a small silver model railway, which »served« the food on the huge dining table.
Mohammed Ghaus Mausoleum	The mausoleum in honour of the saint and author Ghaus Mohammed (died 1563) was built shortly after his death. A voluminous dome rises up above the impressive tomb. A veranda leads around the central burial chamber, which is covered by a lattice wall.
Tansen tomb	A nearby small garden contains the tomb of Tansen, a famous court musician under Akbar. It is the scene of an annual music festival in honour of Tansen (Nov/Dec). The festival is a tribute to traditional Hindi music and a venue for traditional musicians form all over India.

Around Gwalior

The former maharajas' hunting ground of Gwalior (approx. 100km/ 60mi south of Gwalior) has been made a national park. The park, which is a good 160 sq km/62 sq mi in area, consists mainly of dry broad-leaved forests and has large populations of chinkara, nilgai antelopes and sambar deer. Birdwatchers will enjoy the many different species around the artificial lake. There is also good accommodation in Shivpuri Tourist Village.

Shivpuri National Park

Indore

D 8

State: Madhya Pradesh
Population: 1.6 million

Altitude: 567m/1860ft
Distance: 806km/500mi south of Delhi

The up-and-coming industrial and commercial town of Indore is also known as the »Detroit of India« – several important companies like Bajaj, Honda and Hindustan Motors have their production facilities here.

VISITING INDORE · MANDU · UJJAIN

INFORMATION

MP Tourism
Shop NO. 10 & 11
Jhabua Tower, Indore
R. N. T. Road
Tel. 07 31 – 252 86 53

or at the station in Ujjain
Tel. 07 34 – 256 15 44
www.mptourism.com

GETTING THERE

There are various air and rail connections to Indore. It is easy to take a train to Ujjain 55km/34mi north of the city. In contrast Mandu (100km/ 60mi southwest of Indore) is best reached by taxi.

WHERE TO STAY / WHERE TO EAT

► Luxury / Mid-range
Fortune Landmark
Near Meghdoot Garden

Indore
Tel. 07 31 – 255 77 00
This modern hotel has every creature comfort, including a swimming pool, a fitness suite and an elegant restaurant serving international dishes.

► Mid-range / Budget
Malwa Resort
Mandu
Tel. 072 92 – 26 32 35
The resort's 20 bungalows are situated in a lovely garden with sea views. A restaurant and bar are also available.

Shipra Residency
University Road
Ujjain
Tel. 07 34 – 255 14 95
The Shirpa has large, comfortable rooms, a bar and a restaurant with a pleasant atmosphere.

History The city by the rivers Sarasvati and Kham only acquired significance in the 18th century under the Hokar dynasty, when King Malhar Rao received this territory from the Maratha rulers for his services. The city had its golden age under his daughter Ahalya Bai, who was often compared to Queen Victoria. She expanded the city of Indore and built numerous cities and dharamsalas. After her death there were violent conflicts amongst her grandchildren, which ultimately led to them having to give a large part of their kingdom to the British. Until India's independence Indore was a loyal vassal of the British Raj. Its kings adopted much in the way of British architecture and lifestyle.

What to See in Indore

Lal Bagh Palace Lal Bagh Palace (Nehru Centre) is the result of the attempt to build a lavish palace designed on the European model in India. The palace of the Scindias of Gwalior completed several years previously had a significant impact on the building. The Holkar rulers adopted the Western architectural style with Doric columns, stucco ceilings and crystal chandeliers and so the building is more reminiscent of a European court than it is of a Maharaja's palace. Today it houses a museum with a coin collection, miniatures and paintings.

Kanch Mandir (Glass Temple) The Jain temple is generously decorated with mirrored mosaics. The entrance area has drastic images depicting the fate of those who do not follow the right path in life.

Museum Central Museum has several exhibits from the period between 10,000 and 5000 BC, which were discovered at digs in Bhimbetka in 1957 (open: daily except Mon 10am–5pm).

Ujjain

One of the seven holy cities Like ▶ Varanasi, Ujjain, 50km/30mi to the north, is an ancient city with a history going back several thousand years. It is one of India's famous seven holy cities. Every twelve years – next time in 2016 – the impressive **Kumbha Mela** pilgrimage takes place here, which is attended by hundreds of thousands of pilgrims.

In the third century BC the great Indian emperor Ashoka spent a short time in Ujjain as the viceroy of the Maurya dynasty. Chandragupta Vikramaditya later moved his capital from Pataliputra, modern-day Patna, to Ujjain. At this time the city was a centre of art and literature. Chandragupta's court was attended by the great poet Kalidasa and other scholars such as Bhavabhuti and Varahmihara. In the ninth and tenth centuries Ujjain became the capital of the Parmer kings. After the Mughals, the Maratha dynasty obtained control of the city in 1750 and for 50 years Ujjain was the capital of the Maratha Empire.

Today Ujjain appears more like a sleepy provincial town primarily visited by Indian pilgrims. There are many temples and buildings from different periods. Mahakala Temple is Ujjain's most important temple.

The sanctum of **Mahakala Temple** (mahakala = ruler of time) has one of the twelve Jyotir lingams (light lingams or flame lingams) that represent the god Shiva, and is highly revered in all of India. The temple was destroyed by Altamish in 1235 and later rebuilt by the Scindia dynasty (18th century).

As in Varanasi, pilgrims come to Ujjain all year round in order to bathe in the Kshipra river, which is thought to be sacred. They perform ritual cleansing and make sacrifices in the location where Shiva is said to have destroyed

Mahakala Temple, Ujjain's holiest place

the demon Tripura. It is extremely interesting to walk along the bathing ghats and many small temples and watch the goings-on.

✱ **Bathing ghats**

Upon request of the scientifically-minded Mughal ruler Mohammed Shah, the king of Jaipur, Jain Singh II, an enthusiastic astronomer, built one of his famous observatories in Ujjain in 1730. Both the idiosyncratic shapes and the precision of the calculation of the astronomical processes are still unparalleled in India. According to traditional Indian astronomy the prime meridian runs through Ujjain. Compared with the observatories in Jaipur and Delhi, this one is modest but still well worth a visit because of its romantic location on the banks of the Kshipra.

Jantar Mantar

✱ Mandu

The town of Mandu (100km/60mi southwest of Indore), which has a deserted air, is located on a plateau of the Vindya mountains and was once considered a town of joy and love. The architectural remains of the fort, palaces, canals and pavilions give a good idea of their former size. The town was originally protected by a 75km/47mi wall interspersed by twelve entrance gates. Today only fragments of its former magnificence remain. The fort is better preserved and makes Mandu the largest walled town in the world. Since Mandu lies off the main travel routes it does not get many tourists. However, Mandu's plain but impressive Islamic architecture was the **inspira-**

Flower markets appeal because of their colours and scents

tion for many Indian buildings, from the Taj Mahal to the buildings by Louis Kahn at the Indian Institute of Management in Ahmedabad.

History In the tenth century King Raja Bhoja founded a town in this place, where there had already been forts since the sixth century. Mandu soon flourished as the capital of the Malwas, the rulers of Paramara. The town was considered the gateway to the Deccan plateau; it was conquered by the Delhi sultans in the 14th century and was given the name Shadibad, city of joy. One of the appointed vassals, Dilwar Khan Ghuri, made himself independent and his son Hoshan Shah built important monuments such as Jama Masjid and the Delhi Gate during his long reign; Mandu was the capital of his kingdom. When Ghiyath-ud-din assumed power in 1469, palace life with a harem of 15,000 women and a special guard of 1000 female soldiers from Turkey and Abyssinia reached its final climax. The town was subsequently conquered by Gujarati rulers, Rajput kings and Mughal emperors. Jehangir spent several years in the town of Mandu during his military campaigns and was so taken with its architecture that he had some of the buildings restored.

The sprawling area containing the ruins is divided into three parts: the royal enclave, the village complex and the Rewa Kund complex. In order to enjoy the entire complex in peace and quiet, visitors should aim to spend at least half a day here.

Complex

The area, which begins immediately beyond the Alamgri Gate, is home to the Jahaz Mahal and the Hindola Mahal, its two most important structures. The Jahaz Mahal is a narrow palace built between two artificial lakes. It only unfolds its full magnificence during the monsoon period, when the lakes are brimming with water. During full moon nights the ship-like building is reflected on the still water. It served as the accommodation for the harem of Ghiyath-ud-din. The complex was a place of festivals and celebrations.
The **Hindola Mahal**, the swaying palace, was given its name because of the walls, which lean outwards and appear to sway. The large main hall of the T-shaped building can be accessed via a specially-made ramp that could even be used by the king's elephants.

Royal Enclave

Continuing southwards from the royal enclave, visitors reach the village complex. Jama Masjid, which was built in 1454 on the model of the Great Mosque in Damascus, is a masterpiece of Islamic architecture. The harmonious structure houses a prayer hall covered by three large domes and more than fifty small domes. The entire complex stands on a 4.5m/15ft plinth.
Behind Jama Masjid is the **cenotaph for Hoshang Shah**, who started construction on the mosque. The mausoleum, built under Mahmud I (1436–69), is thought to be India's first marble building. The domed structure rises up over the square walls, which are accessed via particularly nicely decorated entrances.

Village complex

This complex is located at the southern end by the fort walls. The largest building, Baz Bahadur Palace, was built in 1508 by Nasir-ud-din but is named after the later ruler Baz Bahadur, who assumed power in 1554. Baz Bahadur was a great fan of the arts and loved the beautiful Hindu singer Roopmati, for whom he built several structures.
The **Pavilions of Roopmati** are located somewhat further up on the highest point of Mandu's fort. They are reminders of the great love of the strangely matched couple. According to popular legend Baz Bahadur is said to have built these pavilions on the highest point of the palace for her so that Roopmati would be able to see the Narmada river, which was sacred to her. Their romantic love came to an abrupt end when Akbar's troops conquered Mandu in 1601 and Baz Bahadur had to flee. According to a widespread legend the loyal queen Roopmati committed suicide so that she would not fall into the hands of Akbar, who had heard of her beauty and wanted to win her for his harem. To this day many legends sing of this story of love and death.

Rewa Kund complex

Nilkanath Palace is also worth seeing. It was built by Budah Khan, one of Akbar's officers, in 1574–75. The palace is built on a slope and blends into the beautiful landscape. In order to produce a pleasant climate, the water was channelled through the palace. One of the palace's sides was kept open for the view. The small Shiva temple within the palace is evidence of Akbar's well-known religious tolerance. Inscriptions on a wall give precise details about one of Akbar's military campaigns on the Deccan plateau (1600–01).

★★ Khajuraho

F 7

State: Madhya Pradesh
Population: 7000

Altitude: 217m/712ft
Distance: 598km/372mi southeast of Delhi

To this day Khajuraho is a small, sleepy town in an isolated location, making it a great place to escape the hustle and bustle of the cities. The sole attraction consists of the more than 50 well-preserved Hindu and Jain temples of the Chandella dynasty. This wonderful example of the union of architecture and sculpture in medieval India is well worth seeing.

Characteristic of the temples is their wealth of figures, both on the façades as well as in the interior. Khajuraho's sculptures are a world of their own, populated by divine nymphs, demons, gods and copulating couples. It is these sensual, erotic depictions of lovers that attract many visitors.

History The Chandella dynasty traced its origins from the lunar god (Chandra). Under the ruler Dhanga (around 950) these people obtained independence from the Gurjara Pratiharas, whose vassals they had been. Their symbol was two palm trees, from which the town got its name Khajuraho (Kajur = palm tree). The capital Khajuraho gradually developed into a fortified town with more than 50 Jain and Hindu temples. Most of them were built during the golden age of the Chandella dynasty in the tenth and eleventh centuries. It is thought that hundreds of sculptures and stonemasons were employed here during that time.

★★ Temples of Khajuraho

Nagara style The prevailing style amongst the Khajuraho temples is the Nagara style. Walk through the decorated portal (ardamandapa) to get to a

*The most impressive temple in the complexes of Khajuraho →
is Kandariya Mahadeva Temple (western group)*

▶ VISITING KHAJURAHO

INFORMATION

MP Tourism
Chandela Cultural Centre
Tel. 076 86 – 27 40 51
or at the bus station
www.mptourism.com

GETTING THERE

Khajuaraho is best reached by plane and is a good place for a stopover on the flight route Delhi – Agra – Khajuraho – Varanasi. Another option is to travel via Jhansi railway junction, from where visitors can take a bus or a taxi.

EVENTS

Khajuraho Dance Festival
Classical dances from all over India against an impressive backdrop (every year in February / March)

WHERE TO STAY / WHERE TO EAT

▶ **Luxury**
Hotel Chandela
Khajuraho
Tel. 076 86 – 27 23 55
After visiting the temples relax by the pool in the nicely landscaped garden or enjoy a good meal in one of the restaurants or cafés.

▶ **Budget**
Hotel Casa di William
Near the western temple group
Tel. 076 86 – 27 45 50
Basic hotel with a terrace and restaurant serving international cuisine.

hall (mandapa) connected to a vestibule (antarala). Larger temples then have a transept (mahamandapa). Finally there is the sanctum (garbhagriha) surrounded by a colonnade (pradakshina). The entrance hall and side halls form an unparalleled organic unit. Parabolic towers and turrets arch above these sections and they in turn are in the shadow of the shikara (main tower) above the cella. It is easy for observers to see the temples **as symbolic representations of the earthly Mount Meru** in the Himalaya, the home of the Hindu gods. The temples are not surrounded by a wall, as they would be in southern India for example; instead they were built on a high pedestal.

Sculptures During a visit to the temples of Khajuraho visitors are inevitably fascinated by the many sculptures along the exterior façades. Those who choose to immerse themselves in this world of figures will discover heavenly creatures, depictions of gods, musicians, dancers, animals and copulating mithuna figures. The diverse figures can be divided into five groups. They include the three-dimensional depictions of **deities** and semi-relief depictions of **less significant gods** and their relatives, which were produced using the canonically fixed measurements. The **apsaras and surasundaris** (nymphs and heavenly creatures) are amongst the largest, third group. They are either fully sculpted or can be found on the exterior walls and columns in semi-

Gods and fabulous beasts

relief and were freely designed by the artists. They are amongst the best representations in Khajuraho. There is the sense that visitors have caught these female figures by surprise as they were about to write a love letter, look at themselves in the mirror or remove a thorn from their foot. **Earthly creatures** such as teachers, dancers, musicians and erotic depictions of couples or groups can also be admired here as can the final group consisting of **animals and fabled creatures**.

The sheer number of temples in Khajuraho allows visitors to follow the **development** and slow decline of the sculptural tradition. Lakshmana Temple and Parasvanatha Temple have classical, discreetly modelled figures with serious expressions. The Khajuraho style seems to have fully developed in the sculptures of Vishvanatha Temple with their wonderfully balanced proportions. This style finds its most consummate expression in the magnificent Kandariya Mahadeva Temple.

By comparison the figures on Jagadamba Temple and Chitragupta Temple seem narrower and unnaturally contorted in their posture. The narrow figures with their long legs and eccentric movements can also be found on the Jain temples Vamana and Adinatha. On Javari and Chaturbhuja temples, by contrast, the figures seem lifeless and already herald the decline of the sculptural tradition.

Lastly, Duladeo Temple stands out because of its richly adorned figures, which seem mannered and no longer express the strength and beauty of the earlier sculptures.

EROTICISM SET IN STONE

Art historians have had a hard time doing justice to the revealing Mithuna sculptures (couples in the act of lovemaking) in Khajuraho. If they are addressed at all, they are often condemned as pornographic.

Nevertheless travellers come from all around the world to look at these figures, which often seem like the picture book to go along with the *Kama Sutra*. Western visitors are generally used to seeing depictions of erotic scenes in Indian miniature painting, but they tend to be confused to find some of the most revealing sculptures on the **exterior façades of religious buildings**. However, life and love have always been closely connected to the Hindu religion.

It is not just the god Krishna, who has always been known as the darling of all women, and his love life that are described and depicted in detail in the temples. The polarity of opposites and the strength of their union is the central subject of stories around Shiva and Shakti, which culminates in their symbols, the lingam and the yoni (as phallus and vulva). In a famous legend about Shiva it is said that he withdrew to the mountains to meditate after his wife Sati had committed suicide. Subsequently the entire world started to wither, since the divine power of creation had been extinguished. Thus the divine council deci-

ded to get Shiva to fall in love with the goddess Parvati with the help of the god of love Kama. Through the union of Shiva and Parvati life was created again on Earth.

Generally speaking all of the Indian deities have wives, lead family lives and beget children. They fall in love, they are jealous and they thus **reflect human life**, in which love plays a very significant role.

No taboo

Naked human bodies, buxom women or couples entwined in the act of lovemaking can often be found in Jain and Hindu temples. The art of the Sunga period was already depicting Mithuna figures and they appeared again later in the art of Mathura and Amaravathi, which were shaped by Buddhism. As examples of erotic sculptures in temples there are those in Ranakpur, Modhera and Darasuram. The figures there are only small and are to be found in corners and edges, not in any central location. In Khajuraho on the other hand the **erotic depictions are the central subject**. Everywhere there are entwined

couples, ecstatic, rapturous faces and lovemaking positions that seem like circus acrobatics.

There is no satisfactory explanation as yet as to why specifically Khajuraho has so many striking Mithuna figures. Are they supposed to warn people of a debauched life or are they an encouragement? Are they meant to be symbolic of the strength that is created from the union of the lovers? Why did kings spend enormous sums to have these sculptures made and have temples decorated with them?

Tantra cult

It is assumed that the Chandellas, who had the temple complex built in the tenth–eleventh centuries, were followers of the Tantra cult. Tantrism, which developed around Shaktism, is the counter-movement to Buddhism, preaching asceticism, as well as to various tendencies of Shaivism. According to Tantrism it is not just the spiritual exercises (yoga) but also the physical pleasures (bhoga) that are a path to salvation.

A central point is that reality is seen as the result and expression of the symbiosis of the male (= Shiva) and female (= Shakti) principle. Opposites such as male/female, microcosm/macrocosm, sacred/profane and Shiva/Shakti are to be brought into synthesis.

In the tantric Panchtatwa ritual the student is instructed by a guru to indulge in five forbidden pleasures: wine, meat, fish, drugs and sex. The aim of breaking these taboos is to penetrate the opposites of the artificially divided world and to experience unity. Kali (an aspect of Shiva) is the central deity of this tendency. In this context the Mithuna figures, as a glorification of the ideas of the Tantra cult, could be a **symbol of the unification of the individual soul with the world soul**, of transcendence. Regardless of any interpretation, the erotic sculptures allow the conclusion that the people of Khajuraho 900 years ago saw love and physical joys as one of the many goals in life (purusharthas) and that they **neither condemned it nor made it a taboo**.

Indian society today is far from having a relaxed relationship to love and sexuality. While the depictions of sex in film and television are becoming ever more liberal and codes of behaviour in the large cities ever freer, the prudish moral stance of the middle class stands in the way of this trend.

Khajuraho Map

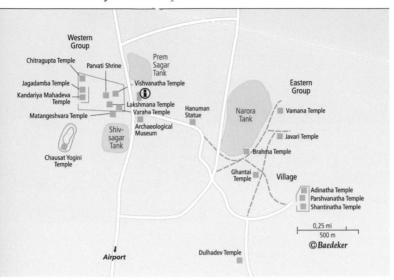

Western Group

The complex known as the Western Group includes Matangeshvara Temple outside of the walls as well as Lakshmana Temple (950), Vishvanatha Temple (1002), Chitragupta Temple and the particularly beautiful Kandariya Mahadeva Temple (1025–50). The Western Group is accessed via a gate and visitors have the option of seeing the five most important temples on a specially designed circuit.

✳ Lakshmana Temple

Lakshmana Temple illustrates the architectural concept of Khajuraho's temples the best since it is almost fully preserved in its interior, too. It is the only temple **still extant in its original form with the four corner shrines**. In a small hall in front of it is a Varaha, the wild boar incarnation of Vishnu. The temple's exterior walls bear depictions of gods, tightly embracing couples and many nymphs. The plinth is surrounded by a finely worked frieze, which also contains erotic depictions.

One of the friezes is dotted with many elephants, all of which are staring strictly ahead. There is an amusing depiction of an elephant, which is laughing and looking to the side so he can get a better look at a copulating couple. One of the best-known reliefs is the scene depicting a man amusing himself with his horse. The ceiling construction in the temple interior is held up by supports in the shape of women. Originally the ceiling had been adorned to an even greater extent and some of these figures can now be found in the Indian Museum in Kolkata. The sanctum contains a Vishnu figure with lion's head and a boar's head.

Kandariya Mahadeva Temple with its 31m/102ft tower is the **largest and most beautiful temple** in Khajuraho. It can be found at the far southwest corner of the park. Its entrance is crowned by a very nice stone arch and both the frieze around the temple and the main hall contain **wonderful sculptures**. The total number is said to be almost a thousand, of which many are a metre (three feet) tall. Some sculptures are of copulating couples, some of which are in quite acrobatic positions. The sculptural compositions seem very rhythmic and blend into the temple's overall architecture. Depending on the visitor's location the temple will reveal different perspectives. From the side visitors can see the gradual rise of the entrance halls, climaxing over the Garbagriha. From the front the temple resembles a narrow mountain surrounded by many small mountains, a representation of the mythical world-mountain, Meru. The Shiva Temple's sanctum has a large lingam on display.

★★ Kandariya Mahadeva Temple

On the sameplatform as Kandariya Mahadeva Temple is the smaller Jagadamba Temple consecrated to Parvati. It has some very nice sculptures. Between these temples are the remains of the Mahadeva shrine.

Jagadamba Temple

At the northwestern corner stands the eleventh-century **Chitragupta Temple**. It is dedicated to the sun god Surya, who is depicted on his chariot in the interior. Almost at the exit, at the northeastern side by the road is **Vishvanatha Temple** with the pavilion for Shiva's vehicle, Nandi, in front of it. It was built in 1002 and can, with its successively aspiring shikaras on the sculptural frieze running around the temple in three bands, be considered a prototype for all the other temples. Outside the surrounding wall on the left-hand side is the plain **Matangeshvara Temple**, which is the only one from the Western Group to be visited by believers on a daily basis.

Further temples

The museum opposite the Western Group allows visitors to see some of the figures depicted on the temple friezes at eye level. It should be remembered, however, that the sculptors designed the figures with their higher elevation in mind, thus some of them can seem somewhat out of proportion at eye level. The **dancing six-armed Ganesha** from the eleventh century in the entrance hall is particularly outstanding. Every one of his arms is adorned with a symbol that characterizes him. In his left lower hand he is holding a bowl with laddhus, sweets he likes to eat. Even while he is dancing he is using his trunk to eat a laddhu. Another interesting sculpture is that of **Shiva and Vishnu in a single figure**, known as Hari Hara. This sculpture illustrates the monotheistic understanding of Hinduism, which sees Vishnu, Shiva and other deities as mere facets of a single god.

Archaeological Museum
Opening hours:
daily except Fri
9am–5pm

The temples of the Eastern Group can be visited on a walk or by rickshaw. Of these temples the group consisting of the three Jain temples is particularly worth taking a look at.

Eastern Group

✷
Parshvanatha
Temple ▶

Parshvanatha Temple was originally consecrated to the first Jain ford-maker, Adinath, but it was later dedicated to the 23rd fordmaker Parshvanatha. The sculptures on its exterior façade contain very attractive depictions of Hindu deities (Hanuman, Sita, Rama) Particularly remarkable are the two female figures that can seemingly be observed applying kohl pencil or pulling a thorn from a foot.

Shantinatha Temple houses a huge 4.5m/15ft statue of Adinath, which completely fills the room in which it stands. The room next door contains a small photographic exhibition about the various Jain temples in India.

The neighbouring **Adinatha Temple** is somewhat smaller but it also has some very nice sculptures.

✷ ✷ Mumbai

C 10

Capital of Maharashtra	**Altitude:** Sea level
Population: 16 million	**Distance:** 1408km/875mi from Delhi

»Our Bombay: it looks like a hand but it's really a mouth, always open, always hungry« wrote author Salman Rushdie, seeing the geographical extent and the economic growth of the city of his birth.

25% of India's industry is concentrated in the conurbation of Mumbai. A third of the state's income tax is generated here and the city has an ever increasing number of resident dollar millionaires. It also boasts 20 of the world's billionaires (London is home to 36). However, half of its 16 million inhabitants live in shanties along the rail tracks and slums such as Dharavi, the largest in all of Asia. Apartment blocks whose rents can be compared to those of European cities and exclusive residential areas such as Malabar Hill, Juhu and Bandra lie side by side with the slums. Land is constantly being reclaimed from the sea at the southern tip of the 2km/1mi–5km/3mi wide and around 30km/20mi long peninsula in order to create the space for new banks, office blocks, apartments and shopping centres in the city centre. Property prices in downtown Mumbai are currently booming more than anywhere else in the world.

Like no other place in India, Mumbai on the subcontinent's west coast attracts people. Every day many new arrivals come to the city,

! **Baedeker TIP**

Mumbai in literature

There is a long list of authors who have been inspired by the city in their work. Some of the best examples are Salman Rushdie's *Midnight's Children*, Kiran Nagarkar's *Ravan and Eddie* and Manil Suri's *The Death of Vishnu*.

lured in by its dubious reputation of being able to provide everyone with work and their daily bread. However, »Bom Bahia« (the good bay), as it was first called by the Portuguese, is a gold mine only for a certain portion of the population: money flows into Nariman Point, Mumbai's bank and business district in Dalal Street, where Asia's oldest stock exchange has its headquarters, into the studios of Bollywood (► Baedeker Special p.112), where most of the world's films are produced, and into Navi Mumbai, the new satellite town at the eastern end of this great city, where many foreign companies have located.

Science and culture

Mumbai is a **centre of science**. Many universities, colleges and research institutions such as the renowned Tata Institute for Social Sciences are based here. In addition the city enjoys a colourful and extremely **lively arts and culture scene**. The National Center for Performing Arts (NCPA) at Nariman Point has regular performances and concerts of international standing playing in several theatres. In addition to the permanent exhibition in the new Gallery of Modern Arts on MG Road there are several galleries with changing exhibitions featuring works by modern artists. They give an insight into the extremely diverse and active Indian arts scene. The best-known is Jehangir Art Gallery, also on MG Road.

Marine Drive: the impressive six-lane coastal road

Mumbai Map

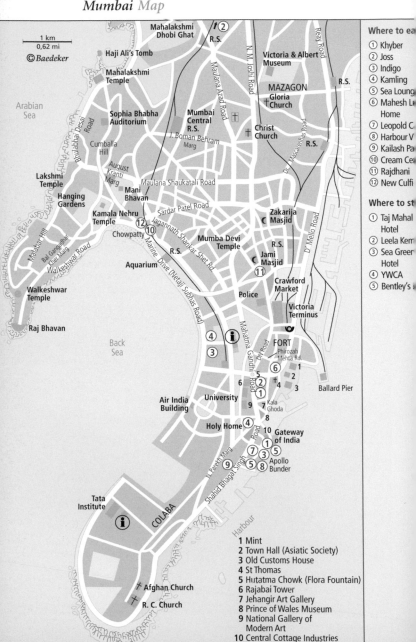

1 km
0,62 mi
©Baedeker

Mahalakshmi
Dhobi Ghat
R.S.

Haji Ali's Tomb

Mahalakshmi
Temple

Arabian
Sea

Victoria & Albert
Museum

MAZAGON
Gloria
Church

N.M. Josh Road

Reay Road

R.S.

Sophia Bhabha
Auditorium

Mumbai
Central
R.S.

Cumballa
Hill

J. Boman Behram
Marg

Christ
Church

R.S.

Maulana Azad Road

Dr. Mascarenhas Road

Lakshmi
Temple

August
Kranti
Marg

Maulana Shaukatali Road

Mani
Bhavan

Hanging
Gardens

Kamala Nehru
Temple

Bhulabhai Desai Road

Sardar Patel Road

Zakarija
Masjid

Jagannath Shankar Shet Rd.

Mumba Devi
Temple

R.S.

Jami
Masjid

D'Mello Road

Lakshmi
Temple

Walkeshwar Road

Bal Gangadhar Khar Marg

Chowpatty

Marine Drive (Netaji Subhas Road)

R.S.

Aquarium

Police

Crawford
Market

Victoria
Terminus

Walkeshwar
Temple

Malabar Hill

Back
Sea

Mahatma Gandhi Road

Dr. Road

FORT
Phirozah
Mehta Rd.

Raj Bhavan

1
6
2
3
Ballard Pier

Air India
Building

University

5
2
6
9
1
4
+
7
8
Kala
Ghoda

Holy Home

4
10 Gateway
of India

Tata
Institute

COLABA

N Parekh Marg

Shahid Bhagat Singh

7
3
5

9
5
8

1
5
Apollo
Bunder

Harbour

Afghan Church

R. C. Church

1 Mint
2 Town Hall (Asiatic Society)
3 Old Customs House
4 St Thomas
5 Hutatma Chowk (Flora Fountain)
6 Rajabai Tower
7 Jehangir Art Gallery
8 Prince of Wales Museum
9 National Gallery of
  Modern Art
10 Central Cottage Industries

Where to ea
① Khyber
② Joss
③ Indigo
④ Kamling
⑤ Sea Loung
⑥ Mahesh Lu
   Home
⑦ Leopold C
⑧ Harbour V
⑨ Kailash Pa
⑩ Cream Ce
⑪ Rajdhani
⑫ New Culfi

Where to st
① Taj Mahal
   Hotel
② Leela Kem
③ Sea Green
   Hotel
④ YWCA
⑤ Bentley's

▶ VISITING MUMBAI

INFORMATION

Government of India Tourist Office
123, Maharishi Karve Road
(opposite Churchgate station)
Tel. 022 – 22 03 31 44
Here visitors can obtain a copy of the regularly published information brochure about cultural events in Mumbai (open Mon–Fri 8.30am–6pm, Sat 8.30am–2pm).

Maharashtra Tourism
near the Gateway of India
Tel. 022 – 22 84 18 77
Organized city tours start here; at the weekends they also take place at night in red double-decker buses. General information can also be found on the website of the state of Maharashtra (www.mtdcindia.com).

»Time Out Mumbai«
Fortnightly city listings magazine

FESTIVALS

Mumbai is a Mecca for fans of classical Indian music. Between December and February countless festivals are held in the city. The most important ones are: St Xavier's Festival, Banganga Festival (first weekend in January), Elephanta Festival (end of Jan / beginning of Feb) and Kala Ghoda Festival (Jan / Feb). The exact dates can be obtained from the Tourist Office or in the Rhythm House music shop (see below).

SHOPPING

One of the most important shopping streets is Shahid Bhagat Singh Road (Colaba Causeway) in the district of Colaba, and its side streets; there are also many interesting shops in Mahatma Gandhi Road and in Phirozah Mehta Road in the district of Fort.

During the Ganesh Chaturthi (Aug / Sept) statues of the gods are brought to the sea and dunked under water

Further shopping streets can be found around the intersection of Kemps Corner / Bhulabhai Desai Road (previously Warden Road) and in Linking Road in the district of Bandra. The bazaar streets around Abdul Rehman Street in Mumbai's old town are also very interesting.

Not far away is Chor Bazaar, a quarter with many antique shops; every Friday a street market also takes place here.

Baedeker recommendation

Fabric heaven
Silk, linen, cotton in every colour, scarves, fabric and printed blankets can all be found in Mangaldas Market, a large textiles market in the heart of the old town (near Crawford Market). This is several hundred square metres of absolute heaven for fans of Indian fabrics.

Rhythm House
Kala Ghoda; Fort district
Excellent music shop; concert tickets can also be bought here.

The Bombay Store
Phirozah Mehta Road
A good place to buy nice presents for the folks back home.

Strand Book Stall
Diagonally opposite Bombay Store. Very well organized little book shop with knowledgeable staff. Upon request books can be sent home by mail.

Fab India
MG Road / Kala Ghoda
Indian textiles of all different varieties, from shirts to scarves to curtains.

Nalanda Book and Record Shop
Inside the Taj Mahal Hotel
This shop also has a good selection of books and CDs.

Bombay Khadi Village Industries Emporium
286 D. N. Road, Fort
Goods from the Gandhi production sites, from hand-woven cotton fabrics to honey.

Chimanlals
A-2, Taj Building
210 D. N. Road, Fort
Continuing along D. N. Road from the Gandhi shop towards VT station, visitors can find this wonderful paper shop in a somewhat hidden location in a side street to the left.

Cottage Industries Emporium
State-run shop with a large selection of arts and crafts, Chhatrapati Shivaji Marg, Colaba, near Gateway of India

GOING OUT
Mumbai has the largest number of bars, lounges, discos and nightclubs in the whole of India. Juhu and Bandra are two quarters considered particularly chic. However, the south of Mumbai, where most tourists are based, also has a good selection in this regard, such as:

Geoffreys
In the Marine Plaza hotel on Marine Drive
Serves tasty cocktails and the Indian treats are addictive.

Not just Jazz by the Bay
Next to »The Pizzeria«, also on Marine Drive, with live music or karaoke

Indigo
This restaurant in Colaba (see below) has a very nice lounge.

List of the hip eateries
www.explocity.com/mumbai/nightlife

WHERE TO EAT
▶ Expensive
① *Khyber*
145, Mahatma Gandhi Road
Kala Ghoda
Tel. 022 – 22 67 32 27
One of the best restaurants for northern Indian cuisine.

② *Joss*
30 K, Dubash Marg
Kala Ghoda, tel. 022 – 66 35 69 08
Excellent Southeast Asian specialities, tasty starters.

③ *Indigo*
4, Mandlik Road
Colaba
Tel. 022 – 56 36 89 80
Mediterranean cuisine in a stylish

ambience with a garden and a roof terrace.

④ *Kamling*
84, Veer Nariman Road
Churchgate
Tel. 022 – 22 04 26 18
Excellent Chinese cuisine, very good starters and soups.

⑤ *Sea Lounge*
In the Taj Mahal hotel
visitors can enjoy a »high tea« or a cappuccino as well as good snacks while taking in the first-class views of the sea.

► **Moderate**
⑥ *Mahesh Lunch Home*
8-B, Cawasji Patel Street
a side street of Phirozah Mehta Road
Fort
Tel. 022 – 22 87 09 38
Fish specialities prepared southwest-coast style; the pancakes (neer dosa) should definitely be tried as a side dish!

Relaxing by the pool of the Taj Palace Hotel

⑦ *Leopold Café*
Shahid Bhagat Singh Road
Colaba
Tel. 022 – 22 82 81 85
Multicuisine restaurant and bar, traditional meeting place for travellers.

⑧ *Harbour View hotel*
Apollo Bunder
opposite Radio Club
Tel. 022 – 22 84 11 97
Roof-terrace restaurant with great views of the port; best for long evenings accompanied by music and good tandoori dishes.

► **Inexpensive**
⑨ *Kailash Parbat*
1st Pasta Lane
Side street of Shahid Bhagat Singh
Road
Colaba
Tel. 022 – 22 87 48 23
North Indian vegetarian cuisine, local snacks such as Bhelpuri and Dahi Puri, many different sweets.

⑩ *Cream Center*
Fulchand Niwas
Opposite Chowpatty beach
Tel. 022 – 23 67 92 22
Large selection of flat breads and northern Indian vegetarian snacks.

⑪ *Rajdhani*
Opposite Mangaldas Market
near Crawford Market
Tel. 022 – 23 44 90 14
Vegetarian thalis (various dishes served on a single plate) in the styles of cuisines from Rajasthan and Gujarat.

⑫ *New Kulfi Center*
By Aaren Bridge opposite Chowpatty beach
This establishment serves Mumbai's best ice cream (kulfi); visitors should not miss the pistachio almond ice cream (badam-pista) and the mango ice cream.

WHERE TO STAY
▶ Luxury
① *The Taj Palace Hotel*
Apollo Bunder; Colaba
Tel. 022 – 66 65 33 66
One of the most famous and traditional hotels in Asia, directly next to Mumbai's landmark, the Gateway of India. Several very good restaurants and bars make life here even sweeter for its guests. The hotel was targeted during the 2008 terrorist attacks.

② *The Leela Kempinski*
Sahar, near the international airport
Tel. 022 – 66 91 12 34
Luxury hotel with all the creature comforts and good restaurants, very popular amongst business people because of its location.

▶ Mid-range
③ *Sea Green Hotel*
145 Marine Drive
Tel. 022 – 66 33 65 25
www.seagreenhotel.com
Spacious, clean rooms with balcony and magnificent views of the sea and the promenade.

▶ Mid-range / Budget
④ *YWCA*
18 Madame Cama Road; Fort
Tel. 022 – 22 02 50 53
Clean and very well run hotel with a small dining room (breakfast and dinner included in the price). Centrally located, book in good time!

⑤ *Bentley's Hotel*
17, Oliver Road; Colaba
Tel. 022 – 22 84 14 74
www.bentleyshotel.com
Rooms of varying sizes, centrally located, breakfast is included.

History	up until the 14th century	Home of the Koli people, Hindu and Muslim rulers
	1534	Portuguese colonial rule
	1661	British rule: Bombay is expanded into a trading centre of the Indian west coast, immense immigration
	1885	Founding of the Indian National Congress in Bombay
	1996	Official renaming of the city to Mumbai
	2008	Terrorists attack several targets in Mumbai

Originally Mumbai consisted of seven islands inhabited by the Koli fishing people. These were Colaba, Mahim, Mazgaon, Parel, Worli, Girgaum and Dongri, from which districts in the city still get their names. The city's name **Mumbai**, which has now been reintroduced, probably comes from Mumba Devi, the Koli patron goddess. The fishing community still makes up a part of Mumbai's population, albeit a small one. The Koli people also still live from fishing as well as the processing and sale of fish.

During the European Middle Ages the area was governed by both Hindu and Muslim rulers and in 1534 it fell into the hands of the Portuguese colonial power, which gave it the name **Bom Bahia** (good bay) because of its excellently protected natural harbour along this stretch of coastline. Bom Bahia fell into the hands of the rival colonial power, the British, in 1661, in the shape of a dowry which the Portuguese Infanta Catherine of Braganza brought to her marriage with Charles II of England. He leased the land for a symbolic ten pounds to the East India Company, whereupon the new trading post was developed under Governor Gerald Aungier. Marshes were drained and the various islands were connected to each other by filling in the land between them. Bom Bahia became the English **Bombay**. This new settlement attracted people from far and wide: merchants (mostly Parsi and Jains) from Surat further to the north, Muslims from Persia and the western stretch of coastline, Jews, Christians, Sikhs and even Chinese traders. The bulk of the necessary labourers and craftsmen came from the Marathas of the surrounding area, who were predominantly Hindus. This created a colourful mix

Highlights *Mumbai*

Prince of Wales Museum
Particularly famous for its lovely miniature and sculpture collections
► page 480

Marine Drive and Chowpatty beach
A walk along the promenade to the beach at sunset is a must.
► page 485

Taj Mahal Hotel
Tea break in the Taj, India's most famous hotel (fig. p.420, 477)
► page 489

Elephanta Island
Visit the island and the rock caves by boat.
► page 488

Gateway of India
Whether at sunrise, noon or in the late evening, there is always something going on here!
► page 483

Chhatrapati Shivaji (Victoria Terminal)
The station combines colonial architecture and the bustle of city life.
► page 481

MG Road and DN Road to CST station
Mumbai's busy centre with many nice shops and restaurants
► page 481

Chor Bazaar
The »Thieves' Market« has a large selection of antiques.
► page 485

Crawford Market and Mangaldas Market
A shopping Mecca
► page 484

of peoples, which made Bombay the most multicultural city in India. It is the point of origin of many economic, political and cultural impulses.

The city continued to grow after a connection to the newly accessed island of Salsette was created in 1776. In the mid-19th century its population was around a quarter of a million. At that time the Maratha hinterland with its cotton plantations was opened up by the construction of a railway line. This contributed the fast growth of the textiles industry. Bombay's great hour came when the British were no longer able to cover their cotton needs from America as a result of the War of Independence. This sudden wealth was also reflected in the cityscape and found expression in the many representative buildings by the state, the administration and affluent citizens, while the negative consequences of colonization, industrialization and urbanization also afflicted Bombay. It was no coincidence that the Indian National Congress was founded here in 1885 and to this day the immediately obvious social differences dominate both politics and the streets.

In November 2008 Mumbai was targeted in a series of coordinated terror strikes. The terrorists, allegedly from the Pakistan-based militant group Lashkar-e-Taiba, raided a number of the city's institutions in more than ten shooting and bombing attacks in which at least 173 people lost their lives.

The District of Fort

Streetscape

The district of Fort is home to a large number of buildings dating from the British colonial period. Its name goes back to the fort the British built here. The walk described below leads past the most important attractions and gives some tips for the many shopping opportunities.

★ ★
Chhatrapati Shivaji Vaastu Sanghralaya (Prince of Wales Museum)

The circuit is best started at the upper end of Mahatma Gandhi Road at the Prince of Wales Museum. Mumbai's most important museum, it was built in 1905 by the architect George Wittet in imitation of the Mughal style. Set in an attractively landscaped garden, the building contains a large collection of sculptures, an archaeological department and a natural history department, a collection of India weapons, brocades and precious saris as well as Chinese porcelain. The museum's pride and joy are its **miniatures** on the first floor, featuring some particularly beautiful animal depictions by the Mughal school as well as portrayals of Shiva, Parvati and Krishna from the Pahari school of the 19th century (open: daily except Mon 10.15am–6pm).

Jehangir Art Gallery

To the left of the museum is the Jehangir Art Gallery, which, with its changing exhibition, provides insights into the modern Indian art scene. Visitors can stop for a break directly opposite in the Chetana, a restaurant serving tasty vegetarian Gujarati dishes, or stop by in

The Prince-of-Wales-Museum

Rhythm House, a very well organized music shop to the left of the restaurant, to listen to the sounds of Ravi Shankar and the newest Bollywood hits.

On the other side of MG Road is the **National Gallery of Modern Art** with paintings by the best-known Indian artists of the 20th century (open: daily except Mon 11am–6pm).
North of it are a number of prestige buildings from the 19th century. The traditional Elphinstone College, various university buildings constructed in 1874 in the French Gothic style, the **David Sassoon Library** and the **High Court** of Mumbai with its 170m/186yd façade featuring Venetian and Early-English Gothic styles.

Next visitors will come to the busy Hutatma Chowk (Place of Martyrs), named in remembrance of those who fought for an independent Maharashtra. This place used be called **Flora Fountain**, after the fountain erected in honour of Governor Sir Henry Frere in 1869.

Hutatma Chowk

Leave Mahatma Gandhi Road now and turn into the main shopping street, Dr Dadabhai Navroji Road (DN Road), which leads directly to Chhatrapathi Shivaji Terminal (CST). To the right and left of the road are further neo-Gothic buildings, beneath whose arcades merchants offer their goods for sale. Everything from silk scarves to wood carvings and dried fruit to French perfume can be bought here.

DN Road

Take the left-hand side street and walk past the Thomas Cook bureau de change to get to the well known Khadi Village Industries Emporium a few metres further on. Here visitors can buy hand woven Gandhi cotton shirts and handicraft products.
To the right of DN Road towards VT is **Phirozah Mehta Road**, a further important shopping street, where Strand Book Stall, one of Mumbai's best book shops, and various state-run shops for arts and crafts are located.

Khadi Village Industries Emporium

Continue along DN Road for five minutes to get to Nagar Chowk, a large square dominated by the imposing Chhatrapathi Shivaji Terminus (formerly Victoria Terminus) built between 1878 and 1887. The station is the most beautiful of the buildings in the Indo-Gothic mixed style and, with its magnificent dome reminiscent of the late Gothic style, it can be seen from a great way off. The model for the **largest building of British India** was St Pancras station in London. The façades, ornamented with lavishly decorative details, combine a

Nagar Chowk

◄ Chhatrapathi Shivaji Terminus (Victoria Terminus)

Imposing: the largest building of British India was a station, Chhatrapati Shivaji Terminus (formerly Victoria Terminus)

large number of animals and fabulous creatures. The work was executed by the Mumbai Art School under its director John Lockwood Kipling, father of the famous author.

General Post Office

Directly opposite stands the tower of the Municipal Corporation, another building with neo-Gothic, oriental features. Anyone wanting to send letters, postcards and parcels back home can quickly get to the General Post Office (GPO), by going past the south side of Chhatrapati Shivaji Terminus and crossing the station's taxi entrance. The post office is the next building, and it also has an oriental appearance.

Horniman Circle

From here there are several options for exploring this part of Mumbai further: the first route leads from Nagar Chowk via Walchand Hirachand Marg to Sahid Bhaghat Singh Road, just a few metres beyond Walchand Hirachand Marg on the right-hand side. This route leads to Horniman Circle, around which there are a number of former British buildings: the Mint, built in 1829, to the east the Town Hall (1833), now the seat of the Asiatic Society, and further south the old Custom House of 1720. This place is also one of the small, quiet oases in the middle of the busy centre: the attractively landscaped **Horniman Gardens**, where there are plenty of benches on which to sit down and relax.

Leave the park in a westerly direction to get to Veer Nariman Road, which leads back to Hutatma Chowk. On its south side is the old St Thomas Cathedral dating from 1718. Its interior not only invites visitors to spend some time in quiet contemplation, it also takes them into the lost world of the British Raj. Several commemorative plaques were set up in remembrance of the fates of the former servants of the British crown.

St Thomas Cathedral

⊙ Opening hours:
daily 6.30am–6pm

Those wanting to see the old university or obtain information in the Tourist Office should go back from Chhatrapati Shivaji Terminus to Hutatma Chowk and turn right into Veer Nariman Road (VN Road). VN Road crosses Bhaurao Patil Marg and leads directly to Churchgate Station. The tourist office is opposite.

Tourist Information

Go back to B. Patil Marg and turn right to get to Mumbai University, which was founded in 1857 and completed in 1874. The complex, with its 80m/262ft neo-Gothic Rajabai Tower, is situated in an attractive garden and was designed by the architect Sir Gilbert Scott. Leave the university behind and head in a southward direction to get to Madame Cama Road. To the left is the huge building of the Indian Institute of Science on the corner to Mahatma Gandhi Road.

University and Rajabai Tower

The District of Colaba

The district of Colaba, whose name is still reminiscent of Mumbai's old inhabitants the Koli fishing people, is the peninsula's southernmost tip. Souvenir shops and hotels have clustered in this area. The most famous Indian luxury hotel is also located here, the traditional **Taj Mahal Hotel**, built in 1903 and extended in 1972 by the Taj Intercontinental. On 26 November 2008 the hotel was damaged in a terrorist attack on a number of Mumbai institutions that killed at least 173 people. The hotel reopened in December 2008 and is in the process of being rebuilt. A visit to »Nalanda«, the book shop on the ground floor, is recommended.

Streetscape

Just a few metres away is the Gateway of India, the best-known of Mumbai's buildings. It was built in 1911 as a plaster pavilion on the occasion of the visit to India by King George V and Queen Mary. It was later redesigned by English architect George Wittet as a massive archway made of yellow basalt. The Gateway is now **a meeting place for tourists, jugglers, sweets sellers and drug dealers**. Boats to Elephanta depart from here and visitors can also go on small boat trips of the harbour.

★ ★
Gateway of India

Mumbai's emblem: the Gateway of India

Afghan Church Apart from the Gateway and the Taj Mahal Hotel, Colaba has one other, older attraction: the Afghan Church at the end of Sahid Bhaghat Singh Road. It was built in 1847 in the neo-Gothic style and commemorates those who fell in the first Anglo-Afghan War.

Shopping This part of town is particularly interesting to tourists because of its shopping opportunities. Many shops are located on S. B. Singh Road and its side streets. On Shivaji Maharaji Marg, which leads from the Gateway to Mukherji Chowk, is Central Cottage Industries, the large state-run shop for handicrafts with a very good selection of Indian products.

Old Town

Streetscape An excursion to Mumbai's old town is definitely worthwhile because it is only down the narrow alleys and along the bazaar streets that visitors will get a real impression of life in an Indian city. Since it is easy for outsiders to get lost in the labyrinthine streets it is a good idea to be accompanied by a knowledgeable local. Guides can be found through the tourist office in M. Karve Road.

★
Crawford Market A stroll through this part of town is best begun at Mahatma Phule Market, also known under its old name Crawford Market. It can be reached in just a few minutes from the Chhatrapathi Shivaji Termi-

nus by walking northwards up Navroji Road. Before diving into the half-light of the extensive market halls, take a look at the semi-circular **frieze above the main entrance**. It depicts heavily laden farmers returning home from the harvest and was designed by John Lockwood Kipling. Crawford Market is particularly turbulent in the early mornings when the fruit and vegetable sellers pick up their goods. The interested buyer will be able to find everything here: in addition to mountains of fruit and vegetables, the entire spectrum of Indian spices as well as colourful parrots, chickens and other small animals (see recommendation p.481) can also be bought here.

North of the market is the beginning of the »real« old town with its bazaars such as the gold and silver bazaar, the textile bazaar and many more. Its streets are overflowing with cars honking their horns, heavily laden carts, ranting load carriers making their way through the congested streets and bored-looking cows. The bustling markets are particularly busy during the cooler evening hours when the many lamps come alight in the Muslim quarter around Mohammed Ali Street and Abdul Rehman Street. Quite nearby is Jama Masjid, the city's largest mosque.

Bazaars

> ! **Baedeker** TIP
>
> ### Delicacies during Ramadan
> During the Islamic month of fasting, Ramadan, some Muslim quarters turn into a gourmet's dream. It gets particularly busy around Abdul Rehman Street and Jama Masjid: exquisitely cooked goats' tongues, syrup pancakes (malpua) and firni (spiced rice pudding) are now considered fancy treats amongst connoisseurs.

Another attraction is Chor Bazar (Thieves' Market) located in the district of Bhendi Bazaar, where everything from used portable radios to old gramophones, Chinese vases and Indian miniatures can be bought. On Fridays a street market is also held.

Chor Bazar

Mumba Devi Temple, built in honour of Mumbai's patron goddess is also nearby. It is around 200 years old and houses a statue of the goddess from whom the city gets its name.

Mumba Devi Temple

Western Mumbai

The route in the west of the city can be completed partially on foot, partially by taxi or bus or in several stages.

Tip

The well-known Air India Building at Nariman Point, the banking and business district, is a good starting point for a round trip. This is also the beginning of Marine Drive, an approximately 1.5km/1mi semicircular promenade along the seafront.
It used to also be called **»the Queen's Necklace«**, after the sparkling fairy lights that can already be seen when flying into Mumbai at night. Going for a walk here during the hour of sunset is particularly

★
Marine Drive

nice as it can be seen from here. Passing peanut and coconut sellers, snake charmers and joggers, visitors will reach the city beach Chowpatty just in time for dusk.The city's inhabitants meet here in the evenings to refresh themselves over bhelpuri, ice cream or freshly pressed fruit juice. It is best however, not to go for a dip.

✳
Chowpatty ▶

Mani Bhavan (Gandhi Museum)

🕐
Opening hours:
Museum daily
9.30–6pm
Library Mon–Fri
9.30am–6pm, Sat
9.30am–2pm

Looking eastwards from Chowpatty in the Gamdevi district, there is a remarkable little museum, the Mani Bhavan, showing India's fight for independence and featuring particularly its leading figure, **Mahatma Gandhi**. Gandhi spent some time living in this building. In addition to the museum it houses a library containing 47,000 volumes, including works by the Mahatma and books on the history of the independence movement. The room in which Gandhi lived, and glass cabinets in which the most important stages of his life have been recreated, are two of the main tourist attractions. At the entrance visitors can buy extracts from the great man's works and further reading.

Malabar Hill

North of the sandy bay of Chowpatty is Malabar Hill, one of the preferred addresses for high society. There is a Jain temple at its foot on the south side. Further west is Walkeshwar Temple. Its origins go back to the eleventh century.

From **Kamala Nehru Park** (also known as the Hanging Gardens) visitors can enjoy an attractive view of Marine Drive and the southern part of the peninsula. From the park visitors can also see the **»Towers of Silence«**, where the Parsi religious community dispose of their dead by exposing the corpses to the vultures and the elements.

In the western section of Malabar Hill is the attractive pool known as **Banganga Tank**, surrounded by small temples.

Kemps Corner

B. G. Kher Marg leads back down the hill to the busy Kemps Corner, where Bhulabhai Desai Road (formerly Warden Road) begins. It is one of Mumbai's shopping streets.

Haji Ali Tomb

Follow the road northwards to get to the narrow walkway that leads to the tomb of the Muslim saint Haji Ali. The tomb and the small mosque are built on a rock in the sea. To the right of the walkway is the Haji Ali Juice Center with excellent, freshly pressed fruit juices. A few metres along the wide Tardeo Road opposite visitors will find »Cross Walks«, the big new shopping centre.

Mahalakshmi Temple

On the rock above the sea somewhat south of Haji Ali's tomb stands Mahalakshmi Temple. It is best accessed via an alley off Warden Road. The temple is consecrated to the goddess Lakshmi; the current building dates back to the 18th century.

Mahalakshmi Dhobi Ghat

A more profane but no less interesting outfit also bears the name of the goddess Mahalakshmi. Located near the Metro station of the same name, the Mahalakshmi Dhobi Ghat is a typically Indian institution, namely a **large laundry quarter**. Every day the launderers (dhobis) wash, dry and iron mountains of dirty laundry in long rows of brick basins. It is particularly busy here during the morning. The hustle and bustle can be observed from a bridge leading over this quarter.

Suburbs

Mumbai's northern districts have hardly any classic attractions to offer. However, those interested in the city's history should visit the old Victoria and Albert Museum, now called **Veermata Jeejamata Museum**. It can be found in a botanical garden in the district of **Byculla**. It has an interesting photographic exhibition on the development of Mumbai.

Veermata Jeejamata Museum
🕐
Opening hours:
daily except Wed
10am–5pm

The suburb of Juhu near the airport, where many film stars own villas and a large proportion of tourists find hotels, is an attraction be-

Juhu beach

At Mahalakshmi Dhobi Ghat the men from the Dhobi caste wash and iron laundry

cause of Juhu beach, which gets particularly busy during the weekends. Riding horses and camels is particularly **enjoyable for children**. Food and drink can be bought from one of the countless stalls or beach restaurants. However, visitors should also abstain from bathing here.

✴ ✴ Elephanta

Temples chiselled into the rock

Only 10km/6mi northeast of the Gateway of India is the small island of Elephanta, which should not be left out of any longer stay in Mumbai. The 8 sq km/3 sq mi island is home to mango, tamarind and carissa trees and its **Shiva cave temple** is worth taking a look at. Originally known by the name of Gharapuri, the island has been called Elephanta since the Portuguese occupation. It got its name because of a huge stone elephant the Portuguese found when they landed here. Its remains can now be found in the Victoria Gardens in Mumbai.

Elephanta has a total of **five rock caves**, which were presumably created by Buddhist monks as their shape is reminiscent of the many other rock viharas all over Maharashtra. This cave was later made into Shiva temples. Opinions vary as to the exact date this occurred. Estimates range from the seventh to the tenth centuries. Unfortunately many of the temples are severely damaged, which probably happened during the period of Portuguese occupation, when the sculptures were degraded to targets for shooting practice.

Main cave
🕐
Opening hours:
9am–5.30pm

The main cave with the famous three-headed Shiva is best reached from the Sheth Bunder landing stage via a stairway that makes its way up the hill. The cave is about 5m/16ft high and supported by 36 columns (approx. 48 sq m/57 sq yd). It consists of a central hall that can be accessed via three entrances at the east, north and west sides. Opposite the main entrance in the north is the shrine with the three-headed Shiva, west of it is the central shrine with the Shiva lingam. Leave the cave via a side passage to get to further secondary shrines.

✴ ✴
Three-headed Shiva ►

The temple's actual focal point is the panel with the three-headed Shiva (Shiva Mahashamurti), flanked by two guards (dvarapalas). The 6m/20ft sculpture depicts the god Shiva as Maheshamurti, as great lord in all three aspects, namely as **creator, preserver and destroyer of the world**. This is one of the most impressive depictions of the trimurti, which are usually found on the three highest gods of the Hindu pantheon, namely Brahma (creator), Vishnu (preserver) and Shiva (destroyer).

To the left of it is a very fine sculpture of Shiva as Ardhanarishvara, as**half man, half woman**, which is very well preserved because of its protected location. To the right is a depiction of the well-known myth of the descent of Ganga to Earth (►Baedeker Special p.290). The various side wings and secondary shrines have further depictions from the countless stories of the Shiva myth, some of which are damaged.

East of the main hall are two further severely damaged caves, whose **Viharas** shape is quick to reveal their original function as viharas for Buddhist monks. Behind the last cave there is a small path to the right leading up to the top of the small hill, into which the temples were carved. From there visitors will have a wonderful panoramic view of the island. The other small hill has the two remaining caves, which are, however, in very bad condition.

Boats depart for the island every hour, except during the monsoon **Getting there** season. They dock directly at the Gateway of India. Visitors can take advantage of fully organized sightseeing tours as well as of simple boat trips, which are best for those who want to explore the island on their own. Tickets can be bought on the boats. Those who can should avoid going to Elephanta on Sundays and on public holidays, since the small island gets extremely busy during those times.

Around Mumbai: Near Vicinity

No protected area anywhere in India borders so closely (35km/22mi **Sanjay Gandhi** north of Mumbai's city centre) to the outskirts of a city as **Sanjay** **National Park** **Gandhi National Park**, also known as Borivili Park. Visitors can take the train (Western Railway from Churchgate to Borivili) all the way to the national park entrance. The 94 sq km/36 sq mi park contains two lakes and the Buddhist caves of Kanheri, which should not be missed. The hilly forested area is home to **various deer species** such as sambar deer and chital as well as to monkeys and wild boars and a sizable number of leopards. Ornithologists have counted more than 250 different bird species here. Mugger crocodiles also live in one of the two lakes.

The Kanheri Caves in Sanjay Gandhi National Park consist of **109** **Kanheri Caves** **Buddhist caves** that have been carved into the rock at various heights. The first ones were presumably created during the second century, while the most recent date back to the ninth century. Most of the monks' cells are relatively small but possess a columned veranda that is connected to the forecourt via a stairway. The complex cannot be compared to the caves in Ajanta or Ellora but still provides an insight into Buddhist architecture across several periods.
The uncompleted cave temple (chaitya no. 3) right at the beginning ★ of the small valley, presumably from the second century, is worth ◄ Cave temple seeing. A richly ornamented stone fence surrounds the forecourt. Guards (dvarapalas) stand on both sides of the entrance, which has recently been given the extra support of concrete columns. To the left and right of the central entrance are Mithuna couples and above them sitting Buddhas. The temple's interior is divided into a central

hall and two narrow side aisles by 34 columns, some of which are decorated with artistically chiselled capitals.

Further northeast is the **Maharaja Cave** or Durbar Hall, the largest of the viharas (no. 10). After passing the forecourt there is a stairway leading up to the entrance of the cave, which is one of the complex's most recent. There are twelve cells on its east and south sides. Opposite the entrance is a sitting **Buddha statue** with companions. Those who are interested can discover further fine sculptures during a more extensive tour, such as the statue of the eleven-headed Avalokiteshvara in no. 41. Caves nos. 64, 66 and 67 are also decorated with impressive depictions from the Mahayana period. Somewhat further south, above the Chaitya Hall, is vihara no. 90. It also contains a sitting Buddha statue with his companions Padmapani and Vajrapani in high relief.

Nashik with its hundreds of temples and ghats attracts many pilgrims

Around Mumbai: Further Afield

Nashik (187km/116mi northeast of Mumbai, population 730,000) is **Nashik** not usually on the itinerary of foreign tourists. Visitors with a bit more time on their hands can make a stop in this town on the way from Mumbai to Aurangabad. The Buddhist caves of Pandu Lena 8km/5mi away are worth seeing. Visitors will also get an impression of the busy goings-on in one of the centres of Indian pilgrimage. For pious Hindus a trip here is a real highlight, particularly when the **Kumbha Mela** takes place here as it does every twelve years (►Baedeker Special p.392). Like Varanasi, Allahabad, Ujjain and Haridwar, this town on the river Godavari is one of India's holiest places.

As is the case for many holy sites, the river in Nashik is also lined by **ghats**, temples and shrines. According to official figures there are more than 200 religious sites here. The oldest is Kapaleshvara Temple from the 14th century. Nearby there is another sought-after destination for pilgrims, namely Ram Kund. This water basin is said to have been used by Shiva to cleanse himself of his sins. Other major Hindu attractions are Kala Ram Temple and Sita Cave. According to legend Sita was abducted from here by the demon Ravana and taken to Lanka.

Time and again groups of caves have been discovered in Maharashtra **★** and a particularly large number of them are **Buddhist rock temples**, **Pandu Lena** such as the ones in Pandu Lena (8km/5mi southeast of Nashik). Carved into the hill at a height of 90m/295ft are one chaitya and 22 viharas. The oldest were presumably created as early as the first century BC, while the most recent ones date back to the sixth and seventh centuries. In addition to the chaitya (no. 18) with a magnificent, partially destroyed façade and the interior with an apse and stupa, vihara no. 3 is particularly impressive as a nice example of early Buddhist rock architecture. Of the remaining viharas, nos. 8, 10, 15, 17 and 20 are the most worthwhile. Cave no. 17, next to the chaitya hall, dates from the late Mahayana period.

Lonavala (90km/55mi southeast of Mumbai), on the train line from **Lonavala** Mumbai to Pune, is one of the hill stations in the Western Ghats and a **popular holiday destination** for the stressed inhabitants of Mumbai. Lonavala is a good base for a visit to the early Buddhist cave complexes of Karla, Bhaja and Bedsa, because all of these attractions can be visited by taxi or motorized rickshaw. In addition the mountain town boasts a **large yoga centre** (Kaivalyadhama S. A. D. T. Gupta Yogic Hospital and Health Care Centre, www.kdham.com).

The cave complex of Karla (12km/7mi northeast of Lonavala) is **★** amongst the most impressive examples of early Buddhist art. It con- **Karla cave** sists of a temple and several monasteries. After a small climb visitors **complex** will be able to admire the chaitya from the first century, which is considered the largest and best-preserved in the whole of India. Its imposing multi-storey façade is decorated with large sculptures of its sponsors between the entrances. The Buddha sculptures that were added later date from the sixth century. On the left-hand side is a sixteen-sided pillar with a lion capital. It resembles the columns of the great emperor and supporter of Buddhism, Ashoka, and to this day it is India's national emblem (see p.67)

The well-proportioned, finely decorated interior is considered a **masterpiece of Hinayana Buddhism**. Two rows with 15 columns each divide the large hall into a wide central nave and two narrow aisles. The octagonal columns stand on a vase-shaped base and are finished off with a richly adorned capital, consisting of kneeling elephants with riders. Seven further plain columns surround the stupa in the cave's apse. The wooden ceiling construction is largely still extant.

There are several viharas grouped around the temple, some of which consist of two storeys carved into the rock and have sleeping-cells. Some of them contain Buddha statues of the later Mahayana period. In contrast the new, colourful Hindu shrine built in honour of the goddess Ekviri seems somewhat garish. It attracts many pilgrims from the surrounding area, who come to sacrifice chickens and goats on festive days.

Bhaja
Opening hours:
daily 9am–6pm

Even older than the Karla Caves are the caves near the village of Bhaja (12km/7mi southeast of Lonavala). They too have been carved into the rock and can only be reached after a bit of a climb. It is not just a visit to the complex that is worthwhile, the view of the surrounding area and the nice walk from Bhaja village (approx. half an hour) are also very pleasant.

The chaitya hall was presumably built during the second century BC. Unfortunately its formerly magnificent façade has been largely destroyed. 27 columns structure the interior into a central nave and two narrow aisles. Although this rock temple cannot be compared to the impressive chaitya of Karla visitors have the peace and quiet here to study the old wooden construction method of the early complexes. Many of the old teak beams in the ribbed ceiling are still preserved. Of all the viharas no. 12 to the south is the most interesting. It houses two nicely chiselled flat reliefs with figures interpreted as the gods Surya on the sun chariot and Indra.

Bedsa

The twelve caves on a mountain near the village of Bedsa(23km/14mi east of Lonavala) can only be reached after a climb. Since the path is not signposted it is best to enquire in the village. The chaitya hall can be accessed via a veranda decorated with two high octagonal pillars. Sculptures of horses, elephants and other animals, all with riders, can be found above the bell capital. The façade with the large chaitya window does not have any Buddha figures, a typical example of the temples of the Hinayana period. The interior has an aisled nave with an apse and a stupa.

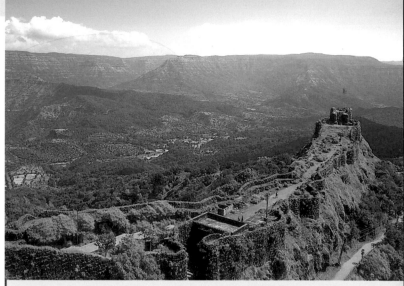

The old Maratha fort of Pratapgarh

The **hill station of Matheran** (139km/86mi southeast of Mumbai) is a very popular weekend destination amongst visitors from Mumbai, being within easy reach of the city. The small town extends in a north-south direction on the plateau of a free-standing mountain ridge. Trains run from Mumbai to the small town of Neral at the foot of the mountain. It is a breathtaking journey on the small narrow-gauge railway, which makes its way round countless bends up to Matheran. The guests' most popular pastime in this health resort, known for its good air, is sightseeing from one of the 23 viewpoints. On clear days it is possible to see all the way to Mumbai. Panorama Point in the north has the best view of the surrounding area.

Hill stations of Matheran and Mahabaleshwar

The popular little holiday town of **Mahabaleshwar** (230km/143mi southeast of Mumbai, 120km/75mi southwest of Pune) is located where the Western Ghats drop off over deep, rugged gorges and valleys to the coastal plain of Maharashtra. Extensive walks to the various viewing points, boat trips on the local lake and excursions to the historic sites of the surrounding area are amongst Mahabaleshwar's main attractions. Just 6km/4mi north of the small town is the village of **Old Mahabaleshwar** with various fairly old temples. Panchaganga Temple (Five Ganga Temple) is situated beside a basin whose water is considered holy.

Another interesting excursion leads to the old Maratha fort of Pratapgarh (20km/12mi west of Mahabaleshwar). Raigarh, the old fortified Maratha capital in which their leader Shhivaji had himself crowned king, can be found about 70km/45mi to the north.

Pratapgarh

Coastline between Mumbai and Goa

Tip
Those who do not want to go straight from Mumbai to Goa's beaches in one go by ship or plane, but would rather see some of the country on the way, can hire a taxi and travel southbound along highway 17. Small side roads lead to the coast, which often has empty beaches, making it a wonderful place to go swimming.

Murud
There is a worthwhile excursion to the coast to Murud (165km/103mi south of Mumbai). Around 2km/1mi to the north is the dilapidated palace of the Nawabs of Janjira, descendants of Abyssinian seafarers who had a small kingdom here.
In front of the bay of the small town is Kasa Fort, the old naval fort built by the Maratha leader Shivaji.

Janjira
6km/4mi to the south on an island in Rajpuri Bay stands the imposing naval fort of Janjira, which is said to have been built by the Siddi rulers as early as the 15th century and extended at a later date. Boats go to the fort where visitors can explore the grass-and-creeper-covered ruins hidden behind a magnificent gate. Good accommodation can be found in the Golden Swan beach Resort in Murud (www.goldenswan.com).

Ganapatipule
The attractive beach of Ganapatipule (290km/180mi south of Mumbai) now possesses a fine holiday complex set up by Maharashtra's tourism authority. Visitors will also find a well-known temple dedicated to the god Ganesha (Ganapati).

Ratnagiri
The large port of Ratnagiri (approx. 30km/20mi south of Ganapatipule) is particularly famous for being the **home of the Alphonso mango**, which is considered the best variety of this fruit. The last king of Burma also lived in Ratnagiri when he was in exile. His palace and the old fort of Ratnadurg by the sea are the city's most important sights. Those wishing to spend the night in the area should check into the Landmark hotel (tel. 023 52 – 22 01 20).

Nagpur

F 9

State: Maharashtra	**Altitude:** 312m/1024ft
Population: 2.1 million	**Distance:** 861km/535mi northeast of Mumbai

Imagine a straight line running from Delhi to Chennai, and one from Mumbai to Kolkata. Nagpur is situated almost exactly where they cross.

This city lies right in the heart of India and in the northeastern tip of Maharashtra. It does not have any particular tourist attractions but is a good starting point for visiting various interesting sites in the surrounding area. Nagpur's oranges are famous throughout India and visitors should definitely try them if in the city during the right season.

By the tenth century this area was already under the control of the kings of the Gond, the local tribal population. In the 15th century the strip of land briefly fell into the hands of the Bahmani sultans, but the Gond were able to get it back. In 1740 the area was conquered by the Marathas, who were making their way eastwards. They in turn had to hand it over to the British in 1853. Under the colonial power Nagpur was the capital of the Central Province. Today it is still the district capital and one of the busiest centres in the state.

 NAGPUR

INFORMATION
MTDC Tourist Office
Dr. Munji Margi Road
Tel. 07 12 – 252 33 24
www.maharashtratourism.gov.in

WHERE TO STAY / WHERE TO EAT
► **Mid-range / Budget**
Hardeo
Dr. Munji Margi Road
Tel. 07 12 – 252 91 15
Centrally located three-star hotel with a good restaurant and bar.

What to See in Nagpur

Right in the city centre on a hill stands the old Maratha fort (built in 1818), which was further extended by the British in 1857. It is not, however, accessible to the public.   **Fort**

There are still some other remains dotted around the area from that same period, such as the old palace gate (Nagar Khane) of the Maratha Bhonslas' palace, which burned down in the 19th century. The rulers' tombs can be found in a garden in the district of Shukrawari.   **Old palace gate**

Around Nagpur

A **much-visited place of pilgrimage** is Ramagiri (Mount Rama) near the small town of Ramtek 47km/29mi northeast of Nagpur. The mountain rising up above the plain is said to have served Rama, Sita and Lakshmana as a resting place on their return from Lanka. That is how it is told in the Ramayana. Foreign visitors only rarely find their way to this remote part of central India. Several snow-white temples and shrines have been built on the hill's plateau. Most of them date back to the 18th century, but are built on older foundations, some of them dating as far back as the fourth / fifth centuries. The famous poet Kalidasa (fifth century) used the inspiration of this place in order to pen one of his most famous works here. Pilgrims   **Ramagiri**

On the way home from the fields

usually combine their stay with a visit to the holy bathing site of Ambala north of the hill. Steps lead down from the temples to the lake. Around the water basin there are also some small temples, donated by wealthy believers.

Ashrams

In order to get to the ashrams, take a bus or train to the small town of **Wardha**, which is 77km/48mi southwest of Nagpur. It is approximately 10km/6mi to Sevagram and 10km/6mi to Paunar.

For Gandhi, **Sevagram** was the ideal place to coordinate the freedom movement from a central location (with train connections in every direction) on the one hand, and on the other to develop his ideas and programmes further in the tranquillity and loneliness of this remote town. In 1933 he built an ashram here with his followers. To this day the Mahatma's followers try to keep up his ideas and values. Those who are interested can visit the **museum** with a documentary about his life's work, and his small house. The ashram also has ac-

Opening hours:
daily 10am–6pm

commodation available for those who want to participate in the life of the community. Various institutions in the surrounding area are also associated with Gandhi's spirit: the Kasturba Hospital, the M. Gandhi Research Institute for Medicine and the Centre of Science for Villages.

Vinobha Bhave, one of Gandhi's comrades-in-arms and an active fighter for the rights of the landless, founded a second ashram on the banks of a stream in **Paunar** in 1938. Spinning, weaving and organic farming are the main activities of the local inhabitants. Those wishing to familiarize themselves with the life of the ashram can find accommodation here if it is not already full. Further accommodation is available in Wardha.

★ Orchha

State: Madhya Pradesh
Distance: 119km/74mi southeast of Gwalior

Population: 8500

Orchha is one of those tranquil places away from the main tourist routes that need some looking for but show travellers a piece of original India.

Dotted in and around the small town there are magnificent palaces, old temples and tombs, as well as lively bazaar. Orchha has a picturesque location on the river Betwa amongst forests that are home to countless flocks of green parrots. The town was founded in the 16th century by the Bundela Rajput clan. The ruler of the time Rudra Pratap built his new capital here and erected a fort on an island in the river between 1525 and 1531. It was extended under his successors into a complex consisting of several palaces. A massive bridge connects the town and the fort with its palace complex, which now also houses a romantic hotel.

What to See in Orchha

The complex's best building is the Jehangir Mahal, which Raja Bir Singh Deo had built at the beginning of the 17th century. Its **imposing façade with an eastward orientation** and many decorative balconies, turrets and domes as well as a massive, richly adorned entrance gate is a good example of the mixture between Islamic and Hindu architecture typical of that time. Beyond it is the multi-storey palace with its courtyard and fountain around which a total of 136 royal suites are grouped over several floors. Many of the niches and balconies are now home to hundreds of pigeons and bats. The Jehangir Mahal is named after the great Mughal ruler in Delhi, to whom

★
Palace complex

▶ VISITING ORCHHA

INFORMATION

Madhya Pradesh Tourism has an office in its Sheesh Mahal Hotel in the palace of Orchha.

GETTING THERE

Orchha is only 16km/10mi from the railway hub of Jhansi. All of the trains between Delhi and Mumbai as well as Delhi and Chennai stop here. There are regular buses from Jhansi to Orchha and a taxi can also be taken. The small town is a few miles from the main road connecting Jhansi with the temple city of Khajuraho and visiting it is a good excursion on the way to these highlights. The closest airport is Gwalior.

WHERE TO STAY / WHERE TO EAT

▶ Mid-range

Orchha Resort
Kanchanghat
Tel 076 80 – 526 77 / 78

customercare@orchharesort.com
Those who prefer more modern surroundings should stay in the Orchha Resort. The well maintained hotel has a garden with a swimming pool and is situated on the Betwa river near the chhatris. The restaurant serves good vegetarian cuisine.

▶ Mid-range / Budget

Hotel Sheesh Mahal
Jehangir Mahal Road
Tel. 076 80 – 25 26 24
hsmorcha@sancharnet.in
This hotel, run by Madhya Pradesh Tourism, has accommodation in every price category and to suit every taste, from small, cheap, but cosy rooms to luxurious suites equipped with furniture owned by the maharajas as well as huge bath tubs and panoramic views from the toilet. The restaurant is excellent. Book in good time!

the Bundelas of that time felt connected. Visitors will be able to hear and smell the resident fauna of the neighbouring Raj Mahal too. This part of the complex is older than the Jehangir Mahal and was commissioned by Bharti Chand, the son of the first ruler, and his successor Madhukar Shah. Its interior still has surviving miniature paintings in the typical Bundela style. The small Praveen Mahal to the north belonged to the musician and poet Praveen, Raja Indramani's favourite courtesan. The palace was built in around 1675. The Sheesh Mahal, a further palace, was built a century later. Madhya Pradesh Tourism now has a hotel in this palace with rooms of varying prices, where visitors can enjoy the tranquillity of this place.

Temple Cross the bridge from the fort to the town to get to a street with small shops selling handicrafts, particularly ones from Madhya Pradesh. To the left is the lively market square from where visitors can climb up to **Ram Raja Temple**. According to legend it was originally a palace, but was later transformed into a temple. Dedicated to the god Rama, it is the destination of many pilgrims. The towers of **Cha-**

turbhuj Temple reach up high into the sky. It, too, is dedicated to the god Rama, since the Bundela rulers were followers of this deity. **Lakshmi Temple** also houses a rich treasure of paintings in the Bundela style. Raja Bir Singh Deo had it built at the beginning of the 17th century.

The 15 chhatris (cenotaphs) picturesquely located along the Betwa river are definitely worth taking a look at. Hidden between bushes and high grass they commemorate the former rulers of Orchha. The tower of the chhatri for Raja Bir Singh Deo is the highest. From the town centre it is a nice 0.5km/0.3mi walk southwards along the river to reach the chhatris. There are several other ruins around Orchha, some of which are overgrown with grass and bushes. They can all be explored on pleasant walks.

★ Cenotaphs of the Bundela rulers

★ Pune (Poona)

C 10

State: Maharashtra
Population: 3.7 million

Altitude: 750m/2460ft
Distance: 170km/105mi southeast of Mumbai

During the 1970s and early 1980s it was not the Taj Mahal that was the destination of many travellers to India. Instead, they came to visit the ashram of the late guru Bhagwan Sri Rajneesh. This is where the journey in search of enlightenment ended for many visitors from the West.

Pune's pleasant climate, caused by its altitude at the western end of the Deccan plateau, along with its great proximity to Mumbai were probably crucial factors for the city's speedy development in recent years. Around the narrow old town is the spaciously built former cantonment or residential district of the British. The formerly independent town of Kirkee and the areas on the left bank of the Mutha and Shivajinagar rivers have also been incorporated.

Pune's significance is closely connected to the rise of the Marathas in the 17th–18th centuries. Shivaji (1627–80) had managed to unite the different tribes and rebel against the Deccan sultans. Marathi, their common language, was a unifying factor, and together with the weakness of the Islamic ruling states this created favourable conditions for the formation of a new regional power. Using guerrilla tactics, the Maratha subdued large parts of India. During the first half of the 18th century their influence in the north temporarily reached all the way to Lahore, in the south all the way to the region of modern-day Bangalore and in the east all the way to Orissa. Thus the originally centrally organized Maratha state developed into a confed-

History

eration of small states with their own rulers during the 18th century. The government and coordination of these states was in the hands of the Peshwas (ministers), whose position was hereditary. They had their seat in Pune. In 1817, however, they too had to give way to the British. The colonial rulers occupied the city and soon moved their government during the monsoon months from hot and humid Mumbai to Pune with its more pleasant climate.

Today it is not just a modern industrial centre; several research institutes, universities and cultural institutions are also located here. New estates are shooting up because high rents, pollution and overpopulation are causing more and more people to leave Mumbai in favour of Pune.

 VISITING PUNE

INFORMATION

Maharashtra Tourism
Tel. 020 – 26 12 68 67
www.maharashtratourism.gov.in

SHOPPING

One of the main shopping streets is MG Road; this is also the location of the Bombay Store with a good selection of gift items.

The bazaar atmosphere can be taken in on Lakshmi Road or on Tulsi Bag in the old town. Metal goods, paper shops, textiles, jewellery and much more can all be found there.

WHERE TO EAT

► **Moderate**

① *Blue Nile Restaurant*
4, Bund Garden Road
Tel. 020 – 26 12 52 38
Northern Indian specialities and very good biryanis.

► **Inexpensive**

② *Shreyas Hotel*
1242 B, Apte Road
Deccan Gymkhana
Tel. 020 – 25 53 12 28
Very tasty thalis with many different vegetarian dishes in the style of Maharashtra, good pickles and chut-

neys. A must for all those in search of a taste experience.

WHERE TO STAY

► **Luxury**

① *Blue Diamond*
11, Koregaon Road
Tel. 020 – 66 02 55 55
www.tajhotels.com
This elegant hotel, which has all of the amenities of the Taj group, is located in Koregaon Park, Pune's green lung. Polite staff in saris, stylish interior and exclusive restaurant.

► **Mid-range**

② *Woodland*
Sadhu Vaswani Circle
Tel. 020 – 26 12 61 61
This three-star hotel with a vegetarian restaurant is located in the vicinity of the station.

► **Budget**

③ *Swaroop Hotel*
Prabhat Road, Lane No. 10
Tel. 020 – 25 67 87 42
This is also the hotel chosen by the well-known film academy to house its guests. It is situated in a quiet area west of the Mutha river. It has a pleasant, small restaurant.

Pune (Poona) *Map*

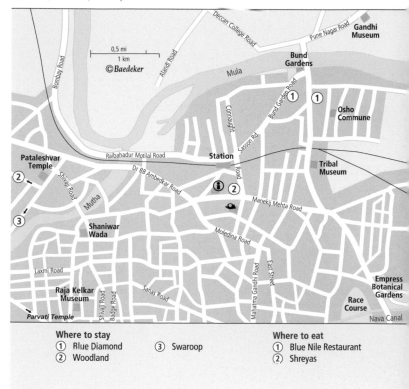

Where to stay				Where to eat	
① Blue Diamond		③ Swaroop		① Blue Nile Restaurant	
② Woodland				② Shreyas	

What to See in Pune

The old town, in which a few districts are named after the days of the week, contains the remains of Shaniwar Wada (Saturday Palace), which was built by Peshwa Baji Rao I in 1736. Several fires have destroyed most of the building. All that remains are some walls and a gate, whose towers are fitted with iron spikes to protect it from elephant attacks.

Somewhat further south is the very worthwhile Raja Kelkar Museum. The poet and art collector Raja Kelkar (1896–1990) gave everything he owned to Maharashtra's government in 1975. The collection contains bronzes and miniature paintings and a **large selection of everyday utensils**, from oil containers to a noodle machine. Musical instruments and regional dresses are also on display (open: daily 9.30am–6pm).

Shaniwar Wada
🕐
Opening hours:
daily 8am–6pm

★★
Raja Kelkar Museum

🕐

Pataleshvar Temple

The western district of Shivajinagar is home to Pataleshvar Temple, located on the busy Jangli Maharaj Road. The city's oldest temple (eighth temple) was carved out of a granite hill. The central shrine contains a Shiva lingam, while the side cells are consecrated to Lakshmi, Ganesha, Rama and Sita as well as Rama's brother Lakshmana. In front of the temple is a small, square courtyard with a round Nandi pavilion.

✱
Parvati Temple

🕓 Opening hours: daily 8am–12pm, 3pm–6pm

In the far south of the city is Parvati Hill, on which Parvati Temple stands. It was built under Peshwa Balaji Baji Rao (1740–61). Next to the main shrine for Shiva, Parvati and Ganesha there are several secondary shrines. The small Peshwa Museum on the history of the Marathas can also be found here. The **panoramic view** of the city and the surrounding area from the hill's highest point is by no means unimpressive.

Gandhi Museum

🕓

The former palace of Aga Khan now houses the small Gandhi Museum. In 1942 Mahatma Gandhi, his wife Kasturba and other freedom fighters were detained within these walls. A memorial commemorates Kasturba Gandhi, who died here (open: daily 9am–12.30pm and 1.30pm–6pm).

The view of Pune from Parvati Temple is lovely

The museum of the Tribal Research and Training Institute, with an interesting documentary about the various tribal cultures in Maharashtra, (open: daily 10am to 5pm), is also worth a visit.

Tribal Museum

Those who want to visit the ashram, which has now been renamed Osho Commune, for more than just a one-hour tour have to provide an HIV test that is less than 30 days old.

Osho Commune

SOUTH INDIA

**STATES
AND UNION TERRITORIES**
Andhra Pradesh: capital Hyderabad
Karnataka: capital Bangalore
Kerala: capital Thiruvananthapuram
Lakshadweep: union territory
Puducherry: union territory
Tamil Nadu: capital Chennai

The states of Tamil Nadu, Andhra Pradesh, Karnataka and Kerala are part of the region making up South India. In addition to their geographic location they are grouped together through another characteristic: their languages are all of Dravidian origin. The same is also true of a large proportion of the population. Lakshadweep and Puducherry are also part of South India. Each of these union territories will be addressed in detail under its own heading.

India's four southernmost states form the apex of the triangular subcontinent. The long sandy beaches of Kerala and Karnataka make up its western end. Bordering the extremely fertile, narrow strip of coastline are the mountains of the Western Ghats. This is where the clouds of the southwest monsoon empty themselves, giving the coastal region immense quantities of water every year as well as its typically humid, tropical climate.
The drier Deccan plateau covers large parts of Karnataka and Andhra Pradesh. It is bordered in the south by the Nilgiris (Blue Mountains), on whose slopes many different spices grow. The green river and coastal plains of Tamil Nadu are located in the east.

Natural environment

Rice cultivation dominates in the fertile coastal and river regions in the east and west, while cultivation on the drier Deccan plateau revolves around the cereal crop sorghum, oleiferous fruits and cotton.
Tea, coffee and spice plantations are located in the Nilgiri mountains and in the hills of the Western Ghats. In addition to the agricultural sector, the textile and metal processing industries also play an important role, particularly in Tamil Nadu. Rubber and plastic processing as well as chemical production sites can be found in Karnataka and Tamil Nadu. The regions around Bangalore and Hyderabad are the south's **new industrial centres**. The electrical industry and computer and, in particular, software production dominate in this area.

Economy

← *Harvesting coconuts*

History   At least parts of southern India remained unaffected by the many invasions by foreign conquerors. This is especially true of Tamil Nadu and southern Karnataka. Countless temples remind visitors of the great southern Indian dynasties of Hindu rulers who controlled the country long ago. Amongst them are the Pallavas and Cholas in Tamil Nadu as well as the Hoysalas in southern Karnataka. Hampi, the impressive city of the Vijayanagar rulers on the central plateau of Karnataka, is also evidence of past greatness. At times the arm of the northern Indian conquerors even reached this far. Towns like Bijapur and Gulbarga in northern Karnataka are cited as evidence for this theory.

India's southwest coast was a **scene of special historical significance**. Many wanted to share in the wealth of this tropical land, particularly in its spices. The Chinese, Arabs, Jews and Christians arrived here early on. Later, various European colonial powers also attempted to profit from the country's wealth. Their legacy shapes the region and its people to this day.

Attractions   Beaches, attractive landscapes and national parks, as well as the wealth of cultural treasures, are all on the list of South India's attractions. For many the region, less subject to outside influences, is the »**original**« **India**. The significant temple sites of Tamil Nadu are a great attraction for those interested in the country's history and culture. The highlights are the complexes of Madurai, Mamallapuram, Kanchipuram and Thanjavur. In addition there are countless other temples, but a detailed description of all of them would be beyond the scope of any travel guide on India.

The sites in Karnataka of the early western Chalukyas (sixth–eighth century) in Badami, Aihole and Pattadakal display a pleasure in architectural experimentation as well as highly developed craftsmanship. The temple buildings of the Hoysalas, who ruled much later from the tenth to the 13th century, in Belur, Halebid and Somnathpur stand out because of their special architectural form and their impressive sculptures. The ruins in Hampi and central Karnataka are evidence of the claim to power asserted by the last Hindu empire in the south. Its downfall was sealed by the power of the Muslim Deccan sultanates. The towns of Gulbarga, Bidar and Bijapur in particular have held on to the rich heritage of those dynasties.

Attractive and diverse natural landscapes shape the appearance of southern India. Its tropical forests are home to many animals. The reserves of Bandipur, Nagarhole, Mudumalai and Wyanad are grouped together into Jawahar National Park, which is the largest connected protected area in India. The diverse flora and fauna attract visitors every year, from both home and abroad. Periyar National Park in Kerala is particularly popular because of its large elephant population.

Thanks to its plentiful wellness facilities and the Ayurvedic medicine practised there, Kerala, the state on the southwest coast, is enjoying

Kathakali, one of the oldest forms of dance, is typical of Kerala.
Before the performance the dancers have to put on large amounts of make-up

growing popularity amongst travellers from all around the world. Beaches lined by palm trees, such as in Kovalam, the fascinating world of the Backwaters and regular traditional festivals such as the Elephant March of Thrissur and the snake boat race in Alapuzzha are further attractions of the region.

The cities of the south, the more traditional Chennai, the Western-oriented boom town of Bangalore and Muslim-oriented Hyderabad, which has recently also been discovered by the software industry, are popular starting locations for trips through the south. The old maharaja's city of Mysore is also amongst the favourite places for a stopover for many tourists in South India.

✴ The Backwaters

State: Kerala   **Altitude:** sea level

In the subcontinent's extreme south, at the base of the Western Ghats, nature has created one of India's most breathtaking landscapes in the form of the Kerala Backwaters, known to the locals as Kuttanad.

The green labyrinth of canals, rivers and lagoons, lined by palm trees and paddy fields, begins directly beyond the coast and extends between the towns of Kochi in the north and Kollam in the south. The network of the Backwaters covers an area of 1900 sq km/735 sq mi. The waterways were used as far back as 1000 years ago as trading and transport routes. In the past, like today, Kettuvallams, the traditional barges filled with coconut shells and copra, glide soundlessly through the water. They are interspersed by noisy masses using the vessels of progress: motor boats, used as buses and water taxis, take children to school every day and adults to the larger towns for shopping, as well as ferrying amazed tourists through a region that is neither fully water nor fully terra firma. A **boat trip through this seemingly endless brush** is one of most enjoyable experiences in Kerala. Narrow canals covered by palm trees quickly expand into huge lagoons. Rivers, crossed by small bridges, are lined by the light green of the paddy fields. Dotted across the landscape are individual houses or small settlements, churches, mosques and temples. Sometimes a red flag can be seen blowing in the wind; this announces the seat of the local office of the Communist Party. The people mainly live from rice cultivation, fishing and palm trees, from which the famous palm wine known as Toddy is made. In some places visitors can still witness women doing traditional foot-fishing. They wade through the water

The Kerala Backwaters: a network of lakes, rivers and lagoons

and use clay pots to hunt down tasty karimeen, a species of fish that lives in the waters here. The apparent paradise that unfolds before the eyes of visitors is viewed with less idealism by its inhabitants. Annual floods caused by the monsoon, long, time-consuming trips to the nearest town and, not least, unemployment problems are just a few of the burdens troubling the people here. More and more people are finding work in the growing tourist industry. The old cargo barges are being converted into houseboats for holidaymakers and hotel chains are opening better-class holiday resorts along palm-fringed lagoons.

★
Snake boat races

Every year in August during the Onam Festival Alapuzzha hosts a special spectacle: the snake boat race, for which the prize is the Neh-

One of Kerala's biggest attractions: the snake-boat race of Alapuzzha

ru Cup. Narrow, artistically decorated boats, called chundan vallams (snake boats), with crews of up to 100, compete to win the race. It is thought this spectacle goes back to old, bellicose traditions; these days, winners are »only« awarded the Nehru Cup, which the former prime minister donated when he was in office. Cheered on by excited spectators following the race on bamboo stands from the shore, the happy victors accept their prize.

Places to Visit in the Backwaters

One of the main starting points for a trip in the Backwaters is the busy port of Kollam, located between the sea and Lake Ashtamudi. It was founded in the ninth century as the seat of government of the Chera dynasty. Previously one of the centres of the international spice trade, it was frequently visited by Arab, Jewish and particularly by Chinese traders. In 1330 the town became an episcopal see under Jordanus, India's first Roman Catholic bishop. **Kollam (Quilon)**

During a walk through the city visitors will see plenty of the **typical wooden Kerala houses** with their attractive tiled roofs. In the alleyways visitors can watch coconut fibres being processed into ropes and mats. Other industries flourishing here are pottery, aluminium, cashew-nut processing and of course fishing.

▶ VISITING THE BACKWATERS

INFORMATION
www.keralatourism.org

DTPC Office
Alappuzha
near the boat jetty
Tel. 04 77 – 225 33 08

HOUSEBOATS
The best way to explore the Backwaters is in a hired boat. Many operators have specialized in trips in kettuvallams, traditional cargo barges transformed into houseboats.

Allepey Tourism
ATDC, Komala Road
Alappuzha
Tel. 04 78 – 224 34 62

Eco Trails Kerala
Tel. 094 – 46 43 92 52
www.ecotourskerala.com or
www.thehouseboatskerala.com

CGlt Earth
Kochi, tel. 04 84 – 301 17 11
spicecoastcruise@cghearth.com

FERRY CONNECTIONS
The Backwaters can also be explored by ferry. The best-known route is the public ferry link between Alappuzha and Kollam. Boats travel this route every day; the trip takes 8½ hours. Kochi and Kottayam can also be reached this way.

FESTIVALS
From June to September, during the well-known Onam Festival, Alappuzha hosts the famous snake boat races.

WHERE TO EAT / WHERE TO STAY
Homestay Programme
In addition to a large number of very nice hotels there is also plenty of other accommodation of all price categories in the Backwaters, often in the traditional wooden houses of Kerala, which can be found through the Homestay Programme (www.homestaykerala.com). The hotels run by Kerala Tourism are also pleasant (www.ktdc.com).

▶ Luxury
Marari Beach Resort
Mararikulam
Alappuzha
Tel. 04 84 – 301 17 11
www.cghearth.com
This attractive hotel complex is located not in the Backwaters, but on the beach north of Alappuzha. Guests can doze in hammocks under palm trees, enjoy the white sandy beach or participate in the rich cultural programme. This feel-good oasis also has an Ayurvedic centre and several very good restaurants.

Ashtamudi Lake Resort
Chavara
Tel. 04 76 – 288 22 88
Guests stay in comfortable bungalows on Ashtamudi Lake; it has an Ayurvedic centre and a good restaurant that also serves Ayurvedic food.

Coconut Lagoon
Kumarakom
Tel. 04 84 – 301 17 11
www.cghearth.com
Between palm trees and small canals, the bungalows owned by Coconut Lagoon can only be reached by boat. This highly distinguished resort is committed to ecologically and socially sustainable tourism, as are all cghearth hotels. Ayurvedic treatments, a yoga centre and cooking

classes are only three of the many services available. An excellent restaurant ensures that guests always have good food and the service is excellent.

Kumarakom Lake Resort
Kumarakom
Tel. 04 81 – 252 49 00
www.klresort.com
Absolute luxury can be enjoyed in this attractive complex. The wooden bungalows built in the traditional style are fitted with every amenity. The »Meandering Pool Villas«, i.e. those with direct access to the water, are the resort's architectural gems. There are two good restaurants and of course here too guests can enjoy Ayurvedic treatments, yoga classes and cruises on the Backwaters.

▶ Mid-range
Mottys Homestay Villas
Alappuzha

Tel. 04 77 – 226 05 73
www.mottys.uniquehomestays.com
Guests live here in rooms with antique furniture in the host's house.

Anamika The Villa
Tel. 04 78 – 224 20 44
Heritage Hotel in an old villa in the centre of Alapuzha. Dance performances are staged in the evenings.

▶ Mid-range / Budget
Tharavad Heritage Resort
West of the north police station
Tel. 04 77 – 24 45 99
www.tharavadheritageresort.com
Typical Kerala-style building; excursions are also organized.

Anjali Park
KK Road, Kottayam,
Tel. 04 81 – 256 36 69
Inexpensive hotel, good cuisine.

Kottayam

The town of Kottayam at the Backwaters' eastern end, located at the foot of the Western Ghats, is a further main ferry landing. **The boat trip from here to Alappuzha is particularly attractive and varied**; it takes around 2½ hours. The town was once a centre for Syrian Christians. Keeping their memory alive are two churches from the 13th century, which can be found around 3km/2mi outside of the centre: Valliapalli, the large church, and Cheriapalli, the small church. The former, later given a Baroque façade, houses two stone crosses with Syrian and Pahlavi writing. Cheriapalli contains some attractive wall paintings. Kottayam is also a good starting point for trips to ▶Periyar National Park.

✱ Kumarakom bird sanctuary

It is only 16km/10mi from Kottayam to Kumarakom bird sanctuary near Lake Vembanad. The reserve is home to many duck and cuckoo species. Several migratory bird species from Siberia overwinter here.

✱ Alappuzha (Aleppey)

Alappuzha is one of Kerala's most important ports and also one of the main landings for the ferries from the Backwaters. The city lives from **processing coconut fibres** from which ropes and mats are produced, amongst other things. During the entire day there are busy comings and goings along the many canals where products are loaded and unloaded. Alappuzha only gained significance as a port during the 19th century; today the Backwaters' largest inland harbour is located here. During the snake boat race (see p.509) in August the city is the destination of many tourists from home and abroad.

✶ ✶ Badami · Aihole · Pattadakal

D 11/12

**Sites of the early
Western Chalukyas**

State: Karnataka
Distance: 450km/280mi–500km/310mi
southeast of Mumbai

In a valley surrounded by a rocky landscape, in the very remote southern Bagalkot district, are the small, sleepy villages Badami and Aihole, each several miles away from the old temple city of Pattadakal, which lies between the two.

It is hard for the so far small number of tourists arriving in slow-paced Badami to imagine that a long time ago this was the location of one of the most powerful centres of the Deccan plateau, the capital of the early Chalukyas, Vatapi (AD 543–754). More than 50 temples and cave temples have survived the centuries in this remote corner of India. They are magnificent pieces of evidence of the early period of religious architecture, which can be found in such wealth and diversity in no other place on the subcontinent.

History Pulakeshin I (543–566) is considered the Chalukya dynasty's founding father. He laid the foundation stone for the fortification of the settlement by the river Malaprabha, and his successor Kirtivarman I (566–583) built it up to be the capital of the expanding empire. The new rulers summoned the best architects and sculptors to Badami so that they could demonstrate their abilities in the neighbouring towns of Pattadakal and Aihole. The countless Hindu and Jain temples that were subsequently built turned out to be **models for the architecture of both northern and southern India**.

The Chalukyas ruled large parts of the Deccan plateau for almost 200 years. Their military campaigns took them to the coast of the Arabian Sea and, in the east, to the heart of the Pallava dynasty, Kanchipuram. In 753 the Rashtrakuta dynasty delivered the crucial blow to the influential rulers of the central plateau under their leader Dantidurga and captured Badami. Another 200 years were to pass before their successors, the Western Chalukyas, of formerly so influential a dynasty, once again had an important position in the power play of southern India's Hindu kingdoms.

Various rulers took possession of the sites by the river Malaprabha over the centuries. For some time the region was part of the Vijayanagar Empire; later it belonged to the Adil Shahis of Bijapur, Haider Ali from Mysore, the Maratha Empire and finally the British. It is surprising that despite the region's eventful history so many of the old buildings have remained.

Badami

The small town of Badami (108km/67mi from Hospet, 132km/82mi south of Bijapur) has a picturesque location at the foot of red sandstone rocks, which ruggedly tower up into the blue sky. The small, artificial Lake Agastya east of the centre was presumably created during the town's founding phase.

The worthwhile cave temples and the remains of a fort can be reached via a steep path south of the town. In the north there are further interesting temples from the Chalukya period as well as the ruins of a second fort. Along the shores of the artificial lake, where women come to wash their laundry on the ghats, there are also shrines from ancient times.

Ghats on Agastya Lake

✶✶
Cave temples

Badami's oldest monuments are the four cave temples of varying sizes carved out of the red sandstone to the south above the town. All four temples consist of a columned veranda, a hall and a sanctum. **Cave no. 1** is consecrated to Shiva, whose impressive form as Nataraja with 18 arms can be seen in the right-hand part of the veranda. Harihara (Shiva / Vishnu), the wives Parvati and Lakshmi and the vehicles Nandi and Garuda are also part of this ensemble. Beyond it is the columned hall with the small, square sanctum. The god Vishnu resides in **cave no. 2**. His incarnations as Varaha (wild boar) and Vamana (dwarf), who in three steps grows to be a giant striding through the universe, decorate the left and right sides of the veranda. Richly ornamented columns and a finely carved ceiling with a lotus and 16 fish are amongst the cave's further highlights. Cave

✶
Cave no. 3 ►

no. 3 is the largest and is also considered the most beautiful of the temples. The lavishly decorated veranda, supported by six columns, extends over an area of 23m/75ft by 6m/20ft. The façade is **richly adorned with sculptures of gods, humans, animals and plant ornaments**. Looking at the walls visitors will see Vishnu, to whom this shrine is also consecrated; he is resplendent in his avatars, to the right as Narasimha and to the left as Narayana, as he sits on the world-serpent Shesha. The ceiling of the inner hall also shows some nice craftsmanship; beyond it is the small sanctum.

Cave no. 4 is a Jain place of worship. Though its set-up corresponds to that of its predecessors, it is much smaller. Tirthankaras, the Jain fordmakers, are chiselled into the stone. The view from up here of the temple pool and the town is quite attractive. Those willing to make another ascent come to the remains of the old southern fort. East of it, hidden in the rocks, are several reliefs depicting Vishnu with Shesha amongst other things.

▶ VISITING BADAMI · AIHOLE · PATTADAKAL

INFORMATION

KSTDC Tourist Office
Ramdurg Road
Badami, tel. 083 57 – 22 00 46
www.karnatakatourism.org

GETTING THERE

Badami can be reached by bus or train from several towns and cities, including Bijapur, Hubli and Bangalore. There is a regular bus connection from Aihole to Badami and to Pattadakal.

WHERE TO EAT / WHERE TO STAY

▶ Mid-range

Hotel Badami Court
Located on the outskirts of town towards the station in Badami
Tel. 083 57 – 22 02 30
The best hotel in town with a pool and garden.

▶ Budget

KSTDC Hotel Mayura Chalukya
Ramdurg Road, Badami
Tel. 083 57 – 22 00 46
Small garden, restaurant and bar

On the other side of the valley are several temples displaying southern influences, expressed in the Vimana, the Dravidian temple tower, for example. On the slope of the northern hill, which also contains the remains of a further fort, stands the **Lower Shivalaya temple** and up on the peak, which can be reached via steep paths and steps, is the **Upper Shivalaya temple**, which was built at the beginning of the seventh century. The temple is decorated with scenes from the life of the god Krishna. The **Malegitti Shivalaya temple** was built on a rock below the fort. It too is crowned by the Vimana tower so typical of southern Indian temples. On the shores of the artificial lake there are several shrines. The oldest is **Bhutanatha Temple** on the eastern side. The local **museum** on Bhutanatha Temple Road houses a collection of finds from the area (open: daily except Fri 10am– 5pm). **Jambulinga Temple** in the town centre dates from the year 699 and has three shrines for the great deities Brahma, Vishnu and Shiva.

Temple complex

🕐

Aihole (Aivalli)

Aryapura or Ayyavole (46km/29mi from Badami, 17km/11mi from Pattadakal) was what the Chalukyas called the town that they founded here many centuries ago. Even today there are still many temples from the sixth, seventh and eighth centuries in Aihole. Entire temple groups can be found within the town, in the surrounding fields and on the rocks and hills. Aihole was also a **place of experimentation for new styles in temple architecture**, as can be seen by the fact that although the structures are very close in space and time they are sometimes extremely varied. Excavations continue to bring new discoveries to the surface.

Within the walled town there are several temples or temple groups worth visiting. Some of them lie hidden between homes and some of them were also used by the village inhabitants as accommodation. The town's largest temple, Durga Temple, is in the far north. It is **not, however, consecrated to the goddess Durga**, as its name suggests, but to Vishnu. The nearby fortification wall (durga) led to its confusing name. It is not just the shape of the temple that is unusual, the lavish ornamentation on its exterior façades is too. The aisled hall with its semicircular sanctum stands on a high plinth, while a row of columns runs around the building. The stylistic borrowings from the Buddhist Chaitya halls are unmistakable.

Temple groups

★

 ◄ Durga Temple

Somewhat further south is **Surya Narayana Temple** with a cult image of the sun god, Garuda Temple, a Durga shrine, and Lad Khan Temple. It is inhabited by the god Shiva, but the shrine's Muslim name dates back to one of its earlier human residents. The square hall and columned porch of this structure built in the seventh–eighth centuries are reminiscent of a Buddhist vihara. At the centre of the interior is a Nandi and the cella contains a lingam, Shiva's attributes. **Chakra**

Living within old temple walls: in Aihole and the surrounding area there are hundreds of temples

Gudi Temple somewhat further south was built in the northern Indian Nagara style, as can be seen by the way its tower was constructed. Right at the centre of town is the **Konti group**, four temples, presumably built in around 700. They consist of a columned hall and a cultic cell. Visitors should pay attention to the pillars, some of which are ornamented, and the attractive ceiling panels. The only building that can be dated with accuracy is **Meguti Temple**, which according to its inscription was built in 634. It is located on a hill in the southeast part of town. The original building, which consisted of the sanctum, a square columned hall and a porch, was later extended. The cult image, a tirthankara, reveals the shrine to be a Jain temple.

In the far northeast is the **Ravana Phadi** rock cave, which was probably created as early as the sixth century. Its interior is dominated by a wealth of highly expressive figures. Shiva is the master of the house.

Museum
🕐 Aihole's small museum near Durga Temple in the northeast houses a collection of sculptures from the surrounding area (open: daily except Fri 10am–5pm).

Pattadakal (Patadkal)

Some of the best examples of early religious buildings can be found in Pattadakal (22km/14mi from Badami, 17km/11mi from Aihole). The Chalukyas' temple city saw new rulers being crowned and religious festivals being held. Most of the temples within an enclosure were built during the reigns of King Vijayaditya II (696–733) and his successor Vikramaditya (733–746). As is the case in Badami and Aihole, **buildings in northern Indian and southern Indian styles stand side by side in harmony**. The Dravidic temples bear the unmistakable traits of Kanchipuram's Pallava art, as Kanchipuram had been conquered by the Chalukyas and its sculptors temporarily earned a living under the new rulers.

In the complex's centre is Sanghameshvara Temple from the early eighth century; it is presumably the oldest in this group. Above the sanctum stands a Vimana tower, a visible symbol of its southern Indian architectural style.

Sanghameshvara Temple

Further south is Virupaksha Temple, the largest here, situated within a surrounding wall along with 32 more shrines. It too is fitted with a Dravidic vimana above its sanctum. In front of the sanctum is a large columned hall with three entrances as well as a Nandi pavilion. The **sculptural ornamentation** on the walls and columns is rich. The latter display scenes from the Mahabharata and Ramayana epics. The temple was donated by Vikramaditya's wife Loka Maha Devi in commemoration of his victory over the Pallavas of Kanchipuram.

★ **Virupaksha Temple**

In the immediate vicinity visitors will also find Mallikarjuna Temple, the smaller version of Virupaksha Temple. It too was built in honour of Vikramaditya's victory. The donor is considered to be Loka Maha Devi's sister Trailoka Maha Devi, another of the ruler's wives. This temple also has many sculptures, including scenes from the life of Krishna.

Mallikarjuna Temple

Built in the northern Indian style are the adjacent Kashivishveshvara Temple and three temples in the north: Galaganatha Temple, which was never completed, Jambulinga Temple and Kada Siddeshvara Temple. They are all crowned by a Shikhara, a tower in the northern Indian style.

Further temples

Some distance from the group to the south stands Papanatha Temple, built in around 750. Two columned halls lead to the sanctum, which gives it an unusual length. Its implementation reflects a combination of northern (e.g. the shikhara) and southern (e.g. the entrance area) forms.
The exterior walls are artistically decorated with scenes from the Mahabhrarata and the Ramayana.

★ **Papanatha Temple**

★ Bangalore (Bengaluru)

E 13

Capital of Karnataka
Population: 6.5 million

Altitude: 920m/3018ft
Distance: 334km/208mi west of Chennai

Back in the 1950s, former prime minister Nehru prophesied that Bangalore would be »India's city of the future«. At the time it was still a provincial backwater.

Indeed the capital of the state of Karnataka has grown from a population of 2.5 to 6.5 million in the past twenty years. The city owes its boom partly to the machine construction and aviation industries, but above all to the software industry. 1500 businesses in the IT sector have locations here and a third of India's software exports and IT services come from the city, which has the reputation of being the southern Indian **»Silicon Valley«**.

However, Andhra Pradesh's capital Hyderabad is increasingly claiming this reputation for itself. Bangalore's infrastructure development was unfortunately not able to keep up with the economic explosion, and many now complain about the constant traffic jams and congested roads. Nevertheless the largest city on the Deccan plateau also has other facets. **Nice parks and gardens** as well as an impressive tree population are also features of Bangalore. Even though the city does not have any outstanding attractions it is a very good starting point for an exploration of South India because of its excellent tourist infrastructure and its pleasant climate. The numerous often very good hotels, restaurants, pubs and cafés, as well as a large number of shopping facilities, invite visitors to spend some time in the city. In addition Bangalore is the starting point for trips to tourist highlights in the surrounding area.

History Bangalore was founded in 1537 by Kempegowda, a vassal of the Vijayanagar Empire. He built a clay fort here. During the following centuries various rulers established themselves, including the princes of Mysore. The Muslim ruler Haider Ali and his son Tipu Sultan built a stone fort in the 18th century in the place where the clay fort had stood, using it to defend themselves against the British. After the victory over Tipu Sultan in 1799 the town fell into the hands of the British, who used it as a place to station their garrisons and visit during the summer months because of its pleasant climate. To this day many of the names, such as those of some of the quarters such as Cox Town or Fraser Town, and the sizable number of Anglo-Indians, bear witness to the city's colonial past. In the spirit of a return to native terms, the city was renamed **»Bengaluru«**, a name that has not yet managed to establish itself. It means »City of Cooked Beans« and refers to a local legend.

Bangalore *Map*

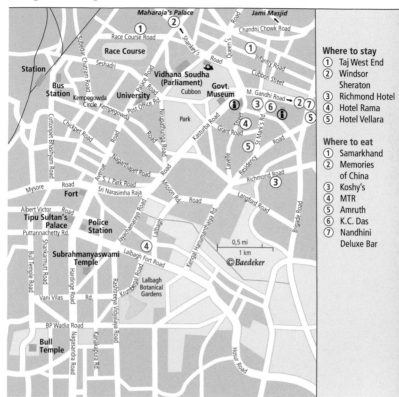

Where to stay
1. Taj West End
2. Windsor Sheraton
3. Richmond Hotel
4. Hotel Rama
5. Hotel Vellara

Where to eat
1. Samarkhand
2. Memories of China
3. Koshy's
4. MTR
5. Amruth
6. K.C. Das
7. Nandhini Deluxe Bar

Cityscape

The lively city centre is definitely worth visiting. Anyone with a little more time should also go on a walk through the parks, especially Lalbagh Gardens. The historic monuments, which are dotted all over the city, can be viewed within the context of an organized city tour. Bangalore's old city centre extends southwest of Cubbon Park around the old bazaar quarter of Chikpet and the busy Kempegowda Road; not far away, somewhat further to the west, visitors will also find the rail and bus stations. Most of the tourist hotels are in the area around Mahatma Gandhi Road. This wide avenue goes through the modern part of the city centre.

What to See in and around Bangalore

Cubbon Park and museums

At the western end of Mahatma Gandhi Road is Cubbon Park, one of the city's green oases. Government Museum, Venkatappa Art Gal-

⏵ VISITING BANGALORE

INFORMATION

Tourist Office
48, Church Street
Tel./fax 080 – 25 58 54 17

Karnataka Tourism House
No. 8, Papanna Lane
St Mark's Road
Tel. 080 – 41 32 92 11/222
www.karnatakatourism.org

SHOPPING

Clothes, shoes and Western brand-name goods can be found in Mahatma Gandhi (MG) Road, Brigade Road and St Mark's Road and around Richmond Circle. Commercial Street and its side streets lure in shoppers with Indian textiles, jewellery and shoes. The »Safina Plaza« shopping centre is also not far away (Infantry Road). Busy bazaars can be found in the old town, particularly around Kempegowda Road and Citymarket/Chickpet. The city quarter of Indira Nagar is considered the new hip part of town, particularly 100 Feet Road and some of its cross roads with their furniture shops, arts and crafts, bars, cafés and galleries.
Residency Road, which branches off from MG Road, is home to many government shops with goods from the various states. Especially recommended is »Gujari« with products from the state of Gujarat.

Cauvery Crafts Emporium
Corner Brigade Road / MG Road
State-run shop for handicrafts, great selection of sandalwood products.

Cottage Industries Emporium
144, MG Road
Large selection of handicrafts and souvenirs.

WHERE TO EAT

► Expensive

① *Samarkhand*
Gem Plaza
66, Infantry Road
Tel. 080 – 41 11 33 64
Excellent northwest Indian cuisine and Tandoori dishes.

② *Memories of China*
In the Taj Residency
41/3, MG Road
Tel. 080 – 25 58 44 44
Top-quality Chinese specialities.

► Moderate

Baedeker recommendation

③ *Koshy's – an institution*
39, St Mark's Road
Tel. 080 – 22 21 37 93
Where do artists, kids and the people of Kerala meet? In Koshy's! The bar has been a the centre of Bangalore's scene for many decades and its waiters and cooks still com from Kerala. Be it beer, coconut soup, fis curry or chips: this place is sure to have i and it all tastes fantastic.

⑦ *Nandhini Deluxe Bar and Restaurant*
100 Feet Road
(near the turn-off to Airport Road)
Indiranagar
Tel. 080 – 25 28 88 81
Specialities from Andhra Pradesh, good biryanis and tandoori dishes.

► Inexpensive

④ *MTR*
(Mavalli Tiffin Rooms)
14, Lalbagh Road

Tel. 080 – 22 22 00 22
Very popular vegetarian restaurant, good southern Indian breakfasts and tasty thalis. The shop next door sells Mavalli Tiffin Room or MTR products (particularly sweets, snacks and pickles).

⑤ *Amruth*
14, St Mark's Road
Tel. 080 – 221 49 88
Here visitors can sample the southern Indian rice pancakes (dosa); there is a large selection of southern Indian and northern Indian vegetarian dishes.

⑥ *K.C. The Sweet Shop*
3, St Marks Road
Opposite Koshy's Restaurant
Very famous for its Bengali sweets and yoghurts. Try them with a tea or coffee.

WHERE TO STAY
► Luxury
① *Taj West End*
Race Course Road
Tel. 080 – 66 60 56 60
www.tajhotels.com
In the Taj West End Hotel guests reside in the middle of a park in pleasantly situated bungalows and enjoy the attractive pool and the very good cuisine.

② *ITC Hotel Windsor Sheraton & Towers*
26, Golf Course Road
Tel. 080 – 22 26 98 98
www.welcomgroup.com
This hotel offers every creature comfort imaginable and has five restaurants and two bars.

► Mid-range
③ *The Richmond Hotel*
88/2, Richmond Road
Tel. 080 – 22 23 36 66
The Richmond has a very central location; all of its 44 rooms have air conditioning. A restaurant serving international cuisine and a bar are also part of the package.

④ *Hotel Rama*
40/2, Lavelle Road
Tel. 080-222 733 11
Also very centrally located. The hotel has 55 rooms with air conditioning. There are two restaurants, one of which is the Charcoal, a lovely roof terrace restaurant.

► Budget
⑤ *Hotel Vellara*
283, Brigade Road
Tel. 080 – 25 36 91 16
Basic, clean hotel with a vegetarian restaurant.

---

lery and the Technological and Industrial Museum can all be found here. The Government Museum houses a collection of sculptures from the times of various southern Indian dynasties. In addition it exhibits miniatures and musical instruments. In the adjacent Venkatappa Art Gallery visitors can see pictures by modern Indian artists.

Opening hours:
Open: daily except
Wed 10am–5pm

At the northwest end of Cubbon Park is the imposing Vidhana Soudha, the seat of Karnataka's state parliament. The five-storey granite building, in which many different Indian architectural styles are reflected, was built in 1956.

Vidhana Soudha

★
Lalbagh Botanical Gardens
🕐
Opening hours:
Open: daily
8am–7.30pm

Further south of Cubbon Park, Lalbagh Botanical Gardens occupy an area of 96ha/237ac. The city's most popular park can be traced back to the Muslim rulers Hyder Ali and Tipu Sultan in the 18th century. Take a look at the **many, occasionally very rare, trees** here, some of which are already several hundred years old. Lotus ponds, lakes and a glasshouse, in which flower shows are held on a regular basis, can also be found in the gardens. From the park's highest point the **views of Bangalore are lovely**.

Fort

In the busy City Market quarter northwest of Lalbagh Botanical Gardens visitors can see the remains of a stone fort built under Hyder Ali and Tipu Sultan.

★
Tipu Sultan's Palace
🕐
Opening hours:
Open: daily
8.30am–5.30pm

Southwest of City Market is a further relic of the times of Muslim rule, Tipu Sultan's Palace. Construction of this two-storey building was begun under Hyder Ali in 1778 and completed in 1789 by his successor, after whom it was named. The ground floor contains an interesting exhibition about the ruler.

Bull Temple

On a hill in the south of Bangalore stands Bull Temple, dedicated to the god Shiva. It dates back to the days of the city's founding and houses a large **Nandi monolith**, Shiva's vehicle.

The glass pavilion of the botanical gardens

Anyone wanting to explore this area should hire a motorized rickshaw to get to the intersection Mahatma Gandhi Road / Brigade Road. MG Road can be explored to the east or the west. Those choosing the eastern direction will come across the Cauvery Crafts Emporium after just a few metres, where shoppers can buy handicrafts of all kinds – the sandalwood products are particularly famous. Residency Road branches off to the right a few metres further on. It is home to the very well organized shops run by the various states. Further still down MG Road is the large Cottage Industries Emporium with an excellent choice of handicrafts. Those choosing to follow MG Road in a westerly direction from Brigade Road will reach the Thomas Cook bureau de change almost immediately. Beyond it are department stores old and new as well as shops, all the way to Cubbon Park.

★
MG Road and side streets

Visitors can hire a motorized rickshaw to get to the lower end of Commercial Street with its many textile and jewellery shops. At the other end of the street is Jama Masjid Road with its mosque. Keep to the right to get to the old Muslim quarter of Shivaji Nagar with its bazaar streets. In order to get to Russell Market, one of the city's major fruit and vegetable markets, turn left off Jama Masjid Road into Minakshi Koil Street.
The church of **St Mary** can be seen from quite far away and to its left there is a busy bus station. Immediately in front of it an alleyway branches off from Minakshi Koil Street to the right, which leads to the indoor markets (approx. 150m/165yd).

Commercial Street, Shivaji Nagar and Russell Market

In Whitefield (22km/14mi to the east) is an ashram run by the world-famous but controversial guru Sai Baba, who has his headquarters in Putaparthi in the neighbouring state of Andhra Pradesh.

Whitefield

Banerghatta National Park is situated 21km/13mi south of Bangalore. It possesses a lion park, a crocodile farm and a snake farm amongst other things (open: daily except Tue 9am–5pm).

Banerghatta National Park
🕐

★ Lepakshi

A small gem lies hidden in the village of Lepakshi, 125km/78mi north of Bangalore. During the Vijayanagar dynasty the village received a significant temple for **Virabhadra**, a terrifying incarnation of Shiva. It contains not just wonderful sculptures, but also quite excellent ceiling paintings. Lepakshi is located in the south of Andhra Pradesh and can be reached from Bangalore via the highway towards Hyderabad in just under three hours.

A columned wall surrounds the temple, which is built in the classical southern Indian style. It stands on a rock in the south of the village. Even though the main entrance is in the north it is thought to bring

Papanasesvara Temple

good luck to enter the inner temple complex through the south gate. There, visitors will come across a large sculpture of the elephant god Ganesha. Further to the east is a huge stone cobra with seven heads.

Virabhadra is worshipped in the sanctum, which contains a 13m/42ft image of the god on the ceiling. In front of the sanctum is the impressive dance hall. It is supported by 70 columns, which have some wonderful sculptures. Lepakshi's distinctive feature is its excellent and well-preserved paintings on the ceiling of the dance hall. They depict scenes from various epics and legends. They illustrate life at court during that time with great mastery and fine brushwork. Thus the images also give insight into the fashions and hairstyles of that period and they also contain a portrait of the architect Virupanna as well as of his brother.

★ ★
Temple paintings ▶

At the eastern entrance there is also a huge **Nandi**. The bull which is the vehicle of Shiva, has been carved from a piece of rock and is 8m/26ft long and 4.5m/15ft tall.

★ ★ Belur · Halebid

D 13

Temples of the Hoysala dynasty
Distance: 200km/125mi west of Bangalore

State: Karnataka

The many relief friezes, large sculptures and fine ornamentations make the temple buildings of Belur and Halebid the most significant in India from an artistic standpoint.

History of the Hoysalas

The Hoysalas, an initiallyinsignificant ruling family from the western Deccan plateau, obtained considerable power during the 12th and 13th centuries. This was mainly at the expense of the Chola kings from Tamil Nadu, who had defeated the Hoysala ruler Vishnuvardhana in around AD 1117. Originally a follower of Jainism, Vishnuvardhana (1110–52) converted to Vishnuism under the influence of the famous Tamil philosopher Ramanuja. In the following two years the Hoysalas had countless temples built in honour of Vishnu. The most famous of them are the temples of Belur and Halebid in the area around Mysore, and the temple complex of Somnathpur.

Temple complexes

The first temple to be built during Vishnuvardhana's reign was that of Belur in 1117. The complex in Halebid followed in 1121, but it took 100 years to complete. Keshava Temple in Somnathpur (▶My-sore, Surroundings) was built in around 1268 and has, unlike the other temples, remained undamaged. The temples of the Hoysala dynasty came to fame as a result of their unusual shape and their magnificent ornamentation, which reveals great craftsmanship.

▶ VISITING BELUR · HALEBID

INFORMATION

KSTDC
Velapuri Hotel (Belur) or
AVK College Road (Hassan)
www.karnatakatourism.org

GETTING THERE

Visitors can get here from Mysore by
bus or train via the provincial town of
Hassan 118km/73mi to the northwest.
From there all of the sites can be
visited by bus or taxi (Belur: 37km/
23mi, Halebid: 32km/20mi from
Hassan, can be combined into a single
day). Sravana Belgola is situated approx. 50km/30mi southeast of Hassan.

WHERE TO EAT / WHERE TO STAY

▶ Luxury
Hoysala Village Resort
Belur Rd. (approx. 3km/2mi outside
Hassan)

Tel. 081 72 – 25 67 64
www.trailsindia.com
Nice bungalow complex with a
swimming pool and Ayurveda centre.

▶ Mid-range
Southern Star
BM Road, Hassan
Tel. 08 17 – 25 18 16
Centrally located good middle price
range hotel with a bar and restaurant.

The small provincial town of Hassan does not possess any attractions   **Hassan**
of its own, but is of interest to tourists as a starting location for visits
to the temples of Belur and Halebid, which are around 30km/20mi
away. Hassan has several hotels.

★ Belur

Chennakeshava Temple in Belur (16km/10mi from Halebid), built   **Chennakeshava**
under Vishnuvardhana in remembrance of his victory over the   **Temple**
Cholas, is one of the most significant examples of Hoysala architecture. It is situated in the middle of a large courtyard. An entrance in
the east flanked by two imposing towers leads to the complex's interior. The cruciform temple has entrances in the east, south and
north. The sanctum is located in the west. The structure is raised up
on a 1.5m/5ft platform, which has the same shape as the temple and
gives believers the opportunity to walk round it.
Artfully worked friezes decorate the temple's foundations. The **masterfully sculpted supporting statues, covered in rich ornaments**,
have achieved particular fame. They can be found along the temple's
exterior façades. Every one of the female statues has a different pose:

one is looking in the mirror, another is playing a musical instrument. The statue of the woman searching for a scorpion in the folds of her garment, revealing parts of her body in the process, is particularly attractive.

Here the Hoysalas' art is expressed in concentrated form; lavish body shapes blend with detailed features such as hairpieces and jewellery. The figure is embedded in ornaments and is defined by gestures and posture rather than facial expression. The greatest artistic precision and love of detail were used to chisel the images into the soft stone, which earned Hoysala art much admiration but also a lot of criticism, as it was claimed that it created soulless creatures in a sea of Baroque trivialities.

As was the case in the later temples, a lot of attention was given to the design of the **temple interior**: here there are further impressively worked supporting sculptures, and columns turned precisely on the lathe hold up a richly adorned ceiling.

The temple consecrated to Vishnu, the only one of the three used as such, is also open to non-Hindus. The courtyard also contains two further small temples and several secondary shrines.

Indian tourists visiting Chennakeshava Temple

✳ Halebid (Halebidu)

Even though King Vishnuvardhana converted to Vishnuism, Jainas and Shaivas were still allowed to practise their religions unhindered. For that reason his capital Dvarasamudra, which later became Halebid (»old capital«; 16km/10mi northeast of Belur, 32km/20mi north of Hassan), had temples dedicated to many different deities. The Hoysala kings ruled from Halebid from the 10th–14th centuries until their reign came to an end as a result of the Muslim conquest of the south.

Former capital

In the year 1310 and again in 1326, Muslim troops destroyed the town and a large proportion of the temples. Hoysaleshvara and Kedareshvara temples have survived the centuries.

Hoysaleshvara is a double temple, dedicated to the god Shiva and his wife Parvati. It was commissioned by Ketamalla, one of King Vishnuvardhana's generals, in 1121. The temple, which was not completed despite being under construction for almost 100 years, is now situated in the middle of a park. Like the other Hoysala structures Hoysaleshvara Temple is also built on a platform, which gives visitors the opportunity to walk round it. Both shrines are laid out in the typical **star-shaped** Hoysala style. As was the case with the temple in Belur, friezes run around the exterior walls. At the bottom there are elephants, on the higher bands there are lions, horses, fabled creatures, legends from the epics and finally wild geese.

Hoysaleshvara Temple

Above all of this is the entire world of the gods. Fantasy figures and human creatures also mingle amongst them in smaller guises. The shrines in the interior contain depictions of Shiva and Parvati with a Nandi, Shiva's vehicle, in front of both of them. Here too turned columns hold up the ceiling, which is populated by a dancing Shiva as Nataraja and by several other gods.

To the east of this building is the smaller Kedareshvara Temple, which is also consecrated to Shiva and was built under King Ballala II in 1219. It is star-shaped and bears the typical characteristics of Hoysala architecture.

Kedareshvara Temple

The Archaeological Survey of India maintains a small museum with a gallery of sculptures within the temple complex (open: daily except Fri 10am–5pm).

Museum
⊙

✳ Sravana Belgola (Shravan Belgola) E 13

Sravana Belgola is one of the major places of pilgrimage for Jains and the most important cult site of the **digambaras**, the »air-clad«, within the sect. The small peaceful town (approx. 50km/30mi southeast of Hassan) is located between two granite hills, the higher Indragiri (also Vindhyagiri) and the lower Chandragiri. Between the two

Important Jain place of pilgrimage

is a temple lake with ghats, which gave the site its name: Sravana Belgola means »White Pond«.

The town's history can be traced back to the third century BC. At that time the Maurya emperor Chandragupta, together with the saint Bhadrabahu, under whose influence he stood, came here to practise asceticism. Followers of the saint spread his teachings all over southern India and thus contributed to Jainism's firmly taking hold of this part of the country. The religion found powerful patrons in the Ganga dynasty, who proved to be generous patrons when it came to the construction of temples (called basti here). It was also during their ruling period that the statue of Bahubali or Gomateshvara (981) was built, which made this place so famous. **History**

It is necessary to ascend 614 steps carved into the rock to get to the top of the 160m/525ft Indragiri. It is a good idea to visit it early in the morning since climbing this hill in the blazing heat creates a more of a desire for something to drink than for culture. Those travellers who are unable to climb to the top of the hill by themselves have the opportunity to use the available **transport litters**. **Indragiri**

The destination of the hoards of pilgrims and the tourists is the 17.5m/57.5ft statue of Bahubali or Gomateshvara, son of Vrishadeva, who is considered the founder of Jainism. It is believed that the donor of **India's largest monolithic sculpture** was Chamunda Raya, a minister of the Ganga king Rachamalla II, who had the statue erected in 981. Since it represents a cult image of the digambaras, it is naked. Climbing plants around the arms and legs reveal the **typical ascetic**, who meditated in the same spot for years until his body was covered by nature.

★
◄ Statue of Bahubali

Every day believers lay offerings at the saint's feet. Every twelve years the entire statue is rubbed down with a mixture of milk, ghee, fruits and spices in a ceremony for which a scaffolding has to be built specially. During this time the small town is bursting at the seams, because the sect's followers go on pilgrimages to this place from all over India. The sculpture stands outside, surrounded by temple walls, which were built in later centuries. Here visitors will also find the cult images of the 24 tirthankaras (fordmakers) as well as reliefs of the eight guardians of the world.

Legend has it that the Maurya emperor Chandragupta and the saint Bahubali retreated to Chandragiri (Moon Hill) opposite to be ascetics. At the top of the hill is a group of bastis, with the stepped roof typical of southern India. The oldest one probably dates back to the eighth century. The architectural style of the Gangas and the Hoysalas can be recognized in some of the other temples. **Chandragiri**

← *Water is poured over Bahubali's feet as a sign of worship*

Bijapur · Gulbarga · Bidar

D/E 11

Capitals of the Deccan sultanates   **State:** Karnataka
Distances: 640km/400mi–750km/465mi
southeast of Mumbai

Magnificent Muslim buildings, relics of the capitals of the Deccan sultanates, can be admired in Bijapur, Bidar and Gulbarga in northern Karnataka.

History   In 1327 Mohammed ibn Tughluq moved his seat of government from Delhi to the fort of Daulatabad on the Deccan plateau in order to be able to have better control of his southern provinces. Nevertheless a rebellion erupted in 1347 and the independent Bahamani sultanate was founded by Sultan Bahman Shah.

The hostile disposition towards the central Muslim power meant that the new rulers of the Deccan plateau focused on contacts with the Islamic world outside India. Many foreigners, particularly from Persia, were employed in the army and administration, which occasionally led to rivalries between the Shiite »foreigners« and the local Sunnis. **Persian influence** also found its way into the new realm's arts and culture, and its capitals of Gulbarga (1347–1423) and Bidar (1423–1538) were at the centre of Islamic scholarship and artistic creativity. At the end of the 15th century the sultanate fell apart and five successor states formed: Berar, Ahmednagar, Bidar, Bijapur and Golconda, of which Bijapur still has the most evidence of the splendour of days gone by.

✳ Bijapur

»Agra of the South«   Its landmark, the huge mausoleum **Gol Gumbaz**, has earned Bijapur (population 200,000; 145km/90mi from Gulbarga) the noble name of »Agra of the South«. Although it can be seen at first glance that this is no serious competitor for the Taj Mahal, this town, which is somewhat off the beaten track, still has a lot to offer.

As if in a huge open-air museum, the countless, partially very well preserved monuments from the time of the Adil Shahi dynasty are dotted all over town. They can be found hidden in parks and gardens, inhabited by flocks of green parrots.

History   The town's foundation was already laid in the tenth–eleventh centuries under the Chalukya dynasty. They named their seat of government Vijayapura, i.e. City of Victory, to which the current name, Bijapur, can also be traced back. At the end of the 13th century the town came under Muslim influence, at first as part of the sultanate of Delhi and then later under the reign of the Bahmanis. Bijapur experienced its golden age as one of the five successor states of the fall-

▶ VISITING BIJAPUR · GULBARGA · BIDAR

INFORMATION

Tourist Office
Next to the hotel Mayura Adil Shahi
Annexe, Station Road, Bijapur
Tel. 083 52 – 25 03 59
www.karnatakatourism.org

GETTING THERE

Bijapur
Rail connections to Bijapur from
Gadag and Badami, bus connection
with many towns (such as Aurangabad, Hubli and Bangalore).

Gulbarga
Gulbarga is situated along the railway
line between Mumbai and Hyderabad / Bangalore / Chennai; many
trains stop there.

Bidar
Bidar is located on the railway line
Mumbai / Hyderabad / Chennai, but
beware: only Slow Passenger Trains
stop here; otherwise there are buses
from Gulbarga, Hyderabad and Bijapur.

WHERE TO STAY / WHERE TO EAT

▶ Mid-range / Budget
Madhuvan International
Station Road, Bijapur
Tel. 08 35 – 25 55 71
Comfortable hotel in Bijapur with a
restaurant and a bureau de change.

▶ Budget
KSTDC Mayura
Adil Shahi Annexe
Anand Mahal Road, Bijapur
Tel. 08 35 – 22 04 35
Four basic rooms right in the centre
of town.

Adithya
2–244 Main Road, Gulbarga
Tel. 084 72 – 22 40 40
Best hotel in town with a good
vegetarian restaurant.

Hotel Mayura Lodge
Opposite the bus station, Bidar
Tel. 08 48 – 22 81 42
Basic, centrally located.

en Bahmani Empire. Its founder, Yusuf Adil Shah, was the son of a
Turkish sultan. In the Bahmani Empire he was thrown into slavery
but still managed to advance all the way to becoming the ruler of a
new state. From 1489 onwards he and his successors ruled Bijapur
until Emperor Aurangzeb conquered the town in 1686, thereby ending the 200-year rule of the Adil Shah dynasty.
The rich heritage from that time consists of countless mosques,
tombs and palaces built in a very unique style. Anyone familiar with
the Mughal art of northern India will be surprised at the differences
here: the architects were not just influenced by Ottoman and Persian
ideas, the Hindu art of the neighbouring Vijayanagar Empire also
found its way to Bijapur.

A 10km/6mi, thick, oval wall containing nine entrance gates sur-   **Townscape**
rounds the town. At its centre is the citadel connected to the gates

via several roads. The attractions are concentrated in the western part of town, with the exception of Gol Gumbaz in the east and the mausoleum Ibrahim Rauza, which can be found outside of the town walls.

★ ★
Gol Gumbaz

Long before the traveller reaches Bijapur, the mausoleum's huge dome announces that the town is not far off. A massive tomb, Gol Gumbaz was built for Mohammed Adil Shah (1627–56), who wanted to eclipse all of his predecessors' final resting places. The complex covers an area of 1700 sq m/2033 sq yd. In addition to the actual tomb it contains a mosque, a music gallery and a dharamsala. Four seven-storey corner towers frame the 51m/167ft dome. Its interior diameter of 37m/120ft makes it the **world's second-largest roof dome** after St Peter's in Rome (38.5m/126ft).

Under the dome are the graves of the sultan and a few family members. In a gallery directly below the dome there is a »whispering gallery« with echo effects: it is the preferred destination of all children who visit. The structure's corner towers provide magnificent views of the town with its extensive parks.

Gol Gumbaz mausoleum was built for Mohammed Adil Shah

The Archaeological Survey of India maintains a small **museum** in front of Gol Gumbaz, exhibiting sculptures, manuscripts, carvings and very worthwhile **paintings of the Bijapur school** (open: daily except Fri 10am–5pm).   ⏰

On the way back to the centre it is possible to do a detour to Jama Masjid. This, the largest place of worship in Bijapur, was largely built during Ali Adil Shah's reign, but never completed. The complex's entire area covers 10,800 sq m/12,900 sq yd and has room for 2250 believers. Above the prayer hall in the west is the semicircular dome, which resembles the bud of a flower. The uncompleted building, which is missing two minarets, was later extended under Aurangzeb.   **Jama Masjid**

Take the road westwards towards the citadel to get to the Mithari Mahal, a richly ornamented gate flanked by two minarets, which leads to the mosque beyond it. East of it, in front of the Citadel, is the **Asar Mahal**, built in around 1646 under Mohammed Adil Shah. It once served as a courthouse. Some of the prophet's beard hairs were also kept here.   **Mithari Mahal**

On an area with a diameter of 500m/550yd, the Citadel contained the palaces and gardens as well as the kings' audience hall. Even though many of the structures have fallen into ruin, there are still some interesting remains of its former glory to be seen, such as the **Gagan Mahal**, built under Ali Adil Shah I in 1561. Its façade is adorned with three wonderful ogives. Remains of a further palace complex, the originally seven-storey Sat Manzil, are also still extant. Immediately opposite is a small water pavilion. There are also two old mosques inside the citadel: Karimuddin mosque in the south, presumably built at the start of the 14th century, and Mecca mosque further to the east, from the time of Ali Adil Shah II.   **Citadel**

The final resting place of Sultan Ali Adil Shah II, which remained uncompleted, and the tomb of the last ruler Sikander can be found in the western part of town. The saint Abdul Razzaq Quadir is also buried there.   **Further tombs**

In order to get to the mausoleum, leave the town to the west. An inscription reads: »Full of wonder the heavens watched the construction of this building and it could be said a second heaven was created as it grew from the ground.« The tomb praised in this way consists of a mausoleum and a mosque, which lie opposite each other in a garden. It was commissioned by Ibrahim Adil Shah (1580–1627) and contains the graves of the ruler, his wife Taj Sultana and further family members. The mausoleum resembles Gol Gumbaz in its floor plan, but is much smaller and adorned with finer ornamentation, features considered the typical characteristics of the Bijapur style.   ★
Mausoleum Ibrahim Rauza

Malik-i-Maidan One of the world's largest cannons can be found on the western side of the town wall: its imposing name Malik-i-Maidan means »Master of the Field«. It is 4.45m/4.87yd long, has a diameter of 1.5m/5ft and weighs around 5.5 tons. Its muzzle, in the shape of a wide open lion's mouth crushing an elephant, is aimed warningly at the would-be enemy.

Gulbarga (Kalburgi)

District capital Gulbarga (population 320,000) is situated along the railway line between Mumbai and Bangalore. A stop here is particularly worthwhile for those interested in Islamic art. In this area the town, which is a fair way away from the major tourist routes, has a lot to offer.

Townscape Hassan Bahman Shah made Gulbarga the capital of the Bahamni Empire, a sultanate that was independent of the central power, in 1347. During the 80 years that followed the town was fortified and equipped with plenty of prestigious buildings. It is surrounded by a thick wall and a 30m/33yd-wide ditch. Within the walls are the citadel, Bala Hisar, a rectangular block without windows, and Gulbarga's most famous building, the Friday Mosque.

✱ ✱
Jama Masjid The Friday Mosque owes its fame to **its architecture, which is unique in all of India**. The mosque's inner courtyard was entirely covered by domes, probably to protect believers from the blazing sun.
Accordingly, along with the large main dome over the prayer hall, the building is also crowned by 75 smaller and four somewhat larger corner domes. The otherwise open courtyard was thus transformed into a columned hall. Open ogives on all sides of the surrounding wall except to the west serve as light sources. The restrained architecture and the clever use of natural light create a spatial effect not achieved by mosques built in the conventional style. The mosque was begun as early as 1367 under the direction of a Persian architect, but it was not completed until 100 years later.

Domed tombs In the east of town visitors will find the domed tombs of the Bahmani sultans, including the group known as Haft Gubmaz, meaning »seven domes«.

✱
Dargah of Saint Gisu Daraz Some way away to the northeast is the burial complex (Dargah) of St Gisu Daraz, who came to Gulbarga to study in 1413. The complex comprises a school, mosques, tombs and accommodation. To this day it is a centre of religious activities.

Bidar

Rarely visited by tourists The town of Bidar in the far northeastern corner of Karnataka (110km/70mi northeast of Gulbarga) is visited by few tourists even

Selling white caps in front of Muslim temples in Gulbarga

though it possesses plenty of remains from the time when it was capital of the Bahmani Empire (1423–1538) and seat of government of the Barid Shahi dynasty (1492–1609). Powerful battlements surround the centre, which is home to mosques, palaces, tombs and an Islamic university.

The town's most famous mosque is Solah Khamba Mosque within the fort. It originally dates back to the year 1327, but was later renovated using Gulbarga's mosque as a model.

★
Solah Khamba Mosque

Of the many palaces, only a few remains are still extant. The best preserved is the **Rangin Mahal** from the time of the Bariden dynasty. It contains some wonderful mother-of-pearl inlay works. The Takht Mahal is older. Its decorations of colourful tiles bespeak the one-time magnificent interior of the royal residences.

★
Palaces

One piece of evidence revealing the Persian influence at the court of the Bahmani sultans is the madrasah, which was built under the scholar Khwaja Mahmud Gavan in 1472. The three-storey building, which surrounds a rectangular courtyard, houses classrooms, student accommodation and a library and is flanked by minarets on three sides. The minarets as well as the façades and walls are still covered in places in richly decorated colourful tiles.

★ ★
Madrasah of Khwaja Mahmud Gavan

Tombs In the northeast of town are the tombs of the Bahmani sultans. They are built in the style of the buildings in Gulbarga, but they exhibit an increasing Persian influence. The **tomb of Alauddin Ahmad Bahmani** (1436–58), which is richly decorated with tiles, is particularly worth a visit. At the western end of Bidar are the tombs of the later Baridi rulers. The most interesting is the tomb of Ali Barid.

✴ Chennai (Madras)

G 13

State: Tamil Nadu
Population: 6.5 million

Altitude: sea level
Distance: 334km/208mi east of Bangalore

Chennai, the capital of Tamil Nadu, is now one of India's largest cities. Just 300 years ago there was nothing here but sleepy villages, which have grown to become the various districts of Chennai.

Like Mumbai and Kolkata, Chennai is a relatively young city founded by the British colonial rulers. Its location made it a good harbour from which goods could be shipped to and from India. Since then Chennai has been developing constantly and is now an important industrial city. It is also a centre of film production that does not just have great economic significance but is also very closely linked with the political sector. Important politicians in India often come from the film industry.

The city does not have many attractions, but with its excellent hotels and good transport connections it is a good starting location for a trip through southern India. As the **cultural centre of the Tamils**, Chennai's many cultural events and museums allow interested parties to learn more about classical Indian music, classical temple dance (Bharata Natyam) and the masterpieces in stone and bronze.

History Even though the city's history only goes back 300 years, the area where Chennai now stands was already of significance before that time. One of the most important Tamil poets, Thiruvalluvar, lived in Mylapore 2000 years ago; it is now a district of Chennai. The Tirukkural, an anthology of couplets written by Thiruvalluvar, is among the great works of world literature. The apostle Thomas, who founded one of the first Christian communities in the world in Kerala, also died in the region of modern-day Chennai. The mountain near the airport is called Mount St Thomas in his honour.

In the past there was even a Christian settlement with a church in Mylapore; they were, however, reclaimed by the sea. Marco Polo also visited this region in the 13th century. When the Portuguese settled here in 1522 they found only a few small fishing villages. The first

Chennai *Map*

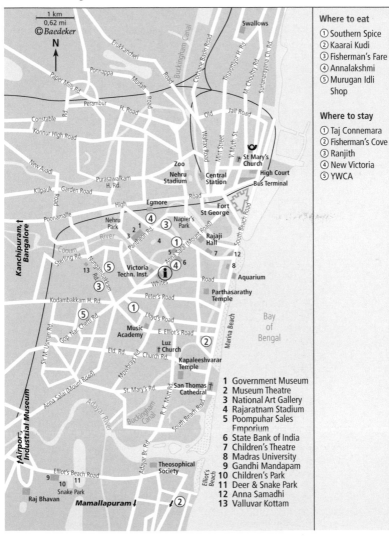

1 Government Museum
2 Museum Theatre
3 National Art Gallery
4 Rajaratnam Stadium
5 Poompuhar Sales Emporium
6 State Bank of India
7 Children's Theatre
8 Madras University
9 Gandhi Mandapam
10 Children's Park
11 Deer & Snake Park
12 Anna Samadhi
13 Valluvar Kottam

British settlement was founded in 1639 by the East India Company in the small village of Chennapatnam. After just two years the British built Fort St George, from where they exported clothes to England. North of the fort another settlement established itself, Madraspatnam (the »black town«), where the dark-skinned Indian population

▶ VISITING CHENNAI

INFORMATION

Tamil Nadu Tourism Complex
2 Wallajah Rd.
Tel. 044 – 25 36 83 58
www.tamilnadutourism.org

India Tourism
154, Anna Salai
Tel. 044 – 284 64 59

FESTIVALS

Chennai is a centre of classical South Indian music and dance. Information is available at www.kalakshetra.in and www.kutcheribuzz.com.

SHOPPING

One of the main shopping streets is Anna Salai: handicrafts can be bought in the Cottage Industries Emporium and the Victoria Technical Institute; the traditional book shop Higginbotham's is also recommendable. The famous Kanchipuram silk can be obtained in Vardharams in Harrington Road, Chetput or from Co-optex in Egmore. Well known local bazaars can be found in T. Nagar, such as Pondi Bazaar and Pangal Park, as well as in George Town.

WHERE TO EAT

▶ Expensive

① **Southern Spice**
In Taj Coromandel
MG Road
Tel. 044 – 55 00 28 27
Specialities from southern Indian cuisine, very good fish and seafood.

② **Kaarai Kudi**
10, Sivaswamy Street
Mylapore
Tel. 044 – 281 11 89
Spicy Chettinad cuisine serving wildfowl, fish and seafood.

▶ Moderate

③ **The Fisherman's Fare**
24, Casa Major Road
Egmore
Good fish dishes.

▶ Inexpensive

④ **Annalakshmi**
Anna Salai
Opposite Higginbotham's
Tel. 044 – 28 52 51 09
Tasty vegetarian dishes.

⑤ **Murugan Idli Shop**
77/1A, G.N. Chetty Road
T. Nagar and Elliot Beach
Tel. 044 – 28 15 54 62
Great selection of southern Indian snacks such as idlis and dosas.

WHERE TO STAY

▶ Luxury

① **Taj Connemara**
Binny Road, tel. 044 – 66 00 00 00
www.tajhotels.com
Chennai's only Heritage Hotel in the heart of the city with good cuisine and all the amenities.

② **Fisherman's Cove**
Covelong Beach
Tel. 041 14 – 67 41 33 33
For those who want luxurious accommodation by the sea, this hotel, also part of the Taj group, lies approx. 30km/20mi south of the city on Covelong beach.

▶ Mid-range / Budget

③ **Ranjith**
15, Mahatma Gandhi Road
Tel. 044 – 28 27 05 21
51 rooms (some of them with air conditioning) as well as a good roof garden restaurant serving international cuisine.

④ *New Victoria*
3, Kennet Lane
Egmore
Tel. 044 – 28 19 36 38
All of the rooms have air conditioning; there is also a restaurant and an
internet café.

► **Budget**
⑤ *YWCA*
1086, Poonamallee High Road
Tel. 044 – 25 32 42 51
www.ywcachennai.com
Nice rooms, pleasant atmosphere,
restaurant and breakfast buffet.

settled. In the 18th century the French and British competed for
control of the harbour town. The French even managed to occupy it
for a short time (1746–49), but after a battle in Arcot the town was
returned to British rule. Until India's independence in 1947 Chennai
was a centre of British rule in India and since then it has been the
capital of the state of Tamil Nadu.

Fort St George and Surroundings

The fort was built by Francis Day and Andrew Gogan and was the
centre of British Madras. Since its construction in 1640 it has been
renewed several times. It was from here that Robert Clive led the
Carnatic War against the French in 1744–54. The East India Company made its profitable business dealings in colonial India from
forts such as this.

Fort St George and the Fort Museum

The Exchange Building, Chennai's first bank, now houses the **Fort
Museum**. It exhibits an extensive collection of coins, medals, flags
and letters from the colonial period. The first floor, the Art Gallery,
contains portraits of important personages. North of the fort is the
old lighthouse from the year 1844.

🕐
Opening hours:
Open: daily except
Fri 9am – 5pm

South of the Fort Museum is Asia's oldest Anglican church, which
was consecrated in 1679. The church's thick walls attest to times during which the city was besieged by the French and British. During
the war it served as a storage facility and a shelter.

St Mary's Church

The district to the north of the fort was renamed Georgetown in
honour of King George V's visit to India. Today it is a busy part of
town, home to the High Court and two churches. The **High Court**
was built by the architect Henry Irwin in the Indo-Saracenic style
in 1892. The very attractive red building bestows a sense of majesty
on a square now completely taken over by traffic. West of the High
Court on the other side of the busy street is the **Armenian Church**
from the year 1772. The East India Company held the Armenians in
high regard as merchants. They enjoyed the same rights as the British and lived in the part of town reserved for white people. Immediately north of the Armenian Church stands **St Mary of the Angels**
(1642).

Georgetown

Marina beach is a popular meeting place

Marina Beach

Chennai's beach is 18km/11mi long. Extending along it for more than 5km/3mi from the harbour in the north to the church of St Thomas in the south is the popular Marina Beach. The new **memorial sites for Tamil Nadu's prime ministers**, built on the left-hand side of Marina Beach when looking from the fort, are particularly impressive. The monument for one of them, Dr C. N. Annadurai, has an entrance in the shape of two large elephant tusks. In the evenings the beach is populated by countless snack vendors and people going for strolls. It is particularly worthwhile to watch the hustle and bustle of traders and shell sellers on Sundays.

Madras University

The university with its pleasant Indo-Saracenic buildings is on the opposite side of the beach. To the south of the somewhat dilapidated Marina Swimming Pool is an aquarium, opposite which stands the ice house. This is where ice brought over by sailing boats in huge blocks from North America was stored 150 years ago.

Continue southbound along the road by the beach to get to the lighthouse, then to St Thomas's Cathedral. This road then leads to Mylapore, where visitors will find Kapaleeshvarar Temple and the Theosophical Society.

Mylapore

St Thomas's Cathedral

This Roman Catholic church was originally built in the Gothic style in 1504, but it was remodelled in 1893. It is said the relics of the apostle Thomas are in this church.

Kapaleeshvarar Temple in the district of Mylapore is a Shiva temple built in the 16th century. There had been a cult site consecrated to Shiva here as early as the seventh century. A 37m/121ft gopuram towers over the main entrance. Its countless stucco figures are colourful depictions of the many gods populating the Hindu pantheon. The temple courtyard has a **small temple for Parvati**, Shiva's wife. She is worshipped as a peahen in this temple. Apparently Shiva cursed her, transforming her into this guise; he returned her to her original form only after serious repentance. It is for this reason that the district is named Mylapore (peacock city).

★
Kapaleeshvarar Temple

West of Kapaleeshvarar Temple stands Chennai's oldest church, which was built by the Portuguese in 1582.

Luz Church

Anna Salai and Surroundings

With its many shops, Anna Salai or Mount Road is the main artery of the city of Chennai. The most important section of this road begins at the roundabout with a statue of Conjeevaram Annadurai, one of Tamil Nadu's former chief ministers, and runs in a dead straight line to Anna Flyover in the southwest. The road subsequently turns south to the airport.

Anna Salai

Banks and airlines have their offices in Mount Road and there are handicraft shops, book shops and much more. The state-run Poompuhar handicraft shop with its excellent bronze figures deserves special mention, as does the well-known book shop called Higginbotham's. From the Annadurai statue, take Ellis Road and go past the Great Mosque to get to the district of Triplicane and Parthasarathy Temple. Drive southeast along Mount Road and turn right into Binny Road, then cross the Coleroon river to get to Pantheon Road and the museum complex located there.

Parthasarathy Temple is dedicated to one of Vishnu's incarnations, Parthasarathy, Arjuna's royal charioteer in the Mahabharata. It was built in the eighth century by the Pallavas and later extended under the Pandya, Chola and Vijayanagar dynasties.

Parthasarathy Temple

The museum, which was founded in 1857, is spread over several buildings. Amongst its exhibits are discoveries from the Stone Age, musical instruments, objects from India's tribal population and portraits of famous British personages. The museum's greatest attraction, the **masterpieces of southern Indian bronze art**, are located in a new building, the Bronze Gallery. These figures were cast out of five metals (pancha dhatu) and are considered to be amongst the best works of their kind. The different depictions of **Nataraja**, dancing Shiva, are particularly impressive. Also worth seeing is the Art Gallery, which is housed in a pleasant Indo-Saracenic building. The fascinating exhibits here include Mughal and Rajput miniatures

★ ★
Government Museum and Art Gallery

⊙
Opening hours:
Open: daily except Fri 9.30am–5pm

as well as glass pictures from Thanjavur. The main items of interest in the archaeological department are the sculptures of the great stupa in Amarvathi.

Further Attractions

Valluvar Kottam The monument for the great Tamil poet Thiruvalluvar is a stone replica of the famous temple chariot of Thiruvarur. Its stone walls are engraved with all 1330 couplets.

Snake Park In Snake Park in Guindy there is a small zoo, which mainly keeps snakes.

Theosophical Society The Theosophical Society has its seat in a huge park in the southern city district of Adyar and is a place of calm in hectic Chennai. It was founded by Henry Steel Olcott and Helena Blavatsky in the United States in 1875 and in 1882 its headquarters were moved to Chennai. The building contains an impressive library with religious and philosophical literature. A further attraction on the complex is a huge ⊙ banyan tree, which is believed to be the largest in the world (open: daily except Sun 8.30am–10.30am and 2pm–4.30pm).

Kalakshetra This centre was founded in 1936 by Rukmini Devi Arundale, who wanted to develop the classical arts further. Her dancing school for Bharata Natyam is now world famous; music and textile design are also taught. Dance and music events are regularly held on the pleasant complex. Kalakshetra is located in the south of Chennai near Elliot beach.

Around Chennai

★
Vedanthangal 86km/53mi southwest of Chennai is India's oldest bird sanctuary. During the breeding season from November to February there are ⊙ more than 100 different species to be seen here (open mid-Nov–end of April daily 6am–6pm).

Tirupati and Sri-Venkateshvara Temple In the forested mountains around Tirumala (approx. 100km/60mi northwest of Chennai), at an elevation of 900m/2950ft, visitors will find Sri-Venkateshvara Temple, one of India's most important temples of pilgrimage. Since the temple is very popular with the merchant caste and millions of pilgrims flock here every year it is also the richest in India. Dating from the tenth century, it does not possess any architectural attractions but does provide the opportunity to experience the workings of a busy temple close up. It is attended by up to 4000 visitors every day. Many pilgrims have their hair cut off here in the hope that this sacrifice will bring them the fulfilment of their wishes. At the foot of the mountains lies the town of **Tirupati**, which is home to the 16th-century Govindarajaswami Temple.

In South Indian temples believers can have themselves »blessed« by temple elephants

Located in the surrounding area is **Chandragiri**, home to the palace of the Vijayanagar kings. After their defeat in Talikota in 1564 they retreated to this place and built the palace on a 180m/590ft rock.

★ Kanchipuram

The temple city of Kanchipuram (70km/45mi west of Chennai) is one of the Hindus' seven sacred cities. In contrast to the other cities it is sacred to both Shaivas and Vaishnavas. Kanchipuram's significance lies in the numerous temples more than 1000 years old that are dotted all over the city. Kanchipuram is also known for its heavy, hand-woven **silk saris**, which have been produced here for almost a millennium.

Former capital of the Pallava Kingdom

Kanchipuram was founded by the Pallava dynasty and was their capital for almost half a millennium. Under the successive kingdoms of the Cholas, Pandyas and Vijayanagar rulers it remained a religious centre. It is thought that it was under the important Pallava king Narasimhavarman II (around 680–720) that the magnificent Kailasanatha Temple was built; its gopuram, resembling a step pyramid, shaped temple architecture all over southern India. At the time Kanchipuram was considered the religious centre for followers of different faiths, such as Jainism, Buddhism and Hinduism.

★★
Kailasanatha Temple

🕑 Opening hours: Sanctum closed from 12.30pm–4pm

The entire complex is surrounded by a wall with 58 shrines. They enclose the central temple, which is crowned by a four-storey Vimana. Opposite it is the small Mahendravarmeshvara shrine with a two-storey roof. The temple's main entrance is located on the east side and is crowned by a pagoda-like structure, a construction that was to develop into the classical **gopuram towers** in later temples.

A walk clockwise along the inside of the surrounding wall reveals the heights attained in the art of sculpture under the Pallava dynasty. Its lively, dynamic use of forms is outstanding. The wall has niches with lovely sculptures of Shiva, Parvati and other gods. In addition the remains of original paintings can still be discerned in some places. In

Silk processing in Kanchipuram

the central temple's sanctum Shiva is worshipped in the form of a 16-sided lingam. It also contains a very interesting depiction of the legendary dance competition between Shiva and Parvati. The temple is considered a **milestone in the development of the South Indian temple type**. The temples built at a later date in Chidambaram and Sri Rangam and Ekambareshvara Temple in Kanchipuram have larger complexes and their gopurams have become landmarks visible from great distances.

Kanchipuram's largest temple (1509) with its 58m/190ft gopuram is a highly visible symbol of the Vijayanagar dynasty and an example of the later South Indian temple type. The entire complex covers 10ha/25ac and has five courtyards, all of which are separated from each other by walls. The believers walk once or three times around these courtyards in a clockwise direction, thus slowly making their way to the sanctum with its cult figure.

Ekambareshvara Temple (Ekambara-Natar Temple)

The complex is entered from the south through the largest temple tower, whereupon visitors enter the fifth courtyard with the Thousand-column Hall and a pond (Kampai Tirtta), which is said to contain the water of an underground holy river. The fourth courtyard contains a small Ganesha temple and a large temple pond. The inside of the third courtyard's surrounding wall is decorated with many small shrines. A holy mango tree, which is said to bear four different mango varieties, can be found behind the cella in the second courtyard. According to legend Shiva is said to have transformed the Vedas into a mango tree with four branches and settled down below it in the form of a lingam. The actual temple is in the first courtyard and has two vestibules and the sanctum containing the lingam cult figure. **This temple is not open to non-Hindus.**

Vaikuntha Perumal Temple was built by Nandivarnam II in the eighth century. It is considered an example of the Pallavas' highly developed temple architecture. Three cellae have been built one above the other in the temple. They contain depictions of Vishnu in various guises. The temple is accessed via an attractive columned hall. Fabulous lion-like beasts make up the columns' bases. On the inside of the temple wall, reliefs depict the Pallavas' history. The **sanctum is open only to Hindus.**

Vaikuntha Perumal Temple

This monumental Vishnu temple from the twelfth century is protected by a high wall. Its lovely 100-column hall is open to non-Hindus.

Varadaraja Perumal Temple

Kanchipuram is also home to one of the three most important temples in India for Shakti, Shiva's wife in the form of **Kamakshi**. According to legend Kamakshi once lured Shiva to Kanchipuram, where she married him. For that reason a big festival is held in her honour in the months of February and March each year.

Kamakshi Amman Temple

Chidambaram

F 14

State: Tamil Nadu
Population: 70,000

Altitude: 6m/20ft
Distance: 250km/155mi south of Chennai

Chidambaram, located in the fertile Kaveri river delta 60km/35mi south of Puducherry, is an agricultural region that has been used for the intensive cultivation of rice for millennia. This area was the heartland of the Chola dynasty (880–1267), during which time many temples were built and Tamil literature flourished.

The Cholas traded a lot with Southeast Asia and influenced the cultures there. To this day the region is covered by paddy fields and during the monsoon it is transformed into a green carpet on which there are many villages surrounded by palm trees. Chidambaram is now an **important place of pilgrimage for Shaivas**, who come here to visit the famous Nataraja Temple. In February / March an interesting dance festival takes place here.

One of Shiva's 108 classical dance poses

Chidambaram is also called Thillai, because a forest of thillai trees is said to have stood here once. The Cholas, who considered themselves »as bees at the lotus feet of Nataraja«, started building the temple in the tenth century; it later developed into the focus of the town. It was constantly expanded by Pandya king Kulottunga III (1178–1216), the Vijayanagar rulers and the Nayakkars (17th century). Today Nataraja Temple is one of Tamil Nadu's best-known temples.

★ ★
Nataraja Temple

With its four large gopurams, Nataraja Temple covers an area of 16ha/40ac. The western one is the oldest and also the most beautiful. It presumably served as a model for the other temple towers, which were built in subsequent centuries. On the side walls of several towers visitors can see **dance positions from the Natyashastra**, the classical treatise on the art of dance. Shiva himself is said to have invented 108 dance positions and to this day dances are performed in Chidambaram in his honour.

Non-Hindus are allowed to enter the temple's inner courtyard, where there are four halls (sabhas): Deva Sabha (Divine Hall), Chit Sabha (Hall of Wisdom), Kanakha Sabha (Golden Hall) and Nritta Sabha (Dance Hall). There is a bronze Nataraja in Chit Sabha, but tourists may not access its cella. An invisible Akasa Lingam is also worshipped here. Kanakha Sabha and Chita Sabha have gilded roofs that sparkle in the afternoon sun. The **Dance Hall** (Nritta Sabha) with its 56 masterfully carved columns and exceptional depictions of dance is designed as a temple chariot, which is highlighted through the wheels and horses on the side walls. In addition to the temple itself, the extensive grounds are home to a large temple pond (the Shivaganga Tank) surrounded by colonnades, the large Thousand-Column Hall (Raja Sabha) and temples for Vishnu, Ganesha and Muruga. Muruga, also known as Subramaniam, is Shiva's younger son and very popular in Tamil Nadu. Amongst the temple's particular riches are the **deities' gemstone jewellery**, which was donated by a large number of believers.

In the tenth century the Chola kings chose Shiva in his form of Nataraja (»Lord of Dance«) to be the family deity and built the current temple in exactly the place where the centre of the universe was said to be and where Nataraja purportedly performed the Ananda Tandawa, the Dance of Delight. The name Chidambaram (heavenly space) refers to this legend to this day. However, it is assumed that a tree and a pond were here before, and that these were associated with a mother deity and worshipped as sacred before the Cholas connected this place with Shiva. Thus Chidambaram is a good example of how pre-Aryan religious sites were appropriated through the construction of a Hindu temple.

Nataraja

► VISITING CHIDAMBARAM

INFORMATION
TTDC Tourist Office
Railway Feeder Road
Tel. 041 44 23 87 39
www.tamilnadutourism.org

GETTING THERE
Chidambaram lies 58km/36mi south of Puducherry and can be visited from there in a day excursion. There are also rail connections with Chennai and Bangalore and buses go from Madurai, Thanjavur and Puducherry.

FESTIVALS
Markashi Tiruvathirai, a temple festival, is celebrated in December / January.

WHERE TO EAT / WHERE TO STAY
▶ **Budget**
Saradharam
19 Venugopal Pillai St.
(opposite the bus station)
Tel. 041 44 – 22 13 36
There is a choice of three restaurants here. Some of the rooms have air conditioning, and there is a garden.

★★
Gangaikonda
Cholapuram

Today, Gangaikonda Cholapuram (42km/26mi southwest of Chidambaram) is a forlorn village with a few tea stalls. King Rajendra built an elegant temple here at the beginning of the eleventh century. To this day it is **one of the most beautiful in Tamil Nadu**. He also temporarily moved the capital from Thanjavur to Gangaikonda Cholapuram and for a short while the town flourished. It soon sank into oblivion again, however. The temple is said to have been built in honour of Rajendra's victory over the kings of the northern Indian empires. The tributary kings had to send water from the Ganges to Rajendra, which he then had filled into a temple pond. The town's name also means »the Chola town that Ganga brought« (►Baedeker Special p.290).

The temple tower rises up above a 30m/33yd square and its concave curve gives it an elegant appearance. It was in Gangaikonda Cholapuram that an assembly hall (Mahamandapa) was built with 150 columns for the first time. It served as the model for the later Thousand-Column Halls of many southern Indian temples.

★★ Hampi (Vijayanagara)

E 12

State: Karnataka

Distance: 350km/215mi northwest of Bangalore

Although India spoils its visitors with countless monuments of its eventful past, only a few places attest to the splendour and transience of an era as much as the ruins of Vijayanagara near the village of Hampi.

»City of Victory« is the name the rulers gave to their capital, which was once the centre of the most powerful kingdom in southern India, a flourishing trading town and the centre of diverse cultural activities. From 1343 to when they were totally destroyed in 1565, the Vijayanagara kings controlled the entire southern part of the subcontinent from here and travelling merchants compared the town to Rome with regard to both its magnificence and its population. To this day the **more than 1000 buildings distributed over an area of 26 sq km/10 sq mi** convey an unforgettable impression of the size of the old royal city.

Vijayanagara lies on the Deccan plateau in Central Karnataka near the town of Hospet. The plateau is blessed with little rainfall but is traversed by several rivers. One of them, the Tungabhadra, forms the northern border of the old town. The predominantly flat land dotted with small hills has a special surprise in store here: a sea of granite rocks of all sizes, forming entire hills, forms the backdrop for the ruins hidden amongst them.

The ruins of Hampi are situated in the middle of a bizarre rockscape

Legend

Many legends mention this rocky landscape that has such a mysterious air. According to local tradition it was the location of a shrine for Shiva, who was worshipped as Virupaksha here. Virupaksha, the three-eyed Shiva, also later became the patron god of the Vijayanagara rulers. Episodes from the epic Ramayana are also closely connected to this place, which finds mention in it as Kishkindha. Several temples were erected for Rama and the monkey king Hanuman in Vijayanagara; the most famous of them is the big Ramachandra Temple in the heart of the city's royal centre.

History

The city was founded in the Middle Ages. After the retreat of the sultans and their troops from southern India, around 1330 various Hindu rulers attempted to take control of the land under Muslim administration. In this endeavour the brothers Harihara and Bukka from the Sangama family, who were warriors in the service of a local prince, proved particularly successful. Just two decades later, after many small wars against Muslim and Hindu rivals, they were clearly the most powerful rulers on the Deccan plateau. **In 1336 they founded the capital Vijayanagara**. For one and a half centuries, from 1336 to 1485, the successors of the victorious brothers occupied the throne of Vijayanagara, to be followed by the Saluva dynasty (1485–1506) and the Tuluvas (1505–65). During this time the empire

● VISITING HAMPI

INFORMATION

KSTDC Tourist Office
In Hampi Bazar
Tel. 083 94 – 22 85 37

In Hospet
Taluk Office Circle
Tel. 083 94 – 42 85 37
www.karnatakatourism.org

GETTING THERE

From Bangalore and Hyderabad there are rail connections to Hospet, from Goa via Hubli; in addition there are express buses from Goa and Bangalore. For the journey from Hospet to Hampi it is best to take a bus or taxi (13km/8mi).

FESTIVALS

The Hampi Festival takes place at the beginning of November.

WHERE TO STAY · WHERE TO EAT

▶ **Mid-range**

Malligi
6/143 JN Road; Hospet
Tel. 083 94 – 22 81 01
Pleasant hotel with a nice interior, a pool and a vegetarian restaurant.

KSTDC Mayura Bhuvaneshwari
Kamalapuram (4km/2.5mi from Hampi Bazar)
Tel. 083 94 – 24 15 74
Some of the rooms here have air conditioning. There is a pleasant garden and a restaurant.

▶ **Budget**

Shanti Guesthouse
North of Virupaksha temple
Tel. 083 94 – 24 15 68
Very basic, clean hotel, highly popular amongst backpackers.

extended to the Bay of Bengal in the east and to the Arabian Sea in the west as well as all the way to the tip of the subcontinent. Particularly during the first half of the 16th century under Tuluva ruler Krishnadevaraja (1510–29) and his successor Achyutadevaraja (1529–42) the empire flourished. Many new temples dedicated to various aspects of Vishnu were built, since the Tuluvas were Vaishnavas.

However, the day came when even Vijayanagara's auspicious name could no longer help. Domestic tensions as well as undiplomatic policies towards the empire's Muslim neighbours in the north caused the latter to join forces against the Tuluvas. On 26 January 1565 the united armies of the sultanates of Bijapur, Golconda, Bidar and Ahmadnagar defeated the troops of the kingdom a few hundred miles northwest of the capital. After the death of the military leader Ramaraja the remaining soldiers fled back to Vijayanagara, which they then left to their pursuing enemies to plunder and destroy. The Vijayanagara Empire survived the destruction of its centre for some time, but it was never able to recover properly. With the fall of the »City of Victory« the glorious days of its rulers also came to an end.

Hampi *Map*

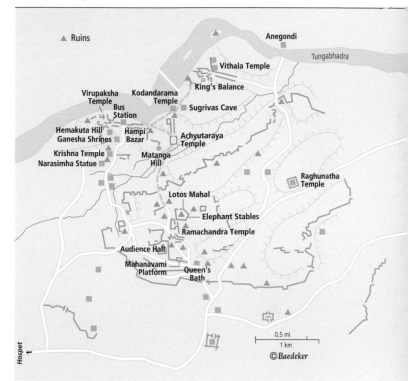

▲ Ruins

Anegondi

Tungabhadra

Vithala Temple

King's Balance

Virupaksha Temple   Kodandarama Temple

Sugrivas Cave

Bus Station

Hemakuta Hill Ganesha Shrines   Hampi Bazar

Achyutaraya Temple

Krishna Temple
Narasimha Statue

Matanga Hill

Raghunatha Temple

Lotos Mahal

Elephant Stables

Ramachandra Temple

Audience Hall

Mahanavami Platform   Queen's Bath

0,5 mi
1 km
©Baedeker

Hospet

Visitors should take at least two days to visit the architectural monuments. It is possible to register for guided tours at the tourist bureau or directly at the tourist information centre in Hampi Bazar. Area maps are also available there. There is a bus connection between Hampi Bazaar and Hospet, as well as between Hampi Bazaar and the village of Kamalapuram, which is situated south of the royal centre. Most tourists use the provincial town of Hospet as their base for a Hampi excursion.

Tip

Religious Centre

At the western end of Hampi Bazar is Virupaksha Temple, Vijayanagara's most important temple. To this day **Shiva is worshipped here in his guise of Virupaksha**. The complex in fact consists of two separate temple complexes surrounded by walls and linked to each other by a gate; these complexes are laid out on an east-west axis. The temple complex's main entrance points eastwards and is crowned by a

✱ Virupaksha Temple

52m/171ft gopuram from the time of Krishnadevaraja. This entrance leads through the first courtyard, a rectangular square surrounded on all four sides by columns and smaller shrines. The central shrine with the sanctum is located in the complex's western part, which is accessed via another gate. An inscription indicates the date of completion (1510) of this rather modest 15m/50ft gopuram. The individual sections of the main temples were also built at different times. The small, square sanctum at the heart of the complex dates back to the Rashtrakuta period in the ninth–tenth centuries. The temple itself was built in the 14th century, shortly after the foundation of the capital, and in two further construction phases (15th and 16th centuries) it was expanded by the addition of a further vestibule and another Mandapa adorned with artfully carved pillars. The drawings on its ceiling probably date back to the 18th century.

Manmatha Tank

Walk through the gopuram at the northern end of Virupasha temple to get to a rectangular pond known as the Manmatha Tank.

Hemakuta Hill

South of Virupaksha Temple lies the sacred Hemakuta Hill, which is surrounded by fortifications. More than 30 larger and smaller temples are dotted around the hill, most of which were built in the ninth and tenth centuries.

Ganesha shrines

At the eastern and southern sides of Hemakuta Hill are two small shrines for Ganesha, Shiva's son. The eastern shrine houses a 4.5m/15ft statue of the elephant god carved from a single lump of rock. Somewhat further south, in the middle of an airy pavilion, is the second Ganesha sculpture. It depicts the god in a sitting position.

Krishna Temple

Somewhat further south is the Krishna temple complex, completed under Krishnadevaraja in 1515. Large parts of the temple were, however, destroyed after the city's occupation. Two large surrounding walls enclose the main temple, which is situated in a courtyard along with many secondary shrines.

✱ Narasimha figure

A few steps south of Krishna Temple is the imposing sculpture of Vishnu's incarnation as Narasimha. This statue, which was also carved from a single lump of rock, is 6.7m/22ft tall, making it the **largest of its kind in Vijayanagara**. An inscription reveals it to have been a donation by Krishnadevaraja in 1528. The wild-eyed god with a lion's head is sitting as a yogi with crossed legs under an archway crowned by a many-headed cobra.

Matanga Hill

Returning to Hampi Bazar, follow the processional road in an eastbound direction to find Matanga Hill on the right. Steps lead up to

Not scared of big gods! →
Vishnu as Narasimha

the top of the hill. The shrine there is consecrated to Virabhadra, a bellicose form of Shiva. The wide **panorama** from this highest point of the entire complex is particularly impressive.

Achyutadevara-jas Temple

The complex lies in a valley with a north-south orientation, which explains the temple's own unusual orientation towards the north. It was consecrated to Vishnu in his form as Tiruvengalanatha in 1534 and was a donation by Hiriya Tirumala, the king's chief minister. The temple, also known as Achyutadevarajas Temple, is amongst Vijayanagara's larger complexes. It is surrounded by two walls, both of which allow visitors to enter through large gopurams on their north side. The inner enclosure has additional gates in the east and west. At its centre is its central shrine as well as a secondary shrine.

Kodandarama Temple

Leave Hampi Bazar at the eastern end and take a small path in a northbound direction to get down to the river and to the Chakratitha ghats. Higher up, on the northern slopes of Matanga Hill, stands Kodandarama Temple. Its sanctum is built against a large rock, out of which the standing figures of Rama, Sita and Lakshmana were carved.

Narasimha Temple

Further to the northeast is Narasimha Temple, probably the oldest structure in this part of the religious centre. According to an inscription in the rock in its courtyard it dates back to the year 1379. Between the temple and the river protruding rocks form a deep cleft known as **Sugriva's Cave**. Ochre and white bands painted on to the rock mark this place as holy.

King's Balance

On the path along the southern riverbank leading to Vithala temple visitors go through a high, two-storey gate. A few metres further on there is an unusual construction, known as the King's Balance. It consists of two slender pillars adorned with reliefs as well as a lintel to which three fastenings are attached. The scales which originally hung from it have long since disappeared.

★ ★
Vithala Temple
🕐
Opening hours:
Open: daily
6am–6pm

Vithala Temple is considered the finest example of religious architecture in Vijayanagara. The once severely damaged temple has seen extensive restoration and now impresses even visitors tired from long sightseeing trips on foot. The structure dates back to the 16th century and is dedicated to Vishnu in his form as Vithala. High walls, interrupted in the east, south and north by entrance gates, surround the spacious courtyard, where the main temple, its vestibules and secondary shrines can be found. The sanctum is a small, square structure with a brick tower and a gallery, which is connected to a further vestibule in the east.

The temple's jewel is the open mandapa in front of it. According to the inscription it dates back to the year 1554. It rises up on a pedestal, whose frieze is decorated with elephants, horses and riders. Small

A stone temple chariot in front of Vithala Temple

niches contain statues of gods. The partly destroyed roof is supported by 56 columns, many of which are engraved with animals, fabulous beasts, dancers and musicians. East of the main temple is one of the complex's further gems, a **shrine for Garuda in the form of a temple chariot**. Its superstructure was unfortunately destroyed at the end of the 19th century.

Royal Centre

It is no coincidence that Ramachandra Temple, consecrated to the god Rama, can be found at the heart of the Royal Centre. Rama was the second most important deity after Virupaksha with whom the Vijayanagara rulers identified. The complex mainly dates back to the 15th century. Within a rectangular walled courtyard are a larger and a smaller temple, various columned halls and pavilions. The design of the walls surrounding the courtyard is remarkable: on their exterior, on the sides facing the secular buildings, they are covered in friezes depicting life at court, while the walls facing the temple contain episodes from the Ramayana. The temple itself consists of a square sanctum with a vestibule and a columned hall. The column shafts with depictions of Vishnu in his various incarnations are particularly beautifully worked.

The temple's exterior walls are covered in finely worked friezes depicting fabled creatures and stories from the Ramayana. The smaller temple, which possesses two sanctums, also illustrates the great epic and its characters. The columned hall in the courtyard's northwestern corner is a later addition dating back to the time of Krishnadevaraja in 1513.

★ ★
Ramachandra Temple

Royal living quarters The ruins of the royal palaces lie to the southwest and northwest of Ramachandra Temple. These buildings are large and rectangular and most of them are surrounded by walls; however, all that is generally left of these buildings are foundation walls, the remains of staircases, balustrades and stone floors.

Virupaksha Temple West of the palace area is a further temple consecrated to the patron god Virupaksha. Since it was covered with earth for a long time it is also known as the underground temple. The original shrine dates back to the 14th century, but it was extended in the 15th century.

Public Area

Hundred-Column Hall Of the building that presumably served as the king's audience hall, only the foundation walls are left. Immediately south of the Hundred-Column Hall an underground chamber was discovered in which the state treasure may have been hidden. Its interior is covered with green chlorite plates.

Interested visitors at the queen's bath

The multilevel stone platform was presumably the foundation of a now destroyed wooden tower. From here the king had the opportunity to watch festivities such as the Mahanavami festival. The structure was built in four successive phases between the 14th and 16th centuries. Well-preserved flat reliefs depict war and hunting scenes as well as courtly entertainments such as dancing, music and sports.

Mahanavami Platform

The royal family's bathing site was presumably the pool somewhat further south of the platform. Its symmetrically laid out ghats covered in chlorite plates produce interesting geometric patterns.

Bathing site

Hidden beyond the plain exterior is a courtyard with a pool surrounded by arcades and overhanging balconies. There are still traces of the original covering with its stucco ornaments.

The Queen's Bath

Northeast of Ramachandra temple, within an enclosure, is a further group of buildings. The highlight is an elegant, two-storey pavilion, which is known as the Lotos Mahal by the locals. It is considered a **particularly fine example of the blend between Hindu and Islamic architectural styles**, which can also be seen on other buildings in Vijayanagara.

★
Lotos Mahal
⊙
Opening hours:
Open: daily
6am–6pm

The largest building of the public area is northeast of the Lotos Mahal, outside the surrounding walls. This is where the king's elephants were housed. The stables consist of five square chambers each, to the left and right of a central pavilion. They are covered by domes of different shapes.

Elephant stables

The archaeological museum exhibits sculptures, coins, paintings and a model of Vijayanagara (open: daily except Fri 10am–5pm).

Museum
⊙

City Centre

Vijayanagara's large population lived east of the royal centre. The most important structure in the city centre is Ragunatha Temple on the flat summit of Malyavanta Hill. Its style indicates that it was built in the 16th century. Walls with gopurams in the south and east surround the main temple as well as a smaller secondary temple. The central shrine houses a large rock, from which the figures of Rama and Sita, accompanied by Hanuman and Lakshmana, were carved.

Ragunatha Temple

The village on the opposite bank of the Tungabhadra is believed to be Vijayanagara's predecessor. Anegondi is framed by fortifications with gates in the north and south. A pleasant walk leads from Hampi Bazar along the river to Anegondi. Small rowing boats bring visitors across the river.

Anegondi

★ Hyderabad

Capital of Andhra Pradesh
Population: 5.5 million

Altitude: 545m/1788ft
Distance: 713km/443mi southeast of Mumbai

For some time now Hyderabad has had a new nickname: Cyberabad. But the city of more than five million inhabitants in the central Deccan plateau is not only attractive for software companies.

As a result of its – by Indian standards – very well developed road network and better developed infrastructure, the former stronghold of the Mughals and Nizams has long since overtaken the software metropolis of Bangalore further to the south. The result has been a fascinating mix of tradition and modernity. While old Hyderabad can be seen in its many Muslim buildings, bazaars and of course its famous cuisine, the new cyberworld can mainly be found on the outskirts of the city.

Hyderabad Map

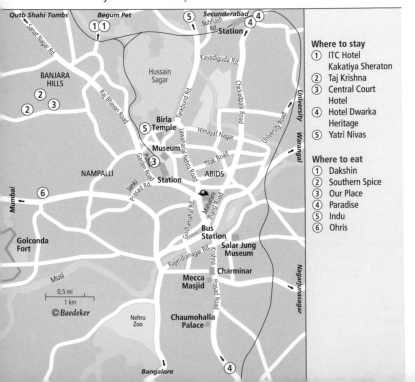

Where to stay
1. ITC Hotel Kakatiya Sheraton
2. Taj Krishna
3. Central Court Hotel
4. Hotel Dwarka Heritage
5. Yatri Nivas

Where to eat
1. Dakshin
2. Southern Spice
3. Our Place
4. Paradise
5. Indu
6. Ohris

©Baedeker

▶ VISITING HYDERABAD

INFORMATION

Andhra Pradesh Tourism Development Corporation (APTDC)
Tank Bund Road
Tel. 040 – 23 45 30 36 or 23 45 01 65
www.tourisminap.com

»Channel 6«
City magazine

SHOPPING

The bazaar streets around Charminar are the place to go to find Hyderabad's famous pearls. Bangle Street, which is also close to the four-towered gate, is known for its glass bangles of all colours. Further along there are some good perfume shops. The streets in the vicinity of Abid Road and in the General Bazaar in Secunderabad are all good for shopping. A large selection of gifts, sculptures and textiles can be found in »Kalanjali, Arts and Crafts« on Hill Fort Road in the district of Saifabad.

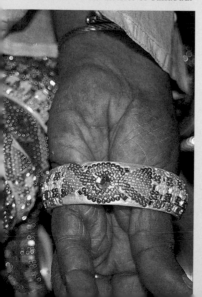

WHERE TO EAT
▶ Expensive
① *Dakshin*
In the ITC Hotel Kakatya Sheraton & Towers, Begumpet
Tel. 040 – 23 40 01 32
The »Dakshin« is considered one of the best restaurants for southern Indian cuisine in the whole of Asia.

▶ Moderate
② *Southern Spice*
8-2-350/3/2, Rd. No.3
Banjara Hills
Tel. 040 – 23 35 38 02
Authentic southern Indian cuisine, a great selection of specialities from Andhra Pradesh and Tamil Nadu. Highly recommended. No alcohol served.

③ *Our Place*
8-8-602/E, Charan Pahaadi
Rd. No.10
Banjara Hills
Tel. 040 – 23 35 34 22
Restaurant serving international cuisine, with a bar outside. The right place for long evenings!

⑥ *Ohri's*
Opposite the Old Gandhi Medical College, Basheerbagh
Tel. 040 – 23 29 88 11
In the basement diners can eat northern and southern Indian cuisine in a replica metro, on the ground floor the restaurant serves ice cream and pizza and upstairs guests can expect Chinese and Pakistani cuisine as well as a bar.

④ *Paradise*
Paradise SD Rd.
Secunderabad-3
Tel. 040 – 27 84 31 15

Famous for its Hyderabad biryanis, grilled chicken and a lot more.

▶ **Inexpensive**

⑤ *Indu*
Secretariat Road
Next to Thomas Cook
Tel. 040 – 23 24 41 89
Tasty thalis Andhra Pradesh-style, but very spicy; the chicken should be tried. No alcohol.

WHERE TO STAY

▶ **Luxury**

① *ITC Hotel Kakatiya Sheraton & Towers*
6-3-1187 Begumpet
Tel. 040 – 23 40 01 32
www.welcomgroup.com
Considered the best establishment in Hyderabad; excellent cuisine and all the amenities as well as four restaurants and two bars.

② *Taj Krishna*
Road No. 1, Banjara Hills
Tel. 040 – 55 66 23 23
www.tajhotels.com

Centrally located in the fancy district of Banjara Hills, with four good restaurants and two bars.

▶ **Mid-range**

③ *Central Court Hotel*
Public Garden Rd.
Hyderabad
Tel. 040 – 23 23 23 23
www.thecentralcourt.com
Stylish boutique hotel with a good coffee shop and a multi-cuisine restaurant.

▶ **Budget**

④ *Hotel Dwarka Heritage*
116 Chenoy Trade Center Parklane
Secunderabad-3
Tel. 040 – 27 84 50 20
50 rooms, some of them with air conditioning.

⑤ *Yatri Nivas*
1-8-180B, S.P. Road
Secunderabad-3
Tel. 040 – 23 46 18 55
Basic, clean hotel run by Andhra Pradesh Tourism with a garden restaurant.

History India's fifth-largest city was founded by Muhammad Quli Qutb Shah under the old name Bhagnagar in 1591, since the old Mughal fort on the Golconda Hills suffered from a constant water shortage and the inhabitants were the victims of several plagues. His successor, however, was already driven off by the Mughal ruler Aurangzeb (1656). Aurangzeb's death lead to a crisis amongst the Delhi sultanates and the governor put in place by the Mughals, Asaf Jah, used the window of opportunity to make himself independent. The Nizam dynasty he founded cooperated alternately with the French and the British. The fifth Nizam Ali was a British confidant. During his day he was not just India's highest-ranking prince, he was even considered the richest man in the world. In 1948 the Nizams' kingdom was incorporated into independent India. When the union states were reorganized on a linguistic basis, Hyderabad was made the capital of the new state of Andhra Pradesh. The twin city of Secunderabad founded by the British has now merged with Hyderabad.

What to See in Hyderabad

The Charminar is the **emblem of Hyderabad** and lies in the heart of the city. It was built by Sultan Muhammad Quli Qutb Shah as a centre of learning in 1591. There was originally a mosque on its roof, in which children were taught the Qu'ran. The Charminar owes its name to the **four (char) towers (minar)**, which are all almost 55m/180ft tall. The four magnificent 15m/50ft arches of the three-storey main building create a pleasant flow of air in the inner hall.

The roads around the Charminar are full of shops. They mainly sell pearls, embroidery and perfume.

★★
Charminar

★
◄ Bazaar

Construction of Mecca Masjid was begun as early as 1614 by Muhammad Quli Qutb Shah, but it was Aurangzeb who managed to complete this monumental mosque in 1687. It got its name because some of its bricks were fired using clay from soil brought from Mecca. A number of Nizams from Hyderabad are buried in the tombs to the left of the mosque. India's sixth-largest mosque has room for 10,000 people in its courtyard.

Mecca Masjid

! *Baedeker* TIP

Pearl paradise

Leaving Hyderabad without going to one of the pearl shops north of the Charminar would almost amount to sacrilege. Such a large selection at these prices will be hard to find anywhere else. However, bartering is the order of the day in the bazaar!

The **zoo** in Hyderabad is the largest in India. It is particularly exciting for bird lovers as it is home to 240 different species. It also has a lion safari park, a prehistoric park with models of dinosaurs, a natural history museum and an aquarium.

The Salar Jung Museum possesses a huge collection of antiques (35,000 items), collected by a former prime minister of the Nizam of Hyderabad. From Belgian glass to Bidri works from Hyderabad, Chinese porcelain, old miniatures and manuscripts to European paintings, the collection assembled by Mir Yusuf Ali Salar Jung III has it all.

Salar Jung Museum

Cahumohalla Palace near the Charminar is the place where the Nizams celebrated their festivals. A part of the complex built during the late 18th century is open to the public. The palace, set in the middle of a beautiful garden, is open every day except Friday from 11am–5pm.

★
Chaumohalla Palace
◷

This Hindu temple built by the Birla foundation in white Makrana marble on a hill in 1976 is consecrated to Venkateshwara, one of Vishnu's incarnations. It can be visited by people of any faith. The Birlas are amongst the richest industrial magnates of modern India. They also built the Birla Planetarium next to the temple. There is a good view to be had of the city from this hill.

Birla Temple

At the Chaminar, Hyderabad's landmark

Hussain Sagar Hyderabad's largest lake was created by King Ibrahim Quli Qutb Shah (16th century). Along its dam is a promenade with 33 statues of some of Andhra Pradesh's well-known personages. In the middle of the lake is a fairly recent, enormous statue of Buddha. The artificial lake and the surrounding parks are the city's green lungs. There are many restaurants and cafés here.

Immediate Surroundings

★
Golconda Fort

⊕
Opening hours:
Open: daily
9am–6pm
then a sound and
light show

The fort built on granite hills after the models of Bidar and ►Gulbarga is now a rambling ruin. It is located around 10km/6mi west of Hyderabad. Visitors should plan to spend at least three hours exploring the **large fort with the remains of palaces, baths, bazaars and mosques**. Golconda Fort was founded as long ago as the 13th century by the Kakatiya King Ganapathy. At the time it was only a small fort with mud ramparts. Later the Islamic Qutb Shah kings extended it to create a large fort with stone ramparts and different buildings, and the kings also moved their capital from Warangal to Golconda. The fort city, with its seven gates and sophisticated water system for the »hanging gardens«, was known for diamond manufacture and trade. In 1687 Aurangzeb's troop conquered it. The famous **Koh-i-Noor diamond** stolen by Aurangzeb was later broken down into smaller pieces which have been incorporated into the British crown jewels.

Today many of the former buildings are no longer extant, but their ruins are still impressive evidence of what the fort must once have been like. It used to be protected by a triple wall. Eight great gates, of which four have survived, gave access to the city. Within the city walls there is not just the fort, but also several mosques, of which Jama Masjid is the most important.

When coming from Hyderabad the complex is entered on its eastern side through the attractive Balahisar gate, beyond which visitors will enter the large vestibule with its **surprising acoustics**: every word spoken here can be heard in Durbar Hall high up in the palace. The areas of the fort the most worth seeing are the three-storey palace in which visitors will find the said Durbar Hall and in which the sultans

View of the well-fortified Golconda Fort

regularly held court, the ruins of the private chambers, and the queen's quarters. Clever water systems brought water to the highest point, from where it was then channelled to the individual taps. The Shahi Mahal, the royal sleeping chamber, is said to have once had a vaulted roof. The view from the **citadel** over the surrounding area is stunning.

✱
Qutb Shahi tombs

A little under 1km/550yd north of Golconda Fort are the tombs in which six sultans and other members of the royal family lie buried. A total of 82 tombs were built here; they were modelled on the tombs of the Bahmani dynasty in Bidar.

Every tomb is crowned by an onion-shaped tower, and this rests on a round drum which in turn sits on a square foundation. The large towers have two floors and are surrounded by decorative ogive arcades, while the smaller, plainer ones only have a single floor. The towers were originally decorated with colourful tiles on white plaster. Few of them have remained. Texts from the Qu'ran have been engraved into the archways.

Further Afield

Warangal

The capital of the district of the same name, Warangal (population 460,000, 130km/80mi northeast of Hyderabad), was the **capital of the Kakatiyas**, a local dynasty, in the 12th and 13th centuries before it fell into the hands of changing Muslim rulers. The remains of the town and the surrounding area mainly date back to the Kakatiya period. The **Thousand-Column Temple**, commissioned by Kakatiya king Rudra Deva in 1163, is famous. The star-shaped temple is consecrated to the gods Shiva, Vishnu and the sun god Surya. Unfortunately its roof has collapsed. On the outskirts of town is **Bhadrakali Temple**, dedicated to the goddess Kali. It has a picturesque location by a small lake. As is so often the case in southern India, the beautiful sculptures in its interior are colourfully painted. The temple is very popular and attracts many believers.

✱
Warangal Fort ▶

The clear highlight of any visit to Warangal is Warangal Fort, which was located a few miles out of town. It was built in the 13th century under King Ganapati Deva. The fort's ruins are scattered over an area of 19 sq km/7 sq mi, which was enclosed by a wall. The best pieces are now exhibited in a kind of large open-air museum. They include the fort's **magnificent entrance gates** as well as exquisitely worked fragments of temples and sculptures.

✱
Ramappa Temple

The well-preserved Rama Lingeshvara Swami Temple, also known as Ramappa Temple, the name of its architect, is worth an excursion. It is located near the village of Palampeta. It lies 65km/40mi north of Warangal and can be reached on a very picturesque journey through paddy fields, palm trees and lakes. The temple the Kakatiya rulers had built in the 13th century **is one of Andhra Pradesh's most at-**

tractive temples. It is dedicated to the god Shiva, as is indicated by the great Nandi opposite the main entrance. Inside the temple visitors will find black, finely turned columns with excellent sculptures. The base and the temple's exterior walls also contain excellent friezes and lovely supporting statues.

Anyone wishing to spend the night in Waranagal should give the Punnami Hotel (tel. 0870 – 257 79 55) a try.

Jawahar National Park

D/E 13/14

The name Jawahar National Park denotes the merging of Bandipur National Park, Rajiv Gandhi National Park (Nagarhole) in Karnataka, Mudumalai Game Preserve in Tamil Nadu and Wyanad Game Preserve in Kerala. The reserve was created to protect India's largest elephant population and is considered the country's largest continuous game preserve.

Unfortunately there are few large elephant populations left in India.
Jawahar National Park gives visitors a chance to observe the animals in the wild

VISITING JAWAHAR NATIONAL PARK

INFORMATION
Forest Department Bangalore
Tel. 080 – 23 34 68 46
www.karnatakaforestdepartment.org
Budget accommodation can also be
booked here.

GETTING THERE
*Rajiv-Gandhi-NP
(Nagarhole)*
Bus connections from Mysore to
Bandipur and Mysore to Hunsur

WHERE TO STAY
▶ **Luxury / Mid-range**
Kabini River Lodge
Karapura

near Nagarhole Park
Tel. 082 28 – 26 44 02
www.junglelodges.com
Well-known jungle lodge by the
Kabini river, consisting of an old
colonial house, cottages and tents.

▶ **Mid-range / Budget**
Tusker Trails
Mangala Village
Chamarajanagar
near Bandipur National Park
Tel. 08 21 – 263 60 55
Along with the accommodation in
cottages there is also a swimming
pool and a tennis court.

✳ **Mudumalai
Game Preserve**
Mudumalai Game Preserve (230km/145mi southwest of Bangalore)
was founded in 1938 and covers an area of 322 sq km/124 sq mi at
the northern edge of the Nilgiri mountains. It borders on Bandipur
National Park in Karnataka and on Wyanad in Kerala. Mudumalai
(malai = mountain) lies at an altitude of 1000m/3280ft and is dominated by dense mixed-forest vegetation. Since precipitation within
the mountainous preserve varies enormously between 2000mm/
78.7in and 500mm/19.7in, the wetter southwest is covered in rainforest, which then becomes a dry broad-leaf forest and then brush
vegetation towards the east. Swamp forests and bamboo forests can
also be found here. The preserve's main attraction consists of the
many **Indian elephants**, which traverse the park in herds. A further
attraction is Moyar waterfall, which descends more than 150m/500ft.
The elephant camp in Teppakadu is involved in breeding elephants
to be used as working animals. The reception centre in Teppakadu,
on the road between Ooty and Mysore, permits excursions of a very
special kind: the forests can be explored from the back of an elephant. The best time to go is March–April.

✳ **Bandipur
National Park**
Bandipur National Park (80km/50mi south of Mysore), which bor-
ders the northern foothills of the Nilgiris, is **one of India's tiger re-
serves** and was also once in the possession of Mysore's maharajas.
The park covers an area of 865 sq km/334 sq mi to the south of the
Kabini river. Mountains, gorges, forests and grass landscapes provide

refuge for many different kinds of animals. As is the case in Nagarhole Reserve (see below) visitors can watch herds of Indian elephants, many different deer species, and, with a lot of luck, predators such as tigers and leopards, as well as different species of monkey here. There is a wonderful view of Mysore Ditch, a deep gorge, from the Rolling Rocks. There are a number of different places to spend the night in the park, from where Jeep tours and elephant rides are organized. It is a good idea to make reservations in advance. It is best to avoid the park at weekends. Season: September–May.

North of Kabini is Rajiv Gandhi National Park, also known as Nagarhole after the river Nagarhole (»snake's foot«). The former hunting area used by the rulers of Mysore was made into a national park in 1955 (96km/60mi southwest of Mysore), then expanded in 1975 and now it covers an area of 640 sq km/247 sq mi.

★★
Rajiv Gandhi National Park

The forests and grass landscapes provide ideal living conditions for Indian elephants, sambar deer and chitals. Gaurs, the largest feral cattle, which move around in herds, can also be watched very nicely here. Various beasts of prey also feel at home in the park, such as leopards, striped hyenas and dholes, a wild dog. Many different bird species such as herons, cormorants, ducks, osprey and numerous species of buzzard and hawk live by the **Kabini river** and its backwaters. The waters are inhabited by mugger crocodiles and countless fish species, including the large mahseers. Accommodation is available in Nagarhole and Karapura. Karapura, where the comfortable Kabini River Lodge (see Where to Stay) is located, also offers Jeep tours and boat trips on the Kabini reservoir. It is a good idea to book accommodation in advance and avoid the park at weekends, since it gets very full. The best time to visit is from September to May.

Wyanad Game Preservelies in the state of Kerala, around 110km/70mi from Kozhicode. Here too visitors can see elephants and many other wild animals. Entrances are located in Tholpetty and Muthanga.

★
Wyanad Game Preserve

★ Kanyakumari (Cape Comorin)

E 15

State: Tamil Nadu
Population: 12,000

Altitude: sea level
Distance: 674km/419mi south of Bangalore

Kanyakumari is the place where the Arabian Sea, the Bay of Bengal and the Indian Ocean meet. The town's viewing points are great for watching lovely sunrises and sunsets. Since the sun is worshipped by Hindus in the form of the god Surya, many people flock here every day.

▶ VISITING KANYAKUMARI

INFORMATION

Tourist Office
Beach Road, tel. 046 52 – 24 62 76
www.tamilnadutourism.org

GETTING THERE

There are rail connections with Thir-uvananthapuram, Bangalore, Mumbai and Delhi, amongst other places. Buses go from Kovalam, Madurai and Chennai. Kanyakumari can also be visited in a day trip from Kovalam.

WHERE TO EAT / WHERE TO STAY

Kanyakumari is a place of pilgrimage. It is therefore advisable to book in advance.

▶ Budget

TTDC Hotel Tamil Nadu
Tel. 046 52 – 24 62 57
Basic rooms, some of them with air conditioning and ocean views. There is a restaurant.

What to See in Kanyakumari

Kanya Kumari Temple

According to a legend Kanya, an incarnation of Parvati, did great penance here in order to marry Shiva. When her plan was not successful she decided to remain a virgin (kumari). The town was named Kanyakumari after its patron goddess. The temple consecrated to her is open to all visitors, but the sanctum can only be accessed by Hindus.

Gandhi Mandapam

The **unadorned memorial for Gandhi**, the »Father of the Nation« (▶ Famous People), stands directly by the sea. It was built in the place where an urn filled with Gandhi's ashes was kept for the public, before they were scattered on the three seas. The building, which resembles a temple, is designed in such a way that sunlight reaches its interior on Gandhi's birthday, the 2 October. There is a nice view of the rocks and the island in front of them from the first floor.

Vivekananda Memorial

The Vivekananda Memorial, on a rocky island around 400m/440yd from the mainland, can easily be reached in one of the boats leaving every half hour. The memorial site for the Indian philosopher **Swami Vivekananda** was built in 1970 using different architectural styles. The philosopher from Bengal swam to this island in 1892 in order to meditate prior to his trip to America, where he was to give a lecture about Hinduism. Vivekananda was, alongside Ram Mohun Rai, Ramakrishna and Dayananda, one of the leading modern reformers of Hinduism. The island is also known as Sri Pada Parai, since it is located in the place where the goddess Kumari repented. Her footprints (pada) attract many Indian pilgrims.
To the west is another rock, on top of which is a statue of the Tamil scholar and saint Thiruvalluvar.

India's southernmost point: Kanyakumari

Kerala (State)

Area: 38,864 sq km/15,005 sq mi **Population:** 31.8 million
Capital: Thiruvananthapuram

As legend has it, Kerala came into existence when Parasuram, an incarnation of Vishnu, flung his axe from the Western Ghats. By all accounts he created a veritable paradise, with rivers, forests, beaches – and pepper, which is indigenous to Kerala. Add to that the high rate of literacy and the low rate of poverty here, and the epithet »God's Own Country« was never more fitting.

India advertises the small state of Kerala on the subcontinent's southwest coast as paradise on earth. But the elongated strip of land between the Western Ghats and the Arabian Sea with its stunning tropical landscape is not just the home of the pepper plant. When Kerala's inhabitants proudly declare that their home is **»God's Own Country«**, they have the perfect legend handy to confirm just that: Parasuram, Vishnu's sixth incarnation, is considered Kerala's creator. He was chosen to give the Brahmins, who were besieged by warriors, a

 Baedeker TIP

Kerala in literature
Not only the colours and smells of Kerala, but also its contradictions and incomprehensibilities come alive in Arundhati Roy's award-winning novel *The God of Small Things*.

Paradise under the hammer-and-sickle

new home. Varuna, the god of the sea, gave him permission to take some land from the ocean to this end. However, the land was only allowed to be as wide as the distance the god was able to throw his axe from the Western Ghats. Parasuram threw his weapon, the water receded and Kerala was born: a land with 41 rivers, evergreen forests and sandy beaches. In the west it opens to the sea, in the east it is separated from the rest of the subcontinent by mountains. Kerala's tropical climate allows pepper, cardamom, cinnamon, ginger and nutmeg to be cultivated. The coast was once considered a treasure trove for pearl fishers.

The special geographic location coupled with lush vegetation have always influenced the fate of India's southwesternmost tip and given the development of the region its own direction. The legendary treasures here were already attracting merchants in antiquity. The large port of Muziris (now: Craganore) was a **reloading point and meeting place** for Chinese, Egyptians, Phoenicians and Babylonians, Arabs, Jews and Romans from

History the third century onwards. In the fourth century Kerala saw its first Jewish and Christian settlements. Some time later Muslims arrived, assuming an important role as middlemen in the spice trade. The various religious communities peacefully coexisted with the Hindu majority, united by common economic interests.

Greater changes only took place with the arrival of the European powers, particularly the Portuguese, at the end of the 15th century. In 1498 **Vasco da Gama** arrived in India for the first time, prepared for the task of breaking the Arab monopoly of the spice trade. At that time there were many lesser princes in Kerala as well as the Kolathiri rajas in the north, the Zamorin in Calicut (modern-day Kozhicode) and the Venad rulers in the south. The new arrivals knew how to make good use of the rivalries amongst the different princes. By means of promises and then forced contracts they bagged a large portion of the trading rights for the valuable products in very little time. In 1503 the Portuguese settled in Cochin (modern-day Kochi), from where they extended their sphere of influence to cover the hinterland and the coast. They planted the first coconut palms and laid the foundation for a pronounced monoculture. Cultivating cashew nuts and tobacco was also introduced. In the early 17th century the Dutch arrived, driving out the Portuguese and the few British people who had settled here. They now became the rulers of this land and its wealth for a considerable period even though Raja Martanda Varma and the Muslim ruler Tipu Sultan from Mysore managed to win back some of the land in the 18th century. However, it was only a matter of time before the strong arm of the British would reach into this corner of India and defeat their rivals. The year 1800 saw this change take place and Kerala was incorporated into the British Madras Presidency.

After independence

After India's independence, in the course of the country's restructuring according to linguistic borders, the state of Kerala was formed with Malayalam as the official language. To this day **this area is still different from the rest of India in many ways**. In 1957 Kerala became the first state in which a **Communist government** came to power through democratic elections. With the exception of a short break they have determined Kerala's fate ever since. Kerala's inhabitants point proudly towards the state's literacy rate, which, at 90%, is far above the country's average. Healthcare in this state is also exemplary and radical land reforms as well as the money earned by migrant workers in the Gulf states have cut back on the poverty that is so visible elsewhere in India. The women here also have fewer obstacles than they do in other parts of the subcontinent. Good training with a job to follow is no rarity in Kerala and a school education goes without saying. The fact that they are doing better than their sisters in the north in every regard is something the women of Kerala are very familiar with, because until not too long ago several castes followed matrilineal inheritance law, meaning that family property was passed on from mother to daughter.

Economy

32 million people now live on the 580km/360mi strip of land, which is not even 100km/60mi wide in many places. Houses upon houses line the roads; there is hardly a spot that is not built up in some way. Most people work in agriculture. In addition to coconuts, which dominate everything, the other main crops are rice and, in the hinterland, bananas, mangos, tapioca and the sought-after pepper. The humid, green mountain slopes are not just home to spices such as cardamom and cinnamon. Here visitors will also come across coffee, tea and rubber plantations, as well as sandalwood forests. Fishing also has a long tradition. To this day men go out with dugout canoes and simple boats to go fishing. Competition from industrial fishing businesses and deep-sea fishing fleets is making it increasingly difficult for the local population. Nonetheless fish and seafood are still amongst Kerala's main exports. A not insignificant proportion of the population work in the **Gulf states**, contributing to the family income in that way.

Tourism   Tourism has recently discovered these southern regions of India. The white sandy beaches, tropical palm-tree landscapes and clean, peaceful towns, as well as the absence of the abject suffering and political unrest that can be found in other parts of the country, have meant that the small state has been drawing in an increasing number of visitors. Paradise is opening its gates and, once again, people are flocking to »God's Own Country« from all over the world.

✶✶ Kochi · Ernakulam

State: Kerala
Population: 1.35 million

Altitude: sea level
Distance: 546km/339mi southwest of Bangalore

To compare Kochi with Venice would be overdoing it just a little, but not completely off the mark. Like the old merchant city on the Adriatic, Kochi (Cochin) is a large port built on several islands.

It was not rare for goods to be sent from here to Kochi's Italian sister city. Only one of the seven city districts is built on the mainland, namely Ernakulam, now the largest and most modern district. The other six are on islands and peninsulas.

Playing the drums through the streets of Kochi

► VISITING KOCHI

INFORMATION
Tourist Office
At the bus station in Fort Cochin
Tel. 04 84 – 221 66 54
or at the tourist desk of the main ferry
landing in Ernakulam. Introductory
information can be found on the
website of Kerala Tourism
(www.keralatourism.org).

GETTING THERE
By air from Mumbai, Delhi, Bangalore and the Gulf states. In addition
there are many rail and bus connections, to Bangalore, Mumbai, Margao
(Goa) and other places.

SHOPPING
Handicrafts, jewellery and antiques,
or deliberately aged furniture, masks
etc. can be found around the synagogue and Mattancherry Palace on
Fort Cochin. The bookshop opposite
the synagogue has a great selection.
The long, busy Bazar Road nearby is
worth a visit. Spices are loaded and
sold here. The roads around Princess
Street near the Chinese fishing ncts
have also developed into a shopping
district. In Ernakulam the modern
MG Road is known for its many
jewellery shops, but there are also
clothes shops, shoe shops and much
more.

WHERE TO EAT
► Expensive
① Fort Cochin
In the casino hotel
Willingdon Island
Tel. 04 84 – 266 82 21
Serves Kochi's best fish and seafood
specialities.

② Malabar Junction
Parade Road, Fort Cochin

Tel. 04 84 – 221 66 66
Excellent restaurant with Mediterranean and Indian cuisine situated in
the picturesque court of the Malabar
House hotel.

► Inexpensive
③ Gopuram
Trust Tower
Near the Medical Trust Hospital
near MG Road
Ernakulam
Tel. 04 84 – 301 23 81
A large menu offers specialities from
Kerala, served on banana leaves. The
duck curry and the coconut pancakes
(vellayappam) are delicious.

④ Kashi Art Café
Burgher Street
Fort Cochin
Tel. 04 84 – 221 57 69
The cosy Kashi Art Café is a gallery
and café in one. Here patrons can
obtain snacks, chocolate cake and
good coffee.

WHERE TO STAY
► Luxury
① The Brunton Boatyard
Fort Cochin near the fishing nets
Tel. 04 84 – 361 17 11
www.cghearth.com
Stylishly rebuilt hotel in the place
of the old Brunton boatyard with
22 rooms and suites. The view of
the harbour entrance and the neighbouring islands is unique. In
addition there is a lovely pool and
good food. Ayurvedic treatments are
available.

The Malabar House see ②
Parade Road
Fort Cochin
Tel. 04 84 – 221 66 66

Kochi • Ernakulam *Map*

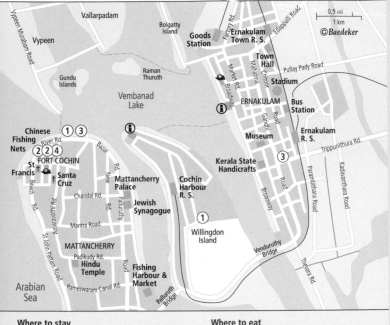

Where to stay
1 The Brunton Boatyard   3 The Fort House
2 The Old Courtyard

Where to eat
1 Fort Cochin   3 Gopuram
2 The Malabar House   4 Kashi Art Café

www.malabarhouse.com
Elegant boutique hotel with an enchanting courtyard. Every room is furnished with hand-picked items. There is also a gallery and a swimming pool in the courtyard.

► Mid-range
② *The Old Courtyard*
Princess Street
Fort Cochin
Tel. 04 84 – 221 63 02
www.oldcourtyard.com
The old Portuguese villa offers its guests a nice courtyard and pleasantly furnished rooms with a veranda.

► Budget
③ *The Fort House*
Calvathi Road
Fort Cochin
Tel. 04 84 – 221 71 03
www.forthousecochin.com
One of the small bungalows situated in the middle of a lovely garden makes a wonderfully comfortable place to stay. There is a lovely atmosphere on the hotel's terrace, where guests are served right by the sea.

A flood created the natural harbour in 1341 and it was soon to become the largest reloading point for the sought-after spices of the Malabar Coast. Merchants, traders and rulers certainly left their mark on this place. They have created a unique mixture of very different cultural monuments in a very small space, something not found in this form anywhere else in India.

Fort Cochin, the most interesting island, has Chinese fishing nets next to Dutch villas and Portuguese churches; a Maharaja's palace borders on the Jewish quarter with its synagogue. Small canals and roads criss-cross the elongated island. The low homes with their colourful façades get a severe battering by the monsoon every year. Spice traders compete with jewellers and barbers. Visitors amble along the streets with washing blowing in the wind, hens clucking and bicycle bells ringing, because despite the many historical remains here, which undoubtedly give the island a cosmopolitan flair, it has held on to its village character.

History

By 1405 the raja's family moved from Muziris, the port somewhat to the north, to Kochi. In 1500 the Portuguese seafarer Pedro Alvarez Cabral arrived in the lagoon. Two years previously his fellow countryman Vasco da Gama had reached the Indian coast near Calicut (modern-day Kozhicode) for the first time. Disputes with the ruler there, the Zamorin, who did not want to bow to the pressure of the new arrivals, forced the Portuguese to look for a new base for their trading endeavours. Kochi was the ideal location. The shallow bay with its many islands offered protection for the ships and Kochi's ruler welcomed the new arrivals because he hoped they would help him in his fight against his enemy in Calicut.

Two years later, **Vasco da Gama** appeared in Kochi with further ships and the **Portuguese founded their first trading post**. In 1503 they founded Fort Manuel, the first defensive castle of a European power in India. In the following 160 years the Portuguese were the town's undisputed rulers. They built palaces, trading posts, churches and the port. The local rajas were degraded to puppets and the Jewish community, most of them merchants, were constantly subjected to reprisals and persecution.

The **Dutch** developed into serious rivals over the course of the 17th century and in 1663 they finally drove the Portuguese out of the town. The churches became Protestant, and the Jews saw better times ahead. In addition the new rulers took over the entire trading network their predecessors had laboriously built up over many years. The Dutch ruled Kochi's fate for more than 100 years until finally they too had to leave in 1795 with the arrival of the British. In 1800 the town and all the surrounding areas were annexed to the Madras Presidency. In the 1920s the **British** expanded the port to make it suitable for ocean shipping. To this day spices, fish and other products are loaded here and Ernakulam has become Kerala's most modern city.

Fort Cochin

Tip   Most of the sights are in the districts of Fort Cochin and Mattan-cherry, both of which are on the island of Fort Cochin. Both quarters have a jetty and can easily be reached by ferry. There are also regular ferry connections to the other islands and to Ernakulam.

★
Chinese
fishing nets   Those taking a ferry to Fort Cochin, where Fort Manuel once stood, will be able to see the long row of Chinese fishing nets from afar. They are still in use. It is said they were introduced in the 14th century by Chinese fishermen who were accompanying merchants from the court of Kublai Khan. At least four people are necessary to operate the levers of the heavy wooden constructions on which the nets hang.

A tourist attraction:
nevertheless the Chinese fishing nets are still used today

Immediately beyond, by the beach, there is a **small fish market**, and merchants there also sell coconuts, postcards and soft drinks. Not far from the market are the old villas of the Dutch and the Portuguese. To this day the island's northern tip is a preferred residential area. The city's new elite lives between ancient trees and bougainvillaea bushes, breathing in the fresh sea air.

This is also where visitors will find St Francis, the oldest church exhibiting European architecture in India. Franciscan friars who came to Kochi with Cabral first built a wooden church, replacing it with a stone building in 1516. It contains Vasco da Gama's tombstone. He was buried here in 1524, though his remains were later moved to Portugal. The **forerunners of modern fans** with which the church is equipped are also interesting. Woven mats, hung on poles and moved from outside of the building, fan fresh air towards the sweating church-goers during the service. The small church was originally consecrated to St Anthony; it was only renamed St Francis in the 19th century. Today the building belongs to the Church of South India.

✱
St Francis

Somewhat further south, near St Francis, is the later cathedral, Santa Cruz, a Catholic church with a nice interior.

Santa Cruz

Mattancherry

To get to the district of Mattancherry take a bus, rickshaw or ferry from the landing in Fort Cochin or go on foot. Those who decide to walk should be aware that the trip is several miles long.

Not far from the landing is Mattancherry Palace, built by the Portuguese in 1557 and handed over to Raja Vira Keralavarma in exchange for trading privileges. The plain, two-storey structure with its square floor plan is built around a small temple and seems very unassuming from the outside. It does, however, contain **some of Kerala's best wall paintings**.

✱✱
Mattancherry Palace
🕐
Opening hours:
Open: daily except
Fri 10am–5pm

The entrance, which can be reached via some stairs, leads straight into the coronation hall, which has a teak ceiling and portraits of various rulers. The room to the left is covered with the finest wall paintings from the 16th century. The main colours used are ochres, reds and greens and the pictures tell stories from the Ramayana in copious detail.

The side room to the right contains old maps of the Malabar Coast, historic town plans and stamps. To the right of the coronation hall are some remarkable depictions of Lakshmi, Shiva and Vishnu. Hanging in the king's audience hall beyond hangs the ruler's swing. Visitors can also see a weapons collection here.

A further gem in this palace is the painting in the ladies' sleeping quarters, which can be reached via a staircase leading to a lower floor. Erotic depictions of Krishna surrounded by gopıs, as well as Vishnu and Shiva with their playmates, created the right atmosphere in the sleeping quarters. The depiction of Shiva and Parvati kissing is particularly bold: it is a pose that was banned from Indian cinema until quite recently.

✻
Old Jewish Quarter

Only a few metres away the city's former Jewish quarter begins. Jewish merchants and traders settled here very early on. During the period of Portuguese rule the community was the victim of severe persecution, but was able to re-establish itself under their successors. Today **hardly any Jews** are left in Kochi. Most of them left for Israel in the 1950s. Walking through the small quarter in which many antiques dealers have settled, visitors will come across the old house signs providing insights into the buildings' former occupants.

✻ ✻
Synagogue
⏱
Opening hours:
Open: Sun–Thu
10am–12pm and
3pm–5pm

At the end of a cul-de-sac, in a somewhat hidden location, stands the old synagogue from the year 1568. It was partially destroyed by the Portuguese in 1662, but was renovated two years later, after the Dutch moved in. Another 100 years later the rich merchant Ezekiel Rahabi had the tower on the other side built. He also had the synagogue fitted with Chinese tiles he had brought with him from Kanton. The large windows brighten up the synagogue's interior. The light is reflected off the countless chandeliers and glass lamps. The scrolls of the Torah are kept at the back end of the room. Visitors can also see a copper plate from the tenth century, which is believed to have been Raja Bhaskara Ravi Varmas's record of the gift to the Jewish community. In a small room to the right, next to the synagogue's entrance, ten picture tablets tell the history of the Jews on the Malabar Coast.

Further Attractions

Bolgatty Island

The small Bolgatty Island is joined to the mainland by a bridge. An old park covers the area between the boat landing and Bolgatty Palace, which was built in 1774 by the Dutch; for this reason it is also known as the Dutch Palace. The former residence has been transformed into a hotel.

Willingdon Island

Willingdon Island, which can be reached from the mainland by a bridge, is a product of the port expansion of the 1920s. At the island's tip visitors will find the Taj Malabar hotel, which boasts an extremely attractive location.

Ernakulam

The modern city of Ernakulam is on the mainland. Ernakulam's main road, Mahatma Gandhi Road, is a very busy thoroughfare on which the cinemas, shops and restaurants are concentrated. The Indian Arts Performing Centre and the Cochin Cultural Centre often hold Kathakali performances here.

Market in Ernakulam

The Cochin Museum on Darbar Hall Road exhibits collections of the Cochin rajas, including oil paintings from the 19th century, coins and sculptures (open: daily except Mon 9.30am–12pm and 3pm–5.30pm).

Cochin Museum

🕐

Around Kochi

Those leaving Kochi northbound towards ► Thrissur could make a detour to Kalady (48km/30mi northeast of Kochi) in the hinterland. Passing banana and coconut plantations, it takes around two hours to get to the small town on the Periyar river. It is the birthplace of the famous philosopher Shankaracharya, to whom several temples are dedicated here. He lived in the eighth–ninth centuries and made a not insignificant contribution to Hinduism's revival through his interpretation of Vedic texts. At the four philosophical schools he founded in various parts of the country his texts are still studied today.

Kaladi

The town's most famous structure is the 46m/151ft, nine-storey octagonal tower, the **Adi Sankara Kirti Stambha Mandapam**, which is the destination of many pilgrims. It contains illustrations depicting the important events in the life of the great thinker Adi Sankara. Somewhat outside of town on the riverbank is a further complex with several temples, one of which is dedicated to Sri Shankaracharya. The town also has an ashram run by the Ramakrishna Mission with a temple, three schools and a large Ayurveda centre (Nagarjuna Ayurvedic Centre).

Kozhicode (Kozhikode, Calicut)

D 14

State: Kerala
Population: 420,000

Altitude: sea level
Distance: 378km/235mi southwest of Bangalore

Little is now left to bear testimony to the turbulent times Kozhikode has gone through over the centuries. Nevertheless the port does have some interesting traces of its old history.

Bustling activity is the order of the day at the harbour, where the fishing boats sway in the water. The old Muslim quarter of Kuttichera with its old mosques and narrow alleyways brings the past back to life. In addition there are some interesting destinations in the surrounding area.

History The town's origins presumably go back to the 14th century, when it was laid out according to the guidelines for a Hindu ruler's seat. The still extant Tali Shiva Temple once formed the town centre. at one time, the powerful Zamorins (Masters of the Sea) ruled large parts of the country from Kozhicode. In 1498 the Portuguese seafarer Vasco da Gama arrived at Kappad beach, a few miles north of the town. The ruler's initially friendly welcome was soon followed by severe confrontations, since the Zamorin was not willing to simply bow to the pressure of the foreigners and their greed for loot. There were frequent military exchanges between the rajas of Kozhicode and the Portuguese as well as their successors, the Dutch. Unacceptable conditions of surrender and misunderstandings caused the Zamorin to burn himself along with his entire palace in front of his enemies. The colonial rulers were only defeated in 1766 by Tipu Sultan, the Muslim prince from Mysore, who managed to conquer large parts of

 VISITING KOZHICODE

INFORMATION
District Tourism Promotion Council
Mananchira Sq., tel. 04 95 – 272 00 12
www.keralatourism.org

WHERE TO STAY / WHERE TO EAT
▶ **Mid-range**
The Beach Heritage Hotel
Beach Road, Kozhicode
Tel. 04 95 – 36 53 63,
www.beachheritage.com

The bungalow contains eight stylishly renovated rooms with sea views and balcony / veranda. The hotel has a restaurant too.

▶ **Inexpensive**
Zain's Hotel
Convent Cross Rd. (north of the Muslim quarter Kuttichera)
Tel. 04 95 – 236 63 11
Well-known eatery, serving regional Muslim specialities.

Building ships as in days gone by in the boatyards of Beypore

Kerala. After a short period of Muslim rule the British took over the town in 1792.

What to See in and around Kozhicode

Two museums can be found in the east of town on East Hill. The Pazhassirajah Museum exhibits copies of various wall paintings, coins and bronzes. Right next to it is the **Krishnamenon Museum** with souvenirs of the popular politician V. K. Krishnamenon and works by various artists including the painter Raja Ravi Varma (opening times for both museums: Tue–Sun 10am–12.30pm and 2.30pm–5pm, only in the afternoon on Wed).

Pazhassirajah Museum

🕑

During a walk through the picturesque old Muslim quarter of Kutti-chera in the south of town visitors will come past several old mosques that were built with a lot of wood in the typical Kerala style. Standing tall next to the Kuttichera Tank is the large Mishkaal Mosque and further to the northwest in a side street are Jama'at Palli Mosque and Muchandi Palli Mosque, both of which contain interesting wood carvings.

Kuttichera

At the mouth of the river of the same name (11km/7mi south of Kozhicode) lies the old port of Beypore, which is steeped in tradition. Here, the Muslim community of ship-builders still make wooden boats according to the traditional method. A walk from the harbour towards the river mouth leads past the wharves and visitors can stop and watch the sawing, hammering and assembly of the boats.

Beypore

The busy harbour is also worth a visit. Tons of tuna and other seafood is loaded here and sent all around the world. Between mountains of fish and ice, visitors can wander through the market halls and watch sales being made. Beypore can be reached from Kozhicode by bus or taxi.

Kappad beach (fig. p.73)
In 1498, **Vasco da Gama** set food on Indian soil around 16km/10mi north of Kozhicode. A column commemorates his first landing on the subcontinent. The attractive, palm-fringed beach is a lovely place to go swimming or take a stroll. There is a hotel right by the beach (Kappad Beach Resort) with an Ayurvedic centre.

Kottakal
Kottakal (48km/30mi south of Kozhicode) is **one of the most famous centres of the traditional Ayurvedic medicine** (▶ Practicalities, Ayurveda). It has a research centre, a clinic and a laboratory in which medications are produced. A botanical garden with the most important traditional medicinal plants is open to the public.

Kannur (Cannanore)
Kannur (93km/58mi north of Kozhicode) with its landmark, Fort San Angelo, and the many mosques, indicative of the large Muslim population, is one of Kerala's northernmost coastal towns. Like many other ports Kannur was also a base for the various rulers, merchants and conquerors. The Kolathiri rajas had their port here. In 1505 the Portuguese settled in Kannur and built Fort San Angelo until they were driven out in 1663 by the Mopla ruler Ali Raja, who was allied to the Dutch. Later the British took over the town and set up a military base in the fort.
Kannur is a good place for a stopover on the way north or south. Several hotels are available. The walk to Fort San Angelo, which lies on a rocky outcrop, affords some nice views.

Lakshadweep (Union Territory)

D 13–15

Population: approx. 60,000

Distance: 200km/125mi–400km/250mi west of Kerala's coast

Those who felt that Kerala's beaches were not white enough, the water not clear enough and life not quiet enough can escape to Lakshadweep, providing the extra cost for this holiday is not an issue. The Lakshadweep islands are 200km/125mi–400km/250mi from Kerala's coast in the Arabian Sea.

Coral reefs, populated by iridescent fish, lagoons with fine sand, quiet palm tree groves, so far without the typical souvenir shops and beach bars like those in Goa or Kovalam, make Lakshadweep ideal for some rest and relaxation. Of the 36 islands, only ten are in-

● VISITING LAKSHADWEEP

INFORMATION
www.lakshadweeptourism.com
bangaramisland@cghearth.com

GETTING THERE
Regular flights from Kochi to Agatti,
from there by boat to Bangaram
Island (8km/5mi). The season lasts
from October to March.

Entry regulations
The Lakshadweep islands are part of
the Indian state's union territories.
Their centre lies on Kavaratti. Entry is
subject to several restrictions. So far
foreigners are only allowed to come to
the uninhabited island of Bangaram.
The Casino Hotel group has built a
holiday resort there, the Bangaram
Island Resort.

WHERE TO STAY / WHERE TO EAT
► Luxury
Bangaram Island Resort
Reservations via Casino Group of
Hotels in Kochi
Tel. 04 84 – 301 17 11
www.cghearth.com
This smart resort has a diving school;
visitors can also snorkel, go deep-sea
fishing and dabble in some yoga. An
Ayurvedic centre, a restaurant and a
bar are also available of course.
Guests staying here will also have the
visitor-permit issue taken care of for
them.

---

habited. Their population of 60,000 or so largely consists of descendants of Muslim emigrants from Kerala. The main sources of income
here are fishing and the processing of coconut products.

★ Madurai

State: Tamil Nadu
Population: 1.2 million

Altitude: 100m/330ft
Distance: 461km/286mi southwest of
Chennai

**The ancient temple city of Madurai on the banks of the Vaigai river
can look back on a history of more than 2000 years. There are
many legends about this city, which takes its name from the Tamil
word madhuram, meaning »sweetness«.**

The city allegedly got its name because Shiva scattered nectar over it
when it was founded. Today Madurai is an important trading and industrial city that sees constant growth.

Madurai's history goes back around 2000 years. Holy ascetics lived in   **History**
the caves in this region and the powerful Pandyas ruled their kingdom from here for almost a whole millennium until the tenth cen-

tury. Madurai was an important, flourishing trading centre at the time. Goods were moved from here via Poompuhar harbour to other continents. In the tenth century the Chola king Parantaka conquered Madurai. Four centuries later a large part of the city was destroyed when it was conquered and plundered by the armies of the Delhi sultanate under the leadership of Malik Kafur. After just a short while Madurai joined the Vijayanagara Empire and the Nayaks, governors appointed by Vijayanagara, became Madurai's new rulers. Under the Nayaks, who made themselves independent of the Vijayanagara Empire in 1565, the town flourished a second time. Madurai was laid out in accordance with the classical architectural teachings in the shape of a lotus around the new temple. Meenakshi Amman temple and the palace of Thirumalai Nayak were also built during this time. The wide streets around the temple were made in such a way as to accommodate the huge temple chariots pulled by thousands of people during the annual festival.

What to See in Madurai

★ ★
Meenakshi Sundareshwarar Temple

In contrast to many other temples in India, the **main deity of this magnificent temple complex is a goddess: Meenakshi**. She is said to have been a Pandya king's daughter whom Shiva desired. After her wedding with him she also became a goddess. Only a small temple

A sadhu with a trident-like Trishul, one of Shiva's insignias

► VISITING MADURAI · CHETTINAD

INFORMATION
TTDC (Tamil Nadu Tourism Development Corporation)
1, West Veli Street
Madurai – 625001
Tel. 04 52 – 233 47 57

GETTING THERE
By air from Chennai, Mumbai or Thiruvananthapuram; rail and bus connections to all larger towns in southern India.

FESTIVALS
Colourful temple festivals
In Jan / Feb the temple raft festival is celebrated on the temple lake Vandiyur Mariamman Teppakulam: during a full moon the figures of many important deities from the temples of Madurai are pulled around the island in the lake on illuminated rafts. The ten-day Chitrai festival (April / May) serves to commemorate the wedding between Shiva and Meenakshi, during which the temple chariot is pulled around the temple.

SHOPPING
Karaikudi, Chettinad's main town, is famous for its woven fabrics and antiques. The latter can be found in Muneesvaran Temple Street for example.

WHERE TO EAT / WHERE TO STAY
► Mid-range
Fortune Pandiyan Hotel
Race Course
Madurai – 625 002
Tel. 04 52 – 253 70 90 or 435 67 89
www.fortuneparkhotels.com
Modern rooms with air conditioning, pool and internet as well as a very good restaurant with a recommendable buffet.

Baedeker recommendation

The Bangala
Karaikudi, Chettinad
Devakottai Road, Sanjai
Tel. 045 65 – 22 02 21, 25 02 21
www.thebangala.com
Top class regional cuisine in an old Chettinad bungalow in Karaikudi. On the outskirts of town Mrs Meyyappan has developed an old family bungalow for guests, who are spoiled by twelve lovingly and individually furnished double rooms, a lovely garden and a comfortable lounge, as well as great food. The Bangala also organizes sightseeing tours of the surrounding area, which include visits to the various particularly worthwhile Chettiar houses and workshops.

was built in honour of her husband **Shiva in the form of Sundareshwarar**. Meenakshi Temple has some very old sections but the largest part dates back to the 17th century. The extensive temple complex, which is surrounded by a high wall with four entrances, above which there are four huge gopurams up to 49m/161ft high, is one of the largest in India. The four towers are decorated with many figures from the Hindu pantheon; they can be seen from great distances. The temple grounds contain many temples, temple halls and a

The colourful sculptures portray the Hindu pantheon

temple lake. The **diversity of the depictions of the gods**, in granite and in stucco, of which there are apparently 33 million (!) is at times bewildering. Since shoes have to be taken off before entering the temple tower it is best to enter the complex via its eastern gate. After viewing the temple visitors can carry on to the Pudhu Mandapam further east.

✳
Pudhu Mandapam

The Pudhu Mandapam (new hall) is supported by **124 columns**. The hall's sculptures are amongst the best in Madurai. Since there are several retail stalls in the hall it is somewhat difficult to admire the figures' craftsmanship. However, the hall full of merchants still has its special appeal. Visitors will find a lot of tailors, who can run up made-to-measure clothes for tourists in just a few hours. Behind the Pudhu Mandapam is the ruin of a gopuram that was never completed. It has the huge dimensions of 64m/210ft x 36m/118ft.

✳
Thirumalai Nayak Palace

Only a section has remained of the Nayaks' once large palace complex, whose monumentality is still impressive. The throne room is more than 20m/68ft in height and is crowned by a huge dome, while the colonnades around the courtyard are decorated by 12m/40ft pillars. A light-and-sound show takes place here in the evenings. The dancing hall is particularly worth taking a look at.

Mariamman Theppakulam

Around 5km/3mi to the east is the Mariamman Theppakulam, the largest temple pond in India with a multi-storey pavilion in the middle. It is visited by thousands of pilgrims once a year during the raft festival (Jan/Feb). During the festival statues of gods are put on floats and pulled around the pavilion in the pond. For most of the year the pond is without water, however, even though it has a connection to the Vaigai river.

Mahatma Gandhi Memorial

The museum on the northern side of the Vaigai river, which divides the town, provides a good overview of the independence movement led by Gandhi in India. In addition to photographs there are also some of Gandhi's personal effects on display.

Chettinad

Named after the merchant caste of the Chettiars

The region of Chettinad (90km/55mi east of Madurai) is considered a **new destination on Tamil Nadu's tourist map**. The 75 villages and small towns between Madurai and Tamil Nadu's coast mainly owe their reputation to two things: their **exceptional architecture and their outstanding cuisine**. Both go back to the merchant caste of the

Chettiars who have their home here. The Chettiars achieved great wealth in the 19th and at the beginning of the 20th century through their business dealings with various Southeast Asian countries, particularly Burma and Indonesia. The men invested their money where their families were living, i.e. in their birthplaces, the towns and villages of Chettinad. Between 1850 and 1940 they built magnificent houses here, every one of them bigger and more beautiful than the next, with large courtyards tiled with marble, carved teak columns and Belgian glass. Many of these buildings are now empty for the majority of the year since their owners live in Chennai or in other Indian cities. Chettindas is the southern Indian counterpart of the region of Shekhawati in Rajasthan where, during the same period, the Marwari merchant caste also showed its status by building the palatial homes known as havelis.

Karaikudi

Chettinad's largest town is Karaikudi. There are several hotels and restaurants here as well as very good shopping opportunities. Karaikudi is a good place from which to explore the area. The main attractions are the palace of the Raja of Chettinad in the small town of Kanadukathan and the small museum of everyday utensils in the house next door. The raja's private station not far from here is also worth a visit.

Villages

The villages of Chettinad have countless magnificent houses; most of them can only be admired from the outside, however, except on guided tours. The temples dedicated to the patron deity Ayyanar (one of Shiva's incarnations) with their terra cotta horses as votive gifts are also typical of this region.

✶ Mamallapuram (Mamlapuram, Mahabalipuram)

G 13

State: Tamil Nadu
Population: 10,000

Altitude: sea level
Distance: 60km/37mi south of Chennai

The wonderful white sandy beach and the temple complexes, caves and reliefs, most of which have now been uncovered and are amongst the oldest and most beautiful artworks in India, and have made the somewhat sleepy town of Mamallapuram one of the most important centres of tourism in southern India.

Mamallapuram is an ideal place to find some rest and relaxation and to get to know Indian culture at the same time. It is definitely worth staying here for several days. The government art academy for sculptors and stonemasons is based here and the many workshops produce statues of deities for the entire South Indian market.

▶ VISITING MAMALLAPURAM

INFORMATION

Tamil Nadu Tourist Office
East Raja Street
Tel. 044 – 27 44 22 32
(Mon–Fri 10am–5.45pm)
or www.tamilnadutourism.org

GETTING THERE

Bus and rail connections with
Chennai

SHOPPING

Mamallapuram is famous for its
figures carved from granite and
soapstone. High-quality handicrafts
and antiques can be bought in
Southern Arts & Crafts (72 East Raja
Street).

WHERE TO STAY / WHERE TO EAT

► Luxury

① **Sterling Mahabalipuram**
Shore Temple Road
Tel. 044 – 27 44 22 87
www.sterlingmahabalipuram.net
Why not relax after a tour of the
temples in the pleasant hotel garden
by the pool or in the nice restaurant
or even by having an Ayurvedic
massage.

► Budget

② **Greenwoods Beach Resort**
Ottavadi Cross Street
Tel. 044 – 27 44 22 12
Friendly hotel with a pleasant roof
restaurant and garden.

History The town's name, Mamallapuram, comes from the sobriquet Maha-malla (great warrior) given to the important Pallava king Narasimha-varman I. During his reign (630–668) he founded a port here, where the god Vishnu is said to have defeated the demon king Bali, and had many temples, reliefs and caves carved from the rocks and mountains. The town briefly flourished as a trading and military port. Narasimhavarman launched two successful military campaigns to Lanka (modern-day Sri Lanka) from here. After the decline of the Pallava Empire the town quickly lost its importance. The harbour silted up, Mamallapuram fell into complete oblivion. Over time, the temple complexes were covered by sand. They were only uncovered during the 20th century, after which they were restored and secured.

? **DID YOU KNOW ...?**

■ ... that the devastating tsunami of December 2004 caused some of the sculptures of the Pallava dynasty that had been hidden in the sand to be uncovered? Further temples were also discovered in the sea.

What to See in Mamallapuram

★★
Five rathas
South of the centre is a group of five small temples called rathas (temple chariots) because they resemble the processional chariots used during temple festivals. The five monolithic temples are named after the Pandava heroes (Dharmaja, Bhima, Arjuna and the twins

Mamallapuram *Map*

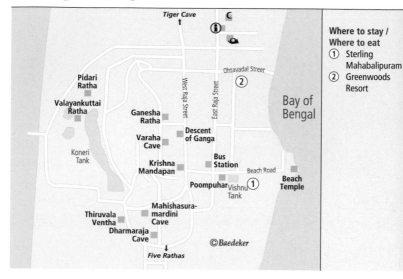

Tiger Cave

Ohtavadal Street

Pidari
Ratha

Valayankuttai
Ratha

West Raja Street

East Raja Street

Ganesha
Ratha

Varaha
Cave

Koneri
Tank

Descent
of Ganga

Krishna
Mandapan

Bus
Station

Beach Road

Bay of
Bengal

Poompuhar Vishnu ①
Tank

Beach
Temple

Thiruvala
Ventha

Mahishasura-
mardini
Cave

Dharmaraja
Cave

©Baedeker

Five Rathas

**Where to stay /
Where to eat**
① Sterling
Mahabalipuram
② Greenwoods
Resort

Nakula and Shadev) as well as their joint wife Draupadi. These temples, which all vary in their architecture, were never used and their purpose is not fully understood. They were probably a collection of models of different temple types.

Dharmaraja Ratha resembled a three-stepped pyramid with a square ground-plan. Its base is richly adorned with depictions of Harihara, Brahma, Skanda, Ardhanarishvara and Narasimhavarman I, who commissioned it. **Arjuna Ratha**, with its richly ornamented façade, resembles Dharmaraja Ratha; on its eastern side is a very fine depiction of the Vedic god Indra riding on his white elephant Ariavata. Next to this ratha is a monolithic Nandi. The rectangular **Bhima Ratha** has a gallery on its long side flanked by four lion columns on either side. The small, plain building with empty apses on the façade is **Nakula Shadeva Ratha**, beside which is a monolithic elephant. The square **Draupadi Ratha**, which houses a depiction of the mother goddess Durga, looks more like a straw-covered hut than a temple.

Mamallapuram has several cave temples, of which only a small number were carved out of the hard granite until they were complete. The most important cave temple is consecrated to the goddess **Mahishasuramardini, an incarnation of the great goddess Durga**. According to legend she killed the hitherto invincible demon Mahisha, whereupon she was given the name Mahishasuramardini (conqueror of Mahisha). The cave's interior is decorated with a relief depicting the highlight of the battle. The goddess, riding on a lion, has several arms and is holding a bow and arrow with which she is storming

Cave temples

The beach temple is showing its battle scars from fighting wind and weather

ahead, while the demon Mahisha retreats from her strength together with his followers.

★ ★
Beach temple

Right on the beach stands the granite Shiva temple, which shows clear signs of centuries of weathering. It was built by Narasimhavarman II (around 690–715). The temple is decorated with two slender Vimanas and contains three cult cells. In addition to Shiva, Vishnu was also worshipped in this temple. The entrance of the main cell is directed towards the east, to the sea, so that the sun's morning rays can illuminate the lingam. Many Nandi figures adorn the low surrounding wall of the temple complex, which has still not yet been fully uncovered. The beauty of this beach temple lies less in its size than in its **harmonious proportions and the wonderful work of the entire façade**. It is an impressive experience to visit the temple in the early hours of the morning. The sun rising over the sea washes it with a golden glow.

★ ★
Descent of
Ganga

In the middle of the old town is one of the world's largest reliefs (12m/39ft tall, 33m/110ft long), which initially confuses beholders with its wealth of figures. Its creators composed a masterpiece with gods, humans and animals, which is interpreted as the descent of the river goddess Ganga from heaven to earth. Ganga was, according to this legend, moved by the strict meditations of the ascetic Bagiratha to come down to earth and give the people wealth and riches (►Baedeker Special p.290).

The large relief is divided into two pieces by a large, vertical gap in the middle, through which water once flowed. There are nagas sym-

The large relief describes the myth of the creation of the Ganges

bolizing fertility and affluence in the gap. To the left of the gap is a depiction of the ascetic meditating and somewhat above him the god Shiva can be made out in a blessing position. Gods, nobles, saints, musicians and animals all populate the scene. The elephants, which are almost life-size, are amongst the **best animal depictions in the whole of India**. The sculptors did not just express this divine subject in a magnificent manner, but also with humour. It can be seen that the monkeys on the right-hand side of the gap are having fun imitating the ascetic's yoga exercises.

According to an alternative interpretation the depiction is called »Arjuna's penitence«. The meditating yogi is believed to be Arjuna, the hero of the Mahabharata, who was given the miracle weapon Pasupatha by Shiva after intensive meditation on the banks of the Ganges.

Further temples

In addition to those already described, Mamallapuram has many reliefs and small cave temples that are nice to stumble across when going for walks in the area. On the road of the five rathas heading towards the large relief »Descent of Ganga«, visitors will come across **Dharmaraja Mandapa**, an incomplete relief, **Krishna Mandapa** with nice depictions from Krishna's life and **Pancha Pandava Mandapa** with lion columns, in this order.

Handicrafts

The road leading from the town centre to the five rathas is lined by workshops selling figures of granite and soapstone. It is a special treat to watch these artisans at work, and to observe how they use the simplest tools to recreate the diverse Indian pantheon out of the hard granite.

Beach North of Mamallapuram there is a nice hotel-lined beach, where visitors can swim and relax.

Around Mamallapuram

Saluvankuppam Tiger Cave Around 6km/3.5mi north of Mamallapuram visitors will find Tiger Cave, a Durga temple, by the beach. The entrance of this impressive cave is designed as a mouth surrounded by grimacing tigers.

Crocodile farm After looking at temples for several days, a visit to Madras Crocodile Bank Trust 20km/12mi north of Mamallapuram, where different crocodile species are bred, may make for a welcome change of scene (open: Tue–Sun 9am–5.30pm).

Mangalore

D 13

State: Karnataka
Population: 430,000

Altitude: sea level
Distance: 347km/215mi west of Bangalore

The attractive coastal town of Mangalore, with its introspective air, is bedded in a sea of palm trees and stretches out over several hills. Interesting churches, a lively fish market and good hotels and restaurants invite visitors to take a closer look at the town. It is a good base from which to visit the old temple sites in the hinterland.

Mangalore was an important port in days gone by. Even today all kinds of goods, particularly coffee and cashew nuts, are exported from here.

Around Mangalore

Excursion A nice tour that can easily be followed in a taxi in a single day heads inland. The drive on relatively good roads leads through fertile green hills and fields to Mudbidri, then onwards to Karkal, back to the coast to Udupi and from there back to Mangalore again. This trip can be extended by a detour to Sringeri somewhat further away with its worthwhile temples.

The small town of **Mudbidri** (30km/20mi northeast of Mangalore) is an important place of pilgrimage for Jains. There are 16 temples here that were built between the 12th and 15th centuries. The largest of

VISITING MANGALORE

INFORMATION

Tourist Office
Tel. 08 24 – 244 29 26
www.karnatakatourism.org

GETTING THERE

Flight connections to Mumbai and Bangalore; many rail and bus links, for example with Bangalore, Margao (Goa), Mumbai and Kochi

WHERE TO EAT / WHERE TO STAY

► **Luxury / Mid-range**
Manjarun Hotel
Old Port Road, Mangalore
Tel. 08 24 – 566 04 20
www.tajhotels.com
Nice rooms, some of them with sea views, a restaurant and a 24-hour coffee shop.

them is **Chandranatha Temple, also known as Thousand-Column Basti**. It consists of several halls, one beyond the other. They are supported by richly adorned granite columns. The palace of the local ruling dynasty, the Chautas, can also be visited. The carvings on the wooden columns in the complex from the 17th century are particularly impressive. In **Karkal** (30km/20mi north of Mudabidri) there is another group of Jain temples. The 14m/46ft statue of **Bahubali** (Gomateshvara) is similar to the statue in Sravana Belgola (►Belur · Halebid, Around) and dates back to the year 1432. It too represents the ideal ascetic of the Digambaras (air-clad), naked and covered in climbing plants as a result of incessant meditation outdoors.

◄ Udupi

Udupi (58km/36mi north of Mangalore) is a picturesque little town with narrow streets and old houses. It is considered the **religious centre of the Madhva sect**, named after its founder Madhvacarya (13th century). The pilgrims' destination is the Krishna temple in the heart of town as well as Anandeshvara Temple next to it. Here too visitors will be fascinated by the **vibrancy of temple life so typical of Krishna shrines**. A walk through the temple's interior is definitely worth it, even though it does not contain any valuable treasures from an art-historical perspective. Every two years at the end of January a large temple festival (Madhva Sarovara) is held with a procession of wonderfully decorated temple chariots.

Richly adorned temple chariots

Only 5km/3mi from Udupi, where the pace of life is leisurely, is the new town of **Manipal** with its modern research and educational institutions.

Sringeri   Located in the evergreen rainforests of the Western Ghats is the small town of Sringeri (90km/55mi east of Udupi), the **centre of Shaiva Amnaya Matha community**, founded by the great reformer Shankara. The drive from Udupi along winding roads through dense forests and coffee plantations is very attractive. The main destination in Sringeri for pilgrims and visitors alike is **Vidyashankara Temple**, commissioned by Harihara and Bukka, the founders of the Vijayanagara dynasty, and completed in 1356. The reddish granite temple consists of a sanctum and mandapa, which are connected via a double apse. The temple is built on a pedestal, which imitates the temple's elliptical shape. Plant and animal friezes, panels with mythical stories and more than 60 figures in total adorn the building's exterior walls. The central shrine houses the Vidyashankara lingam and three further secondary shrines for Brahma and Sarasvati, Vishnu and Lakshi and Shiva as Maheshvara and Uma. The columned hall stretching to the east is supported by twelve pillars decorated with roaring Vyalas and elephants, where each one represents a sign of the zodiac. In the vicinity of the main temple there are several other temples; Sharadoka Temple is the main one sought out by the pilgrims.

✶ Mysore

E 13

State: Karnataka	**Altitude:** 770m/2526ft
Population: 870,000	**Distance:** 135km/84mi southwest of Bangalore

Mysore, the former capital of the state of Mysore (now Karnataka) and the one-time residence of the maharajas of Mysore, is four hours' drive southwest of the state's current capital ▶ Bangalore. Its location in Karnataka's hills gives it a pleasant climate, and this, combined with its many parks, palaces, gardens and avenues, has earned Mysore the name »Garden City«.

Largely spared the hustle and bustle of other Indian cities of this size, it is an ideal starting point for trips to the many sights in the closer and more distant surroundings, even though Mysore itself does not have any outstanding attractions to offer. Once a year, however, in October / November, Mysore is visited by half a million tourists who come to see the colourful **Dussehra procession** (▶Baedeker Special p.392), which is famous all across India.

History   According to legend, Mysore was founded in the place where the goddess Durga defeated the buffalo demon Mahisha after a nine-day fight. Durga, called Chamundi in Mysore, was also the patron goddess of the ruling Wodejar dynasty. They worshipped their goddess during the annual Dussehra celebrations, which last for ten days and culminate in the great procession on the final day. The Wodejars, the successors of the Rajputs who had gone southwards, ruled their empire from Mysore, and occasionally also from the nearby island of Srirangapatna, from the beginning of the 17th century until they were deposed by their own general Haider Ali in 1761. After the British victory over Haider Ali and his son Tipu Sultan in the legendary Battle of Seringapatam in 1799, large parts of the former empire

VISITING MYSORE

INFORMATION

KSTDC Tourist Office
In the Mayura Yatri Nivas Hotel
2, Jhansi Laxmi Bhai Road
Tel. 08 21 – 242 34 92

Information also on the website of Karnataka Tourism (www.karnataka-tourism.org)

GETTING THERE

Train connections to Bangalore, countless bus links (with Bangalore, Hassan, Hospet, Kochi and Panjim in Goa, for example)

FESTIVALS

The Dussehra Festival is celebrated with a great procession (Oct / Nov, a more exact date can be found in the festival calendar under www.india-tourism.com). Accommodation must be booked in advance for this period.

SHOPPING

Mysore is famous for its sandalwood products and its silk.

WHERE TO STAY / WHERE TO EAT

► Luxury

① *ITDC Lalitha Mahal Palace*
Siddhartha Nagar
Tel. 08 21 – 247 04 70

Sophisticated Heritage Hotel, located on a hill above Mysore; it once served as the maharaja's guesthouse.

► Mid-range

② *Reegalis*
Vinobha Road
Tel. 08 21 – 242 64 26
Comfortable and modern with a pool and two restaurants.

⑤ *Sandesh The Prince*
3, Nethra Nivas
Nazarbad Road
Tel. 08 21 – 243 67 77
Modern middle of the range hotel with a restaurant.

► Budget

③ *Hotel Mayura Hoysala and Mayura Yatri Nivas*
2, Jhansi Laxmi Bhai Road
Tel. 08 21 – 242 53 49
The somewhat more expensive (Mayura) and inexpensive variety (Yatri Nivas) of the hotel chain run by Karnataka Tourism. Basic, clean rooms, terrace, restaurant.

④ *Hotel Mayura Riverview*
In Srirangapatna
Tel. 082 36 – 21 74 54
Attractive location by the river with restaurant and bar.

Mysore Map

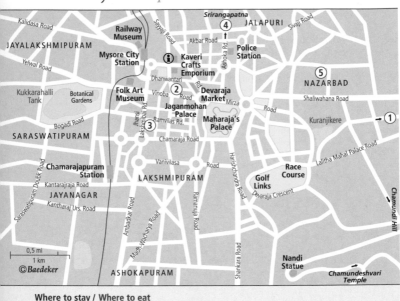

Where to stay / Where to eat
① ITDC Lalitha Mahal Palace
② Reegalis
③ Mayura Hoysala and Yatri Nivas
④ Mayura Riverview
⑤ Sandesh the Prince

were put under British administration, while the ruling family was re-established in the now very much smaller remaining state with the residency of Mysore. They ruled until the state became incorporated into the Indian Union; they did this from Bangalore, however, which had steadily grown in significance. The old capital of Mysore with its palaces remained the residence of the royal family and a centre of cultural activities.

What to See in Mysore

★ ★
Amba Vilas (Maharaja's palace)

⏱
Opening hours:
Open: daily
10.30am–5.30pm

In the city centre and within the fort is Amba Vilas, the residence of the former rulers, whose successors still inhabit parts of the palace. The Indo-Saracenic palace was built between 1897 and 1912 under the guidance of British architect Henry Irwin in the place of the building that had previously burned down. The structure with its many onion domes and its access balconies taken from the Rajput palaces is illuminated at night with thousands of lamps. Its interior boasts lavish magnificence and abundance: artistically painted columns bear filigree lattice work, above which there are vaulted ceilings made of multicoloured Scottish window-glass. Marble floors, crystal chandeliers, mirrored walls and heavy velvet curtains transport visitors into the atmosphere of a late-Baroque palace and give an idea of what the grandiose way of life was like for the maharajas around 1900. The »**Lion Throne**« in the Wedding Hall (Kalyana Mandapa), carved from fig wood and covered in gold leaf, is particularly interesting. According to legend it was the throne of the Pandavas (heroes of the Mahabharata). It was probably a gift from Emperor Aurangzeb to Cikkadevaraja.

The Sri Jayachamarajendra Art Gallery located in **Jaganmohan Palace** exhibits miniature paintings from the Mysore school, pictures by Raja Ravi Varma and a collection of musical instruments (open: daily 8.30am–5pm).

Sri Jayachamarajendra Art Gallery ⏱

Mysore's fruit and vegetable market in the city centre is very worthwhile. Beguiling floral scents from jasmine and other flowers sold here in long garlands attract many buyers and sightseers.

Devaraja Market

The Kaveri Arts and Crafts Emporium has a large selection of sandalwood products for sale. Mysore is one of the processing centres of this precious wood. In addition to carvings, visitors can also buy the

Kaveri Arts and Crafts Emporium

Evening atmosphere at Mysore's palace

famous »Mysore Incense Sticks«, **which are made of real sandalwood**. Anyone wishing to watch how sandalwood oil is extracted can visit the government **Sandalwood Oil Factory** in the south of the city (open: Mon–Sat 9am–11am and 2pm–4pm).

Chamundi Hill

Approx. 3km/2mi southeast of the city centre is Chamundi Hill (1065m/3494ft), whose highest point can be reached via a 10km/6mi winding road. Halfway up is a 5m/16ft monolithic **Nandi** (Shiva's vehicle) carved from the rock. It dates back to 1659.

A gigantic monolith as a Nandi

On the top of the hill is **Chamundeshvari Temple**, consecrated to Durga, the goddess who defeated the buffalo demon. It is accompanied by a summer residence of the maharajas. The view of the city and the surrounding area from the terrace of the summerhouse is very attractive.

Around Mysore

Srirangapatna

Various ruling dynasties governed their area of influence from the 5km/3mi-long island in the Kaveri river. A fort was built here back in the time of the kings of Vijayanagara who secured their supremacy over this region by forming alliances. After their decline they were succeeded by the Wodejars, the maharajas of Mysore. They made Srirangapatna (16km/10mi northeast of Mysore) their capital in 1610. One and a half centuries later, in 1761, the Muslim ruler Haider Ali conquered the island and fought his relentless war against the British, until they took this island fort in 1792. His son Tipu Sultan was able to continue ruling after making great concessions, but only for seven years.

The **fort**, surrounded by a double wall, is in the western part of the island. An obelisk marks the place where the British penetrated in 1799 by breaching the wall, thereby surprising the enemy. Within the walls visitors will find Sri Ranganathasvami Temple, probably dating from the 12th century, a popular temple dedicated to Vishnu. This is also where the place takes its name from. Further east is the Friday Mosque, Jama Masjid, which was built under Tipu Sultan in 1784.

Tipu Sultan's summer palace ►

Further east still, outside the fort, is what is probably the most interesting building remaining of the period of Muslim rule: Tipu Sultan's summer palace, Daria Daulat (Wealth of the Sea), stands in the middle of a small park. Like the Friday Mosque, it also dates back to 1784. Both the interior and the exterior walls of the two-storey building are richly painted. The building itself stands on a square platform and is surrounded by a columned veranda. It has now been transformed into a very worthwhile museum, in which visitors can admire wall paintings with battle scenes from the time of the wars with the British. The Gumbaz mausoleum of the ruling family in the eastern part of the island houses the tombs of Haider Ali, Tipu Sultan and his mother. On the opposite side of the road is a small church of Abbé Dubois, dating from 1800.

The small but wonderful Ranganathittu Bird Sanctuary lies 2km/1mi west of Srirangapatna. Many bird species breed on a lake and on several islands, particularly between November and March. The species include painted stork, herons and cormorants. The lake is also home to crocodiles.

✳ Ranganathittu Bird Sanctuary

On the shore of the Krishnarajasagar Dam (19km/12mi northeast of Mysore) is a further attraction: the Brindavan Gardens. The Kaveri was dammed here in 1932 to create a reservoir 2621m/2866yd long and 39m/128ft high. On one side terraced gardens were laid out with fountains, a lake and colourful illumination at night.

Brindavan Gardens

The temple in Somnathpur (30km/20 east of Mysore) is one of a group of the famous, still well-preserved temples of the Hoysala dynasty. The others are to be found in ►Belur and Halebid.
Keshava Temple lies in a courtyard measuring 75m/82yd by 60m/66yd and lined by 64 cells. It consists of a vestibule and assembly hall, from which three sanctuaries, all dedicated to different aspects of Vishnu, lead off. The special shape of their exterior walls is striking: the usually square sanctum became a **star-shaped structure** by the rotation of the square, which has created a multi-angular exterior façade, greatly increasing the surface area. This created an amazing space for the sculptors: a total of **194 large sculptures** populate the temple's exterior walls. The base's star-shape continues in the 11m/36ft high temple roof and gives it an overall bell-like shape. The entire complex is built on a wide 1m/3ft platform allowing believers to walk around the building. Both the platform and the temple's foundation and hall display a strong horizontal structuring by means of bands and sculptural friezes. The exceptional finesse and precision with which the artists were able to work here is thanks to the material of which the temples in ►Belur and Halebid were also made: chlorite, a type of stone with a grey-green shimmer, is very easy to work with. The **six friezes** at the base of the temples are particularly impressive. At the bottom there is a row of elephants, the animals who hold the universe on

✳ Somnathpur ✳ ✳

◄ Keshava Temple

Keshava temples are laid out in a star-shaped pattern

their shoulders in Hindu cosmology and who symbolically support the temple as a symbol of the universe. Above them are bands with mythological creatures, while flowers wind around the temple and with a great love of detail stories from the great epics Mahabharata and Ramayana are told – when visitors walk around them in the right way the stories unfold in front of their very eyes. The final frieze depicts marching geese. Above it are filigree stone windows (jalis) that let air and a little light into the temple's interior. The effort put in by the craftsmen did not end with the exterior façades. The **temple's interior** also contains ample proof of their ability. The three-dimensional design of the ceiling in the main hall and the columns, turned on lathes, are particularly striking. As in many other Hoysala temples, the sculptors have immortalized themselves on some of their works by name. The original figure of Vishnu in the main cella was stolen and replaced by a new one. The northern sanctum houses an attractive figure of Janardana and the southern one a figure of Krishna as Venugopala (flute-playing shepherd).

Madikeri

Madikeri (125km/78mi west of Mysore) is the capital of the district of Kodagu (Coorg) and was only made part of the state of Karnataka in 1956. Since the 17th century the Hindu dynasty of the Lingayats ruled here, interrupted by several occupations by the Muslim rulers Haider Ali and Tipu Sultan, who briefly brought the area under their control in the 18th century.

The small town in this mountainous region, part of the Western Ghats, is now a **popular destination** for Indian tourists, particularly during the dry winter months. Visitors can also get here by bus from Bangalore or Mangalore, but the route from Mysore to Madikeri is particularly picturesque. The narrow road winds upwards, lined by countless coffee plantations and evergreen forests. A walk through the town's steep alleys and a viewing of Omkareshvara Temple are both particularly worthwhile. The remains of the old fort date back to a period of Islamic rule.

Madikeri is ideal for a short stop to relax in the fresh air and enjoy some peace and quiet. There are a few hotels including the »Mayura Valley View« run by Karnataka Tourism (see Tip box). In addition, the KSTDC Tourist Office (tel. 082 72 – 22 85 83) provides extensive information about the region. Anyone not coming here in the winter should definitely bring wet weather gear, as it rains for the large part of the year.

! *Baedeker* TIP

Spending the night in Madikeri and Kodagu

Orange Country Resort (near Siddapur, Kodagu, tel. 082 74 – 25 84 81, fax 25 84 85, www.trail-sindia.com) is an exquisite resort hotel in the middle of a great coffee plantation with an Ayurveda centre and a pool. A more inexpensive option is the attractively situated Mayura Valley View Hotel in Madikeri (tel. 082 72 – 22 83 87). Visitors can also choose homestays, because many plantations in the region offer accommodation (www.travelcoorg.com).

Nagarjunakonda

F 11

State: Andhra Pradesh

Distance: 534km/332mi northwest of Chennai

Located on the river Krishna, Nagarjunakonda has been a site of human habitation for thousands of years, as discoveries from the Stone Age prove. The region flourished under the Ikshvaku dynasty from 275 to 350.

This dynasty made itself independent from the Satvahanas, who controlled the region from Amaravathi. At the time Nagarjunakonda was **one of the most important Buddhist centres of southern India**. Later the town was renamed Nagarjunakonda after the Buddhist monk Nagarjuna.

The first king of the Ikshavuks was a worshipper of the god of war Karttikeya, the son of Shiva. The king's sister, Chamsatri, on the other hand, was a follower of Buddhism. This concurrent worship of different religions by the ruling family led to the construction of both Hindu temples and Buddhist stupas. In addition Nagarjunakonda developed into a very famous university town. It fell into oblivion and was only rediscovered in 1926, by A. R. Saraswathi.

 NAGARJUNAKONDA

INFORMATION

Andra Pradesh Tourism Office
Hyderabad
Tel. 040 – 23 45 30 36
www.aptourism.com

APTDC offers tours that include Srisailam, Kurnool and Alampur.

GETTING THERE

By bus or taxi from Hyderabad

WHERE TO STAY

Punnami Vijay Vihar
Nagarjunasagar
Tel. 086 80 – 27 73 62

What to See in and around Nagarjunakonda

Systematic digs in Nagarjunakonda brought Buddhist Chaitya halls, stupas, monastic complexes as well as Hindu temples and even amphitheatres to light. They helped in forming a better understanding of Buddhist architecture.   **Digs**

The large Stupa of Nagarjunakonda is an attempt to develop the stupa as a symbol of Buddhist teaching. Around the central column three concentric rings made of brick were built. The gaps were filled with earth. The rings were connected by radial walls, symbolizing the spokes of a wheel. The stupa is fitted with platforms in four directions on which there are five columns. These five stambhas repre-   **Stupa** sent the five great stations of the Buddha's life: birth, renunciation, enlightenment, first sermon and death.

Since the Indian government decided to create a reservoir on the site of the excavation, a few important buildings were rebuilt on the nearby hill and smaller objects brought to a museum. The hill of Nagarjunakonda is now an island because of the reservoir and can only be reached by ferry.

Museum ⏲ The museum has a good collection of Buddhist sculptures and coins (open: daily 9am–4pm).

Nagarjuna Dam One of India's largest reservoirs lies behind Nagarjuna Dam. The Indian government wanted this construction to help modernize the country's agriculture after independence. The water serves both electricity generation and the irrigation of the fields in the surrounding area.

✱ Srisailam Temple Srisailam Temple (100km/62mi northeast of Kurnool) is an important place for Indian pilgrims because one of the Jyotir Lingas (light lingams) is worshipped here. The Shiva temple from the Vijayanagara period has countless flat reliefs as an extra attraction. They decorate the complex's 6m/20ft-high exterior walls. This stone picture-book tells stories from Shiva's life.

Kurnool and Alampur The district capital of Kurnool (120km/75mi southwest of Nagarjunakonda, 230km/143mi south of Hyderabad) is a good starting location for visiting the temples of Alampur.

Alampur is a small town at the confluence of the Tungabhadra and the Krishna rivers which is mainly visited by pilgrims coming through on their way to Srisailam. Those interested in the development of the South Indian temple style can go and see a group of temples from the Chalukya dynasty here. Every one of the nine eighth-century temples was named after Brahma. Despite the names, all of the temples are in fact dedicated to Shiva, which is why they contain lingams.

✱ Ooty (Udagamandalam, Uthagamandalam, Ootacamund)

E 14

State: Tamil Nadu	**Altitude:** 2286m/7500ft
Population: 82,000	**Distance:** 260km/162mi south of Bangalore

Thanks to its altitude, the town in the Nilgiris is relatively cool even in summer. Ooty is therefore an ideal place to take a break when it gets too hot for comfort in the rest of South India. There are many walks in the area and visitors can also go on boat trips on the lake.

The small train of the Blue Mountain Railway runs every day between Mettupalayam and Ooty (46km/29mi). The journey takes almost five hours, but the winding route through the forest with its numerous tunnels is a special experience.

✶
◄ Blue Mountain Railway

The region around Ooty was »discovered« by the British district governor of Coimbatore, John Sullivan, in 1819. He created the lake of Ooty, which today endows the entire town with a pleasant atmosphere. Many British people set up their summer homes here in the time that followed. In 1840 the botanical gardens were created, as were golf courses, polo fields and tennis courts. After 1869 Ooty rose to become the official summer residence of the government in Chennai. Today the **»Queen of the Hill Stations«** is a popular destination for wealthy southern Indians, and is especially busy during the months of April and May.

What to See in Ooty

The **Botanical Gardens** laid out by the Marquis of Tweeddale in terraces in 1847 cover an area of almost 20ha/50ac. More than 1000 different plant species

On the Ooty train

🕐
Opening hours:
Open: daily
8am–6pm

grow here. It is considered to be one of India's most beautiful gardens. Beside a small pond stands a fossilized tree, thought to be around 20 million years old. The neighbouring office sells plant seeds.

Ooty's oldest place of worship, St Stephen's Church, was built in the Gothic style in 1829.

St Stephen

Many maharajas used to have their summer residences in Ooty. Some of these palaces have followed the general trend in India and been transformed into hotels, as is the case for the palaces of the maharajas of Mysore and Jodhpur.

Palaces

The small artificial lake is an inviting place to take a boat trip or do some fishing. On its banks the obligatory small ponies wait to take customers for rides around it. The lake, which was initially designed for irrigation, has been shrinking for years.

Lake

There are plenty of places to go hiking in the area around Ooty. The route to the Wenlock Downs (6km/3.5mi), the Kalahatti Falls and

Hiking

⊙ VISITING OOTY

INFORMATION

Tamil Nadu Tourist Office
Wenlock Road
Tel. 04 23 – 244 39 77
www.tamilnadutourism.org

GETTING THERE

The scenic train journey on the narrow-gauge Nilgiri Blue Mountain Railway from Conoor or Mettupalayam to Ooty is recommendable. In addition there are buses from Mysore, Bangalore and Chennai, amongst other places.

WHERE TO STAY / WHERE TO EAT

▶ **Luxury**
Fernhills Palace
Ooty

Tel. 04 23 – 244 56 83
www.welcomheritagehotels.com
Guests live in Fernhills Palace, the former summer palace of the maharajas. The reopened complex is surrounded by a huge garden with a sizable tree population. Ayurvedic treatments are available and there is plenty of opportunity to enjoy such sports as horseback riding, golf and trekking; there is also a gym.

▶ **Budget**
YWCA »Anandagiri«
Ettines Road
Tel. 04 23 – 244 22 18
Hours of relaxation await in the »English Parlour«, and the pleasant rooms also contribute to lovely ambience here.

the peak of Dodabetta (around 12km/7mi) are particularly popular. The almost 3000m/10,000ft-high mountain peak can be reached by bus and the 10km/6mi to Ooty can be completed on foot. The path leads past tea gardens and eucalyptus plantations.

⋆ ⋆ Periyar National Park

E 15

State: Kerala
Distance: 600km/373mi southwest of Chennai

Altitude: 1000m/3280ft–2019m/6624ft

The green rainforests of the Cardamom Hills, part of the southern Western Ghats, are home to one of the most popular and attractive nature reserves in the whole of India: Periyar National Park.

Within the large park, which extends 190km/120mi to the southeast of ▶Kochi, there is a reservoir with several branches. The Periyar river was dammed for the first time in 1895 to irrigate parts of the neighbouring state of Tamil Nadu with the masses of water brought by the two annual monsoons. The Maharaja of Travancore was the first to attempt to protect the forest by implementing a hunting ban in 1934. In 1950 the area was expanded to 777 sq km/300 sq mi and in 1982 a core zone of 350 sq km/135 sq mi was declared a national park. It has been one of India's tiger reserves since 1977 . Periyar is one of the few parks with a »real« jungle. The local rainforest where trees can grow up to 50m/165ft is called Shola. It covers around 40% of the terrain. The rest consists of broad-leafed forest, particularly of eucalyptus trees, and grassland.

✶ ✶
◀ Animal reserve

The park is known for its large elephant herds; many deer species, such as chitals and sambar deer can be found here, too. Wild boar, various monkey and prosimian species are also amongst Periyar's inhabitants. In order to encounter a leopard or one of the approximately 50 tigers a great deal of luck is needed, as is the case everywhere in India. The protected area is a paradise for ornithologists in particular. 275 bird species have been recorded here, including a dozen cuckoo and woodpecker species, 29 species of raptor and eight species of owl. On the shores of the reservoir, cormorants, darters, kingfishers and osprey can be seen.

Animal population

Elephants at the Periyar reservoir

The decorated temple elephant touches believers with its trunk and blesses them

MASTER OF ALL OBSTACLES

Of the 400 mammalian species in India, the elephant is the largest. Indian elephants (Elephas maximus) differ from their larger, heavier relatives, African elephants, in their proportionately smaller head, smaller ears and shorter tusks. An elephant can weigh up to 5000kg/11,000lbs and reach a shoulder height of up to 3m/10ft.

The relationship between elephants and humans goes back thousands of years and is reflected in an even older mythology. The elephant was probably domesticated as a mount 4500 years ago. Elephants can only be used as working animals from the age of 20 onwards. The enormous animals devour up to 250kg/550lbs of grass a day and their strength is used by the **mahouts**, elephant riders, to perform difficult forestry work. It is said no vehicle could manoeuvre and overcome obstacles as well as elephants can. Elephants make paths through almost impenetrable vegetation, they are capable of climbing mountains and of crossing fast-flowing streams. There are currently around 15,000 elephants in India, of which around 6000 inhabit the southern states of Kerala, Tamil Nadu and Karnataka; in

addition there are large numbers of them in Bengal and Assam. However, the significance of elephants in India is not limited to their use as working animals.

Shrouded in myth

Quite the opposite in fact: they are considered sacred and there are many myths about them. It is said about their origin that through the power of song the divine elephant Airavata hatched from one half of the shell of a cosmic egg and seven further elephants followed. From the other part of the shell eight female elephants followed. These sixteen original elephants were the ancestors of all other elephants. Many of South India's large temples have **temple elephants** accompanying the processions of the deities. It is said that laying eyes

on an elephant purifies the soul and if the animal touches a person's head with its trunk that person is believed to have been blessed. This is also the reason why visitors can see parents let the temple elephants touch their children's heads or why they give the mahout a banana or a rupee. In Indian culture elephants are considered a **symbol of affluence and fertility** since they are closely connected to Lakshmi, the goddess of wealth and affluence. Elephants have been attributed with properties of good fortune, such as making rain: elephants are said to be able to magically attract rain clouds and thereby overcome periods of drought.

According to ancient legends elephants once had wings and had been **the clouds' friends**. »Once elephants had wings and moved alongside their companions, the clouds, through the sky and were able to change their shapes. One day several high-spirited elephants settled on a huge tree in the Himalaya. Under this tree an ascetic was just teaching his students. The elephants were too large even for this big branch and so it broke off and buried some of the students under it. The students died on the spot but the elephants carried on flying without concern and sat down on another branch. The ascetic was so angry about the elephants' thoughtlessness that he cursed them. From then on they lost their wings and stayed firmly on the ground, but they have kept the ability to attract clouds filled with rain.« **White elephants**, which are said to be particularly talented in this endeavour, are considered especially holy. In some processions elephants

Strange world: small Ganesha on large rat

are still whited with ash. Kings were always at pains to possess such an animal. A story about Buddha says when he was a king in a past life he gave his white elephant to a neighbouring regent whose land was suffering from drought.

Ganesha, god with the elephant head

Indians' affection for this animal is also expressed in their worship of fat Ganesha with his elephant head. Ganesha is the son of Shiva and Parvati. According to legend Shiva, having returned from a long period of absence, is said to have cut his son's head off because he believed him to be his wife's lover. In order to correct the disaster as quickly as possible he gave Ganesha the head of the animal he had run into first: an elephant. Ganesha is considered the **god of wisdom, scholarship, science and politics**. He is meant to guarantee wealth and business success, which is why Ganesha can be found in many household shrines and entrance ways. He is often depicted as a symbol of fertility together with

Linga and Yoni or as serpentine in the village shrines. Together with his wife Siddhi (success) and Buddhi (wisdom) he also acts as helper to writers because he is said to have written one of the holy books with a broken tusk. This is why no student fails to make a small sacrifice to Ganesha before an exam.

His vehicle is a rat, which does not exactly seem fitting in a physical sense for this huge deity. However, it complements the elephant in an ideal manner through its small size, because what they have in common is that they can both avoid and overcome obstacles well. It is said about Ganesha that he breaks through obstacles as an elephant goes through the jungle, treading on bushes, bending or uprooting trees and wading through rivers. The rat, with its small size and its speed, gets access to locked silos and other larders. Thus they both embody the power of this god to overcome every obstacle on the way to salvation. As a lucky charm and as master of all obstacles Ganesha often decorates the dashboard of buses and lorries.

▶ VISITING PERIYAR NATIONAL PARK

INFORMATION
DTPC
Thekkady Junction, Kumily
Tel. 048 69 – 22 26 20
www.keralatourism.org

Periyar Ecotourism Centre
near the park entrance in Thekkady
Tel. 048 69 – 2245 71
www.periyartigerreserve.org
Reservations for the Periyar Tiger
Trail, one-day treks, night patrols
with gamekeepers etc.

GETTING THERE
Buses go to the national park from
Ernakulam, Kottayam and Madurai.
Since the trip from Ernakulam and
Kottayam is scenically very attractive
and it would be nice to be able to stop
anywhere, it is a good idea to take a
taxi.

SHOPPING
On the main road in Kumily there are
shops selling fresh spices.

WHERE TO EAT/
WHERE TO STAY

▶ Luxury
Spice Village
Kumily, tel. 048 69 – 031 17 11
www.cghearth.com
Spice Village's wooden bungalows
stand between coffee bushes, pepper
and cardamom plants. Excursions to
the surrounding plantations as well as
to Periyar National Park are organized
from here. An Ayurvedic centre, a
pool, two restaurants and a bar are
also part of this outstanding resort.

▶ Luxury / Mid-range
Aranya Nivas
Tel. 04 869 – 922 20 23
www.ktdc.com
The hotel lies in the national park and
there is a lovely view of Lake Periyar
from its terrace.

▶ Budget
Periyar House
Tel. 0486 – 922 20 26, www.ktdc.com.
Basic hotel by Lake Periyar.

Reservoir

One of Periyar's main attractions is a boat trip on the reservoir. Especially during the dry months of March and April such a trip offers a good chance of spotting animals since they come to the lake to drink at this time. The »drowned trees« have an eerie air. Their stumps sometimes protrude from the water and demand great attention on the part of anyone in charge of a boat. Birds often land on them.

Cardamom Hills

The area around Periyar National Park is a famous spice cultivation area, which is why it is also called the Cardamom Hills. However, this is not the only spice that grows in the rainy heights of the Western Ghats. Pepper, coffee and tea plantations can be found here, and cinnamon, cloves and vanilla are also cultivated. In the area around Kumily various plantations can be visited. In addition the town itself has many shops where spices can be bought fresh.

✳ **Puducherry** (Pondicherry, Union Territory)

Altitude: sea level
Distance: 160km/100mi south of Chennai

Population: 400,000

Puducherry (known until 2006 as Pondicherry) is a modern, up-and-coming town on India's southeastern coast. It has some interesting cultural monuments and its Mediterranean charm make it a popular destination for visitors.

Its former role as capital of the area occupied by the French is unmistakable; in fact a lot of the town, not least the strictly grid-pattern streets with houses that have a French air and the, by Indian standards, unusually tidy, even ordered townscape reveal marked European influences. Its particular attraction is based on two institutions that owe their existence to the philosopher **Sri Aurobindo Ghose** (▶ Famous People): Aurobindo Ashram and Auroville. These days Puducherry is the administrative centre of several former French enclaves dotted around the area that were brought together under the umbrella of the union territory of Pondicherry in 1954. During Masi Magham in February / March figures of the gods are taken out of their temples in this region and brought to the sea.

History Not far from Puducherry, which is also called Pudu Ceri (new town) in Tamil, lies the fishing village of Arikamedu. It was once the harbour town from which ships set sail. Finds of many Roman coins prove that Arikamedu's inhabitants were already nurturing trading contacts with the Romans in the first century AD. The French chose this region in 1673 to found a trading post. They acquired a fishing village called Puliceri (Puli = tamarind) from the Sultan of Bijapur, which then became the town of Pondicherry. During the bellicose confrontations between the Dutch, British and French, Pondicherry was conquered several times and almost completely destroyed during the occupation. In the year 1954 the French voluntarily handed over their areas to independent India. The town was given union territory status and to this day forms its own administrative unit, which also oversees the former French enclaves scattered in the area. It was officially renamed Puducherry in September 2006.

✳ Aurobindo Ashram

Genesis The Bengali philosopher **Sri Aurobindo Ghose** (1872–1950; ▶ Famous People) settled in Pondicherry in 1910. His commitment to the Indian independence movement caused him to have to leave his home town of Calcutta in 1909, as it was under British control. A

► VISITING

INFORMATION

Tourist Office Puducherry
40, Goubert Avenue
Tel. 04 13 – 233 94 97
http://tourism.pondicherry.gov.in

Sri Aurobindo Ashram in Auroville
Information on the ashram and its
activities is available at: www.sriaur-
obindosociety.org.in

GETTING THERE

Rail connection via Villupuram to
Chennai, Madurai, Thiruvananthapuram. In addition there are numerous bus services, e.g. to Bangalore,
Chidambaram.

WHERE TO STAY / WHERE TO EAT

► Mid-range
Hotel De L'Orient
17, Rue Romain Rolland

Tel. 04 13 – 234 30 67
www.neemranahotels.com
Stylish hotel in an old villa with a
good restaurant.

► Mid-range / Budget
Kailash Beach Resort
Tel. 04 13 – 233 18 72
www.kailashbeachresort.com
10km/6mi outside Puducherry, directly on the beach, cultural programme, Ayurveda and a restaurant
serving French and Indian cuisine.

► Budget
Park Guesthouse
Goubert Salai
Tel. 04 13 – 233 44 12
This guesthouse has a large garden
and is situated right by the sea. It
offers clean rooms and a cafeteria.

year later he came to the French colony of Pondicherry and dedicated himself to yoga. Together with the Frenchwoman Mira Arfassa,
who lived with him from 1914 onwards, in 1920 he founded an ashram that became one of the richest and most successful in the whole
of India. After 1926 Aurobindo withdrew from the ashram and dedicated himself to »**integral yoga**«. Mira Arfassa continued to run the
ashram and over time became the »mother figure« of this institution.

Current situation

Today the ashram is the spiritual, economic and cultural centre for
around 2000 people, who dominate the formerly »white« part of
town. The ashram's members live and work in around 400 buildings,
and it is an influential institution in the town. The integral yoga developed by Aurobindo still attracts large numbers of visitors from
within India and from other countries. In the ashram's main building is an information office and when there is enough interest a two-
hour tour of the different areas of the ashram is given before noon.
Various shops and production sites have now been incorporated into
the ashram; they too can be visited. The objects produced here, be
they handmade paper, incense sticks or stainless-steel goods, are
some of the best in India.

Samadhis   In the ashram's main building on Rue de la Marine are the tombs (samadhi) of Aurobindo and Mira Arfassa, as well as their living quarters.

Further Attractions

Townscape   The old town of Puducherry resembles an oval and is divided in two by the canal that runs from north to south. The French used to live in the eastern sector by the beach. This »white« town with its beach promenade still has the flair of a Mediterranean town. Along the promenade is the **Gandhi Memorial** with eight columns from the fort

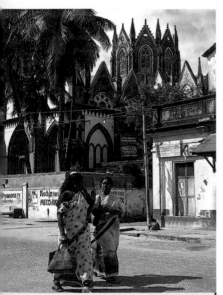
In front of Sacred Heart Cathedral Church

city of Gingee, which the French brought here in 1761. The promenade gets particularly busy with merchants and people going for walks in the evening. Just five minutes from the Gandhi Memorial to the west is **Government Park** with its nice old tree population and several monuments. On both sides of the park are buildings from the French period. To the south is the **Romain Rolland Library** with a collection of more than 50,000 books; to the north is the stately Raj Niwas, the residence of the governor, which can only be admired from the outside. In the southern part of the garden stands the **Pondicherry Museum** with a collection of sculptures and an exhibition about French colonial history.

Puducherry possesses several **churches**, including Notre Dame de la Conception (1865) near the Telegraph Office and Sacre Coeur de Jésus on the town's southern edge. The **beaches** are badly polluted; the only beach section that is relatively clean is in the south near Children's Park. The more than 150-year-old **Botanical Gardens** near the bus station have a nice old tree population; this is a pleasant place to come during the afternoon heat.

Auroville   The foundation of the »town of the future« Auroville (12km/7mi north of Puducherry) goes back to an idea by Mira Arfassa. She wanted to create a place where people could live together **according to the teachings of Sri Aurobindo**. Through the participation of international institutions such as UNESCO, the construction of Auroville was begun on a large area.

The centre of the settlement, laid out in the shape of a mandala, consists of the spherical Matri Mandir and a banyan tree. The people of Auroville live scattered about in individual settlements. They work either in agriculture or in various craft trades such as pottery. Information about the project is available from the visitor centre and on the website www.auroville.org.

★ Thanjavur (Tanjore)

F 14

State: Tamil Nadu
Population: 200,000

Altitude: 59m/194ft
Distance: 334km/208mi south of Chennai

Thanjavur lies in the Kaveri delta, one of Tamil Nadu's most fertile areas of rice cultivation. The former Chola headquarters is now a vibrant town as well as a centre of handicrafts (bronze and glass painting) and raw silk.

The new Tamil university, which was constructed at great expense on a large site outside Thanjavur, is at pains to nurture the old Dravidian language. Visitors to this tradition-steeped town are particularly interested in Brihadeshwarar Temple, a masterpiece of Chola architecture, of which very little still remains in Thanjavur. The second significant attraction is the royal palace of the Nayaks and Marathas, of which only a part is open to the public.

Thanjavur experienced its golden age under King Vijayalaya from the Chola dynasty. He promoted the town to be the capital of the South Indian Empire. Soon afterwards it was destroyed by the Rashtrakutas, but rebuilt by King Rajaraja I a short while later. The Cholas, who were defeated by the Pandyas in around 1279, built many temples in their heartland, the fertile Kaverie plain, which are still extant today. After the Pandyas, the Vijayanagara kings gained control over the region, which they administered through their viceroys, the Nayaks. Like Madurai, Thanjavur was also ruled by the Nayaks and in 1673 conquered by their neighbouring rivals from Madurai. The Maratha king Venkaji and Muhammad Ali, the Nawab of Karnatik, also occupied the town, which was finally taken over by the British. Today Thanjavur is a district capital.

History

> ! **Baedeker TIP**
>
> **Closed midday**
> In all of Tamil Nadu the major shrines are closed from 12.30 to 4pm. In this time the shrines can only be viewed from the outside.

What to See in Thanjavur

Brihadeshwarar Temple is dedicated to the god Shiva and is also the largest monument left behind by the powerful ruler Rajaraja I (985–1012). The texts engraved into the broad base give detailed information about the temple's construction, about the king's gifts and about the temple's administration . The temple employed cooks, gardeners, musicians, dancers, sculptors, painters, guards and of course brahmans. In its heyday the number of temple dancing-girls (devadasis) alone was 400 and the number of brahmans was 200. They were all paid from income derived from donations of land.

The temple is entered through **two gopurams**, of which the first is larger, but the second more impressive thanks to the figures decorating it. The gopuram's panels depict scenes from the lives of the gods, including the wedding of Shiva and Parvati. The two massive, mean-looking dvarapalas (temple guards) framing the entrance of the sec-

Brihadeshwarar Temple is 1000 years old and is considered the most splendid example of Chola architecture

▶ VISITING THANJAVUR

INFORMATION

Tamil Nadu Tourist Office
Hotel Tamil Nadu Complex
Thanjavur
Tel. 043 62 – 23 09 84
www.tamilnadutourism.org

GETTING THERE

Buses depart from Chennai, Madurai, Pondicherry and Tiruchirapalli. There are also train connections, such as to Chennai and Tiruchirapalli.

WHERE TO STAY / WHERE TO EAT

▶ Luxury / Mid-range

Sterling Swamimalai
6/30 Agraharam
Thimmakudy Village
near Kumbakonam

Tel. 04 35 – 24 98 41 14
www.sterlingswamimalai.net
In the pleasantly laid out grounds of an old stately home visitors can listen to concerts, enjoy Ayurvedic treatments and relax at the pool, which is reminiscent of a temple pond. The hotel is situated right in the midst of »temple country« 35km/22mi north of Thanjavur.

▶ Budget

TTDC Hotel Thanjavur
Gandhiji Road, Thanjavur
www.ttdconline.com
Tel. 043 62 – 23 14 21
Hotel run by Tamil Nadu Tourism with basic rooms, some of them fitted with air conditioning.

---

ond gopuram are remarkable. They **are amongst the largest monolithic sculptures in India** and are meant to prevent evil spirits from entering the temple compound. After passing the second gopuram, visitors will come into a temple courtyard measuring 152m/166yd by 76m/83yd, which is surrounded by a large wall and a colonnade attached to it.

Visitors will first enter a hall with **India's third-largest Nandi** (4m/13ft high, 5m/5.5yd long). Shiva's vehicle, carved from a stone block, is looking towards the cella, where there is an equally grand 3.6m/12ft **lingam** called Adavallan (master of dance). The actual **temple with its hall and vestibule** were built on a pedestal. A frieze with animal depictions runs around it. Above the frieze is the above-mentioned inscription. Further up three sides of the temple have figures of deities standing in two rows in niches. The 61m/200ft **Vimana** is crowned by a huge dome that allegedly weighs 81 tons. According to a widespread legend this block of stone is said to have been pushed to its current location over a 6km/4mi ramp that started in the village of Sarapallam. Another tradition says that the dome was pulled by elephants up a helical earth ramp. The temple's interior is only accessible to Hindus.

At the temple complex's northwest corner is the small temple of the war god Subramaniya, which is decorated with attractive sculptures. It was built by the Nayaks in the 16th–17th century and is still visited

★
◀ Subramaniya Temple

by many pilgrims. In addition the complex contains an Amman temple built by the Vijayanagar dynasty and a Ganesha shrine built by the Marathas.

Palace
⏱
Opening hours:
Open: daily
10am–5.30pm

The palace complexes in Thanjavur were built by the Nayaks in the 16th century and later completed by the Marathas. The palace is largely run down and only some parts, such as the Durbar Hall, give an idea of its former glory. From the palace visitors will have a beautiful view of the town of Thanjavur. The Nayak Durbar Hall Art Museum housed in the palace has a wonderful collection of classical southern Indian bronze figures and is definitely worth taking a look at.

✴
Nayak Durbar Hall
Art Museum ▶

Sarasvati Mahal Library

The complex is also home to Sarasvati Mahal Library (Tamil University Library) with a unique collection of old manuscripts accessible only to scholars, and to Rajaraja Chola Museum with a collection of stone sculptures as well as a nice museum shop.

Schwartz Church

This church, situated in a garden, was built in 1799 and was built by a Maratha ruler for the Danish missionary F. C. Schwartz. He had died the previous year in Thanjavur.

Around Thanjavur

Kumbakonam

The old Chola town of Kumbakonam (36km/22mi from Thanjavur) on the banks of the Kaveri is home to many temples, some of which have impressive gopurams and nice sculptures. Every twelve years a significant festival is held in the **Mahamakham temple pond**, when the holy water of the Ganges is said to flow into it. Also of interest are Nagheshvara Temple, Kumbeshvara Temple (a Shiva temple) and Sarangapani Temple consecrated to the god Vishnu, which has a huge, 50m/164ft gopuram. Otherwise the town is famous as a reloading point for stainless steel and silk.

✴ ✴
Darasuram

In the small town of Darasuram (33km/20mi northeast of Thanjavur, 5km/3mi from Kumbakonam) a very nice temple from the time of Rajaraja II (1146–73) is deserving of a visit. Few tourists come to **Airavateshvara Temple**, but its good structural condition and magnificent sculptures make it a real winner. The entire temple contains many depictions illustrating the dance manual Bharata Natyashastra, which was very popular at that time.
Unfortunately the entrance tower typical of this period has been destroyed, even though the rest of the complex is well preserved. The entrance hall is accessed via two very attractively designed stairways in the north and south. The elephants with their riders are quite striking. Found on the stair rail, they are a symbol of wealth. The hall's eight large columns are supported by Yalis (fabled creatures).

Votive gifts →

The pillars are decorated with small reliefs illustrating various mythological subjects. The hall's pedestal is also adorned with niches in which various deities are depicted. They all worship Shiva, the temple's main deity.

The main hall is, like the entrance hall, richly decorated. Many niches are empty, however, since the figures have been lost. Around the shrine is a small wall decorated with lotus motifs and Nandi, which once was the enclosure for a water basin that made the temperature in the temple's interior pleasantly cool. There is a sacrificial hall (yagasala) in the west of the complex.

★
Thiruvarur

After 55km/34mi on the road from Thanjavur to Nagapattinam is the old Chola capital of Thiruvarur. The Cholas and Nayaks spent more than three centuries building Thyagaraja Temple, one of Tamil Nadu's largest temple complexes. The enormous gopurams are particularly impressive.

Point Calimere

The bird sanctuary Point Calimere (Kodikkarai) is 101km/63mi southeast of Thanjavur on the coast and is an important meeting place for waterfowl and migratory birds. The best times for bird watching are the months of January and February.

★ Thiruvananthapuram (Trivandrum)

E 15

Capital of Kerala
Population: 750,000

Altitude: sea level
Distance: 761km/473mi south of Bangalore

Thiruvananthapuram, Kerala's capital, is built on seven hills a few miles away from the coast. Even though its wide streets and prestigious buildings, predominantly from the colonial era, underline its significance as an administrative centre, Thiruvananthapuram has maintained its rather provincial atmosphere.

Name
»Thiru-ananta-puram« means »City of the Holy Snake«, by which is meant Shesha or Ananta, the snake resting on the god Vishnu. It is said to have been born here.

History
The city achieved historical significance under the maharajas of Travancore. The ruler Marthanda Varma (1729–58) was a successful warlord and managed to snare a sizable chunk of the possessions belonging to the Dutch colonial rulers. During his reign Padmanabhaswamy Temple was also extended. Padma-nabha means »lotus navel« and denotes an incarnation of Vishnu that has a lotus growing from the navel. The Travancore maharajas worshipped this form of Vishnu as a domestic god.

Thiruvananthapuram *Map*

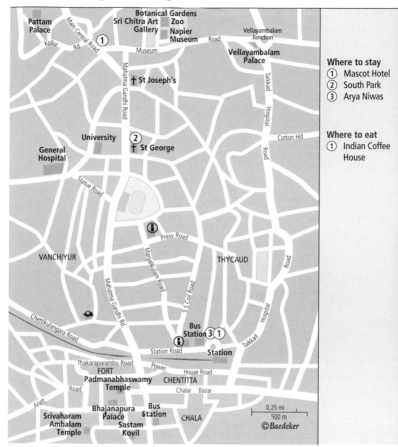

Where to stay
① Mascot Hotel
② South Park
③ Arya Niwas

Where to eat
① Indian Coffee House

The next regent, Karthika Tirunal Rama (1758–98), made Thiruvananthapuram the capital of this empire. During the British Raj the town was part of the Madras Presidency, as was the entire region. Only in 1956, when the states were being reorganized according to linguistic boundaries, did it regain its old significance, this time as the capital of Kerala.

What to See in Thiruvananthapuram

Padmanabhaswamy Temple is located at the southern end of Mahatma Gandhi Road. It is not built in the style of Kerala's wooden temples but in the Dravidian style of Tamil Nadu with a seven-storey,

Padmanabhaswamy Temple

▶ VISITING THIRUVANANTHAPURAM · KOVALAM

INFORMATION

Tourist Offices

can be found at the airport, at the station and next to the Chaitram hotel. The Tourism Directorate is situated across from Napier Museum (tel. 04 71 – 232 11 32). Further information is available at www.kerala tourism.org.

GETTING THERE

By air Thiruvananthapuram can be reached from all major Indian cities, but also from Sri Lanka, the Maldives and the Gulf states. In addition there are plenty of rail and bus connections, from Mumbai, Bangalore, Kochi and Margao (Goa) for example.

SHOPPING

Well-known markets are Connemara (Palayam) Market and Chalai Market. Attractive handicrafts can be found at Kairali Handicrafts (near Statue Junction), products by the Gandhi production sites (Khadi Gramodyog Bhavan) at Ayurveda College Junction.

WHERE TO EAT

▶ **Inexpensive**

① *Indian Coffee House*

Station Road, next to the bus station (Thampanoor)

Good place to breakfast the South Indian way. The restaurant is housed in a red tower and guests have to go up a winding hallway to get upstairs. Idlis, dosas and wadas are eaten on every floor (see p.142).

WHERE TO STAY

▶ **Luxury / Mid-range**

① *Mascot Hotel*

PMG Junction

(MG Road / Museum Road)

Thiruvananthanpuram

Tel. 04 71 – 231 89 90

www.ktdc.com

Guests stay in an old colonial building. There is a swimming pool, an Ayurvedic centre and a good restaurant.

② *South Park*

Centrally located on MG Road

Thiruvananthapuram

Tel. 04 71 – 233 33 33

Amongst the hotel's many facilities are a restaurant (international cuisine), a pub, a bakery, a café and a bookshop. Massages are also available here.

Somatheeram Ayurvedic Health Resort

Chowara (9km/6mi south of Kovalam)

Tel. 04 71 – 226 65 01

www.somatheeram.org

Very highly regarded Ayurvedic resort with a pleasant ambience, direct access to the beach.

Surya Samudra Holiday Resort

Pulinkudi Mullur (Kovalam)

Tel. 04 71 – 226 71 24

www.suryasamudra.com

The resort lies around 10km/6mi south of Kovalam. Guests stay in traditional Kerala houses or in huts. Good restaurant with a stunning view, also Ayurvedic treatments and a pool.

▶ **Mid-range / Budget**

Hotel Rockholm

Lighthouse Road; Kovalam

Tel. 04 71 – 248 03 06

www.rockholm.com

The hotel lies right on the waterfront and has a wonderful terrace restaurant.

Hotel Blue Sea
Kovalam, tel. 04 71 – 248 14 01
Basic rooms in an old wooden Kerala house and comfortable rooms in new buildings. In addition this hotel, which is ten minutes from the beach, offers a pool and a nice garden.

► Budget
③ *Arya Niwas*
Manorama Road, Thampanoor
Thiruvananthapuram
Tel. 04 71 – 233 07 89
Pleasant, clean rooms and an excellent vegetarian restaurant.

17m/56ft entrance gopuram. The interior remains closed to non-Hindus, as with most of Kerala's temples. The only opportunity of seeing the image of the god is during the biannual Arat Festival in March / April and in November / October. Then the figure of Vishnu, accompanied by a large procession led by the maharaja, is brought to the sea to undergo ritual cleansing. Gun salutes, music and evening fireworks accompany the festivities.
The temple complex also has a bathing pool surrounded by pretty, richly adorned brahman houses.

Follow the main shopping street, Mahatma Gandhi Road, northbound to pass the secretariat with its beautiful columns. In the same road visitors will also find handicraft and antique shops. Connemara Market lies to the right in the upper section of MG Road. It sells everything from combs to pineapples. The park complex housing the Napier Museum, the Sri Chitra Art Gallery and the zoo can also be found here.

Mahatma Gandhi Road

The interesting Napier Museum was built in around 1880. Even from afar it attracts visitors with its unusual architectural style, achieved by the British architect Robert Chisholm who combined elements of colonial architecture with those of the traditional Kerala houses. The museum contains several **magnificent ivory and wood carvings**, excellently worked gold jewellery, Chola bronzes from the 12th century, a temple chariot and a lot more.

✷
Napier Museum
⊙
Opening hours:
Open: daily except
Mon 10am–4.45pm

Quite nearby is the worthwhile Sri Chitra Art Gallery. It exhibits miniatures from the Rajput and Mughal schools as well as paintings from the Thanjavur school. In addition it possesses paintings from China, Japan and Tibet, as well as some by the Russian painter Nicolaus Roerich. Several galleries are dedicated to the famous painter Raja Ravi Varma. Theopening hours are the same as those of the museum.

✷
Sri Chitra Art Gallery

Around Thiruvananthapuram

During the past decade the small fishing village of Kovalam (13km/ 7mi south of Thiruvananthapuram) has developed into one of Kera-

✷
Kovalam

la's main attractions. The reason for this lies in two palm-lined bays separated by promontories, which, together, have around **4km/2.5mi of white sandy beaches**. Particularly during the high season from November to February this alternative to Goa is usually full of tourists. Along the more southerly of the two bays, which is bordered by the lighthouse rock, there are beach cafés, restaurants, souvenir shops and small hotels.

Anyone not wanting to spend the day on the beach or in a café can go for a pleasant walk to the fishing village of **Vizhinjam** somewhat further south. The path leads along the road, past the lighthouse, from where there is a lovely view of the coast and the fishing harbour. It is only open to the public in the afternoons from 2pm to 4pm.

The fishing harbour of Vizhinjam is dominated by a large, modern mosque built in an exposed location. On the beach fishermen can be seen fixing their nets or bringing in their catch.

Varkala

One beached praised as an alternative to Kovalam beach is the lovely beach of Varkala (50km/31mi north of Thiruvananthapuram). Visitors should be aware, however, that this place is sacred to Hindus. It is popularly called Papanashini, i.e. the destroyer of sins. Believers bring the ash of their deceased relatives here to hand it over to the sea or in order to pray for the souls of their ancestors. The town itself is home to Janardhana Swamy Temple; this Vishnu temple is the destination of many pilgrims. There are regular buses from Kollam and Thiruvananthapuram to Varkala.

★ **Padmanabha puram**

63km/39mi southeast of Thiruvananthapuram is **Padmanabhapuram**, the impressive wooden palace of the former maharajas of Travancore. From 1550 to 1750 they ruled their empire from here. The town bears the name of the patron deity of the Padmanabha dynasty, one of Vishnu's incarnations. In 1550 the raja at the time assumed the title Padmanabhasa (»Padmanabha's servant«) and subsequently ruled the empire as the god's governor, a traditional way for Hindu rulers at the time to legitimate their power.

Opening hours: Open: daily except Mon 9am–1pm and 2pm–5pm

The palace, which is predominantly built of wood, consists of several interconnected buildings. Their tiled roofs with triangular, occasionally very nicely carved gables show off Kerala's typical architecture, which can be found in many temples and old houses. Narrow stairs connect the complex's various floors. The building is accessed through the veranda-shaped entrance hall. It contains an oil lamp that hangs from a wooden ceiling decorated with 90 different flower motifs. The granite bed in the corner was presumably used by the maharaja to rest on hot summer days. On the first floor is the former assembly hall. Its black, shiny floor was made of a mixture of burnt coconut, egg-white, lime and sand amongst other things, a mixture no longer in use today.

The ruler's bedroom is also well worth taking a look at; the **imposing bed adorned with rich carvings** consists of 16 different medicinal woods. Directly above the bedroom is the meditation room with impressive wall paintings. Two oil lamps have been burning here since its inauguration. A dancing hall and a dining room, in which up to 2000 brahmans could be fed, are also part of the palace.

> **!** ***Baedeker* TIP**
>
> **Great day trip**
> Anyone craving an alternative to life on the beach can hire a taxi and make a nice day trip to Kanyakumari, at India's southern tip. The wonderful wooden palace of Padmanabhapuram and the temple town of Suchindaram should definitely be included on the itinerary.

During the onward journey to Kanyakumari, visitors can make a stop in the small town of Suchindaram with its Shiva temple. The temple, which seems very lively, lies next to an attractive small temple lake surrounded by brahman houses.

Suchindaram

Thrissur (Trissur, Trichur)

E 14

State: Kerala
Population: 300,000

Altitude: sea level
Distance: 472km/293mi southwest of Bangalore

Thrissur, the capital of the former Cochin state, is built around a hill, which at the same time marks its centre. This is also the location of the lovely Vadakkunatha Temple, to which non-Hindus unfortunately have no access.

The town was much fought over in the 18th century, during which time it fell into the hands of both the Zamorin of Calicut and Tipu Sultan from Mysore. The Raja of Kochi, Shaktan Tampuran, gave Thrissur its largest festival, the Puram festival, causing masses of people from all over Kerala and even foreign visitors to flock to the town.

History

What to See in Thrissur

One attraction definitely worth a visit is the 16th-century Vadakkunatha Temple. Even though non-Hindus are not permitted to enter the temple's interior, the walk to the hill in the middle of town is

Vadakkunatha Temple

worth it. The temple dedicated to the god Shiva in his form of Badakkunatha is a **good example of Kerala's temple architecture**. The entire structure is covered in wood. The gabled roof, which has three steps and is made with wooden beams, is deserving of special attention. The stone lamp stand in the shape of a tortoise outside of the temple's main entrance is also typical of Kerala. In addition to the main shrine for Vaddakunatha, the temple houses the Kuttambalam theatre as well as several further shrines for Rama and Krishna, amongst others.

✱
Puram Festival

The temple hill is the scene of the colourful annual Puram Festival. During this time several large temples compete to present the best line-up of **elephants, musicians and fireworks**. In two separate pro-

VISITING THRISSUR

INFORMATION
District Tourism Promotion Council
Palace Road (opposite the Town Hall)
Tel. 04 87 – 232 08 00
www.keralatourism.org

GETTING THERE
By rail from Ernakulam and Kozhicode; by bus from Thiruvananthapuram and Kochi, amongst other places.

FESTIVALS
Puram Festival, Kerala's largest festival with magnificent elephant processions, is celebrated in April / May.

WHERE TO STAY / WHERE TO EAT
▶ **Luxury**
Kalari Kovilakom
Kollengode –678 506
Palakkad (60 km/37mi northeast of Thrissur)
Tel. 04923-263 155
www.cghearth.com
One of Kerala's best Ayurvedic centres is housed in the stylishly refurbished old palace of Kollengode. This is the right address for anyone searching for rest and relaxation, wanting to undergo some Ayurvedic treatment

(including a personal menu and individual yoga classes). Since the house is run like an ashram, guests have to forgo smoking, drinking and the use of mobile phones.

▶ **Mid-range**
Kadappuram Beach Resort
Nattika Beach
(25km/15mi from Thrissur)
Tel. 04 87 – 239 49 88
www.kadappurambeachresorts.com
Bungalows located near a nice sandy beach, Ayurveda centre and restaurant serving Ayurvedic cuisine, smoking is not permitted within the complex.

▶ **Mid-range / Budget**
Casino Hotel
TB Road
Tel. 04 87 – 242 46 99
By the station, with restaurant, bar, internet café and garden.

Siddharta Regency
Tel. 04 87 – 242 47 73
By the station, with pool and restaurant serving northern and southern Indian cuisine. Small, pleasant rooms.

cessions the elephants approach the town, accompanied by the deafening sound of countless drums, cymbals and wind instruments. A cheering mass welcomes the mahouts with their elephants decorated with gold and carrying silk umbrellas in garish colours. The celebrations last until late at night and end with a magnificent firework display. The temples spend a lot of money on this demonstration of grandeur, which has now become the largest festival in Kerala.

Built in 1795, Shakthan Thampuram Palace houses the very worthwhile archaeological museum. The Kerala-style building is situated in the middle of a pleasantly laid-out garden. It contains collections from the possessions of former rulers, including paintings, sculptures, bronzes and discoveries from the region.

Shakthan Thampuran Palace

Line-up of elephants decorated in gold at Puram Festival

State Art Museum   The State Art Museum, which is in the middle of the zoo, exhibits sculptures from the Sunga period, oil lamps and, as a special feature, a 13th-century silver depiction of the snake god Anantha.

Lourdes Cathedral   On College Road stands the Syrian-Catholic Lourdes Cathedral. The crypt contains a replica of the grotto in Lourdes. Amongst the statues there is also one of St Alphonsa, a nun from Kottayam, who was canonized in 1986.

Ring road   Shopping is best done on the ring road in the centre where there are a number of good handicraft shops offering special products from Kerala.

Around Thrissur

Guruvayur   The local Krishna temple makes Guruvayur (32km/20mi north of Thrissur, population 20,000) one of Kerala's most important places of pilgrimage. Every day countless people flock to the famous temple, which is not open to non-Hindus. The temple, whose origin is obscure, was probably built in its current form in the 16th century. There is a real hustle and bustle on the streets in front of the entrance.

Elephant-Training Camp in Punnathur Kotta   The Elephant Training Camp in Punnathur Kotta 4km/2.5mi outside of town is interesting for travellers. Around 60 elephants are kept at the camp, where they are prepared for their tasks at the many processions. Visitors can watch the mahouts feeding the animals and washing them in the pool. A separate section houses the camp's »psychiatric ward«. It is home to particularly aggressive (securely tied up) animals that are treated with Ayurvedic medicine. Within the enclosure there is also the old Maharaja's palace, which has been the backdrop for cinema films on several occasions.

Kodungallur (Craganore)   Kodungallur (35km/22mi south of Thrissur) is situated like an island between the sea, the Kerala Backwaters and two river mouths. It was here that the ancient harbour of Muziris was located, from which Kerala's spices were shipped all over the world. It was also here that the legendary king Cheraman Perumal, who later converted to Islam and emigrated to Mecca, set up his capital. **Thomas the Apostle** is said to have set foot on Indian soil here in AD 52, bringing Christianity to the Indian subcontinent. Kodungallur can be reached by bus or taxi from Thrissur. Traces of this early co-existence of different religions can still be found today. Thus around 1.5km/1mi from the town centre visitors will find **Cheraman Jama Masjid**, which is believed to be India's oldest mosque. The previous building is said to have been donated by Cheraman as early as the seventh century. In the centre itself is the large Hindu temple, **Kurumba Bhagavati Temple**, built in the typical Kerala style.

A few miles away, in Azhicode, St Thomas's Church (Mar Thomas Pontifical Shrine) commemorates the apostle, who is associated with the early days of Christianity in India. The church, framed by colonnades, **a kind of miniature replica of St Peter's in Rome**, contains one of the bones of the saint's forearms as a relic. Since the church has a stunning location by a palm-fringed river mouth, taking the trip by boat or taxi from Kodungallur is worthwhile.

**Mar Thomas
Pontifical Shrine
in Azhicode**

Tiruchirapalli <small>(Tiruchirappalli, Tiruchi, Trichy)</small>

F 14

State: Tamil Nadu
Population: 775,000

Altitude: 88m/289ft
Distance: 320km/200mi south of Chennai

Tiruchirapalli, on the banks of the Kaveri, is the commercial centre of the fertile river delta, considered the breadbasket of Tamil Nadu. The city mainly handles textiles, leather, synthetic diamonds and agricultural machines.

Tiruchirapalli does not have many tourist attractions, but the rapidly expanding city is a good starting point for a trip to the nearby **town of Sri Rangam** with its temples.
Tiruchirapalli's history goes back to the classical Sangam period. Later the Choals developed the fort into a bigger fortification. They were, however, defeated by Muslim rulers in the 14th century. In the mid-16th century the town came under the control of the Nayaks and alternated as capital with Madurai. The town continued to experience an eventful history during the Carnatic Wars as well as during the wars between the French and the British as they fought for dominance in the region.

 ## VISITING TIRUCHIRAPALLI

INFORMATION
Tamil Nadu Tourist Office
Cantonement
Tel. 04 31 – 246 01 36 or
www.tamilnadutourism.org

WHERE TO STAY /
WHERE TO EAT
► **Luxury**
Hotel Sangam
Collector's Office Road
Tel. 04 31 – 241 47 00

hotelsangam@vsnl.com
Modern hotel with a nice pool and good restaurant.

► **Budget**
TTDC Hotel Trichy
Mc Donald's Road,
Tel. 04 31 – 241 43 46
Tamil Nadu Tourism (www.ttdconline.com) provides basic rooms with or without air conditioning. All rooms have a TV.

What to See in Tiruchirapalli

Rising up above the otherwise flat land is an 80m/262ft-high granite rock that has been polished by wind and weather. It is crowned by a

Looking smart for a walk through the streets of Sri Rangam

Ganesha temple. The narrow, roofed stairs allow visitors to make the somewhat laborious **ascent up the 435 steps**, which is rewarded with a breathtaking view of the town and the temple complex of Sri Rangam a few miles to the north. The temple itself is only accessible to Hindus. At the foot of the rock is an artificial lake, Teppakulam, which is surrounded by old houses and countless little shops. In March the raft festival takes place here, during which time deities are put on to rafts and taken to the lake. The former Nayak palace stands at the northeastern corner of Teppakulam, but it is no longer open to the public.

Of the countless **churches** in the town, St Joseph's College Church and Christ Church are the most important. The first is a replica of the church in Lourdes. The construction of the second goes back to the efforts of the missionary Christian Friedrich Schwartz, who died in Thanjavur.

✳ ✳ Sri Rangam

Town

The small town of Sri Rangam is located on the narrow green island between the Kaveri and one of its branches, the Kollidam. The attraction of Sri Rangam 3km/2mi north of Tiruchirapalli is the impressive Ranganatha Temple, which is believed to be **India's largest temple**.

Ranganatha Temple

Ranganatha Temple is consecrated to a form of Vishnu, which is depicted in its sanctum resting on the holy snake Sesha. Parts of the temple were already built by the Cholas and then extended by the Pandyas in the 13th century. The kings of the Vijayanagar Empire and their vassals, the Nayaks, added further extensions, which exceeded the existing temple buildings in size. The last and largest gopuram, through which visitors now access the complex, was only completed in around 1990.

Sri Rangam is the classic example of a **temple town**. Grouped around the relatively small main temple are seven courtyards with a total of 21 gopurams. The first three courtyards contain many shops, brahman accommodation and sleeping quarters for the many pilgrims. The actual temple only begins after the fourth courtyard and visitors will have to remove their shoes to enter it.

It is worthwhile to visit the Horse Hall in the fourth courtyard. Looking at the monolithic columns visitors will discover rearing horses, warriors and fabled animals. The Krishna temple with its nice depictions of gopis (shepherdesses) making themselves pretty is also very nice. The temple, whose sanctum is closed to non-Hindus, is visited by large numbers of pilgrims all year round and is famous for its rich gold and gemstone ornamentation.

✱
◄ Horse Hall

Around 4km/2.5mi east of Ranganatha Temple in the small village of Thiruvannaikaval is Jambukeshwara Temple, a famous Shiva temple. It consists of five courtyards and is crowned by five gopurams. Shiva is worshipped in the sanctum as a lingam, which is under water since the temple was built above a spring. Non-Hindus are not permitted to enter the sanctum.

Jambukeshwara Temple

Rearing horses decorate the columns of the horse hall in Sri Rangam

Vijayawada

G 11

State: Andhra Pradesh
Distance: 433km/270mi north of Chennai

Population: 1.01 million

On the banks of the river Krishna, at an important rail junction, is the up-and-coming city of Vijayawada. Its dam is of immense significance to the economy of the Krishna delta as it can irrigate around 1 million hectares or 2.5 million acres of land, making it possible to grow cereal crops here.

Vijayawada is a good starting point for trips to the region thanks to its central location and the good transport connections. The ruins of Amaravathi are among the most popular destinations from Vijayawada.

History
A community already existed in the Krishna delta 2000 years ago during the Buddhist Vengi Empire. Around 605 the town was conquered by the Chalukya King Vishnuvardhana and Buddhism lost more and more of its significance. In the eleventh century the Cholas managed to get this region under their control for two centuries. In 1323 the town fell under Islamic influence until it was conquered by the British. This Islamic influence was only interrupted by a short period during which the local Reddi dynasty made itself independent. From 1427 the Qutb-Shahi kings ruled from Golconda / Hyderabad and they made Vijayawada into an important inland harbour.

What to See in Vijayawada

Kanaka Durga Temple
Visitors can get a splendid panorama of Vijayawada from Indrakilari Hill in the western part of the city. This is also the location of the temple for the goddess Durga, Kanaka Durga Temple.

Victoria Jubilee Museum
The Victoria Jubilee Museum possesses several sculptures and pictures including a well-known colossal statue of the Buddha.

Further attractions
Vijayawada's other attractions are the cave temple of Mogalrajapuram, two 1000-year-old Jain temples and Mazratbal Mosque built by the Qutb-Shahi rulers, with a relic of the prophet Muhammad.

Around Vijayawada

Undavalli
Around 8km/5mi west on the opposite riverbank lies the small village of Undavalli. There is a series of cave temples here, which date back to the Vishnukundin dynasty (sixth century) and are believed to have been models for the cave temples of the Pallava dynasty in Mamallapuram.

VISITING VIJAYAWADA

INFORMATION

APTDC Tourist Office
Tel. 08 66 – 257 02 55
www.aptourism.com

GETTING THERE

Vijayawada lies on the railway line between Chennai and Kolkata. There are trains to Hyderabad.

WHERE TO EAT / WHERE TO STAY

► **Mid-range**

Hotel DV Manor
MG Road, Vijayawada
Tel. 08 66 – 663 44 55

www.hoteldvmanor.com
Centrally located, modern hotel with an excellent restaurant.

Bhavani Island
Tel. 08 66 – 24180 57
www.tourisminap.com
Situated in the middle of the river Krishna on the island of Bhavani, this hotel is run by Andhra Pradesh Tourism and has bungalows, tree houses and a restaurant. It organizes the necessary transport by boat.

From the second century BC to the second century AD, Amaravathi (30km/20mi northwest of Vijayawada) was the cultural centre of southern Indian Buddhism and the capital of the Satavahanas, who supported both Hinduism and Buddhism. Today visitors find only the remains of India's once largest stupa in the midst of the many ruins.

Amaravathi

The stupa's marble cladding and the enclosure were once decorated with wonderful reliefs. They depict scenes from Buddha's life and are amongst the masterpieces of Indian art. The figures developed from a synthesis of the two religions during a time when the king was a Hindu and the queen a Buddhist. Many finds from Amaravathi are now housed in the Chennai Government Museum and in the British Museum in London. The **Archaeological Museum** also possesses original sculptures from the period from the third century BC to the fifth century AD, as well as plaster casts. The new Amaravathi Museum and Interpretation Centre provides in-depth information about the history of Buddhism in the area.

★
◄ Reliefs

GLOSSARY OF GEOGRAPHICAL, RELIGIOUS AND CULTURAL TERMS

Adinatha first fordmaker (tirthankara) of Jainism
Adivasi aboriginal Indian; name given to tribes
Agni Vedic god of fire
Ahimsa non-violence; not harming another in either words or deeds
Apsara heavenly nymph; half-goddess
Ardhanarishvara Shiva depiction: half man, half woman
Arjuna Pandu prince and hero of the Bhagavadgita
Asana yoga position
Ashram place where a guru and his students live together
Atman individual soul
Avalokiteshvara bodhisattva embodying compassion and thus the one most often evoked, Buddha's helper
Ayurveda »knowledge of life«, one of India's traditional medical teachings
Bagh Park
Bhagavadgita core piece of the Mahabharata
Bhakti religious devotion, pious love of god; is taught in the Bhagavadgita
Bharat India
Bhavan house, garden pavilion
Bodhi tree tree under which Buddha found enlightenment
Bodhisattva »enlightened being«: Buddha, who foregoes entry into ▸Nirvana in order to help humans escape from the constant cycle of rebirth; they are often implored regarding problems of daily life.
Brahma creator of the world, one of the three ▸Trimurti
Buddha Siddharta Gautama Shakya, founder of Buddhism; »enlightened one«, who recognized the invalidity of the world out of his own strength
Buddhas of the three ages past, present and future: common group in the main hall of temples: Shakyamuni to the left and Maitreya to the right
Cantonment administrative and military district of a town/city from the time of the British colonial era
Chaitya original early Buddhist burial mound; developed into a temple with a wide central nave and two narrow side naves at the end of which is the dagoba with a gallery
Chakra disc, Vishnu's symbol, wheel of Buddha's teaching
Chamunda fearsome aspect of the mother goddess Devi
Char Bagh square garden divided into four parts
Chhatri tomb in the form of an open shrine
Chowk open square
Dagoba small inner stupa at the end of the Chaitya Hall
Devadasi temple dancer
Devi goddess; original form of Parvati, Kali etc.
Dharamsala accommodation for pilgrims
Dharma law of existence as well as the teaching of ▸Buddha about it, often depicted as the »wheel of knowledge«, that is passed on and on

Dhoti traditional dress for men

Digambaras »air-clad«, followers of Jainism

Diwali Hindu festival of light (Oct. / Nov.)

Dravidic style architectural style of southern India

Dravidians non-Indo-Aryan aboriginal population of southern India

Durga Hindu mother goddess in many guises, ►Devi

Ganesha Hindu protective deity with the head of an elephant, son of ►Shiva

Ganga Hindu river goddess and name of the Ganges

Garbhagriha womb chamber, the sanctum sanctorum

Garuda sun bird, Vishnu's vehicle

Ghat bathing steps, rising mountains

Ghee clarified butter

Gompa Tibetan monastery, cave

Gopuram temple tower built in southern Indian architectural style located at the entrances of the temple complex

Gumbaz Persian dome

Gopi shepherd girl, Krishna's playmate

Guru teacher, master

Hanuman son of the wind god, monkey lord of the Ramayana

Harem women's wing in a Muslim palace complex

Harijan »children of God«, Gandhi's term for the untouchables

Hatha yoga form of yoga occupied with posture and breathing

Haveli merchant house in northern India with nice decorations (wood carvings, wall paintings)

Hill station climatic health spas founded for their fresh air by the British

Hinayana early, austere form of Buddhism (»small vehicle«)

Jainism Jain religion; founded by Jina, one of Buddha's contemporaries (6th century)

Jama Masjid great mosque, Friday Mosque

Jati Hindu term for the caste as a community, which people are born into

Jauhar mass self-cremation of Rajput women to escape captivity

Kali fearsome form of Devi, particularly worshipped in Bengal

Kamasutra ancient Indian book of love

Karma effect of fate

Krishna Vishnu's eighth incarnation

Kshatriya member of the warrior caste

Kumari virgin, unmarried Hindu girl

Kumbh(a) Mela Hindu celebration taking place at solar eclipses; takes place every four years in different cities

Lakshmi Hindu goddess of affluence and beauty; wife of Vishnu

Lingam phallic symbol for Shiva

Mahabharata greatest epic of India's classical literature

Mahadeva »great god«, popular name for Shiva

Mahal palace

Maharaja »great king«, ruler of a kingdom

Maharani »great queen«, ruler or wife of the maharaja

Mahatma »great soul«, honorary title for Gandhi

Mahavira 24th and last fordmaker of Jainism

Mahayana »great vehicle«, later popular form of Buddhism

Maheshvara Shiva's name

Mahout elephant driver

Maidan public square

Mandala symmetrical diagram using circles and squares symbolizing the cosmos

Mandapa open or closed columned hall of a Hindu temple

Mandir temple

Mantra formula of evocation and prayer

Masjid mosque

Medrese Koran school, Islamic university

Meru sacred mountain, abode of Lord Brahma

Mihrab prayer niche in a mosque

Minaret tower of a mosque

Mithuna couples or groups in the act of lovemaking

Naga snake, snake deity

Nagarastil northern Indian architectural style; stands in contrast to the southern Indian Dravidic style

Nagaraja snake king

Nandi bull, Shiva's vehicle

Narasimha man-lion incarnation of Vishnu

Nataraja Shiva as a cosmic dancer

Nawab (Nabob) Muslim title for a ruler, an independent king, comparable to a maharaja

Nirvana »blowing out«, »extinguishing«; in Buddhist teaching the term given to the state when the wheel of rebirths comes to a halt

Padmapani lotus carrier, form of Avalokiteshvara, constant companion of Buddha from Mahayana Buddhism onwards

Paisa a hundredth of a rupee, smallest unit of currency

Pandit scholarly Brahmin

Paria without caste, impure, outside of the four castes; called Harijans by Gandhi

Parvati Hindu deity, wife of Shiva

Pol gate

Puja Hindu ceremony, where the gods are worshipped

Raja local ruler, also used for the British during the colonial period

Rama hero of the Ramayana, Vishnu's seventh incarnation

Ramayana second-greatest heroic epic (Hinduism) after the Mahabharata

Ratha temple chariot

Sad(d)hu holy man, ascetic

Sagar artificial lake

Samsara cycle of rebirths

Sanskrit oldest Aryan language in India, in which the holy Hindu scriptures are written

Sarasvati goddess of knowledge, Brahma's wife

Sari women's dress (5.5m/18ft–6m/19ft 6in) that is wrapped around the body

Sati burning of widows at the bier of the dead husband, also a label for widows who died in this way

Shakti female mother goddess, female energy

Shikhara tower on northern Indian temples

Shiva one of the three highest gods of Hinduism; destroyer of the world, one of the ►Trimurti

Shivalinga phallic symbol for Shiva

Singh »the lion«, name given to all Sikhs

Stupa Buddhist temple; developed from burial or reliquary mound into a pagoda

Sufi Islamic mystic

Surya sun, Vedic sun deity

Tantrism expressionof the creative power of god; in Hinduism: literature that is connected to Shaktism

Thangka religious scroll image of Buddhism

Tirthankara fordmaker in Jainism

Trimurti three-headed depiction of the highest Hindu gods, Brahma, Vishnu and Shiva, in one figure

Trishul trident, Shiva's symbol

Vahana vehicle of a Hindu deity

Vaishya farmer and craftsperson, member of the third caste

Vajrayana »diamond vehicle«, late developmental phase of Buddhism

Varaha wild boar incarnation of Vishnu

Varna »colour«, term of caste (Brahmins white, Kshatriyas red, Vaishyas yellow, Shudras black)

Vav well, stepped well

Vedas religious scriptures of Hinduism

Vihara Buddhist monastery, already during the early Buddhist rock architecture

Vimana name for the southern Indian Dravidic stepped or terraced temple tower, in contrast to the parabola-shaped shikharas of the northern Indian Nagara style

Vishnu world preserver, one of the ►Trimurti

Yamuna Hindu river goddess, depicted in the form of a turtle

Yatha Hindu pilgrimage

Yoga philosophical teachings containing a number of mental and physical exercises

Yogini female demons who play the central role of Shakti as companions of Durga in the tantric ritual

Yoni symbol for the female genitals; counterpart to the lingam

Yonilingam lingam with yoni, in the shape of a basin with drain for the sacrificial water

INDEX

LIST OF MAPS AND ILLUSTRATIONS

PHOTO CREDITS

PUBLISHER'S INFORMATION

Illustrations etc: 319 illustrations, 48 maps and diagrams, one large map

Text: Karen Schreitmüller, with contributions by Mohan Dhamotharan and Beate Szerelmy

Editing: Baedeker editorial team (Robert Taylor)

Translation: Michael Scuffil

Cartography: Christoph Gallus, Hohberg; Franz Huber, Munich; MAIRDUMONT/Falk Verlag, Ostfildern (map)

3D illustrations: jangled nerves, Stuttgart

Design: independent Medien-Design, Munich; Kathrin Schemel

Editor-in-chief: Rainer Eisenschmid, Baedeker Ostfildern

1st edition 2009

Based od Baedeker Allianz Reiseführer »Indien«, 6. Auflage 2009

Copyright: Karl Baedeker Verlag, Ostfildern
Publication rights: MAIRDUMONT GmbH & Co; Ostfildern

Printed in Germany

BAEDEKER GUIDE BOOKS AT A GLANCE
Guiding the World since 1827

DEAR READER,

We would like to thank you for choosing this Baedeker travel guide. It will be a reliable companion on your travels and will not disappoint you.

This book describes the major sights, of course, but it also recommends the best beaches, surfing and diving, cafés, as well as hotels in the luxury and budget categories, and includes tips about where to eat or go shopping and much more, helping to make your trip an enjoyable experience. Our author Karen Schreitmüller ensures the quality of this information by making regular journeys to India and putting all her know-how into this book.

Nevertheless, experience shows us that it is impossible to rule out errors and changes made after the book goes to press, for which Baedeker accepts no liability. Please send us your criticisms, corrections and suggestions for improvement: we appreciate your contribution. Contact us by post or e-mail, or phone us:

► **Verlag Karl Baedeker GmbH**
Editorial department
Postfach 3162
73751 Ostfildern
Germany
Tel. 49-711-4502-262, fax -343
www.baedeker.com
www.baedeker.co.uk
E-Mail: baedeker@mairdumont.com